De Gruyter Handbook of Personal Finance

# De Gruyter Handbook of Personal Finance

Edited by
John E. Grable
Swarn Chatterjee

**DE GRUYTER**

ISBN 978-3-11-135674-7
e-ISBN (PDF) 978-3-11-072769-2
e-ISBN (EPUB) 978-3-11-072770-8
ISSN 2748-016X
e-ISSN 2748-0178

**Library of Congress Control Number:** 2021950674

**Bibliographic information published by the Deutsche Nationalbibliothek**
The Deutsche Nationalbibliothek lists this publication in the Deutsche Nationalbibliografie;
detailed bibliographic data are available on the internet at http://dnb.dnb.de.

© 2023 Walter de Gruyter GmbH, Berlin/Boston
This volume is text- and page-identical with the hardback published in 2022.
Typesetting: Integra Software Services Pvt. Ltd.
Printing and binding: CPI books GmbH, Leck

www.degruyter.com

# Contents

## Part III: **Financial Security**

## Part V: **Summarization**

# List of Contributors

Forty-three of the world's leading personal finance researchers, financial service professionals, and thought leaders contributed to this handbook. When viewed holistically, those who contributed to this handbook represent some of the leading contemporary figures conducting personal finance research. The work of these individuals has shaped – and continues to affect – the way that personal finance is conceptualized and practiced. The following list shows each contributor, in alphabetical order. A brief biographic sketch for each person is also shown.

**Efthymia (Effie) Antonoudi** serves as an instructor and undergraduate coordinator for all majors and minors in the Department of Financial Planning, Housing, and Consumer Economics at the University of Georgia (UGA). She is responsible for teaching financial planning and consumer economics courses. Effie received a B.S. in Accounting and Finance from the University of Macedonia in Greece and an M.B.A. and M.P.A. from Georgia State University and is currently pursuing a Ph.D. in personal financial planning at Kansas State University. Her current research is focused on behavioral finance, financial issues of young adults, financial therapy, and how policy affects financial decisions. Effie is a certified public accountant (CPA) and a certified financial planner (CFP®) and has more than ten years of experience in business – in financial consulting, marketing, accounting, auditing, and international tax consulting. Prior to joining UGA, she worked for Deloitte and Grant Thornton. She has also worked with the Executive M.B.A. Program at Georgia State University. A Greek native, Effie created and directed the Family and Consumer Sciences (FACS) Greece Study Abroad Program at the University of Georgia. She has created, directed, and taught the FACS Greece virtual studies program for the past two years. Effie has taken the lead on diversity and inclusion, with the Diversity and Inclusion in Financial Planning Symposiums held in 2019 and 2020, and led UGA to be a partner university on the Diversitas financial knowledge symposium with the University of Akron in October 2020. Effie is currently serving on the National Diversitas Advisory Board.

**Kristy L. Archuleta**, Ph.D., LMFT, CFT-I™ is a professor on the Financial Planning program at the University of Georgia. Prior to joining the UGA faculty, she was an associate professor and director of the Personal Financial Planning program at Kansas State University. She is a co-founder of the Financial Therapy Association, the *Journal of Financial Therapy*, the nation's first academic program in financial therapy, and the Women Managing the Farm conference. Dr. Archuleta has garnered national and international attention as a speaker and author who has published numerous scholarly articles and co-edited two books on topics related to financial planning, financial therapy, financial counseling, and mental health. She currently serves on the board of directors for the National Association of Personal Financial Advisors and three editorial review boards. She is commonly featured in podcasts and major news media outlets, such as *The New York Times*, *InvestmentNews*, and CNBC, to name a few, and has won awards for her cutting-edge research. Dr. Archuleta is also a recipient of the Kansas State University College of Human Ecology Myers-Alford Outstanding Teaching Award and the Oklahoma State University College of Human Sciences Distinguished Alumna Award.

**Sarah D. Asebedo**, Ph.D., CFP®, is an assistant professor and director of the Life-Centered Financial Planning graduate certificate program at Texas Tech University. Her research is centered upon evidence-based methods that equip financial professionals to excel in client relationships and for consumers to make sound financial decisions that enhance their financial and overall well-being. She is currently spearheading research focused on the application of positive psychology to personal finance, financial self-efficacy and the psychosocial environment, financial behavior

https://doi.org/10.1515/9783110727692-203

change, and the financial planner/client interaction. Her practice and academic experience have earned notable industry and research recognition including the 2016 Montgomery-Warschauer Award, the 2017 Top 40 Under 40 Award from Investment News, and the 2014, 2017, and 2018 Best Research Award for the *Journal of Financial Planning* and Academy for Financial Services. She is a past president of the Financial Therapy Association and editor of the *Journal of Financial Therapy*.

**Suzanne Bartholomae**, Ph.D. is an assistant professor and extension state specialist in family finance in the Department of Human Development and Family Studies at Iowa State University. Her engaged scholarship focuses on financial education, financial well-being, and financial behavior based in local, regional, state, and national initiatives. Her work has been published in several academic journals and books. She earned her Ph.D. at Ohio State University and currently resides in Ames Iowa where she enjoys reading, cooking, and hiking with her dog Tasha.

**Vicki L. Bogan** is an associate professor in the SC Johnson College of Business at Cornell University. Dr. Bogan is the founder and director of Cornell University's Institute for Behavioral and Household Finance and she is a founding co-editor of the academic journal *Financial Planning Review*. Her research interests are in the areas of financial economics, household finance, behavioral finance, and applied microeconomics, centering on issues involving investment decision-making behavior and financial markets. Dr. Bogan's impactful research has been published in leading economics and finance journals and she has testified before the U.S. House Committee on Financial Services on the gamification of finance. Dr. Bogan teaches finance courses for graduate and undergraduate students. She has received two outstanding educator awards and the SUNY Chancellor's Award for Excellence in Teaching. Dr. Bogan holds a Sc.B. in Applied Mathematics and Economics from Brown University, an M.B.A. in Finance and Strategic Management from the Wharton School of the University of Pennsylvania, an M.A. in Economics from Brown University, and a Ph.D. in Economics from Brown University. She also has held a visiting fellow appointment at Princeton University.

**Swarn Chatterjee** is the Bluerock Professor of Planning at the University of Georgia. He has served as the graduate coordinator and interim department chair for the Department of Financial Planning, Housing and Consumer Economics at the University of Georgia. He currently serves as associate editor for the *Journal of Financial Counseling and Planning* and *Financial Services Review*. He also serves on the editorial review board of the *Journal of Financial Planning*. He has published more than 100 scholarly articles on topics spanning financial planning, household finance, financial decision making, behavioral finance, and financial econometrics. He has previously served as the president of the Academy of Financial Services. For the past decade, Professor Chatterjee has taught classes on Wealth Management, Behavioral Economics, and Personal Finance.

**Isha Chawla** is a Ph.D. student in the Department of Family Science at the University of Maryland, College Park. Her research interests include family financial socialization, behavioral finance, FinTech, and gender-based dynamics in household financial planning. She completed her M.S. in Human Development and Family Studies focused on financial counseling and planning from Iowa State University. Further, she holds an M.B.A. in finance with more than two years of professional experience in the financial service sector. She has worked for the Bank of New York Mellon (BNY Mellon) and the IndusInd Bank, serving both the Indian and the Europe, the Middle East, and Africa (EMEA) markets.

**Chia-Li Chien**, Ph.D., CFP®, PMP®, CPBC, is a director of the Financial Planning Program of California Lutheran University. She is a succession program director at Value Growth Institute. Before her academic and consulting career, she held several senior management positions in Fortune 500 companies, including Diageo, ABB, CIGNA, and RSA Insurance Group. Dr. Chien is a frequent speaker about succession planning and has published three award-winning books (https://bit.ly/dr_chien). Dr. Chien serves on the boards of various national financial service associations. She hosts the NextGen Mentoring Forum webinar series and a succession blog. She holds a doctorate in financial and retirement planning. She is a certified financial planner (CFP®), project management professional (PMP®), and certified professional business coach (CPBC). Dr. Chien and her husband have one daughter. They have residences in Charlotte, NC, and Moorpark, CA.

**Shinae L. Choi** is an associate professor in the Department of Consumer Sciences at The University of Alabama. Dr. Choi received her Ph.D. in Consumer Science from Seoul National University, South Korea. Her research interests center on financial counseling, the cultural dynamics of financial and health-care decision making of families and consumers, psychological and financial well-being in older adults, and public policy evaluation. Dr. Choi has published her research in national and international peer-reviewed journals such as *Aging & Mental Health*, *Journal of Environmental Psychology*, *Journal of Family and Economic Issues*, *Financial Planning Review*, *Journal of Financial Counseling and Planning*, *Journal of Financial Therapy*, and the *International Journal of Consumer Studies*. She has taught classes in consumer marketing management, customer service management, financial counseling, and estate planning.

**Michelle Cull**, Ph.D., is the associate dean, engagement and senior lecturer in the School of Business at Western Sydney University, Australia. Dr. Cull has taught and researched in accounting and financial planning for more than 20 years and has held numerous leadership positions at the University including director of the academic program, head of program and academic course advisor (international). Dr. Cull is co-founder of the Western Sydney University Tax Clinic, developed the WalletSmart App, and has received numerous grants to support her research in financial planning. She has published in peer-reviewed academic journals, practitioner magazines, and textbooks across various areas of financial planning including trust, ethics, and financial literacy, with her research included as recommended reading for all financial advisers by the Financial Adviser Standards and Ethics Authority in Australia. Dr. Cull currently supervises ten Ph.D. students and four MRes students. Dr. Cull is an Allied Professional member of the FPA and a Fellow CPA. She volunteers her time as chair of the Macarthur Advisory Council for the Salvation Army, as an elected member of UniSuper's Consultative Committee, and as NSW Divisional Councillor for CPA Australia. She has previously served on the board of her local Chamber of Commerce and several advisory boards. Prior to becoming a full-time academic, Dr. Cull worked for 15 years in various financial and management accounting positions at ASX-100 listed companies. Dr. Cull has also worked as a consultant. When she is not working, Dr. Cull enjoys spending time with her family and playing field hockey and soccer.

**Leobardo ("Leo") Diosdado**, Ph.D., CFP®, lives atop a mountain just a few steps away from the Appalachian Trail with his loving partner, their intrepid Yorkshire Terrier, and benevolent Goldendoodle. As a first-generation, non-traditional student, he never thought about pursuing education further than his Bachelor of Economics degree, until a faculty mentor encouraged him to pursue financial planning. After completing his M.S. in Personal Financial Planning from Texas Tech University, he worked as a community banker in East Texas. During his tenure as a banker, he was tasked with developing and implementing a financial literacy program. That financial literacy project sparked Diosdado's research interest, which is why he chose to return to Texas Tech to pursue a doctorate. After completing the Ph.D. in Personal Financial Planning, he accepted a position at a university located within the Great Smokeys. Due to Dr. Diosdado's life experience and work exposure, he is able to connect with people from various walks of life, while researching and exploring various economic policies. His research interests include financial literacy, household consumption, the difference between farming and non-farming households as well as the economics associated with the purchase of a consumer's residential home.

**Lu Fan** is an assistant professor in the Department of Financial Planning, Housing and Consumer Economics at the University of Georgia. Prior to joining the faculty at the University of Georgia, she was an assistant professor of financial planning at the University of Missouri. Her research focuses on the financial decisions and behavior and well-being of individuals and households. She is particularly interested in financial advice-seeking, financial capability and literacy, and financial well-being. Dr. Fan received a Ph.D. in Financial Planning, Housing, and Consumer Economics and an M.A. in Journalism and Mass Communication from the University of Georgia.

**Jonathan J. Fox**, Ph.D., is the Ruth Whipp Sherwin endowed professor in the Department of Human Development and Family Studies and program leader in financial counseling and planning at Iowa State University. His research focuses on financial education and financial socialization. He has served as principal investigator (PI) for several financial education evaluations and his publications appear in journals such as *Financial Planning Review*, *Financial Counseling and Planning*, *Journal of Family Issues*, and *Journal of Consumer Affairs*. He teaches consumer economics and personal and family finance and received his Ph.D. in Consumer Economics from the University of Maryland.

**Adrian Furnham** was educated at the London School of Economics where he obtained a distinction in an MSc Econ., and at Oxford University where he completed a doctorate (D.Phil.) in 1981. He has subsequently earned a D.Sc. (1991) and D.Litt. (1995) degree. Previously a lecturer in Psychology at Pembroke College, Oxford, he was a professor of psychology at University College London from 1992 to 2018. He has lectured widely abroad and held scholarships and visiting professorships at, among others, the University of New South Wales, the University of the West Indies, the University of Hong Kong, and the University of KwaZulu-Natal. He has also been a visiting professor of management at Henley Management College. He is currently an adjunct professor of management at the Norwegian School of Management. He has written more than 1,300 scientific papers and 95 books.

**John E. Grable**, CFP®, teaches and conducts research in the Certified Financial Planner™ Board of Standards Inc. undergraduate and graduate programs at the University of Georgia where he holds an Athletic Association Endowed Professorship. Before entering the academic profession, he worked as a pension/benefits administrator and later as an investment advisor in an asset management firm. Dr. Grable served as the founding editor for *Journal of Personal Finance* and co-founding editor of *Journal of Financial Therapy* and *Financial Planning Review*. He is best known for his work in the areas of financial risk-tolerance assessment, behavioral financial planning, and psychophysiological economics. He has been the recipient of several research and publication awards and grants, and is active in promoting the link between research and financial planning practice where he has published more than 150 refereed papers and co-authored several financial planning textbooks, handbooks, and manuals.

**Simmy Grover** holds a master's degree in Biomedical Engineering from Imperial College London, as well as a master's degree with Distinction in Social Cognition from University College London (UCL). She has a Ph.D. in Organisational Psychology from UCL, which was completed under the supervision of Professor Adrian Furnham. Dr. Grover lectures in organizational and consulting psychology at UCL and her research includes individual differences, interpersonal relationships, organizational processes and structure, and their impact on individual and organizational performance. Dr. Grover is an executive coach for individuals in senior leadership positions focused on developing their behavior to become more successful and effective leaders and those looking to transition to the next step in their careers. Prior to her career in occupational psychology, Dr. Grover spent a number of years in financial services. She was honored as one of Financial News' "40 Under 40 Rising Stars of Trading and Technology" in 2011. Together with being widely quoted in the press, in publications including *Financial Times* and *Financial News* and those of Bloomberg, Reuters, and CNBC, she also spoke at key industry events across Europe and Asia, including TradeTech Europe, TradeTech Japan, International Trader Forum, FPL Japan, and FPL EMEA.

**Sherman D. Hanna** is a professor in the Human Sciences Department at Ohio State University, and chair of the Consumer Sciences Program. He received a B.S. in economics from the Massachusetts Institute of Technology and a Ph.D. in consumer economics from Cornell University. He has been the advisor for 37 Ph.D. students. His research has covered many topics in personal finance, including household saving, credit use, retirement adequacy, investment choices, risk tolerance, and racial/ethnic differences in financial decisions. He is an associate editor of the research journal *Financial Planning Review*, and was the founding editor of *Journal of Financial Counseling and Planning*. He was named a Distinguished Fellow of the American Council on Consumer Interests and also of the Association for Financial Counseling and Planning Education, and received the Financial Educator of the Year award from the Association for Financial Counseling and Planning Education. He has received 17 national awards for research papers. In a 2015 article in *Journal of Financial Planning* he was listed as the most prolific author in core financial planning journals from 1985 to 2014.

**Nathan Harness** received his bachelor's degree in finance from the University of Central Arkansas, a master's degree in finance from Texas Tech University, and a Ph.D. in personal financial planning from Texas Tech University. He currently serves as the TD Ameritrade director of Financial Planning at Texas A&M University and teaches the Fundamentals of Financial Planning, Retirement Planning, and the Investments for Financial Planning courses. His research interests include household heuristics and wealth accumulation, gender differences in financial planning, and retirement decision making. He has published in *Applied Economic Letters*, *Financial Services Review*, *International Journal of Business and Finance Research*, *Journal of Financial Services Professionals*, *Financial Counseling and Planning*, *Journal of Financial Planning*, and *Journal of Personal Finance*.

**Deborah C. Haynes** is an associate professor of Consumer and Family Economics at Montana State University. She is currently serving as the acting vice provost of Global Affairs and dean of International Programs at Montana State University. Dr. Haynes is internationally known for her work in consumer economics, small business management, and financial counseling.

**George W. Haynes** is professor and extension specialist in the Department of Agricultural Economics and Economics at Montana State University. His primary line of research is in small business finance, where he studies the financial structure of small businesses, the lending behavior of depository institutions, and the response of small businesses to disasters and disaster assistance. His instructional responsibilities include delivering the Montana agricultural outlook, conducting training for low resource borrowers, and educating farmers and ranchers on agricultural policy issues. Professor Haynes is a past president of the American Council on Consumer Interests, an associate editor for *Journal of Family and Economic Issues*, and an editorial board member for *Entrepreneurship Research Journal*. His research has been supported by the

National Science Foundation, the U.S. Small Business Administration, the United States Department of Agriculture (USDA), and the Montana Agricultural Experiment Station.

**So-Hyun Joo** received her bachelor's and master's degrees from Seoul National University and a Ph.D. degree from Virginia Tech. She was an assistant and associate professor of Personal Financial Planning at Texas Tech University, research associate at Samsung Finance Research Institute, and associate professor at Inha University, Korea. Currently, she is a professor of Consumer Studies at Ewha Womans University, Korea. Her research interests include personal financial wellness, financial help-seeking behavior, behavioral aspects of financial decision-making, and inter-generational/cross-cultural differences in consumer behavior. She has received numerous research awards from academic associations both in the United States (Association for Financial Counseling and Planning Education, American Council for Consumer Interests) and in Korea (Korean Society of Consumer Studies, Gallup Research Award, Korean Society of Consumer Policy and Education, Korean Academic Society of Financial Planning). She has served as a president for the Korean Academic Society of Financial Planning and the Korean Academy of Financial Consumers.

**Josephine Kass-Hanna** is an assistant professor at the Faculty of Business Administration and Management at Saint Joseph University of Beirut, Lebanon. She holds a Ph.D. in economics from the University of Perpignan in France. Her scholarly work revolves around financial inclusion, financial and digital literacy, poverty and inequality, and the economic resilience of vulnerable populations. She has been recently focusing on examining the economic vulnerabilities of Syrian refugees in Lebanon to better inform strategies needed to support them and enhance their overall resilience. She has been contributing, for three years now, to the work of Think 20 (T20), the research and policy advice network of the G20.

**Jinhee Kim**, Ph.D., is a professor in the Department of Family Science, School of Public Health at the University of Maryland. She also serves as assistant director and program leader in Family and Consumer Sciences with the University of Maryland Extension, College of Agriculture and Natural Resources. Her main research areas are financial management, family well-being, and health outcomes. She also evaluates the impact of interventions aimed at improving financial security and family well-being. Her research has been recognized with best paper awards by *Journal of Financial Counseling and Planning* in 2012 and 2013 and by *Family and Consumer Sciences Research Journal* in 2013 and 2017. She has led the development, delivery, and evaluation of extension education programs for various audiences. She has provided more than 2,000 Extension and financial professional trainings and has taught departmental courses addressing family financial management and credit. She is currently serving as associate editor for *Journal of Financial Counseling and Planning* and *Journal of Family and Economic Issues*. Dr. Kim received the Mid-Career Award from the ACCI in 2009. She was recognized as Distinguished Fellow Award by the Association for Financial Counseling and Planning Education in 2019.

**Kyoung Tae Kim** is an associate professor and graduate program coordinator in the Department of Consumer Sciences at the University of Alabama where he teaches on the CFP Board registered undergraduate and master programs. He received a bachelor's degree in economics and a Ph.D. in consumer sciences from The Ohio State University, and a master's degree in economics from Purdue University. He has published more than 50 peer-reviewed research articles including in *Applied Economics Letters, Economics Letters, Economic Modelling, International Journal of Consumer Studies, Journal of Consumer Affairs, Journal of Economic Psychology, Journal of Family and Economic Issues*, and *Journal of Financial Counseling and Planning*. He also serves as a member of the editorial board for *Journal of Consumer Affairs* and *Journal of Financial Counseling and Planning*.

**Michelle Kruger,** Ph.D., CFP® is a financial planner at Elwood & Goetz Wealth Advisory Group in Athens, Georgia. Michelle completed her Ph.D. with a concentration in financial planning at The University of Georgia after graduating magna cum laude with a B.B.A. in finance from the Terry College of Business. Michelle previously held the position of assistant professor of finance at Loras College in Dubuque, Iowa. Michelle has taught a variety of finance and personal finance courses at Loras College and the University of Georgia. During her time at UGA, she served as a financial counselor and supervised undergraduate student financial counselors at the ASPIRE Clinic, an interdisciplinary teaching and research facility, applying marriage and family therapy theories and techniques to her work with financial clients. Michelle has also served as a site coordinator with UGA's Volunteer Income Tax Assistance Program, supervising undergraduate students in preparing tax returns for members of the Athens community. Michelle's research has been published in academic journals such as *Journal of Financial Planning, Journal of Financial Therapy,* and *Financial Services Review.* Her research publications have focused on topics such as the financial satisfaction and financial management practices of couples, risk tolerance, and behaviors associated with building wealth.

**Eun-Jin (EJ) Kwak** is a Ph.D. candidate in the Department of Financial Planning, Housing and Consumer Economics at the University of Georgia. She holds a bachelor's degree in Economics and a master's degree in Business Management with an emphasis in Big Data Analysis. Prior to entering the academic profession, she worked at J.P. Morgan and UBS as an operation analyst. Ms. Kwak is the co-author of several peer-reviewed research papers. She was awarded the outstanding financial planning graduate student at the University of Georgia 2021, and the best research award at the Financial Planning Association/Academy of Financial Services 2020 conference. Her research focuses on financial risk-tolerance/aversion assessment, household finance, behavioral financial planning, and machine learning.

**Sunwoo T. Lee** is an assistant professor in the School of Administrative Studies at York University. She received a B.S. in Consumer Sciences and Business Administration, an M.S. in Consumer Sciences from the Seoul National University, and a Ph.D. in Consumer Sciences from the Ohio State University. She has broad research interests related to household economics, financial behaviors, financial decision making processes, and the personal characteristics affecting those financial decisions.

**Jonquil Lowe,** B.Sc. (Econ), M.Sc. (Social Research Methods), SFHEA, ACSI, is a senior lecturer in Economics and Personal Finance at The Open University (the United Kingdom's largest university and a distance-learning institute), specializing in the areas of retirement provision, investment and taxation, and author/co-author of numerous books, including *Essential Personal Finance: A Practical Guide for Students.* She has a background as an investment analyst and subsequently head of money research at a leading consumer organization. She now combines academic work with running her own business as a freelance personal finance practitioner and consumer advocate, and has worked extensively with regulators, consumer organizations, and financial firms to promote wider access to, and understanding of, financial services.

**Angela C. Lyons** is an associate professor and director for the Center for Economic and Financial Education at the University of Illinois at Urbana-Champaign in the United States. She received her Ph.D. in economics from the University of Texas at Austin. Her research focuses on economic and financial inclusion, financial and digital literacy, FinTech, poverty and inequality, and the economic empowerment and protection of vulnerable populations. Dr. Lyons has assisted more than 40 countries in creating more inclusive and resilient societies around three main pillars – people, planet, and prosperity. She is currently a member of the Think 20 (T20), the research and policy advice network of the G20. She has served on the T20 under three G20 Presidencies (Japan, Saudi Arabia, and Italy).

**Claire Matthews** is an associate professor and Director, Academic Quality for the Massey Business School since 2014, having joined Massey University in 1996 after 12 years in various roles with Trust Bank. Prior to her current role, Claire taught courses in banking and financial advice at both undergraduate and postgraduate levels. She continues to supervise Masters and PhD students. Her research interests centre around consumer's financial behaviour, decisions and attitudes, with a particular interest in payments as well as financial capability and retirement planning, with a particular focus on New Zealand's KiwiSaver scheme. She is the author of the Westpac-Massey Fin-Ed Centre's annual Retirement Expenditure Guidelines report and one of the team of researchers for the Centre's longitudinal study on financial literacy in New Zealand. Claire has a PhD in Banking on the subject of *Switching Costs in the New Zealand Banking Market*. She is a Research Associate with the Westpac-Massey Fin-Ed Centre, a Fellow of the Financial Services Institute of Australasia and a Certified Member of the Institute of Finance Professionals NZ Inc. She is on the board of Pukaha Mt Bruce, a former director of NZCU Baywide and Co-op Money NZ, and a former trustee and chair of the Eastern and Central Community Trust.

**Gianni Nicolini**, Ph.D. is associate professor in Banking and Finance at the University of Rome 'Tor Vergata' (Rome, Italy), Faculty of Economics, Department of Management and Law (DML). His main research interests concern consumer finance and financial literacy, with a special interest on the assessment of financial literacy. He has published books as an author and as an editor with international publishers on consumer-related issues. He has taught in several universities in different countries, including the United States, the United Kingdom, Germany, France, and Italy. He is a Fulbright scholar and has been a member of the American Council on Consumer Interests (ACCI) since 2010.

**Liana Holanda Nepomuceno Nobre** is an adjunct professor of Corporate Finance at Federal University of the Semi-Arid Region-UFERSA (Brazil). Dr. Nobre is currently coordinating the master's program in Business Administration at UFERSA. Dr. Nobre's work focuses specifically on decision making under the perspective of behavioral finance, financing, and investment decisions. She is well known for her work that helped unify definitions of risk tolerance, risk preference, and risk capacity.

**Wade D. Pfau**, Ph.D., CFA, RICP® is the program director of the Retirement Income Certified Professional® designation and a professor of Retirement Income at The American College of Financial Services in King of Prussia, PA. As well, he is a principal and director for McLean Asset Management. He holds a doctorate in Economics from Princeton University and has published more than sixty peer-reviewed research articles in a wide variety of academic and practitioner journals. He hosts the Retirement Researcher website, and is a contributor to *Forbes*, *Advisor Perspectives*, *Journal of Financial Planning*, and is an expert panelist for *Wall Street Journal*. He is the author of the books *Safety-First Retirement Planning: An Integrated Approach for a Worry-Free Retirement*, *How Much Can I Spend in Retirement? A Guide to Investment-Based Retirement Income Strategies*, and *Reverse Mortgages: How to Use Reverse Mortgages to Secure Your Retirement*. His next book is called *Retirement Planning Guidebook: Navigating the Important Decisions for Retirement Success*.

**Abed G. Rabbani, CFP®** is an assistant professor in the Department of Personal Financial Planning at the University of Missouri. He received a bachelor's degree from Khulna University, Bangladesh, and a master's degree from James Cook University, Australia. He also earned a master's degree from the University of Arkansas at Pine Bluff and a Ph.D. in Financial Planning at the University of Georgia. His research is focused primarily on financial risk tolerance, financial knowledge, and financial wellness. He is the lead investigator on the Investment Risk Tolerance Assessment program and a partner administrator of the 2020 Study on Collegiate Financial Wellness (SCFW).

**Cliff A. Robb** is an associate professor of Consumer Science at the University of Wisconsin, Madison. He is the faculty director for the Personal Finance program in the School of Human Ecology. His research interests include financial decision making (with an emphasis on the relationship between financial knowledge and observable financial behavior), college student financial behavior (with an emphasis on student loans), and financial satisfaction and well-being. Dr. Robb has published numerous peer-reviewed academic papers and he serves on the editorial boards for *Journal of Financial Planning*, *Journal of Consumer Affairs*, *Journal of Financial Counseling and Planning*, and *Financial Planning Review*.

**Martin C. Seay**, Ph.D., CFP® is department head and associate professor of Personal Financial Planning at Kansas State University. He is a past president of the Financial Planning Association® (FPA®), the principal membership organization for Certified Financial Planner™ professionals. He received the Kenneth Tremblay Early Career Housing Award from the Housing Education and Research Association in 2016, the Richard L. D. Morse Early Career Award from the American Council on Consumer Interests in 2018, the Distinguished Financial Planning Alumnus Award from the University of Georgia in 2021, and was selected by *InvestmentNews* as a member of their 40 Under 40 class in 2020. His research focuses on borrowing decisions, how psychological characteristics shape financial behavior, and how households receive financial advice. His work has been published in *Journal of Economic Psychology*, *Journal of Behavioral Finance*, *Journal of Financial Counseling and Planning*, *Financial Services Review*, *Journal of Consumer Affairs*, *Journal of Positive Psychology*, *Journal of Family and Economic Issues*, *Personality and Individual Differences*, and *Financial Planning Review*, among others. His research was recognized with the 2014, 2017, and 2019 FPA Annual Conference Best Research Paper Awards, the 2016 CFP Board's ACCI Financial Planning Award, and the 2016 Montgomery-Warschauer Award.

**Derek J. Sensenig**, MBA, CFP® is the senior vice president of Financial Planning for Encompass Advisory Services, LLC in Houston, TX, and is a Ph.D. student at Kansas State University in the Personal Financial Planning Program. Previously, he served as a military training instructor in the United States Air Force. Derek has a B.S. in human resource management from Park University and an M.B.A. from Webster University. In his free time, Derek enjoys playing softball and spending time with friends and family.

**Michael G. Thomas Jr.**, Ph.D. is an accredited financial counselor (AFC®) and a lecturer at the University of Georgia. His research focuses on financial empathy, data visualization's effects on financial behavior, and the connection between brain function and money. Dr. Thomas's philosophy on how to effectively interact with money can be summed up in his Ted Talk: Financial Empathy: Understanding the Story Beneath the Numbers. Utilizing financial empathy as a process for active listening and the creation of client-focused financial recommendations are reflected in two financial literacy and capability programs he helped co-create: Money Dawgs and Discovering Money Solutions. Dr. Thomas's life-long goal is to help underserved communities establish, grow, and sustain their wealth, utilizing an intra- and inter-family wealth-creation process.

**Inga Timmerman** is an associate professor at California State University Northridge and is the Dr. Mary Jean Scheuer Professor of Finance. She has a Ph.D. in Finance from Florida Atlantic University and is a certified financial planner (CFP®). Her research is mostly concentrated on two fields: corporate finance and financial planning. Dr. Timmerman's current projects explore the use and perceptions individuals have about the financial planning profession and the drivers that motivate people to save. Additionally, she is the founder and president of Attainable Wealth, a fee-only financial planning and investment management practice.

**Robert van Beek**, CFP® currently serves on the board of directors for the Financial Planning Association® (FPA®), the principal membership organization for certified financial planner™ professionals and those who support the financial planning process. As the founder and director of his financial planning and investment consulting boutique, About Life & Finance, Mr. van Beek is regularly featured in the media, has authored more than 20 books, and speaks throughout the United States and Europe at various organizations and universities. In addition to this role on the FPA Board of Directors, he currently serves as a member of the editorial board of the *Journal of Financial Therapy* and is a member of CFA VBA Netherlands Behavioral Economics Commission. Until 2019, Mr. van Beek served on local planning and certification organizations, including the DSI Advice Exam Commission, which was responsible for creating and assessing MiFID and ESMA exams for licensed investment professionals. In 2021 he set up a new Financial Life Planning Post Graduate Program at University Colleges Leuven Limburg (UCLL) and joined the Financial Psychology Institute Europe as a member of the Advisory Council. Robert is married and living happily with his wife Liesbet and their two children in Belgium.

**Dee Warmath** is currently an assistant professor of Consumer Economics in the College of Family and Consumer Sciences at the University of Georgia where she teaches courses in consumer well-being, social entrepreneurship, and consumer analytics. She earned her Ph.D. in Consumer Science from the University of Wisconsin-Madison and a master's in Sociology from Vanderbilt University. After a successful 28-year career in industry, Dr. Warmath made the switch to the academic career path. Her research examines the individual's capacity to make decisions and the impact of involving others in those decisions on well-being in the areas of finances and health. She currently serves as a special advisor to the Australian Securities and Investment Commission's longitudinal project on financial hardship and well-being. She served as the principal investigator for the U.S. Consumer Financial Protection Bureau on its project to define and measure financial well-being, as well as test hypotheses of its drivers including financial skill. Her research has been published in numerous journals, including *Journal of Consumer Research*, *Journal of Consumer Affairs, Journal of Public Policy & Marketing, Journal of Business Research, British Journal of Sports Medicine, Journal of Athletic Training, and Sports Health,* and presented at a variety of conferences including the American Council of Consumer Interests, Association for Consumer Research, CFP Academic Research Colloquium, Financial Planning Association, and Frontiers in Service. She is also a fellow of the Center for Financial Security at the University of Wisconsin-Madison.

**Kenneth J. White Jr.** earned his Ph.D. in Consumer Sciences with a focus on Family Resource Management from The Ohio State University and joined the faculty at the University of Georgia as an assistant professor in the Department of Financial Planning, Housing and Consumer Economics. Dr. White teaches undergraduate and graduate students in UGA's CFP® Board Registered Programs. His primary areas of instruction are retirement planning and income tax planning. Dr. White's research interests involve financial literacy, education, socialization, and well-being of historically marginalized populations. His work can be seen in core financial planning journals, such as *Journal of Financial Planning, Journal of Financial Therapy, Journal of Family and Economic Issues, Family and Consumer Sciences Research Journal,* and *Financial Services Review.* He has also published work in international journals, such as *Contemporary Family Therapy* and *Sport, Business, and Management.* Dr. White regularly collaborates across disciplines, with colleagues at universities and colleges nationwide, and often conducts research with current and former graduate and undergraduate students.

**Jing Jian Xiao** is a professor in the Department of Human Development and Family Science, College of Health Sciences, University of Rhode Island. He also serves as the editor of *Journal of Financial Counseling and Planning.* His research interests include how to help consumers increase financial literacy, perform desirable financial behaviors, and enhance financial capability for improving financial and overall well-being. He has published numerous research papers in professional journals in consumer finance and related fields. He published books such as *The Mathematics of Personal Finance, Consumer Economic Wellbeing,* and *Handbook of Consumer Finance Research.* He is also editing a book series entitled *International Series on Consumer Science.* He served as the president of the American Council on Consumer Interests (ACCI) and as the president of the Asian Consumer and Family Economics Association (ACFEA), among others. He received his Ph.D. in consumer economics from the Oregon State University, and M.S. and B.S. degrees in Economics at the Zhongnan University of Economics and Law. He was the inaugural chair holder of TCA Professorship and director of TCA Institute of Consumer Financial Education Research at the University of Arizona in 2005 to 2007 and the editor of *Journal of Family and Economic Issues* in 2001 to 2011.

# Preface

A worldwide pandemic, fears of job loss, forced quarantines, mandated face coverings, political unrest, natural disasters, and a daily need to pivot from one's normal routine provided the backdrop to the development of this handbook. When first conceptualized, our thought, as editors, was to invite the foremost researchers and thought leaders working in the area of personal finance to contribute their ideas and views on some of the foundational elements that comprise the field of personal finance. We were unsure about how our invitations might be received. At first, we were concerned that the concept of this handbook would need to be abandoned or postponed. We prepared for the worst, expecting negative emails.

We were instead overwhelmed with the positive responses to our invitations. To this day, we are not sure if the Covid-19 pandemic heightened our colleagues' awareness of the need to share their thoughts on the importance of studying and practicing personal finance (and helping to increase financial literacy) or whether our colleagues are just, at their core, dedicated, intentional, and productive. In reality, it may be a combination of these factors, but the bottom line is that those who contributed to this handbook are to be congratulated for their fine work and commitment to building and expanding the field of personal finance.

The chapters included in this handbook discuss the main themes and objectives of personal finance. The material included here represents the leading ideas, debates, approaches, and methodologies in the field. As noted in the first chapter of this handbook, the challenge of editing a compilation of chapters of and about personal finance is that the term "personal finance" is an ill-defined concept. The notion of personal finance being a field of study and professional practice is a relatively recent phenomenon. The study of the way individuals and households manage financial resources has historically been the bailiwick of academicians conducting research and teaching about family resource management, consumer economics, family economics, consumption economics, and consumer education. The majority of those studying personal finance topics have traditionally been housed in university home economics units (now known as family and consumer sciences, human sciences, and human ecology). The interest in how individuals, families, and households deal with day-to-day financial concerns began to shift toward mainstream departments of finance and economics beginning in the 1990s. This shift in interest among non-home economists gained strength when John Campbell published his influential treatise called *Household Finance* in 2006. Today, personal finance is emerging as an interdisciplinary field of study informed by economics, psychology, sociology, family economics, resource management, human sciences, education, counseling, and family studies.

The goal of those who conduct personal finance research (and of those who provide personal financial services to consumers) is to better understand how individuals and families (and other households) acquire, develop, and allocate financial resources to meet current and future financial needs. Personal finance encompasses the use of a

https://doi.org/10.1515/9783110727692-204

variety of tools such as financial statements, checking and savings accounts, investment products and strategies, and daily financial management products and services that enhance the management of debt, promote homeownership, reduce bankruptcy, improve risk management, facilitate tax planning, advance retirement planning, improve special needs planning, and facilitate estate planning. The goal of applying personal finance models, tools, and techniques is to improve the financial capabilities (e.g., financial literacy, financial knowledge, financial capacity) and financial security of individuals, families, and households. In this regard – and as highlighted throughout this handbook – personal finance differs from household finance, economics, and traditional finance in that these fields of study generally focus on developing a better understanding of the global macroeconomic and microeconomic environments, market systems, policy, and corporate outcomes. Rather than focus exclusively on consumption patterns, personal finance researchers typically attempt to better understand the determinants of financial well-being. In this way, personal finance research tends to be applied by financial service practitioners in their day-to-day work and by policymakers who are interested in addressing issues related to financial justice.

As editors, we envision this handbook being used as a core reference among researchers, financial service practitioners, educators, and policymakers. We also believe that this handbook provides an excellent supplementary source of readings for those teaching introductory graduate-level classes and senior-level undergraduate courses in personal finance, financial planning, consumer studies, and household finance. In this regard, the handbook includes a robust index, and self-study questions that correspond to each chapter are provided at https://www.degruyter.com/document/isbn/9783110727692/html.

Our sincere hope is that personal finance stakeholders will find this handbook to be a foundational reference source, a guide to the leading ideas, approaches, and methodologies used in the field, and an inspiration for future research and debate. We want to say thank you to everyone who contributed to this handbook and to Eun-Jin Kwak for her outstanding editorial assistance. We are also deeply appreciative of Stefan Giesen and David Repetto for first conceptualizing this project and Jaya Dalal for content editorial assistance.

## Organization and Structure of the Handbook

This handbook is organized into five sections. The first section provides a broad introduction to the discipline of personal finance. The following two sections of the handbook are organized around the core elements of personal finance research and practice: saving, investing, asset management, and financial security. The fourth section of the handbook looks forward by introducing future research, practice, and policy directions. The handbook concludes with thoughts from a journal editor and a summary that provides an educational and research agenda for the future.

The organization and structure of the handbook, and each chapter, was developed using aspects of the seventh edition of the American Psychological Association (APA) formatting guidelines. In most cases, words, terms, and phrases were retained based on the home country of origin of the contributing author(s). Steps were taken to ensure that chapter material retained an international perspective. It is important to note, however, that in some situations material in the handbook, by definition and topic, focuses on U.S. data, rules, regulations, and policies. The intent of sharing this information was not to imply that policies, procedures, and guidelines used in the United States are the "gold standard," or that what occurs in the United States should be modeled worldwide. The intent of including U.S. data and practice standards was to illustrate the commonalities across countries and regions, using U.S. data and information as examples. Each contributor to the handbook was asked to pay close attention to stressing the similarities in customs, laws, and language among those living and working in Africa, Europe, the Middle East, Australia, New Zealand, India, China, and throughout Asia. As editors, we believe that the chapter contributors did an excellent job in this regard. We also believe that the chapter contributions advance the field of study and practice of personal finance.

John E. Grable and Swarn Chatterjee
Athens, Georgia, U.S.A.
August 2021

Part I: **Introduction to the Discipline of Personal Finance**

John E. Grable, Swarn Chatterjee

# 1 Defining Personal Finance

**Abstract:** The purpose of this chapter is to provide a historical review of the development of personal finance over the past 125 years and to provide a definition of personal finance that will spur further discussion about the role of personal finance in the 21st century among the stakeholders in what can broadly be described as the interdisciplinary field (and profession) of personal finance. Based on a historical review of the development of personal finance as an interdisciplinary profession, and a review of the usage of the term "personal finance," this chapter puts forward the following definition of personal finance:

> Personal finance is the study and application of concepts, tools, and techniques associated with the planning and management of personal and household financial activities, including generating income, managing spending and debt, saving, investing, and protecting sources of income and assets in a way that informs practices and policies designed to enhance the well-being of individuals, families, and households.

This chapter concludes with a discussion about the appropriate academic home for those who conduct personal finance research and teach others about personal finance.

**Keywords:** personal finance, interdisciplinary, field of study, history

## Introduction

What is personal finance? The challenge associated with answering this question is that there is no single definition of, or even a consensus opinion about, the term. At best, personal finance is an ill-defined concept. The purpose of this chapter is to provide a historical perspective of the development of personal finance, as something studied and practiced, over the past 125 years. In this regard, one primary objective served as a guidepost in the development of this chapter; namely, when writing about the historical development of personal finance, we strived to unify the separate and unconnected definitions of personal finance into a definition that is both accurate and adaptable enough to meet the needs of researchers, educators, policymakers, and other stakeholders. We hope that this definition will spur further discussion about the role of personal finance in the 21st century among the stakeholders in what can broadly be described as the interdisciplinary field (and profession) of personal finance.

John E. Grable, Swarn Chatterjee, University of Georgia

https://doi.org/10.1515/9783110727692-001

## Historical Perspective

Today, there are more than a dozen personal finance textbooks used in colleges and universities throughout the world. A shopper browsing through any well-stocked bookstore will find numerous general public and trade books and manuals written to help the average consumer improve their household financial situation. The concept of personal finance has permeated popular culture to such a degree that nearly everyone thinks they know what one means when they use the phrase "personal finance," yet when asked, most people cannot summarize the history of this elusive concept.

Although the historical roots of personal finance have been debated, the general consensus is that the beginnings of personal finance, which includes the tracking of income and expenditures at the household level as a means to improving a household's financial position, started when David Davies (1795) undertook a quasi-scientific investigation into the way families in Berkshire, England allocated resources to meet needs and wants (Abdel-Ghany, 2001). In the years following Davies' work, Eden (1797), Engel (1857), Wright (1875), Le Play (1877), and others expanded these analyses to include tests of the associations among well-being, the social environment, income generation, and expenditures on good and services at the household level (Gross et al., 1980). A significant development in this regard occurred in 1862 in the United States. This was the year when the U.S. Congress passed the Morrill Act, which established the U.S. Department of Agriculture. The Act also created the land grant university structure where the focus of education was on the mechanical arts, agriculture, and home economics (many of the largest universities in the United States today are land grant institutions). The teaching of what is generally referred to today as "personal finance" was most often housed in land grant colleges of home economics (Hira, 2009; Liston, 1993).

The adoption of personal finance concepts, terminology, tools, and techniques into home economics curriculums was based on the realities of the 19th century. At that time, nearly all academic research on the topic of economic resource allocation was undertaken at the community or national level rather than at the individual, family, or household unit level, and thus studied in colleges of arts and sciences and departments of economics. More importantly, however, was the notion that household production was split between husbands and wives, with income-production (typically through farm or manual labor) being the domain of husbands and the allocation of household financial resources the primary function of wives (Jones, 2002; McCloat and Caraher, 2018). This resulted in the placement of personal and household finance educational topics in home economics programs.

The strong linkage between home economics and household financial management topics was solidified after the Tenth Lake Placid Conference in 1908 in which the body of knowledge for home economics was organized (Baugher et al., 2000). Under the auspices of the American Home Economics Association (AHEA), household production and allocation decision making were further refined in 1933 when the family economics subdivision of the AHEA was established. This development was a historical artifact. Few women academicians in the 1920s and 1930s were allowed to study business or economics at the doctoral level, and women were rarely hired to fill tenure-track lines in colleges of business or departments of economics. By default, female scholars who were interested in the study of personal finance topics were driven to conduct their work under the umbrella of home economics. Colleges of home economics became the conduit for the first, second, and third waves of feminism (McGregor, 2015).

Beginning in the 1950s, numerous descriptions and subdisciplines of home economics were organized around the "purposeful behavior involved in the creation and use of resources to achieve family goals" (Gross et al., 1980, p. 6). Specializations known as family economics, consumer economics, consumption economics, household management, and family resource management emerged to describe the various research and practice functions associated with household financial decision-making (Abdel-Ghany, 2001; Hira, 2009).[1] By the 1960s, researchers outside of home economics began to take an interest in what, up until that time, had been primarily home economics' activities. According to Becker (1965), "New Home Economics," which was premised on the notion of time allocation, opened up new explorations into the way money is conceptualized, earned, and allocated at the household level. An explosion of work on home production, human and social capital, and the division of labor between women and men took hold in colleges of business and departments of economics, marketing, and other business-related fields. While researchers in home economics – or what is now termed Family and Consumer Sciences – moved in the direction of conceptualizing the family in terms of ecological and resource management models (Deacon and Firebaugh, 1988), those coming from a more traditional business and economic background began explorations of personal finance topics from a strictly household finance and behavioral finance/economics perspective. The reason for this approach, as noted below, is that personal finance has never fit in well within traditional models of finance or economics.

Outside of the family and consumer sciences tradition, the study of personal finance, particularly in departments of finance, is relatively recent. According to Miller (1999), finance as currently conceptualized, has a starting point corresponding to the 1950s. Finance research tends to follow one of two traditions (see Miller, 1999): the business school or an economics department approach. Those with a business school background often use a micro-normative perspective to guide their work. When viewed this way, a decision maker "is seen as maximizing some objective function, be it utility, expected return, or shareholder value, taking the prices of securities in

---

[1] Outside the United States, names like domestic science, living science, home science, practical life studies, household technology, the science of living, and consumer studies have been used to describe traditional home economics activities (Darling, 1995).

the market as given" (Miller, 1999, p. 96). On the other hand, economists tend to use a macro-normative perspective where it is assumed that decision makers are optimizers. With this assumption in place, the goal of research is to infer the evolution of market prices. Personal finance, as a descriptive and sometimes normative field of study, fails to align well with either tradition. As noted by Badarinza et al. (2019), personal finance can better be seen as an extension of household finance when household finance is defined as "the study of how households do (and should) use financial instruments to attain their economic objective" (p. 110). Similar to what has occurred between economics and psychology, it is reasonable to assume that the parameters of what constitutes finance research will change over time as the assumptions underlying finance and economics models are adapted to account for psychological, behavioral, and applied plausibilities (Kahneman, 2003), thus creating more space for personal finance research to occur in more conventional contexts.

It is important to acknowledge that the actual formation of personal finance as a field of study has emerged quite slowly, which aligns with the development of finance as an academic discipline (Miller, 1999). Today, personal finance is sometimes embedded in larger and more established fields of study or assumed to be an element of some other functional field of research and practice. There has been very little cross-disciplinary dialog among those studying personal finance topics. This has resulted, unfortunately, in a lack of appreciation for the long and robust history of the study of the financial situation of individuals, families, and households. Finance, economics, marketing, psychology, and social work researchers who are new to the study of personal finance topics often search their field's core journals for citations on topics of interest. Because much of the early work related to personal finance topics was published in home economics' journals (very few business or economics journals published personal, family, or household finance research prior to Campbell's (2006) introduction of the term "household finance"), key references and theoretical orientations tend to get lost. Additionally, more relevant personal finance papers are often hidden in literature searches because very few personal finance journals are indexed. Thus, sometimes researchers claim that significant gaps in the personal finance literature exist. While certainly true in some situations, these claims are often overstated.

The *Journal of Financial Counseling and Planning* presents an interesting example of this situation. This journal is published by the Association for Financial Counseling and Planning Education (AFCPE). AFCPE was established in the early 1990s by researchers who were primarily interested in personal finance research and practice. Although the journal has been published for more than 30 years, it was only recently that the journal was indexed. Because of the relative obscurity of the journal, few outside of the AFCPE membership actively monitor what has been, and is being, published. This lack of review means that what are sometimes considered gaps in the literature may be more akin to holes that remain to be filled.

# Personal Finance in the 21st Century

This historical sketch leads to today. Before defining personal finance, it is useful to first place personal finance in the context of the modern academy. The goal of those who conduct personal finance research (and of those who provide personal financial services to consumers) is to better understand how individuals and families (and other households) acquire, develop, and allocate financial resources to meet current and future financial needs. According to Schuchardt et al. (2007), personal finance encompasses the study and use of tools such as financial statements, checking and savings accounts, investment products and strategies, and daily financial management products and services (e.g., management of debt, homeownership, bankruptcy, risk-management techniques, tax planning, retirement planning, special needs planning, and estate planning). The goal of applying personal finance models, tools, and techniques is to improve the financial capabilities, financial literacy, and financial security of individuals and households. In this regard, personal finance differs from household finance, economics, and traditional finance in that these fields of study generally focus on gaining a better understanding of the global macroeconomic and microeconomic environment, market systems, policy, and corporate outcomes. Rather than focus exclusively on consumption patterns, personal finance researchers typically attempt to better understand the determinants of financial well-being at the individual, household, or family unit level.

Where does this leave personal finance in the 21st century? We believe, in concordance with Schuchardt et al. (2007), that personal finance is an interdisciplinary field of study, and that the delivery of personal financial services to consumers represents a professional activity. As evidence of this assertion, consider the following definitions: a *discipline* "has a body of knowledge and seeks to discover new knowledge from within its somewhat rigid borders" (Darling, 1995, pp. 371–372). Merriam-Webster (n.d.) describes a discipline as a field of study based on one's education and/or body of knowledge. Although closely related, a *profession* has a defined body of knowledge that is used to serve people. According to Darling (1995), "a profession assimilates and utilizes information from both internal and external sources in order to pursue explanations of socially relevant questions that may or may not be capable of solution" (p. 372). A profession can also be viewed as a vocation or calling. Professionals are governed by codes of ethics and strive to provide services with integrity and in a competent manner (Cruess et al., 2004). Based on these conceptualizations, and as exemplified historically, personal finance can be viewed as an interdisciplinary field of study and profession (Schuchardt et al., 2007), where the body of knowledge in personal finance has been, and continues to be, informed by other disciplines. As illustrated in Figure 1.1, personal finance is informed and shaped by research, pedagogy, and practice standards originating in human sciences, education, counseling, family and consumer sciences, economics, psychology, sociology, resource management, family and consumer economics, finance, marketing, social work, and other related disciplines.

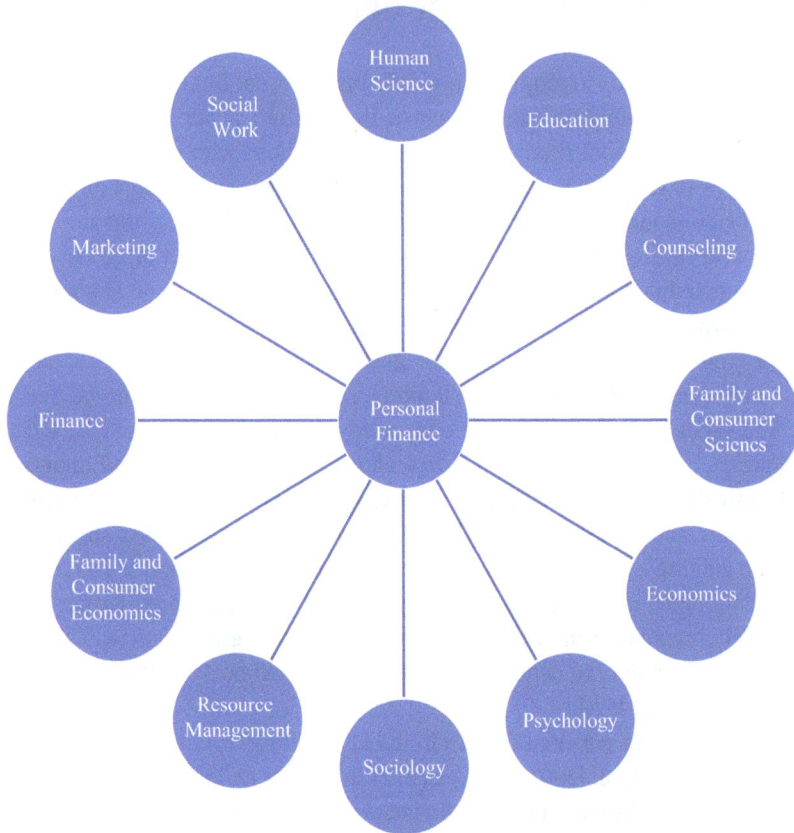

**Figure 1.1:** Personal Finance: An Interdisciplinary Field of Study.

## A Definition of Personal Finance

Identifying an authoritative definition of personal finance is an elusive task. One of the most thorough attempts to conceptualize what is meant by the term "personal finance" was undertaken by Schuchardt and her associates (2007). They made the following observation in relation to the notion of the term (p. 67):

> Personal finance [can be] viewed as an application of the principles of finance, resource management, consumer education, and the sociology and psychology of decision making to the study of the ways that individuals, families, and households acquire, develop, and allocated monetary resources to meet their current and future financial needs.

Schuchardt et al. (2007) went on to note that at the center of all personal finance research and practice is an individual or family unit decision maker. Hira (2009) reiterated this point when stating that personal finance is not a consumer or consumption-focused field of study but, instead, a research and practice discipline that describes, explains, and predicts individual, family, and household attitudes and behaviors. A unifying theme that runs through nearly all personal finance research is an explicit or implied focus on overall and financial well-being. Hira and Schuchardt et al. did acknowledge, however, that financial decision makers are influenced by broader markets, institutions, governments, and socioeconomic trends related to demography and geopolitical events.

While personal finance research has a tendency to be eclectic (Israelsen, 1989), the following research topics tend to be grouped under the personal finance umbrella:
(a) family income source and use
(b) time management
(c) household division of labor
(d) money use
(e) financial management
(f) financial security
(g) retirement preparedness
(h) household risk-taking
(i) marriage and money
(j) saving
(k) debt
(l) household expenditure patterns
(m) financial satisfaction and well-being
(n) financial decision-making
(o) housing and mortgage choices
(p) the effect of money on divorce and marriage
(q) budgeting
(r) insurance
(s) taxation
(t) credit usage

At its most fundamental level, Schuchardt et al. (2007) noted that the interdisciplinary field of personal finance includes a wide number of stakeholders, including:
(a) researchers
(b) educators (community, extension, middle school, high school, and college)
(c) service providers (financial counselors, financial planners, financial advisors, and other financial service professionals)
(d) firms and institutions
(e) policymakers (local, state, and federal)

Given the topics associated with personal finance, the manner in which the interdisciplinary field of personal finance is informed and shaped by other disciplines, and the diverse number and type of personal finance stakeholders, we propose the following definition of personal finance:

> *Personal finance is the study and application of concepts, tools, and techniques associated with the planning and management of personal and household financial activities, including generating income, managing spending and debt, saving, investing, and protecting sources of income and assets in a way that informs practices and policies designed to enhance the well-being of individuals, families, and households.*[2]

## Research and Policy Issues

The notion of personal finance being an interdisciplinary field of study and professional occupation is a relatively recent phenomenon. As already discussed, the study of the way individuals and households manage financial resources has historically been the bailiwick of academicians conducting research and teaching about family resource management, consumer economics, family economics, consumption economics, and consumer education. The majority of those studying personal finance topics have traditionally been housed in university family and consumer sciences units or applied interdisciplinary departments. As noted earlier in this chapter, interest in how individuals, families, and households deal with day-to-day financial concerns is slowly shifting toward mainstream departments of finance, economics, and marketing. This shift in interest among those outside of family and consumer sciences gained strength when Campbell published his influential treatise called "Household Finance" in 2006. Campbell's (2006) work effectively signaled to the broader research community that a shift away from primarily micro-normative and macro-normative analyses toward the incorporation of household financial behaviors and attitudes into models of economic activity is an important and necessary extension of economic thinking and modeling.

In this regard, a need exists to move beyond a strict definition of personal finance to a discussion of theoretical grounding. At the current time, the interdisciplinary field of personal finance does not have a unique theoretical or conceptual model in which research, policy, and educational programming is operationalized (Hira, 2009; Schuchardt et al., 2007). Instead, personal finance, as an interdisciplinary field

---

**2** This definition was informed by descriptions of personal finance from the following sources: (a) Corporate Finance Institute (*Personal finance: The process of planning and managing personal financial activities.* https://corporatefinanceinstitute.com/resources/knowledge/finance/personal-finance/); Hira (2009); (c) Schuchardt et al. (2007); (d) National Financial Educators Council (https://www.financialeducatorscouncil.org/personal-finance-definition/); (e) Consumer Financial Protection Bureau (https://www.consumerfinance.gov/about-us/blog/4-elements-define-personal-financial-well-being/); (f) Oklahoma State Department of Education (https://sde.ok.gov/personal-financial-literacy); and Warschauer (2002).

of study, tends to borrow theoretical concepts from the other disciplines (see Figure 1.1; Black et al., 2002; Cull, 2009; Warschauer, 2002). Some of the most important models and theories used to guide previous research include:
(a)  Behavioral Life-Cycle Hypothesis
(b)  Discounted Utility Model
(c)  Family Systems Theory
(d)  Human Ecological Model
(e)  Life Cycle Hypothesis
(f)  Prospect Theory
(g)  Theory of Planned Behavior
(h)  Transtheoretical Model of Change

While personal finance, as an interdisciplinary field of study and practice, is informed by multiple disciplines, the theoretical and applied study of personal finance topics appears to be coalescing around the field of financial planning, although specialized topics within the domain of personal finance look as if they are being pulled into more traditional business and economics spheres as well. Consider, for example, the concepts of financial knowledge, financial literacy, and financial capability. At one point in time, these topics comprised the foundational elements of personal finance studies. Today, one is just as likely to see a paper about financial literacy in a consumer, economics, marketing, or finance journal as one is to see such a paper in a personal finance, family and consumer sciences, or financial planning journal.[3]

The reason that personal finance meshes so nicely with financial planning is that, as noted by Cull (2009), "Financial planning has been part of everyday life dating back to ancient times" (p. 26), although the modern origins of financial planning harken back to 1969 in the United States and the early 1980s elsewhere in the world (Cowen et al., 2006).[4] Warschauer (2002) defined financial planning as (p. 204):

> [A] process that takes into account the client's personality, financial status, and the socioeconomic and legal environments and leads to the adoption of strategies and use of financial tools that are expected to aid in achieving the client's financial goals.

---

3 The primary journals focused on publishing personal finance research include: *Journal of Personal Finance*; *Financial Planning Review*; *Financial Planning Review* (Korea); *Financial Services Review*; *Journal of Financial Counseling and Planning*; *Journal of Financial Planning*; *Journal of Financial Service Professionals*; *Journal of Family and Economic Issues*; *Financial Planning Research Journal*; *Journal of Financial Therapy*; *Journal of Consumer Affairs*; *Journal of Financial Services Marketing*; *Journal of Financial Services Research*; *Finance Research Letters*; *Financial Analysts Journal*; *Journal of Wealth Management*; and *Journal of Investing*.

4 Personal finance and financial planning are closely related to financial counseling, which Langrehr (1991) defined as: "a holistic [personal finance] approach, [that is focused on] teaching individuals new skills for managing their finances" (pp. 155–156). In this regard, financial counseling can be seen as the applied application of personal finance concepts designed to improve the lives of those who are struggling financially.

This definition highlights the theoretical, technical, and applied nature of financial planning. Financial planning researchers study many of the same topics that are of interest to those who conduct personal finance research, including cash flow and resource allocations, retirement, taxation, estate planning, homeownership, saving and investment planning, debt and risk management, trusts, annuities, and generalized household financial well-being.

## Discussion

Given the historical roots of personal finance, it is reasonable to ask where might personal finance researchers find an academic home? There are certainly many options, including departments and units of financial planning, family and consumer sciences, economics, marketing, and finance. It is also possible that an academic home for personal finance will never emerge. After all, as noted throughout this chapter, personal finance is multidisciplinary, which means, by definition, that the field is informed and shaped by numerous forces. If the trajectory of personal finance over the past 125 years gives insights into the future, then it may be that those who are engaged in personal finance research, education, outreach, and practice will continue to remain in distinct colleges, departments, and units. As illustrated in Figure 1.2, this diversity, when viewed holistically, implies that the same

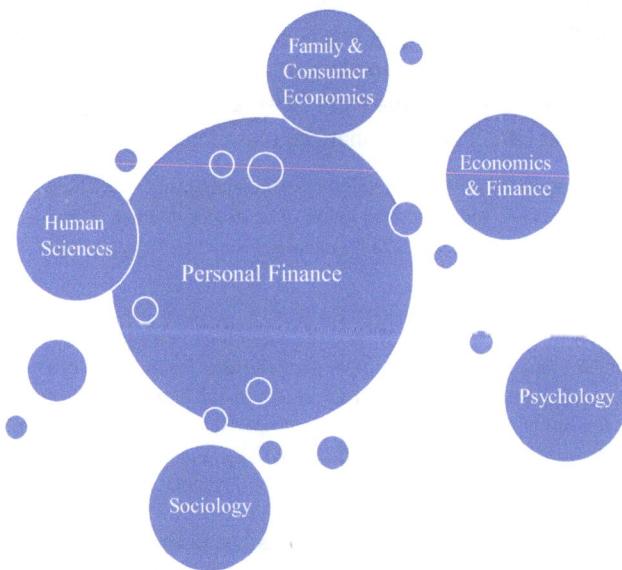

**Figure 1.2:** Research, Education, Outreach, and Practice Diversity Informing and Shaping Personal Finance.

people who address personal finance research questions with an academic-specific grounding can still come together to continue to inform and shape what is termed personal finance.

## Conclusion

We introduced this chapter by asking, "What is personal finance?" We answered the question by pointing out that, to date, there is no single definition of, yet alone a consensus opinion about, the term. This does not mean that researchers, educators, and policymakers have remained silent about the definition or elements comprising personal finance. As noted in this chapter, what is now termed personal finance has a long and robust history in the academy. Beginning in the 1800s, personal finance concepts, tools, and techniques have been described, evaluated, tested, and modeled using numerous theoretical and conceptual frameworks. What originally began as elements of home economics, which was focused primarily on ways to help women manage their household financial and consumption choices, personal finance has emerged into a unique multidisciplinary field of study and professional practice.

Those who conduct personal finance research, and those who teach personal finance, tend to focus on describing tools and techniques that can be used to enhance individual, family, and household well-being, as well as developing models that can be used to explain and predict household-level financial behaviors and attitudes. Policymakers have also developed a keen interest in personal finance topics. Gaining a better understanding of the mechanisms that drive financial behavior at the individual, family, and household level is a uniting factor in bringing researchers, educators, and policymakers together.

Based on our historical review of the development of personal finance as an interdisciplinary profession, and our review of the usage of the term "personal finance," we presented the following definition of personal finance:

> *Personal finance is the study and application of concepts, tools, and techniques associated with the planning and management of personal and household financial activities, including generating income, managing spending and debt, saving, investing, and protecting sources of income and assets in a way that informs practices and policies designed to enhance the well-being of individuals, families, and households.*

As stated at the outset of this chapter, we hope that this definition will spur further discussion about the role of personal finance in the 21st century among the stakeholders in what can broadly be described as the interdisciplinary field (and profession) of personal finance.

# References

Abdel-Ghany, M. (2001). The evolution of research in consumer science: A 200-year perspective. *Family and Consumer Sciences Research Journal*, *30*(2), 223–239.

Badarinza, C., Balasubramaniam, V., and Ramadorai, T. (2019). The household finance landscape in emerging economies. *Annual Review of Financial Economics*, *11*, 109–129.

Baugher, S. L., Anderson, C. L., Green, K. B., Nickols, S. Y., Shane, J., Jolly, L., and Miles, J. (2000). Body of knowledge of family and consumer sciences. *Journal of Family and Consumer Sciences*, *92*(3), 29–32.

Becker, G. (1965). A theory of the allocation of time. *Economic Journal*, *75*(299), 493–517.

Black, K. Jr., Ciccotello, C. S., and Skipper, H. D. Jr. (2002). Issues in comprehensive personal financial planning. *Financial Services Review*, *11*, 1–9.

Campbell, J. Y. (2006). Household finance. *The Journal of Finance*, *61*(4), 1553–1604.

Cowen, J. E., Blair, W. T., and Taylor, S. M. (2006). Personal financial planning education in Australian universities. *Financial Services Review*, *15*(1), 43–57.

Cruess, S. R., Johnston, S., and Cruess, R. L. (2004). Profession: A working definition for medical educators. *Teaching and Learning in Medicine*, *16*(1), 74–76.

Cull, M. (2009). The rise of the financial planning industry. *The Australasian Accounting, Business & Financial Journal*, *3*(1), 26–36.

Darling, C. A. (1995). An evolving historical paradigm: From "home economics" to "family and consumer sciences." *Journal of Consumer Studies and Home Economics*, *19*(4), 367–379.

Davies, D. (1795). *The case of labourers in husbandry stated and considered*. Cambridge University Press.

Deacon, R. E., and Firebaugh, F. M. (1988). *Family resource management: Principles and applications* (2nd ed.). Allyn and Bacon.

Eden, S. F. M. (1797). *The state of the poor, or, an history of the labouring classes in England, from the conquest to the present period: Together with parochial reports relative to the administration of work-houses, and houses of industry; The state of friendly societies; and other public institutions*. B. & J. White.

Engel, E. (1857). Die productions und consumptons-verhaltnisse des konigreichs Sachsen [The production and consumption conditions of kingdom of Saxony]. *Zeitschrift des Statisischen Bureaus des Koniglich Sachsischen Ministeriums des Inners*, *8*(9), 1–15.

Gross, I. H., Crandall, E. W., and Knoll, M. M. (1980). *Management for modern families*. Prentice-Hall.

Hira, T. K. (2009). Personal finance: Past, present and future. *Networks Financial Institute Policy Brief, 2009-PB-10*. https://papers.ssrn.com/sol3/papers.cfm?abstract_id=1522299

Israelsen, C. L. (1989). Family resource management research: 1930–1990. *Journal of Financial Counseling and Planning*, *1*(1), 1–37.

Jones, L. A. (2002). *Mama learned us to work: Farm women in the New South*. University of North Carolina Press.

Kahneman, D. (2003). A psychological perspective on economics. *The American Economic Review*, *93*(2), 162–168.

Langrehr, V. B. (1991). Financial counseling and planning: Similarities and distinctions. *Journal of Financial Counseling and Planning*, *2*(2), 155–168.

Le Play, F. (1877). *Les ouvries Europeens* [European workers] (2nd ed.). Tours, A. Mame Et Fils.

Liston, M. I. (1993). *History of family economics research, 1862–1962: A bibliographical, historical, and analytic reference book*. Iowa State University Research Foundation.

McCloat, A., and Caraher, M. (2018). The evolution of home economics as a subject in Irish primary and post-primary education from the 1800s to the twenty-first century. *Irish Education Studies, 38*(3), 377–399.

McGregor, S. L. T. (2015). The future of family and consumer sciences (FCS) and home economics: An international and intergenerational vignette. *Journal of Family and Consumer Sciences, 107*(3), 9–17.

Merriam-Webster. (n.d.). Discipline. In *Merriam-Webster.com dictionary*. Retrieved February 15, 2021, from https://www.merriam-webster.com/dictionary/discipline

Miller, M. (1999). The history of finance: An eyewitness account. *The Journal of Portfolio Management, 13*(2), 95–101.

Schuchardt, J., Bagwell, D. C., Bailey, W. C., DeVaney, S. A., Grable, J. E., Leech, I. E., Lown, J. M., Sharpe, D. L., and Xiao, J. J. (2007). Personal finance: An interdisciplinary profession. *Journal of Financial Counseling and Planning, 18*(1), 61–69.

Warschauer, T. (2002). The role of universities in the development of the personal financial planning profession. *Financial Services Review, 11*(3), 201–216.

Wright, C. D. (1875). *Condition of workingmen's families. Sixth annual report of the Massachusetts Bureau of Statistics of Labor*. Bureau of Labor Statistics.

John E. Grable, Eun-Jin Kwak

# 2 Personal Finance: A Policy and Institutional Perspective

**Abstract:** Personal finance is often thought of as something most directly associated with the delivery of an educational intervention or the placement of financial products and services. Much of the extant literature in the field of personal finance tends to test hypotheses and models of household consumption and decision making with the goal of assessing and describing individual, family, and household well-being. This narrow view of personal finance does not take into account the profound role that personal finance has in shaping and responding to public and institutional policies. Concepts, tools, and techniques from personal finance have been shown over several decades of analysis to be important descriptors of local, state, regional, and national economic and social outcomes. Public policy has also played an important role in shaping the way personal finance has been defined and applied in practice. Public and institutional policies can have a significant impact, both positive and negative, on the financial well-being of households. In addition to providing a historical review of the relationship between and among public policy, institutional management, and personal finance, this chapter also highlights ten areas with the domain of personal finance that appear to offer the highest impact potential related to public policy and institutional management outcomes over the next few decades.

**Keywords:** public policy, institution, personal finance, productivity, financial literacy

## Introduction

The purpose of this chapter is to provide historical context for the role personal finance[1] concepts, tools, and techniques play in both addressing and responding to

---

[1] As context for this chapter, the use of the term "personal finance," as described in the introductory chapter of this handbook is, "*The study and application of concepts, tools, and techniques associated with the planning and management of personal and household financial activities, including generating income, managing spending and debt, saving, investing, and protecting sources of income and assets in a way that informs practices and policies designed to enhance the well-being of individuals, families, and households.*"

**Note:** We would like to thank Dr. Charles Chaffin for his comments on an early version of this chapter.

**John E. Grable, Eun-Jin Kwak,** University of Georgia

https://doi.org/10.1515/9783110727692-002

public policy[2] and institutional issues, concerns, and outcomes. At the core of this chapter is an attempt to answer the following question: What are the relationships among public policy and institutional policy and personal finance? In an attempt to answer this question, this chapter provides a multi-decade overview of the way personal finance has been conceptualized, studied, and applied in relation to public policy and the management of institutions. This historical sketch also describes how public policy has and continues to influence how individuals, families, and households conceptualize personal finance in day-to-day matters. The chapter provides evidence showing that personal finance concepts, tools, and techniques have had a significant impact on improving the well-being of individuals, families, and households. The chapter concludes with a call for action related to the further development of personal finance as a policy and institutional tool.

## Historical Perspective

The historical study and examination of personal finance topics has its roots in the systematic tracking of household income, expense, and asset data beginning in the late 18th century. Davies (1795) is generally credited with undertaking the first study of household financial behavior. His work was prompted by demands among English policymakers to better understand how households allocated resources, at a time of dramatically changing social and economic events, to meet needs and wants. Policymakers at that time were keenly interested in looking for ways to improve the financial stability of individuals and families (Abdel-Ghany, 2001). The work of Davies spurred additional in-depth studies of personal finance topics. The commonality among all such studies in the 19th century and early 20th was the goal of providing policymakers with information that could be used to improve the financial position of larger segments of the population.

Much of the early academic work related to personal finance topics was limited by a lack of data. This changed following the Great Depression (1929 through 1939), with governmental and private organizations allocating more resources to gather income and expenditure data from households. The number of researchers interested in better understanding personal and household financial topics expanded tremendously during this period. It was not until the early 1960s, however, that steps were taken to systematically gather data and document household financial

---

2 For the purposes of this chapter, a policymaker is defined to include any individual who develops, administers, and/or enforces laws, regulations, and other policies at the local, regional, or national level. In some instances, a policymaker may have jurisdiction over more than one location. Institutions, in relation to this chapter, include for-profit, non-profit, non-governmental and governmental agencies, and other associations that employ individuals.

well-being at a national level. Similar to the earliest academic work on personal finance topics, surveys of consumers and family financial decision makers were launched at the bequest of policymakers who needed additional data to implement policies designed to help individuals, families, and households obtain (and maintain) greater financial stability. In this regard, the first major survey of the financial status of households was undertaken in 1962. The Survey of Financial Characteristics of Consumers (SFCC) was then followed by the Survey of Changes in Family Finances (SCFF) in 1963. These surveys served as the precursors for what later became the Survey of Consumer Finances (SCF).

The SCF[3] serves as a primary source of public policy data on the financial health of American households. According to the Board of Governors of the Federal Reserve System (2021), the SCF is a "triennial cross-sectional survey of U.S. families. The survey data include information on families' balance sheets, pensions, income, and demographic characteristics. Information is also included from related surveys of pension providers and the earlier such surveys conducted by the Federal Reserve Board. Data from the SCF are widely used, from analysis at the Federal Reserve and other branches of government to scholarly work at the major economic research centers." Since its inception, aspects of the SCF have been translated into numerous languages and used as the basis for country surveys worldwide.

Traditionally, data from the SCF and similar surveys (e.g., Consumer Expenditures Survey (CES),[4] National Longitudinal Survey of Youth 1979 (NLSY79),[5] and Survey of Household Economics and Decision making (SHED)[6]) have been used to provide policymakers with general information about the financial health, welfare,

---

**3** This SCF is sponsored by the Federal Reserve Board in cooperation with the Department of the Treasury. Since 1992, data have been collected by the non-partisan and objective research organization at the University of Chicago (NORC). The survey contained a panel element over two periods. Respondents to the 1983 survey were re-interviewed in 1986 and 1989. Respondents to the 2007 survey were re-interviewed in 2009.

**4** The Consumer Expenditure Surveys (CES) provide data on expenditures, income, and demographic characteristics of consumers living in the United States.

**5** According to the Bureau of Labor Statistics (2021), "The NLSY79 is a nationally representative sample of 12,686 young men and women born during the years 1957 through 1964 and living in the United States when the survey began. The survey respondents were ages 14 to 22 when first interviewed in 1979. During the years since that first survey, the participants typically have finished their schooling, moved out of their parent's homes, made decisions on continuing education and training, entered the labor market, served in the military, married, started families of their own, and thought about their retirement expectations. Data collected from the NLSY79 respondents chronicle these changes and provide researchers with a unique opportunity to study the life-course experiences of Americans men and women."

**6** The SHED measures the economic well-being of U.S. households and identifies potential risks to their finances. The survey includes modules on a range of topics of current relevance to financial well-being, including credit access and behaviors, savings, retirement, economic fragility, education funding, and student loans.

and stability of individuals, families, and households. Figure 2.1 illustrates the type
of data, and the visualization format of such data, that have been of interest to
those administering and documenting household financially focused policies. As
shown, data have tended to be aggregated and summarized in a way that provides
a quick overview of trends occurring at the household level.[7]

**Before Tax Family Income by All Families (thousands of dollars)**

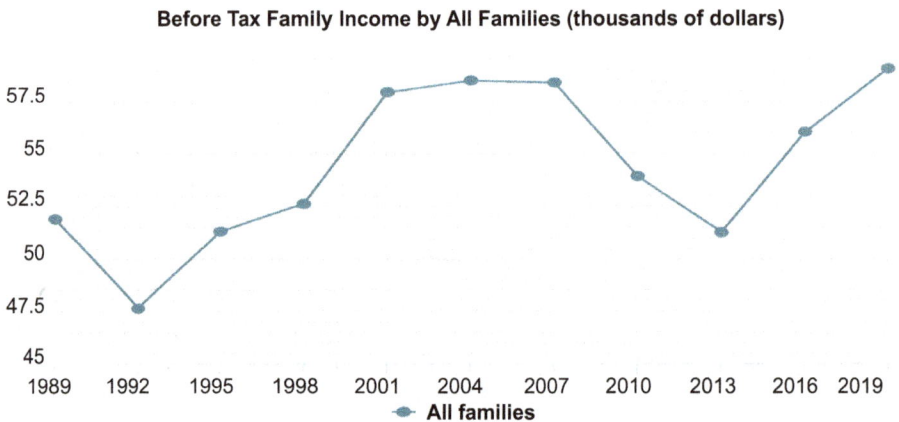

**All families**

**Figure 2.1:** Policy Relevant Data from the Survey of Consumer Finances.
*Source*: Board of Governors of the Federal Reserve System (2021).

A significant shift in the types of personal and household finance questions asked by
policymakers, businesses, and other institutional leaders occurred during the late
1980s through the mid-1990s. Essentially, policymakers and institutions began to demand more robust levels of data analysis, moving beyond simple descriptives like
those shown in Figure 2.1. This period of time in the United States was characterized
by a robust economic environment and increasing global financial interdependence
following the collapse of the Soviet Union. Within this environment, a significant di-
chotomy was emerging. On the one hand, personal and household income and
wealth were increasing; on the other, and at the same time, individuals, families,
and households were facing an increasing number of financial difficulties. While employers were finding it difficult to locate and hire new employees, bankruptcies and
other financial stressors were reaching all-time highs (Luther et al., 1998). In response, policymakers and leaders of large institutions started to question the role
that policy could play in improving the financial situation of the general population.

---

7 Researchers, of course, use the SCF and other survey data to conduct extensive descriptive and
predictive studies of household financial behavior.

While numerous policymakers and institutional thought leaders were asking this question, the U.S. Navy was among the first global institutions to evaluate the degree to which personal finance issues are related to policy and institutional outcomes. By the mid-1990s, the U.S. Navy was facing functional difficulties related to the ability of Navy personnel to deploy and obtain high-level security clearances due to a lack of personal financial stability among enlisted service members.

The Military Family Institute at Marywood University (Luther et al., 1997, 1998) determined the nature of the relationship between personal financial behavior and the U.S. Navy's operational readiness. Institute researchers determined:

- Approximately 60 percent of lost security clearances were directly associated with a service member's financial problems (e.g., a poor credit history can result in a loss of security clearance).
- More than 40 percent of all active-duty U.S. Navy personnel reported facing monthly financial challenges.
- Operational readiness was reduced when a service member's "family experiences financial difficulties while the service member is overseas and the latter functions less effectively" (Luther et al., 1998, p. 176).
- Problematic financial behavior on the part of a service member or their family reduced re-enlistment.
- Married couples who experienced financial stress resulting from problematic financial behavior also experienced marital stress, which reduced operational readiness as the service member's attention became diverted away from operations to the functioning of their family.
- The lack of financial knowledge on the part of a service member resulted in suboptimal loan, grant, credit, and debt choices.
- Lack of financial confidence negatively impacted a service member's ability to perform at a high level.
- Lost productivity was directly associated with "letters of indebtedness, bankruptcies, bad checks, wage garnishments, and requests to the relief society" (Luther et al., 1998, p. 177).

When the costs associated with direct losses, recruiting, training, lost productivity, and other expenses were combined, the Marywood University research team concluded that the U.S. Navy was spending between $172 to $258 million annually as the result of problematic personal financial behavior on the part of service members (Luther et al., 1998). When extrapolated broadly, it was thought that losses associated with problematic financial behavior across the U.S. economy were in the billions of dollars. In response, numerous military and non-profit service providers have since introduced financial wellness, financial counseling, and financial readiness programs to help service members, as well as workers in other institutions, better manage their financial situation.

Employers from all sectors of the U.S. economy, as well as internationally, were also beginning to notice reduced productivity across their respective workforces related to the way employees were managing their personal financial situations. Garman et al. (1996) reported that approximately 15 percent of all employed individuals at that time were experiencing personal financial problems to such an extent that institutional productivity was being reduced significantly. Whether this estimate has improved since the Garman et al. study was disseminated is unknown, but given what has been published since the mid-1990s, it is unlikely that the situation has changed much today. In this regard, consider what Bonner reported in 2016. She noted that while two-thirds of employers offer financial education to their employees, financial stress continues to be a deep-rooted problem in the workforce. Workers tend to be most stressed about debt, saving for retirement, paying for a child's college education, covering basic living expenses, and paying for medical expenses.

Institutional interest in personal finance, like that of policymakers, grew tremendously during the last decade of the 20th century. As world economies peaked, employers found it increasingly difficult to recruit and retain employees (this was the period of the first dot.com bubble). Personal financial education and financial planning were seen as a new type of employee benefit that could be used to enhance recruitment and retention while improving employee productivity. Some large firms even hired in-house financial planning teams to provide financial planning advice and counsel to executives and some rank-and-file employees. In some respects, this period represented a zenith moment in history when policymakers and institutions of all sizes showed a sincere and intense interest in personal finance as both a concept and as a tool to enhance individual, family, household, business, and macro-economic outcomes. Research linking personal finance education and capabilities to employee productivity and wellness showed the following outcomes (Garman et al., 1999, p. 79):

- An increase in participation in and contributions to defined contribution plans
- Improved financial wellness among those who received personal finance education
- Enhanced retirement planning
- Increased employee loyalty and morale
- Significant reductions in employee stress;
- Reductions in employee theft
- Reductions in employee lawsuits

Things changed at the turn of the millennium. As the dot.com bubble burst, the employment market softened, which meant that human resource managers no longer needed to compete for employees. For-profit and non-profit institutions of all sizes began reducing payrolls and eliminating positions. The typical human resource manager at that time had little incentive to provide personal finance education or counseling to employees. Personal financial education outside of colleges, universities, private foundations, and religious organizations effectively disappeared. With the need to recruit and retain highly productive employees dramatically reduced, and productivity concerns no longer of primary interest, nearly all institutions reverted back to viewing personal finance topics and issues as something that was outside the institution's purview or responsibility. Similarly, policymakers were forced to turn their attention away from documenting the benefits associated with having a financially literate and capable population to enacting policies designed to provide baseline financial supports to individuals, families, and households who were facing severe financial stress. During this period, the lessons learned from research conducted by the U.S. Navy and other large employees seemed to have been lost.

A new interest in personal finance from a policy and institutional perspective coalesced in the early 2000s. Researchers like Mitchell and Lusardi (2015), Hastings et al. (2013), and Kumaran (2013) were among the first to point out that while it was true that world economies at that time were contracting, which was a point of engagement for policymakers and institutions, the status of individuals, families, and households was also undergoing significant change and conflict. While global housing prices were rising, the overall financial well-being of consumers and financial decision makers was declining (Brown and Sharpe, 2014). After the onset of the global financial crisis (2007 through 2009), personal finance as a conceptual umbrella that includes financial literacy, financial capability, and other related concepts, reemerged as something of international importance.[8] In this regard, Mitchell and Lusardi (2015), in a retrospective article, made the following observation:

> The modern economy increasingly requires consumers to make many complex and sometimes bewildering financial choices. Almost daily, our students, colleagues, relatives, and even strangers on airplanes ask us difficult questions including: How many credit cards should I have, and how do I select them? Should I borrow for college, and how much is too much to pay? How much should I have in my 401(k) plan, and where do I invest it? Should I lease or buy a car? Should I rent or buy a place, and how much do I need to put down and what can I afford to pay? When can I afford to retire? Obviously, not everyone needs an economics degree, but people do require some financial knowledge to make such decisions . . . financial ignorance can be expensive and even ruinous, for many.          (pp. 107–108)

In 2004, the Health and Retirement Study (HRS)[9] added the following questions, as originally developed by Lusardi and Mitchell (2011) (generally referred to as the "Big Three"), to the survey:[10]

---

**8** The number of *Google Scholar* links with "personal finance" as a key phrase, over the period 2010 to early 2021, was 1,780,000. This was nearly the same number of links identified over the much longer period 1970 through 2009. This suggests that personal finance continues to grow in importance as a topic of study, policy, and practice.
**9** The University of Michigan Health and Retirement Study (HRS) is a longitudinal panel study that surveys a representative sample of approximately 20,000 individuals living in the United States. The survey is supported by the National Institute on Aging and the U.S. Social Security Administration.
**10** The correct answer is indicated by *.

1.  Suppose you had $100 in a savings account and the interest rate was 2% per .
    year. After 5 years, how much do you think you would have in the account if
    you left the money to grow?
    a.  More than $102*
    b.  Exactly $102
    c.  Less than $102
    d.  Do not know
    e.  Refuse to answer

2.  Imagine that the interest rate on your savings account was 1% per year and in-
    flation was 2% per year. After 1 year, how much would you be able to buy with
    the money in this account?
    a.  More than today
    b.  Exactly the same
    c.  Less than today*
    d.  Do not know
    e.  Refuse to answer

3.  Please tell me whether this statement is true or false. "Buying a single com-
    pany's stock usually provides a safer return than a stock mutual fund."
    a.  Ture
    b.  False*
    c.  Do not know
    d.  Refuse to answer

As indicators of personal finance knowledge and the degree to which someone is financially literate, Mitchell and Lusardi (2015) reported that only half of older Americans knew, at the time of their study, the correct answers to the interest rate questions,
whereas only one out of three knew the correct answer for the stock diversification
question. According to Boisclair et al. (2014), the performance of those living in Canada, Germany, the Netherlands, Switzerland, Sweden, Japan, Italy, France, Australia,
and New Zealand was, and continues to be, about the same, which is relatively low.[11]

As the 21st century continues to unfold, the connections between and among
public policy, institutional policy, and personal finance will continue to merge. The
discussion thus far has focused on the way personal finance concepts, tools, and
techniques have been used to inform and guide public policy and institutional outcomes. It is important to note, however, that the associations between and among

---

[11] According to researchers at The Policy Circle (2021), who reported data compiled by the Consumer Financial Protection Bureau and the Financial Industry Regulatory Authority Foundation,
financial literacy has steadily been declining, with only 34 percent to 42 percent of Americans
being financially literate.

these constructs, as illustrated in Figure 2.2, likely have a dual or multi-directional effect. Moving forward, the history of personal finance will be determined in great part by the way governmental and institutional policies impact personal finance.

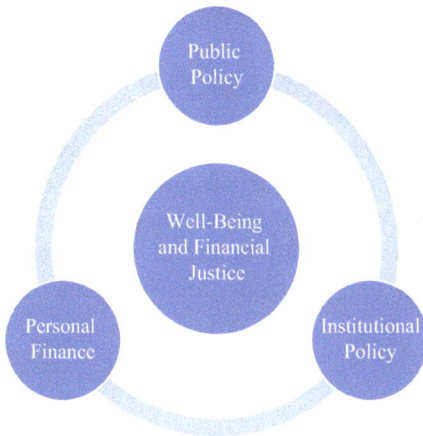

**Figure 2.2:** The Associations between and among Public Policy, Institutional Policy, and Personal Finance Resulting in Individual, Family, and Household Well-being and Financial Justice.

In this regard, it is important to acknowledge that public and institutional policies related to taxes, lending, borrowing, insurance, retirement, and charitable activities will more closely determine the pattern of individual, family, and household financial outcomes over the ensuing decades. Social and economic policies impact groups differently, which often leads to unintended economic, social, and household-level financial consequences across regions and countries. Shifting the way public policy, institutions, and personal finance are conceptualized by gaining a better understanding of the way policy impacts personal finance, rather than determining the manner in which personal finance alters policy outcomes, will likely be the historical narrative of personal finance over the next two decades.

It is reasonable to expect researchers, community activists, and others who are interested in the financial welfare of individuals, families, and households to increasingly demand evidence that governmental and institutional policies do not cause large negative externalities at the state, regional, and national level. Policies will increasingly be evaluated by the degree to which financial justice is achieved and by the way communities of individuals are impacted. As of the early 2020s, the U.S. government, for example, was spending approximately $300 million annually, across 23 federal agencies, on financial literacy and education campaigns. At the same time, private institutions were spending approximately $400 million more annually to improve financial literacy (The Policy Circle, 2021). Whether these expenditures have resulted (or will result) in meaningful outcomes has yet to be fully determined. On top of these direct measures, the impact of economic and social policies will most likely be evaluated with the same lens. The observations of Hall (2014) hint at this increasing level of scrutiny. Hall noted the following:

[G]overnment policy and action have a direct effect on individuals, but they also have an indirect effect on individuals when, for example, they affect business because of the consequences for job creation or the maintenance of employment levels and because of the effect on profitability and the payment of dividends. When the additional expense of higher taxes is passed on to consumers, this reduces their ability to purchase the same levels of goods and service or causes a reduction in the levels of saving if consumption levels are maintained.          (p. 2)

As these notes highlight, the history of personal finance continues to unfold. The era of historically low interest rates at the time this chapter was written, ongoing debates about economic and social justice, tax policies, healthcare costs, foreign currency manipulations, health pandemics, increasing household and national debt levels, and other issues will continue to dominate the way policymakers and institutions act. Actions taken by policymakers and institutions will undoubtedly alter the way personal finance concepts, tools, and techniques are conceptualized and applied in the future.

## Applications

While data about the financial literacy of consumers and financial decision makers helps describe the financial knowledge of people around the world, it is important to ask whether knowledge and the application of personal finance concepts translate into an improvement in the human situation through better financial behavior and a reduction in problematic decision errors? Much of the personal finance, financial literacy, financial capacity, and financial planning literature to date has been focused on answering this important question. When viewed holistically, the answer does appear to confirm the role of personal finance as a key factor that improves individual, family, household, institutional, and national well-being. This is how Mitchell and Lusardi (2015, p. 110) summarized the situation: "there is substantial evidence that more financially savvy people are more likely to plan, save, invest in stocks, and accumulate more wealth." Concepts that comprise the domain of personal finance – when put into practice – are associated with outcomes that reduce burdens placed on policymakers to build systems to enhance social and financial justice.[12] Although somewhat lost in a historical context, this also means that institutions can benefit directly through enhanced employee productivity, lower employee stress, and improved financial well-being when personal finance concepts, tools, and techniques are built into human resource and institutional management processes.

In addition, policymakers and institutions must continue to take steps to safeguard the well-being of consumers and financial decision makers by ensuring that

---

**12** As evidence of this assertion, Lusardi et al. (2017) argued that more than one-third of the wealth inequality observed in the United States is attributable to differences in financial knowledge.

the products, services, and regulations offered by mandate and through private enterprise provide positive outcomes for the largest number of households possible.

## Future Directions

Nearly all personal finance research, to date, tends to be conducted in response to economic, social, and environmental events. In the 1990s, individuals, families, and households were experiencing dualities in financial well-being – increasing wealth and job opportunities concurrently with household budget constraints and stock market volatility. Policymakers and institutions (e.g., U.S. Navy) needed research and educational interventions to improve the outcomes of individuals and families. To some degree, this need was one of self-interest. Researchers and educators responded by documenting associations between personal finance concepts, tools, and techniques and worker productivity and overall financial well-being. In the 2020s, the Covid-19 pandemic prompted new research endeavors to better understand how households dealt with mandatory stay-at-home orders, dramatic reductions in income, and wealth volatility. Again, policymakers and institutions needed information to craft policy and institutional interventions to deal with pandemic-related outcomes. Researchers and educators from a variety of academic disciplines jumped at the opportunity to contribute answers to what policymakers and institutions desperately needed at the time. This type of response on the part of researchers and educators to pressing social, economic, and environmental events will undoubtedly continue into the future.

Policymakers and institutions require up-to-date and meaningful data on the pulse of consumers and financial decision makers.[13] This highlights the ongoing need for the continuation of national and international consumer and household finance surveys. Even so, additional research is needed on the core elements of personal finance. This is true regardless of the way personal finance is defined or conceptualized or the manner in which research questions are addressed, be it with financial literacy, financial planning, or another academic lens. In this regard, the following ten areas within the domain of personal finance appear to offer the highest potential to have an impact on public policy and institutional management outcomes:[14]

---

**13** The U.S. Census Bureau's Household Pulse Survey is an example of how surveys can be used to provide timely data about ways individuals, families, and households deal with financial shocks. The Household Pulse Survey was developed to help better understand the impact of Covid-19 on household financial decisions.

**14** Although this discussion is framed in a way that shows how personal finance topics can potentially affect public policy and institutional outcomes, it is worth noting that public policy can also work to influence the way individuals, families, and households deal with day-to-day issues related to personal finance concepts, tools, and techniques.

– *High School Education*: As noted by Mitchell and Lusardi (2015), "Many employers, teachers, and policymakers have jumped on the financial literacy bandwagon in recent years, offering courses, programs, and new degrees" (p. 113). This highlights the realization that financial literacy, as a key concept embedded in the larger notion of personal finance, is a desired public good. It is known, for example, that students with more knowledge go on to achieve better financial outcomes compared to those with less financial knowledge. However, worldwide, financial knowledge among high-school-age students is very low. Traditional educational models do not appear to be working (Fernandes et al., 2014). A need exists to develop educational interventions that work effectively for those in high school (Kaiser and Menkhoff, 2020).

– *College Education*: Essentially, an investment of time and resources into the delivery of personal finance concepts to college-age youth is an investment in the human capital of a nation. While the evidence regarding the effectiveness of traditional education delivery methods has been questioned, the evidence that those with greater education and training go on to better life outcomes is undisputed. What is needed are national and international standards related to what is an appropriate minimum level of personal finance knowledge and standards related to skill development. This may require a rethinking of the way personal finance education is conceptualized and delivered.

– *Retirement Preparedness*: What started as a trend in the United States has become a worldwide phenomenon – the transition away from private and public retirement pensions to systems that rely on individually managed retirement savings. The knowledge and use of personal finance concepts, tools, and techniques at the individual, family, and household level are essential when the anticipated public policy and institutional outcome is retirement preparedness. Whether or not individuals are prepared financially to retire from paid employment is a subject worthy of additional study. The role of personal finance in providing a foundation for appropriate retirement planning decisions should be a key element of this type of future research.

– *Health and Financial Well-being*: Testing associations between health practices and outcomes and personal finance concepts is likely to be the next important public policy issue for researchers and educators working in the personal finance domain. While studies have been undertaken to explore the relationship between health and individual, family, and household financial well-being, more research is needed (Carr et al., 2015). Such research can contribute to better understanding investments in human and financial capital and unlocking under-recognized relationships between health behaviors and outcomes and economic status. While there is little consensus in the economic and medical literature about conceptual connections between income and health, research in this area will help policymakers and institutions develop more targeted strategies to improve financial and personal well-being.

– *Risk-taking*: The notion of an individual financial decision maker's willingness to take financial risk has been the focus of numerous studies over the past three decades. A need continues to exist to develop frameworks that unite concepts related to financial risk tolerance, risk aversion, and risk preference (Grable et al., 2020) and the manner in which risk attitudes are assessed (e.g., revealed versus stated preferences). At the core of such research is the need by policymakers and institutions to better understand how consumers allocate assets to meet future goals, why men and women appear to make different risk choices, and the degree to which income and wealth inequalities are associated with risky choices made over one's lifespan.

– *Resiliency*: Although rarely stated as an outcome in personal finance research or as a specific policy objective, policymakers and institutions tend to have a keen interest in improving the resiliency of individuals, families, and households. According to Van Breda (2018), resilience refers to "the multilevel processes that systems engage in to obtain better-than-expected outcomes in the face or wake of adversity" (p. 4). The knowledge and use of personal finance concepts, tools, and techniques appear to offer a pathway to enhanced resiliency (Grable et al., 2017); however, more research is needed on this and other related topics (e.g., confidence, self-esteem, mastery, locus of control, and affect).

– *Technology*: Bogan et al. (2020) noted that the emergence of new technologies will continue to have a profound impact on the way households interact with the financial marketplace both locally and globally. Advances in artificial intelligence, the increasing use of robo-advisory services, and machine learning – which are often described jointly as FinTech – will likely change how consumer protection laws and regulations are applied in the future. This will place greater strain on policymakers and regulators to help individuals, families, and households safely utilize new technologies.

– *Decision Making*: Madrian et al. (2017) observed the following: "Low incomes, limited financial literacy, fraud, and deception are just a few of the many intractable economic and social factors that contribute to the financial difficulties that households face today" (p. 27). In their sweeping review of the association between public policy and household financial decision making, Madrian et al. called upon federal governments, as employers and regulators, to take steps to make personal finance decision-making more precise, clearer, and simpler. They noted that interventions that are designed to limit consumer financial mistakes can improve consumer and national welfare. Thinking broadly, Madrian and associates urged policymakers to consider how psychological decision-making processes, tax optimization, retirement planning incentives, and savings proposals can be used to reduce income and wealth inequalities and address other social injustices. Bogan et al. (2020) echoed this thought by noting that the lines between finance, economics, and psychological factors have blurred and will continue to blur, and, as such, policymakers and institutions need to move beyond simple models to frameworks that truly describe, explain, and predict household financial decision-making behavior and outcomes.

– *Impact Investing and Ethics*: As noted in the historical review presented earlier in this chapter, much of the previous research and literature linking personal finance concepts to policy and institutional initiatives and outcomes has been focused on the role of products and services. While quite valuable, this narrow focus has resulted in a gap in the field's understanding of the role moral values, cultural expression, and institutional ethics play in describing individual, family, and household financial behavior. As noted by Bogan et al. (2020), impact investing, environmental, social, and corporate governance (ESG), notions of social responsibility, and ethical decision-making will likely come to dominate discussions related to the best and most appropriate ways public policy and institutional interventions can be used to improve the social condition.

– *Workforce Development*: As if revisiting the past, the notion of workforce development as something positively associated with personal finance is a topic that will ultimately gain importance in the future. As firms struggle to adapt to an ever increasingly complex international market where labor is mobile, institutions will be forced to adopt new strategies when recruiting and retaining employees. Institutions will also be faced with challenges associated with employee productivity. As studies from the 1990s highlighted, the role of personal finance may emerge as a key to helping policymakers and institutions grapple with workforce development issues.

## Discussion

The discussion thus far has implied a causal relationship from personal finance concepts, tools, and techniques to attitudinal and behavioral outcomes. The core assumption is that those who exhibit deeper levels of personal finance knowledge and skill engage in fewer problematic behaviors; they are more likely to save, invest, and plan for the future, all of which contribute to a nation's stock of economic, social, and human capital. The issue of endogeneity immediately comes to mind. It is possible, for example, that better financial outcomes occur for people because they start with an endowment of resources, and that, as such, the depth of personal finance knowledge and skill is less relevant. Lusardi and Mitchell (2014) addressed this issue in a noteworthy study. They concluded that, when controlling for endogeneity issues using econometric techniques, the relationship between personal finance[15] concepts,

---

15 In their study, Lusardi and Mitchell (2014) used measures of financial literacy in their estimations of causality.

tools, and techniques and behavioral outcomes are positive, with a causal path from personal finance to positive outcomes. While more research is needed on this topic, if true, what Lusardi and Mitchell reported has profound implications for public policy and institutional management. This means, for instance, that the more attention paid to personal finance as an intervention tool the more likely policymakers and institutions will observe improvement in financial literacy, financial well-being, and financial justice outcomes. It is important to remember, however, that financial outcomes can also deteriorate when policies are implemented without regard for the negative impact such policies might have on the personal financial situation of individuals, families, and households.

## Conclusion

The manner in which personal finance is studied and used by policymakers and institutions around the world tends to be very fragmented. Research on what are essentially personal finance topics can be found in consumer studies, economics, marketing, education, social work, sociology, and financial planning journals. Some researchers call their work in the area of personal finance financial literacy, financial capability, financial capacity, financial well-being, microfinance, household finance, financial planning, and human sciences. Undoubtedly, personal finance work is being conducted and published in other domains and fields as well. This makes it very difficult for policymakers and institutions to identify best practices when developing educational and regulatory guidelines and targets. In the United States, the Consumer Financial Protection Bureau (CFPB), the Certified Financial Planner Board of Standards, Inc., through the Center for Financial Planning, and the National Endowment for Financial Education, along with other centers and institutes, have attempted to create online libraries of relevant personal finance research. At the international level, the Organisation for Economic Co-operation and Development (OECD), through the organization's Financial Markets, Insurance, and Pensions Division, has also tried to bring together relevant research for use by policymakers and institutions. While these attempts are commendable, significant gaps exist in all such databases. For example, much of the early work showing an association between personal finance capabilities and employee productivity are missing from national and international databases. Research published in specialized education and financial planning journals tends to be missing as well. Until a unified archival system can be developed, policymakers and institutions will continue to be hampered in the use and application of personal finance concepts, tools, and techniques.

Given the importance of personal finance in shaping and responding to public policy outcomes and institutional successes, it is also noteworthy that the number of professional organizations dedicated to personal finance topics is extremely limited.

Much like the way personal finance research is conducted and disseminated, personal finance researchers tend to work in silos defined by their academic training. Economists interested in personal finance attend and present their work at economic conferences. Financial counselors and financial planners share their research at niche conferences, primarily in the United States. Those addressing personal finance topics from diverse fields of study tend to fit their work into the constraints of their discipline. A need exists for a forum where anyone interested in personal finance (e.g., educators, policymakers, institutions, and researchers) can share ideas, strategies, tools, techniques, and successes. In the perfect world, this forum would be international in scope with a journal dedicated to the dissemination of the world's best personal finance insights.[16] One can only imagine the policy and institutional benefits that will emerge once those who are passionate about personal finance topics converge into a body with one unified voice.

# References

Abdel-Ghany, M. (2001). The evolution of research in consumer science: A 200-year perspective. *Family and Consumer Sciences Research Journal, 30*(2), 223–239.

Board of Governors of the Federal Reserve System (2021). *Survey of consumer finances (SCF)*. Accessed July 2021. https://www.federalreserve.gov/econres/aboutscf.htm

Bogan, V. L., Geczy, C. C., and Grable, J. E. (2020). Financial planning: A research agenda for the next decade. *Financial Planning Review, 3*(2), 1–7. https://onlinelibrary.wiley.com/doi.epdf/10.1002/cfp2.1094

Boisclair, D., Lusardi, A., and Michaud, P-C. (2014). *Financial literacy and retirement planning in Canada* (NBER Working Paper No. 20297). Accessed July 2021. National Bureau of Economic Research. https://www.nber.org/papers/w20297

Bonner, P. A. (2016). The impacts of stress on your employees. *Plans & Trusts, 34*(6), 18–24.

Brown, A., and Sharpe, L. (2014, July 7). *Americans' financial well-being is lowest, social highest*. Gallup. Accessed July 2021. https://news.gallup.com/poll/172109/americans-financial-lowest-social-highest.aspx

Bureau of Labor Statistics. (2021). *National longitudinal surveys*. Accessed July 2021. https://www.bls.gov/nls/nlsy79.htm

Carr, N. A., Sages, R. A., Fernatt, F. R., Nabeshima, G. G., and Grable, J. E. (2015). Health information search and retirement planning. *Journal of Financial Counseling and Planning, 26*(1), 3–16.

Davies, D. (1795). *The case of labourers in husbandry stated and considered*. Cambridge University Press.

Fernandes, D., Lynch, J., and Netemeyer, R. (2014). Financial literacy, financial education, and downstream financial behaviors. *Management Science, 60*(8), 1861–1883.

Garman, E. T., Kim, J., Kratzer, C. Y., Brunson, B. H., and Joo, S-H. (1999). Workplace financial education improves personal financial wellness. *Journal of Financial Counseling and Planning, 10*(1), 79–88.

---

16 The first author of this chapter served as the founding co-editor of *Financial Planning Review* (FPR). FPR is an interdisciplinary journal that publishes papers relevant to the field of personal finance.

Garman, E. T., Leech, I. E., and Grable, J. E. (1996). The negative impact of employee poor personal financial behaviors on employers. *Journal of Financial Counseling and Planning*, 7(1), 157–168.

Grable, J. E., Kwak, E-J., Fulk, M., and Routh, A. (2020). A simplified measure of investor risk aversion. *Journal of Interdisciplinary Economics*, 32. https://doi.org/10.1177/0260107920924518

Grable, J. E., West, C. L., Leitz, L. Y., Rehl, K. M., Moor, C. C., Hernandez, M. N., and Bradley, S. (2017). Enhancing financial confidence among widows: The role of financial professionals. *Journal of Financial Planning*, 30(12), 38–44.

Hall, O. (2014, December 28). *Does government policy and action affect personal finance?* Jamaica-Gleaner. Accessed July 2021. http://jamaica-gleaner.com/article/business/20141228/does-government-policy-and-action-affect-personal-finance-0

Hastings, J. S., Madrian, B. C., and Skimmyhorn, W. L. (2013). Financial literacy, financial education, and economic outcomes. *Annual Review of Economics*, 5(1), 347–373.

Kaiser, T., and Menkhoff, L. (2020). Financial education in schools: A meta-analysis of experimental studies. *Economics of Education*, 78, 101,930.

Kumaran, S. (2013). Financial literacy, financial education: A road map personal financial well-being and prosperity. *International Research Journal of Finance and Economics*, 108, 132–143.

Lusardi, A., Michaud, P-C., and Mitchell, O. S. (2017). Optimal financial knowledge and wealth inequality. *The Journal of Political Economy*, 125(2), 431–477.

Lusardi, A., and Mitchell, O. S. (2011). Financial literacy and planning: Implications for retirement well-being. In O. S. Mitchell, and A. Lusardi (eds.), *Financial literacy: Implications for retirement security and the financial marketplace* (pp. 17–39). Oxford University Press.

Lusardi, A., and Mitchell, O. S. (2014). The economic importance of financial literacy: Theory and evidence. *Journal of Economic Literature*, 52(1), 5–44.

Luther, R. K., Garman, E. T., Leech, I. E., Griffit, L., and Gilroy, T. (1997). *Scope and impact of personal financial management difficulties of servicemembers on the department of the Navy* (MFI Report No. 97–1). Military Family Institute of Marywood University.

Luther, R. K., Leech, I. E., and Garman, E. T. (1998). The employer's cost for the personal financial management difficulties of workers: Evidence from the U.S. Navy. *Personal Finances and Worker Productivity*, 2(1), 175–182.

Madrian, B. C., Hershfield, H. E., Sussman, A. B., Bhargava, S., Burke, J., Huettel, S. A., Jamison, J., Johnson, E. J., Lynch, J. G., Meier, S., Rick, S., and Shu, S. B. (2017). Behaviorally informed policies for household financial decision-making. *Behavioral Science & Policy*, 3(1), 27–40.

Mitchell, O. S., and Lusardi, A. (2015). Financial literacy and economic outcomes: Evidence and policy implications. *The Journal of Retirement*, 3(1), 107–114.

The Policy Circle. (2021). *Financial literacy*. Accessed July 2021. https://www.thepolicycircle.org/brief/financial-literacy/

Van Breda, A. D. (2018). A critical review of resilience theory and its relevance for social work. *Social Work*, 54(1), 1–18.

Robert Van Beek

# 3 Personal Finance: A Practice Perspective

**Abstract:** The discussion presented in this chapter represents the perspective of financial advisors who are providing financial advice to individuals and household financial decision makers. In this regard, the purpose of this chapter is to provide an overview of personal finance issues, topics, and future directions from a financial advisor (i.e., practice management) perspective. A key focus of the chapter is on the notion of change – change brought about through regulation, innovation, environmental shocks, and market disruptions. As noted throughout this chapter, the profession of providing financial advice has always been, and will continue to be, impacted by change. Successful financial advisors will be those who are flexible in adapting to change.

**Keywords:** fintech, robo-advisor, behavioral finance, practice management

## Introduction

Every step in life means a change. Big or small. And these changes might lead to a big change in another person's life, which can impact someone's finances. Financial planning, investment planning, and wealth management – as elements of personal finance – are changing. Changes are occurring in basic banking and payment services, borrowing, insurance, taxes, and budgeting and planning. Changes are due to digitalization and more efficient data integration. And more recently, these changes have predominately been driven by new regulations. But changes are also occurring via variations in communication technology and the ongoing integration of psychological sciences into the domain of personal finance.[1]

Regulators worldwide are reshaping the rules of the financial advice profession by issuing a tsunami of new rules. Complianceandrisks.com[2] claims that more than

---

[1] When meeting and talking with private clients, entrepreneurs, investors, and professionals in the financial services and wealth management profession it is always a real pleasure to share expertise, thoughts, experiences, and ideas. It does not matter whether these are well-seasoned senior professionals or students new to the profession. I always try to talk about you. And that is why I am dedicating this chapter to you! It does not matter who you are and where you come from. As long as you are prepared to learn and become a changemaker. You can change your life, and if you are interested in advising others about personal finance topics and issues, this chapter is dedicated to you and your clients.

[2] https://www.complianceandrisks.com/solutions/conquering-the-regulatory-avalanche/.

---

**Robert Van Beek,** About Life & Finance, The Netherlands

https://doi.org/10.1515/9783110727692-003

60,000 regulations, standards, and key documents are included in their C2P library database, all of which have been written since the global financial crisis. New rules can be found in legal frameworks such as the U.S. Dodd-Frank law, Basel III, AIFMD, UCITS, EMIR, and MiFID II, which were predominately introduced to improve transparency, market efficiency, and consumer and investor protection.[3] Whether large or small, businesses will need to invest more resources to ensure they stay compliant.

Traditional software providers have developed not only calculation procedures and financial planning software tools but also Application Programming Interface (API) protocols. In some cases, software firms have since morphed into FinTech companies. PayTech providers, InsureTechies, and WealthTech companies have come to dominate the strategic plans and decision-making processes among business leaders. Big data, robots, and artificial intelligence (AI) have grown in importance. General Data Protection Regulations (GDPR) in Europe are built around a guiding principle called "privacy by design" as an answer to all data collected and stored in the cloud. Compared to "Big Tech," wealth and asset management firms, smaller and midsize independent financial advisors (IFAs), and planning firms have significantly fewer resources available to deal with increased regulations, though both are subject to the same European MiFID II regulations.[4]

Recently, more "new kids on the block(chain)" have entered the traditional financial and investment marketplace with Bitcoin and 900+ other crypto and digital assets available globally. These assets have created new investment opportunities for investors young and old. However, debate continues regarding the true value of these assets. For example, the European Central Bank (ECB) published its monthly *Financial Stability Review* report on May 19, 2021. The report talked about digital assets. Luis de Guindos, vice-president of the ECB, was interviewed on CNBC.[5] de Guindos said, "Crypto assets aren't a 'real investment.'" The ECB said earlier in its Financial Stability Review that the risks posed by Bitcoin to the wider system appear to be limited, even as the surge in prices "[e]clipsed previous financial bubbles like the 'tulip mania' and the South Sea Bubble in the 1600s and 1700s."

The majority of players in the financial advice profession share a real desire to change for the better, even if it does not always look that way. And sometimes, unfortunately, regulators and policymakers feel the need to speed up processes of change due to news in the media. Many people, including those in the media and

---

3 Definitions for each of these acronyms and terms are provided at the end of the chapter.
4 https://www.esma.europa.eu/sites/default/files/library/esma35-43-869-_fr_on_guidelines_on_ suitability.pdf.
5 https://www.bloomberg.com/news/articles/2021-05-19/ecb-s-guindos-says-crypto-assets-aren-t-a-real-investment.

industry, still refer to 10+ years ago – 2008 – as a reference point when developing policies. Nearly everyone was, at that time, in fear of what would come next. These were the questions that dominated the policy debate at that time: (a) would the global financial crisis get worse before it would get better? and (b) what would be the impact on the daily lives of financial decisions makers? Since that time, the world has faced other market challenges, including the Covid-19 pandemic. The one commonality is that society will continue to be challenged. There will be more changes in the future due to bigger and smaller crises. In this regard, personal finance stakeholders are encouraged to rethink the impact of changes by asking how changing models of practice, regulations, and market environments will impact business practices, the advice process, and the types of product solutions used to meet the needs of financial decision makers.

## Historical and Practice Perspective

Vanderhoydonk and Van Beek (2019) noted the following when discussing the future of personal finance advice:

> When you hear media and people talking about FinTech, WealthTech, and InsurTech, the first thing advisors should, according to them, realize, is that there is no future for you as an advisor anymore . . . The financial industry is going through a process of disruption! Bank offices are closed. People don't visit the bank and insurance advisors anymore. Advice will be Robo Advice only in the future for help with their investments, asset allocation, Financial Planning calculations, and future projections. There is no need for face-to-face human advice. And people are not willing to pay for that in the future! Every client will sit in front of his or her computer. Do-it-yourself (DIY) is the future for investing. And for sure, the XY generation and Millennials will be the first! They will make their own assumptions, put in some extra details themselves, use a digital safe for having all paperwork and administration uploaded and stored, handy in one place . . . As long as I am working in the financial and wealth management industry, I have been told these stories. And for the record, that is almost twenty years now! Is the world not changing then? Of course, it is! But instead of thinking of disruption, advisors should embrace the change in my opinion. (p. 166)

This perspective illustrates the adage that "the more things change, the more things stay the same." The demise of financial advice, as a professional activity, and the incorporation of personal financial management into technological platforms has been predicted for decades. While it is true that radical changes have occurred, the practice of providing personal financial advice is just as important as it has ever been. The following discussion provides a brief summary of the financial advice profession, with an emphasis on documenting change factors that have influenced the way personal finance is conceptualized in the 21st century.

## The Future of Financial Advice

Where did consumers historically go if they had a question about their financial situation? The bank. The traditional role of banks is to take deposits and in return pay some rate of interest. And with the same money, together with deposits from other people, banks lend this to other borrowers charging them a higher rate of interest. The spread is where banks make their profits. A bank account being used for daily payments and housekeeping was held traditionally at the same or a competing bank, giving them a better understanding and control of depositors' money coming in and money being spent on all kinds of living expenses.

Those same banks changed their business models through the introduction of a wide range of new products. But at the same time, new providers introduced similar and new products to handle consumer deposits. These market disruptors were not only banks, insurance companies, or other financial institutions, but what has since come to be known as FinTech firms. Today, FinTech services include innovative financial products, services, and distribution models that radically change the way consumers handle money. FinTech is applied in all areas of finance, including payment transactions, lending, credits, and financial software offerings, robo-advice, and reporting and information tools.

The rise of FinTech includes software (using gamification techniques) that can completely take out the human aspect of advice, but as of this writing, FinTech has not been successful at replacing the role of human advisors. Is FinTech driving change? Yes. The first robo-advisors founded in 2008 were focused on rebalancing investor portfolios using a catchy modern, online interface that was directly accessible to investors. Robo-advisors, as service providers and products delivered directly to consumers, changed the personal finance advice business model, but, to date, FinTech has tended to attract mainly execution-only "do-it-yourself" investors. Even so, thanks to these innovative technologies, financial advice is now delivered more efficiently, more transparently, cheaper, and with more client-focused attention compared to offerings provided by traditional private banks and wealth advisors. It is safe to say that FinTech has forever altered existing value chains, products, and services.

# Wealth and Mental Health: Investments, Planning, and Human Behavior

Investment and financial planning advice encompass more than risks, returns, volatility, standard deviation, efficient frontiers, asset allocation, picking and selecting the best investments, and Modern Portfolio Theory. Over the last decade, investment and financial planning (and the entire personal finance field) has embraced concepts from behavioral finance and economics. Today, concepts related to behavior, loss aversion, emotions, irrationality, overconfidence, and regret are embedded in nearly all discussions of personal finance. As noted by Baker and Ricciardi (2014, p. 3), "The field of investor behavior attempts to understand and explain investor decisions by combining the topics of psychology and investing on a micro-level (i.e. decision process of individuals and groups) and a macro perspective (i.e. the role of financial markets). The decision-making process of investors incorporates both a quantitative (objective) and qualitative (subjective) aspect . . . Investor behavior examines the cognitive factors (mental processes) and affective (emotional) issues that individuals, financial experts, and traders reveal during the financial planning and investment management process." The field of behavioral finance is, however, not new. It is possible to trace the study of investor behavior back to at least the 1800s, if not earlier (e.g., to analyses of phenomena like Tulip-Mania).

The blending of traditional investment theory and concepts with elements from behavioral finance has clearly shown that what matters is not so much the products or services offered to meet individual and household financial needs, but rather, the process of financial advice. The financial profession needs a renewed focus on the process of advice, incorporating a focus on behavior, to prevent investors from repeatedly making the same mistakes and wrong decisions.

Consider the situation in the Netherlands. Due to legislation enacted years ago, which introduced a ban on commissions, the practice of being paid for stock picking is now almost a historical footnote. The Dutch regulator, the Authorities Financial Markets (AFM), published several research and white papers describing risk profiling systems and the Know Your Client (KYC) process.[6] In March 2021, the AFM published "Principles for the Use of Consumers Behavioural Insights" that provided interesting insights and also encouraged the advice profession to actively implement behavioral finance techniques when working with clients (e.g., nudging techniques).[7]

While nearly all aspects of the quantitative elements associated with KYC are well documented in practice manuals and in the law, there continues to be something that needs a big improvement: the incorporation of emotional assessments in data-intake questionnaires, particularly in relation to the assessment of risk attitudes and risk tolerance. The FSA in the United Kingdom in 2012, for example, pointed out that traditional ways of risk profiling are flawed. In February 2019, behavioral research experts at the AFM compared some of the most widely used tests and were disappointed, calling them similar to a cosmopolitan magazine test. They also concluded that most of these tests do not work well in describing investor attitudes. A key finding from the report is that those who provide financial advice should incorporate concepts and techniques from behavioral finance, behavioral economics, and investor psychology into their practice.

---

6 https://www.afm.nl/nl-nl/professionals/nieuws/2021/mrt/principes-consumentengedragsinzichten.
7 https://www.afm.nl/~/profmedia/files/publicaties/2021/principles-use-of-consumer-behavioural-insights.pdf?la=nl-NL.

The future of personal finance, from a practice perspective, certainly appears to be linked to behavioral economics, client psychology, and financial therapy. These disciplines fit together since they all seek to understand the "why" behind clients' financial decisions. Behavioral economics seeks to understand the cognitive biases that impact decisions (Chatterjee and Goetz, 2015), whereas client psychology explores the underlying money beliefs that impact decisions (Klontz and Horwitz, 2017), and financial therapy provides techniques for addressing unsaid biases and money beliefs to facilitate healthier financial decisions (Grable et al., 2010). What may emerge over the new few decades is a truly holistic financial planning model that is more than number crunching – one that provides a deeper dive into the mindset of clients that also leads to happier clients (i.e., increased well-being).[8] In the future, more focus on knowledge and skills around integrating insights, theories, and tools from behavioral economics, client psychology, and financial therapy will become an important part of financial planning and improving clients' financial well-being.

## Tools and Techniques for Practice

As noted above, the practice of providing personal finance advice has changed from being a purely product discussion to one focused on the process of behavioral change. Complexity is a real problem for most people when confronted with important individual and household financial decisions. Financial decision making is known to be related to financial literacy. Financial literacy is "a combination of awareness, knowledge, skill, attitude and behavior necessary to make sound financial decisions and ultimately achieve individual financial well-being" (Organisation for Economic Co-operation and Development/International Network on Financial Education, 2012). Research from the OECD shows that financial literacy tends to be low, which can hinder prudent decision making. Countries in the G20, including the Netherlands and Norway, confirmed, in 2017, the importance of developing and sustaining a national strategy of financial education that reaches all segments of the population. One reason for the push to increase financial literacy is that higher levels of financial literacy tend to be associated with greater financial well-being.[9]

---

8 In March of 2021, the Certified Financial Planner Board of Standards, Inc. (CFP Board) announced a new learning outcome category in the U.S.: the CFP curriculum called "Psychology of Financial Planning," which includes not only heuristics and biases (behavioral and financial psychology), but also counseling techniques (e.g., financial therapy).
9 The U.S. Consumer Financial Protection Bureau (CFPB) defined financial well-being as "a state of being wherein a person can fully meet current and ongoing financial obligations, can feel secure in their financial future, and is able to make choices that allow them to enjoy life."

The manner in which consumers will receive financial advice will change in the future. Financial decision makers will continue to need a financial plan, but not all will continue to need a three-inch thick bound financial plan (i.e., book). Financial decision makers still want help. They will continue to need help. Whether this help comes in the form of person-to-person meetings, intelligent apps, red and green flags, or other FinTech tools is less important than the process of making life easier for financial help seekers. People want to live their lives and achieve their goals and dreams. It is up to financial advisors and the financial profession to make the numbers work, to do financial translations, and make sure that people have a future without money worries. The manner in which these tasks are completed should be less important than documenting outcomes.

## How To Do This: Introducing the 7+P Framework

Those who provide financial advice as a professional activity will increasingly face this important question: how does one provide personal finance advice and counsel that is process-oriented rather than product-focused? Little empirical evidence exists in the personal finance literature to address this question. There has been, however, some conceptual work done by practitioners that can be used to answer this question. My colleagues and I, for example, developed a model called the 7+P Framework that we believe can provide insights into the best way to provide financial advice to household financial decision makers. The 7+P Framework incorporates aspects from the following models:

- The 5p model, which is widely used as a strategy or marketing mix tool. The five "Ps" in the model are Product, Price, Promotion, Place, and People.
- The Plan–Do–Check–Act (PDCA) model.
- The financial planning process, which consists of steps ranging from establishing a financial objective and goal to monitoring planning recommendations.

The notion behind the 7+P Framework is that the process of financial advice can be guided by a systematic framework that leads to enhanced outcomes for those receiving advice. The framework is essentially a process where every word or step starts with the letter P. The subpoints under each letter represent conversation starters and domains or points that need to be touched on, discussed, and at the end ticked off if the goal of the advisory session(s) is to help a client reach their financial and life goals, improve financial well-being, and increase financial literacy. Although the 7+P Framework has not yet been empirically tested, the framework has proven to be effective based on work with hundreds of clients. The 7+P Planning Framework looks like this:

**People**
Perfect Picture
Puzzle of Problems and Possibilities: Your Goals
Passion + Purpose = POWER!
Principles and Values
Personality and Psychology
Profiling: Client+Risk+Return

**Plan = Planning**
Priorities
Perspectives
Projections versus Precision
Process and Procedures
Project Management of Your Life!

**Products**
Policy Statement of your Investments (IPS)
Performance
Products: Talking About Returns, Risks and Costs
Portfolio and Solutions that match the Goals

**Professionals and Planet**
Professionals: who to go to!
Platforms: Private, Personal, Wealth and Income
Protection and Rights of Consumers and Investors: Compliance and Regulation

**Practicals**
Paper+Pen+Pencil and More: The Toolbox
Preparation of your meetings
Prints and Pages: One or Multiple pages
Presentation, Reporting, and Monitoring

As noted above, this framework, if applied consistently, should provide more guidance in the "how to . . ." of providing financial advice to individual and household financial decision makers, and through this process, enhance goal-based financial planning and investment planning by placing the client at the center of the process.

# Future Directions: Embrace Change

When FinTech was first conceptualized, all actors in the space had a totally new way of looking at the world of personal finance. Early FinTech companies were convinced that they could do better in serving the needs of individuals and households compared to banks and traditional financial services firms. Having a focus on adding real value for their clients at a significantly lower cost was a disruptive way of doing business. The rise of FinTech, which has since increasingly been incorporated into traditional banking platforms, has brought changes to the advice profession. FinTech has changed the profession at its core, bringing a new focus on the client, more agile delivery models, and an acceptance of new technologies.

For those who provide financial advice to others, now is the time to take the opportunity to update the different process steps in practice. Here are some questions to ask: (a) What changes can be a big advantage for both your client and for you? (b) In what way can automated processes and new algorithms help you in your practice? (c) How can you help your clients with better advice? (d) What monitoring possibilities do you have? and (e) How can you work more efficiently? It is important to look beyond digital changes and improvements when answering these questions. There are a lot of analog techniques that are easy to implement, including visualizing and telling your story and interpreting your clients' stories.[10] A simple plain paper or notebook and pen is all you need. For example, some financial advisors sketch out and jot down complex issues when working through client scenarios. Sometimes financial advisors illustrate solutions using simple diagrams or pictures. Even sticky notes – how simple they are – can work great when creating family trees and when conducting estate planning; you do not need to have Picasso skills for this.[11]

## The Future of the Personal Finance Advisory Profession

With life expectancy continuing to increase, and with governments having to reduce their contributions to retirement and pension schemes, there is a need for people to take more responsibility and direction in savings for later life. Saving more seems

---

**10** For this kind of work, you want (and perhaps need) intelligent (online) solutions, even done by a robo-advisor and software that provides the talking points and conversation starters you need. And it all starts with good listening, asking a lot of questions, and simple but detailed notetaking during meetings, writing down everything that is important for you and your client in the steps of the process.

**11** Some financial advisors use building blocks. They give their clients blocks as homework for discussing and creating cash flow budget plans. When talking about investments, returns, risks, asset allocation, and portfolio building, colorful blocks visualize all the elements. And like how the Periodic Table of Elements works in chemistry, people do understand factor investing better if shown using the same style of visuals. But always be cautious and don't overdo it. A graph with three axes and both left and right showing line graphs in combination with a lot of other data is indeed a way of visualizing finance, but such an illustration may cause confusion. You don't want to make simple graphs so complex that your client does not understand the context of the picture.

like the obvious solution, but with interest rates at or below inflation levels or even negative, clients with safe and familiar savings accounts may end up losing money in the long run. The complexity of financial markets and the uncertainty that comes with investing make choosing this path challenging for many individual and household financial decision makers. Clients need independent advice and want to visit advisors, especially financial advisors who take the time to describe the big picture and who fully understand a client's total situation, and together with clients, can not only define but also achieve client goals. Dreams, wishes, needs, and wants should be prioritized and after setting clear goals and timelines, the process doesn't stop there. A policy statement is a starting point for accumulating and building wealth, enough to finance all the (future) spending that comes with the goals set. All this leads to goal-based financial planning and goal-based investing and creating a portfolio that matches client goals and cash flows, coming in and out of total wealth. And that is when the financial advisor can play an important role in a client's life.

Independent asset management firms (e.g., asset or money managers) are known for developing investment strategies for their clients. This role is likely to grow in the future. Mostly working on an assets-under-management (AUM) business model, more than 4,500 companies are operating in Europe, with about 115,000 people employed directly in the profession. In Europe, almost 85 percent of asset management activity takes place in six countries: the United Kingdom, France, Germany, Switzerland, Italy, and the Netherlands. As shown in Figure 3.1, total fund ownership in Europe amounted to approximately EUR 13.7 trillion at the end of 2020. As shown in Figure 3.2, insurers and pension funds are by far the largest investors in investment funds, followed by other financial intermediaries and households. The five countries with the highest level of fund ownership are Germany, the United Kingdom, France, the Netherlands, and Italy.

**Investment Fund Ownership**
**EUR trillions**

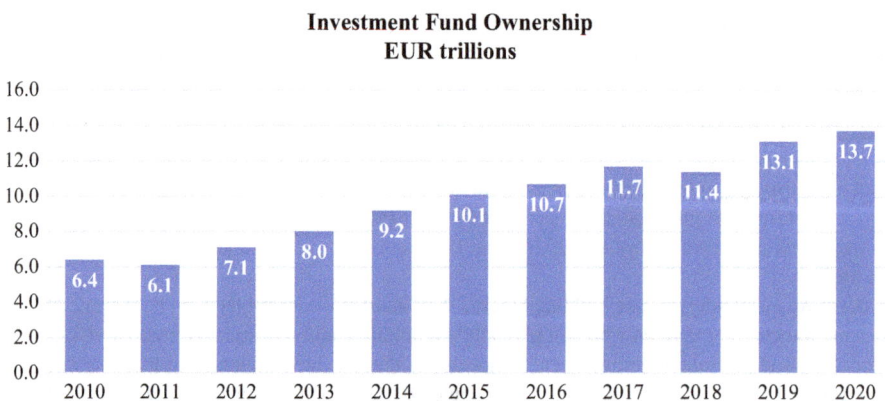

**Figure 3.1:** Investment Fund Ownership in Europe.
*Source*: European Fund and Asset Management Association (https://www.efama.org/about-our-industry/our-industry-numbers).

**Investment Fund Ownership at End 2020**
**EUR billions (%)**

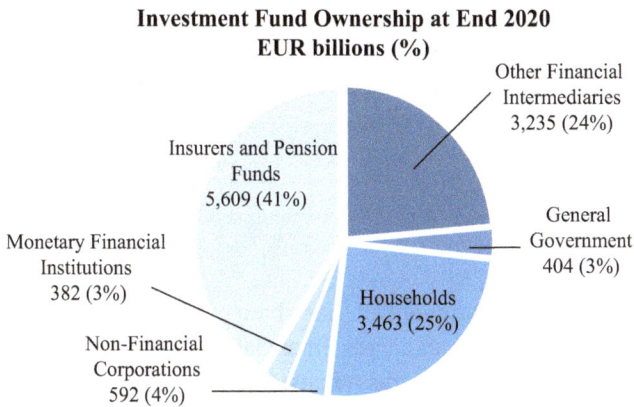

Figure 3.2: Investment Fund Ownership by Entity.
*Source*: European Fund and Asset Management Association (https://www.efama.org/about-our-industry-numbers).

In the Netherlands, which is representative of other European nations, there is a group of about 150 money managers and investment companies that dominate the market. Growing numbers of those employed by these firms become or hire planners registered with the FFP, which is the CFP® Certified Financial Planning Professional certification and membership organization with approximately 3,500 members. Compared to the rest of the world, the majority of these financial planners are not used to giving investment advice as part of their business model and services they deliver.

These advisors do, however, follow the Markets in Financial Instruments Directive II (MiFID II), which has been translated into local laws with the objective to bring much-needed transparency and better access to financial markets in every European country. An unintended consequence of this directive, however, is that the new regulations are making it difficult for smaller and independent advisers to run their business or even expand their current services with investment advice. The reason for this is the added administrative burden. Advisors struggle with how this can be done cost-effectively. This is an issue worthy of research that informs public policy. It is also worth noting that the same MiFID regulation banned receiving commissions by product providers and advisors for advising and selling investments and complex financial products. So, the way of being paid for advice delivered has changed. The Netherlands, for example, followed other countries like the United Kingdom and Australia. All other European countries at this moment have opted out of this option in the EU Directive and most distribution models are still based on selling products that match the needs of the client. Depending on contracts, the advice is delivered by (tied) agents or brokers paid by product providers and the industry. Independent advice is only possible and can only be used by advisors if they or their employers are paid directly by their clients for services as stipulated in MiFID regulations. The average European, in general, will still end up or remain a client of large financial institutions if they want to go for personal investment advice. But in the Netherlands, as well as other parts of Europe and the United Kingdom, a lot is changing.

## Conclusion

The practice of running a financial planning firm has changed dramatically over the past two decades. Independent asset managers, financial planners, and others who provide personal financial advice (i.e., trusted advisors) have been forced to reinvent their business models and their services. Throughout Europe and the world, these changes are prompting new successful business models. Partnerships have been created and advisors have started collaborating. And in this way, they are able to create platforms together using intelligent technologies and integrating soft (i.e., counseling and communication) skills instead of focusing primarily on knowledge and theory. One of the top trends noted by CapGemini[12] in their Wealth Report is the broadening of the financial advice market. Questions remain about the degree to which financial advisors have adapted to changes in the markets and threats from FinTech. More research is needed to determine if financial advisors are ready for changes that loom on the horizon. History suggests that the most successful advisors will be those who are willing to become part of change. Flexibility in adaption will likely be the norm among successful financial advisors.

## Terms and Definitions

Table 3.1 provides a summary of some of the acronyms and key terms used in this chapter and the definitions associated with each term.

**Table 3.1:** Terms and Definitions Used in the Chapter.

| Term | Definition |
| --- | --- |
| AFM | Authority for the Financial Markets (in Dutch: Autoriteit Financiële Markten) |
| AI | Artificial Intelligence |

---

12 https://worldwealthreport.com/wp-content/uploads/sites/7/2020/12/Top-Trends-2021-in-Wealth-Management.pdf.

**Table 3.1** (continued)

| Term | Definition |
|------|-----------|
| AIFMD | Alternative Investment Fund Managers Directive. This is an EU directive that covers funds that are not UCITS and that includes hedge funds, private equity, and real estate funds. |
| API | Application Programming Interface |
| AUM | Assets Under Management |
| ESMA | European Securities and Markets Authority |
| GDPR | General Data Protection Regulation |
| IFA | Independent Financial Advisers |
| InsureTech | Insurance Technology |
| KYC | Know Your Client |
| MiFID | Markets in Financial Instruments Directive |
| MiFID II | A legislative framework introduced in 2018 with the stated aim to increase transparency and regulatory disclosure |
| PDCA | Plan-Do-Check-Act |
| PRIIPs | Packaged Retail and Insurance-based Investment Products. This regulation affects all investment products available to European retail investors and came into effect in 2018. PRIIPs aims to increase the transparency and comparability of investment products through the issue of a standardized information document – the PRIIPs Key Information Document (KID). |
| UCITS | Undertakings for Collective Investments in Transferable Securities. UCITS are investment funds oriented toward retail investors regulated by the European Union. |

# References

Baker, K. H., Filbeck, G., and Ricciardi, V. (2017). *Financial behavior: Players, services, products, and markets*. Oxford University Press.

Baker, K. H., and Ricciardi, V. (2014). *Investor behavior: The psychology of financial planning and investing*. Wiley.

Chatterjee, S., and Goetz, J. W. (2015). Applications of behavioral economics in personal financial planning. In C. R. Chaffin (ed.), *Financial planning competency handbook* (pp. 751–762). Wiley.

Grable, J., McGill, S., and Britt, S. (2010). The financial therapy association: A brief history. *Journal of Financial Therapy, 1*(1). https://doi.org/10.4148/jft.v1i1.235

Klontz, B. T., and Horwitz, E. J. (2017). Behavioral finance 2.0: Financial psychology. *Journal of Financial Planning, 30*(5), 28–29.

Organisation for Economic Co-operation and Development/International Network on Financial Education. (2012). *Measuring financial literacy: Questionnaire and guidance notes for conducting an internationally comparable survey of financial literacy*. https://www.oecd.org/finance/financial-education/49319977.pdf

Vanderhoydonk, K., and Van Beek, R. (2019). Wealth, investments, planning and behavior: K-Y-C Process. *#RegTechBlackBook* (pp. 165–171). About Life & Finance.

So-Hyun Joo

# 4 Personal Finance: An International Perspective

**Abstract:** This chapter outlines a brief history of South Korean financial planning education, research, and practice along with policy issues associated with promoting financial consumer protection and financial resiliency. While South Korea has its own uniqueness with culture, regulations, and economic situation, the stages of development of personal finance discussed in this chapter match, to a great extent, what has been experienced in other countries. Over the past quarter century, policymakers throughout Asia have taken on a growing interest in personal finance issues. This interest aligns with issues of economic justice, market reforms, and financial literacy introduced in Europe, Australia, New Zealand, and North America. For future research, particular areas of need include a better understanding of how changes in technology, the environment, and culture are related to consumer outcomes. In South Korea like other countries in the world, consumers' needs are complicated and diverse. Technological changes can create new opportunities and challenges. Social impacts and sustainability will be primary research topics in the future. Social well-being and sustainability are directly associated with consumer behavior; therefore, research and practice should focus on these issues.

**Keywords:** Asia, South Korea, population aging, consumer financial protection, financial technology, financial education

## Introduction

As a subject of study and practice, personal finance has emerged as a global topic of interest to policymakers over the past two decades. One reason for the growth in the importance of personal finance is the ever-increasing interconnectedness of world economies since the global financial crisis (2008 through 2010). As the Covid-19 pandemic illustrated, financial decision makers in one nation can be influenced by economic issues in another part of the globe. Global events can impact, both positively and negatively, the financial situation of millions of people. With the rapid globalization that has occurred since the 1990s, understanding global perspectives has become an essential element of research and practice. Personal finance is certainly one of the fields that requires a deep understanding of other countries' economic situations. Moreover, to fully understand personal finance

**So-Hyun Joo,** Ewha Womans University, Korea

https://doi.org/10.1515/9783110727692-004

requires glocalization (think globally, act locally) competencies because differences in territorial laws and regulations have become essential tools when identifying cross-cultural differences as key inputs in academic and professional activities. In this chapter, a brief history of personal finance in Asia – specifically South Korea – will be reviewed, along with current issues and concerns. While South Korea has its own uniqueness with culture, regulations, and economic situation, the stages of development of personal finance discussed in this chapter match, to a great extent, what has been experienced in other countries.

## Historical Perspective

A modern economic system and Westernized higher education institutions (e.g., colleges and universities) have existed in South Korea since the late 19th century. In higher education, personal finance, as a field of study, has traditionally been a topic area in home economics. Home economics education in higher education officially started in 1929 when Ewha Womans University, located in Seoul, established the first Home Economics Department as one of its original academic departments. In its original conceptualization, personal finance education focused primarily on family resource management topics and household budgeting. In this regard, the origins of personal finance in South Korea mirror the international foundations of personal finance. In those early days, the home economics field mainly focused on nutrition, hygiene, and clothing. Home management was treated as a minor field where basic economics theories were covered in other college and university departments. The 1930 curriculum in the Ewha Womans University's Home Economics Department included economics as a social sciences topic along with politics and sociology. At that time, there were four classes in clothing, three classes in nutrition, three classes in personal hygiene, three classes in housing, and several science classes offered to students. Later in 1969, the Home Economics Department at Ewha Womans University expanded to a College of Home Economics. Similar expansions of programs were seen across Korean institutions of higher learning, including Seoul National University. Over time, personal finance topics have come to dominate the curriculums of what are now called Departments of Consumer Studies or Departments of Consumer and Child Studies. While traditional topics like consumer decision-making, budgeting, family resource management, and consumption and expenditure analyses are still taught, beginning in the mid-1990s and early 2000s, personal finance classes, including investments, insurance, financial planning, retirement planning, and real estate planning have emerged as popular classes in most consumer studies curriculums.

Throughout Asia, the concept of financial planning and financial planning practices has come to dominate what some describe as personal finance. The first financial planning curriculum was introduced in South Korea in 2000 when two life insurance companies started providing certified financial planner (CFP®) training. The Financial Planners Association (FPA), Korea signed a memorandum of understanding (MOU) with the U.S. CFP Board of Standards, Inc. to help launch the CFP marks in South Korea. In 2004, the Financial Planning Standards Board, Korea separated from the FPA, Korea. Currently, FPSB Korea is the sole certifying body of the CFP marks. As of this writing, there are about 4,000 CFPs and 20,000 AFPK (Associate Financial Planner Korea, the pre-designation of CFP) in South Korea.

## South Korean Products and Services

The sophistication of consumers of personal finance products and services in South Korea, and much of Asia, has exploded over the past 25 years. Diverse financial products, such as mutual funds, exchange traded funds, equity linked funds, and equity linked deposits, are now the norm. Before 2000, most households used simple banking products, such as time deposits and installment deposits. Before 2000, interest rates for these banking products were more than 10 percent (the highest interest rates were about 18 percent to 20 percent in 1998); however, these rates started to drop beginning in 1999. Currently, in 2021, bank savings rates are less than 1 percent. Before 2000, bank savings products were highly sought after. It is not surprising that most Korean households utilized bank savings products as their main financial planning tools. The attractiveness of savings products helped South Korea, and other Asian countries, achieve very high savings rates. As shown in Figure 4.1, during the 1990s, the average household savings rate in South Korea was 19.2 percent (Organisation for Economic Co-operation and Development (OECD), 2021). Traditionally, Koreans have considered incurring debt as a bad financial decision. For example, in South Korea, it has traditionally been difficult to obtain a long-term mortgage. This started to slowly change in the 2000s. Prior to this time, nearly all Koreans saved 100 percent of the value of a home when making a purchase. In addition, the Korean version of rent (called Jeon-Sei) requires large deposits, which also influences savings rates. Unlike the United States and Europe, the deposit required for renting a house ranges somewhere between 50 percent and 90 percent of the value of the rented property. Rather than pay rent, renters give up interest on their money; however, renters do receive their deposit (i.e., key money) back when they move out of the rental.

However, the situation has changed since 2000. Household savings rates have dropped dramatically. Today, savings rates in South Korea are lower than rates in the United States. The interest rates on bank products have also dropped dramatically. Consumers' perceptions about debt have also changed in step with (a) the increase in the average age of the population; (b) greater job mobility, which has reduced retirement savings and stability; and (c) consumers' interests in accumulating wealth through non-bank products. The generation of Korean baby boomers who were born from 1953 to 1964 who experienced high-interest rates from banking

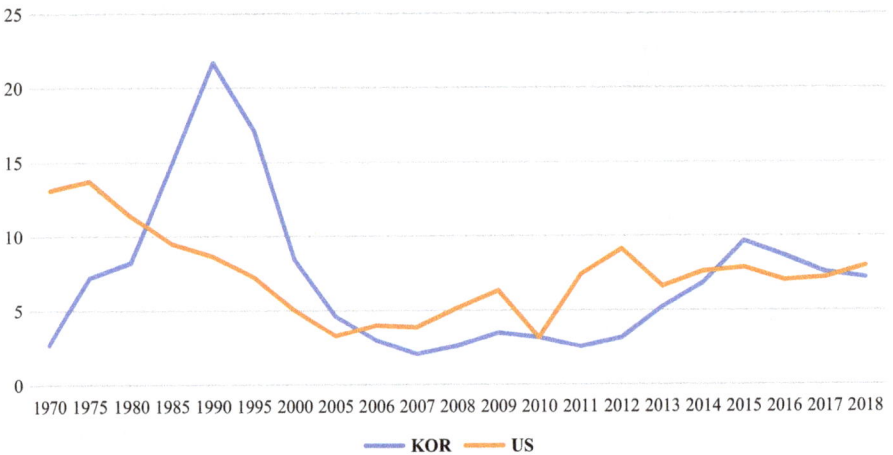

**Figure 4.1:** Household Savings Rate to Disposable Income.
*Source*: Organisation for Economic Co-operation and Development, Household Economics Data (2021).

products has changed their saving behavior. In response, the financial markets have expanded along with the interests of this generation. This can be seen in the growth of the South Korean public fund market. In 2007, the number of mutual fund accounts that were held by individuals (22.95 million accounts) outnumbered the overall number of households (16.42 million) (Son, 2008). On average, those who owned mutual funds held more than five mutual fund accounts (Korea Financial Consumer Protection Foundation, 2010).

In response to the increased interest in investments and financial planning services among Korean households, financial institutions have taken steps to provide differentiated products and services to attract consumers. This is where personal finance concepts, tools, and techniques, and financial planning have come together. The most common financial planning practices – the application of personal finance concepts – tend to be channeled through commercial banks. The professional advice offered by financial planners is provided as part of a sales process. This means that consumers typically do not pay fees for financial advice. In South Korea as of 2021, only a handful of financial professionals charge advice fees to their clients. Nearly all financial professionals work either on salary or via sales commissions. In South Korea, which is similar to other Asian countries, consumers have not yet adopted a fee service model. Unlike payment for legal, psychological, medical, and physical advice, consumers have exhibited an unwillingness to pay directly for personal finance counsel and financial planning advice. The comprehensive professional financial planning market is still in its infancy as of 2021.

## Personal Finance Education and Policy

Since the global financial crisis, financial literacy and consumer protection have been the primary areas of research, policy, and practice for those working in the field of personal finance in South Korea and throughout Asia. With the increased diversity and complexities in financial products and the pursuit of excess returns by consumers, many household financial decision makers have unknowingly entered markets with asymmetric information gaps, resulting in purchases of financial products without full information. Even though the South Korean government enacted the "Financial Investment Services and Capital Market Act" in 2009 (i.e., a law similar to legislation passed in the European Union, Australia, and the United States) – a law that mandates disclosure rules and other investor protection regulations – there have been several media reports over the years describing investment scandals. As a result, and in reaction to urgent and significant needs for consumer protection and fair and transparent practices in financial markets, the South Korean government passed the Financial Consumer Protection Act in 2020. Additional reforms will likely be enacted in response to outcomes associated with the Covid-19 pandemic, dramatic developments in technology, rapid changes in consumer values and lifestyles, and increased uncertainty in the economic outlook of consumers produced by concerns over inclusion, sustainability, generational cohesion, and promotion of social values.

# Research Issues

## Household Finance to Personal Finance

The study of personal finance in South Korea, as in other Asian countries, was subsumed under family economics research that analyzed expenditure or consumption behavior. This changed at the turn of the 21st century. Until the 1990s, research that examined household expenditures, consumption patterns, factors that influence specific expenditures such as durable goods, luxury goods, food consumption, and private education was widely disseminated. Prior research showed that traditionally, in South Korea, human capital investments have been valued highly, so, in general, households tend to exhibit a high propensity to consume for education. Expenditures for private education for South Korean households are higher than that of other countries. As shown in Figure 4.2, private spending on education as a portion of gross domestic product (GDP) for South Korea has been higher than that of the United States until recent years. The decrease in private expenditure on education since 2015 in South Korea is associated with a very low fertility rate – a fertility rate that is calculated by the total number of births per woman was the lowest in the world at 1.09 in 2021 (the fertility

rate for the United States was 1.84 in 2021 [source: www.cia.gov/the-world-factbook
/field/total-fertility-rate/country-comparison]).

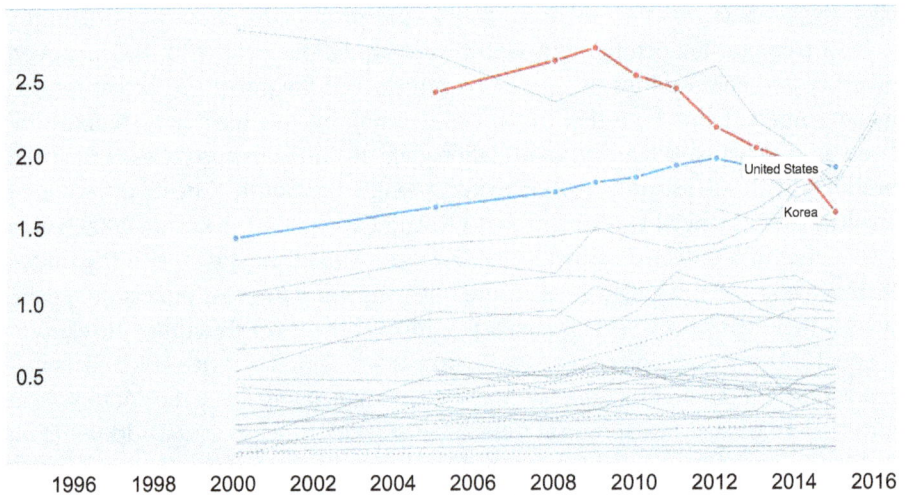

**Figure 4.2:** Private Spending on Education.
*Source*: Organisation for Economic Co-operation and Development (2021).

The types of studies that examined private education expenditures were diverse. Several papers published on the topic compared private education expenditures based on household characteristics including income (Huh, 1995), the marital status of household head (Jeong and Kim, 1999), the number of children (Yang and Lee, 1997), and the sex of child (Yang and Lee, 1997). Prior research also showed that private education expenditure influences household well-being (Kim, 1999), academic performance (Lee and Han, 2016), and economic strains (Lee, 2003). Studies that examined influences on economic factors, like income and economic strain on private education expenditure, showed that there have traditionally been positive relationships between income and private education expenditure. This line of research also showed that households did not reduce private education expenditure when experiencing economic strains during economic downtimes. Other research showed that household expenditures on private education are normally related to a household head's age, which means that private education expenditures are strongly influenced by lifecycle stages. A study by Kim (1999) showed that household well-being is not directly related to the amount spent on private education, but, instead, the subjective burden of private education expenditure is negatively related to household well-being. When examining private education expenditures, some studies (e.g., Joo and Hwang, 2005) included non-economic factors such as non-cognitive factors (e.g., influences of teachers and advertisements) and emotional factors (e.g., involvement with education), and attitudinal factors.

Beginning in 2000, many personal finance researchers have shifted their focus to retirement and investment issues. This line of research was considered novel at the time given cultural traditions in South Korea. Throughout Asia, a traditional family value has been an expectation that younger generations will provide elderly care. However, given the population composition and the work environment, these expectations have slowly been fading. Traditionally, for most South Koreans, children implicitly accepted the responsibility for caring for their older parents, and people generally worked long periods with one employer. However, South Korea has experienced dramatically rapid population aging since 2006 and the values that relate to support for the elderly have changed. A similar change has been seen throughout Asia. In terms of the work environment, people now change employers more frequently, which makes it difficult to accumulate enough severance payments to meet later-life needs. To deal with this issue, employer-sponsored pensions for workers in the private sector were introduced in 2005 with the enactment of the Security of Retirement Income Act. With this Act, employers in South Korea were prompted to establish workplace-based pension programs, such as defined-benefit plans, defined-contribution plans, and Individual Retirement Pensions. Personal finance research topics related to retirement planning now include examining retirement preparedness and adequacy, attitudes toward an employer-sponsored retirement system, savings behavior for retirement, utilization of personal annuity products, and attitudes about annuitization.

More recently, the research focus of those interested in personal finance topics has shifted from the family to the individual. New lines of research related to individuals' behavior in the financial markets, the use of mutual fund investments, stock market participation, and insurance shopping have garnered increased attention. As researchers have shifted to better understand individual behaviors in the financial markets, research using behavioral finance frameworks has come to dominate much of the work being conducted in South Korea. For example, research examining anchoring effects in annuitization decision-making showed that South Korean adults were influenced by anchors that suggested to them how much of their retirement income should be used for annuity products and how much of their retirement income should be provided in an annuity form (Joo and Yun, 2014). Research on stock investments also showed several behavioral heuristics, such as framing and overconfidence. When asked about anticipated returns, investors were found to be influenced by the form of questions, whether they were framed as anticipated price or expected returns. When asked about prices, individuals were shown to anticipate lower returns compared to cases when they were asked for anticipated returns on a percent increase basis (Jeong and Joo, 2019).

## Personal Finance Research Topic Diversification

Since 2010, the personal finance literature has expanded to include diverse research topics. Personal finance culture, prosocial behavior, social enterprise, impact investments, and financial planning technology have emerged as important research topics. With the government's support, the social economy field has grown dramatically since 2007, which was the year that the South Korean government enacted the Social Enterprise Promotion Act. With growing interests in sustainability and sustainable development, social values have become one of the major issues across fields, including social welfare, consumer studies, economics, and management. Several researchers have attempted to examine socially responsible investments and impact investments in South Korea. In addition, ethical and political consumption has been a topic that has caught the attention of many young researchers.

Technological developments continue to dramatically change the lives of consumers. Although this is true worldwide, the effect has been very pronounced in South Korea. South Korea has one of the fastest Internet speeds with extensive coverage. The percentage of smartphone holdings means that South Korea is the number one adopter of smartphone technology – 95 percent of all individuals own a smartphone (the remaining 5 percent of the population have general cell phones) (Silver, 2019). Personal finance researchers have taken an interest in better understanding mobile transactions. It has been shown that technology can produce financial exclusion problems for those who have lower levels of digital literacy. There is a plethora of commercial transaction platforms through personal computers (PCs) and mobile phones, and these new transaction platforms have changed how financial transactions are conducted. Moreover, many banks in South Korea shut down physical branches and offices due to cost increases caused by demographic changes. Consumers were forced to use online banking services because of the inconvenience in using physical branches (consumers who wanted "live interactions" were forced to travel longer, wait longer, and pay more for some services). This situation has created technological exclusion for some older consumers and consumers with disadvantages. Several researchers have examined attitudes and behaviors toward financial technology. Joo and associates (2018) found that the willingness to use financial technology is closely related to attitudes, especially the perceived usefulness of services. Joo et al. (2018) reported that older consumers who are more than 65 years of age are willing to use online and other forms of financial technology when they perceive the services are useful and beneficial.

# Research Data and Methodologies

Research techniques used by personal finance researchers have diversified during the past 30 years. In the 1990s, theoretical and descriptive research was the major research methodology. Conceptual research was also conducted on topics such as consumer rights, consumption ethics, and consumer protection. Until 2006, researchers who wanted to analyze household finance data had to conduct surveys to gather primary data. This changed when large nationally representative datasets became available through the South Korean Statistics Bureau and other organizations. A major advancement in data collection occurred when the National Pension Research Institute under the South Korean National Pension Service launched the South Korean Retirement and Income Study, and when the South Korean Labor Institute started the South Korean Longitudinal Study of Ageing in 2006. In 2008, the South Korea Institute of Public Finance launched the Finance Panel Survey. From 1997 to 2003, many personal finance researchers utilized panel data from the Daewoo Household Finance Panel dataset. Even though the Daewoo Panel stopped data gathering after 2003, the data provided foundational information on household and personal finance and opportunities to examine household financial decision making longitudinally.

The majority of personal finance research conducted in South Korea (and throughout Asia) tends to be quantitative and empirical. Much of the existing literature is based on survey research. In recent years, however, researchers have begun to embrace behavioral finance research through the use of experimental research. One study, for example, reviewed 30 years of consumer research in South Korea. As shown in Figure 4.3, the study showed a huge increase in experimental research during the most recent decade (Joo et al., 2020). Advances in data gathering technology, the establishment of many research companies, and the widespread use of online surveys have provided a platform for a wide variety of research studies. In addition, more government-led large-scale surveys have been introduced, which has opened up new areas of personal finance research. Today, it is possible for researchers who are concerned with issues of sample generalizability to use national data.

# Policy Issues

Over the past quarter century, policymakers throughout Asia have taken on a growing interest in personal finance issues. This interest aligns with issues of economic justice, market reforms, and financial literacy introduced in Europe, Australia, New Zealand, and North America. Several policy issues have garnered particular support among South Korean policymakers, including consumer education, financial literacy and capability, consumer protection in the financial markets, and retirement income security.

**Research Methods in Korean Journal of Consumer Studies**

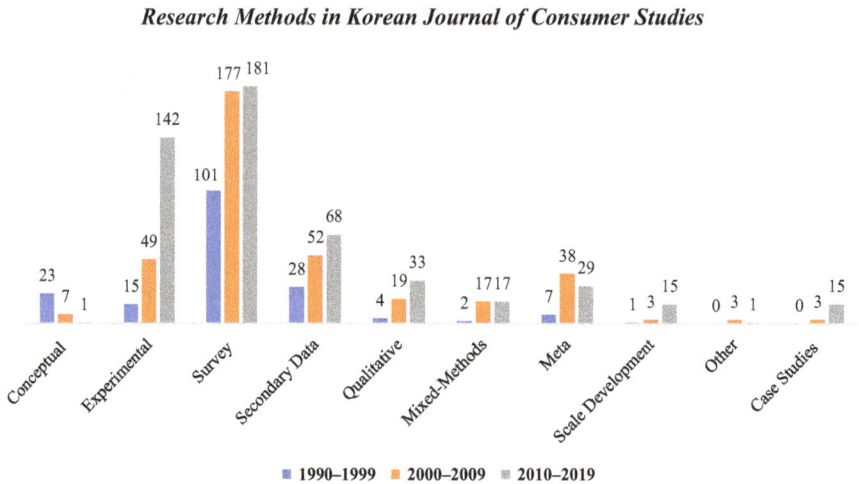

**Figure 4.3:** Research Methods and Data for a 30-Year Period in South Korea (note: figures show the number of manuscripts published using each method).
*Source:* Joo et al. (2020).

## Financial Literacy

The financial literacy among South Koreans has been tested since 2003. Financial literacy was first tested for students enrolled in elementary, middle, and high schools. The first test utilized a modified Jump$tart Financial Literacy test, which showed an average score of only 45.2 out of 100. Financial literacy tests for students have been conducted every three years since 2003, and starting in 2012, the financial literacy of adults aged 18 to 70 has been tested every other year. The National Financial Literacy test uses the OECD/INFE financial literacy test questionnaire. In 2012, the South Korean national average financial literacy score was 62.2 out of 100, which was lower than the OECD average of 64.9. Across the three areas of financial literacy (i.e., knowledge, behavior, and attitudes), South Korean financial literacy scores were highest for knowledge and lowest for behavior, whereas the OECD average was the same with the highest score on knowledge and lowest score for behavior. The financial literacy test scores for South Koreans were lower than the OECD average from 2012 to 2018, but, more recently, financial literacy test scores for South Koreans have been higher than the OECD average. The overall score was 66.8 in 2020, which was up from 62.2 in 2018. The OECD average in 2019 was 62.0. Of particular importance was the upward change in the behavior score. South Koreans' financial knowledge, behavior, and attitudes scores in 2020 were 73.2, 65.5, and 60.2, respectively (Financial Supervisory Services South Korea, 2021). Experts have suggested that important aspects of financial literacy include a functional ability or capability, therefore, behavior should be seen as a key to describing financial literacy. In this regard, improved financial behavior is a desirable change.

However, differences in financial literacy scores based on age have been noted. Those in the younger generation (i.e., ages 18 to 29 years) and older people (i.e., ages 60 to 79 years) exhibited lower financial literacy scores than the national average. However, no gender differences in financial literacy scores have been noted. Even though recent improvements in financial literacy test scores have been noted, it is important to point out that overall levels of financial literacy and competency for South Koreans are not high. Many South Korean consumers lack a basic understanding of personal finance concepts, which leads to suboptimal decision making. Moreover, voice phishing and other financial scams are serious problems in South Korea. Statistics show that, on average, there were about 61 voice phishing scams every day from January 2012 to July 2020, with average fraud amounts per day of $660,000 ($1 to KRW1115) (South Korean Financial News, 2020). These data indicate just a few examples of the need for enhanced financial education.

## Consumer Protection

South Korean policymakers were quick to act in response to increased needs for consumer protection. In 2020, the Financial Consumer Protection Act was passed. This Act provides overarching consumer protection for consumers interacting in the financial markets. The Act specifies consumers' and financial institutions' rights and responsibilities, rules of conduct, (e.g., adequacy and suitability rules), duties to explain, rules for advertisements, prohibitions on unfair transactions, and consumer education frameworks.

## Financial Education

Based on the Financial Consumer Protection Act, the South Korean government formed the Financial Education Coalition in 2020. The government also established the National Strategy on Financial Education. The national strategy outlines ways to improve financial education through the adoption of systematic plans in financial education, quality improvement of financial educators, introduction and strengthening of practical education in the delivery of education, teaching methods (incorporating financial education into formal education), and improvement in the financial education system.

## Financial Markets

Enforcement of The Financial Consumer Protection Act in 2021 has resulted in system-wide changes that positively affect consumers. For example, financial transaction practices have been changed to ensure consumer protection. Financial institutions now have a responsibility to provide explanations when they sell financial investment products. These explanations must be verified and accessible in case of a future dispute. In some situations, this means that consumers have to bear an inconvenience in return for greater protection. This is a great shift in consumer behavior in the financial markets. Traditionally, consumers pursued and valued convenience more than other product and service attributes. With increased protection, however, consumers now must accept some level of inconvenience. The Act also influenced the financial institutional system, governance, and culture. As an industry built on trust – in some ways, trust is their primary good – financial institutions have been forced to change the way business is conducted. Consumer protection clauses and rules are no longer a business cost; consumer protection laws are a foundational element of practice.

## Financial Advice

The Financial Consumer Protection Act introduced a relatively new approach to providing financial advice. The Act defines financial advice and outlines rules, requirements, the scope of businesses, and the responsibilities of financial advice institutions. This means that newly introduced financial advice institutions, by law, could create new opportunities to expand the financial advice marketplace. However, the market situation, especially consumers' views of advice, may limit growth opportunities. Even so, financial advice institutions could be in a position to provide useful services to consumers, especially in reducing the complexities associated with making decisions related to financial products, retirement products, and changing economic and social environments. But how the financial advice market will form in South Korea is not yet clear, which makes this a ripe area of research that can inform public policy.

## Retirement Preparedness

Retirement preparedness and retirement income security are also very significant policy issues throughout Asia and South Korea. Due to rapid population aging, South Korea is anticipated to have the largest portion (37 percent of the total population) of elderly citizens in the world in 2047 (South Korea Statistics Bureau, 2019). Rapid population aging creates significant challenges for any society. For example, due to dramatically low birth rates in South Korea, the number of school-aged children is declining sharply, which can lead to serious financial problems for colleges and universities in South Korea. The number of empty villages in rural areas is increasing and this leads to unequal development and lowered levels of living and problematic conditions in some places. It is clear that the rate of increasing costs for elderly care will be higher than other future costs for the government. And yet, the system for retirement income security is still in its early stages. The workplace pension system has less than 20 years of history (as of 2021) and workers have yet to accumulate enough for their retirement. Research opportunities abound for those interested in shaping public policy related to retirement products, pensions, and old-age issues.

# A Case Study for Retirement Preparedness – An Advanced Example

Personal finance issues, topics, and concerns faced by Asian countries in the 21st century mirror those of the European Union, Australia, New Zealand, and North American in the 20th century. The following case study illustrates how what has been learned internationally can be applied in the context of a country like South Korea.

The Australian Superannuation system – the national pension system – provides insights into how the complementary fields of personal finance and financial planning can inform public policy. In Australia, there are three pillars to retirement income. The first pillar is the Social Security Age Pension, the second pillar is a mandatory superannuation guarantee, and the third pillar is personal savings.

Australia was one of the first countries to establish a modern pension system. In 1908, the Australian government passed the Invalid and Old Age Pension Act to provide pensions for older adults. The first pension was limited to people with special characteristics (e.g., year of work, residency, and means). The pension age was 65 years for both men and women. In just two years, the eligible pension age for women was lowered to age 60. In a short period of time, the superannuation system had evolved to expand coverage (including relaxed means testing) and provide tax benefits (tax deduction for employer contribution). Despite these evolutions, by 1972, only 32 percent of workers were covered by the program. In 1974, The Australian Bureau of Statistics published a national survey of superannuation coverage that showed 58 percent in the public sector and only 24 percent in the private sector were covered by the superannuation program. The Australian government tried to expand pension coverage through further relaxation of means tests (by 1975, means tests were removed for those aged 70 and older). In 1987, the Australian government enacted the Occupational Superannuation Standards Act, which included vesting, benefits, and management provisions.

In 1992, the Australian Labor department introduced a Superannuation Guarantee, which required employer contributions, and, by 1995, 80.5 percent of workers were covered by the superannuation program. To deal with aging and increased pension payments, the pension age of women was increased to age 65 starting in 1994. Retirement savings accounts were introduced in 1997 along with the adoption of a superannuation surcharge. Additionally, the maximum contribution age increased to age 70. Since then, the Australian Superannuation program has changed in response to demographic and regulatory requirements, such as increased contribution rates by employers.

Financial planning, as the applied practice of personal finance, was developing alongside the Australian Superannuation system. Cull (2009) noted that the growth of the middle class, an aging population, changes in lifestyle (e.g., retiring early, prolonged education, larger burden of child-rearing) set the backdrop for the development of financial planning. Cultural factors, including materialism and technological developments, also played an important role in the development of financial planning. For political, economic, and institutional factors, Australian superannuation played significant roles in the development of financial planning. For example, since 1980 the increased participation and contribution to superannuation and the mandatory Superannuation Guarantee since 1992 caused the financial planning industry, especially insurance companies, to introduce more products. Superannuation legislation also encouraged consumers to seek help from financial professionals because of the various choices that can be utilized by the system, such as super choice, super co-contribution, and changes in coverage.

A survey by the Australian Securities and Investments Commission (2019) showed that Australian consumers' experience and expectations with financial planning are quite broad. Among the surveyed 27 percent of the consumers had financial planning advice in the past but 41 percent of survey consumers answered that they would seek financial advice in the future. Moreover, 37 percent of participants who had recently thought about getting financial advice, but had not done so, were open to using digital advice. Topics that Australian consumers want are investment (47 percent), retirement planning (37 percent), growing superannuation (31 percent), and budgeting/cash flow management (22 percent).

As with other countries, Australia also experienced increased demand for digitalization in financial planning services and retirement and later life planning are the key concerns for consumers.

# Future Research Directions

Future directions in personal finance and financial planning in South Korea can be summarized as follows: Research is needed to better understand changes in consumer needs, new technology, and social impacts. First, consumers' needs are complicated and diverse. South Korea, like many other Asian countries, tends to be culturally homogeneous. Even so, South Korea is changing to a multi-cultural society. Younger generations do not share the same values espoused by the older generation. The number of consumers who have different ethnic backgrounds is also increasing. This implies that consumers will increasingly require individualized micro-targeted services. The voice of consumers and the power of individual groups are getting stronger. This creates new challenges for policymakers, personal finance practitioners, and researchers. Future research that expands the understanding of consumers should be continuously promoted. To improve the rigor of research, methodological and analytical techniques should be advanced; however, the application of sound theoretical frameworks may be even more important. Personal finance, as an applied field of study and practice, should attempt to incorporate theories from other fields with more valid reasoning and strive for the development of original theories. Practitioners need to focus more on providing micro-customized services to their clients. Following the concept of financial planning, the nature of personal finance practices should be conceptualized based on individualization.

Second, technological changes can create new opportunities and challenges. Artificial intelligence (AI), machine learning, big data, blockchain data, and other technological advancements can be the key to future research success. Technology is one of the things that society cannot ignore or avoid. Firms that have a competitive advantage in technology are increasingly entering the personal finance domain through product and service offerings. In South Korea, some big technology companies, such as NAVER (the largest information portal company in South Korea), already provide financial services. While consumer protection is a necessary requirement for financial practitioners, consumers still demand convenience. With convenient access and familiarities in other transactions (e.g., shopping, entertainment, and information searching), consumers may view big tech companies' platforms as something appropriate for financial transactions. One underexplored research area is related to understanding the positive and negative outcomes associated with financial information search behaviors by consumers. For example, consumers are continually exposed to various non-verified financial information through online platforms. Whether this information is useful, truthful, or appropriate, and how consumers view and use such information, is something that is understudied.

Third, social impacts and sustainability will be primary research topics in the future. Social well-being and sustainability are directly associated with consumer behavior; therefore, research and practice should focus on these issues. Practitioners need to examine the process of services to ensure positive social impacts and social values. Throughout Asia, and in South Korea in particular, the concept of ESG, i.e., E(Environment), S(Social), G(Governance), has come to dominate business practice. Consumers are closely watching to see if businesses are keeping their socially responsible promises. Additional studies of the associations between and among ESG and investment behaviors and expectations are needed.

# Conclusion

This chapter provided a brief overview of how personal finance is conceptualized and practiced in Asia, with a focus on South Korea. While the situation in South Korea is very similar to that of other countries, including the United States, several differences make the Asian experience unique. For example, South Korea (and many other Asian countries) has experienced significant demographic changes due to extremely low fertility rates. This situation has placed, and continues to place, strains on the country's ability to fund and care for those in or nearing retirement. More personal finance research is needed to inform policy and practice. Particular areas of need include research focused on better understanding how changes in technology, the environment, and culture are related to consumer outcomes. As mentioned in the introduction to this chapter, the world economic system is becoming increasingly intertwined with the personal financial situation of individuals and households. This connectedness is likely to become more deeply rooted in the future. As such, gaining a better understanding of cultural similarities and differences in relation to personal finances is something all personal finance researchers and practitioners, as well as policymakers, should be cognizant of.

# References

Australian Securities and Investments Commission. (2019). *19-223MR consumers see value in financial advice, but lack of trust remains an issue.* https://asic.gov.au/about-asic/news-centre/find-a-media-release/2019-releases/19-223mr-consumers-see-value-in-financial-advice-but-lack-of-trust-remains-an-issue/

Cull, M. (2009). The rise of the financial planning industry. *Australasian Accounting, Business and Finance Journal, 3*(1), 26–37.

Financial Supervisory Services South Korea (2021, March 30). *Report for 2020 national financial literacy survey.* Accessed July 2021. www.fss.or.kr/fss/kr/promo/bodobbs_view.jsp?seqno=23778

Huh, K-O. (1995). A comparison of child rearing expenses between single parent family and both parent family. *Korean Journal of Consumer Studies, 6*(1), 1–19.

Jeong, J-H., and Joo, S H. (2019). Framing effects of price and return forecasts on investor's stock investment decision. *Financial Planning Review, 12*(3), 1–27.

Jeong, S-H., and Kim, H-J. (1999). Support for child rearing expenses for divorce family. *Korean Journal of Consumer Studies, 10*(4), 23–40.

Joo, M., and Hwang, D. (2005). The effect of noncognitive factor on attitude toward private education expenditure. *Korean Journal of Consumer Studies, 16*(2), 147–165.

Joo, S-H., Koh, E-H., and Yoo, M-S. (2018). Exploring factors related to FinTech acceptance in financial transaction. *Korean Journal of Consumption Culture, 21*(2), 175–202. 10.17053/jcc.2018.21.2.008

Joo, S-H., Suk, K., and Rha, J-Y. (2020). Journal of consumer studies: Retrospects and prospects. *Korean Journal of Consumer Studies, 31*(6), 1–30. 10.35736/JCS.31.6.1

Joo, S-H., and Yun, M. (2014). Annuitization decision making and anchoring effect. *Korean Journal of Consumer Studies*, *25*(5), 147–166.

Kim, S. (1999). Private education expenses, burden, and economic well-being of households. *Korean Journal of Consumer Studies*, *10*(3), 101–121.

Korea Financial Consumer Protection Foundation (2010). *Survey of fund investors in 2009.* Accessed July 2021. http://www.invedu.or.kr/research/ir_result_report.jsp

Lee, S. S. (2003). The effects of household financial system on private education expenses: Focused on income classification. *Journal of Korean Home Economics*, *41*(11), 151–169.

Lee. S., and Han, Y. (2016). Private education expenditure and academic performance of child: Focusing on middle school students. *Korean Journal of Consumer Studies*, *27*(2), 85–100.

Organisation for Economic Co-operation and Development. (2021, June 20). *Household savings.* 10.1787/cfc6f499-en.

Silver, L. (2019). *Smartphone ownership is growing rapidly around the world, but not always equally.* Pew Research Center. https://www.pewresearch.org/global/2019/02/05/smart phone-ownership-is-growing-rapidly-around-the-world-but-not-always-equally/

Son, H. R. (2008, January 4). *2007 Fund market reviewed by statistics.* DongA. Accessed July 2021. www.donga.com/news/article/all/20080104/8529949/1

South Korea Statistics Bureau. (2019). *2019 Anticipation of future populations.* Accessed July 2021. https://meta.narastat.kr/metasvc/index.do?confmNo=101033&inputYear=2019

South Korean Financial News (2020, September 30). *Voice phishing scam reached 240 billion KW for the past 9 years.* https://www.fnnews.com/news/202009291318204375

Yang, S-J., and Lee, Y. (1997). Analysis of factors for child rearing expenses: Focusing on number of children and sex of child. *Korean Journal of Consumer Studies*, *8*(2), 81–101.

Sarah D. Asebedo
# 5 Theories of Personal Finance

**Abstract:** This chapter provides an overview of the theories used in personal finance research, practice, and education. Personal finance encompasses financial planning, financial counseling, financial psychology, and financial therapy resulting in a diverse set of theoretical perspectives underpinning personal finance. This chapter highlights the theories unique to financial planning, financial counseling, financial psychology, and financial therapy, in addition to the theories that span across these areas. Lastly, this chapter addresses opportunities, challenges, and future directions for theoretical development within personal finance.

**Keywords:** financial counseling, financial planning, financial psychology, financial therapy, personal finance theory

## Introduction

Personal finance is an interdisciplinary profession that encompasses broad research, practice, and education topics (Schuchardt et al., 2007). Specifically, Schuchardt et al. proposed that personal finance is "an application of the principles of finance, resource management, consumer education, and the sociology and psychology of decision making to the study of the ways that individuals, families, and households acquire, develop, and allocate monetary resources to meet their current and future financial needs" (p. 67). This comprehensive definition of personal finance is an accurate reflection of the varied landscape of personal finance research, practice, and education, as illustrated in Table 5.1. Furthermore, this definition points to the potential for a variety of phenomena to occur within personal finance, which invites theory from multiple disciplines to explain it and inform its future development – including economics, sociology, family studies, psychology, counseling, and therapy (Schuchardt et al., 2007). Consistent with Schuchardt et al., financial planning and financial counseling are two distinct yet overlapping professions within personal finance. Since Schuchardt et al.'s overview of personal finance in 2007, financial psychology (inclusive of behavioral finance) and financial therapy have emerged to make meaningful contributions that deepen our understanding of financial behavior, decision-making, and well-being.

Financial planning, financial counseling, financial psychology, and financial therapy each hold a unique perspective and approach to personal finance with education programs and professional certification paths (see Table 5.1). While each of these

**Sarah D. Asebedo,** Texas Tech University

https://doi.org/10.1515/9783110727692-005

**Table 5.1:** Definitions and Professional Certifications for Areas of Research, Practice, and Education in Personal Finance.

| | Personal Finance | | | |
|---|---|---|---|---|
| | **Financial Planning** | **Financial Counseling** | **Financial Psychology** | **Financial Therapy** |
| **Definition** | "A collaborative process that helps maximize a Client's potential for meeting life goals through Financial Advice that integrates relevant elements of the Client's personal and financial circumstances" (CFP Board, 2018, p. 34). | "A helping profession that assists clients through prevention and intervention services to help them meet their goals. The practice of financial counseling integrates skills and knowledge into the interactions and relationships between the client and counselor and influences the outcomes of the counseling process" (Durband et al., 2019a, abstract). | "Financial psychology draws from behavioral finance and other areas of psychology to help alleviate financial stress and promote healthy financial behaviors. Financial psychology focuses on using psychological research and theory to create micro-basedtechniques to help shape idiosyncratic financial beliefs and behaviors to improve financial health" (Klontz and Horwitz, 2017, p. 29). | "A process informed by both therapeutic and financial competencies that helps people think, feel, communicate, and behave differently with money to improve overall well-being through evidence-based practices and interventions" (FTA, 2020). |
| **Professional Certification** | Certified Financial Planner™ (CFP ®) professional, *CFP Board.* | Accredited Financial Counselor® (AFC®), *AFCPE.* | Certified Financial Behavior Specialist® (FBS®), *FPI.* | Certified Financial Therapist-I™ (CFT-I™), *FTA.* |

*Note.* AFCPE = Association for Financial Counseling and Planning Education; CFP Board = Certified Financial Planner Board of Standards; FPI = Financial Psychology Institute; FTA = Financial Therapy Association.
Source: Doe and Doe (2016)

areas approaches personal finance through a different lens, they also demonstrate considerable synergy through a common goal to help individuals and households achieve financial well-being through sound financial decision making. Therefore, this chapter will provide an overview of personal finance theories through these four unique, yet symbiotic, professions within the broader definition of personal finance according to Schuchardt et al. (2007). Furthermore, this chapter takes a unique approach by reviewing the prevalent theories within financial planning, financial counseling, financial psychology, and financial therapy side by side and within personal finance. Thus, this chapter does not provide in-depth descriptions of each theory; instead, it offers a theoretical map across and within the various professions within personal finance. Readers can find a deeper discussion of each theory in the sources cited in Tables 5.3 through 5.7.

# Historical Perspective

The origins of the professional practice of personal finance date back to 1969 with financial planning emerging from a meeting of financial services industry leaders (Yeske, 2016); financial counseling soon followed in the late 1970s to early 1980s (Archuleta and Grable, 2011) with the Association for Financial Counseling and Planning Education (AFCPE) established in 1983 (AFCPE, 2021). As such, the primary theories informing the early development of personal finance tend to be rooted in financial planning, and therefore consist of finance (i.e., investments), economics, and strategic planning (Overton, 2008). Financial counseling's growth made way for theoretical perspectives from psychology, sociology, and therapy (Durband et al., 2019b). During the 1980s, behavioral finance emerged to explain irrational movements in the stock market due to psychological forces motivating investor behavior (Frydman and Camerer, 2016). Behavioral finance has expanded beyond the investment environment to encompass other financial decision-making domains, such as saving and borrowing, through an area of research and practice known as financial psychology (Klontz and Horwitz, 2017). Financial psychology emerged in the mid- to late 2000s as a way for psychologists to extend their reach and practice expertise (Klontz, 2010). Today, financial professionals are also expanding their skill repertoire by seeking education and certification in financial psychology (Financial Psychology Institute, 2021). Financial psychology has deepened the theoretical foundation for the psychology of money and aligns with Schuchardt et al.'s (2007) definition of personal finance. Similarly, financial therapy was formed in 2008 and has expanded the scope and theoretical map of personal finance even further by integrating the financial, cognitive, relational, emotional, and behavioral aspects of money (Grable et al., 2010; FTA, 2021).

Financial psychology and financial therapy have gained momentum since the 2007–2009 global financial crisis and, more recently, the Covid-19 health pandemic;

research has shown that households have struggled financially and with adversity across multiple life domains due to these events (Afifi et al., 2018; Polizzi et al., 2020). Evidence also suggests that financial professionals faced significant challenges during the global financial crisis and Covid-19 health pandemic given the number of business disruptions, difficult client situations, and personal stressors (Klontz and Britt, 2012). Overall, these notable global economic events were a catalyst for personal finance to integrate counseling, psychology, and therapy (Archuleta et al., 2021; Chaffin, 2018). Financial planning has realized a similar progression over time and has begun to embrace the research and practice insights derived from counseling, psychology, and therapy (Chaffin, 2018). Figure 5.1 depicts the origin and expansion of personal finance over time.

**Figure 5.1:** Origins and Expansion of Personal Finance Over Time.

## What is Theory?

A discussion of theory requires an understanding of what theory is. Researchers often use the word *theory* colloquially to refer to a set of ideas that explain phenomena. Given the variation in theories within personal finance, it is essential to clarify the definition of theory and recognize the different types of theories informing practitioners, researchers, and educators. Doherty et al. (2009) specifically defined theory broadly as both a process and a product that varies in the level of abstraction and the scope of content. Specifically, "Theorizing is the process of systematically formulating and organizing ideas to understand a particular phenomenon. A theory is a set of interconnected ideas that emerge from this process" (p. 20). Based on this definition, a theory is carefully constructed according to a process that emphasizes clarity, coherence, and connection of ideas; Doherty et al. also asserted that there are seven different types of theories typically applied to the family that vary based on the scope of content and level of abstraction (Doherty et al., 2009; Turner, 1978): (a) empirical generalizations, (b) causal models, (c) middle-range theories, (d) formal propositional theories, (e) analytical typologies, (f) conceptual frameworks, and (g) metatheories. Theories in personal finance span across these theory types (defined and summarized in Table 5.2).

**Table 5.2:** Theory Type Definitions, Scope, and Abstraction.

| Type | Definition |
|---|---|
| Empirical Generalizations (a) | Summaries or generalizations of empirical research results connected across studies explained by ideas about the content area without an overarching theory to guide or explain the connections. |
| Causal Models (b) | Summaries or generalizations of empirical research results from a single study employing empirical methods and longitudinal or experimental data to test multiple pathways among variables. |
| Middle-Range Theories (c) | Focused on a particular content area but more abstract than empirical generalizations or causal models. Middle-range theories produce a framework that researchers can test across multiple studies. |
| Formal Propositional Theories (d) | Explain a particular phenomenon in a single content area with a series of abstract statements or propositions, ranging from general to concrete. |
| Analytical Typologies (e) | Explain generic features and is applied to a wide array of content areas. |
| Conceptual Frameworks (f) | A conceptual map consisting of assumptions and identifying fundamental parts that other theories and data explain. |
| Metatheories (g) | Consist of an entire field of knowledge comprised of a variety of content areas. |

**Abstraction/Scope of Content**

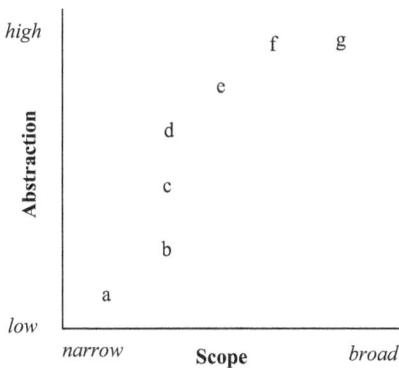

*Sources*: Doherty et al. (2009); Turner (1978).

# Theories in Personal Finance

Theories in personal finance vary in their focus, scope, and level of abstraction across financial planning, financial counseling, financial psychology, and financial therapy. This section outlines the fundamental theories contributing to each area of research, practice, and education that have been documented in the literature while also illuminating the theories that extend across areas. Schuchardt et al. (2007) pointed to fundamental theories from sociology, economics, psychology, and finance that generally underpin personal finance (see Table 5.3). These theories provide a basis for the interdisciplinary nature of personal finance as a helping profession that integrates household finances and economics with human behavior impacted by an individual's psychology and the social environment. These fundamental theories informing personal finance range from very specific and narrow in scope (e.g., household finance) to highly abstract and broad in scope (e.g., human ecological model).

**Table 5.3:** Theories from Sociology, Economics, Psychology, and Finance that Generally Underpin Personal Finance.

| Discipline | Theory (Citation) | Source |
|---|---|---|
| Sociology | Human Ecological Model (Bronfenbrenner, 1979) | Schuchardt et al. (2007) |
| Economics | Life-Cycle Hypothesis of Savings (Ando and Modigliani, 1963) Behavioral Life-Cycle Hypothesis (Shefrin and Thaler, 1988) | |
| Psychology | Theory of Reasoned Action and Theory of Planned Behavior (Ajzen, 1991; Ajzen and Fishbein, 1980) Transtheoretical Model of Behavior Change (Prochaska et al. 1992) | |
| Finance | Household Finance (Campbell, 2006) | |

## Financial Planning

Financial planning is "a collaborative process that helps maximize a client's potential for meeting life goals through financial advice that integrates relevant elements of the client's personal and financial circumstances" (CFP Board, 2018). This definition from the CFP Board emphasizes that financial planning is a *process* that integrates an individual's (client's) personal and financial environments. Overton (2008) built upon Altfest (2004) to summarize the core theories that have shaped financial planning. In addition to the general personal finance theories articulated by Schuchardt et al. (see Table 5.3), Overton and Altfest observed that economics, family studies (e.g., Becker, 1965), and finance theories (e.g., modern portfolio theory (MPT) and strategic planning) primarily inform financial planning research and practice. Overton also noted that strategic planning, management, and thinking specifically served a fundamental role in shaping the financial planning process. However, both Overton and Altfest argued that it is necessary to develop financial planning-specific theories to ground financial planning research and practice and articulate its unique effects. At the time of this writing, three papers have aimed to develop theories that explain phenomena within the context of the professional practice of financial planning: (a) Finding the Planning in Financial Planning (Yeske, 2010), (b) A Conflict Resolution Framework for Money Arguments (Asebedo, 2016), and (c) Financial Planning Client Interaction Theory (Asebedo, 2019). Yeske (2010) summarized themes from the empirical financial planning literature generated from the strategic management field to explain varying approaches to strategy-making in client relationships. Asebedo (2016) incorporated models and concepts from the mediation literature to create a conflict resolution conceptual framework that financial planners can apply to money arguments that surface within the financial planning process. Lastly, Asebedo (2019) utilized a household economics framework to develop a formal propositional theory that explains the unique client interaction effects resulting from a relative interaction between financial planner and client attributes and resources (psychological, social, relational, technical, financial, etc.) that create varying levels of value. Financial planning theory development must continue to advance as researchers, practitioners, and consumers recognize it as a helping- and client-centered profession that reaches beyond the traditional economic and financial domains (Asebedo, 2019; Chaffin, 2018).

**Table 5.4:** Financial Planning Theories.

| Discipline | Theory (Citation) | Source |
| --- | --- | --- |
| Economics and Family Studies | A Theory of the Allocation of Time (Becker, 1965) Human Capital (Becker, 1975) | Altfest (2004); Overton (2008) |
| Finance | Modern Portfolio Theory (Markowitz, 1952) Capital Asset Pricing Model (Black et al., 1972) Efficient Market Hypothesis (Fama, 1970) Strategic Planning and Management (Hill et al., 2014) | |
| Financial Planning | A Conflict Resolution Framework for Money Arguments (Asebedo, 2016) Finding the Planning in Financial Planning (Yeske, 2010) Financial Planning Client Interaction Theory (Asebedo, 2019) | – |

## Financial Counseling

Financial counseling is "a helping profession that assists clients through prevention and intervention services to help them meet their goals. The practice of financial counseling integrates skills and knowledge into the interactions and relationships between the client and counselor and influences the outcomes of the counseling process" (Durband et al., 2019a, abstract). The theories informing financial counseling identified in Table 5.5 were drawn from Durband et al. (2019b) and are theories informing financial counseling above and beyond the general personal finance theories articulated by Schuchardt et al. (see Table 5.3). The aforementioned definition of financial counseling, in addition to the fundamental theories offered by Durband et al. (2019b), suggests that financial counseling focuses on integrating psychology, sociology, and therapeutic approaches within personal finance.

**Table 5.5:** Financial Counseling Theories.

| Discipline | Theory (Citation) | Source |
|---|---|---|
| Psychology | Psychoanalytic Theory (Freud, 1973)<br>Adlerian Theory (Dinkmeyer and Sherman, 1989)<br>Person-Centered Approach (Rogers, 1979)<br>Rational Emotive Behavioral Therapy (Ellis and Dryden, 2007)<br>Solution-Focused Brief Therapy (Iveson, 2002)<br>Motivational Interviewing (Miller and Rollnick, 2013)<br>Well-Being Theory (Seligman, 2012) | Durband et al. (2019b) |
| Sociology | General Systems Theory (Doherty et al., 2009) | |
| Therapy | Appreciative Inquiry (Whitney and Trosten-Bloom, 2010)<br>Gestalt Therapy Theory (Corey, 2001) | |

## Financial Psychology

According to Klontz and Horwitz (2017), "Financial psychology draws from behavioral finance and other areas of psychology to help alleviate financial stress and promote healthy financial behaviors. Financial psychology focuses on using psychological research and theory to create micro-based techniques to help shape idiosyncratic financial beliefs and behaviors to improve financial health" (p. 29). While behavioral finance integrates investments, biology, and psychology (Byrne and Brooks, 2008), Klontz and Horwitz argued that behavioral finance is more accurately described as the application of cognitive psychology to finance. Financial psychology, therefore, encompasses behavioral finance and then expands its application to finance through multiple subspecialties within psychology, including social psychology, personality psychology, multicultural psychology, positive psychology, humanistic psychology, and development psychology (Klontz et al., 2018). Researchers and practitioners have also applied psychotherapeutic strategies within financial psychology, including cognitive-behavioral, motivational interviewing, solution-focused, and positive psychology strategies (Klontz et al., 2018). Lastly, biases and heuristics are the hallmark of behavioral finance that stem from dual-process theories (Evans, 2003; Evans and Curtis-Holmes, 2005; Stanovich, 1999, 2004). Agrawal (2012) further explored behavioral biases in finance and developed a conceptual framework to explain the interaction between biases, their causes, and their outcomes. It is clear from Table 5.6 that in addition to the personal finance theories proposed by Schuchardt et al., financial psychology offers depth for the application and research of psychology within personal finance.

**Table 5.6:** Financial Psychology Theories.

| Discipline | Theory (Citation) | Source |
|---|---|---|
| Psychology | Cognitive Behavioral Therapy (Beck, 2011) Solution-Focused Brief Therapy (Iveson, 2002) Motivational Interviewing (Miller and Rollnick, 2013) Well-Being Theory (Seligman, 2012) | Klontz et al. (2018) |
| | Big Five Trait Theory (John and Srivastava, 1999) | Asebedo (2018) |
| | Dual Process Theory of Reasoning (Evans, 2003; Evans and Curtis-Holmes, 2005; Stanovich, 1999, 2004) Bounded Rationality (Simon, 2000) | Hirshleifer (2015) |
| Behavioral Finance | Prospect Theory (Kahneman and Tversky, 1979) | |
| | A Conceptual Framework of Behavioral Biases in Finance (Agrawal, 2012) | – |
| Therapy | Experiential Therapy (Greenberg et al., 1994) | Klontz et al. (2018) |

## Financial Therapy

Financial therapy is "a process informed by both therapeutic and financial competencies that helps people think, feel, communicate, and behave differently with money to improve overall well-being through evidence-based practices and interventions" (FTA, 2020). Financial therapy emerged with a comprehensive and diverse set of theories forming its foundation, reflecting the broad input in the development of financial therapy from mental health and personal finance practitioners, researchers, and educators (Grable et al., 2010). The Financial Therapy Association's (FTA, 2021) competency handbook for the Certified Financial Therapist-I™ professional designation provided the financial therapy theories in Table 5.7. These theories underscore the comprehensive nature of financial therapy that spans fundamental finance theories (e.g., MPT), sociology (e.g., general systems theory), psychology (e.g., psychoanalytic theory), and therapeutic approaches (e.g., narrative theory). Moreover, Klontz et al. (2014) provided an overview of financial therapy theory along with research-based models for use in practice such as the Ford Financial Empowerment Model, Solutions-Focused Financial Therapy, and psychodynamic financial therapy.

**Table 5.7:** Financial Therapy Theories.

| Discipline | Theory (Citation) | Source |
|---|---|---|
| Finance | Modern Portfolio Theory (Markowitz, 1952) | FTA (2021) |
| | Capital Asset Pricing Model (Black et al., 1972) | |
| Sociology | General Systems Theory (Doherty et al., 2009) | |
| Psychology | Psychoanalytic Theory (Freud, 1973) | |
| | Object-Relations Theory (Fairbairn, 1954; Winnicott, 2018) | |
| | Self-Psychology Theory (Kohut, 1971, 1977) | |
| | Attachment Theory (Ainsworth, 1978) | |
| | Cognitive Behavioral Therapy (Beck, 2011) | |
| | Solution-Focused Brief Therapy (Iveson, 2002) | |
| | Motivational Interviewing (Miller and Rollnick, 2013) | |
| | Neo-Freudian Psychodynamic Theories (Guntrip, 2018) | |
| | Well-Being Theory (Seligman, 2012) | |
| Therapy | Experiential Therapy (Greenberg et al., 1994) | |
| | Gestalt Therapy Theory (Corey, 2001) | |
| | Narrative Theory (Currie, 2010). | |
| | Strategic Therapy (Stanton, 1981) | |
| | Emotionally Focused Therapy (Greenberg and Johnson, 1988) | |
| | Imago Therapy (Hendrix and Hannah, 2012) | |

## Summary of Theories in Personal Finance

Table 5.8 summarizes the various theories supporting personal finance and demonstrates the considerable theoretical overlap across financial planning, financial counseling, financial psychology, and financial therapy (see grey shaded areas) that stems from sociology, economics, psychology, and therapy. These multidisciplinary theories provide theoretical evidence for the comprehensive definition of personal finance proposed by Schuchardt et al. (2007). Despite this synergy, financial planning, financial counseling, financial psychology, and financial therapy are also markedly different in their purpose, aim, and scope. This variation is a strength; however, it also creates ambiguity for consumers, policymakers, educators, researchers, and regulators regarding terminology, professional designations, compensation models, services, and the scope of practice and education within personal finance. This variability and ambiguity present a challenge for personal finance growth and development.

**Table 5.8:** Summary of Theories in Personal Finance.

| Discipline | Personal Finance | | | |
| --- | --- | --- | --- | --- |
| | Financial Planning | Financial Counseling | Financial Psychology | Financial Therapy |
| Sociology | | Human Ecological Model | | |
| | | General Systems Theory | | General Systems Theory |
| Economics | | | Life-Cycle Hypothesis of Savings | |
| | | | Behavioral Life-Cycle Hypothesis | |
| | A Theory of the Allocation of Time | | | |
| | Human Capital | | | |
| Finance | | Household Finance | | |
| | Modern Portfolio Theory | | | Modern Portfolio Theory |
| | Capital Asset Pricing Model | | | Capital Asset Pricing Model |
| | Efficient Market Hypothesis | | | |
| | Strategic Planning and Management | | | |

(continued)

Table 5.8 (continued)

| Discipline | Personal Finance | | | |
|---|---|---|---|---|
| | Financial Planning | Financial Counseling | Financial Psychology | Financial Therapy |
| Psychology | | Theory of Reasoned Action and Theory of Planned Behavior | | |
| | | Transtheoretical Model of Behavior Change | | |
| | | Psychoanalytic Theory | | Psychoanalytic Theory |
| | | Adlerian Theory | | |
| | | Person-Centered Approach | | |
| | | Rational Emotive Behavioral Therapy | | |
| | | | Solution-Focused Brief Therapy | |
| | | | Motivational Interviewing | |
| | | | Well-Being Theory | |

| Therapy | Cognitive Behavior Therapy | | Appreciative Inquiry |
|---|---|---|---|
| | Big Five Trait Theory | Object-Relations Theory | Gestalt Therapy Theory |
| | Dual Process Theory of Reasoning | Self-Psychology Theory | Experiential Therapy |
| | Bounded Rationality | Attachment Theory | Gestalt Therapy Theory |
| | | Neo-Freudian Psychodynamic Theories | Narrative Theory |
| | | | Strategic Therapy |
| | | | Emotionally Focused Therapy |
| | | | Imago Therapy |

(continued)

**Table 5.8** (continued)

| Discipline | Personal Finance | | | |
| --- | --- | --- | --- | --- |
| | Financial Planning | Financial Counseling | Financial Psychology | Financial Therapy |
| Financial Planning | Conflict Resolution Framework | | | |
| | Finding the Planning in Financial Planning | | | |
| | Financial Planning Client Interaction Theory | | | |
| Behavioral Finance | | | Prospect Theory | |
| | | | Behavioral Biases in Finance | |

## Conclusion: Future Directions

While personal finance has breadth and depth, it also lacks unification and clarity. From a theoretical perspective, Altfest (2004) argued that financial planning-specific theory is necessary to set it apart from other professions and articulate client outcomes and benefits. Similarly, it may be that a metatheory that captures all dimensions of personal finance is necessary to communicate its value, synergy, and unique professional practices through financial planning, financial counseling, financial psychology, and financial therapy. A significant challenge to theory development within personal finance is a lack of longitudinal, experimental, and qualitative data within a practice setting that provides information about the professional and the client; without this data, researchers cannot effectively investigate personal characteristics, relationship effects, and client outcomes (Asebedo, 2019). While personal finance has developed quickly and robustly, it remains in its infancy for theory development. Altfest (2004) noted that theory development is necessary for financial planning – and in this case, the broader practice of personal finance – to achieve professional standing and distinction. It may be that a lack of data generated from within personal finance is a significant barrier to this endeavor and likely due to a scarcity of substantial funding sources committed to supporting it. However, a lack of funding and data should not stymie theory development. As Doherty et al. (2009) noted, theory development is a systematic process of formulating ideas and organizing them to understand a particular phenomenon; theory emerges as a product of this process. As such, research producing evidence-based outcomes that falsify and refine theory should naturally follow the dissemination of theoretical works in a peer-reviewed outlet. Furthermore, theory development necessitates an open mind as it requires researchers to take risks and entertain propositions even though the methods and data to generate empirical support may not yet be possible.

Personal finance has become the focal point of productive interdisciplinary research with several rigorous peer-reviewed journals, broad readership, and talent generated from high-quality doctoral programs. Given this momentum, meaningful theoretical contributions and breakthroughs within personal finance are likely on the horizon. A continued commitment to collaborative research, practice, and discussion is essential to making this a reality.

## References

Afifi, T. D., Davis, S., Merrill, A. F., Coveleski, S., Denes, A., and Shahnazi, A. F. (2018). Couples' communication about financial uncertainty following the Great Recession and its association with stress, mental health and divorce proneness. *Journal of Family and Economic Issues, 39*(2), 205–219.

Agrawal, K. (2012). A conceptual framework of behavioral biases in finance. *IUP Journal of Behavioral Finance, IX*(1), 7–18.

Ainsworth, M. D. S. (1978). The Bowlby-Ainsworth attachment theory. *Behavioral and Brain Sciences, 1*(3), 436–438.

Ajzen, I. (1991). The theory of planned behavior. *Organizational Behavior and Human Decision Processes, 50,* 179–211.

Ajzen, I., and Fishbein, M. (1980). *Understanding attitudes and predicting behavior.* Pearson.

Altfest, L. (2004). Personal financial planning: Origins, developments and a plan for future direction. *The American Economist, 48*(2), 53–60.

Ando, A., and Modigliani, F. (1963). The life cycle hypothesis of saving: Aggregate implications and tests. *American Economic Review, 53,* 55–84.

Archuleta, K. L., Asebedo, S. D., Durband, D. B., Fife, S. T., Ford, M. R., Gray, B. T., Lurtz, M. R., McCoy, M. A., Pickens, J. C., and Sheridan, J. (2021). Facilitating virtual client meetings for money conversations: A multidisciplinary perspective on skills and strategies for financial planners (Equal authorship contribution in alphabetical order). *Journal of Financial Planning, 34*(4), 82–101.

Archuleta, K. L., and Grable, J. E. (2011). The future of financial planning and counseling: An introduction to financial therapy. In J. E. Grable, K. L. Archuleta, and R. R. Nazarinia (eds.), *Financial planning and counseling scales* (pp. 33–59). Springer.

Asebedo, S. D. (2016). Building financial peace: A conflict resolution framework for money arguments. *Journal of Financial Therapy, 7*(2), 1–15.

Asebedo, S. D. (2018). Personality and financial behavior. In C. Chaffin (ed.), *Client psychology* (pp. 137–153). Wiley.

Asebedo, S. D. (2019). Financial planning client interaction theory (FPCIT). *Journal of Personal Finance, 18*(1), 9–23.

Association for Financial Counseling and Planning Education (AFCPE). (2021). *About us.* https://www.afcpe.org/about/

Beck, J. S. (2011). *Cognitive behavior therapy: Basics and beyond* (2nd ed). Guilford Press.

Becker, G. S. (1965). A theory of the allocation of time. *Economic Journal, 75*(299), 493–517.

Becker, G. S. (1975). *Human capital: A theoretical and empirical analysis, with special reference to education* (2nd ed.). Columbia University Press.

Black, F., Jensen, M., and Scholes, M. (1972). The capital-asset pricing model: Some empirical tests. In M. Jensen (ed.), *Studies in the theories of capital markets* (pp. 79–121). Praeger.

Bronfenbrenner, U. (1979). *The ecology of human development.* Harvard University Press.

Byrne, A., and Brooks, M. (2008). Behavioral finance: Theories and evidence. *The Research Foundation of CFA Institute Literature Review,* 1–26.

Campbell, J. Y. (2006). Household finance. *The Journal of Finance, 61*(4), 1553–1604.

Certified Financial Planner Board of Standards (CFP Board). (2018). *Side-by-side comparison of code of ethics and standards of conduct to current standards of professional conduct.* https://www.cfp.net/-/media/files/cfp-board/standards-and-ethics/compliance-resources/cfp-board-code-and-standards-side-by-side-comparison.pdf

Chaffin, C. (ed.). (2018). *Client psychology.* Wiley.

Corey, G. (2001). *Theory and practice of counseling and psychotherapy* (6th ed.). Wadsworth Publishing Co.

Currie, M. (2010). *Postmodern narrative theory.* Macmillan Press Ltd.

Dinkmeyer, D., and Sherman, R. (1989). Brief Adlerian family therapy. *Individual Psychology, 45*(1), 148–158.

Doherty, W. J., Boss, P. G., LaRossa, R., Schumm, W. R., and Steinmetz, S. K. (eds.). (2009). Family theories and methods: A contextual approach. In *Sourcebook of family theories and methods* (pp. 3–28). Springer.

Durband, D. B., Carlson, M. B., and Stueve, C. (2019a). The financial counseling profession. In D. Durband, R. LaW, and A. Mazzolini (eds.), *Financial counseling* (pp. 1–16). Springer. https://doi.org/10.1007/978-3-319-72586-4_1

Durband, D. B., Law, R. H., and Mazzolini, A. K. (eds.). (2019b). *Financial counseling*. Springer.

Ellis, A., and Dryden, W. (2007). *The practice of rational emotive behavior therapy* (2nd ed.). Springer.

Evans, J. S. B. (2003). In two minds: Dual-process accounts of reasoning. *Trends in Cognitive Sciences, 7*(10), 454–459.

Evans, J. S. B., and Curtis-Holmes, J. (2005). Rapid responding increases belief bias: Evidence for the dual-process theory of reasoning. *Thinking & Reasoning,11*(4), 382–389.

Fairbairn, W. R. D. (1954). *An object-relations theory of the personality*. Basic Books.

Fama, E. (1970). Efficient capital markets: A review of theory and empirical work. *The Journal of Finance, 25*, 383–417.

Financial Psychology Institute. (2021). *Certified financial behavior specialist® (FBS®)*. Accessed July 2021. https://www.financialpsychologyinstitute.com/CertifiedFinancialBehaviorSpecialist

Financial Therapy Association (FTA). (2020). *Financial therapy*. Accessed July 2021. https://financialtherapyassociation.org

Financial Therapy Association (FTA). (2021). *CFT-I™ practitioner handbook*. Accessed July 2021. https://www.financialtherapyassociation.org/wp-content/uploads/2020/12/Financial-Therapy-Association-CF-T-I%E2%84%A2-Practitioner-Handbook-2.pdf

Freud, S. (1973). *The complete introductory lectures on psychoanalysis*. In A. Richards (ed.) and J. Strachey (trans.), The Pelican Freud library, Penguin Books.

Frydman, C., and Camerer, C. F. (2016). The psychology and neuroscience of financial decision making. *Trends in Cognitive Sciences, 20*(9), 661–675.

Grable, J., McGill, S., and Britt, S. (2010). The financial therapy association: A brief history. *Journal of Financial Therapy, 1*(1), 1–6.

Greenberg, L. S., Elliott, R., and Lietaer, G. (1994). Research on experiential psychotherapies. In A. E. Bergin, and S. L. Garfield (eds.), *Handbook of psychotherapy and behavior change* (4th ed., pp. 509–539). Wiley.

Greenberg, L. S., and Johnson, S. M. (1988). *Emotionally focused therapy for couples*. Guilford Press.

Guntrip, H. Y. (2018). *Personality structure and human interaction: The developing synthesis of psychodynamic theory*. Routledge.

Hendrix, H., and Hannah, M. T. (2012). *Imago relationship therapy*. Routledge.

Hill, C. W., Jones, G. R., and Schilling, M. A. (2014). *Strategic management: Theory: An integrated approach*. Cengage Learning.

Hirshleifer, D. (2015). Behavioral finance. *Annual Review of Financial Economics, 7*, 133–159.

Iveson, C. (2002). Solution-focused brief therapy. *Advances in Psychiatric Treatment, 8*(2), 149–156.

John, O. P., and Srivastava, S. (1999). The big five trait taxonomy: History, measurement, and theoretical perspectives. In L. A. Pervin, and O. P. John (eds.), *Handbook of personality: Theory and research* (2nd ed., pp. 102–138). Guilford Press.

Kahneman, D., and Tversky, A. (1979). Prospect theory: An analysis of decision making under risk. *Econometrica, 47*(2), 263–292.

Klontz, B. (2010). Consulting with financial planners. In S. Walfish (ed.),*Earning a living outside of managed mental health care: 50 ways to expand your practice* (pp. 141–144). American Psychological Association.

Klontz, B., and Britt, S. L. (2012). Tactical asset management or financial trauma? Why the abandonment of buy-and-hold may be a symptom of posttraumatic stress. *Journal of Financial Therapy, 3*(2), 14–27. https://doi.org/10.4148/jft.v3i2.1718

Klontz, B. T., Britt, S. L., and Archuleta, K. L. (eds.). (2014). *Financial therapy: Theory, research, and practice.* Springer.

Klontz, B. T., and Horwitz, E. J. (2017). Behavioral finance 2.0: Financial psychology. *Journal of Financial Planning, 30*(5), 28–29.

Klontz, B., T., Zabek, F., and Horwitz, E. (2018). Financial psychology. In C. Chaffin (ed.), *Client psychology* (pp. 253–270). Wiley.

Kohut, H. (1971). *The analysis of the self.* International Universities Press.

Kohut, H. (1977). *The restoration of the self.* International Universities Press.

Markowitz, H. (1952). Portfolio selection. *Journal of Finance, 7*(1), 77–91.

Miller, W. R., and Rollnick, S. (2013). *Motivational interviewing: Helping people change.* The Guilford Press.

Overton, R. H. (2008). Theories of the financial planning profession. *Journal of Personal Finance, 7*(1), 13–41.

Polizzi, C., Lynn, S. J., and Perry, A. (2020). Stress and coping in the time of COVID-19: Pathways to resilience and recovery. *Clinical Neuropsychiatry, 17*(2), 59–62.

Prochaska, J. O., DiClemente, C. C., and Norcross, J. C. (1992). In search of how people change: Applications to addictive behaviors. *American Psychologist, 47*, 1102–1114.

Rogers, C. R. (1979). The foundations of the person-centered approach. *Education, 100*(2), 98–107.

Schuchardt, J., Durband, D., Bailey, W. C., DeVaney, S. A., Grable, J. E., Leech, I. E., Lown, J. M., Sharpe, D. L., and Xiao, J. J. (2007). Personal finance: An interdisciplinary profession. *Journal of Financial Counseling and Planning, 18*(1), 61–69.

Seligman, M. E. (2012). *Flourish: A visionary new understanding of happiness and well-being.* Simon and Schuster.

Shefrin, H. M., and Thaler, R. H. (1988). The behavioral life-cycle hypothesis. *Economic Inquiry, 26*, 609–643.

Simon, H. A. (2000). Bounded rationality in social science: Today and tomorrow. *Mind & Society, 1*(1), 25–39.

Stanovich, K. E. (1999). *Who is rational? Studies of individual differences in reasoning.* Lawrence Erlbaum Associates Inc.

Stanovich, K. E. (2004). *The robot's rebellion: Finding meaning the age of Darwin.* Chicago University Press.

Stanton, M. D. (1981). Strategic approaches to family therapy. In A. S. Gurman, and D. P. Kniskern (eds.), *Handbook of family therapy* (pp. 1361–1402). Brunner/Mazel.

Turner, J. H. (1978). *The structure of sociological theory* (4th ed.). Dorsey Press.

Whitney, D., and Trosten-Bloom, A. (2010). *The power of appreciative inquiry* (2nd ed.). Berrett-Koehler Publishers.

Winnicott, D. W. (2018). *Psycho-analytic explorations.* Routledge.

Yeske, D. (2010). Finding the planning in financial planning. *Journal of Financial Planning, 23*(9), 40–51.

Yeske, D. (2016). A concise history of the financial planning profession. *Journal of Financial Planning, 29*(9), 10–13.

Part II: **Saving, Investing, and Asset Management**

Michael G. Thomas

# 6 Budgeting and Cash Flow Management

**Abstract:** Budgeting and cash flow management are often viewed as mundane, trivial, restrictive, and time-consuming household financial tasks. However, individuals who consistently engage in these activities experience higher levels of financial well-being and are more likely to create wealth. Budgeting involves setting clear financial goals and planning how and when financial resources will be allocated before they are spent. Cash flow management is the process of monitoring all sources of cash inflows and outflows necessary to achieve budgetary aims. Both, in tandem, are paramount to feeling a sense of financial control, having the flexibility to make choices, developing the capacity to absorb economic shocks, and confidently planning for the future. Failing to engage in both of these processes may lead to adverse and unforeseen financial consequences. The purpose of this chapter is fivefold. First, the chapter provides a foundational understanding of budgeting and cash flow management. Second, historical and contemporary perspectives on budgeting and cash flow management are explored. Third, research and policy issues are presented. Fourth, practitioner tools and techniques are examined. Fifth, the chapter concludes with a discussion on budgeting and cash flow management's future direction and applications.

**Keywords:** budgeting, cash flow management, financial well-being, net worth, wealth

## Introduction

Establishing wealth or net worth is a process by which a household has more assets than liabilities. In the accounting discipline, this estimate is based on the following equation: Assets − Liabilities = Net Worth. As a result, a household can either have positive, neutral, or negative wealth given this equation, all of which is a direct reflection of the way a household manages its finances. Consequently, effective budgeting and cash flow management strategies are essential to generating and maintaining wealth creation. Kholilah and Iramni (2013) described financial management behaviors as how households plan, budget, and manage their financial resources based on their situation. Heck and Trent (1999) expanded this concept further by identifying nine domains of financial behavior: (a) establish financial goals, (b) accurately estimate costs, (c) estimate income appropriately, (d) planning and

---

**Michael G. Thomas,** University of Georgia

https://doi.org/10.1515/9783110727692-006

budgeting, (e) consider alternatives when making financial choices, (f) adjust to meet financial emergencies, (g) pay bills on time, (h) successfully fulfill financial goals, and (i) successfully implement a budget. Managing household resources is not a one dimensional activity. It is a multilayered process that households must engage with to achieve some level of utility, satisfaction, or well-being.

Notions of financial satisfaction vary from household to household, region to region, and country to country. Financial satisfaction must be measured objectively and subjectively to fully understand a household's sentiment (Joo and Grable, 2004). For instance, consider Heck and Trent's (1999) nine categories of financial management. Financial satisfaction may be derived objectively by creating a budget and subjectively in the way one feels by sticking to their budget. An objective sense of financial accomplishment can come from learning how to establish clear financial goals and the subjective emotional relief from having a more transparent financial direction. The household's intersectionality (i.e., culture, race, socio-economic status), conditions (i.e., economic conditions, location, education), and attitudes and beliefs about finances play an important role in understanding financial management behavior.

The recognition of financial satisfaction as being multifaceted is also consistent with recent findings on financial well-being. The Consumer Financial Protection Bureau (2015) identifies financial well-being as a household's ability to (1) have a sense of financial freedom, (2) pay current bills on time, (3) plan for the future, and (4) have the ability to not worry about unexpected financial shocks. Keywords such as "worry" and "sense" are subjective attitudes dependent on a household's perspective on its objective financial circumstances, as are feelings of financial satisfaction. In short, a sense of financial satisfaction or well-being depends on financial management (Adiputra, 2021).

How a household goes about budgeting and managing its cash flows is vital for long-term financial success. And, as aforementioned, success is not purely an objective reality of a household's financial position. Financial satisfaction or a sense of financial well-being is also subjective. A household's attitudes about where they are financially are just as important as what they have done. Managing one's household affairs to optimize standard practices, such as budgeting and cash flow management, to optimize its utility is not as objective as it was once considered in the past – it is subjective, too.

## Historical Perspective

Household resource allocation has long been an area of interest of researchers. The empirical study of household resource allocation dates back as early as the 19th and 20th centuries. During the 20th century, the classical economic theory of choice was the prevailing assumption behind household resource management. Classical economic theory posits that households are rational actors that can make firm predictions about optimizing their utility within perfectly competitive markets (Simon, 1959). Thus, economists at that time assumed that if households were given information and resources, those households would make logical decisions to improve their financial circumstances – hence, the emergence of the term 'home economics' (Pexiotto, 1927).

Two of the leading voices in home economics were Margaret Reid and Dorothy S. Brady (Overton, 2008). They were economists and focused on household consumption behaviors. As with many micro-economists during the 1930s, Reid's and Brady's work sought to understand household dynamics as a way to provide tools and resources to improve household production and consumption in the pursuit of optimizing a household's utility. Moreover, their work was a pressing matter as national conversations held by the American Economic Association about the strength and viability of household budgets were becoming more of a debate for discussion (Pexiotto, 1927).

From there, other theoretical frameworks emerged to understand household financial management behavior – most notably, the work of Gary Becker. Gary Becker, a theoretical economist, established the New Home Economics paradigm from his work on the theory of the allocation of time. In his seminal work on the theory of time, Becker (1965) made the argument that "the allocation of efficiency of non-working time may now be more important to economic welfare than working time." (p. 493). Consequently, this fundamental assumption led to additional assertions about household consumption and production.

In 1974, Becker produced an article titled, "On the relevance of the new economics of the family," which explored how the allocation of time influences household consumption and production behaviors. Becker (1974) argued that a household consumes commodities of personal choice, time included, based upon wage generation, availability of time, and other factors. For instance, given that time is regarded as a scarce resource within this line of thought, Becker claimed that a non-working spouse might assume more financial management responsibilities than the working spouse based upon these new assumptions. Although working versus non-working time allocation was an essential distinction between Becker's new home economics and classical economic emergence, it was not the only one.

Another significant departure in Becker's new home economics was to detangle household choice from monetary market ideology. In other words, household production and consumption behaviors did not solely revolve around optimizing one's utility in the marketplace. Instead, households were constantly considering things such as their capacity to increase their family size, the potential for labor force participation, political behaviors, and investments in human capital (Becker, 1974). Instead, Becker recognized that financial decisions made within a household were more complex and were not adequately captured under classical economic theory.

Becker's work set the foundation for future work designed to explore household decisions on human capital investment (Becker and Tomes, 1976) and how financial management decisions within a household are not made unilaterally but rather through negotiation and consensus (Becker, 1992). Before Becker's (1974) work, other theories described household consumption behavior, such as Modigliani and Brumberg's (1954) life cycle theory. The life cycle theory argues that household consumption in the present is based upon expected future earnings and consumption. In other words, a household may make a choice to consume beyond its means today based on the expectation of greater earnings in the future. Milton Friedman's (1957) permanent income hypothesis held a similar stance. The permanent income hypothesis postulates that a household sets current financial management decisions based on an expectation of receiving a permanent income level over its lifetime. Whether it's Becker, Modigliani and Brumberg, or Friedman, each of these individuals has made considerable contributions to understanding financial management behaviors.

The work done in economics gets a considerable amount of attention regarding household financial management; however, in the 1970s, some researchers began to look at the fields of psychology and sociology to explain financial management behavior (Muske and Winter, 1999). As a result, systems theory emerged as an effective way to understand household financial management behavior. Systems theory considers the cause-and-effect relationship of elements within a system (Bertalanffy, 1968). For example, assume a household decides to drop out of the labor market. Without understanding the context behind this decision, it is impossible to ascertain why the household made this choice. However, upon closer examination, it could be discovered that concerns for safety due to the Covid-19 pandemic, lockdowns, and supplemental income provided by the federal government influenced the household's decision. Thus, systems theory provides a process by which to understand financial management choices through the interactions that are occurring within the household and the world around it (Rettig and Mortensen, 1986; Titus et al., 1989).

More currently, a significant amount of attention has turned to behavioral economics. Behavioral economics is a subset of economics that seeks to understand psychological, emotional, cognitive, cultural, and social perspectives on household decision making. Although the first references to behavioral economics date back to 1958, behavioral economics as it is known today did not begin to gain notoriety until Kahneman and Tversky's articles "Judgement Under Uncertainty: Heuristics and Biases" and "Prospect Theory: An Analysis of Decision Making Under Risk" were published in 1974 and 1979, respectively.

Khamenman and Tversky's (1974, 1979) earlier works diverged from expected utility theory, which was the accepted way economists were accustomed to explaining human behavior. Utility theory posits that a rational actor will behave in a certain way given a complex situation or uncertain outcomes. On the other hand, prospect theory argues that actors make risky or uncertain decisions based upon their reference point or perspective (Kahneman and Tversky, 1979). Kahneman and Tversky were interested in describing the underpinnings of household behaviors instead of prescribing choice selection based on the axioms set by utility theory. Their work has led to the current day understanding of risk and loss aversion, which is the propensity of a household to desire certainty over uncertainty and that one's reference point plays a pivotal role in the way a household frames choice.

The historical perspectives presented here describe an evolution in the way academics and society have come to understand household financial decision making. Household financial management is neither a particular function of micro nor macroeconomics. It is both. External systems do not singularly influence the choices of households. Internal systems do as well. Understanding the inherent complexity and context from which families make financial decisions is imperative to optimizing wealth-creating behaviors such as budgeting and cash flow management.

# Research and Policy Issues

Conceptually, budgeting and cash flow management are similar constructs with slight differences. Godwin (1994) described cash flow management as how a household establishes and implements a financial plan of action to achieve a financial goal or objective. As Leimberg et al. (1993) explained, budgeting is a household's ability to clearly and effectively allocate the use of money over a given period. Cash flow management can be regarded as the financial vision and ongoing maintenance toward said vision. Budgeting is the process by which the financial vision is operationalized from one period to the next.

However, in much of the literature relating to financial literacy efforts, budgeting and cash flow management activities are seen as one function or behavior. Remund (2010) found that the most frequently cited core financial literacy concepts taught to household financial decision makers were cash flow management, debt management, and risk management. In either case, budgeting and cash flow management are essential to financial well-being and wealth creation.

Without a clear financial vision and a process to manage cash inflows and outflows, it can prove challenging for a household to make any meaningful financial progress. Much of the literature attributes a lack of financial advancement to low levels of financial knowledge. Similar to the work of Margaret Reid and Dorothy Brady (see Overton, 2008) during their time, proponents of financial literacy believed that a household's economic instability is due to a lack of financial knowledge. And, as a consequence, if a household knows better, it will do better. Financial literacy researchers have found that low levels of financial literacy lead to having insufficient savings for retirement (Lusardi, 1999), an inability to pay bills on time (Abendroth and Diehl, 2006), and the propensity to overspend (Sotiropoulos and d'Asous, 2013). The literature suggests that these are all counterproductive to building financial stability and creating wealth.

Higher levels of financial literacy have been shown to be positively associated with outcomes directly related to budgeting and cash flow management. A study conducted by Allen et al. (2016) reported that employees who participated in employer-sponsored seminars had higher participation rates in their company's investment plans than those who did not. Research has also shown that households with higher levels of financial literacy are more likely to save and avoid risky lending services (Hilgert et al., 2003; Jappelli and Padula, 2013; Kim and Lee, 2018) and improve credit card management (Disney and Gathergood 2013; Mottola, 2013; Xiao et al., 2012).

Conversely, Fernandes et al. (2014) found that financial literacy efforts have a relatively small effect size on household outcomes and that effects diminish over a 22-month time horizon. Other researchers have reported very weak linkages to no connection between financial literacy efforts and behavioral outcomes (e.g., Carpena et al., 2011; Willis, 2009). Porto and Xiao (2016) suggested that information asymmetry, nontraditional behaviors, and heuristics, rather than low levels of financial literacy, influence consumer behavior.

The financial literacy literature is inconclusive on the impact knowledge has on financial behaviors. As a result, researchers have identified that knowledge alone is not enough to promote behavioral change. Although psychographic variables (e.g., beliefs, attitudes and goals, confidence) have been overlooked in the past (Huhmann and McQuitty, 2009), researchers and policymakers are starting to understand that a holistic approach will be needed to help families engage in optimal financial management behaviors.

Worldwide, thought leaders and policymakers have made concerted efforts to improve the financial welfare of the world's population; however, many of these efforts place the onus of improvement on the household to gather the appropriate information to ward off information asymmetry in the markets. In some cases, systems within a country may produce contradictory messages. For instance, in the United States, national initiatives are underway to help improve the economic conditions of households. However, for every message a household receives about saving "for a rainy day" or its future, the same household receives another message on the importance of spending money in its community to strengthen the local economy. These messages can induce anxiety within households and present a challenging choice architecture for households to navigate with limited resources.

In 2017, Richard Thaler, an acclaimed economist, was awarded the Nobel Memorial Prize in Economic Sciences. This honor validated and confirmed the need to understand household decision making from a broader and more holistic perspective – Thaler's work built upon the efforts of Kahneman and Tversky's (1979) prospect theory. Thaler (1999) also introduced the notion of mental accounting, which is how individuals cognitively process and keep track of financial activities. Thaler and Sunstein (2009) presented the argument for libertarian paternalism. They claimed that it was necessary to nudge individuals to make optimal financial choices. Thaler and Suntein (2009) pointed out that inconsistencies in intertemporal choice, maladaptive heuristics, and instances of preference reversal have adverse effects on household decision making. Their solution was to encourage well-designed choice architectures that would make it easier for households to make better financial decisions.

With the emergence and recognition of behavioral economics, policymakers are beginning to understand the importance of psychology and decision-making systems. A lack of knowledge is not always the cause of a household's inability to budget and manage its cash flow situation. Families must also have sufficient income and the emotional, psychological, and mental capacity to engage in optimal financial behaviors. As a result, more and more interdisciplinary and holistic methods will emerge in how policymakers design programs to improve household financial well-being.

# Practitioner Tools and Techniques

Many practitioners enter into the space of personal financial advising eager to help their clients achieve their financial goals. Unbeknownst to the adviser, they may be unequipped with the tools to address their clients' emotional and psychological needs. Their training, in many instances, focuses on how to develop creative financial strategies and not how to handle unexpected financial behavior(s). Managing client behavior is an essential skill. Kinniry et al. (2019) explained in a Vanguard white paper that behavioral coaching provided the highest value proposition to their clients with 150 basis points of value. The second and third highest value propositions were helping a client develop a spending strategy and assisting a client in establishing their asset allocation, 100 and 75 basis points of value-added, respectively.

## Models of Practice

Understanding this, personal finance advice practitioners must adopt a framework by which to engage with their clients holistically. Helping a client walk through a cash flow management activity and establish a budget is not always as straightforward as it seems. When behavioral issues arise, it is essential to have a strategy that frames how one interacts with their client. There are several therapeutic methods from which to choose. The most common are appreciative inquiry, cognitive-behavioral, and solution-focused techniques.

Appreciative inquiry (Cooperrider and Whitney, 2000) is a process of guided questions by the practitioner to help their clients identify goals and execute them. This process involves the following phases:

(1) Discovering: this occurs when a practitioner asks questions that help determine what activities a client enjoys most when it comes to finances (e.g., what aspect of cash flow management of budgeting brings you the most joy?).

(2) Dreaming: this occurs when a practitioner asks questions about the positive impact associated with creating a cash flow management strategy and what sticking to a budget might mean.
(3) Designing: this occurs when a practitioner helps clients identify multiple strategies that they can employ to achieve their financial objectives within their current financial circumstances.
(4) Deploying: this occurs when a practitioner nudges a client to consider what they can do to take immediate action on their financial goals.

The process of appreciative inquiry is not only beneficial to a client. It also helps a practitioner frame their language in a way that is positive and focused on what is possible as opposed to limitations. Another well-established therapeutic method similar to the appreciative inquiry process is the solution-focused approach.

Solution-focused therapy aims to orient client communications around a future goal. Practitioners who employ this approach focus conversations on a client's strengths, skills, and available resources to achieve said goals. For example, a common line of questioning for solution-focused therapy is as follows:

Practitioner: On a scale from 1 to 5, 1 being poor and five being excellent, how would you rate your ability to stick to your budget?

Client: I would give myself a two.

Practitioner: Why would you give yourself a two instead of a one?

Client: Well, I can stick to my budget on most days. I tend to go off track on the weekends.

Practitioner: What is happening when you are sticking to your budget?

Client: I am working. When I am working, I tend to spend less time on my phone. I do all my shopping on my phone.

Practitioner: Can you identify when you were not working and stuck to your budget?

Client: Yes . . .

With the solution-focused approach, the practitioner frames questions to identify strengths and patterns of behaviors that have already proven effective for the client. Once specified, the practitioner does not have to motivate or convince the client to engage in unfamiliar activities to achieve their goals. When a practitioner finds that a client is resistant to focusing on positive outcomes and chooses to focus on the negative consequences of their past mistakes, cognitive-behavioral therapy is a practical approach that can be used in these instances.

Cognitive-behavioral therapy allows more space for clients to explore their past circumstances or the systems that are influencing their behaviors. With this approach, practitioners help clients target their financial management shortcomings and identify potential strategies to address the emotions and thoughts associated with maladaptive behaviors (Gaudiano, 2008). In many instances, a practitioner can help a client by actively listening and reassuring the client that their thoughts and feelings are valid and will be considered when finalizing a financial recommendation.

Employing a therapeutic approach to client interactions is essential to client rapport building and behavioral financial management. Appreciative inquiry, solution-focused, and cognitive-behavioral techniques can be used across a multitude of disciplines to promote positive outcomes for clients. These approaches also transform the way practitioners internalize their work and the multilayered impact it has on the lives of the people they serve.

## Establishing Goals

Households are inundated with hundreds if not thousands of marketing messages each day. This constant stream of solicitations can make it difficult to organize one's thoughts and clearly define one's financial goals without the influence of external voices. Personal finance advice practitioners can provide considerable value by helping clients walk through the SMART goal process.

A SMART goal (Doran, 1981) is a mnemonic acronym aimed at helping individuals achieve their goals. There are five elements of a SMART goal. A goal must be specific, measurable, attainable, relevant, and timely. A specific goal identifies what a client wants to achieve (e.g., "I would like to save $2,000 for my emergency fund by the end of the year"). Measurable or measurement is how a client will track their process toward their goal (e.g., "I will track my progress toward this goal on Sunday of each week."). To ensure that a financial goal sticks, households should join a community or identify an accountability partner with whom the goal can be shared and there be a sense of accountability. Harkin et al. (2016) found that tracking one's goals and having social accountability help sustain efforts in behavioral change and improve the likelihood of goal attainment.

Moreover, attainability provides an opportunity to identify whether a stated goal is achievable given the circumstances of a household. Matching a stated goal with client capacity is an essential element of goal attainment. Relevance helps a client understand their attentions and the implications for achieving a financial goal. Suppose a goal is not relevant or meaningful to the financial decision maker. In that case, it is unlikely that they will have the motivation to stick with the financial activities associated with achieving their goal.

A timely or time-bound plan identifies when a client must achieve their goal. As with other elements of a SMART goal, a personal finance advice practitioner must ensure that the time horizon of a goal is in alignment with a client's financial capacity. It is an effective strategy to nudge clients to modify long-term financial objectives into smaller tasks. Doing this helps clients maintain focus, motivation, and a sense of meaningful financial progress. In summary, creating a financial

SMART goal is an effective tool to help clients successfully engage in cash flow management and budgeting activities.

## Developing a Budget

Once a household has established a clear financial direction, it is easier to assist the household in establishing a budget. Without a clear path forward, budgeting is commonly associated with restrictiveness and rigidity. Households tend to view budgeting as a reminder of where they've been instead of where they are going.

Budgets take many forms. There are traditional budgets, zero-based budgets, and value-based spending plan budgets, all of which can be operationalized via paper or pencil, computer software, or through the use of apps (e.g., You Need A Budget, Mint, and Every Dollar). A traditional budget identifies all sources of income and spending on a daily, weekly, or monthly basis. A traditional budget projects whether a household operates at a surplus (i.e., has more income than expenses) or a deficit (i.e., has more expenses than income).

A zero-based budget encourages households to spend every dollar on paper, so there is neither a surplus nor a deficit. If a household has a surplus, the household will identify how to allocate those additional resources so that the difference between cash inflows and outflows equals zero. If a household is operating at a deficit, the household needs to increase its income or minimize its expenses so that the difference between cash inflows and outflows equals zero. Given a household's financial circumstances, a zero-based budget may not be practical; however, it serves as an excellent tool to encourage mindful spending practices.

A values-based budget is another way to encourage better financial management behavior. Households can establish a values-based budget utilizing traditional or zero-based budget approaches. The values-based budgeting process creates the space for a household to think thoughtfully and deeply about what aspects of life bring it a sense of joy and satisfaction. Once the family has identified these items, the household then prioritizes those items in its budget. Conversely, a household will determine how it spends money in ways that do not align with its values. Over time, a household will gradually eliminate unnecessary expenditures from its budget to allocate more funds to what it finds valuable. A values-based budgeting process is a useful tool that establishes a positive emotional connection to goal attainment and household management. In addition, it provides a self-sustaining reward mechanism that allows households, especially those with limited resources, to see and experience a strong positive association between sound financial management and greater financial freedom from one monthly budget to the next.

Regardless of how a household decides to budget its resources, budgeting increases financial awareness. And, as a result, it encourages behavioral change. Thus, the primary issue is getting households to engage in the budgeting and cash flow management process, as avoidance is a natural tendency of household financial management practices. Presenting many options increases the likelihood that a household may self-identify with a budgeting practice that it can consistently implement to achieve its financial goals.

# Future Directions

Paradigm shifts in how household financial management is understood have evolved considerably from the 20th century to the 21st. Researchers have characterized budgeting and cash flow management from a function of household utility to understanding the psychology of human behavior. The next logical step is to understand, more specifically, the implications of neuroscience on consumer choice.

With recent advancements in technology, more work is emerging from the field of neuroscience. Neuroscience is the study of the human nervous system. The nervous system involves a complex system of neural circuits and neurons prompted by our senses (i.e., hearing, taste, touch, smell, sight). In other words, how a household experiences the world around it will influence how these experiences affect brain development and cognition.

Dr. Bruce Perry (2009) categorized the brain into four sections: brain stem, diencephalon, limbic, and neocortex. The brain stem regulates blood pressure, heart rate, and body temperature and is connected directly to the spinal cord. The diencephalon regulates sleep, consciousness, and alertness, while the limbic system is responsible for social attachment, reward mechanisms, and the "fight or flight" response. Finally, the neocortex is the section of the brain that allows individuals to think and process information in concrete and abstract terms (Perry, 2009).

Given that many factors influence household financial management behaviors, it is becoming possible to understand how these factors influence brain function with current technologies. A clear understanding of these complex internal and external interactions may lead to more effective ways to engage households with financial information and promote optimal financial behaviors. Current studies in household management have focused on the effects of knowledge on resource management and how to work around the inconsistencies of human behavior. An exploration in neuroscience may lead to interventions that change brain function toward more favorable financial outcomes.

Moreover, the emergence of artificial intelligence (AI) challenges the need to understand brain function. In essence, technology is advancing at such a rate where automation may become the prevailing way households manage their financial resources. For instance, a household can currently use financial applications to organize and track household finances. Advances in AI will soon make it easy for households to automate the expenditure side of their budgets completely. In short, families will set their financial goals and income parameters and allow for the technology to do the rest. Therefore, understanding AI in connection to household resource management will be an essential aspect of family resource management in the not too distant future.

AI cannot improve a household's cash inflows. This is because a family can only reduce their cash expenditures to a certain extent. Focusing on the expense side of a household budget may be insufficient. In many instances, a personal finance advice practitioner will find that households have already reduced their cash outflows as much as possible. As a result, it becomes clear that insufficient income is the primary issue. Due to this reality, efforts must be made to understand the efficacy of a Universal Basic Income (UBI), improved worker wages, and other benefits that make it possible for households to establish financial stability and plan for their future.

## Conclusion

Research in the area of household financial management is still taking form. New ideas about effectively engaging households in budgeting and cash flow management activities have picked up traction. As noted in this chapter, research is redefining educational outreach, developing a more concrete understanding of household motivations, gaining clarity on internal and external systems that affect household behaviors, and exploring dynamic technical and therapeutic approaches to behavioral change. The question is not whether budgeting and cash flow management are essential to household financial management. These financial management activities are invaluable concerning economic stability and wealth creation. The better question is how those who provide financial advice and counsel to households can help clients develop the confidence and capacity to engage in optimal financial behaviors routinely. The content within this chapter provides an overview of using a holistic and forward thinking approach to achieve this end.

## References

Abendroth, L. J., and Diehl, K. (2006). Now or never: Effects of limited purchase opportunities on patterns of regret over time. *Journal of Consumer Research*, *33*(3), 342–351.

Adiputra, I. G. (2021). The influence of financial literacy, financial attitude and locus of control on financial satisfaction: Evidence from the community in Jakarta. *KnE Social Sciences/7th International Conference on Entrepreneurship*, 636–654.

Allen, S., Clark, R., Maki, J., and Morrill, M. (2016). Golden years or financial fears: How plans change after retirement seminars. *Journal of Retirement*, *3*(3), 96–115.

Becker, G. S. (1965). A theory of the allocation of time. *The Economic Journal*, *75*(299), 493–517.

Becker, G. S. (1974). On the relevance of the new economics of the family. *The American Economic Review*, *64*(2), 317–319.

Becker, G. S. (1992). Human capital and the economy. *American Philosophical Society*, *136*(1), 85–92.

Becker, G. S., and Tomes, N. (1976). Child endowments and the quantity and quality of children. *Journal of Political Economy*, *84*(4, Part 2), S143–S162.

Bertalanffy, L. V. (1968). General systems theory as integrating factor in contemporary science. *Internationalen Kongresses fur philosophie*, *2*, 335–340.

Carpena, F., Cole, S. A., Shapiro, J., and Zia, B. (2011). *Unpacking the causal chain of financial literacy* (World Bank Policy Research Working Paper No. 5798). The World Bank. http://dx.doi.org/10.1596/1813-9450-5798

Cole, S., Sampson, T., and Zia, B. (2011). Prices or knowledge? What drives demand for financial services in emerging markets? *Journal of Finance*, *66*(6), 1933–1967.

Consumer Financial Protection Bureau. (2015). *Financial well-being: The goal of financial education*. Accessed July 2021. http://consumerfinance.gov/financial-well-being

Cooperrider, D. L., and Whitney, D. (2000). A positive revolution in change: Appreciative inquiry. In R. T. Golembiewski (ed.), *Handbook of organizational behavior, revised and expanded* (2nd ed., pp. 633–652). Routledge.

Disney, R., and Gathergood, J. (2013). Financial literacy and consumer credit portfolios. *Journal of Banking and Finance*, *37*(7), 2246–2254.

Doran, G. T. (1981). There's a SMART way to write management's goals and objectives. *Management Review*, *70*(11), 35–36.

Fernandes, D., Lynch Jr., J. G., and Netemeyer, R. G. (2014). Financial literacy, financial education, and downstream financial behaviors. *Management Science*, *60*(8), 1861–1883.

Friedman, M. (1957). The permanent income hypothesis. In M. Friedman (ed.), *A theory of the consumption function* (pp. 20–37). Princeton University Press.

Gaudiano, B. A. (2008). Cognitive-behavioural therapies: Achievements and challenges. *Evidence-Based Mental Health*, *11*(1), 5–7.

Godwin, D. D. (1994). Antecedents and consequences of newlyweds' cash flow management. *Journal of Financial Counseling and Planning*, *5*, 161–190.

Harkin, B., Webb, T. L., Chang, B. P., Prestwich, A., Conner, M., Kellar, I., Benn, Y., and Sheeran, P. (2016). Does monitoring goal progress promote goal attainment? A meta-analysis of the experimental evidence. *Psychological Bulletin*, *142*(2), 198–229.

Heck, R. K., and Trent, E. S. (1999). The prevalence of family business from a household sample. *Family Business Review*, *12*(3), 209–219.

Hilgert, M., Hogarth, J., and Beverly, S. (2003). Household financial management: The connection between knowledge and behavior. *Federal Reserve Bulletin*, *89*, 309–322.

Huhmann, B. A., and McQuitty, S. (2009). A model of consumer financial numeracy. *International Journal of Bank Marketing*, *27*(4), 270–293.

Jappelli, T., and Padula, M. (2013). Investment in financial literacy and saving decisions. *Journal of Banking & Finance*, *37*(8), 2779–2792.

Joo, S. H., and Grable, J. E. (2004). An exploratory framework of the determinants of financial satisfaction. *Journal of Family and Economic Issues*, *25*(1), 25–50.

Kahneman, D., and Tversky, A. (1979). Prospect theory: An analysis of decision under risk. *Econometrica*, *47*, 263–291

Kholilah, N., and Iramani, R. (2013). Studi financial management behavior pada masyarakat surabaya. *Journal of Business and Banking*, *3*(1), 69–80.

Kim, K. T., and Lee, J. (2018). Financial literacy and use of payday loans in the United States. *Applied Economics Letters*, *25*(11), 781–784.

Kinniry Jr, F. M., Jaconetti, C. M., DiJoseph, M. A., Zilbering, Y., and Bennyhoff, D. G. (2019). Putting a value on your value: Quantifying Vanguard adviser's alpha. *Vanguard.* Accessed July 2021. https://advisors.vanguard.com/insights/article/IWE_ResPuttin

Leimberg, S. R., Satinsky, M. J., LeClair, R. T., and Doyle, R. J. (1993). *The tools and techniques of financial planning* (4th ed.). The National Underwriter Co.

Lusardi, A. (1999). Information, expectations, and savings for retirement. In H. J. Aaron (ed.), *Behavioral dimensions of retirement economics* (pp. 81–115), Brookings Institution Press.

Modigliani, F., and Brumberg, R. (1954). Utility analysis and the consumption function: An interpretation of cross-section data. *Franco Modigliani, 1*(1), 388–436.

Mottola, G. (2013). In our best interest: Women, financial literacy, and credit card behavior. *Numeracy, 6*(2), 1–15.

Muske, G., and Winter, M. (1999). Cash flow management: A framework of daily family activities. *Journal of Financial Counseling and Planning, 10*(1), 2–13.

Overton, R. H. (2008). Theories of the financial planning profession. *Journal of Personal Finance, 7*(1), 13–41.

Perry, B. D. (2009). Examining child maltreatment through a neurodevelopmental lens: Clinical applications of the neurosequential model of therapeutics. *Journal of Loss and Trauma, 14*(4), 240–255.

Pexiotto, J. (1927). Supplement, papers and proceedings of the thirty-ninth annual meeting of the American association. *The American Economics Review, 17*, 132–140.

Porto, N., and Xiao, J. J. (2016). Financial literacy overconfidence and financial advice seeking. *Journal of Financial Service Professionals, 70*(4), 78–88.

Remund, D. (2010). Financial literacy explicated: The case for a clearer definition in an increasingly complex economy. *Journal of Consumer Affairs, 44*(2), 276–279.

Rettig, K. D., and Mortenson, M. (1986). Household production of financial management competence. In R. E. Deacon, and W. E. Huffman (eds.), *Human resources research* (pp. 137–145). College of Home Economics.

Simon, H. A. (1959). Theories of decision-making in economics and behavioral science. *The American Economic Review, 49*(3), 253–283.

Sotiropoulos, V., and d'Astous, A. (2013). Attitudinal, self-efficacy, and social norms determinants of young consumers' propensity to overspend on credit cards. *Journal of Consumer Policy, 36*(2), 179–196.

Thaler, R. H. (1999). Mental accounting matters. *Journal of Behavioral Decision Making, 12*(3), 183–206.

Thaler, R. H., and Sunstein, C. R. (2009). *Nudge: Improving decisions about health, wealth, and happiness.* Penguin.

Titus, P. M., Fanslow, A. M., and Hira, T. K. (1989). Net worth and financial satisfaction as a function of household money managers' competencies. *Home Economics Research Journal, 17*(4), 309–318.

Tversky, A., and Kahneman, D. (1974). Judgement under uncertainty: Heuristics and biases. *Science, 185*(4,157), 1124–1131.

Willis, L. E. (2009). Evidence and ideology in assessing the effectiveness of financial literacy education. *San Diego Law Review, 46*(2), 415–458.

Xiao, J. J., Sherido, J., and Shim, S. (2012). Financial education, financial literacy, and risky credit card behavior of college students. In D. J. Lamdin (ed.), *Consumer knowledge and financial decisions* (pp. 113–128). Springer.

Gianni Nicolini

# 7 Patterns of Asset Ownership

**Abstract:** The aim of this chapter is to describe how individuals use different patterns of asset ownership to develop and manage their wealth. The chapter analyzes the main theories behind the spending versus saving behaviors and summarizes the key results from a set of empirical studies. The factors that influence the decision to save, and that drive the choice of the assets used to allocate personal resources, are diverse. Some of the key variables include socio-demographic characteristics like age, gender, income, and education. Other sources of influence regard taxation and social welfare. The way individuals develop the structure of their asset ownership depends on a mix of factors that evolves over time. Many of the factors interact with one another. The awareness of the different patterns and the role of different factors able to shape those patterns can help researchers, educators, and policymakers understand the real needs of financial decision makers and provide a clearer view of the possible reactions of individuals to certain policies.

**Keywords:** life-cycle hypothesis, maslow's theory, asset ownership, financial literacy

## Introduction

Wealth can be defined as an "abundance of valuable material possessions or resources" (Merriam-Webster, n.d.). The accumulation of wealth and its management are strictly related to the personal needs and the achievement of the personal goals of individuals and households. From basic needs like food, water, or security and safety, to more sophisticated needs related to the self-fulfillment of individuals, the availability of the resources needed to satisfy those needs involves the development of wealth, its allocation between different assets, and the management of those resources over time.

The way people plan to develop their wealth, the targets they define, and the strategies they use to achieve their goals differ from individual to individual and shape different patterns of asset ownership. Differences between peoples' saving behaviors and investing decisions are often related to their time horizon, risk attitude, and financial literacy, which differ by age, income, gender, family structure, personal beliefs, and other factors. Preferences for real-estate properties related to homeownership, the relevance of financial assets in the asset ownership structure, or the willingness to participate in the stock market are a few examples of how the

**Gianni Nicolini,** University of Rome "Tor Vergata", Rome, Italy

https://doi.org/10.1515/9783110727692-007

wealth of an individual can develop following different paths. The purpose of this chapter is to describe the main patterns of asset ownership of individuals and households and the factors that contribute to shaping those patterns.

# Historical Perspective

To address the patterns of asset ownership it is first necessary to develop a theoretical background and then to analyze results from empirical studies. The following discussion highlights some of the most important theoretical models used to describe and predict household-level asset ownership patterns.

## The Life-Cycle Hypothesis (LCH)

The economic theory of consumption related to the saving and consuming behaviors of individuals is often premised on two fundamental frameworks to address the asset ownership of individuals and households. These are models developed by Modigliani and Brumberg (1954) and Ando and Modigliani (1963). These models are based on the assumption that individuals shape their decision to spend or save their present resources, not referring to current income but to "permanent income." This concept can be approximated as the average income over a lifetime, accounting for the time value of money assuming that individuals are aware of (or can forecast) their future levels of income and that individuals are able to anticipate their future spending power or to postpone their actual spending using borrowing and saving tools.

The theory related to these models is referred to as the life-cycle hypothesis (LCH). According to the LCH, individuals tend to smooth differences between their current income and permanent income by borrowing and saving. They should borrow when their current income is below their permanent income, and they should save when their current income exceeds their permanent income. In the standard case of an individual who works until retirement age, when they will be out of the job market, and income during the working life increases over time, the LCH predicts that the individual will tend to borrow in the first stage of their life, thanks to the chance to use future income to repay debts. In the meantime, this individual should be aware of the need to save for retirement during their working stage of the life cycle in an effort to balance the lack of income in retirement. According to the LCH, the typical time distribution of income over a lifetime follows a humped shape, with the income in the first stage of the working life being lower than the next one, and the post-retirement income being lower than the pre-retirement one.

## The Hierarchy of Needs

The LCH is a good starting point to address the analysis of the pattern of ownership of assets because it provides a solid theory about the amount of resources accumulated and decumulated over time, and it describes the wealth accumulation process. However, while the LCH pays attention to the amount of resources it does not address the allocation of this wealth across different assets. Household financial decision makers could accumulate their wealth by buying houses or other real estate properties, or they could use banking products like saving accounts or certificates of deposit (CDs), or they could invest their savings in the stock market, or they could invest their money in a small business. The analysis of the patterns of asset ownership regards individual decisions to spend vis-à-vis saving, the decisions about how to save, what kinds of assets are used to save, the correlation between the ownership of different assets, and the evolution of the role of certain assets in the wealth composition of individuals. It follows that the study of asset ownership requires analyzing the decision making process of individuals, their preferences, and the key factors that affect their economic behavior.

The decision to spend or save current income or the decision to borrow in case of an unexpected need is related to the will to satisfy some personal needs or to achieve personal goals. For instance, the decision to go on vacation, to buy a new television, to save for retirement, or to take out a mortgage in order to buy a house are examples of how personal decisions affect current and future individual wealth. A model that provides an interpretation of how individuals prioritize their needs, and by consequence how they shape their spending and saving behavior over time, was developed in the 1950s by Maslow (1954). Maslow stated that there is a hierarchy of needs and individuals start by paying attention to the group of needs located in a lower rank of this hierarchy only after they have satisfied all the needs of the previous one. This theory can be visualized as a pyramid where to reach the top people must step up from the bottom. At the bottom of the pyramid there are the highest-priority needs – Physiological needs – referred to as food, water, warmth, rest, etc. The assumption is that people will not focus on other needs until they struggle to achieve physiological needs. The next step concerns Safety needs and involves the need for safety and security. Together with the Physiological needs, Security needs represent the so-called Basic needs. Once people are able to satisfy their basic needs, they will start dealing with the second group of needs called Psychological needs. The first needs that belong to the psychological category are Belongingness and Love needs (e.g., friendship, intimate relationship), which is followed by Esteem needs (e.g., need to achieve prestige and to feel accomplishment). At the top of the pyramid, there are the Self-fulfilment (sometimes referred to as Self-actualization) needs. The needs that belong to this group are related to the achievement of one's full potential, including creative activities.

Maslow's (1954) proposed hierarchy of needs helps to predict what people look for at a specific time of their lives and how priorities will affect their asset ownership composition. Saving for retirement, for example, cannot be a priority for individuals who struggle to make ends meet. This does not mean that those who struggle to pay for regular meals every day are not aware of the need to save for retirement, but the higher priority of meeting physiological needs (e.g., food) will dominate other needs (e.g., Safety needs like saving for retirement). The theory suggests that physiological needs cannot be taken for granted. Following the same logic, people should prioritize buying a home before investing in other assets due to the high priority of Safety needs.

## The Behavioral LCH

When thinking about the allocation of wealth and the different patterns of asset ownership of individuals, there are several contributions from behavioral economics that inform patterns of asset ownership. Thaler (1988) proposed a "behavioral" LCH where consumers mentally divide their assets into different accounts for different specific purposes. The behavioral LCH stresses how different asset categories may have different meanings to household financial decision makers. As such, assets cannot be treated as homogeneous when saving behavior is examined. Shefrin and Thaler (1988) and Weagley and Gannon (1991) categorized household assets into four groups: (a) savings, (b) housing, (c) financial securities, and (d) retirement investments. Xiao and Olson (1993) focused on households' financial assets and divided them into three groups. The first group included checking, savings, money market accounts, and certificates of deposit (CDs) – assets used to meet daily and emergency financial needs. The second group included individual retirement accounts, employer-sponsored profit sharing, thrift, and other savings plans, trusts, and other financial assets – assets used to meet future financial needs. The third group included bonds and stocks (including stocks in mutual funds but excluding money market or individual retirement accounts [IRAs]) – assets used to meet social and personal developmental needs. In practice, household financial decision makers place different constraints on these types of accounts.

# The Determinants of Asset Ownership

To understand how people tend to follow different paths in the development and management of their wealth, it is necessary to identify the key factors that affect peoples' financial behaviors. The first characteristic that affects asset ownership is the age of an individual. Age is a key variable of the LCH that assumes people will tend, on average, to go into debt in the first stage of their life, to pay back their loans and to save in the middle, and to dissave when in retirement. However, age can be relevant not only to estimate the amount of accumulated wealth. Xiao (1996) found that young individuals are less likely than middle-aged individuals to own checking accounts, CDs, IRAs, life insurance, bonds, and stocks. In the meantime, older individuals are more likely than middle-aged individuals to own each of these assets. Ameriks and Zeldes (2001) showed that age matters not only when estimating the amount of wealth but even when describing the composition of wealth. What they found is that when age increases people tend to reduce the share of risky assets in their portfolios. This result confirms a report by Guiso and Jappelli (2000) who found that, over the life cycle, the share of risky assets has a hump-shaped profile. They estimated a probability to invest in risky assets that increases by four percentage points from age 25 to age 40 and declines by eight percentage points from age 40 to age 70.[1]

Another variable that affects the composition of wealth is income. The connection between income and asset ownership has been studied since the 1950s. Atkinson (1956) found that lower-income groups prefer saving deposits or bonds, while higher-income groups prefer corporate stocks. Moreover, Atkinson showed how income and financial asset ownership are positively associated. Xiao and Anderson (1993) identified a pattern that links income levels to different asset ownership. They found that the share of checking accounts on total assets decreases when the income goes up. In the meantime, the curves of shares of CDs and money market accounts, IRAs, and life insurance are reversed U-shape. Xiao and Anderson noted that the curves of shares of bonds, stocks, and other financial assets were in a J-shape. More recently, the relationship between income and asset ownership has been confirmed by Alessie et al. (2004). They, however, found that the positive relationship that exists between income and stock investments is not confirmed for mutual funds. Yumna and Marta (2021) found a clearer relationship between income and financial assets for transaction needs (e.g., checking accounts) rather than investment assets (e.g., stocks).

Xiao (1996) analyzed the role of education on asset ownership and noted that education has a positive effect on the ownership of financial assets. In particular, Xiao identified two patterns. Households with less than a college education were found to be significantly less likely than otherwise similar households with a bachelor's degree to own several types of assets (e.g., checking accounts, saving accounts, CDs, IRAs, life insurance, bonds, and stocks). The ownership of financial assets was found to be greater for those with a post-college education compared to those who had four years of a college education, confirming that higher levels of attained formal

---

[1] This study was based on repeated cross-sectional and panel data drawn from the 1989 to 1998 Bank of Italy Survey of Household Income and Wealth.

education are positively associated with the ownership of financial assets, total wealth, and an increased likelihood of owning liquid assets.

Gender is another variable that seems to shape patterns of asset ownership. Shorrocks (1982) studied the portfolio composition in the United Kingdom, considering 17 assets from cash and saving deposits to residential buildings, including stocks and insurance policies. The study found that for the majority of asset variation in household portfolio compositions by age differs significantly between genders. The personal wealth of females was, on average, about half of that of the males. A gender bias in asset ownership was also found by Jefferson and Ong (2010). Using data from Australia, they found gendered dimensions to both the value and composition of asset holdings. Women had lower asset holdings, and their portfolios were relatively overweighted in the primary home.

Another socio-demographic characteristic able to shape the asset ownership of individuals is marital status. Xiao (1996) found that being married significantly increases the chance of owning checking accounts, saving accounts, CDs, IRAs, life insurance, and stock. Xiao did not find a correlation between marriage and bond ownership. Another interesting effect of gender and marital status in asset ownership was found by Iwaisako et al. (2005). Using data from Japan, these researchers found that wealth for singles was a little more than half that enjoyed by couples and that there is an asset decumulation late in life for both males and females, but it is particularly marked for females. Related to this is the presence of a child in the household. Xiao (1996) found a positive correlation with bond ownership, while the correlation was negative for the ownership of IRAs and stocks.

The effect of the employment patterns of asset ownership was studied by Alessie et al. (2004). Using data from the Netherlands, Alessie et al. found that the self-employed are much more likely to hold stocks than others, but they do not have a different ownership rate in terms of mutual funds. In another study, Blau and Graham (1990) found support for the hypothesis that those who do not have a permanent job, and those who perceive a high risk of becoming unemployed, tend to invest more in liquid assets (i.e., assets to be used in case of emergency).

Among socio-demographic variables, the ethnicity of individuals appears to be quite relevant in explaining wealth distribution and asset ownership. Blau and Graham (1990) analyzed Black–White differences in wealth and asset ownership and found that Blacks' wealth is lower than Whites even after controlling for other factors. A possible explanation provided by Blau and Graham is the presence of barriers for Blacks to acquire certain assets, like businesses and housing, which historically have paid among the highest real rates of return. Another possible explanation proposed by Blau and Graham is the chance that Blacks could face higher unemployment and greater income uncertainty, which could increase the demand of Blacks for more liquid assets, with negative consequences for the overall return of their portfolios. Xiao (1996) analyzed data from the United States and found that households with White heads were more likely to own all financial assets (e.g., bonds, stocks, and mutual funds).

Keister (2000) analyzed the ownership of seven assets in the United States[2] and found that Whites are more likely than Blacks to buy high-risk/high-return assets. In 1986, 77 percent of White families and only 56 percent of Black families owned their own homes, and the differences were larger for higher-risk assets. The percentage of White families with stocks in their portfolios was 32 percent, while the same percentage for Black families was 8 percent.

In a similar vein of research, Keister (2015) looked at the financial asset ownership of Chinese and Indian immigrants and found that Chinese and Indian immigrants to the United States have a high level of wealth and high propensities to own financial assets compared with other immigrant groups (e.g., Cuban, Mexican, other Latinos). Fontes and Kelly (2013) studied the wealth accumulation of Hispanic households, finding that to be Hispanic was not per se a difference, but the differences with White households can be explained by the fact of belonging to disadvantaged groups. In 2004, Hispanic households were roughly 2.5 times more likely to have zero or negative net worth than similar White households. Estimates for 2004 indicated that homeownership rates were 50 percent for Hispanic households and 76 percent for White households (Cortes et al., 2007). Although if the analysis was restricted to households with a net worth greater than $50,000, the differences in the rates of homeownership disappeared. Hispanic households also tend to report lower levels of participation in the stock market (Choudhury, 2001). Another interesting insight is that within Hispanic households at-home English usage and U.S. citizenship appear to be the most important factors associated with increasing the likelihood of ownership for both a home and stocks.

Religion is another variable that can shape people's financial decisions. According to Keister (2003), religion directly affects wealth accumulation by defining the goals people identify as important, by creating a repertoire of skills and knowledge that people draw on when making decisions, and by determining the nature of people's social contacts. Using data from the United States,[3] Keister (2003) found that Jews are more likely to achieve big gains in wealth ownership, while conservative Protestants accumulate relatively little wealth. In contrast, mainline Protestants and Catholics are indistinguishable from each other and the general population in terms of wealth accumulation. The author highlighted the importance of family processes in shaping wealth accumulation by underscoring the importance of culture in shaping economic behavior.

In another study, Keister (2004) analyzed the effect of childhood family structure on subsequent adult asset ownership. The results from the study showed that the presence of siblings strains material and nonmaterial resources during childhood and decreases adult homeownership, stock ownership, and total assets. The

---

**2** Data for this study came from the 1983–1986 panel of the Survey of Consumer Finances.
**3** Data for this study came from the National Longitudinal Survey of Youth 1979 cohort.

author proposed that family size, the presence of extended family, and family disruption during childhood all contribute to adult wealth ownership. Parental resources and human capital improve a child's later adult wealth, while siblings and extended family dilute family resources and reduce wealth attainment. Similarly, Keister argued that family disruption during childhood reduces adult wealth, although extended family can minimize the negative impact of divorce and separation. Blake (1981) studied the relationship between family size and asset accumulation, finding that family size is likely to reduce the resources available to each family member and to diminish the attainment these resources can produce. In larger families, parents have fewer resources to invest in each child, and each child consequently fares worse both immediately and over time. As family size increases, there will be fewer financial resources available during childhood. Financial resources improve educational opportunities, make educational resources such as books and other materials more readily available, provide support during college, and ease life transitions. Financial resources make college more feasible and can prevent children from having to acquire debt as they complete higher education. Moreover, family size reduces inter-vivos transfers and inheritance (Keister, 2003).

Asset ownership changes even according to the size of wealth. Guiso and Jappelli (2000), using data from Italy,[4] noted that the weights of financial assets as a percent of total assets decline with wealth in favor of investments in real estate and business equity. Moreover, wealthy investors tend to invest a much larger share of their wealth in risky assets. Investments in all risky financial assets (e.g., stocks, mutual funds, long-term bonds) increase sharply with wealth.

Asset ownership is affected by financial literacy as well. Van Rooij et al. (2011) showed how people with low financial literacy are much less likely to invest in stocks. Moreover, Van Rooij et al. (2012) reported a strong positive association between financial literacy and net worth, even after controlling for many determinants of wealth. The authors discussed two channels through which financial literacy might facilitate wealth accumulation. First, financial knowledge increases the likelihood of investing in the stock market, allowing individuals to benefit from the equity premium. Second, financial literacy is positively related to retirement planning, and the development of a savings plan has been shown to boost wealth.

Other factors can affect asset ownership. Two important factors are social security benefits and taxation. The presence of tax incentives on certain assets can influence the asset allocation of individuals (Alessie et al., 2004; Poterba and Samwick, 1997). Regarding social security, the awareness of individuals about, for instance, a high social pension benefit is a disincentive to save for retirement (Black, 2001). At the same time, in case a corporate pension will be paid as a lump sum at retirement

---

4 The study is based on repeated cross-sectional and panel data drawn from the 1989 to 1998 Bank of Italy Survey of Household Income and Wealth.

age, people could be more prone to borrow (e.g., to buy a home), being aware they will be able to pay back the loan using this lump sum (Iwaisako et al., 2005). In the meantime, social security benefits can impact the housing market and change the financial behavior of individuals. Wind et al. (2020) identified three possible consequences of low public pensions on the housing market. In the model, "passive asset-based welfare" people buy their house to avoid paying rent in retirement, which may be difficult to do because of a low pension. In the "active asset-based welfare" model, people sell properties when in retirement or use reverse mortgages to fill the gap between a low public pension and their personal needs. In the "proactive asset-based welfare" model, people invest in real estate properties in order to use rental income to compensate their low pension income when retired. It follows that the composition of asset ownership and the willingness to invest in property (e.g., a primary or secondary home) is affected by public policies on pension and social housing.

Differences in asset ownership are also associated with housing location (i.e., urban vis-à-vis country living location) and the presence of an inheritance. Han and Si (2020) used data from China to show how people who live in urban areas are more likely to invest in financial assets than those who live in the countryside. This result matches a study by Duasa and Yusof (2013) that found the higher risk tolerance of those who live in cities, compared to those who live in rural areas, may be associated with investments in risky assets. The presence of an inheritance or any intra-vivos transfer, especially when received at a young age, can change the asset ownership of individuals. These changes cannot be referred only to the presence of the inherited asset, but to the shift in the priorities of the person who stands to inherit assets. For instance, Iwaisako et al. (2005) noted a quite different asset composition for those who inherited a house at a young age. It is thought that those fitting this profile do not need to plan for their housing as a first goal. Blau and Graham (1990) highlighted the role of inheritance in explaining the differences between wealth and asset composition between Whites and Blacks, arguing that the smaller wealth of Blacks and the following smaller intergenerational transfers affect the wealth composition of the two groups, due to the different money relevance of the inheritance.

## Correlation and Patterns of Asset Ownership

The discussion thus far has shown how different factors can affect the financial decision making process of individuals. Now it is time to look at how the ownership of a certain asset is related to the ownership of another one and how the asset ownership of individuals evolves over time.

First, some assets tend to be more common than others in describing individual wealth, due to their role in satisfying more common needs. Xiao (1995), using a national representative sample, reported that in the United States 75 percent of households owned checking accounts, 44 percent owned savings accounts, and 35 percent owned cash value life insurance. In the meantime, other financial products were less frequently owned: 28 percent owned bonds, 24 percent retirement accounts, 22 percent employer-sponsored savings plans, 22 percent money market accounts, 20 percent certificates of deposits, and 19 percent stocks. In the same study, Xiao noted how the ownership of some assets is strictly correlated with the ownership of other assets. For instance, those who have a checking account are more likely to own savings accounts, CDs, bonds, stocks, and life insurance. The rationale behind this correlation could be that a checking account is a basic product that is needed to deal with the financial sector, even before buying other financial products. However, there are even other correlations between asset ownership. Some assets seem to be a complement, while others are a substitute. To own bonds increases the chance to own stocks and life insurance. But to own stocks decreases the chance to own saving accounts. Also, there is a negative correlation between the ownership of retirement plans (i.e., individual retirement accounts) and saving accounts. Negative correlations can be interpreted as an indication of an attitude to change one asset with the other when they are "allocated" to the same financial goal (e.g., long-term investments). Alessie et al. (2004) analyzed the correlation between the ownership of an asset at time "t" with the ownership of another asset in time "t+1." They found that there is a positive relationship between the ownership of stocks in time "t" with the ownership of mutual funds in "t+1," but the ownership of mutual funds in time "t" is negatively related with the ownership of stocks in "t+1." This evolution over time of the composition of the investment portfolio can be explained by an increase in the financial literacy of the individual or the presence of shifting costs from funds to stocks. The latter hypothesis is coherent with the results of the authors that found an increased probability to own stocks when income increases, whereas the probability of owning mutual funds does not.

Correlations do not exist only between financial assets. Black (2001) used data from the United Kingdom to find evidence that financial assets and housing are substitutes, as are housing and personal pensions. For Black (2001), a personal pension was shown to have a strong replacement effect on saving. When an individual can rely on a generous welfare system, they have less incentive to save, increasing their level of consumption. That is, the personal pension is discounted and incorporated in the total wealth of the individual who may feel that they do not need additional savings. In the meantime, a more generous pension can make the payment of housing rent during retirement more affordable, reducing the incentive to buy houses and to become a homeowner. The negative correlation between housing and financial assets was noted by Iwaisakto et al. (2005). These authors analyzed data from the Japanese housing market that provided evidence that especially when the housing market is expensive, the need to save in order to afford a down payment required by lenders (in case the purchase of the house is financed by a mortgage) generates different effects on the asset ownership of individuals. The first effect is the lack of houses in the asset ownership for individuals at a young age. The high prices of houses require more time to save for the down payment, making the asset ownership of young individuals less likely to include house properties. The second effect is the preference for liquid assets for saving, due to the awareness that this money will have to be used in the future to guarantee the down payment of a mortgage. A third effect is the overweight of housing investments on the total assets of individuals after the purchase of a home, and the small amount of financial assets in the years following the housing purchase, due to the need to pay back the mortgage. Iwaisakto et al. highlighted how high property prices and higher mortgage down payments alter patterns of asset ownership.

## Asset Ownership Over Time

Data on asset ownership can be used to illustrate how peoples' financial behavior and financial decisions have changed over time. Table 7.1 shows the evolution of asset ownership in the United States from 1989 to 2016 (Bricker et al., 2019). The percentage of families who hold financial assets has systematically increased from 88.9 percent (1989) to 98.5 percent (2016). However, the relevance of some financial assets has decreased. Stocks were directly owned by 16.8 percent of American families in 1989, while only 13.9 percent did so in 2016. Bonds were included in portfolios by 5.7 percent of American families in 1989, while only 1.2 percent of American families directly owned bonds in 2016. In the meantime, mutual funds became more popular (from 7.2 percent to 10.0 percent), and equity investments (directly or indirectly owned) grew from 31.8 percent to 51.9 percent. The changes in the welfare system can probably be used to explain the growth of individual retirement accounts, which represented 37.1 percent of total assets of Americans in 1989, becoming more than 52.1 percent in 2016. The homeownership rate remained stable over time, with 63.9 percent of the Americans owning their primary residence in 1989 and 63.7 percent doing so in 2016.

**Table 7.1:** Percent of Families that Held Assets 1989–2016.

|  | 1989 | 1992 | 1995 | 1998 | 2001 | 2004 | 2007 | 2010 | 2013 | 2016 |
|---|---|---|---|---|---|---|---|---|---|---|
| Any asset | 94.7 | 95.8 | 96.4 | 96.8 | 96.7 | 97.9 | 97.7 | 97.4 | 97.9 | 99.4 |
| Financial asset | 88.9 | 90.3 | 91.2 | 93.1 | 93.4 | 93.8 | 93.9 | 94 | 94.5 | 98.5 |
| Liquid asset | 85.5 | 86.9 | 87.4 | 90.6 | 91.4 | 91.3 | 92.1 | 92.5 | 93.2 | 98 |
| CDs | 19.9 | 16.7 | 14.3 | 15.3 | 15.7 | 12.7 | 16.1 | 12.2 | 7.8 | 6.5 |
| Mutual fund (dir.) | 7.2 | 10.4 | 12.3 | 16.5 | 17.7 | 15 | 11.4 | 8.7 | 8.2 | 10 |
| Stocks (dir.) | 16.8 | 17 | 15.2 | 19.2 | 21.3 | 20.7 | 17.9 | 15.1 | 13.8 | 13.9 |

**Table 7.1** (continued)

|  | 1989 | 1992 | 1995 | 1998 | 2001 | 2004 | 2007 | 2010 | 2013 | 2016 |
|---|---|---|---|---|---|---|---|---|---|---|
| Bonds (dir.) | 5.7 | 4.3 | 3.1 | 3 | 3 | 1.8 | 1.6 | 1.6 | 1.4 | 1.2 |
| Managed acct. | 3.6 | 4 | 3.9 | 5.9 | 6.6 | 7.3 | 5.8 | 5.7 | 5.2 | 5.5 |
| DC pension or IRA | 37.1 | 40.1 | 45.3 | 48.9 | 52.8 | 49.9 | 53 | 50.4 | 49.2 | 52.1 |
| Other financial | 55 | 51.2 | 50 | 45.1 | 43.7 | 41.5 | 38.5 | 33.1 | 30.7 | 30.9 |
| Equity (dir. or indir.) | 31.8 | 36.9 | 40.5 | 48.9 | 53 | 50.3 | 53.2 | 49.9 | 48.8 | 51.9 |
| Directly held equity | 19.9 | 21.1 | 22.3 | 27.6 | 29.9 | 27.7 | 23.8 | 19.4 | 18.2 | 19.7 |
| Non-financial | 89.3 | 90.8 | 90.9 | 89.9 | 90.7 | 92.5 | 92 | 91.3 | 91 | 90.8 |
| Primary residence | 63.9 | 63.9 | 64.7 | 66.2 | 67.7 | 69.1 | 68.6 | 67.3 | 65.2 | 63.7 |
| Second + home | 13.1 | 12.7 | 11.8 | 12.8 | 11.3 | 12.5 | 13.8 | 14.3 | 13.2 | 13.8 |
| Business | 21.1 | 20.8 | 19.2 | 18.7 | 19 | 19.1 | 19 | 18.5 | 16.7 | 17.4 |
| Other nonfin. | 84.5 | 86.4 | 85 | 83.6 | 85.5 | 87 | 87.7 | 87.2 | 86.8 | 85.8 |
| Any debt | 72.3 | 73.2 | 74.5 | 74.1 | 75.1 | 76.4 | 77 | 74.9 | 74.5 | 77.1 |
| Mortgage | 39.5 | 39.1 | 41 | 43.1 | 44.6 | 47.9 | 48.7 | 47 | 42.9 | 41.9 |
| Mortg. ($2^{nd}$ + home) | 5.1 | 5.7 | 4.7 | 5 | 4.6 | 4 | 5.5 | 5.3 | 5.2 | 5.6 |
| Credit card balance | 39.7 | 43.7 | 47.3 | 44.1 | 44.4 | 46.2 | 46.1 | 39.4 | 38.1 | 43.9 |
| Other installment | 52.5 | 50.2 | 50.3 | 48.5 | 48.5 | 49.8 | 49.8 | 49.2 | 50 | 52.4 |

*Source*: Bricker et al. (2019).

Figure 7.1 shows the average composition of American households' asset holdings. It can be seen how the composition of asset ownership changed from 1989 to 2016. Non-financial assets accounted for more than 60 percent of total assets in the first time slot (1989–1995) while they represented a bit more than 50 percent in the last period (2013–2016). In the meantime, assets related to the financial market grew, as did financial assets related to retirement.

Figure 7.2 illustrates the different patterns of asset ownership between and among individuals according to their total wealth. The weight of the housing-related assets ("Non-Financial – Residences") decreases when household wealth grows. Housing-related assets account for more than 60 percent of the total for the 50 to 60 asset percentile, whereas they represent less than 15 percent for the top 1 percent. For this latter group, "Non-Financial – Business" assets represent the main asset category. The comparison between the average (on the left) with each of the asset percentile groups provides additional evidence of the differences in the asset ownership for different levels of wealth.

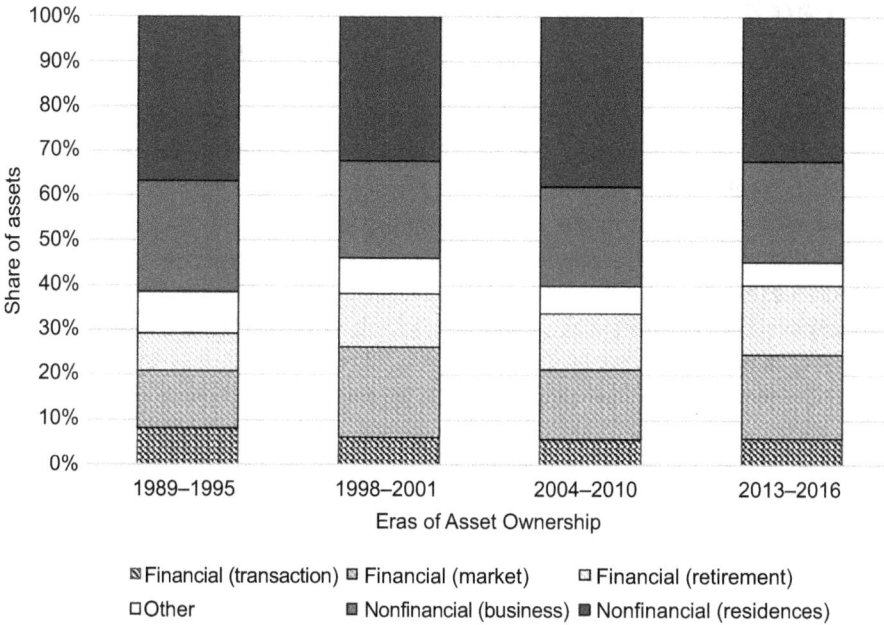

**Figure 7.1:** Average Composition of Household Assets.
*Source*: Bricker et al. (2019).

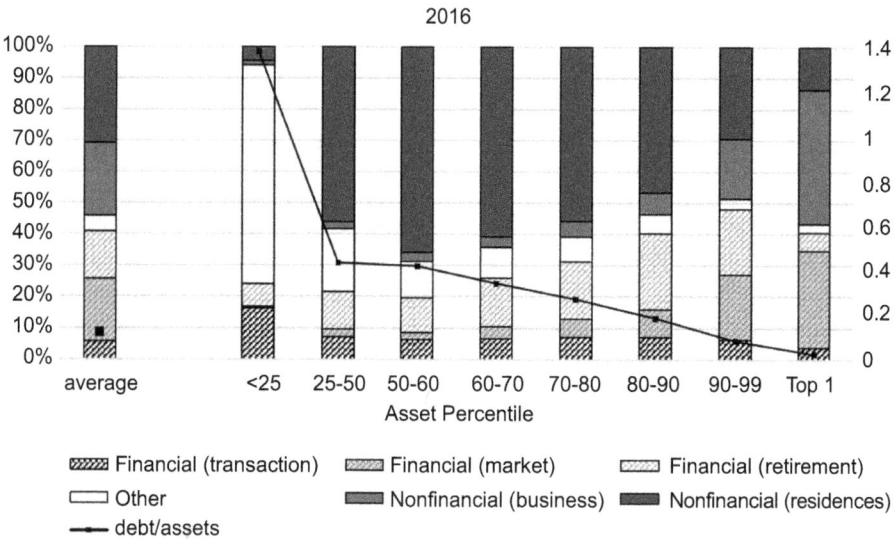

**Figure 7.2:** Share of Assets in Household Asset Portfolios 2016.
*Source*: Bricker et al. (2019).

# Research and Policy Issues

The awareness of peoples' patterns in asset ownership can help policymakers to shape their interventions and researchers to identify new research topics. For instance, the low liquidity nature of assets owned by individuals or the complete lack of savings freely usable in case of a need (so-called "rainy days funds" or emergency funds) raise attention to the potential financial fragility of individuals and households when and if a financial shock occurs. The Covid-19 pandemic represented an example of how an exogenous factor can jeopardize the personal financial management of individuals. Moreover, the effect of the Covid-19 pandemic on the patterns of asset ownership could be related to the propensity to save for the future. People could become more aware of the need to save for the future and re-shape their saving behavior and the types of assets used to save.

An additional area of interest for both policymakers and researchers involves estimating how the asset ownership of people in the long-term is being influenced by low (or zero) interest rate policies practiced by some central banks over the last decade. The effects on the bond markets (with negative yields at least in the short-term) risk compromising the wealth accumulation of individuals due to the lack of the compound interest effect on financial assets returns. In the meantime, the chance that people will change their asset allocation, orienting their savings toward different assets (e.g., deposits, stocks, alternative investments) can generate new patterns in the asset ownership and can affect the functioning of other markets (e.g., money market, stock market, etc.). This possibility is worthy of future study.

# Practitioner Tools, Techniques, and Applications

The different behaviors of individuals in their asset ownership decisions provide useful tips to financial planners and other personal finance advice practitioners. If it is true that age, income, and education are key variables associated with patterns of asset ownership, then it behoves practitioners to understand the financial needs of a new client through appropriate data gathering, including obtaining information and evidence about additional factors that may impact asset choice decisions (e.g., the family structure in childhood, religious beliefs, or urban versus country living). These types of factors may affect the chance that a client will be more prone to follow certain recommendations. In the meanwhile, the roles of cultural background and ethnicity need to be included in advice-giving models. Taking account of a client's cultural background and ethnicity will allow for more precise advice when identifying different strategies to best satisfy client preferences and priorities (housing, children's education, preparedness for retirement, intergenerational transfer of wealth, etc.). Moreover, the fact that the ownership of some assets tends to follow the ownership of other assets can provide useful insights when proposing changes to a client's assets ownership structure.

## Future Directions

Previous studies have addressed the role that single factors can play in the definition of patterns of asset ownership. A potential new area of research concerns the simultaneous role of these factors in the explanation of individual financial behaviors. The interaction of different factors can provide additional details in the explanation of people's financial decision making processes and can shed light on the relevance of each factor related to others.

An additional interesting area concerns the chance that new generational patterns of asset ownership may not exactly replicate the ones of previous generations. An analysis of a cohort effect can help refine knowledge about patterns of asset ownership and incorporate new scenarios. The use of cryptocurrencies as a trading tool or asset needs to be examined in the context of building diversified portfolios. The influence of social media on trading decisions, and the rise of "financial influencers," are just two examples of how the presence of new assets and differences in the way people receive information about market trends can affect the way people interact when developing asset allocation strategies.

## Discussion

The types of assets held by individuals and households are diverse. Traditionally, studies on personal finance have focused on documenting patterns of ownership related to financial securities, housing, other real-estate properties, businesses, vehicles, jewelry, collectibles, etc. As noted in this chapter, different patterns of asset ownership vary based on wealth, income, education, financial literacy, and other factors. In the future, new factors will likely emerge as descriptors and predictors of asset ownership. It follows that recommendations that work for someone will not be as good for another, and the development of a single standard methodology to support individuals in the development and management of their wealth is not possible. However, what may be more workable (and interesting) is a more holistic approach in personal finance, where the study of saving behaviors and the understanding of how people decide to allocate their savings will be based on models that incorporate environmental threats and correlational data as indicators of appropriate asset usage.

# Conclusion

This chapter provided a discussion about the determinants of peoples' decisions to allocate their resources in different ways, developing different patterns of asset ownership. Individual goals vary when some personal needs are satisfied and a new set of needs arise, and the amount of the individual wealth and the composition of the asset ownership change following these new circumstances. The variables that help to explain changing behaviors are many and include socio-demographic characteristics of individuals (age, gender, income, marital status, presence of children, etc.) and external factors like taxation and social security. However, to understand peoples' asset ownership behavior, there are additional components to account for, like the family structure in childhood, personal beliefs, and familiarity with the financial markets. Hence, the asset ownership structure at a certain time can be seen as the result of a mix of decisions that are driven or influenced by a diverse set of factors. Practitioners and policymakers should keep in mind that their actions or recommendation will have different effects when their counterparts differ in terms of asset ownership structure, even in terms of the paths that have led to them.

# References

Alessie, R., Hochguertel, S., and van Soest, A. (2004). Ownership of stocks and mutual funds: A panel data analysis. *The Review of Economics and Statistics*, 86(3), 783–796.

Ameriks, J., and Zeldes, S. P. (2001). *How do household portfolio shares vary with age?* (Columbia University Working Paper). Columbia University, 1–87.

Ando, A., and Modigliani, F. (1963). The "life cycle" hypothesis of saving: Aggregate implications and tests. *The American Economic Review*, 53(1), 55–84.

Atkinson, T. R. (1956). *The pattern of asset ownership: Wisconsin individuals 1949* (NBER Working Paper No. atki56-1). Accessed July 2021. National Bureau of Economic Research. http://www.nber.org/books/atki56–1

Black, D. (2001). *How does pension wealth affect asset composition, savings and retirement behaviour?* Pensions Institute Birkbeck College, University of London.

Blake, J. (1981). Family size and the quality of children. *Demography*, 18, 421–442.

Blau, F. D., and Graham, J. W. (1990). Black-White differences in wealth and asset composition. *The Quarterly Journal of Economics*, 105(2), 321–339.

Bricker, J., Moore, K. B., and Thompson, J. (2019). *Trends in household portfolio composition* (Research Department Working Paper No. 19–9). Federal Reserve Bank of Boston. https://doi.org/10.29412/res.wp.2019.09.

Choudhury, S. (2001). Racial and ethnic differences in wealth and asset choices. *Social Security Bulletin*, 64, 10–15.

Cortes, A., Herbert, C. E., Wilson, E., and Clay, E. (2007). Factors affecting Hispanic homeownership: A review of the literature. *Cityscape*, 9, 53–92.

Duasa, J., and Yusof, S. A. (2013). Determinants of risk tolerance on financial asset ownership: A case of Malaysia. *International Journal of Business & Society*, 14(1), 1–16.

Fontes, A., and Kelly, N. (2013). Factors affecting wealth accumulation in Hispanic households: A comparative analysis of stock and home asset utilization. *Hispanic Journal of Behavioral Sciences, 35*(4), 565–587.

Guiso, L., and Jappelli T. (2000). Household portfolios in Italy (Vol. 2549). *Centre for Economic Policy Research Working Papers, 43*. Accessed July 2021. https://ideas.repec.org/p/sef/csefwp/43.html

Han H., and Si F. (2020). How does the composition of asset portfolios affect household consumption: Evidence from China based on micro data. *Sustainability, 12*, 2946; doi:10.3390/su12072946.

Iwaisako, T., Mitchell, O., and Piggott, J. (2005). *Strategic asset allocation in Japan: An empirical evaluation* (Wharton Pension Research Council Working Paper No. 375). The Wharton School, University of Pennsylvania.

Jefferson, T., and Ong, R. (2010). *Profiling gender differentials in asset and debt portfolios in Australia* (Working Paper No. 201004). Center for Research in Applied Economics.

Keister, L. A. (2000). Race and wealth inequality: The impact of racial differences in asset ownership on the distribution of household wealth. *Social Science Research, 29*(4), 477–502.

Keister L. A. (2003). Religion and wealth – The role of religious affiliation and participation in early adult asset accumulation. *Social Forces, 82*(1), 175–207.

Keister, L. A. (2004). Race, family structure, and wealth: The effect of childhood family on adult asset ownership. *Sociological Perspectives, 47*(2), 161–187.

Keister, L. A. (2015). Financial asset ownership: The case of Chinese and Indian immigrants to the United States. *Business Economics Journal, 6*, 1–19.

Maslow, A. H. (1954). The instinctoid nature of basic needs. *Journal of Personality, 22*, 326–347. https://doi.org/10.1111/j.1467-6494.1954.tb01136.x

Merriam-Webster. (n.d.). Wealth. *Merriam-Webster.com dictionary*. Retrieved June 15, 2021, from https://www.merriam-webster.com/dictionary/wealth

Modigliani, F., and Brumberg, R. (1954). Utility analysis and the consumption function: An interpretation of cross-section data. *Franco Modigliani, 1*(1), 388–436.

Poterba, J., Samwick, A. (1997). *Household portfolio allocation over the life cycle* (NBER Working Paper No. 6185). National Bureau of Economic Research. http://www.nber.org/papers/w6185

Shefrin, H. M., and Thaler, R. H. (1988). The behavioral lifecycle hypothesis. *Economic Inquiry, 26*, 609–643.

Shorrocks, A. F. (1982). Inequality decomposition by factor components. *Econometrica, 50*(1), 193–211.

Thaler, R. H. (1988). Anomalies: The ultimatum game. *Journal of Economic Perspectives, 2*(4), 195–206.

Van Rooij, M., Lusardi, A., and Alessie, R. (2011). Financial literacy and stock market participation. *Journal of Financial Economics, 101*(2), 449–472.

Van Rooij, M., Lusardi, A., and Alessie, R. (2012). Financial literacy, retirement planning and household wealth. *The Economic Journal, 122*(560), 449–478. https://doi.org/10.1111/j.1468-0297.2012.02501.x

Weagley, R. O., and Gannon, C. F. (1991). Investor portfolio allocation. *Journal of Financial Counseling and Planning, 2*(1), 131–154.

Wind, B., Dewilde C., and Doling, J. (2020). Secondary property ownership in Europe: Contributing to asset-based welfare strategies and the "really big trade-off." *International Journal of Housing Policy, 20*(1), 25–52. https://doi.org/10.1080/19491247.2019.1573961.

Xiao, J. J. (1995). Patterns of household financial asset ownership. *Journal of Financial Counseling and Planning, 6*(1), 99–106.

Xiao, J. J. (1996). Effects of family income and life cycle stages on financial asset ownership. *Journal of Financial Counseling and Planning, 7,* 21–30.

Xiao, J. J., and Anderson, J. G. (1993). A hierarchy of financial needs reflected by household paper assets. In T. Mauldin (ed.), *The proceedings of American council on consumer interests 39th annual conference* (pp. 207–214). American Council on Consumer Interests.

Xiao, J. J., and Olson, G. I. (1993). Mental accounting and saving behavior. *Home Economics Research Journal, 22*(1), 92–109.

Yumna, A., and Marta, J. (2021) Understanding the factors influencing banking customers' financial asset ownership. *Journal of Islamic Monetary Economics and Finance, 7*(1), 107–126.

Inga Timmerman

# 8 Approaches to Saving

**Abstract:** Theories on savings range from the classic life cycle and permanent income hypotheses to the newer strands of literature that focus on the psychological aspect. There are several factors that influence the personal savings rate. Among the most often cited are individual demographic characteristics such as age and race, education level, financial knowledge and literacy, and wealth. Lower-income families save less than higher-income families; the same is true for less-educated families. The financial literacy literature points to a strong positive link between financial knowledge and savings behavior. Cultural and geographical differences also have an impact on savings rates, especially when explaining differences in saving across countries. Increasing the personal savings rate has an impact not only on individual wealth but also on the overall economy; therefore, research into saving strategies is imperative. The savings landscape in the future could change by incorporating the psychological aspects of money into traditional financial planning models and focusing on how people actually behave rather than how traditional economic theory predicts they will behave. Providers of personal finance advice have a role in managing and increasing household savings. This means that by focusing on what they can change and influence, such as a focus on clients' human capital and the development of clients' financial knowledge, financial advisors can enhance the wealth of their clients.

**Keywords:** savings, retirement savings, factors influencing savings, increasing savings

## Introduction

The basic choice to save is a trade-off between current and future consumption. A relatively low personal savings rate is an important social and policy issue and getting people to save more is an important policy goal. The savings rate is not constant; rather, it is cyclical. For example, before the 2008 financial crisis, the savings rate was trending down. From 2008 to 2012, the rate went up, making some economists predict a structural change in savings behavior. The change, however, was not permanent. From 2012 to 2020, the savings rate fell, only to result in a savings shock during the 2020 Covid-19 pandemic. Over the period of December 2010 through February 2020, the savings rate

**Inga Timmerman**, California State University, Northridge

https://doi.org/10.1515/9783110727692-008

in the United States was 7.4 percent.[1] To test the pattern and its stability, Ouliaris and Rochon (2018) used financial modeling and concluded that the financial crisis of 2008–2009 did not result in any permanent change in behavior. Rather, increased savings were a result of negative income shocks, employment, and wealth.

Personal savings rates have a broad impact not only on household balance sheets but also on the overall economy, job market, and, potentially, international trade. Increased savings means less consumption, which, in turn, might slow down the growth of a country's gross domestic product (GDP). At the same time, it means more domestic money and potentially, a lower reliance on foreign capital, thereby reducing deficits. In this chapter, I will explore the theories used to explain personal savings rates, the factors that drive savings, the current main research topics, and the opportunities for both researchers and financial advisers as they relate to increasing and optimizing personal savings.

# Historical Perspective

## Definition

Before exploring savings-related theories and their historical perspective, it is important to define the term "savings." Walden (2012) pointed out that "savings behavior" can be defined either at the individual level or the national level. At the macro (national) level, the rate is measured in a specific way, depending on the country. For example, in the United States, it is measured by the U.S. Bureau of Economic Analysis from the National Income and Product Accounts (NIPA). This is normally disposable personal income minus personal outlays expressed as a percent of disposable personal income. There is debate on the quality of this measure. Alternative measures exist from the Federal Reserve and from the Survey of Consumer Finances. The focus of this chapter, however, is on the individual savings rate.[2] Although variations in measurements exist, the micro (individual) savings rate is defined as money coming in minus money going out, be it in terms of income or wealth. Despite the debate on the quality of measures, at a basic level, savings is what is left after consumption (see Bostic et al., 2009).

---

1 https://fred.stlouisfed.org/series/PSAVERT.

2 Individual savings rates can be compiled from the Survey of Consumer Finances and the Consumer Expenditure Survey from the U.S Bureau of Labor Statistics. The Panel Study of Income Dynamics, which can be used to obtain similar data, is available from the University of Michigan.

## Theories of Saving

Throughout the last half-century, two main rational models have been used to explain savings behavior. The theories have their roots in the 1957 permanent income hypothesis work by Friedman that explains savings as the difference between permanent and temporary income changes (Friedman, 1957) and in the 1963 Ando and Modigliani life-cycle hypothesis (LCH) (Ando and Modigliani, 1963).

Both theories assume that rational individuals will borrow against future income if they expect their income to increase or their consumption to decrease in the future. This translates into asset accumulation (savings) in the earlier years, followed by asset decumulation (spending) later in life. The main assumption in the LCH is that individuals go through two primary phases throughout their lifetime: accumulation of assets in the early part and decumulation of assets in the later part based on their individual preferences and utility maximization function. As such, the savings rate (and consumption) will change if changes in income are expected to be permanent rather than temporary. The LCH has been used extensively to explain savings behavior both in the United States and internationally.

The LCH was initially applied only to developed countries but was later expanded to include lesser developed countries like China or countries in Southeast Asia. For example, the relationship between the age composition of a nation and its savings rate was used to explain savings behavior in 16 Asian countries from 1952 to 1992. Modigliani and Cao (2004) used the hypothesis to explain data for China. However, Schultz (2005) questioned the findings, re-estimating savings to be about 25 percent of the original study and proposing other explanations, such as considering lifetime savings as a substitute for children. The LCH explains savings behavior better in some countries than in others. For example, it follows the patterns of savings well in Japan (see Chen et al., 2007; Horioka and Watanabe, 1997). The evidence in the United States is mixed. After an extensive review, Lusardi et al. (2001) concluded that they could not account for the shifts in the U.S. demographic to support the LCH.

A variation of the classic permanent income hypothesis is Mayer's (1972) certainty equivalence model. The savings and consumption trade-off is an equilibrium of the marginal utility of consumption. The trade-off between consumption and savings will be driven by keeping the marginal utility constant over time. Thus, people will borrow if the marginal utility of consumption is higher in the present and save if it is expected to be higher in the future. In other words, households do what brings them the highest marginal utility.

However, as stated by Benartzi and Thaler (2007), standard economic theory assumes that individuals can easily solve optimization problems and have the willpower to execute the optimal plan when it comes to savings behavior. The reality, even in professional circles, is very different. Few people solve math problems to decide on their optimal savings rate; instead, they use biases and heuristics to arrive at that decision. Savings, especially for retirement, is a difficult problem for which most individuals need help from outside sources such as financial planners. This chapter will explore the psychological theory of savings in the next section.

The explanatory power of savings extends beyond traditional economic theory or behavioral economics. Alternative explanations are used to explain individual savings behavior. In a non-traditional setting, Barnea et al. (2010) used a study of identical twins, identifying that genetic variation explains about 35 percent in savings rates across individuals. Nevertheless, individual life experiences, such as the savings behavioral transmittal from parents to children, is a very strong explanatory variable as well. Canare et al. (2019) focused on fear and savings, arguing that negative emotions increase current consumption; in other words, the authors found that the emotional fear of crime has a negative effect on savings. The results do not extend to cognitive or rational fear. More focus should be put on these alternative theories when explaining savings behavior in the future.

## The Psychology of Saving

Warneryd (1989) outlined the psychological savings literature over the last few centuries. He pointed out that psychological theories were discussed during the 19th century, and "in the context of savings, economic principles such as anticipation, uncertainty, self-control, impatience and time preference" (p. 213) were first identified. Bohm-Bawerk (1890) and Fisher (1930) developed their theories by focusing heavily on the psychological aspect of saving. Despite the obvious influence of psychology on savings behavior, the psychological aspect almost disappeared from saving behavior modeling after Keynes (1936) proposed the income theory of savings and the dominance of the life-cycle hypothesis. Ironically, Keynes himself focused on the psychological factors, but the idea has slowly been eliminated from the economic literature over many decades.

Newer strands of literature focus on the psychological aspect of sentiment. Thaler (1994) pointed out that individual psychological intervention would not be necessary if the life-cycle theory would hold as it would be impossible to undersave. Furthermore, he argued that "life-cycle theories failed to describe actual household savings" (p. 186). When the classical theories of savings cannot explain behavior, supplemental theories, including ones that focus on the psychology of savings, tend to fill in the gap. Laibson and Vaitilinga (2008) emphasized that savings behavior and investment decisions need to be viewed from an integral approach where economics is combined with psychology.

Thaler (1994) suggested supplementing classical theory with psychological theories, which, in turn, could result in policy changes. Ewing and Payne (1998) used psychology to explain actual behavior, concluding that households decrease their savings rate when sentiment is high and increase it when sentiment is low. For example, while the decade-long savings rate in the United States was 7.4 percent before March 2020 (beginning of the Covid-19 pandemic), it increased to as high as 33 percent. When there is more uncertainty about the future, individuals tend to keep more assets liquid. Drawing on life-history theory, Griskevicius et al. (2013) linked the response to scarcity, and thus the propensity to save, to their early life experiences and the childhood socioeconomic status. As a result, people whose early life was in a higher socio-economic status were less impulsive and more risk averse. These qualities emerge especially during periods of economic uncertainty. DeVaney et al. (2007) focused on the hierarchy of needs to explain the psychology of savings behavior.

In the last three decades, the study of psychology and personal finance extended to financial therapy. Although it is still an emerging field, it is successfully combining economic theory with human behavior. Archuleta et al. (2012) developed the theoretical framework and the assumption of financial therapy. The authors formalized the ten tenants of financial therapy, starting with the "integration of cognition, behavior, emotion, relationship and finance" (for a complete list, see page 73). The discipline is a combination of behavioral and emotional health and financial health. One of the main differences between financial therapists and financial advisers revolves around the outcomes of financial therapy. While financial therapists look at the overall life improvement of an individual, in which financial health is just a part, financial planners focus almost exclusively on the improvement of finances. The authors pointed out that it is a new discipline, and that future direction should evaluate the effectiveness of interventions, as well as best practices, on which practitioners can base their work.

## Factors Associated with Saving

Savings behavior is often studied along with financial knowledge and education by stratifying the population along different demographic characteristics and by using the framework of a traditional lifecycle savings theory. There are several factors that influence personal savings rates. Among the most often cited are demographic characteristics (e.g., age and race), education level, interest rates, inflation, employer contributions for retirement accounts, net worth, and income. Using the Survey of Consumer Finances (SCF), Hogarth and Hilgert (2002) found that education, race, and age correlate with financial literacy. Lusardi and Mitchell (2007a, 2007b) confirmed the link between knowledge and race/gender using the Health and Retirement Study (HRS).

Specifically, these studies found that individuals who are more educated, are White, and are from the ages of 36 to 65 are more financially literate. Wealth/Social class has also been associated with savings. Karlan et al. (2014) focused on the savings rate of the poorer population, identifying the constraints that preclude poorer individuals from savings. These constraints include transaction costs, lack of trust, information and knowledge gaps, social constraints, and behavioral issues. Overall, it is known that both lower-income families (Bucks et al., 2009) and lower-educated families (Hubbard et al., 1995) save less than higher-income families. Many low-income families can save if their levels of education and financial literacy are higher (see Fry et al., 2008; Schreiner et al., 2006). As consistently reported in the literature, age, education, and income have been identified as strong predictors of savings. In an early study in Great Britain, Furnham (1985) pointed to age and education as strong predictors of savings behavior, with age, sex, and income being the strongest discriminators of savings.

There is also a difference in saving by gender. Sevak et al. (2003) showed that when the husband dies, women are more likely to slide into poverty faster. Low-risk tolerance and poor health reduce the savings rate for women while increased education increases the savings for men (Fisher, 2010).

Focusing on ethnic and racial differences, Dal Borgo (2019) showed that racial inequality could be explained at least partially by income in general and education for passive savings. Lim et al. (2015) added investor optimism to the list of factors associated with savings rates. These authors concluded that optimistic individuals who expect to live longer are more likely to be savers compared to pessimistic individuals. Bloom et al. (2003) added health and longevity to the life-savings model, showing that including these factors leads to increased savings at every age. The effect has been found across countries, not just in the United States.

Cultural and geographic differences also have an impact on saving rates. Unfortunately, traditional economic theory does not clearly explain savings behavior across countries. Costa-Font et al. (2018) looked at the savings rates in the United Kingdom. They used the argument that savings respond to specific cultural norms to analyze the savings rates of multiple generations of immigrants in the United Kingdom, pointing out that cultural differences add strong explanatory power to savings behavior across nations. In a more specific context, Wei and Zhang (2011) looked at the savings rate in China. They concluded that during the 1990s and 2000s, Chinese parents who had a son were led to save more, in order to improve the son's attractiveness in marriage. Grossbard and Pereira (2010) identified traditional gender roles as a factor associated with higher savings rates for young men and lower savings rates for young women. In less traditional countries, the opposite is true; the savings rate of married women is higher than that of married men. Fuchs-Schundeln et al. (2019) also concluded that culture is a significant determinant of savings behavior.

Financial literacy is another factor that has a strong relationship with savings. Many households do not even attempt to calculate their retirement needs. Lusardi and Mitchell (2007b) estimated that only about one-third of older Americans have attempted to calculate their retirement needs. The lack of knowledge extends to pensions and Social Security. Gustman et al. (2011) estimated that about half of the population is not aware of the type of pension and the amount of money available.

Additionally, based on the Retirement Confidence Survey, 18 percent of respondents in 2007 were aware of the age at which they are eligible for Social Security. Lusardi and Mitchell (2007a) argued that the lack of knowledge is linked to low levels of financial literacy and the lack of understanding of concepts such as interest compounding, inflation, or diversification. Generally, the financial literacy literature points to a strong positive link between financial knowledge and savings behavior. Due to the availability of data, many financial literacy studies tend to focus on high-school/college students (e.g., Schuchardt et al., 2009). Other researchers (particularly those based on SCF) have examined working adults with relatively little education/income compared to broader samples or people in a specific age bracket (see Lusardi and Mitchell's (2007a) work based on HRS studies). Consequently, the differences in questions asked in the administered tests/surveys are relatively small. Most of the questions asked focus on textbook economics and applied personal finance material. One of the main conclusions found in many studies is that individuals are not adequately prepared for retirement because they do not possess the financial knowledge and/or because they do not plan for retirement (see Lusardi and Mitchell, 2007a).[3] Many college-educated individuals have been exposed to a basic course in economics and have a basic understanding of (or at least familiarity with) concepts such as interest rates, compounding, and financial markets. Understanding the link between what educated individuals know and their actual saving behavior could offer insights into the use and value of financial education for retirement savings for other segments of the population.

There is disagreement about whether specialized education or financial education on-demand matters more. Overall, there is a strong link between increased financial literacy and increased savings. Bernheim et al. (2001) focused on general education. Even high-school mandated financial literacy programs have a positive relationship with asset accumulation later in life. Bernheim and Garrett (2003) argued that it is the type of financial education that matters. For example, they found that employer-based financial education leads to increased savings, both in general and for retirement. Joo and Grable (2005) showed a link between higher education/ higher income and the existence of workplace retirement savings. Using a sample of highly educated individuals, Beck and Chira (2017) found that, overall, the level and depth of savings knowledge is adequate, at least theoretically. Highly educated individuals are aware they should be saving and when presented with multiple scenarios, are likely to choose an optimal portion of income to save. Despite the knowledge, in practice, participants save less than they say they should. Nevertheless, increasing financial literacy does in fact increase actual savings for highly educated

---

3 For example, Lusardi and Mitchell (2007a) provided a review of current financial education and literacy programs concluding that "many households are unfamiliar with the most basic economic concepts needed to make investment and savings decisions" (p. 205).

consumers, which means that it is a tool that could be used to increase awareness and have a long-term impact on savings behavior.

Financial instability has been shown to have a strong relationship with personal savings rates. Individuals tend to curtail spending and increase savings in unstable periods, such as a financial crisis. For example, the U.S. Bureau of Economic Analysis (2011) estimated that savings in the United States went down by more than 2 percent from 2007 to 2009 and that the personal savings rate rose from less than 2 percent in 2007 to more than 7 percent in 2009. This is normal and expected as individuals try to account for potentially unstable income in the future and is part of the economic cycle. Similar results are starting to emerge as research appears on the Covid-19 crisis. For example, Heo et al. (2020) identified a downward shift in risk during extreme events such as the Covid-19 crisis during early 2020.

Another factor worth mentioning is the cyclical approach to savings as driven by economic shocks such as a financial crisis or a health crisis. The factors that affect savings will matter in different degrees depending on the period. Dos Santos Felipe (2018) used the 2007 and 2013 SCF to build a two-period consumption and savings model and to examine the impact of crisis on savings behavior. He concluded that the 2008 financial crisis resulted in the accentuation of the relevance of some factors and the diminishing of others. For example, number of children, age, education level, and income were more relevant after a crisis while others, like financial risk tolerance, equity or homeownership were less relevant. Future research should put further emphasis on the factors, resulting in targeting recommendations that financial advisors could provide to their clients.

## Research and Policy Issues

One of the main goals of policymaking is to improve the standard of living of a nation's population. Increasing savings is a vehicle that can be used for that purpose. Therefore, identifying factors outside of the individual's power, factors that contribute to savings, is imperative for establishing sound policy. The personal savings rate has a strong impact on the quality of life of a country's citizens, especially in an aging population. Much of the developed world is currently seeing an increase in the older population. Hakkio and Wiseman (2006) pointed out that an aging population means more pressure on social systems like Social Security and Medicare, at a time when the personal savings rate is especially low. Similar declines have been observed in other developed countries, like Australia and Canada. This could result in a crisis in which neither the social net nor personal savings are available to support a large aging population.

Employer contribution has a strong impact on retirement savings. In an experiment by Duflo et al. (2006) with H&R Block, about 14,000 tax clients were offered either a 20 percent, 50 percent, or 0 percent contribution to their IRA when they prepared their taxes. As expected, higher matches raised the voluntary savings significantly from 3 percent in the 0 percent control group to 14 percent in the 50 percent match group. Thus, one way to address the savings shortage is to incentivize employers to contribute more to the employee accounts, increasing the desire of the employees to do the same.

As mentioned earlier, there is a significant difference in the savings rate of wealthy and poor households. Klawitter et al. (2012) explored how, in the absence of easy access to institutional structures like work retirement plans, nonprofits and governments can step in to create and encourage savings. Programs such as Individual Development Accounts (IDAs) are supposed to act as replacements for individual savings. While these programs have had some success, they cannot replace individually driven savings because of the number of things that lower-income families lack.

Devising the best vehicles for savings is a major goal of public policy as it relates to savings. Using tax treatment to incentivize/change behavior is a tool that has been used for decades. For example, the introduction of traditional IRAs/401(k)s and the introduction of Roth 401(k)s in the United States has arguably changed the savings landscape. A major reason for the introduction of IRAs was to increase retirement savings. For pre-tax IRAs to be successful at increasing savings, the actual savings has to be greater than the benefit derived from tax savings. Early research (Gravelle, 1991) argued that IRAs were not successful at increasing savings by decreasing consumption. These results were further reinforced by Gale and Scholz (1994). Using a dynamic utility maximization model, they concluded that IRA savings are a consequence of shifting taxable savings into IRAs instead of a true increase in national savings – hardly the public intention of devising such plans in the 1980s. Newer studies (e.g., Attanasio and DeLeire, 2002) concluded the same; the increase in IRA savings results from shifting assets or from existing savings that would have happened anyway. Furthermore, these findings extend to outside the United States. Attanasio et al. (2004) paralleled these findings, showing that the shifting in savings has also happened in the United Kingdom, after the introduction of IRA-type accounts.[4] Overall, these types of accounts have been an expensive way for governments to encourage savings, which, in effect, did not happen.

On the post-tax landscape, Beshears et al. (2017) examined the impact of the introduction of the Roth 401(k) on savings behavior after such plans were allowed in 2006. The authors found no change in overall 401(k) contributions because of the tax treatment and the availability of the Roth 401(k). Given the post-tax treatment of the Roth accounts, this means that overall, the amount of retirement consumption increases as employees do not adjust for the tax differential. They concluded

---

4 The equivalent of the IRA in the United Kingdom is known as TESSA and ISA.

that "government may be able to increase after-tax private savings while holding the present value of tax collected roughly constant" (p. 95), an argument that contradicts the usual belief that pre-tax pans provide more incentive to employees to save.

## Practitioner Tools and Techniques

As already described in this chapter, savings behavior is moderated by several factors. Generally, higher income and higher satisfaction with one's financial situation results in more savings (Traut-Mattausch and Jonas, 2011). Zagorsky (2013) looked at the use of inherited wealth, concluding that only about half of inherited assets are saved; the other half is either spent or lost. Increasing savings is a main goal for many financial advisors. However, the rate of savings can fluctuate based on factors that provide alternative access to wealth and resources. Walden (2012) pointed out that a negative relationship between savings rates and home equity can be expected. Home equity is an alternative to personal savings and, as a result, could be used by households to enhance savings. A similar result has been found for human capital. Timmerman and Volkov (2020) argued that, in most cases, human capital accounts for the majority of an individual's wealth portfolio for most of an individual's life. Furthermore, the authors showed that by including human capital in the traditional theoretical portfolio choice framework, the choice of career and education level has a significant effect on the Sharpe ratio of an individual's overall wealth portfolio. This means that by focusing on human capital, financial advisors can enhance the wealth of their clients.

One of the areas financial advisors, and others who provide personal finance advice to others, could focus on to further develop their skills is financial therapy and counseling. Dubofsky and Sussman (2009) pointed out that 89 percent of the respondents in a survey of financial planners provided some kind of financial counseling that goes beyond traditional financial planning, but that 40 percent had not taken any courses in the field. As a result, financial advisors may be offering advice they are not qualified to offer. Britt et al. (2008) specifically pointed out this problem. Financial advisors should be aware of the expertise they can offer and not overstep their professional boundaries.

One way to integrate financial therapy into financial advice is to use two professionals, each with their own area of expertise. Kim et al. (2011) analyzed a team of financial planners and marriage therapists co-counseling their clients, concluding that the approach is successful. Financial therapy is an area where additional training may be very useful, as it would enhance both, the advisor's and the client's experience. Combining financial advice with counseling in one individual is an approach that might become dominant in the future.

Another way financial advisors can help their clients optimize savings is by the approach they take to savings: linear versus cyclical. Tam and Dholakia (2014) used a cyclical savings method to increase savings in the United States. They reported the results to be about 78 percent more in savings, on average, compared to the linear savings method. Exploring the cyclical aspect of savings may result in behavior changes. Financial advisors are the perfect vehicle to guide this approach, as they can slow potentially irrational client behavior during internal and external financial crises.

# Applications

Much of the research on personal savings revolves around the reasons for the low savings rate around the world. Some explanations are statistical, such as issues surrounding the measurement of the rate (Guidolin and Jeunesse, 2007), while others are philosophical. As the rate had declined to almost zero in the United States before the 2007 financial crisis, economists have been considering the implications to society. It seems that the country overall has crossed into spindrift territory, structurally changing to a nation that consumes more than it makes in income. From a macroeconomic point of view, the low savings rate might imply the reliance on foreign savings in the form of account deficits, which arguably is not sustainable over long periods of time. According to Guidolin and Jeunesse (2007), a long-run equilibrium should have enough private savings to cover investments; this is practically impossible when the personal savings rate is negative for extended periods of time.

Incorporating psychology into economic theory is another direction that could result in future behavioral change in savings. A good starting point is leaning away from a purely economic train of thought that individuals are solving optimization problems to determine their optimal savings rate toward the more realistic assumption that people act differently than the economic theory predicts. Incorporating the psychology of self-control is another improvement that could be added to traditional savings theories.

Soman and Zhao (2011) pointed out that focusing savings behavior on one goal is more effective than saving for multiple goals. Drawing from marketing research, they argued that multiple goals result in tradeoffs and competition among different goals, which results in less behavior change. Those who provide personal finance advice can focus on prompting their clients to focus on the main savings goal first. A drawback to such an approach is the long-term impact on retirement savings. Given the multiple (and often competing) savings goals clients have, focusing on one goal at a time may result in postponing retirement until it is impossible to accumulate enough savings. It is important for the financial advisor to evaluate each client's needs and adjust the plan according to individual parameters.

# Future Directions

Although few could argue that maintaining savings is a very important personal and policy decision, research could be more focused on individual decision making in the context of variable factors that affect savings. Much of the research has been (and continues to be) focused on promoting savings when the trade-off is seen as a present versus future consumption decision, where income is discretionary. This is hardly the case in all instances. For example, Sussman and O'Brien (2016) looked at the use of savings when present consumption is not discretionary. Looking at six studies, the authors concluded that, in some cases, people tend to preserve their savings and instead borrow from high-interest rate sources, primarily based on the savings intended uses. Nuanced research such as this is needed in the future, to understand how to optimally modify one's behavior.

Another direction in which to focus the field's research to understand savings is to study how to change behavior. Although the extant literature concentrates on explaining savings behavior, less literature addresses how to achieve the desired behavior when individuals may have the desire, but not the knowledge to do so. Using a social marketing approach, Lusardi et al. (2009) devised a plan to help new employees at a not-for-profit institution save in supplement retirement plans with the result of a significant increase in such savings. Similar interventions can be used to create an easy environment for employees to save. The easier the set up for such savings, the higher the potential impact on the savings rate.

Incorporating finance, savings, and individual psychology is another direction that research can take. As mentioned by Archuleta et al. (2012), incorporating the biological (neurological) and psychological aspects of money into traditional financial planning, research could be of use both to practitioners and researchers to understand how to pair financial advice with financial therapy in the future. Focusing on how people behave and how to change their behavior, rather than assuming that individuals are very good at making complex money decisions, could change the savings landscape in the future.

# Discussion

Is a low savings rate bad? There are arguments against emphasizing low rates. One possible explanation is built around the idea of how the savings rate is measured. Lusardi (2000) pointed out that for some segments, such as retired individuals, focusing on assets and selling those assets to finance consumption in retirement may be a solution. Including capital gains in the savings rate displays a much better picture of savings. Using those capital gains to supplement cash flow is a solution for some individuals. Another argument against the low savings rate points out that personal savings is not and should not be the main savings component in a country. For example, Barney et al. (2009) examined individual personal savings in light of corporate savings, concluding that the alarm expressed over falling personal savings rate may not be warranted and that individuals are sophisticated enough to adjust their personal savings rate based on the corporate savings rates, finding the optimal point.

The "wealth effect," which exists when high capital gains are present in equity, may also account for the current savings rate. A high stock market and a strong housing market mean unrealized wealth that would contribute to a lower savings rate (see Dynan and Maki, 2001; Lusardi et al., 2001). Another explanation for the lower savings rate has modified the original permanent income hypothesis. As technology advances, so does the permanent expectation of one's productivity, efficiency, and income. Any type of expectation of future increases in income, be it from improved technology or Social Security, would normally translate into a lower savings rate.

Solutions to the low savings rate range from incorporating automatic savings into employment-type retirement plans to increasing on-demand financial education. For example, opting out of a retirement plan rather than opting in has been shown to be very successful in increasing savings (Choi et al., 2006; Madrian and Shea, 2001).

Another direction to explore in the future is the impact of semi-retirement on savings. The research on the topic is minimal despite the shifting patterns in retirement. More than ever, individuals transition through stages to retirement instead of going from full employment to full retirement, which could have an impact on how much they draw from retirement sources like Social Security, existing pensions, or defined contribution type accounts. Incorporating the shifting timing of retirement is a direction that could help the personal finance field understand how and when to save beyond the standard calculations financial advisors employ today.

# Conclusion

This chapter has addressed several topics, such as the low current saving rate around the world, mechanisms to increase it, and the direction that could result in behavior changes. Although much focus in the literature has been put on the characteristics associated with savings, more work remains to be done on the topic. There is a discrepancy in savings by education, wealth, gender, and race, which ultimately needs to be changed/minimized to increase the overall savings rate of a country.

Savings mobilization is imperative in the functioning of society. It is not an individual "problem"; rather it has a wide social impact on a country's welfare and development. Future economic growth is associated with increased savings rates within the country's population. Despite the obvious argument that overall saving more is beneficial, it is not completely clear as to who should save more, and which savings mechanism(s) should be used. There is an obvious benefit from encouraging savings, but not everyone should save at the same rate. Focusing on the who and the why of savings is an important step in segmenting the research on savings in the future.

# References

Ando, A., and Modigliani, F. (1963). The "life-cycle" hypothesis of saving: Aggregate implication and tests. *American Economic Review*, *53*(1), 55–84.

Archuleta, K. L., Burr, E. A., Dale, A. K., Canale, A., Danford, D., Rasure, E., Nelson, J., Williams, K., Schindler, K., Coffman, B., and Horwitz, E. (2012). What is financial therapy? Discovering mechanisms and aspects of an emerging field. *Journal of Financial Therapy*, *3*(2), 57–78.

Attanasio, O. P., Banks, J., and Wakefield, M. (2004). *Effectiveness of tax incentives to boost (retirement) saving: Theoretical motivation and empirical evidence* (IFS Working Papers No. 04/33). Institute for Fiscal Studies. Accessed July 2021. https://www.econstor.eu/bitstream/10419/71528/1/475312120.pdf

Attanasio, O. P., and DeLeire, T. (2002). The effect of individual retirement accounts on household consumption and national savings. *The Economic Journal*, *112*(481), 504–538.

Barnea, A., Cronqvist, H., and Siegel, S. (2010). Nature or nurture: What determines investor behavior? *Journal of Financial Economics*, *98*(3), 583–604.

Barney, L. D., Schooley-Pettis, D. K., and White, H. (2009). Substituting corporate saving for personal saving: An explanation for falling personal saving rates. *Managerial Finance, 35*(8), 682–690.

Beck, K., and Chira, I. (2017). Expected vs. actual retirement savings behavior of highly educated individuals. *Journal of Personal Finance*, *16*(1), 51–65.

Benartzi, S., and Thaler, R. (2007). Heuristics and biases in retirement savings behavior. *Journal of Economic Perspectives*, *21*(3), 81–104.

Bernheim, B., and Garrett, D. (2003). The effects of financial education in the workplace: Evidence from a survey of households. *Journal of Public Economics*, *87*(7–8), 1487–1519.

Bernheim, B., Garrett, B., and Maki, D. (2001). Education and saving: The long-term effects of high school financial curriculum mandates. *Journal of Public Economics, 80*(3), 435–465.

Beshears, J., Choi, J. J., Laibson, D., and Madrian, B. C. (2017). Does front-loading taxation increase saving? Evidence from Roth 401(k) introductions. *Journal of Public Economics*, *151*, 84–95.

Bloom, D., Canning, D., and Graham, B. (2003). Longevity and life-cycle savings. *The Scandinavian Journal of Economics, 105*(3), 319–338.

Bohm-Bawerk, E. V. (1890). *Capital and interest: A critical history of economic theory* (W. Smart, Trans). Macmillan and Co.

Bostic, R., Gabriel, S., and Painter, G. (2009). Housing wealth, financial wealth, and consumption: New evidence from micro data. *Regional Science and Urban Economics, 39*(1), 79–89.

Britt, S., Grable, J., Goff, B., Nelson, S., and White, M. (2008). The influence of perceived spending behaviors on relationship satisfaction. *Journal of Financial Counseling and Planning, 19*(1), 31–43.

Bucks, B., Kennickell, A., Mach, T., and Moore, K. (2009). Changes in U.S. family finances from 2004 to 2007: Evidence from the Survey of Consumer Finances. *Federal Reserve Bulletin, 95*(2), A1–A55.

Canare, T., Francisco, J.P., and Jopson, E. M. M. (2019). Fear of crime and saving behavior. *Review of Economic Analysis, 11*, 293–323.

Chen, K., Imrohoroglu, A., and Imrohoroglu, S. (2007). The Japanese saving rate between 1960 and 2000: Productivity, policy changes, and demographics. *Economic Theory, 32*(1), 87–104.

Choi, J., Laibson, D., Madrian, B., Metrick, A., McCaffrey, E., and Slemrod, J. (2006). Saving for retirement on the path of least resistance. In J. McCaffery and J. Slemrod (Eds.), *Behavioral public finance: Toward a new agenda* (pp. 304–351). Russell Sage Foundation.

Costa-Font, J., Berkey, P., and Berkay, Ö. (2018). The cultural origin of saving behavior. *PLOS One, 13*(9). Accessed July 2021. https://journals.plos.org/plosone/

Dal Borgo, M. (2019). Ethnic and racial disparities in saving behavior. *The Journal of Economic Inequality, 17*(2), 253–283.

DeVaney, S., Anong, S., and Whirl, S. (2007). Household savings motives. *Journal of Consumer Affairs, 41*(1), 174–186.

Dos Santos Felipe, I. J., (2018). Economic crisis and savings behavior. In W. Mendes-Da-Silva (ed.), *Individual Behaviors and Technologies for Financial Innovations* (1st ed., pp. 47–67). Springer Nature.

Dubofsky, D., and Sussman, L. (2009). The changing role of the financial planner part 1: From financial analytics to coaching and life planning. *Journal of Financial Planning, 22*(8), 48–57.

Duflo, E., Gale, W., Liebman, J., Orszag, P., and Saez, E. (2006). Saving incentives for low- and middle-income families: Evidence from a field experiment with H&R Block. *The Quarterly Journal of Economics, 121*(4), 1311–1346.

Dynan, K. E., and Maki, D. M. (2001). Does stock market wealth matter for consumption? http://dx.doi.org/10.2139/ssrn.270190

Ewing, B., and Payne, J. (1998). The long-run relation between the personal savings rate and consumer sentiment. *Journal of Financial Counseling and Planning, 9*(1), 89–96.

Fisher, I. (1930). *Theory of interest: as determined by impatience to spend income and opportunity to invest it.* The Macmillan Company.

Fisher, P. J. (2010). Gender differences in personal saving behaviors. *Journal of Financial Counseling and Planning, 21*(1), 14–24.

Friedman, M. (1957). *A theory of the consumption function.* Princeton University Press.

Fry, T. R. L., Mihajilo, S., and Brooks, R. (2008). The factors influencing saving in a matched savings program: Goals, knowledge of payment instruments, and other behavior. *Journal of Family and Economic Issues, 29*(2), 234–250.

Fuchs-Schundeln, N., Masella, N., and Paule-Paludkiewicz, H. (2019). Cultural determinants of household saving behavior. *Journal of Money, Credit and Banking, 52*(5), 1035–1070.

Furnham, A. (1985). Why do people save? Attitudes to, and habits of saving money in Britain. *Journal of Applied Social Psychology, 15*(5), 354–373.

Gale, W., and Scholz, J. K. (1994). IRAs and household saving. *The American Economic Review, 84*(5), 1,233–1,260.

Gravelle, J. G. (1991). Do individual retirement accounts increase savings? *Journal of Economic Perspectives, 5*(2), 133–148.

Griskevicius, V., Ackerman, J. M., Cantú S. M., Delton, A. W., Robertson, T. E., Simpson, J. A., Thompson, M. E., and Tybur, J. M. (2013). When the economy falters, do people spend or save? Responses to resource scarcity depend on childhood environments. *Psychological Science, 24*(2), 197–205.

Grossbard, S. A., and Pereira, A. M. (2010). *Will women save more than men? A theoretical model of savings and marriage* (CESifo Working Paper No. 3146). Center for Economic Studies and Ifo Institute. http://hdl.handle.net/10419/39849

Guidolin, M., and La Jeunesse, E. A. (2007). The decline in the U.S. personal saving rate: Is it real and is it a puzzle? *Federal Reserve Bank of St. Louis Review, 89*(6), 491–514.

Gustman, A., Steinmeier, T., and Tabatabai, N. (2011). *How did the recession of 2007–2009 affect the wealth and retirement of the near retirement age population in the health and retirement study?* (NBER Working Paper No. 17547). National Bureau of Economic Research. Accessed July 2021. http://www.nber.org/papers/w17547

Hakkio, Craig S., and Wiseman, E. J. (2006). Social Security and Medicare: The impending fiscal challenge. *Economic Review Federal Reserve Bank of Kansas City, 91*(1), 7–41.

Heo, W., Grable, J. E., and Rabbani, A. G. (2020) A test of the association between the initial surge in COVID-19 cases and subsequent changes in financial risk tolerance. *Review of Behavioral Finance.* https://doi.org/10.1108/RBF-06-2020-0121

Hogarth, J., and Hilgert, M. (2002). Financial knowledge, experience, and learning preferences: Preliminary results from a new survey on financial literacy. *Consumer Interest Annual, 48*(1), 1–7.

Horioka, C. Y., and Watanabe, W. (1997). Why do people save? A micro-analysis of motives for household saving in Japan. *The Economic Journal, 107*(442), 537–552.

Hubbard, R., Skinner, J., and Zeldes, S. (1995). Precautionary saving and social insurance. *Journal of Political Economy, 103*(2), 360–399.

Joo, S-H., and Grable, J. E. (2005). Employee education and the likelihood of having a retirement savings program. *Journal of Financial Counseling and Planning, 16*(1), 37–49.

Karlan, D., Ratan, A.L., and Zinman, J. (2014). Saving by and for the poor: A research review and agenda. *The Review of Income and Wealth, 60*(1), 36–78.

Keynes, J. M. (1936). The *general theory of employment, interest and money*. Macmillan.

Kim, JH., Gale, J., Goetz, J., and Bermudez, J. (2011). Relational financial therapy: An innovative and collaborative treatment approach. *Contemporary Family Therapy, 33*(3), 229–241.

Klawitter, M., Anderson, L., and Gugerty, M. K. (2012). Savings and personal discount rates in a matched savings program for low-income families. *Contemporary Economic Policy, 31*(3), 468–485.

Laibson, D., and Vaitilingam, R. (2008). *The psychology of savings and investment* (CentrePiece – The Magazine for Economic Performance Paper No. 243). Centre for Economic Performance.

Lim, H., Hanna, S., and Montalto, C. (2015). Consumer optimism and savings behavior. *Proceedings of the Academy of Financial Services.* https://ssrn.com/abstract=2622810

Lusardi, A. (2000). *Precautionary saving and the accumulation of wealth* (JCPR Working Paper No. 204). Northwestern University/University of Chicago Joint Center for Poverty Research.

Lusardi, A., Keller, P. A., and Keller, A. M. (2009). *New ways to make people save: A social marketing approach* (NBER Working Paper No. 14715). National Bureau of Economic Research. Accessed July 2021. http://www.nber.org/papers/w14715.pdf

Lusardi, A., and Mitchell, O. (2007a). Baby boomer retirement security: The role of planning, financial literacy and housing wealth. *Journal of Monetary Economics, 54*(1), 205–224.

Lusardi, A., and Mitchell, O. (2007b). Financial literacy and retirement preparedness: Evidence and implications for financial education. *Business Economics, 42*(1), 35–44.

Lusardi, A., Skinner, J., and Venti, S. (2001). Saving puzzles and saving policies in the United States. *Oxford Review of Economic Policy, 17*(1), 95–115.

Madrian, B., and Shea, D. (2001). The power of suggestion: Inertia in 401(k) participation and savings behavior. *The Quarterly Journal of Economics, 116*(4), 1149–1187.

Mayer, T. (1972). *Permanent income, wealth and consumption*. University of California Press.

Modigliani, F., and Cao, S. (2004). The Chinese saving puzzle and the life-cycle hypothesis. *Journal of Economic Literature, 42*(1), 145–170.

Ouliaris, S., and Rochon, C. (2018). *The U.S. personal saving rate* (IMF Working Paper No. 18/128). International Monetary Fund. https://ssrn.com/abstract=3221212.

Schreiner, M., Ng, G. T., and Sherraden, M. (2006). Cost-effectiveness in individual development accounts. *Research on Social Work Practice, 16*(1), 28–37.

Schuchardt, J., Hanna, S. D., Hira, T. K., Lyons, A. C., Palmer, L., and Xiao, J. J. (2009). Financial literacy and education research priorities. *Journal of Financial Counseling and Planning, 20*(1), 84–95.

Schultz, T. P. (2005). *Demographic determinants of savings: Estimating and interpreting the aggregate association in Asia* (IZA Discussion Paper No. 1479). IZA-Institute of Labor Economics. https://ssrn.com/abstract=639187

Sevak, P., Weir, D. R., and Willis, R. (2003). The economic consequences of a husband's death: Evidence from the HRS and AHEAD. *Social Security Bulletin, 65*(3), 31–44.

Soman D., and Zhao M. (2011). The fewer the better: Number of goals and savings behavior. *Journal of Marketing Research, 48*(6), 944–957.

Sussman, A. B., and O'Brien, R. L. (2016). Knowing when to spend: Unintended financial consequences of earmarking to encourage savings. *Journal of Marketing Research, 53*(5), 790–803.

Tam, L., and Dholakia, U. (2014). Saving in cycles: How to get people to save more money. *Psychological Science, 25*(2), 531–537.

Thaler, R. (1994). Psychology and savings policies. *The American Economic Review, 84*(2), 186–192.

Timmerman, I., and Volkov. N. (2020). Career and educational choice as central elements in long-term financial planning. *Financial Services Review, 28*(3), 179–200.

Traut-Mattausch, E., and Jonas, E. (2011). Why do people save? The influence of financial satisfaction and income on savings. *Zeitschrift fur Psychologie, 219* (4), 246–252.

U.S. Bureau of Economic Analysis. (2011). *National income accounts, real personal consumption expenditures*. Accessed July 2021. http://www.bea.gov

Walden, M. L. (2012). Will households change their saving behaviour after the "Great Recession"? The role of human capital. *Journal of Consumer Policy, 35*(2), 237–254.

Warneryd, K. E. (1989). Improving psychological theory through studies of economic behavior: The case of saving. *Applied Psychology: An International Review, 38*(3), 213–236.

Wei, S., and Zhang, X. (2011). The competitive saving motive: Evidence from rising sex ratios and savings rates in China. *Journal of Political Economy, 119*(3), 511–564.

Zagorsky, J. L. (2013). Do people save or spend their inheritances? Understanding what happens to inherited wealth. *Journal of Family Economic Issues, 34*(1), 64–76.

Abed G. Rabbani, Liana H.N. Nobre

# 9 Financial Risk Tolerance

**Abstract:** The purpose of this chapter is to provide an overview of the different ways financial risk tolerance can be measured and applied in the context of personal and household finance research and practice. The chapter begins with a definitional framework to understand the critical elements of financial risk tolerance. Additional discussion regarding the regulatory environment relating to risk-tolerance assessment is also presented. A review of different measurement tools is provided. Major issues associated with the measurement of financial risk tolerance are discussed. The chapter concludes with a summary of additional research needed to understand financial risk tolerance measurement better.

**Keywords:** risk, uncertainty, risk tolerance, prospect theory

## Introduction

Albus Dumbledore of *Harry Potter* fame once said, "Words are, in my not so humble opinion, our most inexhaustible source of magic" (Rowlings, 2007). Words and numbers are codes used to inform one's perception of reality, but they usually do not capture reality's complexity or nuances. Taking the fictitious wizard's comments into a decision context, translating the complexity of a situation into words, and communicating it is not an unbiased activity. Understanding risk in a certain context depends on the way that the situation is framed. When it comes to risk, the way someone captures it reflects the individual's background and values. A single search of the term "risk" at the Web of Science or Scopus highlights the almost limitless use of the concept ranging from health issues, safety, engineering, and investing, to a myriad of different subjects that deal with the notions of uncertainty or probabilities inference. Consider the Merriam-Webster dictionary's definition of risk. According to Merriam-Webster, risk has four main definitions: (1) the possibility of loss or injury or peril; (2) someone or something that creates or suggests a hazard; (3) the chance of loss or the perils to the subject matter of an insurance contract or the degree of probability of such loss; and (4) the chance that an investment (such as a stock or commodity) will lose value. When scholars apply these general definitions of risk to research frameworks, they shape the words to fit the context, considering the complexity and the main variables that affect the desired outcome.

**Abed G. Rabbani,** University of Missouri
**Liana H. N. Nobre,** Universidade Federal Rural do Semi-Árido (UFERSA)

https://doi.org/10.1515/9783110727692-009

The first thing to do before defining risk in a specific matter is, therefore, pinning the target outcome and the chance of undesirable outcomes.

# A Definitional Framework

## Financial Risk

The classical definition of financial risk refers to the uncertainty of future outcomes. The main problem with this definition is that it considers the amount of return that exceeds the target outcome. For classical decision theory, the concept of risk is referred chiefly to a variation of possible outcomes (March and Shapira, 1987), including the full range between positive and negative expected values, while the most accepted axiom of risk is associated with possible negative outcomes. In a general sense, understanding possible positive values above the expected return as risk is almost akin to complaining about the possibility of winning the lottery.

Back to the idea of pinning the target outcome for understanding the idea of risk, financial risk encompasses the chance of obtaining an outcome below a desired return. So, in terms of defining financial risk, the main idea to keep in mind is the peril of not achieving the target return. It is this variability of undesired returns that is risk – the variability is not really known, as expressed in the Knightian expression "an estimate of an estimate" (Nobre et al., 2018). It means that under uncertainty, an individual would estimate possible outcomes – which is a projection – and try to predict the probability of the occurrence, which is another estimation. Risk is projected. As such, it is subject to one's view of the complexity of variables affecting the decision (i.e., how uncertain someone assumes a situation to be). This perspective matches Keynes's (1937) notion of uncertainty, which is based on the level of knowledge about future events that, by its nature, cannot be expressed in terms of a quantifiable probability distribution. The level of uncertainty of an event is not necessarily an attribute of reality but an attribute of one's knowledge or awareness about reality (Nobre et al., 2018). In that way, decisions made in an uncertain context are then based on a limited, fallible, and contingent knowledge about the present with an estimate of results in an indeterminate future (Andrade, 2011; Lawson, 1988). Taking the definition of financial risk from Investopedia as "the possibility of losing money on an investment or business venture" as a starting point, it is possible to state the concise definition of financial risk as to the chance of loss in an investment, understanding that there is nothing in an objective reality that can be measured into probabilities for this unsuccess.

### Financial Risk Tolerance

Moving to financial risk tolerance, Rabbani et al. (2017) pointed out that there is a consensus among researchers that risk tolerance involves the willingness to trade off the possibility of incurring an almost certain small gain with the potential of making a larger gain with an equally high potential of losing wealth (Grable and Joo, 2004; Pan and Statman, 2012). Financial risk tolerance deals with the acceptance of the variability of outcomes below a desired return, remembering that financial decision makers are not likely to complain about achieving outstanding positive returns.

Assessing potential wealth loss depends on how each person frames objective reality, acknowledging and accepting the variables that may affect and mitigate future returns. Some questions emerge from this insight, such as: How do decision makers frame reality? Which factors are being considered to project future scenarios that drive individuals to be financially risk-tolerant? And, most importantly, which core elements from the decision context are excluded when estimating someone's willingness to take a risk? Another point to add is that ignoring factors that might mitigate future returns happens when someone ignores them by not recognizing their importance and deliberately not considering their variability relevant to the decision context, matching what economists call *ceteris paribus*. The *ceteris paribus* fallacy refers to the deliberate and undue transformation of relevant variables in the context of a decision into a constant to simplify reality and make it mathematically measurable – but not necessarily accurate (Shope, 1978). Finally, not addressing all the core elements that might affect financial risk tolerance does not make someone more tolerant of financial risk; it turns out that this type of decision maker is likely misinformed and that is a condition that can be overcome.

## The Regulatory Environment Relating to Risk-Tolerance Assessment

Financial services regulators, both in the United States and internationally, consider financial risk tolerance (FRT) to be a critical element associated with quality investment advice. The Financial Industry Regulatory Authority (FINRA) in the United States defined "risk tolerance" in Regulatory Notice 11–25 as, "A customer's ability and willingness to lose some or all of [the] original investment in exchange for greater potential returns." Under FINRA Regulatory Notice 12–25, a financial advisor must measure a client's risk tolerance before making a recommendation. Recent proposed regulatory changes, such as the Department of Labor (DOL) Fiduciary Rule and the Securities and Exchange Commission's (SEC) Regulation Best Interest (BI), have stressed the importance of risk tolerance to ensure the client's best interest. Under these rules, a financial professional must make investment recommendations that serve the client first and foremost. When finalized, financial advisors must document the client's risk attitude and the client's goals, financial situation, and need to shape a piece of specific investment advice.

Similar, if not more stringent requirements, are in place in the European Union, Australia, New Zealand, Canada, and many parts of Asia. For example, in Europe, the Markets in Financial Instruments Directive (MiFID), which has been in effect since November 2007, requires European financial services providers to categorize investors and their suitability for each investment product type. Financial service professionals in the European Union are now required to have a "reasonable basis" to provide investment advice on a specific product. In Australia, the Financial Services Reform Act (FSRA) 2001 requires that all financial advice on asset allocation and portfolio selection (investment products) must conform to "reasonable basis." A "reasonable basis" of advice is essentially related to each client's tolerance of risk. In Canada, Rule 1300 of the Dealer Member Rules of the Investment Industry Regulatory Organization of Canada (IIROC) requires that financial advisors must meet the requirements of the "Know Your Client" (KYC) rule to ensure their advice is suitable for their clients in terms of their financial situation, investment knowledge, investment objectives, and risk tolerance.

Although these regulatory frameworks stress the importance of risk-tolerance assessment as a means to provide quality investment advice, assessment of risk tolerance is left to individual financial advisors and firms. As of this writing, no regulatory authority prescribes the manner in which someone's financial risk tolerance should or must be assessed. As a result, by assessing risk tolerance using currently available tools, some advisors and firms may be merely fulfilling regulatory compliance obligations. The effectiveness of these assessments may not be given adequate importance.

## Measuring Financial Risk Tolerance

When one realizes that financial risk tolerance has an inherent knowledge component, the next question involves evaluating techniques to measure financial risk tolerance. When it comes to measuring financial risk tolerance, there is a general lack of a standard approach. However, it is important to understand that there is a large volume of studies describing risk tolerance measurement. Researchers typically rely on one of six methods to assess someone's willingness to take a risk: (a) personal or professional judgment, (b) heuristics, (c) objective evaluations, (d) single-item questions, (e) risk scales (e.g., propensity and revealed preference measures), and (f) mixed measures. It is reasonable to ask whether these methods adequately address the knowledge or awareness of the reality of financially risky decisions? In terms of exemplifying these methods, consider the following generic example of two skydivers, a novice and an expert. If both skydivers are similar in age, gender, and other sociodemographic characteristics, and both decide to make a jump on the same day and under the same circumstances, one can conclude that they are both risk-takers. This does not mean, however, that the skydivers share the same risk tolerance level. While it is true that they share a risky behavior, it is possible that their risk tolerances differ. The following discussion reviews the six methods typically used to evaluate risk tolerance.

## Personal or Professional Judgment

Personal or professional judgment approaches use of one of four mechanisms to assess other people's risk tolerance (Grable, 2008; Hsee and Weber, 1997). The first method – known as "same as me" – assumes others have the same risk tolerance as the person making the assessment. The second method – called risk as value – involves perceiving others as less risk-tolerant. The third method – known as risk as feelings – predicts that others have only slight differences in risk tolerance compared to the judge. The final approach – called stereotype – depends on categorizations to arrive at a judgment (e.g., the person is a female and females are more risk-averse – therefore, this person has low-risk tolerance; or the person is an entrepreneur and entrepreneurs are risk-takers – therefore, this person has high-risk tolerance; or this person is an American and Americans are more likely to seek risk – thus, this person has a high-risk tolerance).

The literature has shown that personal and professional judgments are problematic in practice (Roszkowski and Grable, 2005). These methods do not address the knowledge component embedded in the way people conceptualize risk. Those who are tasked with evaluating the risk tolerance of others ought to be cautious when choosing factors such as age or marital status as predicting variables for risk tolerance. Maybe women do exhibit greater risk aversion, but this may be related to being underpaid rather than a biological factor. Considering the correct variable that affects risk tolerance is a key to eliminating the propagation of stereotypes. Consider the problem of using judgment when evaluating the skydiver example. It would be unreasonable to assume that the novice skydiver is the same as the expert skydiver even though both are young males. In fact, the experience and knowledge held by the expert likely make the expert more likely to exhibit a greater tolerance for risk. This assessment is not based on a stereotype but rather an understanding of the true elements associated with being more willing to take a risk.

## Heuristics

Some people use generalized rules or heuristics to assess their own or another person's financial risk tolerance. A heuristic is a simplified rule that relies on a mental shortcut to solve a problem. Risk-tolerance heuristics rely mostly on demographic characteristics such as gender, marital status, age, income, and wealth. For example, some people associate general risk-taking behaviors with financial risk tolerance. They believe that, holding all other factors constant (*ceteris paribus),* skydivers are more likely to take investment risk, scuba dive, or venture into a new business. Others view occupational choice as a heuristic when assessing financial risk tolerance. Previous research has shown that very few heuristic rules can be used reliably (Grable, 1997, 2000) because mental shortcuts are subject to cognitive limitations. The majority of risk-tolerance heuristics can lead to potentially severe miscalculations and incorrect categorizations of individuals into risk-tolerance groups (Grable, 2000). Even valid generalizations may not apply to a specific financial decision maker. A decision maker may fit all the checkboxes for having a high-risk tolerance level but may avoid taking financial risks, like investing in cryptocurrencies. On the other hand, another decision maker may fit a risk avoider's profile but may engage in day trading.

## Objective Evaluations

The objective evaluation method assesses an individual's investment approach and infers risk tolerance from the result. Researchers often use this approach to measure relative risk aversion by a household's ratio of risky assets to wealth (Riley and Chow, 1992). This approach relies on the economic concept of risk aversion. According to this method, a financial decision maker who holds mostly stock in their portfolio would be classified as having a high-risk tolerance, whereas someone who holds mostly bonds would be considered to have a low-risk tolerance. An expert skydiver that has taken more jumps would be considered more risk-tolerant than a novice skydiver, primarily because the novice has not experienced as many risky experiences to attest to their risk tolerance. This assessment method's validity has been criticized (Campbell, 2006; Cordell, 2001) because this approach cannot take into account outside influences, such as emotional biases, when the decision on which the assessment was made. In the context of personal finance, investors tend to underperform indices in both up and down markets (Barber and Odean, 2001). This implies that investment behaviors do not always actually match investors' true risk tolerance.

## Single-Item Questions

Single-item risk-tolerance questions are widely used in personal and household finance research. For example, the Survey of Consumer Finances (SCF) has historically included a four-level subjective risk-tolerance item. This item has been used as the basis of numerous studies, both as an outcome variable and as an independent variable. The question is as follows: "Which of the following statements on this page comes closest to the amount of financial risk that you are willing to take when you save or make investments? The answer choices are (a) Take substantial financial risk expecting to earn substantial returns; (b) Take above-average financial risks hoping to earn above-average returns; (c) Take average financial risks expecting to earn average returns, and (d) Not willing to take any financial risks." The problem with the SCF question and other single-question items is that, while simple to use and assess, one-item risk-tolerance questions may not be a good proxy for people's true level of risk aversion (Grable, 2008). Hanna and Lindamood (2004) found that a large percentage of those answering the SCF question exhibit no risk tolerance. This is highly unlikely. Grable and Lytton (2001) also noted that the question is most closely aligned with investment choice attitudes rather than generalized financial risk tolerance. As SCF possible answers are categorical, discrete, and stackable, this question (and others like it) is a rank choice based on the order of attractiveness of unspecific alternatives. In 2016, the SCF included a new 11-level type measure. Kim et al. (2020) conducted a comparison study between these two measures and concluded that the new SCF measure is seemingly more straightforward than the old measure. The new measure does not have a monotonic relationship with owning stock assets, with a pattern similar to the relation of the old measure to stock ownership. It is likely that some financial decision makers will point blindly to a number when answering this question. Consider again the skydiving example. Assume the following question was asked of the two skydivers: "On a scale from zero to ten, where zero is not at all willing to skydive and ten is very willing to skydive, what number would you be on the scale?" This type of question does not consider any information that could make the answering experience more exciting or more threatening. Rather than generate a risk-tolerance score, answers are really indicating a preference for risk. This conclusion derives from the understanding that risk preference refers to a general situation where the evaluation is based on a feeling that one choice is better than another (Nobre and Grable, 2015).

## Risk Scales

Another method used to assess risk tolerance is a scale. Scales are sometimes referred to as propensity measures. Scaling can be traced back to the late 1950s as proposed by Atkinson (1957). Atkinson hypothesized that risk-taking can be described by six factors: (a) assessment of the subjective probability of achieving success; (b) assessment of the subjective probability of failure; (c) the incentive value of success; (d) the incentive value of avoiding failure; (e) an achievement motive; and (f) the motive to avoid failure. Wallach and Kogan (1959, 1961) used a choice dilemmas questionnaire to measure risk preferences. Their original questionnaire required subjects to advise other individuals regarding 12 choices with two outcomes: a sure gain or a sure loss. An example includes the following: "Mr. A, an electrical engineer, has the choice of sticking with his present job at a modest, though adequate, salary or of moving on to another job offering more money but no long-term security. Please advise Mr. A by deciding what probability of success would be sufficient to warrant choosing the risky alternative" (Wallach and Kogan, 1959, p. 558). Slovic (1962) concluded that choice dilemma measures lack sufficient validity and reliability after examining all forms of the choice dilemma instrument.

Since that time, numerous scales have been developed using classical test theory and item response theory. Grable and Lytton (1999) developed a widely used risk-tolerance scale that was built upon the notion that personal financial risk-taking has three dimensions: (a) investment risk, (b) comfort and experience, and (c) speculation. Their multiple-choice question scale has been tested and shown to offer acceptable validity and reliability levels ($\alpha = 0.75$). The University of Missouri created a website (http://pfp.missouri.edu/research_IRTA.html) to provide users with a risk tolerance score for free based on the Grable and Lytton scale (see Rabbani et al., 2018). Weber et al. (2002) designed a generalized risk-tolerance Likert-type scale that uses a five-point likelihood agreement scale in five content areas: (a) investing versus gambling, (b) health/safety, (c) recreation, (d) ethical, and (e) social decisions.

Outside of personal finance, researchers tend to utilize questions designed to elicit a financial decision maker's revealed preference. Rather than provide a test taker with multiple-choice answers or the ability to indicate an agreement level, revealed preference tests use hypothetical questions based on percentage changes in income (or wealth) that can then be used to estimate a decision maker's relative risk aversion within an Expected Utility Theory framework. For example, questions developed by Barsky et al. (1997) and Hanna and Lindamood (2004) are widely used by those who need a measure of risk aversion as a control or independent variable in models designed to describe behavioral differences among consumers. A relatively new hybrid approach to assessing constant relative risk aversion was introduced by Grable et al. (2020). The Grable et al. measure combines elements from traditional propensity scaling techniques with aspects from expected utility theory.

## Measurement Summary

Brayman et al. (2017) reviewed different risk-tolerance scales and tests used by financial advisors and risk-profiling firms. As shown in Table 9.1, Brayman et al. categorized these scales and tests into three groups. As shown in the table, the mixed approach combines the other five methods. The concept of triangulation, where an answer to a complex question is derived from multiple perspectives (Grable, 2008), which is widely used in the social sciences, indicates that a combination of approaches may produce meaningful results.

**Table 9.1:** Risk Scale Type and Measurement Approach.

| Risk Scale Type | Approach to Measuring Risk |
| --- | --- |
| A) Comprehensive Risk Profile Tool | − These tools combine objective and subjective questions.<br>− Include questions specific to the financial advisor. |
| B) Asset allocation Calculator based on Subjective and Objective Measure | − Utilizes a series of income and/or portfolio preference questions.<br>− Utilizes traditional economic choice theories |
| C) Subjective Risk Tolerance Questions | − Use psychometrically designed questionnaires.<br>− Assess willingness to take financial risk.<br>− Provide a baseline predictive insight into future client behavior. |

As noted by Brayman et al. (2017), there are a plethora of commercial tools available to help those in the personal finance field measure financial risk-tolerance attitudes. According to the Financial Planning 2015 Tech Survey, 44 percent of financial advisors do not use any tools for risk profiling, 30.5 percent use tools provided by their employer or custodian, 8.9 percent use Riskalyze (i.e., a revealed preference assessment tool), 6.6 percent use FinaMetrica (i.e., a propensity measure), 2.2 percent use Pocket Risk (i.e., a propensity measure), and 10.1 percent use another product or service (Brayman et al., 2017). In Europe, the Oxford Risk measure, which is a type of propensity measure, is widely used.

Morningstar's FinaMetrica risk-tolerance questionnaire provides a useful insight into the way propensity measures are designed. The FinaMetrica product is comprised of 25 questions designed to measure a respondent's risk tolerance using a single standardized (0 to 100) Risk-Tolerance Score (RTS). A higher RTS indicates that a respondent can tolerate a higher level of financial risk; conversely, a lower RTS indicates greater risk aversion. The scale has a mean of 50 and a standard deviation of 10. The 0 to 100 range is divided into seven segments or risk-tolerance categories.

There are several other financial risk-tolerance assessment instruments available in the marketplace. For example, Pocket Risk, a web-based questionnaire, assesses a financial decision-maker's FRT. There are a total of 20 questions in the Pocket Risk system. This instrument scores an individual's risk tolerance relative to a sample of the U.S. population. Scores can range from 0 to 100, with lower scores demonstrating low-risk qualities and higher scores demonstrating high-risk qualities. Other measures include: (a) DataPoints (i.e., a Propensity Measure/Psychological Profile), (b) Hidden Lever (i.e., revealed preference/risk profiler), (c) Precise FP (i.e., Propensity Measure), (d) Tolerisk (i.e., propensity measure), and (d) True Profile (i.e., risk profiler).

# Major Issues Associated with the Measurement of Financial Risk Tolerance

The following discussion is focused on measurement issues associated with traditional risk-tolerance measurement approaches. This discussion does not address assessments based on judgments or heuristic or one-item or simplistic items because the research generally shows that these approaches lack validity and reliability.

## Inadequate Focus on Loss Aversion

Outside of personal finance, where the risk scale (i.e., propensity measure) is the popular tool for use when assessing a financial decision-maker's willingness to take a risk, two predominant approaches drive the measurement of financial risk tolerance: (a) the conventional expected utility paradigm that measures risk tolerance through Arrow-Pratt measures (Levy and Levy, 2002) of absolute and relative risk aversion and (b) a behavioral finance framework, which assumes investors place a greater weight on losses from a reference point, otherwise known as loss aversion.

Traditionally, individual risk-assessment questions and assessments have been built on concepts from expected utility theory (Mongin, 1997). The expected utility theory (EUT) concept of risk assessment can be defined as the willingness to accept future consumption variation. Individuals who are more willing to accept variation in future consumption are thought to be more risk-tolerant or less risk-averse. Individuals with a low level of risk tolerance will prefer a less volatile consumption path over their life span compared to someone with a greater level of risk tolerance (Modigliani and Brumberg, 1954). The EUT concept of risk assessment implies that the utility function's slope is the same within gain and loss domains. However, some investors care more about the pain they feel from losses than the satisfaction they derive from gains.

From Prospect Theory (Kahneman and Tversky, 1979) it is known that the idea of losing a value X causes a stronger negative feeling than the joy of gaining the same X value. Prospect Theory describes gains and losses with a value function, similar to a utility function (Figure 9.1). "The value function for losses (the curve lying below the horizontal axis) is convex and relatively steep. In contrast, the value function for gains (above the horizontal axis) is concave and not quite so steep" (Plous, 1993, p. 95).

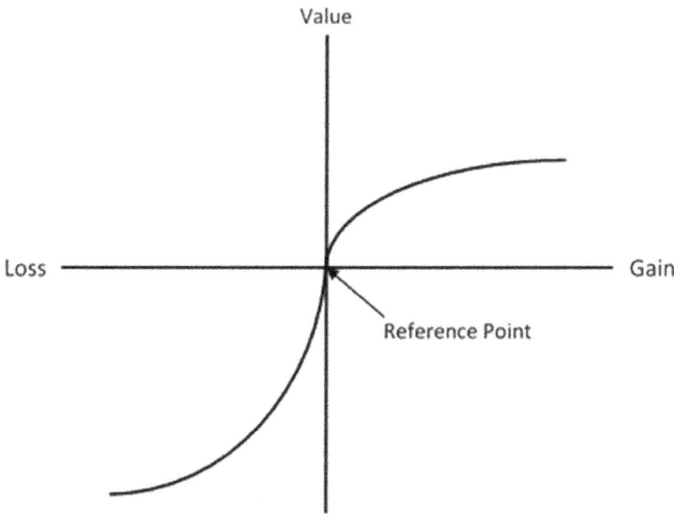

**Figure 9.1:** Value Function of the Prospect Theory.
*Source:* Kahneman and Tversky (1979)

Prospect Theory shows losses to be twice as important as gains in individual decision making regarding risk measurement. Benartzi and Thaler (1995) stated that loss aversion can be estimated by taking the slope of the value function in the loss domain and dividing it by the slope of the value function in the gain domain. One of the primary implications that arises from the notion of loss aversion is that a financial decision-maker's risk tolerance will depend on how a situation or event is framed. Practically, decision makers demonstrate risk-averse behavior when asked to choose an outcome framed as a gain; the same decision maker will often choose a risk-seeking alternative when the choice is framed as a loss (DellaVigna, 2009). Consider the following questions:

– "In addition to whatever you own, you have been given $1,000. You are now asked to choose between: (a) a sure gain of $500 and (b) a 50 percent chance to gain $1,000 and a 50 percent chance to gain nothing."

–  "In addition to whatever you own, you have been given $2,000. You are now asked to choose between (c) a sure loss of $500 and (d) a 50 percent chance to lose $1,000 and a 50 percent chance to lose nothing."

Choices a and c are identical, and so are b and d. However, in laboratory settings, few people choose a; most choose c. As this example illustrates, attitudes toward financial risk depend on the framing of questions.

## The Fallacy of *Ceteris Paribus*

Scholars have debated risk tolerance as a personality trait for decades. Some argue that risk-tolerance is a trait-like factor similar to personality. Others argue that while risk-tolerance appears to be stable, risk attitudes can and do change over time and based on context. In line with this argument, and going a little further, as people do not interpret facts the same way, risk tolerance might change under different comprehension circumstances. With this in mind, each individual would differently recognize elements in reality that can affect their risk tolerance in a certain decision-making environment.

Nearly all risk tolerance assessment tools are composed of questions about specific decisions without any context, either related to economic status or individual status. Compared to the field of physics, questions in those assessment tools were drawn to be answered under Standard Temperature and Pressure (STP) guidelines, but even STP has changed over time and institutions. Having some macroeconomic and individual status parameters, like STP, could facilitate a better definition of the framework in which decisions are made.

Consider how assessments are most often taken. Respondents are tasked with answering questionnaires under different macroeconomic conditions and with varying perceptions of future outcomes. Their scores are calculated and stored in a database with the date the questionnaire was completed. Post-fact research would address scores in the context of macroeconomics conditions, but this seldom occurs in practice. Think about someone who completed a questionnaire in 2008, which corresponded to the Great Recession. Without accounting for the recession, its length, and its consequences, the resulting risk-tolerance score may not be a true indicator of the person's willingness to take a risk. In this case, the respondent answered the assessment while navigating a turbulent financial event. A risk questionnaire taken in 2008, for instance, would likely underestimate a person's risk tolerance because the person may have been unduly influenced by harsh economic events. This implies that conclusions derived from scores may sometimes be inconclusive; at a minimum, it is important to affirm the context in which a risk-tolerance score was estimated, taking into account personal and macroeconomic events. As this discussion highlights, the fallacy of *ceteris paribus* is the deliberate attempt to transform meaningful variables into constants while drawing a decision context.

## Biased Risk Knowledge

Imagine that a researcher asks a seven-year-old child if the child can read. In response, the child promptly admits so. Now assume a researcher gives the child a text and that the child does read it, but only while pausing and stuttering. Next, the researcher asks something about the text, but the child does not know how to answer due to a lack of understanding. In some respects, this is the nature of assessing risk attitudes using traditional revealed preference tests and some types of propensity measures.

As subjective knowledge refers to a perception of how much a person knows about something, knowledge may be affected by heuristics and biases (Carr, 2014). For instance, overconfidence may exist when a decision maker overestimates their knowledge or by the "impostor syndrome," which is a bias in which an individual doubts their skills, and other factors, such as framing, ambiguity aversion, and the illusion of control (Gilovich et al., 2002). Even though objective knowledge and subjective knowledge are correlated (Cordell, 1997), there is often a gap between what someone thinks they know and what they actually do know. Assessing risk knowledge through objective measures, while optimal, can be distorted both by questions that are not process-oriented (Fitzpatrick, 1983) and those that are either irrelevant to a given context of a risky decision and by the pressure and emotions that might affect the individuals while assessing knowledge questions.

Cordell (2001) argued that risk knowledge involves comprehending the trade-offs associated with a risky choice and being savvy enough to make a decision. Individuals who have more knowledge can reduce epistemic uncertainty (Walker et al., 2003). They are more risk-tolerant (Ahmad et al., 2011; Carducci and Wong, 1998; Grable, 2000; Haliassos and Bertaut, 1995; Sung and Hanna, 1996). The effect of a biased assessment of risk knowledge can be the wrong assignment of an actual low FRT decision maker to a high FRT classification. This is especially true if risk knowledge is biased by overconfidence, or the other way if risk knowledge is affected by the impostor syndrome.

## Ignoring the Decision Maker's Situation or Background

When it comes to incorporating client-specific situations or backgrounds in the measurement of risk-tolerance attitudes, current tools mostly address past investment decisions in conjunction with some subjective assessments. However, these tools do not address changes in a test taker's current circumstances, such as income stability, household changes, risk knowledge, and other factors. In other words, current tools generally do not provide a very client-specific risk-tolerance assessment as some client-specific information is not part of the assessment model. Theoretically, these client-specific variabilities in risk-tolerance scores are part of the statistical error component of an assessment. This is an important issue associated with current measurement tools. A solution for those who provide financial advice to others is to move beyond a simple risk-tolerance score and handle situations on a case-by-case basis through client meetings and interviews supplemented with test and scale results.

## Measurement Summary

After taking the entire discussion on the major assessment issues and how those issues are associated with financial risk tolerance, it is helpful to present them first as different risk-taking scenarios (in this case, skydiving), and second, as the presence of these issues in different categories of currently available risk-assessment tools in the academic and commercial marketplace (see Table 9.2). Consider again the skydiving example. How might the limitations associated with current risk-tolerance measurement techniques be related to the skydiving scenario? Here are a few possible answers to this question:

- *Loss Aversion*: Framing the tangible losses of a skydiving jump (e.g., broken bones to death) instead of intangible returns (e.g., adrenaline, lifetime experience) could affect someone's willingness to take the risk.
- *The Fallacy of Ceteris Paribus*: Disclosing variables that are considered standard but might change (e.g., parachute tangling, change in wind speed) might affect a potential skydiver's willingness to take the risk.
- *Biased Risk Knowledge*: Assumed knowledge may not match actual knowledge, especially in relation to skydiving procedures and courses of action to take in an emergency. Helping someone understand the gap in their knowledge could affect their willingness to take the risk.
- *Individual Background*: Differences in the individual background (e.g., prior experience in extreme sports, such as bungee jumping, cliff diving) could affect a potential skydiver's willingness to take the risk.

**Table 9.2:** Major Issues in Risk Scale Types.

| Risk Scale Type | Major Issues |
| --- | --- |
| A) Comprehensive Risk-Profile Tool | These tools are intended to be used as a starting point in matching a client with an appropriate product. As such, these tools are not designed to assess risk scores under a client's varying circumstances. Therefore, although these tools address risk knowledge, they suffer from the Fallacy of *Ceteris Paribus*. |

**Table 9.2** (continued)

| Risk Scale Type | Major Issues |
|---|---|
| B) Asset allocation Calculator based on Subjective and Objective Measure | These tools lack the emotional or behavioral aspect of risk-taking. These tools also minimize the role of risk capacity and the risk needs of individual clients. Therefore, although these tools are likely to cover the objective risk knowledge, they may suffer from the Fallacy of *Ceteris Paribus*. |
| C) Subjective Risk-Tolerance Questions | These personal tools have no way of linking risk scores to optimal portfolios. It is up to the financial advisor to incorporate objective indicators into recommendations. These measures do not put choices in the context of other wealth and investment horizons (Hanna et al., 2013). Therefore, these tools also suffer from the Fallacy of *Ceteris Paribus*; they also lack adequate inputs related to objective risk knowledge. |

# Future Directions

The assessment of financial risk tolerance is a crucial issue for those working in the field of personal finance and for those who oversee the regulatory landscape of investment advice. The review of existing measurement tools and techniques described earlier in the chapter shows a lack of a clear standard for measuring financial risk tolerance. Financial advisors use various assessment tools to fulfill current regulatory investment compliance guidelines. This highlights the need for additional refinement of existing measures of financial risk tolerance by developing a standardized measure of financial risk tolerance. One of the possibilities of standardizing risk-tolerance scores is, for instance, to develop a question addressing how an individual currently evaluates market conditions (i.e., a five-item scale with the continuum bear/bull market). This variable (and others related to risk capacity, for instance) could be used as a weight to adjust the final risk-tolerance score.

As researchers attempt to develop a standardized measure, the question of how those who provide financial advice to others can assist financial decision makers better understand financial risks continues to be of primary importance. Financial risk literacy can play a significant role in answering this question. Literacy refers to signs and codes generally accepted when building words, concepts, and ideas. Risk literacy is about recognizing which variables relate to a decision and how those interact in each context. For instance, a risk-literate individual may not be completely aware of the current macroeconomic situation that will likely impact choice outcomes, but the decision maker may be aware of how the economic environment affects investment outcomes. A risk-literate person will be able to decode and process information and express their perspectives on the amount of risk they are willing to accept. Just like rearranging letters leads to different words, understanding how risk variables work can lead to other risk behaviors.

Unfortunately, few individuals possess financial risk literacy. Most financial decision makers lack knowledge about diversification, and they do not understand the relationship between risk and return (Lusardi, 2015). One finding from the literature stands out: Individuals display very low knowledge of risk in every country studied and across financial contexts. Strikingly, in one study, one-third of decision makers stated that they did not know the answer to questions that measure understanding of risk. This is important because risk literacy is an important component of financial literacy, and financial illiteracy carries significant consequences. Lusardi et al. (2017a) considered an intertemporal saving model with many sources of risk (e.g., income, health, and capital market returns) and incorporated financial literacy into the model. They showed that financial risk literacy can account for more than 30 percent of the wealth inequality in the United States.

The empirical estimates of Lusardi (2015) show that financial risk literacy affects both retirement planning and precautionary savings. Thus, even after accounting for household resources, such as income and homeownership, and individual characteristics such as education, those who are more financially literate are more likely to plan for retirement and to have precautionary savings. Knowledge of risk diversification is the variable that matters most in terms of financial knowledge. Specifically, those who are knowledgeable about risk are 11 percent more likely to plan for retirement and 5 percent more likely to have made provisions to insure against financial shocks. In the Netherlands, those who are knowledgeable about risk were found to be 14 percent more likely to plan for retirement (Alessie et al., 2011). Fornero and Monticone (2011) examined the relationship between financial literacy and pension plan participation in Italy and showed that those who are more financially literate were also more likely to participate in a pension plan; in the case of Italy, simple numeracy was found to matter, which is consistent with the fact that the numeracy question had a deficient proportion of correct answers and is likely to differentiate between levels of financial knowledge.

Heinberg et al. (2014) showed that a simple way to improve knowledge of risk diversification is via a relatively brief written or video narrative designed to be accessible and engaging. In their study, narratives were designed on several well-established principles of psychology and marketing. The concept of risk diversification was embedded in a short story that described the concept verbally and presented the benefits of taking action. The story focused on a few simple takeaway points related to the concept, and the use of complex jargon was minimized. A narrative strategy was adopted, as in commercial advertising, adult education, and public health, as it is a conventional means of creating cognitive involvement and emotional immersion and has been shown to improve comprehension, particularly for poor readers.

Additionally, education research indicates that video narratives can create a fertile opportunity for cognitive engagement. Lusardi et al. (2017b) developed and evaluated a web-based program aimed at explaining the concept of risk diversification. Using the research team's expertise in financial literacy, marketing, and linguistics, they designed an interactive visual tool that effectively demonstrated the workings of risk diversification. According to the project's preliminary evaluation, this type of initiative can improve knowledge of risk and individuals' ability to incorporate that knowledge into financial decision making.

# Conclusion

More research on risk literacy would help the personal finance field figure out how knowledge affects people when they are making financial decisions. Risk literacy can change financial behaviors, which can have positive effects on the financial well-being of households. But right now, most research focuses on financial literacy. Future studies are needed to assess the effects of risk literacy and how well an individual can understand and use risk-related information. Researchers already know that financial advisors should improve communication with clients regarding risk tolerance. But a key question remains unanswered: Does risk communication help financial decision makers make better financial decisions?

The broad field of financial-risk tolerance assessment will offer many research opportunities in the future. Researchers and practitioners interested in this topic have much work to do in upcoming years to understand and apply financial risk-tolerance concepts. Future research directions include answering the following questions:

- What is the regulatory intent of requiring risk-tolerance assessments? Is it just an investment compliance issue or is there more to it?
- Can consistent and valid development guidelines for measuring financial risk tolerance be created, implemented, and enforced?
- What are the key working assumptions underlying a standard financial risk-tolerance measurement?
- How does the compensation model of a financial advisor affect investment recommendations made in response to a risk-tolerance assessment?
- How do composite risk-assessment tools (i.e., those that include elements from different assessment traditions) relate to the notion of relative risk aversion and optimal portfolio allocation?
- What is the relationship between risk capacity, risk preference, time horizon, and risk tolerance?

# References

Ahmad, A., Safwan, N., Ali, M., and Tabasum, A. (2011). How demographic characteristics affect the perception of investors about financial risk tolerance. *Interdisciplinary Journal of Contemporary Research in Business*, 3(2), 412–417.

Alessie, R., Van Rooij, M., and Lusardi, A. (2011). Financial literacy and retirement preparation in the Netherlands. *Journal of Pension Economics & Finance*, 10(4), 527–545.

Andrade, E. B. (2011). Excessive confidence in visually-based estimates. *Organizational Behavior and Human Decision Processes*, 116(2), 252–261.

Atkinson, J. W. (1957). Motivational determinants of risk-taking behavior. *Psychological Review*, 64(6), 359–372.

Barber, B. M., and Odean, T. (2001). Boys will be boys: Gender, overconfidence, and common stock investment. *The Quarterly Journal of Economics*, 116(1), 261–292.

Barsky, R. B., Juster, F. T., Kimball, M. S., and Shapiro, M. D. (1997). Preference parameters and behavioral heterogeneity: An experimental approach in the health and retirement study. *The Quarterly Journal of Economics*, 112(2), 537–579. https://doi.org/10.1162/003355397555280

Benartzi, S., and Thaler, R. H. (1995). Myopic loss aversion and the equity premium puzzle. *The Quarterly Journal of Economics*, 110(1), 73–92.

Brayman, S., Grable, J. E., Griffin, P., and Finke, M. (2017). Assessing a client's risk profile: A review of solution providers. *Journal of Financial Service Professionals*, 71(1), 71–81.

Campbell, J. Y. (2006). Household finance. *The Journal of Finance*, 61(4), 1553–1604.

Carducci, B. J., and Wong, A. S. (1998). Type A and risk taking in everyday money matters. *Journal of Business and Psychology*, 12(3), 355–359.

Carr, N. A. (2014). *Reassessing the assessment: Exploring the factors that contribute to comprehensive financial risk evaluation* [Doctoral dissertation]. Kansas State University.

Cordell, D. M. (2001). RiskPACK: How to evaluate risk tolerance. *Journal of Financial Planning*, 14(6), 36–40.

Cordell, V. V. (1997). Consumer knowledge measures as predictors in product evaluation. *Psychology & Marketing*, 14(3), 241–260. https://doi.org/10.1002/(SICI)1520-6793(199705)14:3<241::aid-mar3>3.0.CO;2-B

DellaVigna, S. (2009). Psychology and economics: Evidence from the field. *Journal of Economic Literature*, 47(2), 315–372.

Fitzpatrick, M. (1983). The definition and assessment of political risk in international business: A review of the literature. *Academy of Management Review*, 8(2), 249–254.

Fornero, E., and Monticone, C. (2011). *Financial literacy and pension plan participation in Italy* (CePR Working Paper No. 111/11). Center for Research on Pensions and Welfare Policies. https://www.cerp.carloalberto.org/wp-content/uploads/2011/03/wp_111.pdf

Gilovich, T., Griffin, D., and Kahneman, D. (eds.). (2002). *Heuristics and biases: The psychology of intuitive judgment*. Cambridge University Press.

Grable, J. E. (1997). *Investor risk tolerance: Testing the efficacy of demographics as differentiating and classifying factors* [Doctoral dissertation]. Virginia Polytechnic Institute and State University.

Grable, J. E. (2000). Financial risk tolerance and additional factors that affect risk taking in everyday money matters. *Journal of Business and Psychology*, 14(4), 625–630.

Grable, J. E. (2008). Risk tolerance. In J. J. Xiao (ed.), *Handbook of consumer finance research* (pp. 3–19). Springer.

Grable, J. E, and Joo, S.-H. (2004). Environmental and biopsychosocial factors associated with financial risk tolerance. *Journal of Financial Counseling and Planning*, 15(1), 73–82.

Grable, J. E., Kwak, E-J., Fulk, M., and Routh, A. (2020). A simplified measure of investor risk aversion. *Journal of Interdisciplinary Economics*. https://doi.org/10.1177/0260107920924518

Grable, J. E. and Lytton, R. H. (1999). Financial risk tolerance revisited: The development of a risk assessment instrument. *Financial Services Review, 8*(3), 163–181.

Grable, J. E, and Lytton, R. H. (2001). Assessing the concurrent validity of the SCF risk tolerance question. *Journal of Financial Counseling and Planning, 12*(2), 43–53.

Haliassos, M., and Bertaut, C. C. (1995). Why do so few hold stocks? *The Economic Journal, 105* (432), 1110–1129.

Hanna, S. D., Guillemette, M. A., and Finke, M. A. (2013). Assessing risk tolerance. In H. K. Baker, and G. Filbeck (eds.). *Portfolio Theory and Management* (pp. 99–120). Oxford University Press.

Hanna, S. D., and Lindamood, S. (2004). An improved measure of risk aversion. *Journal of Financial Counseling and Planning, 15*(2), 27–45.

Heinberg, A., Hung, A., Kapteyn, A., Lusardi, A., Samek, A. S., and Yoong, J. (2014). Five steps to planning success: Experimental evidence from US households. *Oxford Review of Economic Policy, 30*(4), 697–724.

Hsee, C. K., and Weber, E. U. (1997). A fundamental prediction error: Self-others discrepancies in risk preference. *Journal of Experimental Psychology: General, 126*(1), 45–53.

Kahneman, D., and Tversky, A. (1979). Prospect theory: An analysis of decision under risk. In L.C MacLean, and W. T. Ziemba (eds.). *Handbook of the fundamentals of financial decision making: Part II* (pp. 99–127). World Scientific.

Keynes, J. M. (1937). The general theory of employment. *The Quarterly Journal of Economics, 51*(2), 209–223.

Kim, K. T., Hanna, S., and Ying, D. (2020). The risk tolerance measure in the 2016 Survey of Consumer Finances: New, but is it improved? *Journal of Financial Counseling and Planning, 32*(1), 1–28.

Lawson, T. (1988). Probability and uncertainty in economic analysis. *Journal of Post Keynesian Economics, 11*(1), 38–65.

Levy, H., and Levy, M. (2002). Arrow-Pratt risk aversion, risk premium and decision weights. *Journal of Risk and Uncertainty, 25*(3), 265–290.

Lusardi, A. (2015). Risk literacy. *Italian Economic Journal, 1*(1), 5–23. https://doi.org/10.1007/s40797-015-0011-x

Lusardi, A., Michaud, P. C., and Mitchell, O. S. (2017a). Optimal financial knowledge and wealth inequality. *Journal of Political Economy, 125*(2), 431–477.

Lusardi, A., Samek, A., Kapteyn, A., Glinert, L., Hung, A., and Heinberg, A. (2017b). Visual tools and narratives: New ways to improve financial literacy. *Journal of Pension Economics & Finance, 16*(3), 297–323.

March, J. G., and Shapira, Z. (1987). Managerial perspectives on risk and risk taking. *Management Science, 33*(11), 1404–1418.

Modigliani, F., and Brumberg, R. (1954). Utility analysis and the consumption function: An interpretation of cross-section data. *Franco Modigliani, 1*(1), 388–436.

Mongin, P. (1997). Expected utility theory. In J. Davis, W. Handes, and U. Maki (eds.), *Handbook of economic methodology* (pp. 342–350). Eward Elgar.

Nobre, L. H. N., and Grable, J. E. (2015). The role of risk profiles and risk tolerance in shaping client investment decisions. *Journal of Financial Service Professionals, 69*(3), 18–21.

Nobre, L. H. N., Grable, J. E., Silva, W. V., and Nobre, F. C. (2018). Managerial risk taking: A conceptual model for business use. *Management Decision, 56*(11), 2487–2501. https://doi.org/10.1108/MD-09-2017-0892.

Pan, C. H., and Statman, M. (2012). Questionnaires of risk tolerance, regret, overconfidence, and other investor propensities. *Journal of Investment Consulting, 13*(1), 54–63.

Plous, S. (1993). *The psychology of judgment and decision making*. Mcgraw-Hill Book Company.

Rabbani, A. G., Grable, J. E., Heo, W., Nobre, L., and Kuzniak, S. (2017). Stock market volatility and changes in financial risk tolerance during the Great Recession. *Journal of Financial Counseling and Planning, 28*(1), 140–154. https://doi.org/10.1891/1052-3073.28.1.140

Rabbani, A. G., O'Neill, B., Lawrence, F., and Grable, J. (2018). The investment risk tolerance assessment: A resource for extension educators. *Journal of Extension, 56*(7), 3. https:// tigerprints.clemson.edu/joe/vol56/iss7/3

Riley, W. B., and Chow, K. V. (1992). Asset allocation and individual risk aversion. *Financial Analysts Journal, 48*(6), 32–37. https://doi.org/10.2469/faj.v48.n6.32

Rowling, J. (2007). *Harry Potter and the deathly hallows*. Scholastic Inc.

Roszkowski, M. J., and Grable, J. (2005). Estimating risk tolerance: The degree of accuracy and the paramorphic representations of the estimate. *Journal of Financial Counseling and Planning, 6*(2), 29–47.

Shope, R. K. (1978). The conditional fallacy in contemporary philosophy. *The Journal of Philosophy, 75*(8), 397–413.

Slovic, P. (1962). Convergent validation of risk taking measures. *The Journal of Abnormal and Social Psychology, 65*(1), 68.

Sung, J., and Hanna, S. D. (1996). Factors related to risk tolerance. *Journal of Financial Counseling and Planning, 7*, 11–19.

Walker, W. E., Harremoës, P., Rotmans, J., Van Der Sluijs, J. P., Van Asselt, M. B., Janssen, P., and Krayer von Krauss, M. P. (2003). Defining uncertainty: A conceptual basis for uncertainty management in model-based decision support. *Integrated Assessment, 4*(1), 5–17.

Wallach, M. A., and Kogan, N. (1959). Sex differences and judgment processes. *Journal of Personality, 27*(4), 555–564.

Wallach, M. A., and Kogan, N. (1961). Aspects of judgment and decision making: Interrelationships and changes with age. *Behavioral Science, 6*(1), 23–36.

Weber, E. U., Blais, A.-R., and Betz, N. E. (2002). A domain-specific risk-attitude scale: Measuring risk perceptions and risk behaviors. *Journal of Behavioral Decision Making, 15*(4), 263–290. https://doi.org/10.1002/bdm.414

John E. Grable
# 10 Accounting for Time When Saving and Investing

**Abstract:** The purpose of this chapter is to introduce how the conceptualization and study of time correspond to the development of personal finance as an interdisciplinary profession. This chapter describes time in the context of one of four dimensions: (a) time horizon, (b) decision frame, (c) orientation/preference, and (d) perception/perspective. As noted in this chapter, the concept of time is an un-unified concept. Researchers, policymakers, and personal finance practitioners interested in applied financial decision making often focus on goal time horizons. Those interested in decision-maker behavioral tendencies generally limit their inquiries to describing decision time frames or modeling time orientation and time preference. Researchers who are interested in the nonconscious processes underlying human behavior typically focus on evaluating time perceptions and perspectives. To date, these disparate research agendas have not been unified in any meaningful way. This includes, for example, the lack of unified time horizon definitions. This chapter reintroduces the notion that a time horizon definition can be identified and standardized. This chapter concludes with an insight that the future of personal finance will be closely aligned with time horizon, decision time frame, orientation/preference, and perception/perspective research developments that occur over the next few decades.

**Keywords:** time horizon, decision time frame, time orientation, time preference, time perception, time perspective

## Introduction

The opening chapter of this handbook proffered the following definition of personal finance: "The study and application of concepts, tools, and techniques associated with the planning and management of personal and household financial activities, including generating income, managing spending and debt, saving, investing, and protecting sources of income and assets in a way that informs practice and policies designed to enhance the well-being of individuals, families, and households." In this regard, personal finance can be conceptualized as an interdisciplinary profession where the concepts, tools, and techniques used by personal finance researchers, educators, practitioners, and policymakers are informed and shaped by a variety of

**John E. Grable,** University of Georgia

https://doi.org/10.1515/9783110727692-010

professional fields of study. One factor that unifies the interdisciplinary study and application of personal finance concepts, tools, and techniques is the notion of time.

Time itself, however, is a somewhat elusive concept. According to the Merriam-Webster (n.d.) dictionary, time is the indefinite (nonspatial) series of events that occur in sequence from past to present to future. The prevailing thought is that time is a linear function (Sircova et al., 2015). Time has been studied as a religious construct, a philosophical state, and as science (e.g., Einstein, 1931, Theory of Relativity). The advent of the calendar was an attempt to measure time temporally. Clocks were designed to measure time physically. While these examples provide context for what time represents, time, in the context of personal finance, goes beyond these examples. Time can be viewed as a horizon to which goal achievement is measured. Time can also be viewed as the duration over which a decision must be made. Related to this point of view is something called time orientation or a decision maker's degree of preference for short-term, intermediate, or long-term performance feedback. Additionally, time can be seen as a state of perception. The purpose of this chapter is to describe time in relation to these four dimensions – each of which can be conceptualized as an input into personal finance decision-making processes.[1]

# Historical Perspective

Time, when viewed from the perspective of personal, family, and household decision-making, is something that generally must be included in an analysis where projections of future goal achievement must be made (Ebert and Piehl, 1973). As shown in Figure 10.1, the following four aspects of time are most relevant to those tasked with making personal, family, and household financial decisions: (a) time horizon, (b) decision time frame, (c) orientation/preference, and (d) perception. Each of these aspects of time is discussed in more detail below.

## Time Horizon

Among household and managerial decision makers, time is typically conceptualized as a time horizon or the "distance into the future to which a decision maker looks when evaluating the consequences of a proposed action" (Ebert and Piehl, 1973, p. 35). Time horizon has also been described as "the time span associated with . . .

---

1 Although this chapter focuses on these four dimensions of time, it is worth noting that the study of time has multiple branches, including estimates and tests of time attitude, temporal orientation, sense of time, subjective experience, temporal experience, and time structuralization, to name just a few examples (Drake et al., 2008).

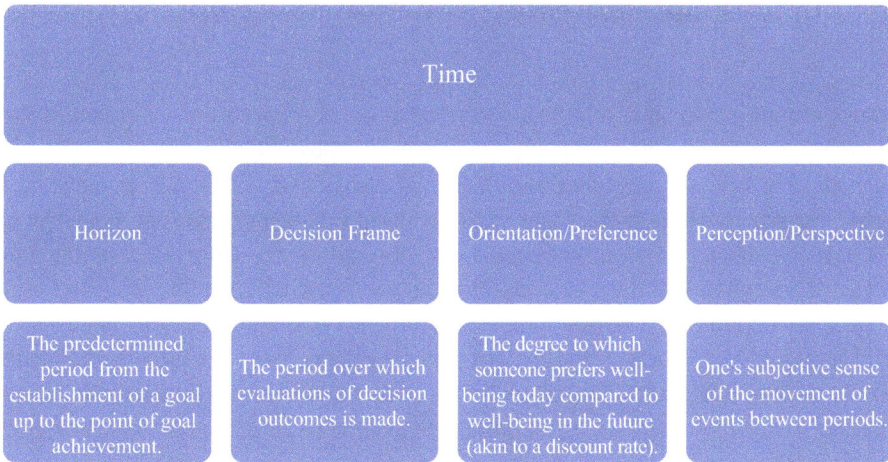

| | | | |
|---|---|---|---|
| | | Time | |
| Horizon | Decision Frame | Orientation/Preference | Perception/Perspective |
| The predetermined period from the establishment of a goal up to the point of goal achievement. | The period over which evaluations of decision outcomes is made. | The degree to which someone prefers well-being today compared to well-being in the future (akin to a discount rate). | One's subjective sense of the movement of events between periods. |

**Figure 10.1:** Aspects of Time.

decision making concerned with the timing of returns" (Reilly et al., 2016, p. 1172), with a person's investment time horizon being forward-looking. When viewed with an applied lens, a general best practice is to assume that when making a personal finance decision, an individual, family, or household decision maker will assign a time duration to an anticipated outcome. In general, researchers have tended to classify time horizons as short-term, intermediate-, or long-term.

## Decision Time Frame

When discussing time in relation to personal finance decision making, a person's goal time horizon is generally the frame of reference. However, decision makers almost always use a secondary measure of time when evaluating goal achievement and outcomes: a decision time frame. Garmaise (2006) described the decision time frame as the period over which decision makers assess the results of an investment or behavior when determining whether to move forward or change tactics. According to Kirby (2005), the decision time frame tends to be short and nearly always shorter than a person's goal time horizon. Intermediate and long-term decision time frames are known to exist, but these have rarely been described in the literature (Reilly et al., 2016), other than to conclude that decision makers tend to use very short decision time frames even when a goal time horizon extends far into the future.

## Time Orientation/Preference

Closely related to a person's time horizon and decision time frame is something called time orientation, which is sometimes referred to as a person's time preference. Time orientation/preference is an economic concept where those with a high time preference tend to focus on their short-term well-being, whereas those with low time preference exhibit greater patience by focusing on their future well-being. A general tendency is for decision makers to emphasize short-term performance and outcomes. Conflict typically arises when two decision makers, who are faced with similar projected outcomes, share differing time orientations. Historically, outside of the personal-finance and household-finance decision-making domains, managerial decision makers tend to rely on their time orientation, rather than a project or investment time horizon, when making judgments about the actual and perceived benefits of a decision (Ebert and Piehl, 1973).

Time orientation has been described in a number of ways. For example, Laverty (2004) used the term "short-termism" to describe actions that aim for desirable near-term outcomes, even when these outcomes may not be optimal. Others have used terms like "present focus" (Cojuharenco et al., 2012), "hyperbolic discounting" (Plambeck and Wang, 2013), and "temporal myopia" (Levinthal, and March, 1993) to describe short-termism and a preference for immediate well-being.

One might assume that the literature on time horizons, decision time frames, and time orientation would be unified. This is not the case. A prevailing assumption is that those with a long-time horizon incur less risk (often measured as a form of volatility) (Jaggia and Thosar, 2000; Lee, 1990),[2] and as such, should invest more aggressively. Another assumption is that those with a short time orientation trade generally too often and thus miss cyclical market gains that occur over time. While these assumptions do appear to correspond to what is observed among financial decision makers in practice, the research suggests that these are, in fact, merely assumptions. Samuelson (1994) noted that someone's investment horizon should not affect the person's portfolio allocation when equity returns are random and when investors exhibit constant relative risk aversion. This insight leads to what Bodie (1995) pointed out as a logical conclusion; namely, rational financial decision makers who want to maximize the expected utility of consumption over their lifetime should make no adjustment for age (i.e., a proxy for time horizon) when investing in risky assets such as stocks. Rather than reduce risk, lengthening the investment time horizon appears to increase risk because the number and types of unknown factors that can negatively impact portfolio

---

2 Risk can be defined in numerous ways, including (a) the probability of a loss, (b) the magnitude of a potential loss, (c) the coefficient of variation, and (d) the standard deviation of outcomes (Klos et al., 2005).

performance increase across time (Bierman, 1997), especially in cases where models of future outcomes are based, in part, on past performance.

However, as noted by Jaggia and Thosar (2000), individuals tend to feel greater comfort allocating investment assets more aggressively if their time horizon (the point in the future where the assets will be needed to fund a financial goal) is long. This implies that a person's willingness to take financial risk will generally be predicted to increase in concordance with the person's time horizon. It is important to note that someone's willingness to take risks may not be tied directly to the reality associated with the riskiness of assets over time. Instead, one's risk tolerance may be more closely linked with perceptions of risk (Klos et al., 2005). It is perception, rather than reality, that often shapes how personal finance decision makers make choices across household tasks (Yakup and Diyarbakirlioglu, 2011). In this regard, perception of time has been found to be correlated with a decision maker's age (those who are older have less time to recoup losses) and the "temporal distance between the initial investment point and the cash-out point" (Jaggia and Thosar, 2000, p. 212).

## Time Perspective

Lewin (1942) was among the first psychologists to lay out the parameters surrounding the notion of time perspective. In 1951, Lewin described time perspective as "the totality of the individual's views of his psychological future and psychological past existing at a given time" (p. 75). Bandura (1997) used elements of Lewin's (1942, 1951) conceptualization of time perspective when developing self-efficacy theory. Zimbardo and Boyd (1999), in what is now the seminal paper on time perspective, further refined the definition of time perspective as follows: "the often nonconscious process whereby the continual flows of personal and social experiences are assigned to temporal categories, or time frames, that help to give order, coherence, and meaning to those events" (p. 1271). The time perspective literature shows that a person's time perspective can "exert a dynamic influence on many important judgments, decisions, and actions" (Zimbardo and Boyd, 1999, p. 1272).

According to Zimbardo and Boyd (1999), time perspective is situationally determined and relatively stable. Time perspective encompasses the following dimensions: (a) past-negative, (b) past-positive (c) present-hedonistic, (d) present-fatalistic, and (e) future.[3] Someone who holds a past-negative time perspective will generally be pessimistic, often depressed, and averse to behavioral change, whereas those with a past-positive time perspective tend to be more optimistic, sentimental, and less

---

**3** Zimbardo and Boyd (1999) introduced the notion that some people hold a future transcendental time preference in which behavior is driven, in large part, by their belief in existence after death. This dimension of time preference has not undergone much empirical testing over the past two decades.

regretful. Those with a present-hedonistic time perspective often exhibit sensation-seeking behavior and act impulsively. On the other hand, those whose time perspective aligns with a present-fatalistic outlook often feel helpless and hopeless (Carelli et al., 2011). A future time perspective is correlated with long-term planning and an ability to resist temptation.[4] Those who actively save and invest typically hold a future time perspective. Zimbardo and Boyd argued that a person's goal should be to develop and maintain a balanced time perspective, which is defined as "the mental ability to switch flexibly among time perspective depending on task features, situation considerations, and personal resources rather than be biased toward a specific time perspective that is not adaptive across situations" (p. 1285).

## Summary

As noted by Carelli et al. (2011), "Time offers an important basis for helping us understand our experiences in the world, including shaping our thoughts, lives, and existence" (p. 220). As noted in this historical sketch, time – from the perspective of a personal finance decision maker – can be viewed as a dimension of someone's time horizon, decision time frame, time orientation/preference, and/or time perspective. Each of these dimensions provides a unique insight into the way personal, family, and household decision makers conceptualize, organize, and utilize time when making a financial decision. However, rather than debate the riskiness associated with shortening or lengthening one's time horizon, or in debating the merits of one time orientation over another, personal finance decision makers (and those who provide advice to those making investments) tend to be more interested in and focused on determining (a) how the decision time frame affects the decision-making process, (b) how the concept of time horizon should be used as a decision-making input, and (c) how to measure time horizon consistently across decision-making scenarios (Bierman, 1997; Grable et al., 2009; Jaggia and Thosar, 2000). The following discussion separates these issues into thoughts for researchers and policymakers and tools for practice.

## Research and Policy Issues

From a research and policy perspective, a person's time horizon, in the context of financial decision making, is of interest because the time horizon is directly associated with the manner in which personal, family, and household assets are allocated.

---

4 A crossover from psychology and economics occurs with the term "future time perspective." Occasionally, future time perspective is referred to as future orientation, patience, time preference, and planning horizon (Jacobs-Lawson and Hershey, 2005).

In this context, resource allocation is correlated with the concepts of risk and uncertainty (Reilly et al., 2016). A short-time horizon is most often associated with less uncertainty and risk, whereas a longer-time horizon introduces greater uncertainty and risk.

As noted by Rolison et al. (2017), a person's time horizon plays an important role in goal setting and financial planning activities. Constraints related to time arise when someone's decision-making orientation (i.e., decision time frame) is shortened and when someone's goal achievement time horizon is limited. Rolison and associates pointed out that as the time horizon shortens, a decision maker's priorities shift toward goal achievement and away from goal preparation and resource acquisition.

It is worth noting a secondary issue that can have a direct impact on research that entails measuring and using a dimension of time. As noted by Blanchet-Scalliet et al. (2008), a decision maker's time horizon itself may not be stable. A decision maker can never be certain when assets allocated for a future objective will be needed. The time horizon can be estimated, but factors such as changes in market conditions, new choice alternatives, changes in someone's financial endowment, and exogenous shocks that negatively impact consumption choices can alter a decision maker's desired time horizon. As noted by Levinthal and March (1993), there are typically no guarantees of short- or long-run survival when a financial decision is made.

The time orientation of a decision maker plays a significant role in the types of behaviors a decision maker engages in. It has been widely reported, for example, that those who are future-oriented exhibit long planning horizons and focus on the future more so than the present or the past (Rolison et al., 2017). Sometimes the literature reports a future time perspective as a temporal orientation (Reilly et al., 2016). Those with a future time orientation are more likely to save for retirement compared to those with a shorter-term or present time orientation (Jacobs-Lawson and Hershey, 2005). Hershey and Mowen (2000) noted a strong correlation between future time orientation and financial knowledge, although the causality of the relationship is still being debated, primarily because time orientation differs across individuals and cultures.

Given the importance of time as a factor that is known to shape the way decisions are made, it may be a surprise that traditional mean-variance optimization models do not account for a decision maker's time horizon, age, time orientation/preference, or time perception (Lenoir and Tuchschmid, 2001). Time horizon, for example, is not needed when it is assumed that expected returns, the variance of returns, and covariances are constant over time. However, if this assumption is violated, then time horizon does become an important situational variable that should be accounted for when allocating assets. These insights are presented as a caution for those who undertake personal finance research that entails a dimension of time. It is important to acknowledge, from the outset of a research project, that there is no consensus that any dimension of time is needed when modeling financial behaviors, tasks, or portfolio choices. This, of course, has policy implications as well. What is presented in the academic literature (i.e., normative models and solutions) may not always align with what is seen in practice.

Consider the work of Hong and Hanna (2014). They were among the first to examine expressed time horizons in relation to a person's time preference. In Hong and Hanna's noteworthy study, they asked whether different planning horizons reflect someone's true time orientation (i.e., preference).[5] They noted that a person's planning time horizon should depend on the discount rate, with a higher discount rate leading to a shorter time horizon and vice-a-versa. Using this logic, numerous researchers have assumed that someone's planning time horizon can be used as a proxy for their time preference. For example, the following question, from the Survey of Consumer Finances, is sometimes used as an indicator of time preference: "In planning (your/ your family's) saving and spending, which of the time periods – the next few months, the next year, the next few years, the next 5 to 10 years, or longer than 10 years – is most important to you/your family?" Hong and Hanna showed that rather than being a proxy for time preference, answers to this question are actually situational and not truly indicative of time preference. In summarizing their work, they noted the following: "a person who is saving for a down payment to buy a home might have a short time horizon, but the same person after the home is purchased might then have a long time horizon, for instance, for retirement."

## Practitioner Tools, Techniques, and Applications

Although the concepts of decision time frame, time orientation/preference, and time perception are important, and in many ways dominate time study research, from a purely practical point of view, the goal time horizon is of most importance for those engaged in making personal, family, and household financial decisions. As noted earlier in this chapter, there is no consensus on what constitutes a given time horizon. What one financial decision maker calls short-term may be an intermediate-term horizon for someone else. Likewise, one person's intermediate-term time horizon may fit another decision maker's definition of long-term. As noted by Grable and associates (2009), those in the academy have avoided the task of standardizing time horizons in the context of personal finance decision making. Those in the academy have focused their research attention primarily on issues related to time orientation and time preference as inputs into decision-making models. However, decision makers, and those who provide advice and guidance to decision makers, need consistent and defensible definitions of time horizon. Consider, for example, the following situation:

---

5 Time preference is the marginal rate of substitution between current and future consumption (Becker and Mulligan, 1997).

A financial advisor is working with a client who is 62 years of age. The client has seven years until retirement. Further, assume that the financial advisor concludes that seven years corresponds to a long-term time horizon. As such, the financial advisor allocates the client's retirement assets aggressively, with equities representing 70 percent of the client's retirement portfolio. If the outcome of the decision matches or exceeds expectations, both the client and financial advisor will be pleased with the allocation decision. However, if the outcome falls below expectations, the client will likely be disappointed and question the allocation decision. Assume this happens and that the client asks another financial advisor to review the initial recommendation. The second financial advisor may respond by stating that the allocation choice was a mistake because, in the financial advisor's opinion, seven years is not a long time horizon; rather, in the eyes of this advisor, seven years is an intermediate time horizon, which means that the initial allocation decision was too aggressive.

In this situation, which financial advisor is correct? It is very difficult to answer this question. Both financial advisors can provide evidence from the academic literature and trade publications supporting their position. In the end, the client is left in a compromised position.

This example illustrates the need for a standardized set of time horizon definitions. Attempts have been taken over the 25 years to address this need, but, to date, few time horizon proposals have been widely adopted (see Droms and Strauss, 2003; Garmaise, 2006; Rattiner, 2003; Schooley and Worden, 2003). The only consistent recommendation to emerge from the literature is that those with a longer time horizon should be able to withstand more volatility in their portfolio, whereas those with a shorter time horizon should reduce risk in their portfolio because they have less time to recoup potential losses. Additionally, it is generally assumed as true that "the longer a client's investment time horizon the more complicated the allocation approach becomes in order to meet the wealth accumulation target" (Grable et al., 2009, p. 52).

One of the most compelling attempts to standardize the language surrounding time horizon definitions was undertaken by Grable et al. (2009). They presented time descriptors associated with specific time horizon definitions. Their guidelines were developed to match what Garmaise (2006) described as an investment time horizon – the period from the establishment of a financial objective or goal through the point in the future when the financial decision maker's assets are needed (Grable et al., 2009, p. 53). The definitions, as shown in Table 10.1, were standardized based on focus group and survey data obtained from a group of seasoned financial service professionals. Twenty-two financial advisors, who each had more than 21 years of financial planning experience, on average, at the time of the focus group activity, provided feedback about what they believed were appropriate time horizon definitional parameters. In general, those in the focus group agreed that "the shorter an investors' time horizon, holding other factors constant, the more conservative the investor should be when making financial decisions" (Grable et al., 2009, p. 53).

What makes these descriptors and definitions unique is that the financial advisor data used to frame the definitions indicated that rather than splitting time horizon into three elements (i.e., short-, intermediate-, and long-term), a financial decision

**Table 10.1:** Time Horizon Definitions.

| Time Descriptor | Time Definition |
| --- | --- |
| Ultra-Short Term | 9 months or less |
| Short-Term | More than 9 months up to 2.5 years |
| Short-Intermediate Term | More than 2.5 years to 5 years |
| Long-Intermediate Term | More than 5 years to 10 years |
| Long-Term | More than 10 years |

*Source*: Grable et al. (2009).

maker's goal time horizon can be seen as ranging from ultra-short-term (i.e., a situation in which no portfolio risk should be taken) to long-term (i.e., when more portfolio risk can be taken). The time between these extremes range from short-term (i.e., more than 9 months to 2.5 years), short-intermediate term (i.e., more than 2.5 years to 5 years), and long-intermediate term (i.e., more than 5 years to 10 years). The practical implication associated with this timing framework is that goals associated with different time frames will have correspondingly different allocations to risky assets. Goals with shorter time horizons should, holding other factors constant, have less exposure to portfolio risk.

# Future Directions

The study of time, as a factor that impacts nearly every personal finance situation and decision task, has yet to be fully exploited by researchers. The study of time horizons, decision time frames, orientations/preferences, and perceptions/perspectives have yet to be codified or modeled jointly. This is an interesting insight because, as noted in this chapter, these four dimensions of time are closely associated. However, each dimension tends to be studied separately in the context of unique disciplines. Those interested in applied financial decision making often focus on goal time horizons. Those interested in decision maker behavioral tendencies generally limit their inquiries to describing decision time frames or modeling time orientation and time preference. Psychologists who are interested in the nonconscious processes underlying human behavior typically focus on evaluating time perceptions and perspectives. An opportunity exists to develop unified models that include these four dimensions. Such models can then be used to inform the literature, policy, and practice.

# Discussion

Upon reflection, it may seem odd that so few papers have been published on the topic of time as it relates to personal finance decision making. It is not so much that a lack of research on time exists, but rather that time studies tend to be focused on particular behaviors or discipline-specific topics, and that time, as a modeling input, is almost always used as a control variable (most often proxied by a decision maker's age) in resource allocation models. To date, for example, there are no unified descriptions or definitions of what constitutes a goal time horizon. This chapter reintroduced a definitional framework proposed by Grable et al. (2009), but more empirical testing of these definitions is needed. It is reasonable to conclude that the future direction of personal finance, as an interdisciplinary profession, will be closely tied to the way time is conceptualized, defined, studied, and modeled across the ensuing decades.

# Conclusion

As noted in this chapter, the concept of time is the one factor that unites all of the disciplines that inform and shape the interdisciplinary profession of personal finance. The problem facing those who (a) conduct personal finance research, (b) use personal finance research when designing public policy, and (c) provide advice and guidance to others related to personal finance topics is that time, although an important input into almost all personal finance decision-making models, is an un-unified concept. Time is thought to be a linear function (Sircova et al., 2015), but when applied, time takes on many dimensions. This chapter showed that time can be seen as a goal time horizon, a decision time frame, an orientation/preference, or a perception/perspective. The notion of goal time horizons has the most relevance for the use of personal finance tools and techniques. The decision time frame and time orientation/preference tend to be studied from an economic perspective, often to describe why some decision makers exhibit myopic behavior while other decision makers focus on long-term goal outcomes. The fourth dimension of time, as described in this chapter – time perception/perspective – is usually studied by psychologists who are interested in explaining why people behave in ways that sometimes appear to be biased or counter to optimal outcomes. The future of personal finance will be closely aligned with research developments, across these four dimensions, that occur over the next few decades.

# References

Bandura, A. (1997). *Self-efficacy: The exercise of control*. Freeman.

Becker, G. S., and Mulligan, C. B. (1997). The endogenous determination of time preference. *The Quarterly Journal of Economics, 112*, 729–758.

Bierman, H. Jr. (1997). Portfolio allocation and the investment horizon. *The Journal of Portfolio Management, 23*(4), 51–55.

Blanchet-Scalliet, C., El Karoui, N., Jeanblanc, M., and Martellini, L. (2008). Optimal investment decisions when time-horizon is uncertain. *Journal of Mathematical Economics, 44*, 1100–1113.

Bodie, Z. (1995). On the risk of stocks in the long run. *Financial Analysts Journal, 51*, 18–22.

Carelli, M. G., Wiberg, B., and Wiberg, M. (2011). Development and construct validation of the Swedish Zimbardo time perspective inventory. *European Journal of Psychological Assessment, 27*, 220–227.

Cojuharenco, I., Patient, D., and Bashshur, M. R. (2012). Seeing the "forest" or the "trees" of organizational justice: Effects of temporal perspective on employee concerns about unfair treatment at work. *Organizational Behavior and Human Development Processes, 116*, 17–31.

Drake, L., Duncan, E., Sutherland, F., Abernethy, C., and Henry, C. (2008). Time perspective and correlates of wellbeing. *Time & Society, 17*, 47–61.

Droms, W. G., and Strauss, S. N. (2003). Assessing risk tolerance for asset allocation. *Journal of Financial Planning, 16*(3), 72–77.

Ebert, R. J., and Piehl, D. (1973). Time horizon: A concept for management. *California Management Review, 15*(4), 35–41.

Einstein, A. (1931). *Relativity: The special and general theory* (R. W. Lawson, Trans.). Crown.

Garmaise, E. (2006). Long-run planning, short-term decisions: Taking the measure of the investor's evaluation period. *Journal of Financial Planning, 19*(7), 68–75.

Grable, J. E., Archuleta, K., and Evans, D. A. (2009). Hey buddy, do you have the correct time (horizon)? *Journal of Financial Service Professionals, 63*(4), 49–55.

Hershey, D. A., and Mowen, J. C. (2000). Psychological determinants of financial preparedness for retirement. *The Gerontologist, 40*, 687–697.

Hong, E. O., and Hanna, S. D. (2014). Financial planning horizon: A measure of time preference or a situational factor. *Journal of Financial Counseling and Planning, 25*(2), 184–196.

Jacobs-Lawson, J. M., and Hershey, D. A. (2005). Influence of future time perspective, financial knowledge, and financial risk tolerance on retirement saving behaviors. *Financial Services Review, 14*, 331–344.

Jaggia, S., and Thosar, S. (2000). Risk aversion and the investment horizon. A new perspective on the time diversification debate. *The Journal of Psychology and Financial Markets, 1*, 211–215.

Kirby, F. (2005). Investment risk from the client's perspective. *Journal of Financial Planning, 18*(12), 42–51.

Klos, A., Weber, E. U., and Weber, M. (2005). Investment decisions and time horizon: Risk perception and risk behavior in repeated gambles. *Management Science, 51*, 1777–1790.

Laverty, K. J. (2004). Managerial myopia or systemic short-termism? The importance of managerial systems in valuing the long term. *Management Decision, 42*, 949–962.

Lee, W. Y. (1990). Diversification and time: Do investment horizons matter? *The Journal of Portfolio Management, 16*, 21–26.

Lenoir, G., and Tuchschmid, N. S. (2001). Investment time horizon and asset allocation models. *Financial Markets and Portfolio Management, 15*, 76–93.

Levinthal, D. A., and March, J. G. (1993). The myopia of learning. *Strategic Management Journal, 14*(S2), 95–112.

Lewin, K. (1942). Time perspective and morale. In G. Lewin (ed.), *Resolving social conflicts* (pp. 103–124). Harper.

Lewin, K. (1951). *Field theory in the social sciences: Selected theoretical papers*. Harper.

Merriam-Webster. (n.d.). Time. In *Merriam-Webster.com dictionary*. Retrieved May 26, 2021, from https://www.merriam-webster.com/dictionary/time

Plambeck, E. L., and Wang, Q. (2013). Implications of hyperbolic discounting for optimal pricing and scheduling of unpleasant services that generate future benefits. *Management Science*, *59*, 1,927–1,946.

Rattiner, J. H. (2003, May). Back to basics. *Financial Planning*, 107–108; 130.

Reilly, G., Souder, D., and Ranucci, R. (2016). Time horizon of investments in the resource allocation process: Review and framework for next steps. *Journal of Management*, *42*, 1169–1194.

Rolison, J. J. Hanoch, Y., and Wood, S. (2017). Saving for the future: Dynamic effects of time horizon. *Journal of Behavioral and Experimental Economics*, *70*, 47–54.

Samuelson, P. A. (1994). The long-term case for equities. *The Journal of Portfolio Management*, *21*(1), 15–24.

Schooley, D. K., and Worden, D. D. (2003). Generation X: Understanding their risk tolerance and investment behavior. *Journal of Financial Planning*, *16*(9), 58–63.

Sircova, A., van de Vijver, F. J. R., Osin, E., Milfont, T. L., Fieulaine, N., Kislali-Erginbilgic, A., Zimbardo, P. G., and 54 members of the International Time Perspective Research Project. (2015). Time perspective profile of cultures. In M. Stolarski, N. Fieulaine, and W. van Beek (eds.), *Time perspective theory; review, research, and application: Essays in honor of Philip G. Zimbardo* (pp. 169–187). Springer International Publishing.

Yakup. D., and Diyarbakirlioglu, I. (2011). A theoretical approach to the role of perception on the consumer buying decision process. *Asian Journal of Business and Management Sciences*, *1*, 217–221.

Zimbardo, P. G., and Boyd, J. N. (1999). Putting time in perspective: A valid, reliable individual-differences metric. *Journal of Personality and Social Psychology*, *77*, 1271–1288.

Nathan Harness, Leobardo Diosdado

# 11 Household Financial Ratios

**Abstract:** Financial ratio analysis enables households and businesses to make quick assessments of their current financial situation and provides metrics for a relative comparison of financial health across households. Numerous financial ratios have been studied in the literature to measure several wellness indicators, such as meeting investment goals, limiting exposure to risks, or ensuring adequate liquidity levels. However, it is debatable which financial ratios are adequate assessments of overall financial health. This chapter aims to narrow the scope of financial ratios analyzed in the existing literature by summarizing a list of the most studied and applicable ratios used in the field of personal finance. A case study approach is used to show the application of ratios and uncover the value of using multiple ratios in concordance to gain insight into a real-world scenario. Opportunities for further study are discussed in terms of developing heuristics to help establish normative standards for the profession of financial planning.

**Keywords:** financial ratio analysis, heuristics, financial wellness, statement analysis

## Introduction

Individuals have always sought ways to shorten the decision-making process either through comparative observation or time-saving tools such as ratios. Financial ratios are heuristics that can serve as an index that enables a household or business to evaluate and analyze their current financial strength and progression toward their financial goals over time (Harness et al., 2008; Lytton et al., 1991; Winger, 2000). The analysis of a simple ratio may provide more than just a glimpse of that particular aspect; it can also paint a comprehensive picture of an entity's overall financial health (Gibson, 1987). Initially, lending institutions were the first to introduce and implement financial ratio analysis to evaluate a prospective borrower's overall creditworthiness (DeVaney and Lytton, 1995; Duca and Rosenthal, 1994). Much of the exploratory work on financial ratios began in the 1980s and continued throughout the mid-1990s but has since declined, even though academic textbooks continue to use financial ratios as recommended household financial management analysis tools (Dalton et al., 2019). This decline in academic ratio research is partly due to the complexities of using ratios as variables in modern statistical techniques rather than simply using the numerator or denominator variables of the ratio as predictors. It is also difficult for researchers to

**Nathan Harness,** Texas A&M University
**Leobardo Diosdado,** Western Carolina University

https://doi.org/10.1515/9783110727692-011

find panel data that provides a complete financial picture of a household to allow for comprehensive ratio analysis across time. This type of panel data often produces spurious results because the data is non-stationary (Ioannidis et al., 2003).

Although these limitations are not unique to datasets comprised of households, the effect is more muted among corporate entities, which explains why modern research within corporate finance continues to use a multitude of ratios to analyze and evaluate an entity's financial health (Beaver et al., 2005) and even forecast corporate stock prices (Ang and Bekaert, 2007; Lewellen, 2004; Pontiff and Schall,1998). Household researchers do not have the luxury of competitive market outcome variables such as a stock price, forcing researchers to use proxies of financial outcomes or normative goals. This does not negate the power of simplicity and replicability that ratios can bring to a household, a financial practitioner, or a macro policymaker to enable financial wellness practices. The following section within this chapter summarizes the current literature regarding the overall usefulness and the definitions of key financial ratios along with the application of those ratios when analyzing a household's or individual's financial conditions.

## Historical Perspective

As corporate financial statements became more common in the early 1900s, financial ratios were used in the accounting profession and the business world to standardize financial performance comparisons (Horrigan, 1968). However, standardization of an entity's financial statements for comparison met some opposition. Welsh and White (1981) suggested that the traditional concepts and methodology of applying financial standardization and ratio measures to businesses of varying sizes needed to be reexamined since it is not practical to compare a small business to a relatively large one without first taking into account the various factors that impact the firm's financial statements. The goal of most business owners and operators is maximizing shareholder wealth, which can be accomplished by growing the business. Thus, an analysis of the firm's financial ratios can be instrumental in enabling managers to obtain that goal. Valuation techniques such as fundamental analysis of a business's financial statements conducted by a security analyst would be much less robust without using and implementing financial ratios to conduct that analysis (Gibson, 1987).

The power of a financial ratio comes from the simplicity of the calculation and relative comparison of large and small entities. Ratios are used in a wide range of applications, from painting and photography (e.g., golden ratio), to the proportion of medicine given to patients of varying weight, and even in how fast people can and should drive cars (e.g., miles per hour). Any heuristic, such as a ratio, can allow for greater ease of decision making by making complex problems tractable and providing ease of visualization of goal progression. Kahneman (2011) famously dichotomized the power and need for heuristics in how people process information in their daily lives within the intuitive "system 1" versus the slower logic and analysis used in "system 2" thinking of dual-process theory. He asserted that "system 1" allows people to make fast, intuitive judgments that leverage their ability to make everyday decisions. However, this sometimes comes at the cost of behavioral bias. Financial ratios themselves are not simply heuristics that provide a pathway toward quick decision making; they can provide comparative guidance to help households understand their cross-sectional and longitudinal economic environments. Financial ratios also provide financial planners and financial counselors with red flags or markers of potentially problematic financial behavior or future goal trade-offs.

Griffith (1985) first mentioned the usage of ratios as decision tools for households, whereas Lytton et al. (1991) was the first to apply financial ratios to case studies built with a household's financial statements. As this stream of research progressed, more studies began to analyze the effectiveness of ratios as predictive indicators of outcomes, such as financial well-being. Financial service professionals currently use financial ratios to make and track financial recommendations made to clients (DeVaney, 1994; Garman and Forgue, 2015; Heo et al., 2020; Lee and Kim, 2016). Financial ratios are also presented as fundamental tools to analyze and evaluate household financial wellness in many financial planning textbooks (e.g., Dalton et al., 2019; Garman and Forgue, 2011; Kapoor et al., 2006). However, financial ratios often serve best as descriptors or markers of a current household's financial situation rather than predictors of future performance or failures (Heo et al., 2020; Medio and Gallo, 1995; Shapiro and Gorman, 2000).

## Commonly Used Household Ratios

Early work identified from 16 to 20 ratios as numeric guidelines for households (Mason and Griffith, 1988; Prather, 1990). In many studies, the numerator and denominator were dictated by the availability of national data sets used to analyze households, which influenced the ratio inputs slightly across studies.[1] There can also be inconsistencies across household balance sheets and income statements since these financial statements are not regulated or prescribed by standard accounting

---

[1] Academic studies on financial ratios have predominately focused on households in the United States; however, ratios have been used internationally to predict outcomes such as financial fragility (La Cava and Simon, 2005). Ratio comparison across countries is confounded by varying tax and economic conditions, perceptions of familiarity, and local preferences for specific asset classes (Badarinza et al., 2016). There is limited research on international financial literacy and household heuristics. Still, the broad application of ratio analysis as a tool for comparison and progress is applicable within a multitude of applications.

practices or regulatory bodies more common to corporate finance. Even given the limitations of previous studies, ratios are still powerful tools used to help household financial decision makers express goal progression and analyze overall comparative wellness. A collection of the most widely used ratios is shown in Table 11.1, along with recommended ratio norms across different academic studies.

**Table 11.1:** Common Ratios and Prescribed Ratio Norms.

| Ratio | Recommend Level | Citation |
| --- | --- | --- |
| Liquidity Ratio = Liquid Assets/Monthly Expenditures | ≥ 2.5 Months | (Greninger et al., 1996; Griffith, 1985) |
| | ≥ 3 Months | (DeVaney, 2000) |
| | 2 to 6 Months | (Prather, 1990) |
| Current Ratio = Liquid Assets/Current Debt (or Current Liabilities) | ≤ 0.5 | (Greninger et al., 1996; Griffith, 1985) |
| Debt Safety Ratio = Monthly Consumer Debt Payment/Monthly Disposable Income | ≤ 0.15 "reasonable" | (Greninger et al., 1996) |
| | ≤ 0.15 "danger point" | |
| | ≥ 0.10 "safe" | (Garman and Forgue, 2011) |
| | 0.11 to 0.15 "reduced financial flexibility" | |
| | 0.16 to 0.20 "fully extended" | (Godwin, 1996) |
| | ≥ 0.20 | |
| Debt Service Ratio = Annual Debt Payments/Annual Disposable Income (including both consumer and mortgage) | ≤ 0.35 "reasonable" | (Greninger et al., 1996) |
| | ≤ 0.45 "danger point" | |
| | ≤ 0.4 | (DeVaney, 2000) |
| | ≤ 0.2 | (Johnson and Li, 2010) |
| House Expense Ratio = Housing Expense/Gross Income | ≤ 0.35 | (Greninger et al., 1996) |
| | ≤ 0.28 | (Blackman and Krupnick, 2001) |
| Solvency Ratio = Total Assets/Total Liabilities | ≥ 1 | (DeVaney, 2000) |

**Table 11.1** (continued)

| Ratio | Recommend Level | Citation |
|---|---|---|
| Capital Accumulation Ratio = Investment Assets/Net Worth | ≥ 0.5 | (Greninger et al., 1996; Yao et al., 2003) |
| | ≥ 0.25 | (DeVaney, 2000; Lytton et al., 1991) |
| Savings Ratio = Annual Total Savings/ Annual Disposable Income | ≥ 0.1 | (Greninger et al., 1996) |
| | Flexible depending on life stage | (Grable et al., 2012) |
| Tax Burden Ratio = Payroll Taxes/Gross Income | 0.20 to 0.30 | (Greninger et al., 1996) |
| | Increasing as household income increases | (Hazan, 2015) |

## Liquidity Ratio

A household's ability to maintain its current consumption level and satisfy its obligations in the short term can be assessed by the liquidity ratio (Gibson, 1987). Garrett and James III (2013) suggested that a liquidity ratio of 2.5 is adequate, which implies that the household has sufficient liquid assets to cover 2.5 months of living expenses after a total loss of a household's income. However, the prior research of Greninger et al. (1996) and Chang et al. (1997) suggested that the denominator of this ratio be a household's monthly income instead of its monthly expenditures. This approach would enable an individual or household to survive a layoff or loss of employment; thus, one could argue that there is a significant difference between 2.5 months' worth of income and 2.5 months' worth of monthly expenses. Financial planners often recommend that clients maintain a liquidity ratio within the range of two to six months as this ratio serves as a proxy to determine the size and resilience of the household's emergency fund (DeVaney, 1994). However, one of the shortfalls of the liquidity ratio is that it fails to identify whether a household manages its debt appropriately (Winger, 2000). In the era of historically low-interest rates, a household may be failing to take advantage of the benefits associated with the use of credit instead of cash since some credit card promotions allow the consumer to make purchases without having to incur egregious interest rate costs and low annual percentage rate promotions to qualified consumers.

## Current Ratio

In corporate finance, the current ratio measures a company's ability to meet its current liabilities, which are those liabilities that are due within a year. However, a household's balance sheet typically does not include inventory or accounts receivable; thus, for this calculation, the numerator will most likely only include the household's cash and liquid assets. A household's current ratio measures the ability to repay a short-term debt if an emergency occurs. If this metric is calculated and collected over various points in time, the household's current ratio can provide a benchmark or average of the degree of liquidity that a household possesses throughout time and serve as an indicator of possible issues regarding the amount of current liabilities that will be due within a year. Both Griffith (1985) and Greninger et al. (1996) noted that households aim to maintain at least two times more in current assets than current liabilities. However, this metric fails to include the amount of long-term liabilities that must be satisfied within the next 12 months. This may underestimate the actual liabilities that a household needs to pay in the event of an income shock or the amount or percentage of capital that must be allocated toward a money market or high-yield checking account since these types of holding accounts are less likely to be exposed to higher levels of volatility.

## Debt Safety Ratio

A household's debt safety ratio is calculated by first determining all consumer debt, which excludes the mortgage and any other debts associated with the purchase of a home, and then dividing the monthly consumer debt payments by the household's monthly disposable income. Greninger et al. (1996) and Godwin (1996) both suggested that no more than 0.15 (or 0.16) of a household's monthly disposable income should be allocated toward the satisfaction of consumer debts; however, Garman and Forgue (2015) used a much lower debt safety ratio of 0.10. They argued that households with debt safety ratios from 0.11 to 0.15 are more likely to experience a reduction in their financial flexibility. As with several of the ratios, it might be more important to track progress on the debt safety ratio than set an initial target, given the conflicting ratio recommendations.

## Debt Service Ratio

The household debt service ratio was first published by the Board of Governors of the Federal Reserve System in 1980 (Luckett, 1980). The ratio measures the share of after-tax income that must be used to satisfy debt repayments, divided by aggregate after-tax income. Greninger et al. (1996) recommend that households strive to maintain a debt service ratio below 0.35, whereas DeVaney (2000) suggested that maintaining the debt service ratio below 0.4 was acceptable. However, Johnson and Li (2010) found empirical evidence indicating that households with a debt service ratio above 0.3 were more likely to be turned down when seeking access to a new or additional credit line. Johnson and Li's (2010) recommendation was significantly lower than that of prior researchers (e.g., DeVaney, 2000; Greninger et al., 1996) since it suggests that households should aim to maintain a debt to service ratio below 0.2 due to the probability that households with higher debt service ratios are more likely to be denied when trying to access new or higher lines of credit.

## Housing Expense Ratio

The housing expense ratio is calculated by adding the cost associated with a home purchase, such as the principal amount due for a mortgage loan and the interest on the loan, property taxes, homeowner's insurance premiums, and any other homeowner dues. Mortgage lenders typically refer to this ratio as the front-end ratio and use it to determine a prospective homebuyer's creditworthiness. Mortgage lenders tend to abide by the heuristic that the purchase of a home should not lead to an excess of 28 percent of the household's income being allocated toward the expenses associated with owning the home (Blackman and Krupnick, 2001). Lenders allow some flexibility with this ratio depending on the borrower's credit report profile and credit score. This ratio tends to be most important for households preparing to purchase a home and is often ignored after a home is purchased because it is assumed that the denominator will remain constant. However, the housing expense ratio is still important to monitor for those who purchase a home using a variable rate and in locations where property taxes or insurance premiums increase significantly over time.

## Solvency Ratio (Debt-to-Assets Ratio)

A household's solvency ratio (or its debt-to-asset ratio) measures a household's ability to satisfy debt obligations through the liquidation or sale of assets (DeVaney, 1994; Kim and Lyons, 2008). This ratio is calculated by dividing all of a household's liabilities (or debts) by all of the household's assets (Garman and Forgue, 2011; Garrett and James III, 2013; Kim and Lyons, 2008; Lee and Kim, 2016). Winger (2000) recommended that this ratio be less than 0.5 as this would imply that the total overall debts do not exceed 50 percent of total assets. If the solvency ratio exceeds one (1.0), this implies that the total liabilities exceed total assets; therefore, the household would be considered insolvent. Chen and Finke (1996) and Mountain and Hanna (2012) suggested that a solvency ratio greater than 1.0 (i.e., a negative net worth) is not necessarily a negative aspect, especially if the ratio describes a younger individual or household that borrowed resources in hopes of capitalizing on the investment, such as human capital, in future.

## Capital Accumulation Ratio (Investment Ratio)

The capital accumulation ratio, sometimes called the investment ratio, is calculated by dividing the fair market value of investments by the household's net worth. Prior research suggests that a household should aim to maintain a minimum ratio of 0.25 (DeVaney, 1994; Lytton et al., 1991). However, this ratio fails to incorporate the proximity to retirement, which is why Yao et al. (2003) argued that older households who are about to enter the retirement phase of the life cycle should consider delaying retirement until this metric either meets or exceeds 0.50. Garman and Forgue (2015) suggested that following the investment ratio over time would serve as a proxy toward determining if a household is adequately accumulating investment assets throughout its life, with the ratio functioning as an indicator of retirement preparation. Assessing the various investment assets and the associated risk classification for each asset class can become rather complex, especially when comparing one household to another. Although this ratio measures the savings a household has accumulated, with the expectation of future consumption, it fails to account for the variability within the numerator. If a household financial decision maker has access to the underlying asset classification or allocation structure, it likely makes sense to segment the capital accumulation ratio into two or three risk categories. This is not currently standard practice because most researchers do not have data this granular across various households to allow for this type of detailed study.

## Savings Ratio

There are two different formulas in the existing research used to derive the calculation of the saving ratio. Greninger et al. (1996) included both employer and employee contributions as well as any additional surplus of income in the numerator, whereas Grable et al. (2012) limited it to the sum of the household savings; however, both versions of the equation use a household's annual gross income in the denominator. Prior research suggests that various social-economic variables are associated with lower savings ratios, such as age, ethnicity, race, marital status, number of children in the household, and levels of education (DeVaney et al., 2007; Kim and Lyons, 2008; Lunt and Livingstone, 1991; Lyons and Yilmazer, 2005; Yuh and Hanna, 2010). Therefore, an individual's savings ratio is more likely to be explained by their current life stage (DeVaney et al., 2007). The savings ratio is a useful ratio to use in tandem with the capital accumulation ratio and a measure of time horizon. If a household has a large capital accumulation ratio, then the savings ratio recommendation may be lower than average. However, if a household has a short time horizon left until retirement and a lower capital accumulation ratio, it might indicate the need to increase the savings ratio above the 10 percent recommendation prescribed by Greninger et al. (1996).

## Tax Burden Ratio

Due to the progressive nature of the United States federal tax rate (and general tax rates worldwide), as income rises, so does the amount owed in income taxes (Piketty and Saez, 2007). Thus, households need to understand and estimate the direct tax burden that they are subjected to. The tax burden ratio is calculated by dividing the total payroll and income tax due by the household's gross annual income. Theoretically, those with higher-level income are burdened with higher income taxes as a percentage of income due to the higher marginal tax rates they must pay on each additional dollar earned. In this ratio, what is not accounted for are indirect tax burdens, which are often more difficult to assess since these taxes are imposed on consumption, which tends to be regressive in nature since lower-income households are more likely to allocate a significant portion of income to consumption (Hazan, 2015). This ratio is sometimes overlooked because it is assumed that households can identify their marginal tax bracket or that the most significant portion of taxes due is beyond the control of the household's ability to reduce or mitigate. Setting a target for this ratio is very difficult because of the variability across time due to tax policy and the differences between households of varying income. However, the tax burden ratio can be an excellent ratio to motivate households to engage in tax-efficient savings or investment strategies and track significant tax burden increases across time.

# Financial Ratio Case Analysis

The following case study of the Katherine and Cody Hicks family provides a practical application of how financial ratios can be used as a personal finance decision making and financial management tool. The case is presented from the perspective of a financial planner working with a client family.

Dr. Katherine Newsom-Hicks and Cody Hicks have come to a financial planner to plan for their financial future and to better understand their overall financial position. Katherine is a 38-year-old emergency room doctor at St. Joseph's Hospital earning $205,000. Cody is a 41-year-old professor of practice in construction sciences at a university earning $100,112 per year. Both Cody and Katherine were married previously, and each has two children from those prior marriages with full custody of all four children. Katherine recently reduced her retirement account elective deferral because of fears concerning market volatility but would like to discuss the potential of increasing her contributions. Cody was frugal with spending before marrying Katherine, which has created some conflict between the two of them. As a married couple, the Newsom-Hicks family has sufficient income and desire to begin working toward their financial future for the first time.

A financial planner would typically work with these clients to collect the relevant data needed to create financial statements and begin the process of analyzing the household's financial health. Financial statements are a powerful tool in themselves as they may indicate areas of overspending or anemic growth of assets. It would not be uncommon for a financial planner to quickly conduct a vertical analysis of a client's income statement and expenses to get an idea of what percentage of income is being spent in each category. As shown in Table 11.2, Katherine and Cody spend approximately 37 percent of their total combined income on personal and family expenses. Without running traditional ratios, a financial planner can begin to understand the allocation of spending resources simply by analyzing this statement.

Table 11.2: Statement of Income and Expenses.

| 20X1 STATEMENT OF INCOME AND EXPENSES | |
| --- | --- |
| Cash Inflows | Annually |
| Katherine's Income | $205,000 |
| Cody's Income | $100,112 |
| Total Cash Inflows | $305,112 |
| Cash Outflows | |
| Savings | |
| Katherine 401(k) Contribution | $9,500 |
| Cody 403(b) Contribution | $11,500 |
| Emergency Fund Savings | $4,000 |
| Total Savings | $25,000 |
| Payroll Taxes | |
| Federal Income Tax | $42,840 |
| Social Security Tax | $15,675 |
| Medicare Tax | $3,666 |
| Total Payroll Taxes | $62,181 |

**Table 11.2** (continued)

| 20X1 STATEMENT OF INCOME AND EXPENSES | |
|---|---|
| **Personal and Family Expenses** | |
| Charitable Donations | $11,200 |
| Child Care | $16,000 |
| Club Dues | $5,600 |
| Credit Card Debt Payment (Katherine) | $3,600 |
| Credit Card Debt Payment (Cody) | $2,400 |
| Dining | $8,200 |
| Entertainment | $2,200 |
| Groceries | $10,800 |
| Hobbies | $24,000 |
| Vacation/Travel | $11,400 |
| Student Loan (Katherine) | $17,586 |
| **Total Personal and Family Expenses** | **$112,986** |
| **Vehicle Expenses** | |
| Loan | $26,165 |
| Insurance | $4,035 |
| Fuel | $2,100 |
| Repairs/Maintenance | $2,000 |
| **Total Vehicle Expenses** | **$34,300** |
| **Home Expenses** | |
| Mortgage | $28,922 |
| Real Estate Tax | $11,275 |
| Homeowner's Insurance | $2,165 |
| Utilities | $8,340 |
| Maintenance | $3,400 |
| **Total Home Expenses** | **$54,103** |
| **Personal Insurance Expenses** | |
| Medical, Vision, and Dental Family | $8,477 |
| Life Insurance Katherine | $3,200 |
| Life Insurance Cody | $1,100 |
| Umbrella Liability | $397 |
| **Total Personal Insurance Expenses** | **$13,174** |
| **Total Cash Outflows** | **$301,744** |
| **Unidentified Cash Flows*** | **$3,368** |

*Unidentified Cash Flow is frequently referred to as discretionary income in personal income statements. This can give a false sense of usable cash flow when planning for clients because these are often funds that are not identified and thus not usable for savings or other areas.

Many of the ratios presented earlier in the chapter use data from both the Statement of Financial Position, often called the Statement of Net Worth, and the Statement of Income and Expenses, frequently referred to as the Income Statement. A
quick vertical analysis of the Statement of Financial Position (Table 11.3) shows that
Katherine and Cody have almost 30 percent of their net worth in short-term liabilities. Although this is not a traditionally studied ratio, it allows for a comparative
understanding of the allocation of debts and assets.

**Table 11.3:** Statement of Financial Position.

| 20X1 STATEMENT OF FINANCIAL POSITION | | |
|---|---|---|
| **Assets** | **Owner** | **Value** |
| **Cash/Liquid Assets** | | |
| Joint Checking | Joint/ROS | $22,196 |
| **Total Cash/Liquid Assets** | | $22,196 |
| **Investment Assets** | | |
| Previous Employer 403b | Katherine | $127,656 |
| St. Joseph 401k | Katherine | $55,517 |
| University 403b | Cody | $145,261 |
| Inherited IRA | Cody | $41,256 |
| **Total Investment Assets** | | $369,690 |
| *Tangible Assets* | | |
| Car 1 | Katherine | $64,658 |
| Car 2 | Cody | $66,454 |
| Primary Residence | Joint/ROS | $499,208 |
| **Total Tangible Assets** | | $630,320 |
| **Total Assets** | | $1,022,206 |
| **Liabilities** | **Owner** | **Value** |
| **Short-Term/Current Liabilities** | | |
| Credit Card | Katherine | $3,000 |
| Credit Card | Cody | $4,100 |
| Mortgage on Primary Residence (12 months)* | Joint/ROS | $28,922 |
| Car 1 Loan (12 months)* | Katherine | $13,082 |
| Car 2 Loan (12 months)* | Cody | $13,082 |
| Student Loan (12 months)* | Katherine | $17,586 |
| **Total Short-Term Debt** | | $79,772 |

**Table 11.3** (continued)

| 20X1 STATEMENT OF FINANCIAL POSITION | | |
|---|---|---|
| Liabilities | Owner | Value |
| **Long-Term Liabilities** | | |
| Mortgage on Primary Residence | Joint/ROS | $404,578 |
| Car 1 Loan | Katherine | $32,696 |
| Car 2 Loan | Cody | $45,813 |
| Student Loan | Katherine | $191,192 |
| **Total Long-Term Debt** | | **$674,280** |
| **Total Liabilities** | | **$754,052** |
| **Net Worth** | | **$268,154** |

*These current liabilities represent the payment portion of 12 months of debt payments attributed to the associated long-term liability.

An analysis of different ratios for these clients reveals some insightful information that can serve to point out potential overall financial health problems and provide them with quick, numeric targets for progress. As seen in Table 11.4, the ratios representing liquidity suggest there may be a few red flags that would imply a need for more investigation and exploration as to why these clients lack liquidity. The liquidity ratio of .88 is below the recommended ratio of 3.0 months, and the current ratio (27.82 percent) indicates that these clients would be unable to cover current liabilities if either of them were to lose their jobs. The clients are also borderline on the debt safety ratio (20.93 percent) but seem in a better condition in relation to the debt service ratio (32.84 percent). Although these are traditionally points of caution, there is more to consider than a single ratio in isolation. These clients are high-income earners, and their balance sheet suggests that their income is not subject to any long-term credit card debt. Second, the Statement of Income and Expenses shows that they are currently contributing to emergency fund savings. The ratio analysis results suggest there may be some opportunities to manage cash flow better and bring awareness to the need for greater liquidity, especially with four children at home. The housing ratio (13.88 percent) appears appropriate for these clients based on prior research recommendations, as does their solvency ratio (1.36), which highlights the healthier amount of investment assets they own.

The household's capital accumulation ratio (137.86 percent) is well above the recommended level, which highlights some of the proportionality issues that arise with the use of financial ratios. The relatively low net worth for these clients is driving an appropriate capital accumulation ratio upwards. A capital needs analysis is likely necessary to determine the total accumulation Katherine and Cody will need to afford their financial goals and supplement the information provided by the capital accumulation ratio. A somewhat common, but unresearched, heuristic calculates a client's investment assets to gross income to determine retirement savings adequacy. Given the age of these clients and anticipating a somewhat similar set of expenses in retirement, it is likely that savings would need to be increased going forward. The capital accumulation ratio has been shown to indicate better retirement preparation for those who meet the 25 percent guideline (Yao et al., 2003). However, Yao et al. (2003) indicated that the capital accumulation ratio is deficient as a singular indicator of retirement adequacy. The savings ratio (10.29 percent) indicates these clients are barely meeting the savings guideline, but, similar to the capital accumulation ratio, the client's current savings and age are also important factors to take into account. Combining the results from the savings ratio and liquidity-based ratios, it is likely these clients need to consider increasing their savings toward both intermediate- and long-term capital. The tax ratio appears to be somewhat useless on the surface because it will vary due to tax policy that might be out of the client's control. However, the tax ratio does an excellent job showing clients just how much they pay in overall taxes as a percentage of income. For many clients, this might be the first time they have ever seen their income taxes shown on a relative basis. This can be an excellent tool to motivate them towards tax deferral strategies or educate them regarding the benefits of how good tax planning can impact taxes across time.

**Table 11.4:** Select Ratio Analysis and Prescribed Recommendations.

| HOUSEHOLD FINANCIAL RATIOS | | | | Cur. | Rec. |
|---|---|---|---|---|---|
| Liquidity Ratio | $\dfrac{\text{Liquid Assets}}{\text{Monthly Expenditures}}$ | = | $\dfrac{\$22,196}{\$25,145}$ | = 0.88% | >3.0% |
| Current Ratio | $\dfrac{\text{Liquid Assets}}{\text{Current Liabilities}}$ | = | $\dfrac{\$22,196}{\$79,772}$ | = 27.82% | > 50% |
| Debt Safety Ratio | $\dfrac{\text{Monthly Consumer Debt}}{\text{Monthly Disposable Income}}$ | = | $\dfrac{\$4,238}{\$20,244}$ | = 20.93% | >20% |
| Debt Service Ratio | $\dfrac{\text{Monthly Consumer + Mort Debt}}{\text{Monthly Disposable Income}}$ | = | $\dfrac{\$6,648}{\$20,244}$ | = 32.84% | < 45% |
| Housing Ratio | $\dfrac{\text{Housing Expenses}}{\text{Gross Income}}$ | = | $\dfrac{\$42,363}{\$305,112}$ | = 13.88% | < 35% |

**Table 11.4** (continued)

| HOUSEHOLD FINANCIAL RATIOS | | | | Cur. | Rec. |
|---|---|---|---|---|---|
| Solvency Ratio | $\dfrac{\text{Total Assets}}{\text{Total Liabilities}}$ | = | $\dfrac{\$1,022,206}{\$754,052}$ | = 1.36% | >1.0% |
| Capital Accumulation Ratio | $\dfrac{\text{Investment Assets}}{\text{Net Worth}}$ | = | $\dfrac{\$369,690}{\$268,154}$ | = 137.86% | > 25% |
| Savings Ratio | $\dfrac{\text{Annual Total Savings}}{\text{Annual Disposable Income}}$ | = | $\dfrac{\$25,000}{\$242,931}$ | = 10.29% | > 10% |
| Tax Ratio | $\dfrac{\text{Payroll Taxes}}{\text{Gross Income}}$ | = | $\dfrac{\$62,181}{\$305,112}$ | = 20.38% | < 30% |

Note. Cur. = Current ratio; Rec. = Recommended Ratio.

# Limitations of Financial Ratios and Future Direction

The study of personal finance continues to evolve. The field is still in its infancy in the development of normative practice standards and empirical evidence around measures of household financial planning success. Numerous complexities arise when researchers attempt to research predictive variables, in this case, ratios. Like most wealth data, ratios used in multivariate studies often need to be transformed due to non-normality. There are also co-linearity issues and proportionality concerns that need to be mitigated when using ratios as predictors. Secondary data used by household researchers are often self-reported and limited in scope. As with any tool, ratios are only as valuable as the data reliability and consistency of the inputs when it comes to setting recommendations and testable hypotheses; thus, it is vitally important to consider the validity of self-reported data and check for consistency of the variables used to define the numerator and denominator of a ratio cumulatively. A single ratio can be significantly impacted by the seasonal effects of a temporary cash-flow change or debt incurred in isolation. Similar to testing the blood pressure of a patient, it is likely wise to estimate multiple ratio measures across time to determine the accurate ratio metrics for a household and consequently help identify areas of concern. Taking multiple measures of ratios across time can help smooth out temporary changes in input variables and give a better picture of overall financial health. There are also off-balance sheet items, such as human capital, that can vary significantly across time and across households that should be considered when providing financial advice. Even with the complexity of measurement and analysis, ratios provide a quantitative measure for both households and those who provide financial advice to households to assess comparative financial health.

It is often said that providing financial advice is both an art and science, and while this is likely the case when prescribing any advice, it is wise to have measurable data to filter through the experience of practice to help counsel or guide households toward attainment of their financial goals. Financial planners and others who help households manage financial resources at the micro-level, and policymakers at the macro level, can use financial ratio heuristics as general guides and standards or thresholds to provide easy-to-understand heuristics households can use to navigate the complex financial environment they face.

## Conclusion

Even with the limitations presented by ratio analysis, financial ratios provide powerful heuristics to simplify and scale financial advice delivery. Financial ratios have become an important tool used by household financial decision makers and those who provide advice to households to determine problems and opportunities within the measurable metrics of financial statements. Ratio analysis provides a formalized mechanism to coach household financial decision makers or uncover relationships across current cash flows and future accumulation. The value of ratios is not limited to financial service professionals; ratios can also be used by households exploring appropriate metrics of financial progress or those that need visual cues to commemorate progress. Some of the power of financial ratios is in the simplicity and repeatability of the values derived from the calculations. Although the personal finance profession needs to refine and tailor practice standards continuously, the most straightforward approach can sometimes be the most prudent.

## References

Ang, A., and Bekaert, G. (2007). Stock return predictability: Is it there? *The Review of Financial Studies*, *20*(3), 651–707.

Badarinza, C., Campbell, J. Y., and Ramadorai, T. (2016). International comparative household finance. *Annual Review of Economics*, *8*, 111–144

Beaver, W. H., McNichols, M. F., and Rhie, J. W. (2005). Have financial statements become less informative? Evidence from the ability of financial ratios to predict bankruptcy. *Review of Accounting Studies*, *10*, 93–122.

Blackman, A., and Krupnick, A. (2001). Location-efficient mortgages: Is the rationale sound? *Journal of Policy Analysis and Management*, *20*(4), 633–649.

Chang, Y. R., Hanna, S., and Fan, J. X. (1997). Emergency fund levels: Is household behavior rational? *Journal of Financial Counseling and Planning*, *8*(1), 47–55.

Chen, P., and Finke, M. S. (1996). Negative net worth and the lifecycle hypothesis. *Journal of Financial Counseling and Planning*, 7, 87–96.

Dalton, M. A., Gillice, J. M., Dalton, J. F., and Langdon, T. P. (2019). *Fundamentals of financial planning*. Money Education.

DeVaney, S. A. (1994). The usefulness of financial ratios as predictors of household insolvency: Two perspectives. *Journal of Financial Counseling and Planning*, 5, 5–24.

DeVaney, S. A. (2000). Using financial ratios. In E. T. Garman, J. J. Xiao, and B. H. Brunson (eds.), *The mathematics of personal financial planning* (2nd ed., pp. 147–161). Thompson Learning/ Dame.

DeVaney, S. A., Anong, S. T., and Whirl, S. E. (2007). Household savings motives. *Journal of Consumer Affairs*, 41(1), 174–186.

DeVaney, S. A., and Lytton, R. H. (1995). Household insolvency: A review of household debt repayment, delinquency, and bankruptcy. *Financial Services Review*, 4, 137–156.

Duca, J. V., and Rosenthal, S. S. (1994). Borrowing constraints and access to owner-occupied housing. *Regional Science and Urban Economics*, 24, 301–322.

Garman, E. T., and Forgue, R. (2011). *Personal finance*. Cengage.

Garman, E. T., and Forgue, R. (2015). *Personal finance*. Cengage.

Garrett, S., and James III, R. (2013). Financial ratios and perceived household financial satisfaction. *Journal of Financial Therapy*, 4(1), 39–62.

Gibson, C. (1987). How chartered financial analysts view financial ratios. *Financial Analysts Journal*, 43, 74–76.

Godwin, D. D. (1996). Newlywed couples' debt portfolios: Are all debts created equally? *Journal of Financial Counseling and Planning*, 7, 57–69.

Grable, J. E., Klock, D., and Lytton, R. H (2012). *A case approach to financial planning* (2nd ed.). National Underwriter.

Greninger, S. A., Hampton, V. L., Kitt, K. A., and Achacoso, J. A. (1996). Ratios and benchmarks for measuring the financial well-being of families and individuals. *Financial Services Review*, 5, 57–70.

Griffith, R. (1985). *Personal financial statement analysis: A modest beginning*. Third Annual Conference of the Association of Financial Counseling and Planning Education, Ames, IA, United States.

Harness, N. J., Chatterjee, S., and Finke, M. (2008). Household financial ratios: A review of literature. *Journal of Personal Finance*, 6(4), 77–97.

Hazan, M. (2015). The change in the household tax burden between 2003 and 2011. *Taub Center State of the Nation Report 2015*, 1–24.

Heo, W., Lee, J. M., Park, N., and Grable, J. E. (2020). Using artificial neural network techniques to improve the description and prediction of household financial ratios. *Journal of Behavioral and Experimental Finance*, 25, 100,273.

Horrigan, J. O. (1968). A short history of financial ratio analysis. *The Accounting Review*, 43, 284–294.

Ioannidis, C., Peel, D. A., and Peel, M. J. (2003). The time series properties of financial ratios: Lev revisited. *Journal of Business Finance & Accounting*, 30, 699–714.

Johnson, K. W., and Li, G. (2010). The debt-payment-to-income ratio as an indicator of borrowing constraints: Evidence from two household surveys. *Journal of Money, Credit and Banking*, 42, 1,373–1,390.

Kahneman, D. (2011). *Thinking, fast and slow*. Macmillan.

Kapoor, J., Dlabay, L., and Hughes, R. (2006). *Personal finance* (8th ed.). McGraw Hill.

Kim, H., and Lyons, A. C. (2008). No pain, no strain: Impact of health on the financial security of older Americans. *Journal of Consumer Affairs*, 42(1), 9–36.

La Cava, G., and Simon, J. (2005). Household debt and financial constraints in Australia. *Australian Economic Review*, *38*, 40–60.

Lee, J. M., and Kim, K. T. (2016). Assessing financial security of low-income households in the United States. *Journal of Poverty*, *20*, 296–315.

Lewellen, J. (2004). Predicting returns with financial ratios. *Journal of Financial Economics*, *74*(2), 209–235.

Luckett, C. (1980). Recent financial behavior of households. *Federal Reserve Bulletin*, *66*, 437.

Lunt, P. K., and Livingstone, S. M. (1991). Psychological, social and economic determinants of saving: Comparing recurrent and total savings. *Journal of Economic Psychology*, *12*(4), 621–641.

Lyons, A. C., and Yilmazer, T. (2005). Health and financial strain: Evidence from the survey of consumer finances. *Southern Economic Journal*, *71*(4), 873–890.

Lytton, R. H., Garman, E. T., and Porter, N. (1991). How to use financial ratios when advising clients. *Journal of Financial Counseling and Planning*, *2*(1), 3–23.

Mason, J. W., and Griffith, R. (1988). New ratios for analyzing and interpreting personal financial statements. *Journal of the Institute of Certified Financial Planners*, *9*, 71–87.

Medio, A., and Gallo, G. (1995). *Chaotic dynamics: Theory and applications to economics*. Cambridge University Press.

Mountain, T., and Hanna, S. D. (2012). Negative net worth and the life cycle hypothesis. https://dx.doi.org/10.2139/ssrn.2116323

Piketty, T., and Saez, E. (2007). How progressive is the US federal tax system? A historical and international perspective. *Journal of Economic perspectives*, *21*, 3–24.

Pontiff, J., and Schall, L. D. (1998). Book-to-market ratios as predictors of market returns. *Journal of Financial Economics*, *49*(2), 141–160.

Prather, C. G. (1990). The ratio analysis technique applied to personal financial statements: Development of household norms. *Journal of Financial Counseling and Planning*, *1*, 53–69.

Shapiro, A. F., and Gorman, R. P. (2000). Implementing adaptive nonlinear models. *Insurance: Mathematics and Economics*, *26*, 289–307.

Welsh, J. A., and White, J. F. (1981). Small business ratio analysis: A cautionary note to consultants. *Journal of Small Business Management (pre-1986)*, *19*(4), 20–23.

Winger, B. J. (2000). *Personal finance on the internet, an interactive guide: Personal finance [to accompany personal finance: An integrated planning approach]*. Prentice-Hall.

Yao, R., Hanna, S. D., and Montalto, C. P. (2003). The capital accumulation ratio as an indicator of retirement adequacy. *Journal of Financial Counseling and Planning*, *14*(2), 1–11.

Yuh, Y., and Hanna, S. D. (2010). Which households think they save? *Journal of Consumer Affairs*, *44*(1), 70–97.

Kenneth J. White, Efthymia Antonoudi

# 12 Income, Income Transfers, and Taxes

**Abstract:** The generation of income, and the taxation of such income, is a keystone element in the study and practice of personal finance. It goes almost without saying, the laws governing the taxation of income can be complex. Research suggests that income is often broadly defined and the taxation of income varies from country to country and taxing authority to taxing authority. In this chapter, we discuss components of income and types of taxes using examples from the United States as well as other taxing authorities. The chapter also provides a discussion of income inequality, as well as the use of governmental transfers and taxes as a means to reduce inequality.

**Keywords:** consumption, flat taxes, income, income inequality, progressive taxes, regressive taxes, taxation, transfers

## Introduction

Fiscal policy, through the use of levying taxes, is the primary way in which countries, localities, and taxing authorities obtain revenue for spending and social transfers. When viewed from a global perspective, the types of taxation policies used vary dramatically by region and country, with differences between and among localities within a particular country also exhibiting variation. The purpose of this chapter is to provide a broad overview of taxation issues from a personal finance perspective. Many of the examples used in this chapter come from the United States. The choice of using the United States as an example source is that while the laws described are unique to the United States, the underlying concepts shaping U.S. tax laws and purported outcomes associated with tax policy are more universal.

## The Legal Basis for Taxation

The Sixteenth Amendment to the United States Constitution states, "The Congress shall have power to lay and collect taxes on incomes, from whatever source derived, without apportionment among the several States, and without regard to any census or enumeration." The U.S. Internal Revenue Code (IRC) adopts the same language in Section 26(a) when it offers a general definition of gross income to be:

**Kenneth J. White, Efthymia Antonoudi,** University of Georgia

https://doi.org/10.1515/9783110727692-012

"Except as otherwise provided in this subtitle, gross income means all income from whatever source derived." The U.S. IRC then immediately lists 14 items that are included in gross income. Nearly all governing political entities around the world provide policymakers with similar legal doctrines to determine what is income and then to tax a portion of stated income. Given broad taxation powers, the tax policy of a region, country, state, and/or municipality can influence the manner in which individuals, families, and households accumulate wealth. It is important, therefore, to have an understanding of income and the taxation of income.

## Income and Wealth Defined

Income is a resource households use to fund consumption. Researchers, economists, and policymakers have defined income in numerous ways based on the various sources from which it is derived (Kendall et al., 2019). In Italy, income is recorded as the sum of four components: employee compensation, pensions and transfers, self-employment income, and property income (Clementi et al., 2010). Differing sources are subject to different tax rates. With so many sources, income can be difficult to ascertain. Worldwide, each source falls into one of two general categories: labor income or non-labor income.

Income from labor includes wages and salaries. Worldwide, labor income is the largest contributor to total income for most households. For example, labor income is the single most important source of income in the United States (Kuhn and Rios-Rull, 2016), and labor income represents nearly 90 percent of the total income in all but the top 1 percent of Spanish households (Garcia-Miralles et al., 2019).

Non-labor income is capital income. Introducing capital income necessitates a discussion of wealth. Income and wealth are highly correlated, and each has a time component (Bricker et al., 2016). First, income determines what a household is able to consume within a certain time period (D'Ambrosio et al., 2020). Wealth, on the other hand, is the accumulation of income over time. Second, income is used to create wealth, and wealth is often used to create additional income. Finally, wealth has the ability to enhance income through access to better education leading to higher-paying jobs and through the acquisition of income-producing assets (Kendall et al., 2019).

Capital income, created by wealth, includes taxable interest, nontaxable interest, dividends, capital gains, and business income as defined by a taxing authority (Bricker et al., 2016). Wealth provides a form of economic security for households, allowing them to absorb negative income shocks, handle emergencies, and maintain a constant level of consumption through the retirement life expectancy (D'Ambrosio et al., 2020).

Income transfers are included in non-labor income. If income is a resource used by households to consume, then other economic benefits received by households must also be considered. Income transfers are part of the total resources available to households that prevent income from becoming zero despite potential drops in earnings (Babiarz and Yilmazer, 2017). After labor income, transfers are the second most important source of income for U.S. households (Kuhn and Rios-Rull, 2016).

The United States and other countries broadly define income transfers as either cash transfers or in-kind transfers (Aizer et al., 2016). Cash transfers, such as Social Security benefits, unemployment insurance, and disability insurance, assist low and middle-income households to soften budget constraints and increase consumption of food and health services. A guaranteed payment in the form of a cash transfer can help families create liquidity, avoid debt, and save and invest (Bastagli et al., 2019). In-kind transfers include government-provided healthcare (e.g., Medicare and Medicaid), housing assistance, temporary assistance to needy families (e.g., food stamps), and higher education tuition subsidies (Bricker et al., 2016; Saez and Zucman, 2020).

Transfers are further categorized as conditional or unconditional and public or private. Conditional transfers require households to have income and assets below certain threshold amounts (Rothwell et al., 2020). Other non-economic conditions may include school attendance or work requirements. Unconditional transfers do not have income, asset, or non-economic requirements. In the United States, Temporary Aid for Needy Families (TANF) and Supplemental Nutrition Assistance Program (SNAP) are two conditional transfer programs. Unemployment insurance and workers' compensation are two unconditional transfer programs. Unconditional transfers are growing in popularity worldwide. Pilot programs such as Supplemented Income Guarantee, Negative Income Tax, and Citizen's Dividend in Kenya and Uganda are being tested for effectiveness (Sircar and Friedman, 2018).

Public transfers are governmental cash payments that include Social Security, disability insurance, unemployment insurance, and withdrawals from retirement accounts (Babiarz and Yilmazer, 2017; Kuhn and Rios-Rull, 2016). Private transfers include retirement income from private pensions and support from family and friends (Babiarz and Yilmazer, 2017).

There is a third category of income transfers that also needs to be considered. Public goods are resources available for collective consumption in society. Spending on education, police, and defense is provided by tax dollars collected by the government (Saez and Zucman, 2020). Although not taxed as income, these transfers do provide a mechanism to produce and secure income in society.

# Income Inequality

A discussion on income and taxation of income would be incomplete without mentioning income inequality. The Gini index is a tool used to measure income inequality (Ardanaz and Scartascini, 2013; Joumard et al., 2013). Capital income, labor income, and business income all contribute to income inequality. In the United States, labor and business income are the main factors associated with income inequality (Kuhn and Rios-Rull, 2016). If upward economic mobility is used as a strategy to decrease income inequality, then transfers tend to be effective for elevating lower-income households (Kuhn and Rios-Rull, 2016). Disposable cash income measures income after taxes and may be the most important in describing income inequality. Disposable cash income reveals the amount of resources available for consumption, saving, and investing.

Income transfers and taxes are two ways that governments address inequality. Worldwide, income transfers seem to be effective in reducing household and child poverty. In particular, public cash transfers have been important in places such as the 37 countries that are members of the Organisation for Economic Co-operation and Development (OECD) (Caminada et al., 2012; Joumard et al., 2013). Similarly, the Universal Child Allowance in Argentina is a fundamental tool providing minimal social and economic guarantees (Groisman, 2015). The United States is an outlier by using the tax code as a means of income transfer (Joumard et al., 2013). Credits such as the Earned Income Tax Credit (EITC), Child Tax Credit (CTC), and the Additional Child Tax Credit (ACTC) are designed to transfer money to households while also encouraging work and promoting labor income (Hoynes, 2019).

When viewed holistically, it is possible to conclude that income stability improves economic security perceptions while contributing most to a household's well-being, mental health, and life satisfaction (D'Ambrosio et al., 2020; Kendall et al., 2019). In particular, when current income is free of negative income shocks and closely aligned with permanent income (e.g., labor income, capital income, and transfers), households generally feel the most satisfaction. While negative income shocks have been found to affect satisfaction, positive gains increase satisfaction little to none at all (D'Ambrosio et al., 2020). Households feel most satisfied when negative income shocks are minimized and income is stable.

## Taxation of Income

The U.S. Internal Revenue Code (IRC), as well as nearly all other worldwide taxation systems, seeks to define income so that it can be taxed. Income is typically broadly defined from whatever source it is derived, including income earned worldwide by the taxpayer. For example, in Spain, worldwide income is subject to personal income tax (Garcia-Miralles et al., 2019). To avoid double taxation, both the United States and Spain have bilateral agreements with other countries to allow offsetting tax credits for taxes paid in another country.

Not all income is subject to taxation. Income can be classified into three broad categories for tax purposes: (1) fully taxable income, (2) partially taxable income, and (3) non-taxable income (Bricker et al., 2016). Each is described in more detail below. Income is also classified into three categories: (1) active, (2) passive, and (3) portfolio income. Active income is received from performing a service. It includes wages, tips, salaries, commissions, and income from material participation in a business. Passive income is received from a business in which the taxpayer is not actively involved. Portfolio income comes from investments and includes dividends, interest, and capital gains.

Fully taxable income is either ordinary or capital, which is taxed at different rates. Ordinary income includes wages earned from work and is most often subject to a progressive tax where higher earners are taxed at higher and more progressive rates. Capital income is often taxed at flat or much less progressive rates. Households earning predominantly labor income bear a much higher tax burden than those with mainly capital income. Social Security benefits are one example of income that is partially taxed since at most 85 percent of the benefit is taxable and it depends on the amount of other income reported by the taxpayer.

The most common source of income exempt from taxes is the value of employer-provided benefits such as health insurance, disability insurance, life insurance, and employer contributions to pension plans (Bricker et al., 2016; Saez and Duncan, 2020). Some government income transfer income is untaxed as well.

## Tax Payments

For employees, taxes are withheld at the source from each paycheck issued by an employer and submitted to the tax authority on the employee's behalf. In the United States, those who are not employees or that have additional income from other sources on which taxes have not been withheld, such as business income from self-employment, passive income, or capital gains from investments during the year, need to make estimated tax payments to the appropriate tax authority every quarter based either on their tax liability paid in the previous year or the estimated tax liability in the current year. Most countries that levy taxes on income use similar tax payment systems that rely on withholdings at the source and estimated payments from a taxpayer on a quarterly or annual basis. Some countries like France also let taxpayers make monthly tax installment payments if they choose to do so over ten months with an additional true-up payment at the end of the year.

Statutory taxes are withheld on dividends, interest, and royalty payments made by companies to residents and non-residents. The statutory withholding rates depend on the country from which the payment originated and the country of residence of the payee. Treaties and double taxation agreements between territories may specify reduced withholding rates. PricewaterhouseCoopers provides world-wide tax summaries and charts with withholding rates of the different territories.[1]

## Tax Policies

For individuals who are considering moving to a different country, an important consideration may be the way their income will be taxed in that country compared to their current country of residence. Two income approaches are generally used around the world. The first is the worldwide income approach also known as a global tax system that taxes income earned from whatever source derived in any location. The second is the territorial income approach that taxes income earned within a country's borders. The worldwide income approach is applicable in 104 countries, whereas the territorial income approach is applicable in 30 countries (Shum et al., 2017).

Countries like the United States that use the worldwide income approach to tax their residents also have provisions like the foreign tax credit, the itemized foreign tax deduction, and the foreign earned income exclusion to help their residents avoid double taxation. The way these rules apply to each resident also depends on the tax treaties in place between the United States and each foreign country when applicable. Hong Kong, Singapore, Taiwan, and Thailand are some examples of countries that use the territorial approach. Countries like Kuwait, Oman, Qatar, and U.A.E. are examples of countries that do not impose personal income taxes on their residents.

There exist three distinct tax systems: (a) progressive taxes, (b) regressive taxes, and (c) flat taxes. As already noted, governments use taxes as their main source of revenue. The progressive tax system is considered a method to reduce income inequality. A progressive tax is a tax in which the tax rate increases as the taxable amount increases. The tax rate progresses from low to high so that the average tax rate is lower than the marginal tax rate. Two examples of progressive taxes are the personal income tax (PIT) and the inheritance tax (INH).

In the United States, a taxpayer's income is divided into brackets or income ranges. In 2021, for example, income tax rates started at 0 percent and went up to 37 percent for those in the highest income tax bracket. The United Kingdom income tax system uses progressive tax rates on income above certain allowances that are different depending on the tax authority (starting at 19 percent and going up to 46 percent in 2021). France uses a progressive tax rate system for income taxes with rates that start from 0 percent and go up to 45 percent as of 2021. Sweden maintains a top statutory income tax rate of 57.1 percent, whereas Denmark's top tax rate is 55.9 percent.

Capital gains are profits from the sale of a capital asset (e.g., a share of stock, a business, a parcel of land, a building, or artwork) (McClelland, 2017). Capital gains

---

1 See https://taxsummaries.pwc.com/quick-charts/withholding-tax-wht-rates.

generally are included in taxable income but are taxed at a lower rate if the capital asset is held for more than one year. For example, in 2021 the U.S. capital gains rates were 0 percent, 15 percent, and 20 percent depending on a taxpayer's income tax bracket. United Kingdom taxes capital gains in 2021 were 10 percent and 20 percent depending on a taxpayer's income level. Not all countries tax capital gains. Examples of countries that do not impose taxes on capital gains are Singapore, New Zealand, Bahrain, Barbados, and Jamaica. Short-term capital gains for assets held less than a year are taxed at the ordinary tax rates discussed above. The imposition of higher tax rates on short-term capital gains and lower tax rates on long-term capital gains is designed to reward long-term ownership of assets and has been shown to increase corporate innovation in a study using a panel of 30 OECD countries (He et al., 2019).

An inheritance tax or estate tax is a tax on the estate (the property, money, and other tangible and intangible possessions) of a deceased person. Across the OECD, 24 countries have an inheritance or an estate tax. There are two different types of taxes that countries use to tax bequests. The first is an estate tax that taxes a deceased donor based on their total wealth. The second is an inheritance tax that taxes the beneficiaries according to the total value of the assets received from the deceased donor. Twenty OECD countries use inheritance taxes to tax the recipients of a deceased person's assets. Denmark, South Korea, the United Kingdom, and the United States impose estate taxes on a deceased person's wealth. All the countries that have an estate or inheritance tax regime also have a gift tax regime in place that most often is beneficiary-based. Some countries never tax inheritances or gifts, including Estonia and Latvia, and some others have repealed their inheritance and gift taxes (e.g., Australia, Austria, Canada, Czech Republic, Israel, Mexico, New Zealand, Norway, Slovac Republic, and Sweden). On average, only about 0.5 percent of total tax revenue comes from inheritance, estate, and gift taxes in the countries that have these tax systems (OECD, 2021). Many OECD countries apply special favorable tax treatment to transfers of certain assets such as businesses, principal residences, private pensions, and life insurance (OECD, 2021).

Fifteen OECD countries use progressive rates where the marginal tax rate rises with the value of the inheritance assets. In 2021, the United States used progressive estate tax rates that started with 0 percent and went up to 40 percent. Seven countries impose flat tax rates on inheritance or estate, and two of those countries impose two separate flat rates based on the relationship between the transferor/donor and the transferee/donee. Flat rates range from 4 percent in Italy to 40 percent in the United Kingdom, whereas progressive rates range from 1 percent in Chile to 80 percent in Belgium (OECD, 2021). The range is less wide on tax rates for spouses and children and is usually lower. The United States offers an unlimited estate tax marital deduction for spouses that are U.S. citizens.

Regressive taxes impose a larger burden on individuals with lower incomes because they constitute a higher percentage of their income compared to higher-income individuals. Examples of regressive taxes are payroll taxes, general sales taxes (GST), value-added taxes (VAT), and various excise taxes. Pigouvian and sin taxes are also examples of regressive taxes that are in place to prevent behaviors with negative externalities. A flat tax imposes the same tax rate on all taxpayers. In practice, regressive taxes discussed in this chapter use flat tax rates for all taxpayers regardless of their income.

## Research and Policy Issues

High economic growth and a more equal income distribution are two primary policy goals of government authorities. In his attempt to explore whether factors that affect a government's performance toward these two goals are conflicting or aligned, Chen (2020) showed that U.S. income inequality began increasing slowly in the early 1980s and has gotten significantly worse since 1987. There is extensive academic literature that has developed models of optimal tax theory to address optimum tax progressivity (Diamond and Saez, 2011).

Whether progressive tax rates translate into progressive tax policies is an issue that has created debate in the literature. Oh (2017), showed how progressive marginal rates serve the interests of wealthy taxpayers. Because taxpayers benefit from rate cuts that occur at levels that are below their own income – called inframarginal tax rate cuts – the rich and middle-class benefit from rate cuts at low levels of income. To shed better light on this, Oh explained that when raising tax revenue, it is best to do so without distorting people's decisions to put in more effort and work harder or longer. To illustrate this, assume that you are running your own company and you make $1,000,000 a year. When you think about whether to take on additional clients to earn extra money, you care about the marginal rate that applies to that extra money you could earn; you do not care about the rate that applies to the first $25,000 made during the year. As such, if tax rates were raised on the lower income brackets, that would not affect the labor decision for a lot of taxpayers, and it would raise additional tax revenue whereas if rates were raised at the top marginal bracket, that would affect the labor decision of those high-income taxpayers and would not result in a considerable amount of extra tax revenue because there are fewer individuals who belong in this high-income category. As such, there is support for the assertion that to promote redistribution, governments should impose relatively flat marginal rates combined with a significant demogrant (Oh, 2017).

The flax tax system that imposes the same rates on all types of income is mostly academic in nature since few governments use a flat income tax. Hall and Rabushka (2013) argued that by taxing different forms of income and different individuals with varying rates, the public would still come up with ways to benefit from the disparity. Hall and Rabushka strongly recommend the simplicity of a flat tax in the form of a consumption tax of 19 percent while exempting the poor from paying the tax and making other taxpayers contribute their share to the tax revenues based on their level of income.

There are differences among studies that have examined the regressivity of VAT. Studies that find VAT to be regressive have evaluated VAT payments as a percentage of current income across the income distribution. Several European country studies (e.g., Leahy et al., 2011; O'Donoghue et al., 2004; Ruiz and Trannoy, 2008) have used this methodology showing support for the view that the VAT is a very regressive tax. On the other hand, studies that analyze VAT payments as a fraction of current expenditure across either the income or expenditure distribution (e.g., Bird and Smart, 2016; Institute for Fiscal Studies, 2011; Metcalf, 1994) have found that VAT taxes are relatively proportional or slightly progressive. Thomas (2020) showed that when the VAT is presented as a percentage of current income, in all 27 OECD countries, it appears to be regressive, but when it is studied as a percentage of current expenditures it appears either proportional or slightly progressive.

Total tax revenues in each country as a percentage of gross domestic product (GDP) can signal the overall focus of governmental policies and the extent of social services provided to its citizens. In 2018, the U.S. tax revenue as a percentage of GDP was 24 percent compared to an average of 34 percent for the other 35 members of the OECD. European countries that provide more widespread government services compared to the United States have higher tax revenue as a percentage of GDP that in many cases exceeds the 40 percent threshold. France's tax revenues, for instance, were the highest at 46 percent of GDP (OECD Revenue statistics comparative tables retrieved 05.12.2019).

## Practitioner Tools and Applications

Practitioners who provide personal finance advice to others often have a fiduciary duty to act in the best interest of their clients. This is especially true when practitioners are engaged in comprehensive financial planning. In these situations, they are expected to take into account the short-term and long-term tax implications of their recommendations. In cases when a client's tax situation has complications that are outside of the practitioner's expertise, the practitioner needs to refer their client to a qualified tax professional.

Advisors should help taxpayer employees optimize their tax withholding at the beginning of each year. A high tax withholding can result in lost spending power throughout the year while a low tax withholding could result in tax penalties and interest. For taxpayers that have other sources of income, appropriate estimated tax payments are also important in order to avoid tax penalties and interest. This can be seen in the example shown in Table 12.1. Simple time value of money calculations for households of different income levels is presented to illustrate the long-term impact of differences in tax rates in additional savings for households.

**Table 12.1:** A Time Value of Money Example Showing the Impact of Taxes.

| | Client with High Income | | | |
|---|---|---|---|---|
| Tax rate levels | 37% | 35% | 32% | 24% |
| Annual income | 1,000,000.00 | 1,000,000.00 | 1,000,000.00 | 1,000,000.00 |
| Effective tax rate | 37% | 35% | 32% | 24% |
| Tax liability | 370,000.00 | 350,000.00 | 320,000.00 | 240,000.00 |
| Net annual income | 630,000.00 | 650,000.00 | 680,000.00 | 760,000.00 |
| Annual expenses | 250,000.00 | 250,000.00 | 250,000.00 | 250,000.00 |
| Annual savings | 380,000.00 | 400,000.00 | 430,000.00 | 510,000.00 |
| Investment rate of return | 7.1% | 7.1% | 7.1% | 7.1% |
| Inflation | 3% | 3% | 3% | 3% |
| Annual rate of return adjusted for inflation | 4.0% | 4.0% | 4.0% | 4.0% |
| Timeframe in years | 30.00 | 30.00 | 30.00 | 30.00 |
| Savings in 30 years | $21,243,279.92 | $22,361,347.28 | $24,038,448.33 | $28,510,717.78 |
| Additional savings due to lower tax rate | | $1,118,067.36 | $2,795,168.41 | $7,267,437.87 |
| | Client with Medium Income | | | |
| Tax rate levels | 22% | 20% | 18% | 12% |
| Annual income | 100,000.00 | 100,000.00 | 100,000.00 | 100,000.00 |
| Effective tax rate | 22% | 20% | 18% | 12% |
| Tax liability | 22,000.00 | 20,000.00 | 18,000.00 | 12,000.00 |
| Net annual income | 78,000.00 | 80,000.00 | 82,000.00 | 88,000.00 |
| Annual expenses | 40,000.00 | 30,000.00 | 30,000.00 | 30,000.00 |
| Annual savings | 38,000.00 | 50,000.00 | 52,000.00 | 58,000.00 |
| Investment rate of return | 7.1% | 7.1% | 7.1% | 7.1% |
| Inflation | 3% | 3% | 3% | 3% |
| Annual rate of return adjusted for inflation | 4.0% | 4.0% | 4.0% | 4.0% |
| Timeframe in years | 30.00 | 30.00 | 30.00 | 30.00 |
| Savings in 30 years | $2,124,327.99 | $2,795,168.41 | $2,906,975.15 | $3,242,395.36 |
| Additional savings due to lower tax rate | | $670,840.42 | $782,647.15 | $1,118,067.36 |

**Table 12.1** (continued)

| | Client with Low Income | | | |
|---|---|---|---|---|
| Tax rate levels | 10% | 8% | 5% | 0% |
| Annual income | 40,000.00 | 40,000.00 | 40,000.00 | 40,000.00 |
| Effective tax rate | 10% | 8% | 5% | 0% |
| Tax liability | 4,000.00 | 3,200.00 | 2,000.00 | – |
| Net annual income | 36,000.00 | 36,800.00 | 38,000.00 | 40,000.00 |
| Annual expenses | 25,000.00 | 25,000.00 | 25,000.00 | 25,000.00 |
| Annual savings | 11,000.00 | 11,800.00 | 13,000.00 | 15,000.00 |
| Investment rate of return | 7.1% | 7.1% | 7.1% | 7.1% |
| Inflation | 3.0% | 3.0% | 3.0% | 3.0% |
| Annual rate of return adjusted for inflation | 4.0% | 4.0% | 4.0% | 4.0% |
| Timeframe in years | 30.00 | 30.00 | 30.00 | 30.00 |
| Savings in 30 years | $614,937.05 | $659,659.74 | $726,743.79 | $838,550.52 |
| Additional savings due to lower tax rate | | $44,722.69 | $111,806.74 | $223,613.47 |

When it comes to portfolio management, Chincarini and Kim (2001) explored the impact of different tax strategies on after-tax investment returns. From the selling of investments in a loss position to avoiding income tax on dividends, to reducing long-term investment turnover, they found that after-tax investment returns can change drastically due to taxation. To illustrate the extent to which taxes can make a difference, they examined a hypothetical investor that bought the Vanguard Index 500 Fund in 1976 and sold it in 2000. The investor ended up paying more than 43 percent of the terminal value in taxes. This was due to fund turnover that created taxable transactions and to stocks entering and leaving the index over time. If the same gross return was attainable with a lower turnover, the investor could have saved a lot of money in taxes. As this example illustrates, taxes can have a significant impact on investment performance, even more significant than transaction costs and management fees. Smart-beta strategies that attempt to increase performance using non-capitalization-weighted portfolio construction techniques result in additional turnover that leads to increased tax bills that can lower the after-tax value added (Vadlamudi and Bouchey, 2014).

When money is invested in international funds and businesses, the tax complications of investing in these funds need to be considered in advance. Investors should consult with a qualified tax professional with expertise in international tax law before implementing transactions. Statutory withholding taxes on dividends, interest, and royalties need to be considered. Even if the investments do not generate dividends, interest, or royalties that may result in withholding taxes, they may generate additional tax reporting obligations for taxpayers, and in some cases, phantom income if, for example, they are investments in passive foreign investment companies (PFICs).

Another way practitioners can help their clients reduce tax liabilities is by encouraging them to save money in tax-advantaged accounts (e.g., qualified retirement accounts). In the United States, when taxpayers save money in retirement plans, either employer-sponsored plans or individual accounts such as traditional IRAs, they can defer paying taxes on the money invested in these accounts. Taxes will be paid when the taxpayer reaches retirement age and starts taking distributions out of these accounts. The value of deferring taxes is essential when taking into account the time value of money throughout the years until retirement. Furthermore, the taxpayer may be in a lower tax bracket in retirement and save additional money in taxes due to the tax rate differential. In the United States, other tax-advantaged accounts that help taxpayers save for retirement are Roth accounts. Taxpayers contribute after-tax money into Roth accounts and can take tax-free distributions out of the accounts at retirement, assuming certain requirements are met. While there is no tax deferral on the money saved in these accounts, taxpayers benefit from tax-free earnings accumulation through the years until retirement. Depending on how investments in the Roth accounts perform in the long run, the tax savings can be considerable. Half of OECD countries (e.g., Canada, Chile, Croatia, Estonia, Finland, Germany, Greece, and others) apply a variant of the Exempt–Exempt–Taxed or EET regime to retirement savings, where both contributions and returns on investment are exempted from taxation while benefits are treated as taxable income upon withdrawal. Other tax regimes are also in place from the Exempt–Exempt–Exempt or EEE (e.g., Bulgaria, Colombia, Mexico, Slovak Republic) regime where contribution returns on investment and pension income are tax-exempt to regimes where two out of three flows of income are taxed (OECD, 2021).

## Conclusion

As discussed in this chapter, individuals use income to satisfy consumption needs. In personal finance, income and taxation law is not only complex but also varies from country to country. Given that each country and taxing authority has its own laws and procedures, what is taxed as income can be different depending on the taxing authority. Nevertheless, there are some similarities. Income comes in the form of wages from work, earnings from self-employment, gains from investments, or transfers from governmental agencies. As income accumulates over time, it creates financial security in the form of wealth. The circular relationship of income and wealth means that wealth then produces more income for the individual that is potentially taxable.

Income can be fully taxed, partially taxed, or exempt from taxation. Wages and earnings from self-employment are each fully taxed. An example of partially taxed income is Social Security benefits in the United States. Although gains from income produced from investments may be taxed, gains earned in Roth accounts may be totally exempt from taxes if certain conditions are met. Further, some income transfers from governmental agencies will never be taxed. Income subject to taxation may face either progressive, regressive, or flat taxes. Progressive taxes are conceptually designed for tax rates to increase as income increases. This is meant to ensure that higher-income individuals pay more of their income in taxes. However, the effectiveness of progressive taxes as a tool to reduce income inequality is debatable. In general, regressive taxes are designed to decrease as the taxable base increases but some taxes like Payroll, GST, and VAT that are considered regressive in practice use flat tax rates for all levels of income. The flat tax is more academic in nature.

# References

Sources used in this chapter apart from those listed here include the Urban Institute, Brookings Institution, and individual authors, 2021. (2020, May). *How are capital gains taxed?* Tax Policy Center. https://www.taxpolicycenter.org/briefing-book/how-are-capital-gains-taxed.

Aizer, A., Eli, S., Ferrie, J., and Lleras-Muney, A. (2016). The long-run impact of cash transfers to poor families. *American Economic Review, 106*(4), 935–971.

Ardanaz, M., and Scartascini, C. (2013). Inequality and personal income taxation: The origins and effects of legislative malapportionment. *Comparative Political Studies, 46*(12), 1636–1663. https://doi.org/10.1177/0010414013484118

Babiarz, P., and Yilmazer, T. (2017). The impact of adverse health events on consumption: Understanding the mediating effect of income transfers, wealth, and health insurance. *Health Economics, 26*(12), 1743–1758. https://doi.org/10.1002/hec.3496

Bastagli, F., Hagen-Zanker, J., Harman, L., Barca, V., Sturge, G., and Schmidt, T. (2019). The impact of cash transfers: A review of the evidence from low- and middle-income countries. *Journal of Social Policy, 48*(3), 569–594. http://dx.doi.org/10.1017/S0047279418000715

Bird, R., and Smart, M. (2016). Taxing consumption in Canada: Rates, revenues, and redistribution. *Canadian Tax Journal, 64*(2), 417–420.

Bricker, J., Henriques, A., Krimmel, J., and Sabelhaus, J. (2016). Measuring income and wealth at the top using administrative and survey data. *Brookings Papers on Economic Activity, 2016*(1), 261–331. https://doi.org/10.1353/eca.2016.0016

Caminada, K., Goudswaard, K., and Wang, C. (2012). *Disentangling income inequality and the redistributive effect of taxes and transfers in 20 LIS countries over time* (MPRA Working Paper No. 42350). Luxembourg Income Study Data Center.

Chen, S. H. (2020). Inequality-growth nexus under progressive income taxation. *Journal of Macroeconomics, 65*, 103, 234. https://doi.org/10.1016/j.jmacro.2020.103234

Chincarini, L. B., and Kim, D. (2001). The advantages of tax-managed investing. *The Journal of Portfolio Management, 28*(1), 56–72.

Clementi, F., Gallegati, M., and Kaniadakis, G. (2010). A model of personal income distribution with application to Italian data. *Empirical Economics*, *39*(2), 559–591.

D'Ambrosio, C., Jäntti, M., and Lepinteur, A. (2020). Money and happiness: Income, wealth and subjective well-being. *Social Indicators Research*, *148*(1), 47–66.

Diamond, P., and Saez, E. (2011). The case for a progressive tax: From basic research to policy recommendations. *Journal of Economic Perspectives*, *25*(4), 165–190.

García-Miralles, E., Guner, N., and Ramos, R. (2019). The Spanish personal income tax: Facts and parametric estimates. *Journal of the Spanish Economic Association*, *10*(3), 439–477. https://doi.org/10.1007/s13209-019-0197-5

Groisman, F. (2015). Social protection to the informal sector: the role of minimum wage and income transfer policies. https://doi.org/10.2139/ssrn.2665225.

Hall, R. E., and Rabushka, A. (2013). *The flat tax.* Hoover Institution Press.

He, E., Jacob, M., Vashishtha, R., and Venkatachalam, M. (2019). The effect of capital gains tax policy changes on long-term investments. https://doi.org/10.2139/ssrn.3383649

Hoynes, H. (2019). The earned income tax credit. *The Annals of the American Academy of Political and Social Science*, *686*(1), 180–203. https://doi.org/10.1177/0002716219881621

Institute for Fiscal Studies. (2011). *A retrospective evaluation of elements of the EU VAT system* (FWC No. TAXUD/2010/CC/104). https://ec.europa.eu/taxation_customs/system/files/2016-09/report_evaluation_vat.pdf

Joumard, I., Pisu, M., and Bloch, D. (2013). Tackling income inequality: The role of taxes and transfers. *OECD Journal: Economic Studies*, *2012*(1), 37–70. https://doi.org/10.1787/eco_surveys-col-2013-4-en

Kendall, G. E., Nguyen, H., and Ong, R. (2019). The association between income, wealth, economic security perception, and health: A longitudinal Australian study. *Health Sociology Review*, *28*(1), 20–38. https://doi.org/10.1080/14461242.2018.1530574

Kuhn, M., and Ríos-Rull, J. V. (2016). 2013 Update on the US earnings, income, and wealth distributional facts: A view from macroeconomics. *Federal Reserve Bank of Minneapolis Quarterly Review*, *37*(1), 2–73. https://doi.org/10.21034/qr.3711

Leahy, E., Lyons, S., and Tol, R. S. (2011). The distributional effects of value added tax in Ireland. *The Economic and Social Review*, *42*(2), 213–235.

McClelland, R. (2017). *Capital gains.* Tax Policy Center. https://www.taxpolicycenter.org/publications/capital-gains

Metcalf, G. (1994). Life cycle versus annual perspectives on the incidence of a value added tax. *Tax Policy and the Economy*, *8*, 45–64.

O'Donoghue, C., Baldini, M., and Mantovani, D. (2004). *Modelling the redistributive impact of indirect taxes in Europe: An application of EUROMOD* (EUROMOD Working Paper No. EM7/01). Institute for Social and Economic Research.

Organisation for Economic Co-operation and Development (OECD). (2021). *Inheritance taxation in OECD countries.* https://doi.org/10.1787/e2879a7d-en

Oh, J. S. (2017). Are progressive tax rates progressive policy? *New York University Law Review*, *92*, 1, 909.

Rothwell, D. W., Giordono, L. S., and Robson, J. (2020). Public income transfers and wealth accumulation at the bottom: Within and between country differences in Canada and the United States. *Social Policy & Administration*, *54*(6), 914–932.

Ruiz, N., and Trannoy, A. (2008). Le caractère régressif des taxes indirectes: Les enseignements d'un modèle de microsimulation [The regressive nature of indirect taxes: Lessons from a micro simulation model]. *Economie et Statistique, 413*(1), 21–46.

Saez, E., and Zucman, G. (2020). The rise of income and wealth inequality in America: Evidence from distributional macroeconomic accounts. *Journal of Economic Perspectives*, *34*(4), 3–26. https://doi.org/10.1257/jep.34.4.3

Shum, C., Fay, J., and Lui, M. C. (2017). Worldwide or territorial approach for individual income tax: Which is more prevalent? *Journal of Modern Accounting and Auditing, 13*(4), 137–151.

Sircar, N. R., and Friedman, E. A. (2018). Financial security and public health: How basic income & cash transfers can promote health. *Global Public Health*, *13*(12), 1878–1888.

Thomas, A. (2020). *Reassessing the regressivity of the VAT* (OECD Working Papers No. 49). Organisation for Economic Co-operation and Development.

Vadlamudi, H., and Bouchey, P. (2014). Is smart beta still smart after taxes? *The Journal of Portfolio Management, 40*(4), 123–134.

Cliff A. Robb

# 13 The Use of Credit in the Consumer Marketplace

**Abstract:** Credit is an essential part of the economic system for American households, as the vast majority of consumers utilize at least some form of credit during their lifetime. Whereas nearly all credit borrowed by consumers is mortgage credit, consumers are increasingly utilizing a variety of other credit products. Aggregate dollars borrowed among products such as auto loans, credit cards, and student loans have grown significantly in the last decade with trillions borrowed. Expanded access to credit presents both challenges and opportunities. Credit may be an effective tool for wealth generation, but in turn, credit might also hinder financial growth and limit opportunities. Despite general trends towards greater access, there remain many inequalities in the credit system, particularly in the United States. Access to fair and reasonable credit is a challenge for many households and an increasing number of consumers are taking on debt that does not ultimately serve to assist in their household's long-term economic growth.

**Keywords:** credit cards, student loans, well-being, inequality

## Introduction

As shown in Figure 13.1, consumer credit has become a natural part of the financial order for most American households, particularly in the last four decades. In this chapter, I will endeavor to (a) explain how consumer credit became so ubiquitous and (b) provide implications about the consequences that occur when broader access to credit for individuals, households, and society occurs. This necessarily entails an understanding of the variety of different consumer credit products in the marketplace and changing trends in consumer utilization of these products. Additionally, I will address some of the fundamentals of lifecycle income management and the role of debt in a complex economy. Finally, I will delve into the role of research and policy in this space while considering the potential future of consumer credit products.

First, it is important to differentiate categories of credit that exist in the United States market. Consumer credit might best be defined as referring to "all kinds of credit employed by individuals that are not collateralized by real estate . . . or by specific financial assets such as stocks and bonds and that are not used for business

**Cliff A. Robb,** University of Wisconsin, Madison

https://doi.org/10.1515/9783110727692-013

**Trillions of Dollars**

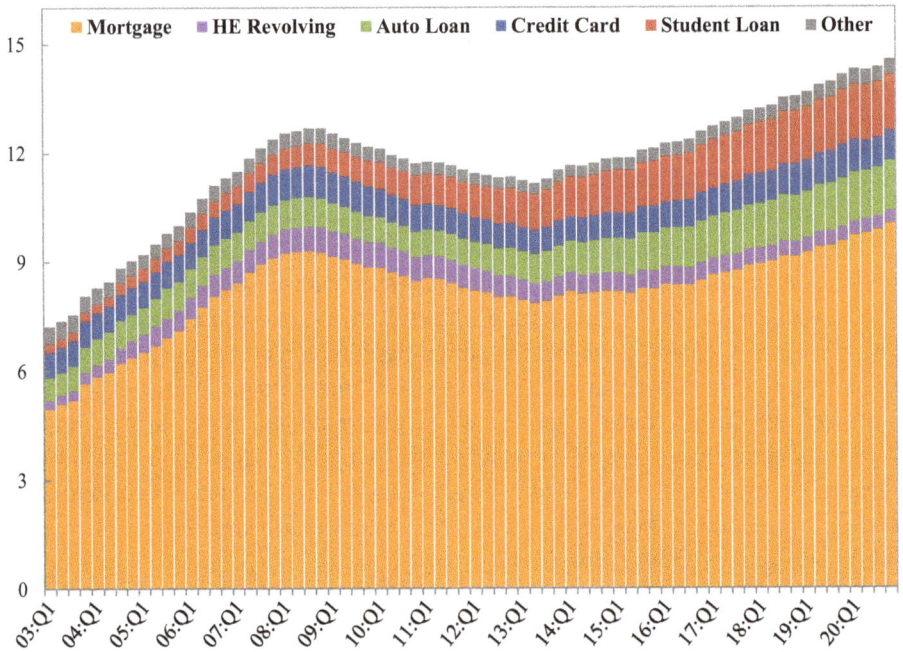

**Figure 13.1:** Total Debt Balance and Its Composition in the United States.
*Source*: New York Fed Consumer Credit Panel/Equifax (2021).

purposes" (Durkin et al., 2014, p. 2). Whereas this definition explicitly excludes mortgage debt, this distinction of consumer credit still leaves a broad array of products (including auto loans, credit cards, and student loans). Each of these products has unique characteristics and can be analyzed in turn. If one considers total household debt (mortgages included), household debt reached an all-time high at more than $14.5 trillion in the United States in 2019–2020 (Federal Reserve Bank of New York (FRB NY), 2020). A significant majority of this debt is mortgage debt (roughly two-thirds). As noted in the debt definition above, the focus of this chapter lies in that remaining one-third of consumer debt, which is composed of a variety of product types. After mortgage loans, student loan debt and auto loans make up the largest shares of consumer debt, with credit cards a not-so-distant third among the consumer credit categories (see Figure 13.1). These figures represent a significant shift in consumer debt holdings over the last decade, as student loan debt has doubled since 2009, to reach an approximate high of $1.5 trillion. In the next section of this chapter, I will explore the history of consumer credit, with a particular emphasis on more recent changes in the United States.

# Historical Perspective

There are a number of excellent overviews of the history of consumer credit that provide a deeper dive than would be possible in a single chapter. If readers are so inclined, I would recommend the book *Consumer Credit and the American Economy* by Durkin et al. (2014). If one is seeking a more comprehensive review of the consumer finance marketplace in the United States, Ryan et al. (2011) is another helpful resource. Like Ryan et al., I will focus on the dramatic changes in the United States consumer marketplace that preceded World War II. Prior to the Second World War, there was a robust market for mortgage and auto financing. However, it is really in the post-Second World War era that saw a dramatic growth in new forms of unsecured installment and revolving loans, including student loans, payday loans, credit cards, and bank lines of credit. Whereas retailers largely pioneered the use of revolving credit in the United States prior to the Second World War, the post-war era saw a massive spike in these offerings with bank credit cards emerging as a general use product over the 1950s and 1960s. This era in consumer finance in the United States was truly transformative, as an increasing number of product options became available to consumers.

This rapid product innovation was driven by numerous factors, including consumer demand, increases in disposable income, and changing policy structures. The trend toward greater inclusion was a major positive of the post-war era. However, it is important to acknowledge that these changes introduced new challenges as well. Emphasis was increasingly placed on consumers' ability to make choices in this complex marketplace. As a result, greater choice on the part of consumers not only created opportunities for consumers to select the exact products that could meet their needs, but it also introduced new risks associated with mistakes or poor decisions by those same consumers. This era saw a significant shift in risk, as consumers took on greater responsibility for their own financial success. This shift can be seen in multiple dimensions of the financial marketplace, including changes to the retirement system. As Ryan et al. (2011) aptly noted, "This risk-taking, enabled by an increase in personal decision making and a growth in the complexity and flexibility of financial options, was not matched by a commensurate rise either in financial capabilities of consumers or in financial advice provided by third parties" (p. 462). The market was creating new opportunities for consumers, but those consumers were not necessarily better equipped, compared to prior generations, to effectively maneuver in this new complex environment.

Building off of the momentum in the 1960s and 1970s, the 1980s and 1990s saw a more rapid expansion of credit card ownership among consumers as companies sought to expand market share. This expansion was further facilitated by key legislative decisions that not only made lending more lucrative for companies but also relaxed lending standards (Garcia, 2007). As a result, credit was more accessible than ever to a broader group of Americans. Recent data suggest that from 70 percent to 80 percent of Americans now have at least one credit card (FRB NY, 2020; Foster et al.,

2019). This is significantly higher than the estimated 50 percent of Americans who had at least one card in 1970 or the estimated 65 percent who held cards in the early 1980s (Castranova and Hagstrom, 2004; Durkin, 2000). Further, ownership rates vary significantly by income, education, and race/ethnicity (FRB NY, 2020). Whereas ownership rates were approximately 69 percent for those with a high-school degree or less in 2018, 95 percent of Americans with a bachelor's degree or more reported holding at least one card (FRB NY, 2020). Among cardholders, revolving behavior has become increasingly common, as only 47 percent of Americans in 2018 noted that they always pay their card in full each month (FRB NY, 2020).

If one focuses on the growth of the consumer credit market in the 1990s and early 2000s, one method of expansion that became increasingly common was marketing to young adults, with a significant emphasis on marketing to college students (Manning and Kirshak, 2005; Nellie, 2002). During the 1990s, ownership rates among undergraduate students grew from roughly 54 percent to about 83 percent (Nellie, 2002). This dramatic shift in credit card ownership among young adults, and subsequent studies on increasing debt holdings, led to more restrictive policies. The Credit Card Accountability Responsibility and Disclosure (CARD) Act of 2009 was specifically designed to limit the marketing of credit cards to young adults, though it did not completely remove credit cards as an option. Whereas the CARD Act served to reduce ownership of credit cards among undergraduates, it is important to recognize that student financial needs did not change as a result, nor did costs of education decline.

Growing costs of higher education have been a significant factor in rising consumer debt over the past two decades, specifically in the area of student loan debt. As noted in the introduction to this chapter, student loan debt is the largest category of consumer debt in terms of magnitude and is the second-largest category of household debt overall when accounting for mortgage debt in the United States. College costs have consistently risen over the last three decades, as average costs for public four-year institutions have tripled, whereas private four-year institutions have more than doubled (Ma et al., 2020). More than half (54 percent) of students reported taking on debt to pay for their education. Overall student loan debt topped $1.6 trillion in 2020 (FRB NY, 2020). As a result of this growth, the overall debt make-up for the average household in the United States is changing, with young adults carrying larger student loan debt balances in lieu of a mix of different debt types.

In recent years, there have been significant increases in non-loan debt that often comes from medical bills, utilities, and other overdue bills. This debt can be generated through income shocks and emergencies. It may also be the result of a household simply struggling to make ends meet over a lengthier period of time. This is in stark contrast to debt that might be taken on for the purchase of an asset or for the development of human capital. As noted in a report by Stark (2018), medical expense shocks are becoming increasingly common. Roughly a quarter of households headed by an adult under the age of 65 years in the United States had some medical debt in 2015 (Karpman and Caswell, 2017). This trend highlights some of the challenges consumers are facing, as debt might increasingly be required for a number of households without providing the potential for growing wealth or improving long-run financial security.

# Research and Policy Issues

## Consumer Credit and the Life Cycle

To best understand decisions around consumer credit, one can first consider theories of consumption and conceptualize borrowing decisions in more detail. One of the key advantages that credit markets offer consumers is the ability to shift resources from one point in time to another. The Life-Cycle Income Hypothesis (LCIH) assumes a general desire for consumption smoothing among consumers (Ando and Modigliani, 1963). Under this framework, consumers are faced with an uneven stream of lifetime income that can be smoothed through the use of capital markets. In effect, individuals can borrow at younger ages when earnings are relatively low and pay back these loans during their peak earning years. Income growth over time can facilitate not only this repayment of previously borrowed funds but also support saving for future needs. Money that is saved during periods of higher earnings can then be utilized in retirement when income is greatly reduced.

Whereas the LCIH serves to provide reasoning for why borrowing might be rational, it is generally agnostic in regards to the method of borrowing or the product being used. Borrowing decisions can be conceptualized as a multi-step process. First, consumers must consider whether or not they are willing to borrow to achieve some goal or to make a purchase. Once the decision to borrow has been made, consumers have to consider options related to products or rates available. Ultimately, a rational decision maker should seek to maximize utility, balancing the marginal costs of any borrowing decision with the marginal benefits. Despite the intuitive appeal of lifecycle income models, existing research points to a number of inefficiencies and potential issues in terms of real-world debt-management decisions. The LCIH generally assumes access to fair credit based on financial factors like income and a credit score. In reality, a number of non-financial factors, including race and ethnicity, play a role in credit access and serve to create an unleveled playing field. Additional evidence suggests that older Americans are carrying more debt into retirement and that a greater number of households are facing greater income volatility, which makes income smoothing more difficult (Pew Charitable Trusts, 2015; Seefeldt, 2015). This income volatility is exacerbated by the general macroeconomic trend of stagnant wages among lower- to middle-income Americans since the global financial crisis. From 2000 to 2018, the average annual rate of income growth was a mere 0.3 percent, and inequalities in income growth between the top 10 percent of earners and the bottom 90 percent grew significantly during this period (Horowitz et al., 2020).

## Borrowing Decisions: Macro and Micro Considerations

If one looks at the past decade, saving and borrowing decisions have taken place in a relatively low-interest-rate environment, with the effective federal funds rate staying at or below about 2.5 percent since the global financial crisis (FRB Saint Louis, 2021a). Independent of any other economic factors, such an environment certainly encourages borrowing and discourages saving. If one considers recent trends, the personal savings rate in the United States was relatively stagnant from 2000 to 2018, rarely exceeding 10 percent, and often hovering at about 5 percent or lower (FRB Saint Louis, 2021b). During this same time frame, if we consider consumer debt as a broad category, aggregate balances have grown significantly since (particularly since the Great Recession of 2009). Whereas 2020 saw a slight decline in credit card debt as compared to 2019, both student loans and auto loans have maintained strong growth. Notably, there has been a recent trend of mortgage debt declining as a share of overall household debt.

At roughly $4 trillion, consumer credit accounts for a significant portion of total household debt in the market. Whether or not this growing debt is a serious problem is a topic of debate among researchers and policymakers. It is broadly recognized that consumer credit offers real opportunities to individuals and can support economic growth. The existence of credit markets provides consumers with greater flexibility in their consumption timing and, if used properly, can assist in wealth generation. These are positive features that should not be ignored. However, a review of the literature and examination of actual consumer interactions in the market suggest a number of problems that should be considered. Many policymakers and consumer advocates have questioned whether consumers are overly reliant on credit as a way to establish or maintain lifestyles that might be unrealistic at the cost of long-term financial security. The most recent statistics from the American Bankers Association (2021) detail some encouraging trends, as overall credit card debt was down in 2020, with only about 41 percent of accounts revolving a balance (compared to 34 percent of accounts that paid in full each month and the remaining 25 percent representing dormant accounts). If one considers active accounts only, roughly 55 percent of accounts were revolving in the third quarter of 2020 (American Bankers Association, 2021). These revolvers are of key interest due to the fact that research suggests many consumers might see the minimum payment as a signal of how much they should pay or simply adopt this amount without actively addressing the long-term costs (Keys and Wang, 2014). These sorts of anchoring or mental accounting errors can serve to exacerbate consumer debt, as expenditures may not be applied efficiently. It is common to see consumers struggle with determining which debts to prioritize and inconsistently apply payments to numerous obligations that they might face. Specifically, research has highlighted a tendency on the part of consumers who face multiple debts to focus on paying down or prioritizing smaller debts first as opposed to focusing on the highest interest debt (Amar et al., 2011; Gathergood et al., 2019).

One method of gauging overall health in the consumer credit markets is to look at default and delinquency rates. Overall, delinquency rates in the United States have fallen since the global financial crisis. The delinquency rate on all consumer loans was at a high of about 4.85 percent in the second quarter of 2009 and fell to about 1.96 percent in the fourth quarter of 2020 (FRB NY, 2021). Credit card delinquency rates demonstrated a similar pattern during this same time frame. However, delinquency rates for student loan debt were far steadier over the same period. About 11 percent of aggregate student loan debt was in delinquency or default at the end of 2019 (FRB NY, 2020).

## Market Inequalities

Many problems in consumer credit markets are a result of inefficiencies, as access to products or reasonable rates is not equal across borrowers. An analysis of borrower characteristics and differences in credit use can help shed further light on these issues. According to Stark (2018), middle-income households borrow most heavily, whereas the lowest income households have the lowest levels of borrowing. This makes reasonable sense, all things considered, but it does not necessarily tell the whole story. Significant differences exist in the types of products being used and the details of the arrangements, as lower-income borrowers are more reliant on credit cards and other high-cost unsecured loans. Beyond inequalities related to income or wealth, research has identified notable inequalities in U.S. credit markets based on age, gender, race, and ethnicity. In essence, households of color are less likely to have debt that supports wealth generation and have higher levels of higher-cost debt (Stark, 2018). Even among debt that is categorized as wealth-generating, like student loan debt, one sees concerning inequalities that demand further exploration.

Early in the 21st century, much of the concern around young adult finances, and college students in particular, was related to ownership and utilization of credit cards (Lyons, 2004; Manning and Kirshak, 2005; Robb, 2011; Robb and Sharpe, 2009). That attention has shifted dramatically to student loans in recent years, as the past decade has seen massive growth in the amount of student loan debt (and as student loan debt surpassed both credit cards and auto loans in magnitude). Student loan debt is often labeled as "good" debt and is framed as an investment in human capital since it offers consumers an opportunity to enhance their market earnings, which can be a path to wealth generation. However, rising higher education costs and a generally more stagnant wage environment have raised serious questions about the sustainability of a model that requires individuals to take on increasing levels of debt. Recent studies have highlighted the potential negative impacts of rising student loan debt. High levels of debt impact not only degree attainment, but also later financial decisions like employment, homeownership, and marriage (Addo, 2014; Bleemer et al., 2017; Robb et al., 2020).

In addition to questions regarding the long-term viability of the student loan market in the United States, serious concerns have been raised over significant inequalities within this market. For many Americans, taking on student loan debt may not sufficiently improve their economic opportunities as degree completion is not a guarantee of future success. Many students are forced to enter the labor force early; they are then saddled with significant debt burdens without the benefit of a degree. Major drivers for inequalities within the student loan market are income and race. Houle (2014) highlighted that Black students often take on more debt during school, all else being equal. Due to a heavier reliance on loans, low income and students of color often carry higher debt-to-income and debt-to-asset ratios when compared to other students (Federal Reserve Board of Governors, 2019). Houle and Addo (2019) followed debt trajectories over time, noting that student loan debt might actually serve to reinforce wealth inequalities between minority and nonminority borrowers. In effect, the burden of student loan debt may actually increase the financial fragility of middle-class minority households rather than serving to enhance wealth generation.

## Practical Applications

The previous section explored numerous micro- and macroeconomic impacts of consumer debt. Whereas these are critical aspects to consider for individuals and society as a whole, it should be acknowledged that a large balance of consumer debt is made up of millions of smaller consumer decisions. Issues such as delinquency and bankruptcy have real consequences for households and society, but it is important to not ignore subtle psychological factors. There is a rich body of research that explores aspects of subjective well-being, stress, and consumer attitudes toward debt, as all of these factors have significant implications for consumer financial markets. Earlier research noted that socioeconomic status and health are strongly related (Adler et al., 1994; Adler and Stewart, 2010), though this early work did not place any special emphasis on debt (and often focused more attention on assets and wealth overall).

A number of studies have been conducted that focus explicitly on connections between debt and psychological well-being. These studies noted that financial strain from having high levels of debt or specific negative events, like a foreclosure, are significant predictors of negative psychological outcomes like stress, depression, and other mental disorders (Brown et al., 2005; Drentea and Reynolds, 2012; Jenkins et al., 2008; McLaughlin et al., 2012). These findings have prompted researchers to consider that debt and financial hardship might have an impact on physical health as well. A study by Sweet et al. (2013) evaluated a sample of 8,400 young adults and noted that higher debt-to-asset ratios were associated with higher self-reported stress, lower self-reported health, and higher diastolic blood pressure. Richardson et al. (2013) conducted a meta-analysis of the literature on health and financial status (over 50 studies), noting that a vast majority of the studies (80 percent) indicated that holding higher debt amounts was associated with poorer health. Similar connections were noted between debt and mental health, indicating a fairly consistent negative association between debt and well-being. Greenberg and Mogilner (2020) looked at several types of debt, noting that life satisfaction was usually lower for those debts that consumers mentally viewed as "debt." Interestingly, survey respondents were less likely to view mortgage and credit card debt as a negative, whereas student loan debt was significantly associated with lower life satisfaction. Other recent studies have indicated similar findings related to the impact of student loan debt on health and well-being (e.g., Poplaski et al., 2019). As a whole, this research raises broader questions about the impact of consumer credit use on health and well-being.

These findings that highlight the importance of consumer perceptions of debt have practical implications. Financial planners and financial counselors who are trying to help people manage money effectively might consider adopting clear strategies for demonstrating what healthy borrowing habits might look like. Particular emphasis can be placed on discussing which debts tend to support long-term growth and why. In many circumstances, there may be a strong disconnect between objective financial status and consumers' stress or psychological state. Some consumers with healthy debt mixes might feel unnecessarily high levels of guilt or anxiety, whereas other consumers who are in much poorer financial health may not recognize the warning signs or potential long-term implications of their present behavior. As noted above, consumers today have access to a wide array of products, and understanding how well they actually understand these products or the decisions they are making is paramount.

## Future Directions

All signs point to the marketplace for consumer debt remaining fairly open and one is likely to see continued growth in terms of the sophistication and selection of products. Although there have been encouraging trends in the use of credit cards, with notable declines in the aggregate revolving amount in 2020, utilization of other forms of credit like student loans continues to grow.

At the present time, it is difficult to know what sort of lasting impact Covid-19, and the resulting worldwide pandemic, might have on consumer credit and the overall financial stability of households. Many consumers are currently able to take advantage of extended forbearance windows on their student loans and mortgage payments. What is unclear, however, is how different households will manage once these forgiveness periods time out. It is likely that many households will face a much slower recovery than others in terms of financial security, and one might see Covid-19 further exacerbate differences in household financial security. Indeed, Covid-19 has shed further light on many of the existing inequalities in the U.S. financial system, and these inequalities should be an area of research emphasis for the future. A lack of equal access to fair credit is a major issue at the present time, and this impacts minority and lower-income consumers most significantly. If these households continue to have limited access to lower-cost credit, the wealth gap in the United States will likely continue to grow.

It remains unclear whether there will be any concerted effort to change the current financing model for higher education expenses. Discussions concerning student loan debt relief highlight the challenges that so many young adults face in choosing to pursue higher education. Whereas supporters of debt relief see immediate benefits to millions of Americans, opponents suggest that such a forgiveness program would disproportionately support middle-upper income Americans, with the same problem existing for the next batch of college students who are currently enrolled. Even if some form of relief is enacted, whether it be complete forgiveness of existing federal student loan debt, or some lesser amount of debt relief, it would not change the fundamental issue of affordability.

## Conclusion

The consumer credit marketplace has evolved significantly over the last several decades. In general, the most consistent trend has been increasing indebtedness across households, although the mix of credit utilized varies significantly based on age, income level, and race/ethnicity. Increased utilization of credit is not problematic in and of itself; however, there are certainly some concerning factors to consider when looking at the current marketplace. First, numerous inequalities can be observed, highlighting a flawed system that could clearly be more effective. Credit markets certainly reach more consumers than they did several decades ago, but not all Americans are equally served by this expansion. Second, many Americans appear to be taking on debt that does not ultimately serve to assist them in generating long-term wealth. This can be seen in the utilization of student loans at for-profit education institutions, excessive borrowing at non-profit institutions, or for degrees that are not completed. It is also apparent from trends in indebtedness based on consumption smoothing that is not necessarily part of an asset acquisition or human capital development. This includes a variety of individuals, including those struggling to meet their regular payments, or responding to income shocks like a major medical expense. In order for consumer credit markets to serve a greater number of Americans more effectively, these systemic problems will need to be addressed in some form. There is little doubt that credit will continue to be an essential tool for economic growth for many households, but ensuring that U.S. households have equal access and opportunity in credit markets must be a central goal of policy and market innovations.

# References

Addo, F. R. (2014). Debt, cohabitation, and marriage in young adulthood. *Demography, 51*, 1677–1701.

Adler, N. E., Boyce, T., Chesney, M. A., Cohen, S., Folkman, S., Kahn, R. L., and Syme, S. L. (1994). Socioeconomic status and health: The challenge of the gradient. *American Psychologist, 49*(1), 15–24.

Adler, N. E., and Stewart, J. (2010). Health disparities across the lifespan: Meaning, methods, and mechanisms. *Annals of the New York Academy of Sciences*, 1,186, 5–23.

Amar, M., Ariely, D., Ayal, S., Cryder, C. E., and Rick, S. I. (2011). Winning the battle but losing the war: The psychology of debt management. *Journal of Marketing Research*, 48, S38–S50.

American Bankers Association (2021). *Credit card market monitor.* https://www.aba.com/news-research/research-analysis/credit-card-market-monitor

Ando, A., and Modigliani, F. (1963). The "life-cycle" hypothesis of saving: Aggregate implications and tests. *American Economic Review, 53*(1), 55–84.

Bleemer, Z., Brown, M., Lee, D., Strair, K., and van der Klaauw, W. (2017). *Echoes of rising tuition in students' borrowing, educational attainment, and homeownership in post- recession America* (Staff Reports No. 820). Federal Reserve Bank of New York. https://www.newyorkfed.org/medialibrary/media/research/staff_reports/sr820.pdf?la=en

Brown, S., Taylor, K., and Price, S. W. (2005). Debt and distress: Evaluating the psychological cost of credit. *Journal of Economic Psychology, 26*, 642–663.

Castranova, E., and Hagstrom, P. (2004). The demand for credit cards: Evidence from the survey of consumer finances. *Economic Inquiry, 42*(2), 304–318.

Drentea, P., and Reynolds, J. R. (2012). Neither a borrower nor a lender be: The relative importance of debt and SES for mental health among older adults. *Journal of Aging and Health, 24*(4), 673–695.

Durkin, T. A. (2000). Credit cards: Use and consumer attitudes, *1970–2000. Federal Reserve Bulletin.* 623–634. https://www.federalreserve.gov/pubs/bulletin/2000/0900lead.pdf

Durkin, T. A., Elliehausen, G., Staten, M. E., and Zywicki, T. J. (2014). *Consumer credit and the American economy.* Oxford University Press.

Federal Reserve Bank of New York (FRB NY). (2020). *Quarterly report on household debt and credit.* https://www.newyorkfed.org/medialibrary/interactives/householdcredit/data/pdf/HHDC_2020Q3.pdf

Federal Reserve Bank of New York (FRB NY). (2021). *Delinquency rate on consumer loans, all commercial banks.* https://fred.stlouisfed.org/series/DRCLACBS

Federal Reserve Bank of Saint Louis (FRB Saint Louis). (2021a). *Effective federal funds rate.* https://fred.stlouisfed.org/series/FEDFUNDS

Federal Reserve Bank of Saint Louis (FRB Saint Louis). (2021b). *Personal savings rate.* https://fred.stlouisfed.org/series/PSAVERT

Federal Reserve Board of Governors. (2019). *Report on the economic well-being of U.S. households in 2018.* https://www.federalreserve.gov/publications/files/2018-report-economic-well-being-us-households-201905.pdf

Foster, K., Greene, C., and Stavins, J. (2019). *The 2018 survey of consumer payment choice: Summary results* (Research Report No. 19–02). Federal Reserve Bank of Atlanta. https://www.frbatlanta.org/-/media/documents/banking/consumer-payments/survey-of-consumer-payment-choice/2018/2018-survey-of-consumer-payment-choice.pdf

Garcia J. (2007, November 7). Borrowing to make ends meet: The rapid growth of credit card debt in America. *Demos*. https://www.demos.org/research/borrowing-make-ends-meet-rapid-growth-credit-card-debt-america

Gathergood, J., Mahoney, N., Stewart, N., and Weber, J. (2019). How do individuals repay their debt? The balance-matching heuristic. *American Economic Review, 109*(3), 844–875.

Greenberg, A. E., and Mogilner, C. (2020). Consumer debt and satisfaction in life. *Journal of Experimental Psychology: Applied*. https://doi.org/10.1037/xap0000276

Horowitz, J. M., Igielnik, R., and Kochhar, R. (2020). *Trends in wealth inequality*. The Pew Research Center. https://www.pewresearch.org/social-trends/2020/01/09/trends-in-income-and-wealth-inequality/

Houle, J. N. (2014). A Generation indebted: Young adult debt across three cohorts. *Social Problems, 61*(3), 448–465.

Houle, J. N., and Addo, F. R. (2019). Racial disparities in student debt and the reproduction of the fragile black middle class. *Sociology of Race and Ethnicity, 5*(4), 562–577.

Jenkins. R., Bhugra. D., Bebbington. P., Brugha, T., Farrell, M., Coid, J., Fryers, T., Weich, S., Singleton, N., and Meltzer, H. (2008). Debt, income and mental disorder in the general population. *Psychological Medicine, 38*(10), 1,485–1,493.

Karpman, M., and Caswell, K. (2017). Past-due medical debt among nonelderly adults, 2012–15. *Urban Institute*. http://www.urban.org/sites/default/files/publication/88586/past_due_medical_debt.pdf

Keys, B., and Wang, J. (2014). *Perverse nudges: Minimum payments and debt paydown in consumer credit cards*. University of Chicago Press. https://www.economicdynamics.org/meetpapers/2014/paper_323.pdf

Lyons, A. C. (2004). A profile of financially at-risk college students. *Journal of Consumer Affairs, 38*(1), 56–80.

Ma, J., Pender, M., and Libassi, C. J. (2020). *Trends in college pricing and student aid 2020*. College Board. https://research.collegeboard.org/pdf/trends-college-pricing-student-aid-2020.pdf

Manning, R. D., and Kirshak, R. (2005). Credit cards on campus: Academic inquiry, objective empiricism, or advocacy research? *Journal of Student Financial Aid, 35*(1), 39–48.

McLaughlin, K. A., Nandi, A., Keyes, K. M., Uddin, M., Aiello, A. E., Galea, S., and Koenen, K. C. (2012). Home foreclosure and risk of psychiatric morbidity during the recent financial crisis. *Psychological Medicine, 42*(7), 1441–1448.

Nellie, M. (2002). *Undergraduate students and credit cards: An analysis of usage rates and trends*. Nellie Mae. http://www.nelliemae.com/library/research.html

Pew Charitable Trusts. (2015). *The complex story of American debt: Liabilities in family balance sheets*. https://www.pewtrusts.org/~/media/assets/2015/07/reach-of-debt-report_artfinal.pdf.

Poplaski, S., Kemnitz, R., and Robb, C. A. (2019). Investing in education: Impact of student financial stress on self-reported health. *Journal of Student Financial Aid, 48*(2), Article 3.

Richardson, T., Elliott, P., and Roberts, R. (2013). The relationship between personal unsecured debt and mental and physical health: A systematic review and meta-analysis. *Clinical Psychology Review, 33*(8), 1148–1162.

Robb, C. A. (2011). Financial knowledge and credit card behavior of college students. *Journal of Family and Economic Issues, 32*(4), 690–698.

Robb, C. A., Schreiber, S. L., and Heckman, S. J. (2020). The role of federal and private student loans in homeownership decisions. *Journal of Consumer Affairs, 54*(1), 43–69.

Robb, C. A., and Sharpe, D. L. (2009). Effect of personal financial knowledge on college students' credit card behavior. *Journal of Financial Counseling and Planning*, *20*(1), 25–43.

Ryan, A., Trumbull, G., and Tufano, P. (2011). A brief postwar history of U.S. consumer finance. *The Business History Review*, *85*(3), 461–498.

Seefeldt, K. (2015). Constant consumption smoothing, limited investment, and few repayments: The role of debt in the financial lives of economically vulnerable families. *Social Service Review*, *89*(2), 263–300.

Stark, E. (2018). *Expanding retirement security through public and private innovation*. Aspen Institute Financial Security Program. https://assets.aspeninstitute.org/content/uploads/2018/08/2018_RetirementSavingsReport.pdf.

Sweet, E., Nandi, A., Adam, E., and McDade, T. (2013). The high price of debt: Household financial debt and its impact on mental and physical health. *Social Science & Medicine*, *91*, 94–100.

Martin C. Seay, Derek J. Sensenig

# 14 Debt and Mortgage Choices

**Abstract:** The home is unique within a household's financial portfolio, generally representing its largest asset, as well as its largest monthly expense. Most homes are purchased using a mortgage, a financial product that has increased in complexity over the last several decades. Given the long-term implications of a mortgage on a household's cash flow and balance sheet, the borrowing decision becomes one of the most critical and complex financial decisions a household will make. Evaluating a mortgage requires an individual to simultaneously weigh economic factors, individual preferences, and an often uncertain time frame. This is complicated by variations in loan types, loan amounts available, financing costs, and ongoing shifts in the ways homeowners live their lives. Historically, people lived in the same house for much of their adult lives; however, in modern times, housing tenures have shortened in response to a more mobile work population and an increased preference to purchase multiple homes to match income over the work life. Consequently, the homeownership decision is one of the most important determinations that a household can make, with the potential to provide long-term benefits to overall financial well-being. However, sub-optimal purchase decisions can lead to significant negative long-term effects both financially and psychologically.

**Keywords:** homeownership, mortgage choice, financial literacy, financial well-being

## Introduction

This chapter provides an overview of the role of homeownership in society,[1] how mortgages have evolved over time, and current theory and research into how borrowers make mortgage decisions. The chapter also provides insights into how financial planners, financial, real estate and mortgage advisors, academics, and government policy can influence optimal mortgage decisions, within the context of individuals' own preferences and financial situations.

Homeownership has been a fundamental tenet of the American Dream for generations (Rohe and Watson, 2007). As Americans recovered from the aftermath of the Great Depression, the federal government began to play a more significant role in developing strategies to support homeownership (Rubinowitz and Trosman, 1979).

---

[1] While the examples used in this chapter involve U.S. and Canadian households, the underlying concepts presented in the chapter apply broadly across regions and countries.

---

**Martin C. Seay, Derek J. Sensenig,** Kansas State University

https://doi.org/10.1515/9783110727692-014

Beginning with the charter of the Federal National Mortgage Association, or Fannie Mae, various mortgage options were developed to provide access to affordable housing (Allen et al., 2012). For many Americans, homeownership represents a household's largest asset, as well as the largest recurring expense (Maroto and Aylsworth, 2017; Nau and Tumin, 2012; Spilerman, 2000). While the mortgage payment itself is usually the most substantial part of this expense, additional expenses may include taxes, insurance, homeowner's association dues, repairs, maintenance, and more.

Given the large role that homeownership plays within a household's financial portfolio, understanding how home purchase decisions are made is increasingly important. The home purchase decision is rather complex, as a wide range of intertemporal factors needs to be considered. Further, due to the relative size of mortgage payments, embedded in the home purchase decision are significant long-term implications on financial well-being and the ability to accomplish other financial goals. Owning a home has traditionally been viewed as a conservative investment; however, the prevalent use of mortgages can create a highly leveraged asset. For example, consider a home purchased for $200,000 with a 20 percent down payment. A subsequent 1 percent increase or decrease in home value is the equivalent of a 5 percent return or loss on the investment. If purchased with a 5 percent down payment, this 1 percent change in home value is equivalent to a 20 percent return or loss on the investment.

Another important consideration is the changing way Americans use their homes. Historically, Americans remained in the same home for their adult life, mortgages were held to maturity, and, most often, paid off prior to retirement. The long-time horizon served to mitigate many of the risks associated with the use of mortgages and negate the impact of short-term market fluctuations. However, societal norms have changed, with increased job mobility and the practice of upgrading homes to match income over the life course becoming prominent. These factors have significantly decreased the average time a home is owned, as well as increasing the proportion of income that is spent on housing.

Moreover, Americans historically have sought to retire debt-free with their mortgages paid off (Rose, 2013). This has proven increasingly challenging based on shifting lifestyles, with overall debt loads increasing rapidly (Lusardi and Mitchell, 2013). The prevalence of mortgages in retirement is challenging for two reasons. From a balance sheet perspective, home equity has historically been viewed as a form of insurance to offset unaccounted for living and health expenses (Munnell et al., 2007). Without this reserve, homeowners are more vulnerable to economic shocks. From a cash flow perspective, the presence of mortgage payments increases the amount of money required at retirement and puts consistent pressure on living expenses. In the 2020 Retirement Confidence Survey, only 27 percent of workers reported that they were very confident in their ability to retire comfortably and 58 percent of workers and 42 percent of retirees stated that debt was a problem in their situation (Employee Benefit Research

Institute, 2020). All of these factors combine to highlight the importance of home-purchase and mortgage decisions on a household's financial well-being.

# Historical Perspective

Homeownership in the United States has been significantly influenced by federal housing policy, particularly as it relates to mortgage requirements (Rubinowitz and Trosman, 1979). Prior to the Great Depression, mortgage repayment schedules typically ranged from five to ten years, with a large balloon payment at the end of that period (DeRitis, 2013). In 1934, the Federal Housing Administration (FHA) was created and expanded how a mortgage could be used. Standard mortgages expanded to include a 20-year repayment period, a 20 percent down-payment, and a maximum loan amount of $16,000. Since then, primary mortgage choices have expanded to include multiple variations of fixed-rate mortgages (FRMs), adjustable-rate mortgages (ARMs), and interest-only mortgages. In recent times, the 30-year fixed-rate mortgage has become the dominant loan type (Lea and Sanders, 2011).

Qualification for a mortgage is largely based on three factors: (a) credit score, (b) the debt-to-income ratio, and (c) down payment. A credit score is a communication of creditworthiness to the mortgage originator, signals the borrower's historical quality of debt repayment, and quantifies the risk associated with mortgage repayment (Avery et al., 1996). It is a key component of the securitization of mortgage-backed securities (MBS) and corresponds to the quality and default risk within the security (Heuson et al., 2001). The credit score is a primary determinant of the mortgage interest rate and conventional mortgage underwriters prefer a credit score of 740 and require a minimum of 680 (Rose, 2011). The debt-to-income ratio is another metric used by loan originators to determine the applicant's ability to repay and the interest rate. This ratio measures the applicant's financial liquidity and ability to handle its other obligations alongside mortgage payments, with banks requiring ratios below 36 percent to 45 percent (Johnson and Li, 2010; Rose, 2011).

The down payment has a multi-faceted purpose in the underwriting process. Conventional lenders typically require a down payment of 5 percent of the home's value, with certain types of loans permitting lower levels. This down payment is used to determine the homeowner's initial loan-to-value (LTV) ratio. Historically, a 20 percent down payment has been used as the gold standard, providing an initial LTV of 80 percent. For homes with LTV's greater than 80 percent, Primary Mortgage Insurance (PMI) is required and is paid by the borrower and protects the lender in the case the borrower quits making mortgage payments. PMI costs about 0.5 percent to 2 percent of the total outstanding balance, typically covers the first 20 percent to 30 percent of the loan balance while the physical home stands good for the remaining portion. It is retained for about five years on average (Johnstone, 2004) and can be removed once a borrower achieves an LTV of 80 percent. To avoid PMI, mortgage companies may offer a piggy-back loan at a higher interest rate (Chambers et al., 2008).

FRMs are characterized by a set monthly payment, with the mortgage being fully paid off at the end of the loan term, most often 15 or 30 years. ARMs also are fully paid off at the termination of the loan; however, mortgage payments vary based on changes in interest rates. While consumers will see lower payments if interest rates decline, they similarly may be subject to increased payments if interest rates rise. To limit the effect of drastic changes in interest rates, ARM payments adjust on a set schedule, with both period and lifetime caps on how much the rate can vary. Interest-only mortgages typically have short durations and are non-amortizing loans. This feature is critically important, as payments only cover the costs of interest accrued, leading to much lower monthly payments but no principal reduction. At the end of the loan term, the full balance of the loan is due, often referred to as a balloon payment.

In addition to the growth in types of mortgages, there has been significant variation in the quality of loans offered. Subprime mortgages, which rose to popularity in the early 2000s, provide loan options to those who may not otherwise qualify, but with less favorable terms. Subprime mortgages are characterized by having lower credit standards, a high loan-to-value ratio, and minimal documentation for qualification (Demyanyk and Van Hemert, 2011). While offering mortgages to those who may not otherwise qualify, these loans have seen significantly higher default rates. For example, subprime loans accounted for 18.7 percent of mortgages in 2002 (Sherlund, 2011) and by 2006 represented more than 60 percent of all foreclosures (Immergluck, 2008). The reduction of underwriting standards resulted in a rapid expansion of mortgage debt, significantly increasing the likelihood of default, and played a significant part in the global financial crisis (Chomsisengphet and Pennington-Cross, 2006; Foote et al., 2021).

While primary mortgages allow for the purchase of homes, secondary mortgages are designed to allow Americans to access their home equity. The two most common secondary mortgages are the home equity line of credit (HELOC) and the home equity conversion mortgage (HECM). A HELOC is a loan that allows a homeowner to borrow against the value of their home as needed, often to pay more costs associated with education, home improvements, weddings, or medical bills. Typically, borrowers can draw money as needed, with the payment amount determined by the current balance of the loan. HELOCs use the home as collateral, meaning foreclosure may be required if payments are not made. A similar type of loan is an HECM, which is commonly referred to as a reverse mortgage, which can be used by an older homeowner to access home equity during retirement without having to risk losing their home (Carswell et al., 2013; Nakajima and Telyukova, 2017). While HELOCs require recurring payments based on principal borrowed, reverse mortgages do not typically require active repayment if the homeowner is alive and living in the residence. To qualify for a reverse mortgage, a borrower must be at least 62 years of age, live in the home as a primary residence, have significant home equity, and complete approved counseling.

# Research and Policy Issues

There are several key themes in research into debt and mortgage choice that are worth highlighting. First, the significance of theory in relation to organization and communication of the constructs and composition of the study. Second, the impact of financial literacy and consumer education on mortgage selection. Third, the influence of homeownership and mortgage characteristics on well-being. After reviewing theoretical considerations commonly used in evaluating home purchase and mortgage decisions, this section will delve into each of the other topic areas.

## Applying Theory to Borrowing Decisions

Theory is fundamental to research issues and provides boundaries, assumptions, and constraints for the structure of a study's constructs (Bacharach, 1989). At a broad level, theory is used when evaluating mortgage decisions to inform two things. First, theory is used to help understand optimal borrowing decisions. Second, theory is used to understand how borrowers make intertemporal decisions in practice and why these decisions deviate from the optimal scenario. Furthermore, theory serves to address the behavioral attributes within the analysis of the decision-making process.

The optimal borrowing decision is often analyzed through the assumptions of the life-cycle hypothesis (LCH) (Ando and Modigliani, 1963). The LCH suggests individuals intend to smooth consumption over their lifetime by borrowing and saving at various stages, with the mortgage decision touching on both aspects. Mortgages deliver an opportunity to use future income to increase current consumption to the appropriate lifetime consumption rate. Optimal borrowing decisions, then, are based on a rational evaluation of current income, current assets, and future income to determine the amount and type of housing that should be purchased. Appropriate borrowing rates must consider age or life-stage, net worth, and the decreasing marginal utility of consumption. Consequently, mortgages smooth consumption and, on the investment side, mortgages can be a way to have a "forced" savings account (Chen and Jensen, 1985), balance risk tolerance (Yao et al., 2005), and enhance net worth (Basciano et al., 2008).

In practice, borrowing decisions tend to deviate substantially from what is predicted by the life-cycle hypothesis. The behavioral life-cycle hypothesis (BLCH) (Shefrin and Thaler, 1988) provides keen insight into why this occurs. The BLCH hypothesis indicates that, although individuals try to act rationally as indicated by the LCH, they are limited by emotional and cognitive factors. Emotionally, individuals face the internal conflict between short- and long-term time consumption, with temptation being the desire for consumption in the short term. Will-power is the effort necessary to overcome this temptation and align behaviors with long-term goals, providing for self-control. The absence of self-control provides context for situations where a household becomes overleveraged with mortgage debt (Agarwal et al., 2017). Similarly, individuals face cognitive barriers in identifying the optimal borrowing decision. Consequently, individuals tend to use mental accounting when making decisions (Kahneman and Tversky, 1984). Rather than viewing wealth as fungible, wealth is categorized into current income, current assets, and future income. Each "bucket" of money is viewed differently, with the propensity to spend being higher for current income. This is revealed as a present-time bias, which has been associated with increased foreclosure activity (Agarwal et al., 2020). Finally, framing posits that individuals frame choices, preferences, and outcomes in relation to a specific and situational reference point rather than purely rational considerations (Tversky and Kahneman, 1981).

## Financial Literacy and Mortgage Choice

Significant research has focused on consumers' ability to properly evaluate mortgage choices. This analysis has most often been based on understanding the impact of financial literacy, which is defined as having both the financial knowledge to understand a given financial scenario, as well as the ability to apply that knowledge (Huston, 2010). It is composed of awareness of facts on personal finances, the ability to comprehend financial terms, and integrate them with financial management behaviors (Garman and Forgue, 2006; Huston, 2010). The influence of subprime mortgages, expansion of mortgage product options, and the subsequent fallout resulting in the global financial crisis have brought forth a renewed concern for greater understanding and financial literacy. The onset of adjustable-rate mortgages, interest-only loans, and other variations have served to obfuscate individuals' understanding of the financial impacts of a mortgage (Bianco, 2008). A lack of financial literacy is a growing concern as empirical evidence suggests that Millennials have lower levels of financial knowledge compared to older generations (Kim et al., 2019b) and those with lower levels of financial knowledge are more likely to use high-cost lending instruments (Robb et al., 2015).

Mortgages are a comparatively rare transaction in an individual's life and experiences from prior transactions may not be applicable or appropriate (Collins, 2009). The selection of a mortgage must consider the ability to handle potentially negative situations, such as market fluctuations, job changes, and income shocks, since the residual effect of foreclosure can have a significant effect on financial well-being. Lusardi and Mitchell (2011) found that, in general, consumers struggle to conceptualize the long-term impact of these events on mortgage choices. Moreover, Bucks and Pence (2008) posited that borrowers do not fully grasp the degree to which interest rates can fluctuate. Fishbein and Woodall (2006) established that decision makers placed a high degree of focus on short-term payment size and discount potential future impacts if the market does not maintain its momentum. Leading up to the global financial crisis, the enticement of lower monthly payments increased the allure of alternative mortgages, particularly for households with lower financial literacy (Seay et al., 2017).

Of particular concern are individuals who exhibit overconfidence in their financial abilities. Overconfidence is known to be associated with higher occurrences of taking on too much mortgage debt (Hauff and Nilsson, 2020) and utilizing subprime loans (Moulton et al., 2013). Overconfident individuals are more likely to overestimate future income prospects to rationalize higher mortgage balances (Atlas et al., 2017), be overleveraged (Johnson et al., 2011), less likely to seek advice on borrowing capacity (Moulton et al., 2013), and have higher default rates (Kim et al., 2019a). On the contrary, homeowners who seek advice and have more accurate evaluations of their financial literacy are less likely to be over-burdened with debt (Bertrand and Morse, 2011). Further, Mountain et al. (2017) found that consumers who take the time to read federal disclosure documents, a form of financial education, are more likely to choose appropriate mortgage options.

## Homeownership, Mortgages, and Well-Being

Historically, homeownership has offered many key benefits and has been shown to increase subjective well-being and increased housing and life satisfaction (Baek and Devaney, 2009; Elsinga and Hoekstra, 2005; Rossi and Weber, 1996). However, there is some evidence this has begun to shift. During the global financial crisis, the volatility of housing prices, the psychological consequences of foreclosure, and overall control of one's housing situation undermined some of the traditional benefits of homeownership (Rohe et al., 2013). While some research found that renters and homeowners exhibited similar levels of financial hardship during the financial crisis (Manturuk et al., 2012), strong evidence still suggests that homeownership remains associated with higher levels of financial satisfaction (Tharp et al., 2020). However, this relationship can be more complicated for individuals who hold a mortgage (Cairney and Boyle, 2004), especially if the mortgage leads to cash flow pressures (Tharp et al., 2020).

Financial satisfaction and well-being can be impacted in various stages of homeownership. For example, the change from renter to homeowner has been shown to improve financial satisfaction (Joo and Grable, 2004) and the transition from having a mortgage to paying off the mortgage further increases financial satisfaction (Baek and Devaney, 2009). These insights support the notion that net home value is a key determinant of financial satisfaction (Plagnol, 2011). As such, the consideration of homeownership must not only integrate mathematical considerations but also the potential influence on psychology and overall well-being. Promoting stability to one's financial situation through homeownership is instrumental to financial satisfaction (Vlaev and Elliott, 2014).

# Practitioner Tools and Application

The mortgage choice, viewed as a singular decision, involves navigating a complex landscape of considerations that includes the comparison of a 15- versus 30-year length, fixed-rate versus adjustable rate, and 5 percent down payment versus 20 percent; however, including intertemporal and emotional aspects of the decision compound the intricacy. The growing prevalence of student loans, credit cards, and consumer debts enhances the need for individually specific, independent advice from a fiduciary to adequately examine the strengths and weaknesses of each option. A financial professional (i.e., financial planner, financial counselor, mortgage counselor) can help their clients discern optimal outcomes for home purchases, refinancing or repayment options, real estate investment, and accessing home equity based on a holistic review of their personal situation, risk tolerance, retirement adequacy, and future goals.

## Home Purchase Decisions

Homeownership decisions are an interconnected decision process that includes residual effects of past choices and prospective future outcomes. Heuristics are a good starting point for determining an affordable percentage of income spent on housing; however, the conversation must go deeper. A mortgage or financial counselor can present side-by-side mortgage comparisons that account for the details of a client's individual situation, stimulating a comparison of the differences between timeframes, interest rates, and total fees and expenses. Empirical research has illustrated that exposure to quality information about different loan choices leads to more optimal decision making (Mountain et al., 2017).

Financial planners can be of particular value in enriching the discussion of homeownership by overlaying a comprehensive financial plan to complement the mortgage analysis. This helps integrate the interconnectedness of other essential variables, like retirement savings and college funding, which can be crucial but not urgent based on the timing relative to the present. More so, the financial planning process provides an opportunity to educate potential and current homeowners and facilitate a conversation to address the emotional aspects of buying a home (Fuscaldo, 2016). A thoughtful deliberation of the potential outcomes of homeownership can help households avoid situations of being overleveraged, accurately ponder future income prospects, and balance other long-term financial objectives.

Homeownership is not always advantageous, and financial professionals can initiate the dialog of whether purchasing a home is fundamentally the right choice for a given individual or household. While research has shown that homeownership is positively associated with financial satisfaction (Garrett and James III, 2013), the psychological impact of bankruptcy has demonstrated that homeownership must be optimal for a household's financial picture to not cause long-term financial strain (Xiao, 2015).

Renting, when viewed as an outcome of patience, allows for short-term control of housing expenses while the fundamental aspects of homeownership and job stability are considered.

## Mortgage Refinance and Repayment Decisions

The mortgage refinance decision has been increasingly common in recent years due to historically low-interest rates. Although the main driver for mortgage refinancing is low-interest rates, homeowners often have one of three motivations when considering a refinance alternative: (a) lower monthly payments, (b) convert a 30-year mortgage to a 15-year mortgage, or (c) consolidate consumer debts. The linear and non-linear relationships related to refinancing and repayment decisions provide another opportunity for holistic planning to accentuate the long-term ramifications of each decision.

Refinancing for the purposes of lowering monthly payments or consolidating debt should be based on a harmonized discussion that includes ideal uses of the increased cash flow. A financial professional can individualize the discussion and provide alternatives that include emotional and financial considerations. For example, the consolidation of high-interest credit card debt into a lower-rate mortgage loan may seem appealing on the surface; however, advisors must advance the conversation to include behavioral dynamics. A consumer's credit card debt may actually be a residual outcome of low levels of self-control or susceptibility to impulsive buying tendencies (Baumeister, 2002; Fenton-O'Creevy et al., 2018). Therefore, a myopic view of behavioral antecedents that underlie credit card debt may result in a consumer consolidating credit card debt into a mortgage and then simply going back into credit card debt. This compounds the negative financial impact and can have a detrimental effect on long-term financial well-being.

There are also strategic repayment decisions to consider. Especially in low-interest-rate environments, postponing the payoff of a personal residence can potentially lead to higher rates of return (Kim et al., 2016), as there may be significant tax benefits and higher net returns achieved by investing money in a tax-deferred retirement account and taking advantage of employer retirement plan matches (Smith and Seay, 2016). Those who provide advice to others about mortgage choices must consider a homeowner's risk tolerance and debt beliefs, as well as whether the household will be able to claim a mortgage interest deduction based on applicable tax laws.

## Real Estate as an Investment

Fiduciaries play a critical role in helping their clients understand the risk and benefits associated with investments in rental real estate. This investment may vary between the purchase of a real estate investment trust (REIT) within an investment portfolio or direct investment in rental property. Prior to the global financial crisis, rental real estate investment was associated with higher net-worth households (Seay et al., 2013); however, the easing of monetary policy and reduction of interest rates provided greater opportunity for those in the lower and middle-class to enter the real estate market as property owners (Baum et al., 2021; DeFusco and Paciorek, 2017). When evaluating a direct investment in rental real estate, three diverse sources of return arise: (a) rental payments, (b) property value appreciation, and (c) state and federal tax benefits (Seay et al., 2018), which must include potential financial and non-financial consequences.

Two areas where a financial advisor can supplement information for a client are in regards to expectations and ancillary investment factors. Many real estate investments take time to become profitable and most do not even turn a profit in the first year (Lereah, 2005). If the discussion begins with outlining the long-term benefits and short-term drawbacks, a potential property owner can be better prepared to handle market fluctuations and have an investment time perspective that is future-oriented. Simultaneously, a financial advisor can augment the conversation with tax and investment elements, such as the expenses associated with insurance, property management, repairs, vacancy, maintenance, liquid reserves, legal costs, depreciation and potential recapture, and availability of 1031 exchange rules (Lederer, 2009).

## Home Equity in a Financial Plan

Historically, the preferred financial standard was to pay off a mortgage and be debt-free prior to retirement (Rose, 2013). However, as the economic environment has gradually become more sophisticated, those in a fiduciary role, when advising others, must also consider discussions with homeowners surrounding reverse mortgages and home equity loans. A reverse mortgage can be a useful tool for accessing home equity for retirees because it does not require repayment until the owner moves, dies, or sells the home; however, it remains a complex financial product that can be difficult to understand and has the potential for fraud (Carswell et al., 2013; Seay et al., 2014). Similarly, home equity lines of credit can provide access to capital to fund other financial objectives in the most efficient manner.

Reverse mortgages within a retirement planning strategy (see Chapter 14) can potentially enhance retirement adequacy in three primary ways: (a) by offsetting market volatility, (2) by providing access to low-cost capital, and (3) by mitigating overall portfolio risk (Pfau, 2017). Retirees may find themselves in a situation where they prefer the long-term growth opportunities presented by equity investments while simultaneously needing to account for the market's volatility. A reverse mortgage can allow a homeowner to access home equity as a source for smoothing retirement consumption in market downturns, which allows investment accounts time to recover to a desired level. Moreover, a reverse mortgage can also allow for tax considerations that enable a retiree to delay accessing tax-deferred accounts and recognize income taxes judiciously.

Accessing home equity also has implications for non-retirees. Similar to refinancing situations, conversations regarding home equity loans must include a discussion on behavioral implications depending on the intended use of the funds (i.e., paying off credit cards or other consumer debt). A review of home equity use can also include topics related to supplementing retirement planning. Equity can be used to amplify retirement savings and provide funding for tax-advantaged retirement savings that can have a multiplicative effect on returns (Smith and Seay, 2016). In a like manner, home equity loans can be used as a tool to increase home value by using the funds to modernize the home, increase the investment's return, and maximize the home sale tax exclusion to avoid capital gains taxes.

## Conclusion

Homeownership remains a critical component of financial achievement and well-being in the United States and around the world, reinforced through government programs and tax policy. However, the paradigm is shifting, and research has shown that the homeownership and the marriage rate of Millennials have decreased and home purchases are being delayed because of debt (Addo, 2014; Mountain et al., 2020). Furthermore, as employers move more aggressively toward defined contribution plans and away from defined benefit plans, the burden of retirement rests on the shoulders of the individual (Benartzi and Thaler, 2007; Broadbent et al., 2006). Therefore, a holistic conversation on situational factors of mortgage choice is imperative. Homeownership likely represents the largest asset, debt, and monthly expense for a family, and it is critical that proper attention be paid to how consumers make their home purchase decisions. Given the complexity involved, as well as the potential long-term impacts, financial services professionals and researchers alike must stay keenly attuned to the factors that promote more informed and appropriate home purchase and mortgage borrowing decisions.

## References

Addo, F. R. (2014). Debt, cohabitation, and marriage in young adulthood. *Demography*, *51*(5), 1677–1701. Accessed July, 2021. https://doi.org/10.1007/s13524-014-0333-6

Agarwal, S., Chomsisengphet, S., and Lim, C. (2017). What shapes consumer choice and financial products? A review. *Annual Review of Financial Economics*, *9*(1), 127–146. https://doi.org/10. 1146/annurev-financial-110716-032417

Agarwal, S., Deng, Y., and He, J. (2020). Time preferences, mortgage choice and mortgage default. *International Real Estate Review, 23*(2), 777–813.

Allen, F., Barth, J., and Yago, G. (2012). *Fixing the housing market: Financial innovations for the future*. Pearson Prentice Hall.

Ando, A., and Modigliani, F. (1963). The life cycle hypothesis of saving: Aggregate implications and tests. *The American Economic Review, 53*(1), 55–84.

Atlas, S., Johnson, E., and Payne J. (2017). Time preferences and mortgage choice. *Journal of Marketing Research, 54*(3), 415–429.

Avery, R., Bostic, R., Calem, P., and Canner, G. (1996). Credit risk, credit scoring, and the performance of home mortgages. *Federal Reserve Bulletin, 82*, 621–646.

Bacharach, S. B. (1989). Organizational theories: Some criteria for evaluation. *The Academy of Management Review, 14*(4), 496–515.

Baek, E., and Devaney, S. (2009). Assessing the baby boomers' financial wellness using financial ratios and a subjective measure. *Journal of Family and Consumer Sciences, 32*(4), 321–348. https://doi.org/10.1177/1077727X04263826

Basciano, P. M., James, A. M., Jackson, P. Z., James, P. M., and Grayson, J. M. (2008). Mortgage choice: A review of the literature. *Journal of Personal Finance, 7*(1), 42–67.

Baum, A. E., Crosby, N., and Devaney, S. (2021). *Property Investment Appraisal*. John Wiley & Sons.

Baumeister, R. F. (2002). Yielding to temptation: Self-control failure, impulsive purchasing, and consumer behavior. *The Journal of Consumer Research, 28*(4), 670–676.

Benartzi, S., and Thaler, R. H. (2007). Heuristics and biases in retirement savings behavior. *Journal of Economic Perspectives, 21*(3), 81–104. https://doi.org/10.1257/jep.21.3.81

Bertrand, M., and Morse, A. (2011). Information disclosure, cognitive biases, and payday borrowing. *The Journal of Finance, 66*(6), 1865–1893. https://doi.org/10.1111/j.1540-6261.2011.01698.x

Bianco, K. M. (2008). *The subprime lending crisis: Causes and effects of the mortgage meltdown*. Wolters Kluwer Law & Business.

Broadbent, J., Palumbo, M., and Woodman, E. (2006, December). *The shift from defined benefit to defined contribution pension plans—Implications for asset allocation and risk management*. Reserve Bank of Australia, Board of Governors of the Federal Reserve System and Bank of Canada, 1–54. Accessed July, 2021. https://www.bis.org/publ/wgpapers/cgfs27broadbent3.pdf

Bucks, B., and Pence, K. M. (2008). Do borrowers know their mortgage terms? *Journal of Urban Economics, 64*(2), 218–233. https://doi.org/10.1016/j.jue.2008.07.005

Cairney, J., and Boyle, M. H. (2004). Homeownership, mortgages and psychological distress. *Housing Studies, 19*(2), 161–174. https://doi.org/10.1080/0267303032000168577

Carswell, A., Seay, M., and Polanowski, M. (2013). Reverse mortgage fraud against seniors: Recognition and education of a burgeoning problem. *Journal of Housing for the Elderly, 27*(1–2), 146–160. https://doi.org/10.1080/02763893.2012.754819

Chambers, M. S., Garriga, C., and Schlagenhauf, D. (2008). The loan structure and housing tenure decisions in an equilibrium model of mortgage choice. *Review of Economic Dynamics, 12*(3), 444–468.

Chen, A., and Jensen, H. (1985). Home equity use and the life cycle hypothesis. *Journal of Consumer Affairs, 19*(1), 37–56. https://doi.org/10.1111/j.1745-6606.1985.tb00343.x

Chomsisengphet, S., and Pennington-Cross, A. (2006). The evolution of the subprime mortgage market. *Federal Reserve Bank of St. Louis Review, 88*(1), 31–56.

Collins, J. M. (2009). *Education levels and mortgage application outcomes: Evidence of financial literacy* (Discussion Paper No. 1369–09). Institute for Research on Poverty.

DeFusco, A. A., and Paciorek, A. (2017). The interest rate elasticity of mortgage demand: Evidence from bunching at the conforming loan limit. *American Economic Journal: Economic Policy, 9*(1), 210–240. https://doi.org/10.1257/pol.20140108

Demyanyk, Y., and Van Hemert, O. (2011). Understanding the subprime mortgage crisis. *Review of Financial Studies, 24*(6), 1848–1880. https://doi.org/10.1093/rfs/hhp033

DeRitis, C. (2013). *Beyond the 30-year fixed-rate mortgage: A plan for reform*. Moody's Analytics. https://www.economy.com/home/products/samples/2013-12-20-Beyond-30-Year-Fixed-Mortgage.pdf

Elsinga, M., and Hoekstra, J. (2005). Homeownership and housing satisfaction. *Journal of Housing and the Built Environment, 20*, 401–424. https://doi.org/10.1007/s10901-005-9023-4

Employee Benefit Research Institute. (2020). *2020 Retirement confidence survey fact sheet #1. Retirement confidence*. https://www.ebri.org/docs/default-source/rcs/2020-rcs/rcs_20-fs-1_confid.pdf?sfvrsn=e3bc3d2f_6

Fenton-O'Creevy, M., Dibb, S., and Furnham, A. (2018). Antecedents and consequences of chronic impulsive buying: Can impulsive buying be understood as dysfunctional self-regulation? *Psychology & Marketing, 35*(3), 175–188. https://doi.org/10.1002/mar.21078

Fishbein, A. J., and Woodall, P. (2006). Exotic or toxic? An examination of the non-traditional mortgage market for consumers and lenders. *Consumer Federation of America*, 1–33.

Foote, C. L., Loewenstein, G., and Willen, P. S. (2021). Cross-sectional patterns of mortgage debt during the housing boom: Evidence and implications. *The Review of Economic Studies, 88*(1), 229–259.

Fuscaldo, D. (2016, March 6). Maybe you shouldn't pay off your mortgage before retirement. *Fox Business*. https://www.foxbusiness.com/features/maybe-you-shouldnt-pay-off-your-mortgage-before-retirement

Garman, E. T., and Forgue, R. E. (2006). *Personal finance*. Houghton Mifflin.

Hauff, J., and Nilsson, J. (2020). Determinants of indebtedness among young adults: Impacts of lender guidelines, explicit information and financial (over) confidence. *International Journal of Consumer Studies, 44*(2), 89–98. https://doi.org/10.1111/ijcs.12549

Heuson, A., Passmore, W., and Sparks, R. (2001). Credit scoring and mortgage securitization: Implications for mortgage rates and credit availability. *Journal of Real Estate Finance and Economics, 23*(3), 337–363. https://doi.org/10.1023/A:1017952120081

Huston, S. J. (2010). Measuring financial literacy. *Journal of Consumer Affairs, 44*(2), 296–316. https://doi.org/10.1111/j.1745-6606.2010.01170.x

Immergluck, D. (2008). From the subprime to the exotic: Excessive mortgage market risk and foreclosures. *Journal of the American Planning Association, 74*(1), 59–76. https://doi.org/10.1080/01944360701702313

James, R. N., and Garrett, S. (2013). Financial ratios and perceived household financial satisfaction. *Journal of Financial Therapy, 4*(1).

Johnson, E., Atlas, S., and Payne, J. (2011). Time preferences, mortgage choice and strategic default. *Advances in Consumer Research, 39*, 178–179.

Johnson, K. W., and Li, G. (2010). The debt-payment-to-income ratio as an indicator of borrowing constraints: Evidence from two household surveys. *Journal of Money, Credit and Banking, 42*(7), 1,373–1,390. https://doi.org/10.1111/j.1538-4616.2010.00345.x

Johnstone, Q. (2004). Private mortgage insurance. *Wake Forest Law Review, 39*. https://heinonline.org/HOL/LandingPage?>handle=hein.journals/wflr39&div=34&id=&page=

Joo, S.-H., and Grable, J. (2004). An exploratory framework of the determinants of financial satisfaction. *Journal of Family and Economic Issues, 25*(1), 25–50. https://doi.org/10.1023/B:JEEI.0000016722.37994.9f

Kahneman, D., and Tversky, A. (1984). Choices, values, and frames. *American Psychologist, 39*(4), 341–350.

Kim, K., Lee, J., and Hanna, S. (2019a). The effects of financial literacy overconfidence on the mortgage delinquency of US households. *Journal of Consumer Affairs, 54*(2), 517–540. https://doi.org/10.1111/joca.12287

Kim, K., Seay, M., and Smith, H. (2016). After the Great Recession: Financial sophistication and housing leverage. *Applied Economics Letters, 23*(18), 1285–1288.

Kim, K. T., Anderson, S. G., and Seay, M. C. (2019b). Financial knowledge and short-term and long-term financial behaviors of millennials in the United States. *Journal of Family and Economic Issues, 40*(2), 194–208.

Lea, M., and Sanders, A. (2011). Government policy and the fixed rate mortgage. *The Annual Review of Financial Economics, 3*(1), 223–234. https://doi.org/10.1146/annurev-financial-102710-144920

Lederer, W. A. (2009). *Ultimate property management handbook.* Wiley.

Lereah, D. (2005). *Are you missing the real estate boom?* Crown Business.

Lusardi, A., and Mitchell, O. S. (2011). *Financial literacy and planning: Implications for retirement wellbeing* (NBER Working Paper No. 17078). National Bureau of Economic Research. https://www.nber.org/papers/w17078

Lusardi, A., and Mitchell, O. S. (2013). *Older adult debt and financial frailty* (Working Paper No. WP 2013–291). University of Michigan Retirement Research Center.

Manturuk, K., Riley, S., and Ratcliffe, J. (2012). Perception vs reality: The relationship between low-income homeownership, perceived financial stress, and financial hardship. *Social Science Research, 41*(2), 276–286.

Maroto, M., and Aylsworth, L. (2017). Assessing the relationship between gender, household structure, and net worth in the United States. *Journal of Family and Economic Issues, 38*(4), 556–571. https://doi.org/10.1007/s10834-017-9521-z

Moulton, S., Loibl, C., Samak, A., and Collins, J. (2013). Borrowing capacity and financial decisions of low-to-moderate income first-time homebuyers. *Journal of Consumer Affairs, 47*(3), 375–403. https://doi.org/10.1111/joca.12021

Mountain, T. P., Cao, X., Kim, N., and Gutter, M. S. (2020). Millennials' future homeownership and the role of student loan debt. *Family and Consumer Sciences Research Journal, 49*(1), 5–23. https://doi.org/10.1111/fcsr.12374

Mountain, T. P., Gutter, M. S., Ruiz-Menjivar, J., and Çopur, Z. (2017). Exploring the role of financial disclosure forms in mortgage type selection. *Journal of Financial Counseling and Planning, 28*(2), 285–299. https://doi.org/10.1891/1052-3073.28.2.285

Munnell, A. H., Soto, M., and Aubry, J. P. (2007). Do people plan to tap their home equity in retirement? *Center for Retirement Research at Boston College.* http://hdl.handle.net/2345/bc-ir:104346

Nakajima, M., and Telyukova, I. (2017). Reverse mortgage loans: A quantitative analysis. *The Journal of Finance, 72*(2), 911–950.

Nau, M., and Tumin, D. (2012). Wealth transfer receipt and later life wealth. *Research in Social Stratification and Mobility, 30*(3), 233–245. https://doi.org/10.1016/j.rssm.2012.01.003

Pfau, W. (2017). *Using reverse mortgages in a responsible retirement income plan.* Retirement Researcher. https://retirementresearcher.com/using-reverse-mortgages-responsible-retirement-income-plan/

Plagnol, A. C. (2011). Financial satisfaction over the life course: The influence of assets and liabilities. *Journal of Economic Psychology, 32*(1), 45–64. https://doi.org/10.1016/j.joep.2010.10.006

Robb, C., Babiarz, P., Woodyard, A., and Seay, M. (2015). Bounded rationality and use of alternative financial services. *Journal of Consumer Affairs, 49*(2), 407–435. https://doi.org/10.1111/joca.12071

Rohe, W., Boshamer, C. C., and Lindblad, M. R. (2013). Reexamining the social benefits of homeownership after the housing crisis. *Joint Center for Housing Studies of Harvard University*, 1–54.

Rohe, W., and Watson, H. (2007). *Chasing the American dream: New perspectives on affordable homeownership*. Cornell University Press.

Rose, C. (2011). Qualifying for a home mortgage in today's mortgage environment. *Journal of Financial Service Professionals, 65*(2), 70–76.

Rose, J. (2013, March 7). 5 debts that can ruin your retirement. *MarketWatch*. https://www.market watch.com/story/5-debts-that-can-ruin-your-retirement-2013-03-07

Rossi, P. H., and Weber, E. (1996). The social benefits of homeownership: Empirical evidence from national surveys. *Housing Policy Debate, 7*(1), 1–35. https://doi.org/10.1080/10511482.1996.9521212

Rubinowitz, L. S., and Trosman, E. (1979). Affirmative action and the American Dream: Implementing fair housing policies in federal homeownership programs. *Northwestern University Law Review, 74*(4), 493–515.

Seay, M., Carswell, A., Nielsen, R., and Palmer, L. (2013). Rental real estate ownership prior to the Great Recession. *Family and Consumer Sciences Research Journal, 41*(4), 363–374. https://doi.org/10.1111/fcsr.12024

Seay, M. C., Anderson, S. G., Carswell, A. T., and Nielsen, R. B. (2018). Characteristics of rental real estate investors during the 2000s. *Journal of Financial Counseling and Planning, 29*(2), 369–382. https://doi.org/10.1891/1052-3073.29.2.369

Seay, M. C., Carswell, A. T., Wilmarth, M., and Zimmerman, L. G. (2014). Exploring HECM counselors' fraud awareness and training. *Journal of Financial Crime, 21*(4), 484–494. https://doi.org/10.1108/JFC-03-2013-0020

Seay, M. C., Preece, G. L., and Le, V. C. (2017). Financial literacy and the use of interest-only mortgages. *Journal of Financial Counseling and Planning, 28*(2), 168–180. https://doi.org/10.1891/1052-3073.28.2.168

Shefrin, H. M., and Thaler, R. H. (1988). The behavioral life-cycle hypothesis. *Economic Inquiry, 26*(4), 609–643. https://doi.org/10.1111/j.1465-7295.1988.tb01520.x

Sherlund, S. M. (2011). The past, present, and future of subprime mortgages. In R. W. Kolb (ed.), *Lessons from the financial crisis: Causes, consequences, and our economic future* (pp. 147–154). Wiley. https://doi.org/10.1002/978118266588.ch20

Smith, H., and Seay, M. (2016). An analysis of the tradeoff between mortgage prepayment and tax-deferred retirement. *Journal of Financial Services Professionals, 70*(3), 64–75.

Spilerman. (2000). Wealth and stratification processes. *Annual Review of Sociology, 26*, 497–524.

Tharp, D. T., Seay, M., Stueve, C., and Anderson, S. (2020). Financial satisfaction and homeownership. *Journal of Family and Economic Issues, 41*(2), 255–280. https://doi.org/10.1007/s10834-019-09652-0

Tversky, A., and Kahneman, D. (1981). The framing of decisions and the psychology of choice. *Science, 211*(4,481), 453–458.

Vlaev, I., and Elliott, A. (2014). Financial well-being components. *Social Indicators Research, 118*(3), 1,103–1,123. https://doi.org/10.1007/s11205-013-0462-0

Xiao, J. J. (2015). Consumer borrowing. In *Consumer economic wellbeing* (pp. 181–198). Springer. https://doi.org/10.1007/978-1-4939-2821-7_10

Yao, R., Zhang, H. H., Ahn, H., Ciochetti, T., Cao, H., Cocco, J., Conrad, J., Coval, J., Gao, B., Ghysels, E., Gomes, F., Reed, A., Shilling, J., Slezak, S., Stanton, R., and Kong, C. (2005). Optimal consumption and portfolio choices with risky housing and borrowing constraints. *The Review of Financial Studies, 18*(1), 197–239. https://doi.org/10.1093/rfs/hhh007

Sherman D. Hanna, Kyoung Tae Kim, Sunwoo T. Lee

# 15 Considerations when Planning for Retirement

**Abstract:** The United States has been experiencing a "gray tsunami" due to its aging population and increased life expectancy. Although this is true in the United States, a similar aging trend is occurring worldwide. These demographic trends will have significant impacts on retirement planning in policy debates such as pension reform, social benefit reform, income tax laws, and retirement pension plans. This chapter provides a comprehensive overview of considerations and salient factors when planning for retirement, discusses some perspectives on various issues related to retirement savings, and planning for later life financial stability. The chapter also provides a discussion of the tools and techniques used in retirement planning, including capital needs analysis and assessment of retirement adequacy.

**Keywords:** retirement planning, retirement savings, retirement adequacy, pensions, social security

## Introduction

Most developed nations have been experiencing a "gray tsunami" due to aging populations and increased life expectancies. As shown in Figure 15.1, the elderly population as a percent of the working-age population in the United States has been increasing rapidly over the last few decades. It is projected that the age 65+ population will outnumber the number of children under 18 in 2034 for the first time in U.S. history (U.S. Census Bureau, 2017). At the same time, the remaining life expectancy at age 65 has grown steadily over the past decades and was at 19.5 years in 2018 compared to 13.9 in 1950 (National Center for Health Statistics, 2021). The life expectancy at birth and the life expectancy at age 65 has increased over the past decades not only in the United States but also in most of the Organisation for Economic Co-operation and Development (OECD) countries (OECD, 2021). These demographic trends will have significant impacts on retirement planning and for policy debates related to private and public pension system reform and income tax incentives.

Federal Old-Age and Survivors Insurance and Federal Disability Insurance (OASDI) is also known as the Social Security program of the United States, and the

**Sherman D. Hanna,** The Ohio State University
**Kyoung Tae Kim,** University of Alabama
**Sunwoo T. Lee,** York University

https://doi.org/10.1515/9783110727692-015

OASDI Trust Fund plus payroll tax revenue covers Social Security benefit payments. According to the 2020 OASDI Trustees Report (Social Security Administration, 2020b), OASDI payments are projected to exceed total payroll tax revenue starting in 2021. The OASDI Trust Fund reserves might become depleted in 2035 if no changes in taxes or benefits are implemented. At that point, benefits could still be paid, but only at 79 percent of benefits estimated under the current benefit structure. To maintain Social Security solvency, lawmakers may be forced to consider some policy options, including (a) increasing the payroll tax rate and (b) implementing a permanent reduction in scheduled benefits. This funding issue is not unique to the United States. Numerous countries are currently grappling with the same issue as their populations age. The old-age dependency ratio, the ratio of population 65 and over to population aged from 15 to 64, is projected to almost double by 2080 in many countries (Devesa-Carpio et al., 2020). A number of countries have been discussing a reform of their public pension systems to control the risk of dependency and depletion (Rosado-Cebrian et al., 2020).

Over the past 30 years, U.S. workers have experienced changes in the retirement pension environment and tax rules. Defined benefit pension plans have been steadily replaced with defined-contribution pension plans. With defined contribution plans workers are tasked with more retirement savings responsibilities. Further, new income tax laws have impacted retirement planning. For example, the Setting Every Community Up for Retirement Enhancement Act of 2019 (SECURE Act) and the Coronavirus Aid, Relief, and Economic Security Act of 2020 (CARES Act) have changed the way U.S. workers choose retirement planning options and implement savings strategies.

In this chapter, we will review and discuss some perspectives on various issues related to retirement savings and planning in the United States. Although this chapter focuses on U.S. data and trends, the personal finance tools and techniques presented throughout the chapter have universal application. We will discuss some trends in projected retirement adequacy and key issues in determining whether workers will be able to maintain an adequate level of consumption after retirement.

# Perspectives on Major Retirement Planning Issues

There are many factors that need to be considered when it comes to retirement planning. In this section, major factors related to retirement planning are discussed. Table 15.1 summarizes the issues related to these major factors.

## Work-Life Expectancy

One of the major considerations embedded in the retirement preparation process is the decision of when to retire. Work-life expectancy, defined as the expected duration

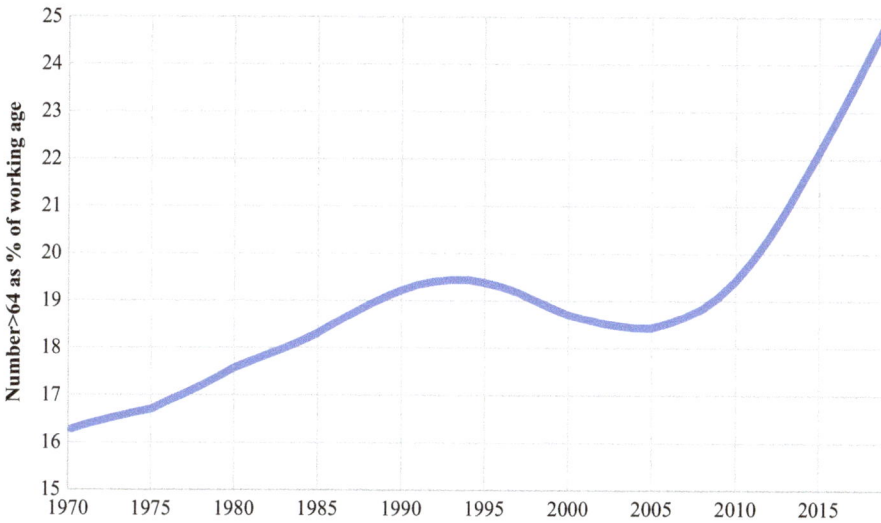

**Figure 15.1:** Number of People Aged 65 or Older as a Percent of the U.S. Working-Age Population 1970–2019.
*Source*: Federal Reserve Bank of St. Louis (https://fred.stlouisfed.org/series/ SPPOPDPNDOLU.S.A).
*Note*. The working-age population is defined as those aged 15–64.

of time between the beginning of labor force participation and retirement, is the period in which individuals can accumulate wealth. The average retirement age has been increasing for the last three decades. The 2017 average was 64 for men and 63 for women (Munnell, 2019). While the average retirement age is slightly lower than the Social Security Administration's designated normal[1] retirement age of 67, the share of the projected labor force of older workers (55 and older) has been growing since the 1990s. The projected annual growth rate in the labor force is almost five times higher among the age 65 or over group compared to younger age groups (Toossi and Torpey, 2017).

The issue of retirement age needs to be approached carefully because actual and expected retirement ages do not necessarily align. Blanchett (2018) found that people tend to retire earlier than they expected, which creates uncertainty in the context of retirement planning. This uncertainty has a significant and negative effect on determining retirement adequacy. In addition, Hanna et al. (2017) suggested that the people who indicate that they are never going to retire might not have indicated their true intention or preference to never retire, but are, in fact, indicating their lack of consideration of retirement and inadequate preparedness.

Workers covered by Social Security need to consider both when to stop full-time employment and when to start receiving their Social Security benefit. Workers

---

1 Also referred to as the "full" retirement age.

can start claiming a Social Security pension when they turn age 62, but those born after 1960 have a "full retirement age" of 67, and if they start collecting their pension at age 62, their pension will be only 70 percent of the level it would be if they waited until age 67. (The pension would be even higher if it were not started until age 70, when it could be 77 percent higher than if started at age 62.) Some workers who plan to retire before age 67 should consider complex factors related to the best choice for when to start collecting their Social Security pension (Alderson and Betker, 2017).

**Table 15.1:** Major Factors to Consider in Retirement Planning.

| Factor | Issues and Estimates |
|---|---|
| Work-life expectancy | Age start working full-time; Interruptions such as education and childcare; Expected retirement age; Actual retirement age |
| Retirement-life expectancy | Retirement age; Remaining life expectancy (accounting for health) |
| Retirement needs | Consumption smoothing; Taxes and employment costs; Medical costs; Bequest goals |
| Inflation | Expected rate; Historical patterns |
| Portfolio allocation | Aggressive (all stocks); or balanced; or target-date fund. Will determine the expected rate of return of the portfolio |
| Income and payroll taxes | Usually, a lower tax rate is expected in retirement, and no payroll tax on income from investments and pensions |
| Sources of retirement income | Social Security; Employer-sponsored retirement plans; Personal savings; Earnings during retirement |
| Withdrawal strategies | The 4 percent rule; generating perpetual income stream; Required Minimum Distribution; Annuitization |

## Retirement-Life Expectancy

Retirement-life expectancy, defined as the expected duration of time between retirement and death, is the period in which individuals should plan to have their resources last. One's remaining life expectancy at retirement can be calculated from tables of government statistics, but generally, life expectancy depends on age, gender, health, and similar factors. For instance, for all people aged 65, the remaining life expectancy in 2018 was 19.5 years, with a life expectancy of 18.1 years for men and 20.7 years for women (National Center for Health Statistics, 2021). However, more sophisticated estimates can produce higher numbers for some people. For instance, based on the calculator at longevityillustrator.org, a non-smoking 65-year-old male with excellent health has an expected remaining life expectancy of 23 years, whereas a similar 65-year-old female has an expected remaining life expectancy of 25 years. If the male and the female were a couple, there is a 50 percent chance that at least one of them will be alive 29 years later, at age 94, and a 25 percent chance that at least one of them will be alive 33 years later, at age 98.

## Retirement Needs

Retirement needs must be considered in retirement planning. Financial advisors generally recommend replacing 70 percent or more of pre-retirement income (Biggs and Springstead, 2008). This advice is based on the concept of the life-cycle savings model (see an overview in Modigliani, 1986). The normative life-cycle model provides an important conceptual basis and can most easily be understood in the original simplified version. For instance, assume that a 25-year-old consumer knows she will live to be 85 and will receive the same amount of utility (satisfaction) from a particular amount of spending at each age. In the original simple version of the model, there are no durable goods – the consumer rents a home, auto, etc. In this simplified model, Modigliani also assumed that consumers would have zero real interest rates on saving and borrowing. While these assumptions are obviously unrealistic, the basic model provides useful insights that hold even with more realistic assumptions. The consumer has some initial level of assets, designated as $N_0$. The consumer expects to have after-tax earnings each year, and then a pension after retirement. The consumer therefore can be considered to have lifetime wealth, $W = N_0 + \sum I_i$ as i ranges from present age to age 100. In Modigliani's original simplified model, he suggested that lifetime satisfaction (what economists refer to as utility) would be maximized by consumption smoothing, which in the simple model implies having the same level of consumption or spending each year. Therefore, spending should be equal to lifetime wealth W divided by the number of years. So, for example, if the consumer expected to earn $50,000 per year for 40 years and then have a pension of $20,000 per year for 20 years, and initially has no assets or debts, then total lifetime wealth = 50,000 × 40 + 20,000 × 20 = $2,400,000. Based on the original simplified model, each year the consumer should spend the same amount, W/N, where N is 60 years, so optimal spending = $40,000, and the consumer should save 20 percent of after-tax earnings each year while employed, in order to accumulate enough to be able to maintain the same level of spending after retirement. The capital needed at retirement would be $400,000, and withdrawals from that would supplement the pension income so that $40,000 could be spent each year in retirement. Hanna et al. (1995) provided illustrations of the implications of the normative life-cycle model when more realistic assumptions are made about interest rates and uncertain life expectancies.

The key to rational thinking about spending needs in retirement is to focus on what components of household expenditures provide satisfaction, rather than just being needed for employment or financing of purchases. For instance, loan payments for home mortgages and vehicle purchases might be eliminated by retirement if loans are paid off. Skinner (2007) discussed many other factors related to what spending should be planned for in retirement. Support for children and other dependents might be reduced as family members become independent. For some workers, commuting costs and other items needed for a job might be substantial, and in retirement, there might be substitution of market-purchased goods with home-production (Hurd and Rohwedder, 2008).

Health-care costs need to be carefully considered as well, as the costs are typically much higher as people age. Older adults are likely in need of more hospital and medical services. Healthcare utilization is known to increase after retirement (Lucifora and Vigani, 2018), and longer life expectancy is the driving force of the increase in current and projected expenses of healthcare (Pokorski and Berg, 2017). Because many workers in the United States rely on group health insurance through employers before retirement, securing an appropriate funding source for health-care-related costs after retirement is crucial. Medicare and Medicaid are the programs provided by the U.S. government to meet this need. Medicare is a federal health insurance plan that covers people who are aged 65 and older while Medicaid provides medical assistance to households with low income and low assets. In addition to those government-sponsored programs, many retirees purchase Medigap insurance, which is private insurance used to supplement costs not covered by Medicare or other forms of private insurances.

Long-term care (LTC) costs should also be estimated as life expectancy increases. According to a report by the U.S. Health and Human Services, adults aged 65 and over have about a 70 percent chance of needing long-term care before death (Johnson, 2019). Low- and moderate-income households may qualify for government programs such as Medicaid to offset LTC costs. On the other hand, middle- and upper-income households need to plan for LTC costs because they might not qualify for Medicaid, which would require them to rely on their own assets for those costs. Recently, in the United States, about 60 percent of those who required LTC services had Medicaid as a payer source for nursing homes and adult day services centers, while Medicaid only covered 10 percent of home health agencies and 17 percent of residential care community users (Harris-Kojetin et al., 2019). Despite the risk of having significant LTC expenses, Johnson (2016) reported that only 11 percent of the age 65 and over population in the United States were covered by private LTC insurance.

While one is employed full-time, income and payroll taxes typically comprise a substantial portion of household income. Payroll taxes are not imposed on unearned income, but the federal income tax will be imposed on most forms of income from investments, and it is difficult to predict whether income tax rates will be higher in the future. When planning for retirement, it is important to remember that some states tax pension income and others do not, so one's location in retirement can make a difference in evaluating spending needs in retirement in the United States. Additionally, bequest goals are very important in retirement planning (Lockwood, 2018). Those who want to leave money or assets to someone else or to institutions, such as a church or university, need to accumulate more than those who do not, and this should be incorporated into a capital needs analysis.

## Inflation

Another important factor that needs to be considered is the inflation rate. Based on the change in the Consumer Price Index (CPI) from 1913 to 2020, inflation has averaged 3.1 percent per year, but it averaged 3.9 percent per year from 1970 to 2020.[2] As Figure 15.2 shows, the five-year moving average in the inflation rate has varied substantially since 1970, with a rapid increase from 1970 to 1980, reaching almost 10 percent per year in 1981. At that time, many households expected that the high inflation rate would persist for a long time; however, rates dropped much more quickly than expected. The inflation rate from 2000 to 2020 averaged 2.1 percent per year, al-

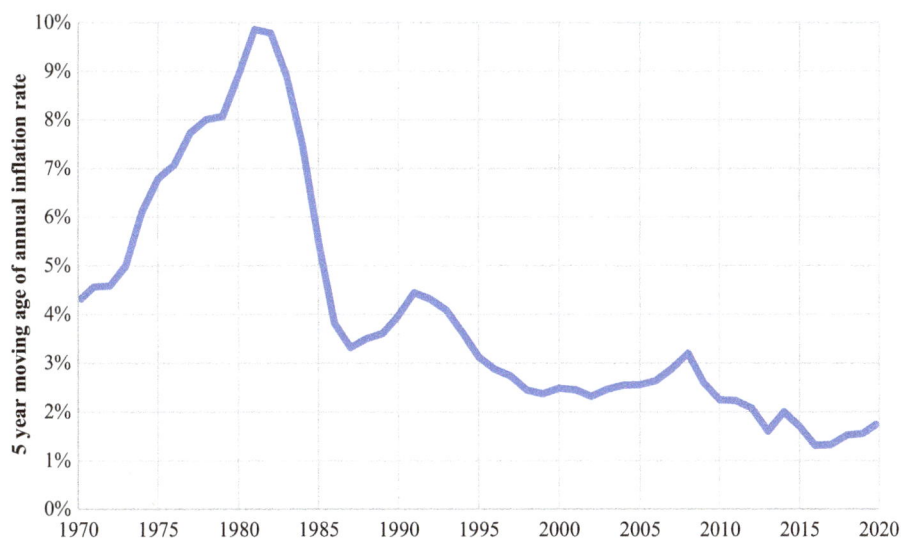

**Figure 15.2:** Five-Year Moving Average of Annual Change in Consumer Price Index.
*Source*: U.S. Bureau of Labor Statistics (https://www.bls.gov).

---

2 The long-term inflation rates reported here are calculated as geometric means.

though the rate might increase substantially in the future. Hanna and Kim (2017) provide additional perspectives on inflation and retirement planning. We discuss approaches to incorporating inflation into retirement planning later in the chapter.

## Portfolio Allocation

Portfolio allocation and investment rates of return by asset classes are also critical as they are directly related to the performance of a retirement portfolio. Historical statistics shown in Table 15.2 illustrate the clear trade-off between mean rates of return and volatility by types of investments, as measured by the annual standard deviation of returns. Taking the power of compounding into account, finding an optimal balance between volatility and returns through portfolio diversification is very important. Diversified stock funds have historically achieved far higher growth than bond or cash equivalent funds over the long run. Over the very long run, the superiority of stock investments is striking – a $1,000 investment in a hypothetical small stock index fund on January 1, 1926 would have grown to almost $2,885,000 in inflation-adjusted dollars by the end of 2020, compared to just over $752,000 in a hypothetical large stock index fund, and under $20,400 in a long-term corporate bond fund (Ibbotson, 2021). Diversification across asset classes can reduce volatility, although for periods of 20 years or more, diversification away from stocks is related to substantial reductions in growth with limited benefits from lower volatility. In this regard, index funds can provide diversification across companies and sectors, and also generally have much lower expenses that reduce growth.

To project expected accumulations in retirement funds, the inflation-adjusted rate of return should be used (Hanna and Kim, 2017). This can be straightforward if a pure type of investment is assumed (e.g., a large stock index fund). Table 15.2 shows long-run mean returns, with both the geometric mean and the arithmetic mean. The arithmetic mean is just the average of the returns from each year over a period of time, while the geometric mean is the rate that would achieve the same accumulation as actually took place for the investment during that period. For volatile investments, the geometric mean return is always lower than the arithmetic mean return, and could be considered a more conservative rate to use in projections. So, for instance, assume that Ann Smith, a worker who initially has nothing in her retirement fund, will be contributing $10,000 this year (including any employer matching contribution) and plans to contribute a constant percent of her salary to her retirement fund each year for the next 30 years. If her salary increases at the same rate as inflation, one can assume that her contributions will be constant in terms of today's prices. It is possible to use a financial calculator to estimate the future value. With a present value of $0, payment of $10,000, geometric real return of 7.2 percent per year (assuming a large stock index fund), and assuming one end of the year payment each year, the projected real accumulation at the end of 30 years would be $979,289. Note that this could buy what that amount would buy today, whereas if the nominal rate of return is used, Ann would need to adjust for inflation to have a meaningful amount to consider.

As noted earlier, given recent trends in the retirement pension market environment (i.e., replacing defined benefit (DB) plans with defined contribution (DC) plans), the responsibility of constructing an investment portfolio is being shifted from employers to employees. To aid individuals when managing their portfolios, Target Date Funds have become a popular choice in 401(k) plans. These funds are expected to improve retirement wealth, compared to common portfolio choices by workers (Mitchell and Utkus, 2020). Target Date Funds automatically decrease the proportion of stocks in the portfolio as the person gets closer to the target date or retirement.

**Table 15.2:** Inflation-Adjusted Annual Returns and Standard Deviation of Returns (%): 1926–2020.

| Asset class | Inflation-Adjusted Returns | | |
|---|---|---|---|
| | Geometric Average | Arithmetic Average | Standard Deviation |
| Large-cap stocks | 7.2 | 9.1 | 19.7 |
| Small-cap stocks | 8.7 | 12.9 | 30.7 |
| Corporate bonds (Long term) | 3.2 | 3.7 | 9.5 |
| Government bonds (Long term) | 2.7 | 3.3 | 10.8 |
| Government bonds (Intermediate term) | 2.2 | 2.4 | 6.6 |
| Treasury bills | 0.4 | 0.5 | 3.7 |

*Source*: Ibbotson (2021).

## Income Tax Issues

The details of income tax rules significantly differ depending on the countries and regions of residence, but there is no doubt that income taxes have significant implications for retirement planning. Many retirement plans and individual retirement accounts offer tax advantages. In traditional retirement plans in the U.S., one can defer part of one's compensation to those tax-advantaged accounts, make a tax-deductible contribution, and only get taxed when the money is distributed. As a result, not only current but also future tax rates must be considered. Households are generally expected to be in a lower tax bracket once they retire, but wealthy households could be in a higher tax bracket even after retirement.

In the United States, the marginal tax rate has been as high as 90 percent (in the 1940s), but after some fluctuations, the rates, as of 2021, range from 10 percent to 37 percent. It is difficult to predict future income tax rules and rates, but one should not assume that that one's income tax rates will be necessarily lower in the future compared to the present. How the tax brackets and rates might change in the future should be carefully approached. Based on projections, one could minimize tax payments by utilizing various tax-advantaged accounts available for retirement asset accumulation. For instance, most tax-advantaged accounts designed specifically for the purpose of retirement savings (e.g., in the United States, 401(k) plans and traditional IRA accounts) allow tax-deferred contribution to the account as well as tax-deferred growth of the earnings. Individuals do not get a tax deduction for contributions to Roth type accounts, such as Roth 401(k)s and Roth IRAs, but they may be able to obtain tax-free payments on qualified distributions. However, the strategies for savings, investments, and withdrawals would be different among countries since the specific details of income tax rules vary substantially.

## Sources of Retirement Income

The next consideration when planning for retirement is accounting for various sources of retirement income. In the United States, there are four primary sources of retirement income: (1) Social Security, (2) employer-sponsored retirement plans, (3) personal savings, and (4) employment after retirement. Each source of income is described in more detail below.

*Social Security.* Whitehouse and Queisser (2007) reported that public pensions of OECD countries have gross replacement rates of about 60 percent for average workers. Social Security benefits function as the fundamental source of income for many households in the United States. Retirement benefits, disability, survivors' benefits, Medicare, and Supplemental Security Income benefits are offered to families in order to secure the financial stability of U.S. households. The Social Security Administration (2017) reported that Social Security constituted about 33 percent of aggregate income among people aged 65 and over in 2015. About 21 percent of married and 45 percent of unmarried elderly Social Security beneficiaries received 90 percent or more of their income from Social Security benefits (Social Security Administration, 2020a). As shown in Figure 15.3, the Social Security pension replacement rate drops significantly as a person's annual wage increases. This fact emphasizes the importance of planning for additional sources of retirement income to supplement Social Security benefits for middle- and high-income households.

One major concern about Social Security benefits is the risk of the trust fund being depleted. The trust fund is projected to run out in 2035, and beginning in 2035, the benefits payable to recipients might drop to 79 percent of the scheduled benefit (Social Security Administration, 2020b) if no major changes such as tax increases are made. The dotted line of Figure 15.3 illustrates the reduced projection after the cliff. A more conservative projection of Social Security benefits is needed to account for the potential risk of depletion. In addition, as noted earlier, public pension systems of many countries are also facing the issue of sustainability with the risk of depleting the funds.

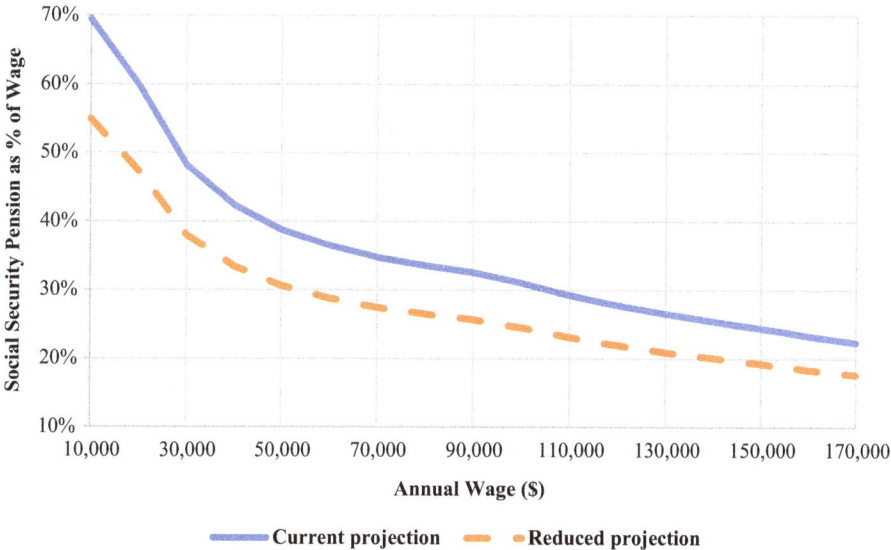

**Figure 15.3:** Social Security Pension as a Percentage of Wage, Based on Current Projections, by Wage. *Note.* Calculated by authors using Social Security Quick Calculator, assuming a retirement age of 67.

*Employer-sponsored plans.* Employer-sponsored retirement plans are also an important source of retirement income. In the past, defined benefit (DB) plans were more commonly offered, but the proportion of employers offering DB plans has decreased over the years while the proportion of employers offering defined contribution (DC) plans has surged. In 2020, about 64 percent of workers had access to DC plans while only 15 percent had access to DB plans (U.S. Bureau of Labor Statistics, 2021). As DC options, such as 401(k) plans, become more prevalent, many workers are now required to make their own choices regarding the amount of and the investment of contributions.

*Personal Savings.* In addition to employer-sponsored retirement plans, there are various forms of tax-advantaged accounts that individuals can use to personally save to fund their retirement, including Individual Retirement Accounts (IRAs). For both IRAs and employer-sponsored plans, workers may be able to choose between traditional accounts with tax-deductible contributions, and Roth accounts, without tax-deductible contributions but with tax-free withdrawals at retirement. However, not everyone can make tax-deductible contributions to traditional accounts. One's ability to deduct contributions to a traditional IRA depends on the person's or household's modified adjusted gross income (MAGI) level. The Internal Revenue Service (IRS) places restrictions on contributions based on whether one (or one's spouse) is an active participant of a retirement plan and one's tax-filing status. If the MAGI is below the phase-out range, the contribution may be fully deductible, and if it is within the range, one may get a partial deduction. If the MAGI is above the phase-out range, none of the contributions to a traditional IRA will be tax-deductible. The optimal choice between Traditional and Roth accounts depends on factors such as current and projected tax brackets (Horan and Al Zaman, 2009). If pre-retirees use these tax-preferred accounts wisely, they could benefit significantly because these accounts generally offer tax-deferred growth on the assets held in the accounts. The assets in the accounts could grow much faster without being taxed and could be subject to a lower marginal tax rate upon withdrawal for those who will be in a lower tax bracket after retirement.

Pre-retirees can also hold financial assets outside of retirement accounts including savings accounts, checking accounts, bonds, mutual funds, exchange-traded funds, and stocks. In addition, academic studies have emphasized the critical role of home equity in building retirement wealth (e.g., Bravo et al., 2019; Poterba et al., 2011), and many studies have considered the value of one's primary residence as a source of retirement income (e.g., Engen et al., 2005; Jacobs et al., 2020; Montalto, 2000; Wolff, 2006). However, tighter restrictions by the U.S. Department of Housing and Urban Development placed on the Home Equity Conversion Mortgage program (HECM) in 2017 have resulted in reductions in what homeowners could borrow against their home equity.

*Employment During Retirement.* The last major source of retirement income is wages. Earning constituted about 34 percent of aggregate income among people aged 65 and over in 2015 (Social Security Administration, 2017). While people might retire from their main job, some continue part-time employment. This may be due to personal preference, caregiving responsibilities, health status, or other reasons. According to the U.S. Bureau of Labor Statistics, the ratio of part-time employment among workers aged 55 and over was 27 percent in 2016, which is a considerably higher rate than the proportion of part-time workers of 18 percent from the ages of 25 to 54 (Toossi and Torpey, 2017).

For households with couples, the partners might retire from full-time employment in different years, so this also needs to be considered when conceptualizing one's retirement plan. Kim et al. (2014) showed the impact of both partners retiring in different years and other causes of substantial changes in income during retirement, such as retiring before eligibility for a pension. They found that a majority of working-age households can expect more than one retirement income stage.

## Withdrawal Strategies

An important consideration for retirement planning involves accurately estimating retirement asset withdrawals. Given that distributions from many tax-advantaged accounts, including employer-sponsored retirement plans and traditional IRAs, are subject to ordinary income tax at distribution, one should carefully plan their withdrawals. When, why, and how much one withdraws could have a considerable consequence on after-tax income. The following discussion highlights some commonly used withdrawal strategies.

*The 4 Percent Rule.* The most well-known rule used to guide retirement asset withdrawal decisions is the "4 Percent Rule." Bengen (1994) suggested individuals could withdraw 4 percent of their initial assets and make sequential withdrawals of the same inflation-adjusted amount, based on historical variations in inflation rates and investment returns, and have a relatively low chance of depleting their investments before death. However, as it will be further noted later in this discussion, the 4 percent withdrawal strategy may not be realistic now because of extremely low returns on savings (Finke et al., 2013).

One approach to more conservatively assess the capital needed to ensure a realistic constant withdrawal strategy is to compute the amount of retirement wealth large enough to generate a perpetual income stream. For example, if $50,000 is assumed as the desired amount needed in addition to pension income in the first year of retirement, a retiree would need the total capital that would yield $50,000 as the first-year earnings. The total capital needed, using the formula below, is $2,500,000 if a 2 percent real return is assumed.

$$Annual\ funding\ amount = Total\ capital\ needed\ at\ retirement \times Real\ return$$

$$Total\ capital\ needed\ at\ retirement = \frac{Annual\ funding\ amount}{Real\ return}$$

*Required Minimum Distributions.* Starting at age 72, individuals in the U.S. must start withdrawals from their traditional retirement accounts. This requirement is enforced through the Required Minimum Distributions (RMD) rule. With RMD rules, distributions based on life expectancy factors must be made once a person attains age 72. This rule applies to many retirement plans and accounts including profit-sharing plans, 401(k), 403(b), 457(b), traditional IRAs, SEPs, SARSEPs, and SIMPLE IRAs. Funds not taken on time are subject to a 50 percent excise tax. Figure 15.4 presents what percentage of a retiree's account balance(s) should be distributed by age. It is clear as one gets older, the percentage of asset that needs to be taken out increases.

If households fail to accumulate enough retirement assets in advance or fail to appropriately manage the assets during retirement, they may be able to remedy the situation by adjusting withdrawals. Scruggs (2019) stated that people have three choice levers when managing retirement outcomes: (1) asset allocation, (2) the

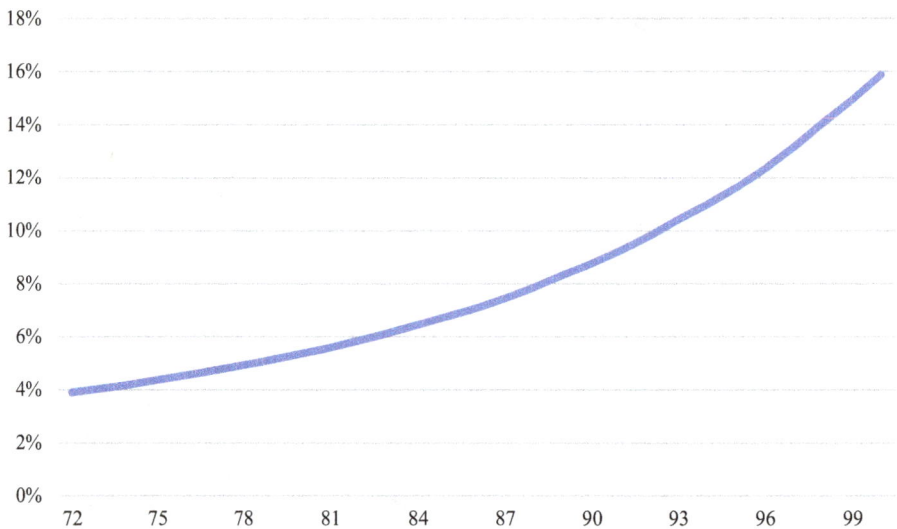

**Figure 15.4:** Annual Required Minimum Distributions (RMD) as Percentage of Balance.
*Note.* Calculated by authors using IRS Uniform Life Table.

initial withdrawal rate, and (3) withdrawal flexibility. Moving these choice levers could have a significant impact on one's future consumption and terminal wealth.

*Annuitization.* Considerable annuitization is preferable in some cases due to longevity risk (Davidoff et al., 2005). In addition, individuals are at risk of mismanaging their retirement assets especially in cases where a retirement account is distributed as a lump sum. A survey conducted by MetLife (2017) found that 21 percent of retirement plan participants chose lump-sum distributions; the report also indicated that these accounts are typically depleted in an average of 5.5 years. Annuitization is a tool that can be used to prevent the risk of outliving retirement savings.

A crude estimation of the cost to purchase an annuity can be determined based on one's projected life expectancy and desired payment level. Consider again the example of the hypothetical worker, Ann Smith. Assume she wants to retire at age 62, and based on her health and family history, she could expect a remaining life expectancy then of 25 years; in other words, on average, 62-year-old women similar to her lives to be 87. Assume also a pessimistic projection of her Social Security pension, and if she started collecting when she turns 62, the benefit would be $20,000 - per year in today's dollars. Assume she also projects that based on her spending needs, she would like to be able to spend $60,000 per year in today's dollars, which means she would need to generate $40,000 per year from her investments. If she had to pay income taxes on withdrawals from her investments, she would need more than $40,000 per year of withdrawals to be able to spend $40,000 per year; however, for simplicity, assume that her retirement fund is a Roth 401k, resulting in tax-free withdrawals. If she wanted to generate a perpetual income stream from her own investments, and she wanted to use a very pessimistic real rate of return on stable investments of 1 percent per year, she would need capital of $4,000,000 at retirement to yield $40,000 of withdrawals every year.[3] However, even with the same pessimistic assumption about the net interest rate on an inflation-projected annuity, she would need capital of only $889,735 at retirement.[4] The reason is that the company selling her the annuity would be spreading the longevity risk across many people.

In the previous example, Ann Smith was projected to accumulate $979,289 by contributing $10,000 per year in constant dollars to her retirement fund; so, by planning to buy an annuity at retirement, she could reach her retirement spending goal if her investments earned the historical real mean rate of return. Keep in mind, however, that increasing her contributions or delaying retirement until age 63 might be prudent since there is a chance her investments will not earn the historic mean real return.

Despite the advantages associated with purchasing annuities, many U.S. households fail to (or choose not to) annuitize their retirement assets when given a choice. The average percentage of households annuitizing all defined benefit (DB) plans is about 70 percent, but when it comes to retirement plans with no restriction on lump-sum distributions, the annuitization rate drops to about 35 percent (Banerjee, 2013). In addition, according to the U.S. Bureau of Labor Statistics (2018), the most common payment option for defined contribution (DC) plans is a lump-sum distribution. This reluctance to annuitize one's retirement asset is referred to as the 'Annuity Puzzle' (Lown and Robb, 2011, p 53). The puzzle may be due to the uncertainty of life expectancy and the hesitancy to pay a lump sum expense to purchase a single-premium annuity.

## Assessment of Retirement Adequacy

Each of the factors discussed thus far is key to determining retirement adequacy. Retirement adequacy is an indicator of retirement preparedness, which is evaluated by comparing projected retirement wealth to projected retirement needs. According to Kim et al. (2014), the proportion of households with adequate projected retirement income to replace their pre-retirement needs increased from 44 percent in 1995 to 58 percent in 2007. However, one of the major concerns with retirement adequacy is that worker perception of adequacy often is not consistent with an objective projection of adequacy. Some workers may not be on track to have enough retirement income but perceive themselves as being adequately prepared; they are, therefore, likely to

---

**3** $40,000/1% = $4,000,000.
**4** PV of $40,000 per year, N=25, i/y=1%, BGN (as an annuity due calculation).

experience shortfalls in retirement (Kim and Hanna, 2015; Lee, 2021; Munnell et al., 2008). According to Lee (2021), in 2016, 72 percent of households perceived themselves to be on track and adequately prepared for retirement, while only 50 percent were projected to have enough retirement income. About 31 percent were unrealistically optimistic in their retirement income projections. For those interested in this topic, Hanna et al. (2016) provided a comprehensive review of empirical studies on retirement adequacy and related issues.

Calculation of projected adequacy at retirement is complex. One approach is to compare the present value of spending needs to the present value of income from pensions and other sources. Social Security benefits include cost of living adjustments and can be considered safe investments, but defined benefit pensions from private employers, and even some government employers, often do not have cost of living adjustments, so the calculation of the present values may require different discount rates. For instance, an inflation-adjusted interest rate for Social Security benefits versus a nominal interest rate for a defined benefit pension from a private employer may be needed. The present value of pension income and other continuing income can be added to projections of investment accumulations, with the total being a projection of wealth at retirement. The present value of spending needed should be calculated with an inflation-adjusted interest rate. If the projected wealth at retirement is greater than the present value of the spending need in retirement, one can conclude that the pre-retiree is on track to meet their retirement adequacy goal, although there could be uncertainty about projections of investments and whether the worker can work as long as expected.

## Conclusion

As noted at the outset of this chapter, the United States has been experiencing an aging boom coupled with increased life expectancies in the population. This phenomenon is being encountered worldwide, where old-age dependency ratios in many countries are projected to considerably increase for the next few decades (Alaminos et al., 2020; Devesa-Carpio et al., 2020). The demographic change combined with other issues led to the increase in average public spending on public pensions in the OECD countries from 6.3 percent of gross domestic product (GDP) in 1990 to 8.0 percent of GDP in 2015 (OECD, 2019). Aging trends can serve as a call to action for personal finance researchers and practitioners, as well as policymakers, by directing greater attention to the growing importance of retirement planning. Workers in the United States and worldwide will continue to face challenges related to public pension deficits and potential social support program insolvency, changes in the retirement pension environment, and evolving income tax laws (e.g., SECURE Act and CARES Act). An opportunity exists to expand the retirement planning literature by empirically testing models of income adequacy, withdrawal rate stability, and savings behavior. Each of the various issues and factors discussed in this chapter is worth further research, practice, and policy considerations.

# References

Alaminos, E., Ayuso, M., and Guillen, M. (2020). Demographic and social challenges in the design of public pension schemes. In P. O. Marta, A. G. Jose, D. F. Inmaculada, and D. Pierre (eds.), *Economic challenges of pension systems: A sustainability and international management perspective* (pp. 33–55). Springer.

Alderson, M. J., and Betker, B. L. (2017). Does the benefit of deferring social security offset the opportunity cost to do so? *Journal of Financial Planning*, *30*(9), 38–47.

Banerjee, S. (2013). *Annuity and lump-sum decisions in defined benefit plans: The role of plan rules* (EBRI Issue Brief No.381). Employee Benefit Research Institute. https://pubmed.ncbi.nlm.nih.gov/23479827/

Bengen, W. P. (1994). Determining withdrawal rates using historical data. *Journal of Financial Planning*, *7*(4), 171–180.

Biggs, A. G., and Springstead, G. R. (2008). Alternate measures of replacement rates for social security benefits and retirement income. *Social Security Bulletin*, *68*, 1–19.

Blanchett, D. M. (2018). The impact of retirement age uncertainty on retirement outcomes. *Journal of Financial Planning*, *31*(9), 36–45.

Bravo, J. M., Ayuso, M., and Holzmann, R. (2019). *Making use of home equity: The potential of housing wealth to enhance retirement security* (IZA Discussion Papers No. 12656). Institute of Labor Economics. https://www.iza.org/publications/dp/12656/making-use-of-home-equity-the-potential-of-housing-wealth-to-enhance-retirement-security

Davidoff, T., Brown, J. R., and Diamond, P. A. (2005). Annuities and individual welfare. *American Economic Review*, *95*(5), 1573–1590.

Devesa-Carpio, J. E., Rosado-Cebrian, B., and Álvarez-García, J. (2020). Sustainability of public pension systems. In P. O. Marta, A. G. Jose, D. F. Inmaculada, and D. Pierre (Eds.), *Economic challenges of pension systems: A sustainability and international management perspective* (pp. 125–154). Springer.

Engen, E. M., Gale, W. G., and Uccello, C. E. (2005). Lifetime earnings, social security benefits, and the adequacy of retirement wealth accumulation. *Social Security Bulletin*, *66*(1), 3–8.

Finke, M., Pfau, W. D., and Blanchett, D. (2013). The 4 percent rule is not safe in a low-yield world. *Journal of Financial Planning*, *26*(6), 46–55.

Hanna, S., Fan, J. X., and Chang, Y. R. (1995). Optimal life cycle savings. *Journal of Financial Counseling and Planning*, *6*, 1–15.

Hanna, S. D., and Kim, K. T. (2017). Treatment of inflation in retirement planning calculations: An improved method. *Journal of Financial Planning*, *30*(1), 44–53.

Hanna, S. D., Kim, K. T., and Chen, S. C.-C. (2016). Retirement savings. In J. J. Xiao (ed.), *Handbook of consumer finance research* (2nd ed., pp. 33–43). Springer.

Hanna, S. D., Zhang, L., and Kim, K. T. (2017). Do worker expectations of never retiring indicate a preference or an inability to plan? *Journal of Financial Counseling and Planning*, *28*(2), 268–284.

Harris-Kojetin, L. D., Sengupta, M., Lendon, J. P., Rome, V., Valverde, R., and Caffrey, C. (2019). *Long-term care providers and services users in the United States, 2015–2016*. U.S. Department of Health and Human Services. https://www.cdc.gov/nchs/products/index.htm

Horan, S. M., and Al Zaman, A. (2009). IRAs under progressive tax regimes and income growth. *Financial Services Review, 18*(3), 195–211.

Hurd, M. D., and Rohwedder, S. (2008). *The retirement consumption puzzle: Actual spending change in panel data* (NBER Working Paper Series No.13929). National Bureau of Economic Research. http://www.nber.org/papers/w13929

Ibbotson, R. G. (2021). *2021 Stocks, bonds, bills & inflation yearbook.* Duff & Phelps, LLC.

Jacobs, L., Llanes, E., Moore, K., Thompson, J., and Volz, A. H. (2020). *Wealth distribution and retirement preparation among early savers.* Board of Government of the Federal Reserve System. https://doi.org/10.17016/feds.2020.043

Johnson, R. W. (2016). *Who is covered by private long-term care insurance?* Urban Institute. http://www.urban.org/research/publication/who-covered-private-long-term-care-insurance

Johnson, R. W. (2019). *What is the lifetime risk of needing and receiving long-term services and supports?* (ASPE Research Brief April 2019). U.S. Department of Health and Human Services Office. https://aspe.hhs.gov/pdf-report/what-lifetime-risk-needing-and-receiving-long-term-services-and-supports

Kim, K. T., and Hanna, S. D. (2015). Do U.S. households perceive their retirement preparedness realistically? *Financial Services Review, 24*(2), 139–155.

Kim, K. T., Hanna, S. D., and Chen, S. C.-C. (2014). Consideration of retirement income stages in planning for retirement. *Journal of Personal Finance, 13*(1), 52–64.

Lee, S. T. (2021). *Financial knowledge, overconfidence, and financial behaviors of individuals* [Unpublished doctoral dissertation]. Ohio State University.

Lockwood, L. M. (2018). Incidental bequests and the choice to self-insure late-life risks. *American Economic Review, 108*(9), 2513–2550.

Lown, J. M., and Robb, D. K. (2011). Attitudes toward immediate annuities: Overcoming the annuity puzzle. *Journal of Consumer Education, 28*, 44–60.

Lucifora, C., and Vigani, D. (2018). Health care utilization at retirement: The role of the opportunity cost of time. *Health Economics, 27*(12), 2030–2050.

MetLife. (2017). *Retirement Plan lump sums being depleted too quickly.* https://www.metlife.com/about-us/newsroom/2017/april/retirement-plan-lump-sums-being-depleted-too-quickly/

Mitchell, O. S., and Utkus, S. (2020). *Target date funds and portfolio choice in 401 (k) plans* (NBER Working Paper Series No.26684). National Bureau of Economic Research. https://doi.org/10.3386/w26684

Modigliani, F. (1986). Life cycle, individual thrift, and the wealth of nations. *Science, 234*(4777), 704–712.

Montalto, C. P. (2000). Retirement savings of American households: Asset levels and adequacy. *Consumer Federation of America, DirectAdvice.com*, 1–11.

Munnell, A. H. (2019). Socioeconomic barriers to working longer. *Generations, 43*(3), 42–50.

Munnell, A. H., Golub-Sass, F., Soto, M., and Webb, A. (2008). *Do households have a good sense of their retirement preparedness?* (Issue Brief No.8–11). Center for Retirement Research at Boston College. http://crr.bc.edu/wp-content/uploads/2008/08/ib_8-11_508x.pdf

National Center for Health Statistics (2021). *Health, United States, 2019.* https://www.cdc.gov/nchs/hus/contents2019.htm

Organisation for Economic Co-operation and Development (OECD). (2019). *Pensions at a glance 2019.* https://doi.org/10.1787/888934042314

Organisation for Economic Co-operation and Development (OECD). (2021). *Life expectancy at 65.* https://data.oecd.org/healthstat/life-expectancy-at-65.htm#indicator-chart

Pokorski, R., and Berg, B. W. (2017). Retirement planning: Coping with higher health care costs. *Journal of Financial Service Professionals, 71*(3), 53–62.

Poterba, J. M., Venti, S., and Wise, D. (2011). The composition and drawdown of wealth in retirement. *Journal of Economic Perspectives*, *25*(4), 95–118.

Rosado-Cebrian, B., Peris-Ortiz, M., and Rueda-Armengot, C. (2020). Adequacy of public pension systems. In P. O. Marta, A. G. Jose, D. F. Inmaculada, and D. Pierre (eds.), *Economic challenges of pension systems: A sustainability and international management perspective* (pp. 173–191). Springer.

Scruggs, J. T. (2019). Asset allocation and withdrawal strategies: Three levers for managing retirement outcomes. *Journal of Financial Planning*, *32*(6), 39–49.

Skinner, J. (2007). Are you sure you're saving enough for retirement? *Journal of Economic Perspectives*, *21*(3), 59–80.

Social Security Administration. (2017). *Fast facts & figures about Social Security, 2017*. https://www.ssa.gov/policy/docs/chartbooks/fast_facts/2017/fast_facts17.pdf

Social Security Administration. (2020a). *Fact sheet: Social Security*. https://www.ssa.gov/news/press/factsheets/basicfact-alt.pdf

Social Security Administration. (2020b). *The 2020 annual report of the board of trustees of the federal old-age and survivors insurance and federal disability insurance trust funds*. https://www.ssa.gov/OACT/TR/2020/tr2020.pdf

Toossi, M., and Torpey, E. (2017). *Older workers: Labor force trends and career options*. U.S. Bureau of Labor Statistics. https://www.bls.gov/careeroutlook/2017/article/older-workers.htm

U.S. Bureau of Labor Statistics. (2018). *Lump sums are the most common payment option for participants in defined contribution retirement plans*. https://www.bls.gov/opub/ted/2018/lump-sums-are-most-common-payment-option-for-participants-in-defined-contribution-retirement-plans.htm

U.S. Bureau of Labor Statistics. (2021). *CPI for all urban consumers (CPI-U): 12-month percent change*. https://data.bls.gov/pdq/SurveyOutputServlet

U.S. Census Bureau. (2017). *2017 National population projections tables*. https://www.census.gov/data/tables/2017/demo/popproj/2017-summary-tables.html

Whitehouse, E., and Queisser, M. (2007). *Pensions at a glance: Public policies across OECD countries*. Organisation for Economic Co-operation and Development. https://doi-org.proxy.lib.ohio-state.edu/10.1787/pension_glance-2007-en.

Wolff, E. N. (2006). *The adequacy of retirement resources among the soon-to-retire, 1983 – 2001* (Working Paper No.472). Levy Economics Institute of Bard College. http://www.levyinstitute.org/pubs/wp_472.pdf

Wade D. Pfau

# 16 Generating Income in Retirement Using Systematic Withdrawal Strategies with Investments

**Abstract:** Retirees seek to fund expenses from their accumulated retirement asset base over an unknown retirement length. Practitioner models developed since the 1990s to understand sustainable spending in the face of longevity and market risk are based on historical data or Monte Carlo simulations. After exploring the assumptions of these basic studies and reasons why they may overestimate potential sustainable spending levels in the historical perspective, this chapter digs deeper into the types of retiree characteristics that may best align with these approaches in research and policy. Those who may be best served by thinking about sustainable withdrawal rates from a total return portfolio will tend to have preferences for probability-based focus on growth, a desire to front-load retirement spending, a preference for time-based flooring, and a view toward technical liquidity. A related "hybrid" strategy of time segmentation shares many of these characteristics, but re-positions bonds to cover early retirement expenses through a safety-first focus on contractual protections. After identifying these characteristics, the chapter continues with practitioner tools and techniques to examine how sustainable spending may be increased for those whose retirement income style is aligned. This chapter lays out the various approaches to using withdrawal rates with investment assets to guide retirement spending.

**Keywords:** retirement income planning, safe withdrawal rate, retirement spending, retirement distributions, the 4 percent rule

## Introduction

The challenge in building an effective retirement income plan is to use available income tools and tactics in a strategic manner to meet the financial goals of retirement while also managing the risks confronting those goals. The primary financial goal for most retirees relates to spending: Maximize spending power in such a way that spending can remain consistent and sustainable without any drastic reductions, no matter how long the retirement lasts. Other important goals may include leaving assets for subsequent generations and maintaining sufficient reserves for unexpected expenses and contingencies in retirement.

**Wade D. Pfau,** The American College of Financial Services

https://doi.org/10.1515/9783110727692-016

Meanwhile, the three major categories of risk for a retirement income plan include longevity, market volatility, and spending shocks. Longevity risk is the possibility of living longer than planned, which could mean not having resources to maintain the retiree's standard of living. Market volatility is the risk that poor market returns are realized, leading to a reduced portfolio value and a reduced ability to maintain the retirement standard of living. Taking distributions from investments in retirement further amplifies market risk by increasing the importance of the ordering of investment returns. This is called sequence-of-returns risk. Finally, spending shocks are the risk that expensive bills materialize, such as for long-term care or healthcare, which require large expenditures that deplete assets and reduce the ability to maintain a lifestyle.

Academics and practitioners have developed a variety of strategies and techniques for building retirement income strategies to manage these risks. This chapter focuses on a subset of techniques related to taking sustainable distributions from investment portfolios throughout retirement without relying on insurance tools to manage longevity and market risk. These retirees face a trade-off with spending in retirement as spending more at the present means creating greater risk for needing to reduce spending in the future. Retirees need to weigh the consequences between spending too little and spending too much—that is, being too frugal or running out of assets. For such retirees, it is important to determine a "safe" withdrawal rate.

This chapter describes practitioner-based research on the question of the safe withdrawal rate from a portfolio of investment assets that extends back to Bengen (1994). This bases retirement spending feasibility on historical data or uses Monte Carlo simulations seeking a high probability of success for withdrawal rate strategies. With U.S. historical data, the rule identified by William Bengen is that for a 30-year retirement period, a 4 percent inflation-adjusted withdrawal rate using a 50 to 75 percent stock allocation should be reasonably safe for retirees to use. After describing this approach, I work through its key assumptions to identify how withdrawal rates may be lower than the possibilities accounted for with his core assumptions.

Next, the chapter considers more thoroughly the question of retirement income styles. There are multiple suitable approaches to building a retirement income plan, and the withdrawal rate methodology described in this chapter is more relevant to some retirement income styles than others. I describe the factors that contribute to determining a style and the strategies that associate with different styles, focusing on sustainable spending strategies from a total-return investment portfolio or time-based segmentation.

From here, the chapter describes more practitioner tools and techniques for managing retirement risks with withdrawal rate approaches. When attempting to fund a retirement spending goal in retirement, there are ways to help manage market risk with investments to help support greater spending in retirement. These include recognizing the potential to take on greater risk when one has more reliable income sources not exposed to market volatility, planning to adjust spending in response to portfolio performance, reducing portfolio volatility at key points in retirement, and drawing from an external buffer asset to temporarily support spending when the portfolio is underperforming.

# Historical Perspective

Withdrawal rate research began in earnest with practitioner approaches in the 1990s that were largely divorced from traditional lifecycle finance models. Early in that decade, William Bengen read misguided claims in the popular press that average portfolio returns could guide the calculation of sustainable retirement withdrawal rates. If stocks average 7 percent after inflation, then plugging a 7 percent return into a spreadsheet suggests that retirees could withdraw 7 percent each year without ever dipping into their principal. Bengen (1994) recognized the naïveté of ignoring the real-world volatility experienced around that 7 percent return, and he sought to determine the impact of volatility on sustainable spending.

Bengen (1994) pioneered the approach of studying sustainable withdrawal rates from investment portfolios by codifying the importance of sequence-of-returns risk. What is known today as the 4 percent rule for retirement spending was calibrated to the highest sustainable initial spending rate for inflation-adjusted spending from the worst-case 30-year period found in the U.S. historical data for stock and bond index returns since 1926. He used the S&P 500 index to represent the stock market and intermediate-term U.S. government bonds to represent the bond market. He constructed rolling 30-year periods from this data (1926 through 1955, then 1927 through 1956, and so on), using a technique called historical simulations. He calculated the maximum sustainable withdrawal rate for each rolling historical period.

His "SAFEMAX" was the highest sustainable withdrawal rate for the worst-case retirement scenario in the historical period. With a fixed 50/50 allocation for stocks and bonds, the SAFEMAX was 4.15 percent, occurring for a hypothetical retiree in 1966 who experienced the 1966–1995 market returns. If the assumption is modified to have withdrawals taken at the start of each year, as opposed to the end of the year, the SAFEMAX falls to 4.03 percent.

Assume you start retirement with a $1 million portfolio; the 4.03 percent withdrawal rate means that you could withdraw $40,300 in the first year of retirement. In each subsequent year, you could increase that spending amount by the realized inflation rate from the previous year, and you would have been able to sustain these distributions for at least 30 years in each historical 30-year period of data. In all but this worst case, you could have spent at a higher rate, or if you did use 4.03 percent then you would have had additional funds remaining at the end of 30 years. Regarding the choice of 30 years, for a 65-year-old, this leads to a maximum planning age of 95, which Bengen (1994) felt was reasonably conservative. His strategy manages longevity and investment risk by assuming a longer than average lifetime and the worst-case sequence of historical market returns.

Despite being conservative for spending, his approach is not conservative for asset allocation. Bengen (1994) concluded that retirees should use a stock allocation from 50 to 75 percent, but as close as possible to the higher end. Higher stock allocations tended to support higher withdrawal rates, with little in the way of downside risk (Bengen, 2006). Those who find value in this approach to retirement income are generally optimistic about the long-run potential of stocks to outperform bonds and provide positive real returns, so investors are generally advised to take on as much risk as they can tolerate to minimize the probability of plan failure.

Bengen's (1994, 2006) work pointed out that sequence-of-returns risk will reduce safe, sustainable withdrawal rates below what is implied by the average portfolio return over retirement. Indeed, the 4 percent rule implies that the retiree only experienced a 1.3 percent real return on their investments in retirement, as defined by the internal rate of return on their sustainable cash flows, while the 30-year period that defined the 4 percent rule (1966 to 1995) experienced an average compounded return of 4.2 percent for a 50/50 allocation (Pfau, 2017). Sequence-of-returns risk amplifies the impact of traditional investment volatility by making retirement outcomes disproportionately dependent on what happens in the early years of retirement (Pfau, 2014).

Cooley et al. (1998) provided a further study that helped to popularize the idea of "safe" withdrawal rates. Their research followed the same methodology used by Bengen in his 1994 article. The key difference was their shift in emphasis away from the SAFEMAX to the idea of "portfolio success rates." The Trinity study tallied up the percentage of times that withdrawal rates fell below or above certain levels. They calculated these portfolio success rates for different withdrawal rates, for different time horizons, and for different asset allocations. What can generally be observed is that success rates increase for lower withdrawal rates, shorter time horizons, and higher stock allocations.

Simplifying assumptions were used in these early research studies, as the purpose was to provide a more realistic assessment of sustainable spending than found when assuming a fixed average investment return. But these studies subsequently took on a life of their own. The 4 percent rule has been widely adopted by the popular press and financial planners and viewed as having almost universal applicability. But the "rule" depends on a very specific set of assumptions.

The basic philosophy and assumptions behind the 4 percent rule include that the objective is to meet an overall lifestyle spending goal. Retirees are assumed to desire smooth spending, but they also have an appetite for market volatility. Retirees do not voluntarily reduce spending as they age or adjust withdrawals in response to realized financial market returns. Withdrawals are constant, inflation-adjusted amounts. Retirees earn the precise underlying investment returns net of any fees for a fixed asset allocation with annual portfolio rebalancing. The investment portfolio is either tax-deferred or tax-free. The two financial assets are large-capitalization stocks (S&P 500) and intermediate-term U.S. government bonds. The 4 percent rule assumes the U.S. historical experience is sufficiently representative of what future retirees may expect.

With this approach, failure in retirement is defined as not meeting the overall spending goal for the assumed planning horizon. The underlying objective is to keep the failure rate (the probability of depleting investment assets) at a reasonably low level. For market risk management, retirees use a relatively aggressive diversified portfolio focused on total returns with spending from income and principal. For longevity risk management, retirees assume a planning horizon well beyond life expectancy. For management of spending shocks, retirees focus on precautionary savings, recognizing that additional assets should be available in all but the worst-case scenarios.

Understanding the many assumptions behind the 4 percent rule is important, as suggested spending rates can vary dramatically by changing assumptions. About the 4 percent rule being potentially too high, the U.S. historical experience does not provide a long time span to be confident about 4 percent as a worst-case scenario withdrawal rate. Pfau (2010) identified that the 4 percent rule has not worked nearly as well with financial market data from other developed countries except for Canada. Internationally, the 4 percent rule worked about two-thirds of the time. As well, the work of Finke, Pfau, and Blanchett (2013) suggests less confidence for 4 percent in a low-interest-rate environment. With low yields, retirees may be pushed to spend principal, digging a hole for their portfolio that will be hard to overcome even if interest rates rise back toward historical averages later in retirement.

Another matter is that the 4 percent rule assumes that investors precisely earn the underlying indexed market returns with annual rebalancing. Due to fees, asset allocation choices, or investor behavior, the portfolios of real-world investors may underperform compared to the underlying index returns. With net returns at 1 percent less than market indices, which could result from fees or underperformance, the safe withdrawal rate falls by about 0.5 percent (Pfau, 2017).

The 4 percent rule is also based on a tax-free or tax-deferred portfolio. For those spending from a taxable portfolio, taxes must be paid on reinvested dividends, interest, and capital gains when they accrue. This limits the opportunity for compounding growth as assets are also removed for tax payments, which reduces the sustainable spending rate.

As well, the 4 percent rule assumes a retiree has no desire to leave a bequest or to build in an additional safety margin for their assets. In the worst-case scenario, wealth depletion can be expected. Building in an additional safety margin for wealth further reduces the sustainable withdrawal rate (Pfau, 2017).

The 4 percent rule is also based on a planning horizon of 30 years. When Bengen (1994) prepared his initial research, this was a conservative assumption for the longest survivor in a couple. Today this is no longer the case. Recent estimates from the Society of Actuaries suggest that 30 years is about the life expectancy for the longest living member of a non-smoking 65-year-old couple in excellent health. A conservative longevity projection may now require 35 to 40 years, suggesting an additional 0.5 percent reduction to the "safe" withdrawal rate (Pfau, 2017).

# Research and Policy Issues

The withdrawal rate question is not the only way to approach retirement income planning. Cooper and Pfau (2016) described two distinct schools of thought regarding retirement income, which they described as probability-based and safety-first. These philosophies diverge on the critical issue of where a retirement plan is best served: In the risk/reward trade-offs of a diversified and aggressive investment portfolio or in the contractual protections of insurance products to fund key spending before turning to investments as well. The withdrawal rate methodologies described are distinctly a probability-based approach. It is worth exploring what types of retirees will be most suited to using these withdrawal rate strategies.

Understanding which retirement income approach is best for any individual means knowing more about that individual's preferences and style. Murguia and Pfau (2021) provided a framework for identifying retirement income styles and linking those styles to specific strategies. They tested and quantified the role of six specific and distinct retirement income factors that make up one's retirement income style. They demonstrated the importance of two main sets of factors, as well as four additional supporting factors.

The first main factor relates to preferences on the *Probability-Based versus Safety-First* dimension. This details how individuals prefer to source their retirement income from assets. Probability-based income sources are dependent on the potential for market growth to continually provide income. This includes a traditional diversified investment portfolio or other assets that have the expectation of growth through realized capital gains. Meanwhile, safety-first income sources incorporate contractual obligations. The spending provided through these sources is less exposed to market swings. A safety-first approach may include protected sources of income common with defined-benefit pensions, annuities with lifetime income protections, and holding individual government bonds to maturity.

The second main factor reflects the dimension of preferences for *Optionality versus Commitment*. Optionality reflects a preference for keeping options open for retirement income. Those with an optionality preference want to maintain flexibility with their strategies to respond to more favorable economic developments or to a changing personal situation. Conversely, commitment reflects a preference for committing to a retirement income solution. The security of having a dedicated retirement income solution outweighs missing out on potentially more positive future outcomes.

The other four factors play a more secondary role for understanding retirement decisions. First, with the *Time-Based versus Perpetuity* dimension, retirees ultimately have two funding strategies for building retirement income floors. They may either fund an income floor for specific time periods or in perpetuity. Time-based funding strategies are used to fund fixed windows of time in retirement. Building perpetual floors uses lifetime income protections with risk pooling.

Next is the *Accumulation versus Distribution* dimension. Wealth management traditionally focuses on accumulating assets without applying further thought regarding the differences that may happen after retiring. It is possible that individuals may approach investing during retirement rather differently from investing for retirement, as retirees may worry less about maximizing risk-adjusted returns and worry more about ensuring that their assets can support their spending goals for the remainder of their lives. As such, the distinction for accumulation and distribution details whether one prefers to focus on portfolio growth while retired even though it will entail a more uncertain and lumpier retirement income stream (Accumulation), or whether one prefers a more predictable retirement income path to maintain a standard of living at the potential cost of not seeking the highest potential investment account value at death (Distribution).

Next, the *Front-Loading versus Back-Loading Income* dimension relates to the amount and pace of income to be received throughout retirement. This factor can be directly linked to the trade-offs identified by the concept of longevity risk aversion described in Milevsky and Huang (2011). Longevity risk aversion represents a fear of outliving assets in retirement, and it will impact some individuals more strongly than others. Does an individual feel more comfortable front-loading portfolio distributions with higher spending early in retirement to better ensure that savings can be enjoyed during the early stages when one is more assured to be alive and healthy (Front-Loading)? Or does an individual prefer to spend at a lower rate in early retirement to better ensure that a particular lifestyle can be maintained without cuts during the later stages of a potentially long retirement horizon (Back-Loading)?

Finally, the *True versus Technical Liquidity* dimension reflects differences between the two ways that liquidity can be defined in financial planning. Those who prefer *True Liquidity* would like to have assets earmarked specifically as reserves for future unknown events that can derail a retirement income plan. To be truly liquid, assets must not already be matched to other financial goals such as planned retirement expenses or a specific legacy goal. True Liquidity can involve the use of cash set-asides, buffer assets, and insurance. Those who prefer *Technical Liquidity* would rather raise cash from investments or assets already earmarked for other goals when necessary to fund unexpected expenses, with an understanding that cuts may then need to be made elsewhere. Technical liquidity refers more to a general sense that there is a pot of assets to draw from for any type of expense.

With these six factors, Murguia and Pfau (2021) described Retirement Income Style Awareness™ (RISA™) Profiles as based on the RISA Matrix™ shown in Figure 16.1. The RISA Profile™ is effectively a replacement for measuring risk tolerance for accumulation that is broader and includes more dimensions to be better suited to the complexities of retirement income planning. The RISA Matrix lays out how scores calculated for each RISA factor can be utilized and matched to appropriate retirement income strategies. This process relies on the idea that even though these six factors are statistically distinct from one another and reflect unique characteristics, there are some correlations found between them that work together to link with retirement income strategies.

The scale for probability-based versus safety-first is aligned horizontally, and optionality versus commitment is aligned vertically. This creates four distinct retirement income strategy quadrants, each of which is based on an individual's scores for these two main RISA factors. Important to this as well is that the probability-based perspective is correlated with a preference for optionality, while those with a safety-first outlook also tend to be more commitment-oriented. The four supporting factors are mixed in as well through their correlations to the main factors to identify strategies more strongly.

From the available retirement income strategies, it is possible to identify four main classes of strategies to match the four quadrants within the RISA Matrix. These are total return, risk wrap, income protection, and time segmentation (or bucketing). In their framework, the strategies described in this chapter largely fit into the "total return" category, with overlap to the hybrid "time segmentation" category.

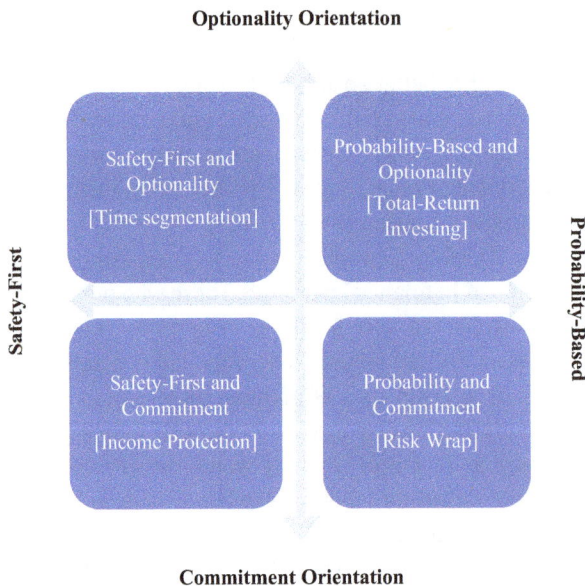

**Optionality Orientation**

| | |
|---|---|
| Safety-First and Optionality [Time segmentation] | Probability-Based and Optionality [Total-Return Investing] |
| Safety-First and Commitment [Income Protection] | Probability and Commitment [Risk Wrap] |

Safety-First · Probability-Based

**Commitment Orientation**

**Figure 16.1:** The Retirement Income Style Awareness™ (2021) Matrix.

Individuals who locate in the upper-right quadrant of the RISA Matrix hold preferences that lean toward both probability-based and optionality. On average, participants with probability-based and optionality preferences identify with drawing income from a diversified investment portfolio rather than using contractual sources to fund their retirement expenses. Investors expect portfolio growth to sustainably support their spending and do not want to feel committed to a strategy. As for secondary characteristics in this quadrant, as identified through their correlations with the two primary factors, these individuals also tend toward an accumulation focus, technical liquidity, front-loading for spending, and time-based flooring. Those who value optionality wish to maintain the ability to consider retirement income withdrawal options on an ongoing basis. They are also more comfortable with seeking market growth despite the volatility. The individual is likely to consider a preference for a more variable income stream with the potential for investment growth rather than a stable retirement income stream with more muted potential investment growth. They want to enjoy their early retirement years and are willing to accept the risk that they may have to make spending cuts later. These retirees are comfortable with investments-centric approaches that rely on earning the risk premium from the stock market.

Also relevant is the upper left quadrant, identified with time segmentation. With this style, an investment portfolio is still the primary focus for funding retirement income, but a different view about asset allocation is used. This is a hybrid case as these are individuals with both safety-first and optionality preferences. These individuals like contractual protections, but they also prefer to keep options open. This quadrant is also correlated with preferences for true liquidity and for front-loading retirement spending. The desires reflected here relate to time segmentation.

A time segmentation strategy usually sources short-term retirement income needs with a rolling bond ladder or other fixed-income assets. Bond ladders are frequently implemented with contractually protected instruments (e.g., cash equivalents or government-issued securities) that can be used for shorter to intermediate income needs, with a diversified investment portfolio designed for longer-term expenses that will gradually replenish the short-term buckets as those assets are used to cover retirement expenses. These strategies address the need for asset safety by including short-term contractual protections while maintaining high optionality for other investment assets. This provides a longer period for volatile assets to recover from market declines before they must be sold as part of funding retirement. Huxley and Burns (2004) explained that the natural way to choose a stock allocation is whatever is left over after creating a bond ladder to lock-in upcoming spending needs for a window of three to ten years.

There is much debate about whether these strategies are materially different from using total-return investing. However, in terms of behavior, these strategies do have an important difference from total returns if they help people displaying the characteristics of this retirement income style to be more comfortable with a growth portfolio by overlaying short-term protections.

## Practitioner Tools and Techniques

From the historical perspective, concerns about defining "safe" withdrawal rates as based on historical data using the Bengen (1994) methodology were identified in this chapter. The objective was to determine how low spending should be so that retirees do not have to worry about depleting their investments while maintaining a fixed (or inflation-adjusted, which is fixed in real terms) spending level throughout retirement. In practice, fixed spending from a volatile investment portfolio is the least efficient way to manage retirement risk. It creates the most sequence-of-returns risk such that initial spending must be low to avoid the risk of outliving assets. Scott et al. (2009) identified these inefficiencies, as retirees will underspend in typical retirement circumstances while still facing the risk of overspending if their assumptions were not conservative enough. For practitioner tools and techniques, I consider modifications to the withdrawal rate methodology that may work to support more retirement spending.

Milevsky and Huang (2011) also summarized the academic criticism of constant spending from a volatile portfolio that seeks to minimize failure. They noted that optimal spending strategies should be dynamic, with spending positively related to survival probabilities and the degree of exogenous pension income, and negatively related to longevity risk aversion. This deviates in several ways from the 4 percent rule assumptions. The first is that one should intentionally plan to spend more when they are sure to be alive, while reducing spending at a time that may never exist. Otherwise, a retiree sacrifices too much by cutting spending in early retirement to allow for the same spending later when survival rates are low. With lower planned future spending, the initial withdrawal rate can be increased. As well, most retirees will have income streams available from outside their financial portfolios, such as Social Security or other pensions. This reduces the impact of financial asset depletion, which could allow a retiree to be comfortable with more aggressive spending above a "safe" rate. Finally, both factors will be tempered somewhat to the extent that a retiree is particularly fearful of outliving their financial assets. Greater longevity risk aversion requires planning for less spending over a longer time horizon. With these factors in mind, it is quite possible that some retirees may be willing to choose a withdrawal rate of 4 percent or higher even if it cannot be considered as "safe."

Relatedly, spending may naturally decline with age. The 4 percent rule assumes constant spending in inflation-adjusted terms throughout the retirement period. But actual retirees do tend to reduce their discretionary expenditures as they age and spend more time at home (Blanchett, 2014). On the other hand, health expenses tend to rise with age. To the extent that spending can be assumed to decline at higher ages as reflected in average spending patterns, a retiree is justified to use a higher initial withdrawal rate at the start of retirement.

Another approach that can help manage sequence-of-returns risk for an aggressively allocated investment portfolio is to allow spending to fluctuate in response to the portfolio performance. Spending adjustments mitigates sequence-of-returns risk by reducing the need for distributions after a portfolio decline. This allows for fewer shares to be sold at a loss and more assets to remain available in the investment portfolio to experience any subsequent market recovery.

Bengen (2001) described fixed-percentage withdrawals as an opposing alternative to constant inflation-adjusted spending. This rule calls for users to spend a constant percentage of the remaining portfolio balance in each year of retirement. This rule never depletes the portfolio. Cotton (2013) also formalized how a constant percentage strategy eliminates sequence-of-returns risk entirely since spending changes proportionately with portfolio changes. As such, it is possible to expect the sustainable spending rate to be higher than with constant inflation-adjusted withdrawals. As for disadvantages, spending can become extremely volatile with this strategy, if combined with volatile investments, and it will be difficult for retirees to budget in advance.

The fixed percentage and the constant (inflation-adjusted) spending rules represent two extremes. Other dynamic spending rules provide a compromise between these two extremes, by having a mechanism to smooth spending adjustments made in response to market volatility. These compromise options seek to balance the trade-offs between reduced sequence-of-returns risk and increased spending volatility by only partially linking spending to portfolio performance. Financial advisors and other researchers have proposed various dynamic spending strategies. Examples include the Bengen (2001) floor-and-ceiling withdrawal method, the decision rules and guardrails developed by Guyton (2004) and Guyton and Klinger (2006), and the Zolt (2013) Target Percentage Adjustment method.

Other variable spending approaches are more related to actuarial methods that generally have clients regularly recalculate their sustainable spending based on the remaining portfolio balance, remaining longevity, and expected portfolio returns. These factors are all updated on an ongoing basis to determine a reasonable ongoing spending percentage rate. A basic form for the actuarial method is to use the Internal Revenue Services' Required Minimum Distribution (RMD) rules as a more general guide for sustainable spending. The RMD rules indicate a by-age percentage that must be withdrawn from tax-deferred accounts in the United States, but they can be applied more generally to define overall retirement spending. Blanchett et al. (2012) and Sun and Webb (2013) both studied the RMD rule as a spending option and found it to be a reasonable strategy that roughly approximates more sophisticated optimization attempts.

Another approach to managing sequence-of-returns risk is to reduce portfolio volatility. A portfolio free of volatility does not create sequence-of-returns risk. However, simply shifting into bonds does not work successfully if the spending goal exceeds what the bond yield curve can support. It is important to consider other aspects of volatility reduction. This chapter has discussed time segmentation as one potential option. Another approach is the rising equity glidepath concept outlined in Pfau and Kitces (2014). A rising equity glide path in retirement starts with an equity allocation that is lower than typically recommended in the "safe" withdrawal rate research literature at the start of retirement, but then the stock allocation slowly increases over time. This can reduce the probability and the magnitude of retirement failures while not giving up entirely on market growth opportunities. This approach reduces vulnerability to early retirement stock market declines that cause the most harm to retirees.

Another possible way to reduce volatility is to use broader portfolio diversification. The 4 percent rule assumes only a few asset classes are used. What matters for sustainable withdrawal rates is the interaction of portfolio returns and volatility. Creating a more globally diversified portfolio can potentially produce return/volatility characteristics supporting a higher withdrawal rate. To provide more flexibility about choosing asset classes and capital market assumptions, Pfau (2012) provided charts that connect sustainable spending rates to portfolio returns and volatilities for different success rates and retirement time horizons.

The final category of approaches to managing sequence-of-returns risk is to have other uncorrelated "buffer" assets available outside the financial portfolio to draw from after a market downturn. Returns on these assets should not be correlated with the financial portfolio, since the purpose of these buffer assets is to support spending when the portfolio is otherwise falling short. To manage sequence-of-returns risk, buffer assets must have the characteristic that they are liquid and must not decline in value along with a general market downturn. They are framed as being held outside of the portfolio and only used temporarily under certain market conditions to be conceptually different from a time segmentation strategy. Three buffer assets are cash holdings (Evensky, 2006), cash value for whole life insurance (Pfau, 2019a, Pfau, 2019b), and a Home Equity Conversion Mortgage (i.e., reverse mortgage) line of credit (Sacks and Sacks, 2012; Salter et al., 2012; Pfau, 2018). In isolation, using buffer assets may look expensive. But the costs can be offset by gains elsewhere in the overall financial plan through their ability to help manage sequence-of-returns risk. Buffer assets can work to protect the investment portfolio from incurring excessive distributions at perilous moments.

## Conclusion

Discussions about retirement income planning can become quite confusing as there are so many different viewpoints expressed in the consumer media. Each individual must ultimately identify the style and its associated strategies that can best support his or her financial and psychological needs for retirement. This chapter has discussed withdrawal rates for retirement income, which link most closely to total return investment strategies and time segmentation.

Bengen (1994) defined the baseline approach for sustainable distributions by seeking constant (inflation-adjusted) spending from a volatile investment portfolio.

This strategy amplifies the sequence of returns risk for retirees, and the chapter considered various reasons why the "safe" withdrawal rate may be less than implied by Bengen's methodology and data. Nonetheless, with practitioner tools and techniques, the chapter also considered various ways to increase spending by changing some of those core assumptions. These include accepting a higher risk of portfolio depletion, reducing spending with age, allowing spending to adjust for portfolio performance, reducing portfolio volatility in the early years of retirement, using broader portfolio diversification, and having buffer assets outside of the investment portfolio.

The Retirement CARE Analysis™ introduced in Pfau (2017) outlines the factors a retiree should consider when choosing an initial spending rate and asset allocation. This framework is based on Capacities, Aspirations, Realities, and Emotions, which relate to the issues described. When determining a withdrawal rate strategy, this chapter explored how retirees may consider a higher initial withdrawal rate as it relates to characteristics including having reliable income sources from outside the portfolio that do not expose spending to downside market risks, having the flexibility to adjust spending and make potential reductions over time, having more optimistic capital market assumptions, managing behavior, fees, and taxes to have less impact on net returns, having less risk aversion for short-term portfolio volatility, and less longevity risk aversion as related to fears about outliving wealth.

# References

Bengen, W. P. (1994). Determining withdrawal rates using historical data. *Journal of Financial Planning, 7*(4), 171–180.

Bengen, W. P. (2001). Conserving client portfolios during retirement, Part IV. *Journal of Financial Planning, 14*(5), 110–119.

Bengen, W. P. (2006). *Conserving client portfolios during retirement.* FPA Press.

Blanchett, D. (2014). Exploring the retirement consumption puzzles. *Journal of Financial Planning, 27*(5), 34–42.

Blanchett, D., Kowara, M., and Chen, P. (2012). Optimal withdrawal strategy for retirement-income portfolios. *Retirement Management Journal, 2*(3), 7–20.

Cooley, P. L., Hubbard, C. M., and Walz, D. T. (1998). Retirement savings: Choosing a withdrawal rate that is sustainable. *American Association of Individual Investors Journal, 20*(2), 16–21.

Cooper, J., and Pfau, W. D. (2016). The yin and yang of retirement income philosophies. *The Journal of Superannuation Management, 7*(1), 39–42.

Cotton, D. (2013, September 20). Clarifying sequence of returns risk (Part 2, with pictures!). *The Retirement Café.* http://theretirementcafe.blogspot.com/2013/09/clarifying-sequence-of-returns-risk_20.html

Evensky, H. (2006). Withdrawal strategies: A cash flow solution. In H. Evensky, and D. B. Katz (eds.), *Retirement income redesigned: Master plans for distribution* (pp. 64–74). Bloomberg Press.

Finke, M., Pfau, W. D., and Blanchett, D. (2013). The 4% rule is not safe in a low-yield world. *Journal of Financial Planning, 26*(6), 46–55.

Guyton, J. T. (2004). Decision rules and portfolio management for retirees: Is the "safe" initial withdrawal rate too safe? *Journal of Financial Planning*, *17*(10), 54–62.

Guyton, J. T., and Klinger, W. J. (2006). Decision rules and maximum initial withdrawal rates. *Journal of Financial Planning*, *19*(3), 49–57.

Huxley, S. J., and Burns, J. B. (2004). *Asset dedication: How to grow wealthy with the next generation of asset allocation*. McGraw-Hill Education.

Milevsky, M. A., and Huang, H. (2011). Spending retirement on planet Vulcan: The impact of longevity risk aversion on optimal withdrawal rates. *Financial Analysts Journal*, *67*(2), 45–58.

Murguia, A., and Pfau, W. D. (2021). A model approach to selecting a personalized retirement income strategy. https://ssrn.com/abstract=3788232

Pfau, W. D. (2010). An international perspective on safe withdrawal rates: The demise of the 4% rule? *Journal of Financial Planning*, *23*(12), 52–61.

Pfau, W. D. (2012). Capital market expectations, asset allocation, and safe withdrawal rates. *Journal of Financial Planning*, *25*(1), 36–43.

Pfau, W. D. (2014). The lifetime sequence of returns: A retirement planning conundrum. *Journal of Financial Service Professionals*, *68*(1), 53–58.

Pfau, W. D. (2017). *How much can I spend in retirement: A guide to investment-based retirement income strategies*. Retirement Researcher Media.

Pfau, W. D. (2018). *Reverse mortgages: How to secure your retirement with a reverse mortgage*. Retirement Researcher Media.

Pfau, W. D. (2019a). *Safety-first retirement planning: An integrated approach for a worry-free retirement*. Retirement Researcher Media.

Pfau, W. D. (2019b). Investigating the role of whole life insurance in a lifetime financial plan. *Journal of Financial Planning*, *32*(2), 44–53.

Pfau, W. D., and Kitces, M. E. (2014). Reducing retirement risk with a rising equity glide path. *Journal of Financial Planning*, *27*(1), 38–45.

Sacks, B. H., and Sacks, S. R. (2012). Reversing the conventional wisdom: Using home equity to supplement retirement income. *Journal of Financial Planning*, *25*(2), 43–52.

Salter, J. R., Pfeiffer, S. A., and Evensky, H. R. (2012). Standby reverse mortgages: A risk management tool for retirement distributions. *Journal of Financial Planning*, *25*(8), 40–48.

Scott, J. S., Sharpe, W. F., and Watson, J. G. (2009). The 4% rule—at what price? *Journal of Investment Management*, *7*(3), 31–48.

Sun, W., and Webb, A. (2013). Should households base asset decumulation strategies on required minimum distribution tables? *The Geneva Papers on Risk and Insurance-Issues and Practice*, *38*(4), 729–752.

Zolt, D. (2013). Achieving a higher safe withdrawal rate with the target percentage adjustment. *Journal of Financial Planning*, *26*(1), 51–59.

George W. Haynes, Deborah C. Haynes

# 17 Small Business Ownership: Impact of the Lack of Transparency and Separation on Small Business Finances

**Abstract:** Small businesses are often viewed as smaller versions of large businesses; however, small businesses possess many attributes distinguishing them from large businesses. This chapter discusses the unique characteristics of small businesses that operate in the United States and examines the influence of the lack of transparency and separation between the family and business on the financial structure and access of small business owners. The chapter explores claims that the lack of financial transparency encourages small business owners to acquire equity and debt capital from internal sources, such as owner savings, family, friends, and other business affiliates. In addition, this chapter explores claims that there is a lack of separation between the family and business. The lack of separation creates challenges for the family business, such as having an undiversified financial portfolio for the owning family, intermingling of financial capital between the family and business, and the lack of liability protection. The lack of transparency and separation are important to recognize when researching small business owners. The challenge for those interested in researching small business owners is utilizing qualitative and quantitative data that enables the analyst to consider a holistic view of the family business.

**Keywords:** transparency, separation, small business, family business, financial structure and access, small business ownership

## Introduction

Small businesses in the United States comprised 99.9 percent of all businesses (13.7 million), employed 47 percent of the private workforce (60.6 million), and accounted for 44 percent of economic activity in 2014 (Kobe and Schwinn, 2018). Small businesses are often viewed as smaller versions of large businesses; however, small businesses, which are largely privately held, are fundamentally different from large businesses, which are largely publicly held. In addition, nearly all small businesses are family businesses, where unraveling the finances of the family and business can be challenging. Ang (1991) addressed these concerns by suggesting, "It is fair to say that the theory of modern corporate finance is not developed with

**George W. Haynes, Deborah C. Haynes,** Montana State University

https://doi.org/10.1515/9783110727692-017

small businesses in mind" (p. 1). This chapter explores two major issues facing small business owners: lack of transparency and lack of separation between the family and small business.

The lack of transparency refers to the inability of lenders to correctly assess the creditworthiness of the business due to the lack of generally accepted management and financial procedures used in small businesses. The lack of separation refers to the fact that small businesses are owned and managed by a family member or family members and therefore have financial and management "spill-over" between the family and business systems.

Until the late 1980s, small business finance was an under-researched area in business and personal finance because very limited data were available. The small business finance research discussed in this chapter depended primarily, but not exclusively, on four datasets: (a) National Survey of Small Business Finances (NSSBF), (b) Survey of Consumer Finances (SCF), (c) National Family Business Survey (NFBS), and (d) Kauffman Firm Survey (KFS). With the advent of the NSSBF in the late 1980s, small business researchers had access to high-quality financial data supplied by the Federal Reserve Board and Small Business Administration. Unfortunately, the NSSBF was discontinued in 2003; however, analysis of these data continues today. Researchers interested in the linkage between the household and small business utilized the SCF and NFBS. And, finally, those researchers focused on entrepreneurship utilized the KFS, which began in 2004. Other research utilized the Call Reports from the Federal Deposit Insurance Corporation (FDIC) and Community Reinvestment Act reports to explore lending behavior by depository lenders.

This chapter will use themes of transparency and separation to discuss what makes small businesses different in the historical perspectives section, explore the impact of these differences on their financial structure and access in the research and policy section, introduce a model designed to address financial challenges faced by these small businesses owners in the practitioner tools and techniques section, present an illustration of a family business financial assessment challenge in the applications section, and examine future directions.

# Historical Perspective

## Transparency

The lack of transparency and separation is thought to be more prevalent in small businesses than in large businesses. Ang's (1991) analysis of the unique characteristics of small businesses is a good starting point to see where transparency and separation issues exist. Ang identified nine characteristics of small businesses: (1) no publicly traded securities, (2) owners have undiversified personal portfolios, (3) limited liability is absent or ineffective, (4) first-generation owners are entrepreneurial and prone to risk-taking, (5) management team is not complete, (6) experience high cost of market and institutional imperfections, (7) relationships with stockholders are less formal, and (8) a higher degree of flexibility in designing compensation schemes. These characteristics identified by Ang have highlighted the challenges small business owners face because their businesses lack financial transparency and lack separation between the family and business. Berger and Udell (1998) suggested that the most important characteristic defining small business finance is informational opaqueness; more recent research has focused on family business characteristics, where an understanding of the family and business is important in analyzing the family business (Stafford et al., 1999).

Several characteristics identified by Ang (1991) made small businesses financially opaque, where it is challenging for equity investors and debt holders to assess the validity (accuracy) of financial information supplied by small businesses. Small businesses typically hold no publicly traded securities or debt (bonds). On the equity side, small businesses do not participate in organized exchanges, such as the New York Stock Exchange, and seldom have access to equity capital through angel or venture capital investors. On the debt side, small businesses do not participate in public bond markets and have a limited set of financing sources. Most importantly, small businesses are not required to produce audited financial statements or other financial information because they are not required to publicly report financial information. Berger and Udell (1998) noted the following: "These private equity and debt markets are often highly structured, complex contracts that are often informationally opaque. In contrast, large businesses utilize public stock and bond markets that are informationally transparent and utilize relatively generic contracts" (p. 614). In addition to the lack of opportunity to participate in publicly traded equity and debt markets, financial reporting and contracting can be hindered by the education, expertise, and experience of the small business' management team.

The management team is often only the owner, who manages the firm. The expertise in finance, marketing, and production resides in the human capital of the owner-manager. Given that the management team has less expertise, lenders and investors are concerned about the quality of financial data they report. In addition, small businesses may face higher costs because of their scale and management expertise, thus making it more costly to comply with regulations where the business owner may provide less accurate information. While large firms may be classified as "too big to fail" small businesses are often regarded as "too small to worry about," which opens up the opportunity to be less transparent. Although in an early study of small and large businesses, small business respondents saw themselves as much more ethical than those owning large businesses (Brown and King, 1982).

Small business owners are less likely to have extensive business experience. Robb (2013) reported that less than 50 percent of small business entrepreneurs had previous startup experience. These entrepreneurs, especially those acquiring debt capital outside of the family, are assuming substantial financial risk in hopes of earning high returns (Ang, 1991). If family equity or debt capital is available, the risk of the small business may be substantially less; however, the lack of experience still makes acquiring equity and debt capital challenging because of a lack of valid and reliable financial information.

Berger and Udell (1998) also suggested that small businesses in operation for a limited amount of time are much less likely to have established a reputation providing a signal of the quality of the firm. Without an established business reputation small business owners may depend on relationships that are more personal and less formal with investors and lenders.

## Separation

In addition to being financially opaque, nearly all small businesses are family businesses, where there is a lack of separation between the family (or personal) and business risks. Recognizing the small business as family-owned suggests that the household likely has an undiversified financial portfolio, intermingles financial capital between the family and business, and has limited liability protection. Small business owners typically have a substantial investment in their business; hence, their personal financial portfolio is likely to have minimal financial diversity (Ang, 1991). Household and business financial resources are often intermingled between the family and business. Research has shown that any financial assessment of business is incomplete without a financial assessment of the household (Haynes et al., 1999; Yilmazer and Schrank, 2010). Additionally, small businesses organized as sole proprietorships or partnerships offer no liability protection to the owners. Those organized as corporations offer only very limited liability protection because owners are required to sign personal guarantees, where the assets of the family are pledged against the business' liabilities (Ang et al., 1995; Avery et al., 1998; Robb and Robinson, 2012).

These characteristics contribute to the lack of transparency and the additional risk of small business ownership and create substantial impacts on small business finances as owners navigate the market for equity and debt capital. The next section examines research on how small business owners have responded to these constraints posed by the lack of transparency and separation.

# Research and Policy

## Transparency

The lack of transparency means that small business owners' relationships with investors and lenders may be more implicit and less formal, as noted by Berger and Udell (1998). With less formal relationships, the demand for transparency may be replaced by personal relationships, where small businesses may be more likely to acquire equity and debt financing from owners, family, and friends, and debt financing from smaller commercial banks, which are more likely to depend on personal relationships than "hard" financial data (Berger and Black, 2011).

## Internal Equity and Debt

The importance of relationships for both equity and debt financing was recognized in the work of Berger and Udell (1998). Utilizing NSSBF data from 1993, Berger and Udell found that total financing of small businesses is evenly split between debt and equity. Nearly 35 percent of equity and debt capital was provided by the business owner. Nearly two-thirds of the equity was invested by the principal owner with angel and venture capital investors contributing nearly 11 percent of total equity. The remaining equity was provided by family and friends and other members of the start-up team. The largest share of debt capital was from commercial banks and trade credit, which held 37 percent and 31 percent of total debt, respectively; and owners provided less than 10 percent of the debt capital (Berger and Udell, 1998).

A study by Robb (2013) examining the financing patterns of young firms during the early years of their existence found a similar financial structure. When just getting started, about 70 percent of total equity was provided by internal (i.e., owners, family members, and personal affiliates of the firm) investors; however, less than 20 percent of total debt was held by internal debt holders. As the small businesses in this study aged, the share of internal equity declined to less than 45 percent and internal debt declined slightly to less than 17 percent. Although it is important to note, the owner will likely have signed a personal guarantee, which makes the owner liable for any loan defaults with commercial lenders and others.

## New options for debt and equity financing

The challenge of acquiring financial capital has taken an interesting turn with the advent of equity and debt capital becoming available through equity crowdsourcing and other avenues. Statista (2021) estimated that total crowdfunding commitments were $5.9 billion in the United States in 2017. Based on FDIC estimates of small business loans outstanding in June of 2017, the $5.9 billion of commitments would be less than 1 percent of the $618.9 billion of small business loans outstanding (FDIC, 2021).

Small firms with the potential to attract external equity investors through an initial public offering, venture capital, or private equity firm are firms with high growth potential and high risk. Robb (2013) noted that investing in these types of firms involves much more than just providing financing. It involves the development and collaboration of a business strategy with the founder to grow the business. The financial risk is high; therefore, these investors demand high returns on their investments. In addition, acquiring external equity can be expensive. A small firm attempting to develop a proposal for an initial public offering (IPO) will find the process expensive, time-consuming, and challenging. Even though there has been substantial interest in the dynamic growth of external equity, Ou and Haynes (2006) suggested that the importance of external equity from angel and venture capitalist for small firms seems to be overstated for most small firms.

With the introduction of a new rule by the Securities and Exchange Commission in 2012, start-up firms now have the ability to raise capital through the issuance of securities, which are known as equity- or lending-based crowdfunding (Fricke et al., 2021). Having the opportunity to raise capital from accredited investors through crowdfunding platforms may be a viable opportunity for small businesses. A recent study (Tiberius and Hauptmeijer, 2021) forecasts that equity crowdsourcing will increase by up to 20 percent over the next five to ten years, albeit, from a very low base. The viability of this financing will likely depend on addressing transparency issues and assessing the importance of relationships between small businesses and potential investors.

## Relationship Lending

The fact that small businesses are less transparent makes it more difficult for large lenders to handle their business; hence, they are relegated to smaller lenders who have the time to develop relationships with the owner. It is a case of where relationship and factor lending compete with relationship lending being the preferred, or perhaps, the only option for small businesses. If lenders have less information about the financial condition of the business, then owners can engage in risky projects, transfer risk toward other creditors, or otherwise misuse funds. Some researchers have argued this is why small and young firms can rarely borrow in the public capital markets, and why one would expect firm–creditor relationships to be especially important (Diamond, 1991).

The seminal paper on relationship lending by Peterson and Rajan (1994) showed that the primary benefits of close relationships are manifest in the expansion of the number of financial services purchased (e.g., checking, saving, credit card, lending, and other services) and increased access to financing. Peterson and Rajan found that relationship lending had minimal effects on the price of credit; however, attempts to widen the circle of financial relationships by borrowing from multiple lenders led to increases in the price and reductions in the availability of credit.

A subsequent study by Cole (2004) found that large and small banks differ in their approaches to evaluating small business loan applications. Because small businesses are more opaque, large banks are more likely to employ a "cookie-cutter" strategy to small businesses, where they can control for agency problems (i.e., asymmetric information between the borrower and lender) and maintain consistent loan standards. Small banks may face less severe agency problems, primarily because they are likely to know more about the small business borrower. Small banks use an approach dependent upon pre-existing relationships that provide insights into the character of a borrower and assign less weight to financial factors (Berger and Black, 2011).

Haynes et al. (1999a) examined whether large banks would loan money to small businesses. Haynes et al. found that large banks did not appear to "cherry-pick" the market by only offering loans to larger, higher-quality small businesses. Although, Haynes et al. did find that the smallest small business borrowers appeared to have less access to financial capital, especially line-of-credit loans, from large banks compared to other small business borrowers. More recently, this basic result was supported in an extensive study by Mkhaiber and Werner (2021) who examined the relationship between bank size and the propensity to lend to small firms.

An analysis of line-of-credit, rather than other traditional, loans is important in this case. Four loan instruments are considered traditional loans: (a) line-of-credit, (b) vehicle, (c) equipment, and (d) mortgage. Three of these traditional loans (i.e., vehicle, equipment, and mortgages) are asset-backed loans and pose a minimal amount of risk to the lender. Line-of-credit loans are not asset-backed loans, so the lender must solicit other forms of capital to secure these loans. A line-of-credit loan requires more confidence in the borrower's ability to repay the loan and more information about the borrower, especially regarding their character.

Based on this literature, one would expect small banks, which are more likely to be relationship lenders, to have the largest share of small business loans. Utilizing the FDIC data on the share of "small loans" (not small business loans) held by lenders of various assets sizes, about 42 percent of small loans are held by banks with less than $10 billion of total assets (small banks) and 58 percent are held by large banks with total assets of $10 billion or more (FDIC, 2021) indicating that large banks are still important to small business borrowers.

## Separation

An additional challenge beyond choosing a lender for small business owners is the lack of separation between the family and business, as previously discussed. Nearly 20 percent of all households in the United States have one or more members who are self-employed or own a business (Ou and Haynes, 2006). Nearly two-thirds of these business-owning households have an owner or manager in the household and one-third are self-employed individuals. These small businesses are typically family-owned businesses, where understanding the interface between the family and business is critical to understanding the family business.

Danes et al. (2016) noted that the financial health of the household and business is inextricably intertwined for business-owning families. This interface between the family and business has two critically important dimensions: interpersonal relationships interface, where tensions between the family members cause tension in business operations; and financial interface, where financial and human resources move between the family and business. The exploration of a research strategy to recognize the interface was addressed initially by Stafford et al. (1999) who proposed the Sustainable Family Business Model (SFBM). The SFBM delineation of the interface between the family and business outlined research methods recognizing the overlap of family and business systems. Subsequent research by Stafford et al. (2010) used the SFBM and National Family Business Survey data to show that family businesses who provided more income for their families, hired more temporary help, owned larger firms, and had more experience were likely to survive longer. In more recent work, McDonald and Marshall (2018) found that cash flow problems increased tension between the household and business, and when the household was faced with cash flow problems, the business did not transfer more cash to the household either because the owner was unable or unwilling to make the transfer. This result suggests that family businesses hold on to financial resources to help the business, rather than the household.

In addition, the close relationship between the business and family presents a challenge for small business owners because the business only has very limited liability protection. In 2003, 56 percent of small businesses were organized as either sole proprietorships or partnerships with no liability protection (Cole, 2013). Even though 44 percent of small businesses were organized as corporations (or other limited liability legal organizations), the corporate structure offers minimal protection against business failure because owners are required by lenders to sign personal guarantees or pledge noncorporate assets as collateral for loans (Robb and Robinson, 2012). Using the NSSBF and SCF, Avery et al. (1998) found that while liabilities of unincorporated firms are implicitly guaranteed by their owners, incorporated firms were more likely to have personal commitments or guarantees with commercial banks. The SBA 7(a) loan-guarantee was created to address the personal commitments issue, where the SBA would guarantee up to 90 percent of the outstanding loan balance. However, the loan guarantee was designed to provide more access to financial capital and protect the lender, not the small business borrower. When considering commercial bank lending, small business owners, regardless of their legal organization, have minimal liability protection because all loans must be personally guaranteed.

This literature shows the importance of recognizing the issues of transparency and family and business separation, as these businesses are not simply smaller versions of larger businesses. Recognizing the importance of these characteristics provides a rationale to explain why the financial structure is dependent upon owner equity and debt financing, why small business owners are more likely to use relationship rather than factor lenders, and why the interface between the family and business is important to understand in determining how these family businesses exchange financial resources and assume financial liability.

# Access and Structure of Women- and Minority-Owned Small Business

The lack of transparency and separation creates important structural challenges for small business owners, which are aggravated by access challenges for some types of small business owners, especially women and minority owners. While the financial structure of small businesses is impacted by small businesses using more internal equity and debt capital and relationship investors and lenders, financial access is impacted by the higher likelihood of being denied credit.

Access to credit is assessed by asking respondents if they have (1) applied for credit; (2) applied, but were fully or partially denied; or (3) wanted credit, but did not apply because they expected to be denied. In a recent study of access by established small businesses in 2010, Kennickell et al. (2016) found that 25 percent applied for credit, 20 percent applied but were partially or fully denied, and 8 percent wanted credit but did not apply. New small businesses were less likely to apply for credit, were more likely to apply but be denied, and less likely to want credit but did not apply than established small businesses (Kennickell et al., 2016). The total demand for credit varies substantially with firm size with the larger small businesses having more access to credit (Kennickell et al., 2016).

Large publicly traded companies are seldom identified by race, ethnicity, gender, and other personal and demographic characteristics of the owners or managers. In most cases, the owners of the business are the shareholders, who have limited or no management responsibilities. However, small businesses are easily identified by personal and demographic characteristics, especially race and gender, because the owners are the managers. Gender and race have been shown to be important determinants in the ability of these small businesses to access capital.

## Women

An important phenomenon in the United States economy since the early 1970s has been the rapid growth in women-owned businesses. In 1972, women owned less than 5 percent of all businesses and produced less than 1 percent of total sales

(Haynes and Haynes, 1999b). Based on more recent estimates of business activity in 2012, women-owned businesses comprised 36 percent of employer businesses and 12 percent of sales in the United States (McManus, 2016). Even though small business ownership by women has increased significantly, many women who own small businesses claim they have less access to the market for financial capital than men-owned small businesses.

Substantial concern exists about discrimination against women-owned small businesses in financial capital markets. After controlling for business quality women-owned small businesses appeared to have very similar access to line-of-credit loans as men-owned small businesses (Haynes and Haynes, 1999b). This result is important because line-of-credit loans were not asset-backed loans; hence, these borrowers were more dependent on the character assessments than borrowers applying for other types of credit. Controlling for business quality was important because women-owned businesses were newer and smaller, more likely to be sole proprietors, and more likely to be engaged in retail and service industries, which have been considered to be less transparent and riskier than men-owned businesses that are more likely to be engaged in construction or manufacturing industries.

Robb (2013) has shown the women-owned small businesses use a different mix of equity and debt capital, rely disproportionately on owner equity investments, and operate with substantially less capital than male-owned firms. Women-owned small businesses were more likely to have a higher proportion of total financial capital from owner equity and debt and insider (family and friends) debt than men-owned small businesses (Table 17.1).

**Table 17.1:** Financial Structure of Women- and Men-owned Small Businesses 2010.

| Type of equity or credit | Gender | | Race | |
|---|---|---|---|---|
| | Women | Men | Black/Hispanic | White |
| Owner equity | 12.7 | 9.1 | 13.1 | 9.1 |
| Insider equity | 0.2 | 2.3 | 0.5 | 2.1 |
| Outsider equity | 3.0 | 12.8 | 7.1 | 11.3 |
| Owner debt | 8.0 | 4.0 | 6.6 | 4.5 |
| Insider debt | 13.6 | 8.3 | 9.1 | 8.8 |
| Outsider debt | 62.5 | 63.5 | 63.6 | 64.1 |
| Total | 100.0 | 100.0 | 100.0 | 100.0 |

*Source*: Robb (2013).

Haynes and Haynes (1999a, 1999b) showed that household financial structure information is a reliable indicator for predicting business financial structure for men-owned, but not women-owned, small businesses. Women-owned small businesses may be secondary businesses for the family; hence, lenders may know less about these businesses and be less interested in extending credit to them. If this information is not a reliable indicator of the borrower's financial structure or expectations for the business, then the woman business owner may face credit rationing and other barriers to financial credit access. Robb (2013) found that women-owned small business owners were significantly more likely not to apply for credit because they feared having the loan application denied. Perhaps, women business owners may benefit from more complete and objective credit analysis using loan scoring algorithms, which could minimize the degree of information asymmetry between women business owners and their lenders (Haynes and Haynes, 1999a).

## Race/Ethnicity

Minority small business owners face many of the same structural and access issues as women small business owners. African-American and Latinx small business owners were shown to utilize a different mix of equity and debt capital than nonminority small business owners (Robb, 2013). They relied disproportionately upon owner equity investments, employed less debt from outside sources, and operated with substantially less capital than Whites (Table 17.1).

Cavalluzzo and Wolken (2005) found large unexplained differences in denial rates between African-American-, Hispanic-, Asian-, and White-owned businesses. In addition, Cavalluzzo et al. (2002) found evidence that denial rates for African-Americans increased with lender market concentration. In addition, Cavalluzzo et al. found that personal wealth, especially homeownership, was important in predicting small business loan turndowns differences between Hispanic- and Asian-owned businesses and White-owned businesses. However, personal wealth did not explain any of the turndown differences between African-American and White-owned businesses.

In short, access challenges are a double whammy for women or minority small business owners. First, because they are small business owners; and second, because they are a woman or minority. The next section turns to examining practitioner tools and techniques for managing the lack of transparency and issues with separation between the family and the business.

# Practitioner Tools and Techniques

Small businesses are essentially households owning small businesses, where the interface between the business and household is very important to recognize. While information asymmetries may be minimized between managers and owners because they are often the same person, information asymmetries between small business owners and those providing financial resources (either equity or debt) may be substantial because of the lack of transparency in business. However, knowledge obtained by the lender or investor about the business and family (or household) helps mitigate the lack of transparency, thus enabling small business owners to secure external capital.

Recognizing the intersection between the family and business is critically important in assessing the survival and success of small (family) businesses. Sustainable Family Business Theory, depicted in Figure 17.1, was developed to better understand how capital is used within the family business to support both the family and business (Stafford et al., 1999). In this model, financial capital includes such tangibles as money, credit, assets (e.g., land and buildings), and investments. The family business finance literature acknowledges the intermingling of family and business resources and acknowledges that intermingling of family and business financial resources occurs (Haynes et al., 1999c; Zuiker et al., 2003). Within family businesses, families and businesses have been found to compete for resources of individual family members to support the family or business (Stafford et al., 1999).

When developing an analytical model of the family business it is important to control for important attributes of the family and business. Family variables, such as the marital status of the owner, number of children, household income, and net worth are important. Business variables such as the legal organization, industrial sector, size, and rural or urban location are important. In addition, the analytical model should consider the interface between the family and business. For instance, it's important to consider the family's dependence on the income generated by the business or business' dependence on the income generated by the household; the use of resources, such as labor and money, in hectic times when resources are exchanged; and, whether the business is a family business or not.

## Application

Successful family businesses depend on having profitable businesses and healthy families. When businesses are unprofitable or families are unhealthy, the probability of survival or success wanes. When assessing the financial condition of a small (family) business being aware of the flow of resources in the intersection is very important. For instance, family capital is often essential for start-up capital for the young entrepreneur. However, when family capital is used to sustain an existing small business, a business assessment based on cash flow and profitability may be misleading. To illustrate, assume a substantial no-interest loan is offered to a small business owner to sustain the firm. On the surface, cash flow looks good; however, no interest is being expensed, so expenses are under-estimated and net profit is inflated; and if

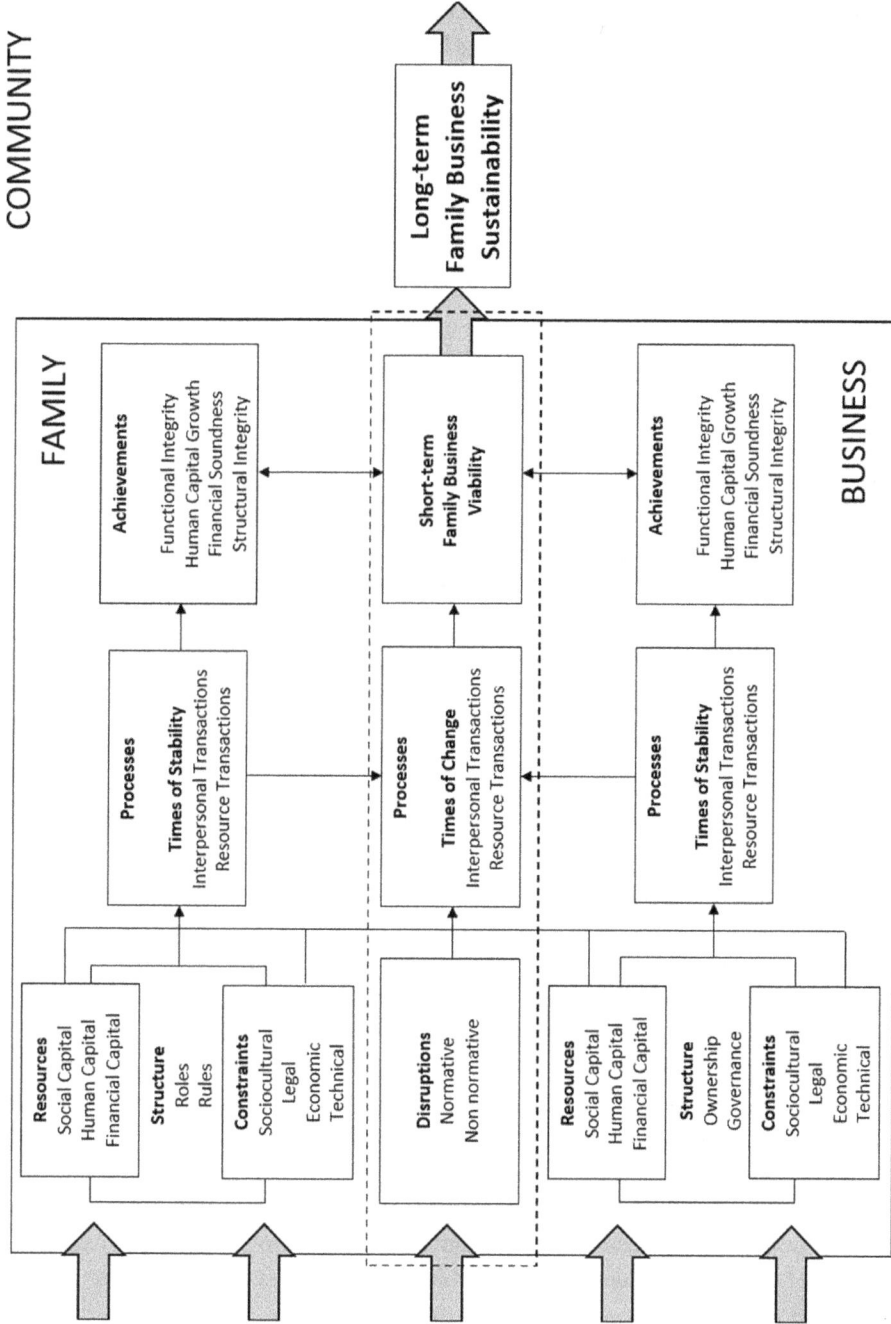

**Figure 17.1:** Sustainable Family Business Theory.
*Source:* Danes et al. (2016).

the loan remains "off-balance-sheet" then liabilities are understated and net worth is inflated. While the business may appear to be doing okay, the family business may be struggling. Clearly, transparency for both the family and business is important in assessing the family business. While it's normal for the business venture to support the family, it is unusual for the family to support the existing business beyond a startup phase.

## Future Directions

The study of small, family-owned businesses is relatively new, as previously stated, with many avenues of inquiry still existing for future work. This chapter has focused on the challenges that transparency and separation create for small business owners. Future directions for this line of research should include the impact of disaster assistance grant programs, challenges of small business owners in developing countries, financial management strategies to enhance sustainability, the impact of family events on business survival, and navigating the regulatory environment. The following topics warrant further research:

- Federal disaster assistance grant programs have been important for agricultural producers; however, small business owners have largely been excluded from similar grant programs until recently. An important research question is the following: Have federal disaster assistance grant programs, such as the Paycheck Protection Program, increased the survival and success of small businesses?
- An extensive literature on small business finance exists for the United States and other more developed countries; however, a dearth of literature on small business finance has been published from developing countries. More research on family businesses from throughout the developing world needs to be introduced to the academic marketplace.
- Small business sustainability is an important issue. More research is needed to further define sustainability and assess the impact of financial management and strategy on sustainability.
- Family events, such as marriage, divorce, disability, and death have important financial impacts on small businesses. More research is needed to assess the impact of these events on the survival and success of the family business.
- Small businesses face challenging regulatory environments, where the cost of compliance with regulations can be substantial. More research is needed to assess the impact of regulations and consider public policy solutions to improve the efficacy of small businesses.

# Discussion

Small business owners are faced with owning and managing a business with unique characteristics, which have profound implications on financial structure and access to debt and equity capital. The availability of the NSSBF, SCF, and KFS data in the 1980s through the 2000s provided the impetus for research on small business finance issues. Research has shown that small business owners adapt to the lack of transparency by utilizing a higher percentage of internal debt and equity capital because public debt and equity markets are not available to them. They rely on relationship lenders, who are willing to take the time to get to know their businesses and families. For some, especially women and minorities, access to credit is more challenging. These small business owners depend on establishing relationships with lenders and investors; and utilize public policy, such as the SBA's 7(a) loan-guarantee program to secure capital. While the loan guarantees help the small business acquire capital, they do not provide financial protection to the small business. More recently, small business owners have been able to participate in a grant program designed to help small business owners survive the economic downturn created by the pandemic. Analysis of this grant program will help policymakers determine if the grant funding, utilized extensively in agriculture, will enhance the sustainability of small businesses.

# Conclusion

As discussed in this chapter, small business owners exist in private equity and debt markets that are often highly structured and involve complex contracts because the financial market is informationally opaque. While information asymmetry challenges may be minimal between owners and managers because they are often the same person, information asymmetry challenges can be very severe between borrowers and lenders because of the lack of transparency of small businesses. The lack of transparency is complemented by recognizing that these business ventures are really family businesses, where the family and business are inextricably intertwined. The challenge for those interested in researching small business owners is utilizing qualitative and quantitative data that enables the analyst to consider a holistic view of the family business. While Ang (1991) was correct in suggesting, "It is fair to say that the theory of modern corporate finance is not developed with small businesses in mind" (p. 1), it is also true that small business finance was not developed with the family business in mind. The use of models such as the Sustainable Family Business Model is important in moving research on small business owners forward.

# References

Ang, S. A. (1991). Small business uniqueness and the theory of financial management. *Journal of Small Business Finance, 1(1)*, 1–13. http://hdl.handle.net/10419/114623

Ang, J. S., Lin, J. W., and Tyler, F. (1995). Evidence on the lack of separation between business and personal risks among small businesses. *Journal of Small Business Finance, 4*(2/3), 197–210. http://hdl.handle.net/10419/114691

Avery, R. B., Bostic, R. W., and Samolyk, K. A. (1998). The role of personal wealth in small business finance. *Journal of Banking and Finance, 22*(6–8), 1019–1061. https://doi.org/10.1016/S0378-4266(98)00016-8

Berger, A. N., and Black, L. K. (2011). Bank size, lending technologies, and small business finance. *Journal of Banking and Finance, 35*(3), 724–735. https://doi.org/10.1016/j.jbankfin.2010.09.004

Berger, A. N., and Udell, G. F. (1998). The economics of small business finance: The roles of private equity and debt markets in the financial growth cycle. *Journal of Banking and Finance, 22*(6–8), 613–673. https://doi.org/10.1016/S0378-4266(98)00038-7

Brown, D. J., and King, J. B. (1982). Small business ethics: Influences and perceptions. *Journal of Small Business Management, 20*(1), 11–17. https://search.proquest.com/scholarly-journals/small-business-ethics-influences-perceptions/docview/210758692/se-2?accountid=28148

Cavalluzzo, K., Cavalluzzo, L., and Wolken, J. (2002). Competition, small business financing, and discrimination: Evidence from a new survey. *The Journal of Business, 75*(4), 641–679. doi:10.1086/341638. https://www.jstor.org/stable/10.1086/34163

Cavalluzzo, K., and Wolken, J. (2005). Small business loan turndowns, personal wealth, and discrimination *The Journal of Business, 78*(6), 2,153–2,178. https://doi.org/10.1086/497045

Cole, R. (2004). Cookie cutter vs. character: The micro structure of small business lending by large and small banks. *The Journal of Financial and Quantitative Analysis, 39*(2), 227–251. https://www.jstore.org/stable/30031854

Cole, R. (2013). What do we know about the capital structure of privately held US firms? Evidence from the surveys of small business finances. *Financial Management, 42*(4), 777–813. https://doi.org/10.1111/fima.12015

Danes, S. M., Haynes, G. W., and Haynes, D. C. (2016). Business-owning families: Challenges at the intersection of business and family. In J. J. Xiao (ed.). *Handbook of consumer finance research* (2nd ed., pp. 179–193). Springer. https://doi.org/10.1007/978-3-319-28887-1_15

Diamond, D. W. (1991). Monitoring and reputation: The choice between bank loans and directly placed debt. *Journal of Political Economy, 99*(4), 689–721. https://www.journals.uchicago.edu/doi/pdfplus/10.1086/261775

Federal Deposit Insurance Corporation (FDIC). (2021). *Statistics on depository institutions* [Data set]. https://www7.fdic.gov/sdi/main.asp?formname=customddownload

Fricke, E., Fung, S., and Goktan, M. S. (2021). Is "accredited crowdfunding" a lemons market? Evidence from 506(c) filings. *Journal of Small Business Management*, 1–25. https://doi.org/10.1080/00472778.2020.1849715

Haynes, G. W., and Haynes, D. C. (1999a). The debt structure of businesses owned by women in 1987 and 1993. *Journal of Small Business Management, 37*(2), 1–19. https://search.proquest.com/scholarly-journals/debt-structure-small-businesses-owned-women-1987/docview/221004665/se-2?accountid=28148

Haynes, G. W., Ou, C., and Berney, R. (1999b). Small business borrowing from large and small banks. *Business Access to Capital and Credit*, 287–327.

Haynes, G. W., Walker, R., Rowe, B. R., and Hong, G. S. (1999c). The intermingling of business and family finances in family-owned businesses. *Family Business Review, 12*(3), 225–239. https://doi.org/10.1111/j.1741-6248.1999.00225.x

Kennickell, A.B., Kwast, M. L., and Pogach J. (2016). Small businesses and small business finance during the financial crisis and the great recession: New evidence from the Survey of Consumer Finances. In J. Haltiwanger, E. Hurst, J. Miranda, and A. Schoar (eds.), *Measuring entrepreneurial business: Current knowledge and challenges* (Volume 75, pp. 291–349). National Bureau of Economic Research. http://www.nber.org/chapters/c13496

Kobe, K., and Schwinn, R. (2018). Small business GDP 1998–2014. *U.S. Small Business Administration Office of Advocacy*, 1–75. https://cdn.advocacy.sba.gov/wp-content/uploads/2018/12/21060437/Small-Business-GDP-1998-2014.pdf

McDonald, T. M., and Marshall, M. I. (2018). Family business responses to household and business cash-flow problems. *Journal of Family and Economic Issues*, 39(1), 163–176. https://doi.org/10.1007/s10834-017-9543-6

McManus, M. J. (2016). Minority Business Ownership: Data from the 2012 survey of business owners. *U.S. Small Business Administration Office of Advocacy*, 13, 1–75. https://archive.mbda.gov/sites/mbda.gov/files/migrated/files-attachments/Minority-Owned-Businesses-in-the-US.pdf

Mkhaiber, A., and Werner, R. A. (2021). The relationship between bank size and the propensity to lend to small firms: New empirical evidence from a large sample. *Journal of International Money and Finance*, 110. https://doi.org/10.1016/j.jimonfin.2020.102281

Ou, C., and Haynes, G. W. (2006). Acquisition of additional equity capital by small firms: Findings from the national survey of small business finances. *Small Business Economics, 27*(2–3), 157–168. https://doi.org/10.1007/s11187-006-0009-8

Peterson, M. A., and Rajan, R. G. (1994). The benefits of lending relationships: Evidence from small business data. *Journal of Finance, 49*(1), 3–37. https://doi.org/10.1111/j.1540-6261.1994.tb04418.x

Robb, A. (2013). *Access to capital among young firms, minority-owned firms, women-owned firms and high-tech firms*. U.S. Small Business Administration Office of Advocacy. https://cdn.advocacy.sba.gov/wp-content/uploads/2019/05/15130241/rs403tot2.pdf

Robb, A. M., and Robinson, D. T. (2012). The capital structure decisions of new firms. *The Review of Financial Studies, 27*(1), 153–179. https://doi.org/10.1093/rfs/hhs072

Stafford, K., Bhargava, V., Danes, S. M., Haynes, G., and Brewton, K. E. (2010). Factors associated with long-term survival of family businesses: Duration analysis. *Journal of Family and Economic Issues, 31*(4), 442–457. https://doi.org/10.1007/s10834-010-9232-1

Stafford, K., Duncan, K. A., Danes, S., and Winter, M. (1999). A research model of sustainable family businesses. *Family Business Review, 12*(3), 197–208. https://doi.org/10.1111/j.1741-6248.1999.00197.x

Statista. (2021). *Total crowdfunding commitments in the United States as of May 2017, by sector*. https://www.statista.com/statistics/621216/total-crowdfunding-commitments-usa-by-sector/

Tiberius, V., and Hauptmeijer, R. (2021). Equity crowdfunding: Forecasting market development, platform evolution and regulation. *Journal of Small Business Management*, 1–33. https://doi.org/10.1080/00472778.2020.1849714

Yilmazer, T., and Schrank, H. (2010). The use of owner resources in small and family owned businesses: Literature review and future research directions. *Journal of Family and Economic Issues, 31*(4), 399–413. https://doi.org/10.1007/s10834-010-9224-1

Zuiker, V. S., Katras, M. J., Montalto, C. P., and Olson, P. D. (2003). Hispanic self-employment: Does gender matter? *Hispanic Journal of Behavioral Sciences, 25*(1), 73–94. https://doi.org/10.1177/0739986303251697

Jonquil Lowe

# 18 Applying Investing Theory to Practice

**Abstract:** This chapter describes theories from economics that are widely used to determine the price it is deemed worth paying for an asset or portfolio of assets, taking account of risk, as well as theories based in psychology that explain why price may deviate from an asset's intrinsic value. These theories underpin the common practitioner techniques of fundamental analysis, technical analysis, and active and passive portfolio management. Individuals and households should normally consider using investments, such as equities, to help them achieve long-term goals. The strategies for managing the risk and return involved are relatively straightforward where the aim is to accumulate assets, but are more challenging during decumulation stages of life, such as retirement. This is particularly so, because monetary and social policies, and also climate change, may increase the volatility of investments.

**Keywords:** discounted cash flow, bubble, modern portfolio theory, efficient frontier, capital asset pricing model, fundamental analysis, technical analysis

## Introduction

In the field of personal finance, investing means the process of using money to acquire assets that generate income and/or a future gain. Assets are often classified into four types: cash (such as savings accounts), fixed interest (loans to governments and companies, often called bonds), property (residential and commercial), and equities (shares in companies). However, any asset that has the capacity to generate income or appreciate in value can function as an investment, including, for example: human capital, meaning the ability of an individual to turn their labor into earnings – which can be enhanced through investment in training and qualifications; commodities, such as energy sources, metals, and foodstuffs; other tangible items, such as fine wines, classic cars, and artworks; and intangible items, such as royalties and patents that generate income. Intangible assets also include derivatives that give the holder the right or opportunity to receive income or gain related to some underlying asset under specified conditions without actually owning that asset.

However straightforward or complex the investment, a fundamental question for investors is: What is its value? In other words: What price is worth paying for it? In one form or another, this question of value is at the heart of investment theory and practice, and the two disciplines that vie most to provide answers are economics and psychology.

**Jonquil Lowe,** The Open University, London

https://doi.org/10.1515/9783110727692-018

# Historical Perspective and Research

Theories about investment value and price broadly split into those that are based on intrinsic value and those that favor behavioral explanations. Each is discussed in more detail below.

## The Intrinsic Value of an Investment

The U.S. mathematical economist Irving Fisher (1867–1947) posited that "capital value . . . is merely the capitalization of expected income" (1930, p. 40) and developed the theory of time preference, which is the notion that individuals place a higher value on income received today than in the future. Thus, an investor needs to be compensated for waiting for future income by receiving interest. In a simple two-period example, the relationship can be written as:

$$FV = PV(1+r)^n$$

Where $FV$ = future value (a payment to be received at a future date)
$PV$ = present value (the value of the income stream today)
$r$ = periodic interest rate
$n$ = number of periods until the future payment is made

For example, if the 100 pounds, dollars, or other currency is to be paid in five years' time and the interest rate available is 2 percent, to be compensated for waiting the investor will want the future payment to be:

$$100(1+0.02)^5 = 110.41$$

where the future payment and the interest rate are known, the equation can be rearranged to find the equivalent value today:

$$PV = \frac{FV}{(1+r)^n}$$

In this format, the interest rate, $r$, is said to be "discounting" (in other words, reducing) the future value and so is called the discount rate.

Moreover, where an investment offers a stream of payments, the various discounted future payments can simply be added together to find the equivalent value today of the whole income stream:

$$PV = \frac{FV_1}{(1+r)^1} + \frac{FV_2}{(1+r)^2} + \cdots + \frac{FV_n}{(1+r)^n}$$

$$= \sum_{i=1}^{n} \frac{FV_i}{(1+r)^i}$$

This is called a discounted cash flow (DCF) equation.

If an investment offers a stream of payments whose amount and timing are known – as is the case with conventional government and corporate bonds – it is a relatively simple task to plug the amounts into the DCF equation in order to find the expected value today (the *PV*) of the income stream and so the amount that it should be worth paying to buy the bond.

However, there is the question of what interest rate should be chosen for the discounting – a point to which I will return later. Moreover, where there is a risk that the provider may fail to make promised payments or when DCF is applied to a stream of payments whose amount and/or timing may fluctuate – as with equities – the inputs into the equation are no longer certain. Instead, the inputs become estimates reliant on assumptions and probabilities. Nevertheless, DCF equations appropriately weighted or modified are still today a widely used basis for estimating the value of many types of investment.

By equating *PV* to the current market value of an asset, the DCF equation can alternatively be used to solve for *r*, the discount rate, also called the "expected return" from the investment.

## The Behavior of Markets

While there is plenty of scope for variation in the assumptions embedded in a DCF equation, it might be expected that those on the pessimistic side would balance those that are more optimistic, and minor deviations up and down over time would similarly cancel out. Thus, for investments traded on a stock exchange at least, there might be a broad consensus about the price at which they should trade, reflecting their intrinsic value, provided stock markets are efficient.

In a seminal paper, U.S. economist Eugene Fama (1939–) reviewed the literature regarding the efficient markets hypothesis and proposed three tests for efficiency (Fama, 1970):

- *Weak form*: Do current prices reflect historical prices? If they do, then past performance cannot be a predictor of future price movements.
- *Semi-strong form*: Do current prices also already reflect all information that is obviously publicly available?
- *Strong form*: Do current prices also reflect all other relevant information, including, for example, "insider information"?

Under the strong form of the EMH, only completely new information can shift prices. All other information – even speculation about possible future announcements – has already been absorbed into the adjustments to the current price. Fama (1970) concluded that stock markets passed the weak and semi-strong tests and that, while a minority of specialists might have usable insider information, for the broad mass of investors, stock markets are efficient.

However, this conclusion sits uncomfortably with observations of events such as the roaring stock markets of the 1920s that preceded the Wall Street Crash, the dot.com bubble of the 1990s (when technology stocks with little or no intrinsic value first soared and then collapsed), and the buoyancy of mortgage-backed securities in the run-up to the 2008 Global Financial Crisis.

At an individual level, investors do not necessarily think or act rationally. Psychologists Stanovich and West (2000) distinguished two types of thinking: System 1, automatic, largely unconscious, intuitive, emotional decision making; and System 2, which is slower, effortful, analytical thinking. Calculating the expected return from investments involves System 2 thinking, but Israeli psychologist Daniel Kahneman (1934–) noted that people tend toward System 1 thinking, conforming to the "law of least effort" (2011, p.35). In other words, they look for mental shortcuts, such as "herd behavior" (following what others do) and "hot hands" (assuming whatever has done well up to now will continue to do so).

This echoes the earlier writings of U.K. economist John Maynard Keynes (1883–1946). Keynes distinguished "enterprise," which he equated to forecasting the expected return from an asset, and "speculation" – by which he meant trying to predict the average opinion of other investors in the hope of making a quick profit (Keynes, 1936, pp. 158–159). Importantly, Keynes observed that speculation is not a problem when the enterprise approach is dominant but becomes disruptive when speculators outnumber enterprise investors.

Speculation may dominate so much that prices may deviate significantly from intrinsic value, in a phenomenon commonly called a "bubble." Economic historian Charles Kindleberger (1910–2003), applying a model developed by fellow U.S. economist Hyman Minsky (1919–1996), described five stages of a typical bubble (Kindleberger and Alber, 2005):
- *Displacement*: There is an external shock that changes previous expectations about the opportunity for and/or extent of future returns from investment.
- *Credit expansion*: Firms and individuals not only invest but also borrow to take greater advantage of the newly perceived opportunity.
- *Euphoria:* The widespread backing for the new opportunity pushes up the relevant asset prices, encouraging yet more investors and lenders to back the new opportunity.
- *Financial distress*: As prices become ever higher, further buyers may start to be deterred and some owners decide to sell to make a profit. This dampens the price and, at some point, selling may turn into a stampede and the bubble collapses.

– *Revulsion*: Sellers may suffer large losses; other investors may be unable to sell at all. Some face bankruptcy if they cannot repay the earlier loans. Creditors become wary of extending loans or lending more.

Bubbles are important for all investors, not just for the holders and would-be purchasers of the particular asset concerned. This is because, when they burst, asset price bubbles may trigger wide-ranging impacts on the stability of the whole financial system and the real economy[1] as well (see, for example, Reinhart and Rogoff, 2011).

## Investments and Risk

Earlier I noted that an important assumption in the DCF equation is the choice of a discount rate. Using the economic concept of "opportunity cost" (meaning the next-best alternative foregone when a decision is made), a rational choice might be the return that could be obtained by investing instead in another investment that is a close substitute.

Importantly, to be a close substitute, the alternative would need to expose the investor to a similar level of risk. There are three high-level risks that most commonly concern investors (Mazzucato et al., 2010):
– *Capital risk*: The risk of losing some or all of the original sum invested (the "capital") or gains previously accrued.
– *Income risk*: The risk that variable payments may be less than expected or not paid at all.
– *Liquidity risk*: The risk of being unable to cash in the investment when needed quickly enough or at an acceptable price.

There are many underlying components of these risks – for example, capital risk may be linked to market prices going down as well as up, insolvency of the issuer, inflation eating into the buying power of the money invested, exchange-rate risk if the asset is priced in another currency, and so on.

Investors need an incentive to be persuaded to take on higher risk. Figure 18.1 illustrates this risk–return relationship by comparing different types of investment according to their typically relative levels of risk and return.

Figure 18.1 includes a risk-free asset. This provides a baseline return for a notional asset that involves no capital, income, or liquidity risks. In practice, such an asset does not exist, but 90-day Treasury bills (a type of very short-term government bond) come close. The extra return from other assets is the "risk premium," in other words, the reward for taking on risk.

---

**1** The "real economy" refers to goods and services produced and consumed.

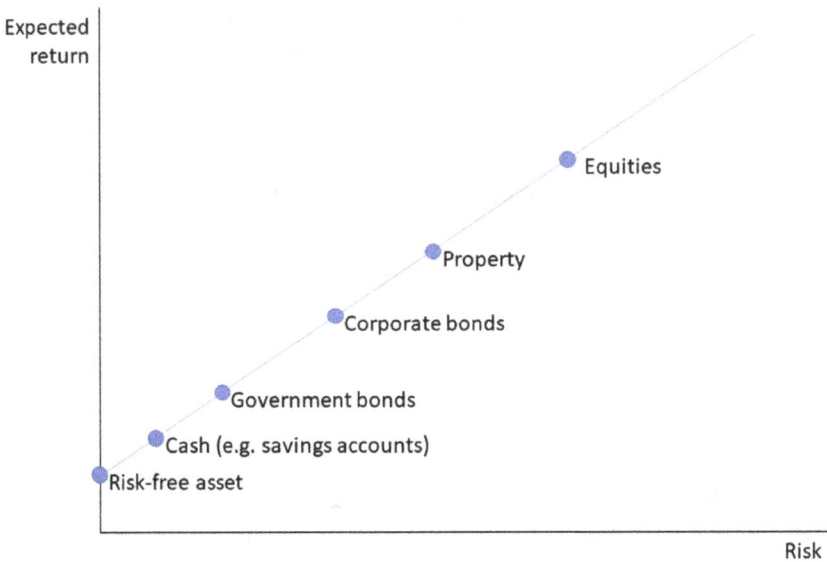

**Figure 18.1:** A Typical Relative Risk–Return Relationship for Selected Assets.

Individual investors have different appetites for risk depending on their psychological make-up (attitude toward risk), capacity for loss, and need to take on risk to improve the chance of achieving their financial goals.

It is unlikely that any one asset will match an individual's risk appetite and full range of goals. Investment strategies usually focus on diversification, which means combining different assets into a portfolio in order to manage the balance between risk and return.

## Building a Portfolio

U.S. economist Harry Markowitz (1927–) set out the principles of Modern Portfolio Theory (MPT) back in the 1950s. He demonstrated mathematically how to construct efficient portfolios, where efficiency is defined as combining assets to produce the maximum return for a given level of risk or alternatively the minimum risk for a given level of return (Markowitz, 1952).

Figure 18.2 gives a visual summary of Markowitz's findings. The chart plots expected return – calculated using a DCF approach – against risk, measured as the variance of the returns over some past period. (Variance is a statistical measure of the extent to which a variable is dispersed around its average value.) Every asset and every possible combination of the assets (so every portfolio) is represented in the cloud of dots in Figure 18.2.

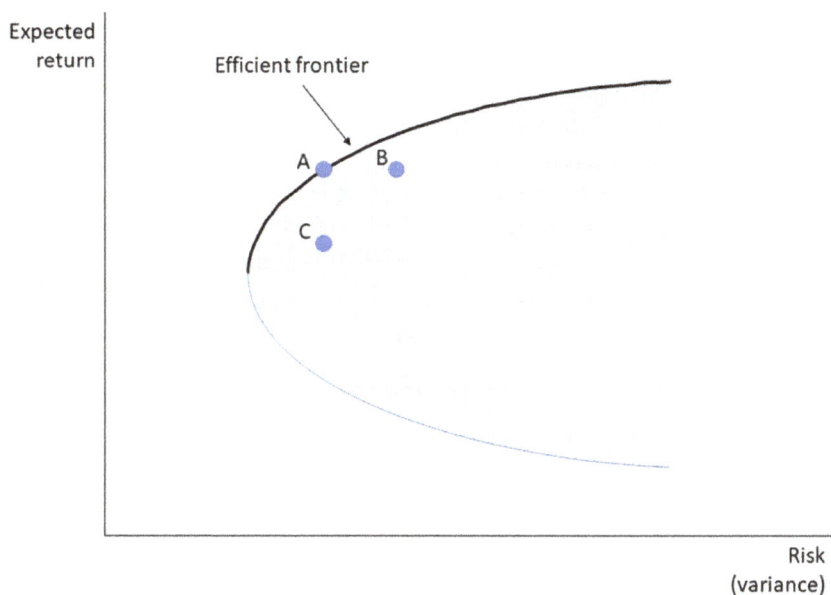

**Figure 18.2:** The Efficient Frontier-Location of Superior Portfolios.

The expected return for a portfolio is simply the weighted average of the expected return for each asset in the portfolio:

$$E_p = \sum_{i=1}^{N} w_i E_i$$

where $E_p$ = the expected value from the portfolio

$w_i$ = the proportion of the portfolio invested in asset $i$

$E_i$ = the expected return from asset $i$

$N$ = the number of assets in the portfolio

In the unlikely event that assets' prices were perfectly correlated, in other words moving exactly in tandem, the calculation of the variance of the portfolio would similarly be the weighted average of the risk of each asset. However, provided the correlation is less than perfect, combining the assets in a portfolio reduces the overall risk to less than the weighted average of the individual risks. In the extreme of assets that are perfectly negatively correlated (exactly offsetting each other's price movements), risk can be eliminated completely. The smaller the positive correlation or, even better, the larger the negative correlation, the more efficient the portfolio.

The most efficient portfolios are found on the highlighted section of the curve in Figure 18.2, called the efficient frontier. For example, rational investors would not choose portfolio B because they could get the same return at lower risk from portfolio

A. Similarly, they would not choose portfolio C, because A offers a higher return for the same risk.

One of the most important further developments of MPT was the Capital Asset Pricing Model (CAPM). It was devised independently by several U.S. economists, including William Sharpe (1934–).

The essence of CAPM is that the expected return from an asset is the excess return due to the risks specific to that asset (such as, whether investing in a new plant pays off) plus its exposure to the risks that impact the market as a whole (such as a change in interest rates, economic downturn, and so on), called systematic risk. This can be expressed in a simple regression equation:

$$E_i - \rho = \alpha + \beta_{im}(E_m - \rho)$$

where $E_i - \rho$ = the risk premium for asset $i$

$\alpha$ = (alpha) the specific risk of asset $i$

$\beta_{im}$ = (beta) asset $i$'s exposure to systematic risk

$E_m - \rho$ = the risk premium for the market as a whole

In an efficient market, the excess returns and risks from alpha would rapidly be diversified away, leaving just the asset's exposure to market risk. The relationship between expected return and beta for every asset and every combination of assets (so every portfolio) can be described by a securities market line (SML), as shown in Figure 18.3. Assets that have:

- a beta of 1 move in line with the market;
- a beta greater than 1 outperform in a rising market but lose more in a falling market (aggressive performance);
- a beta less than 1 lag behind a rising market but drop less in a falling market (defensive performance).

In an efficient market, an asset or portfolio will have a price that produces the expected return suggested by the SML. Assets and portfolios not on the SML are either over-valued (lying beneath the SML) or under-valued (lying above the SML).

There is another important conclusion from the CAPM provided that: The market is efficient and unhindered by any transaction costs or taxes; all investors are rational, interested only in risk and return, have access to all relevant information, and analyze the information in the same way; and every investor can borrow and lend at the risk-free rate. If these assumptions were to hold, investors would all choose the same portfolio. Moreover, any asset not initially in the portfolio would have a low price, but this would increase its expected return, attracting investors to buy it. Conversely, if there was excess demand for another asset, its price would rise making it less attractive, so investors would sell until its price fell back. The upshot is that investors would not just hold the same portfolio but that it would comprise every asset in the market held in proportion to its share of the market by value – this is called the market portfolio and is shown by point M in Figure 18.4.

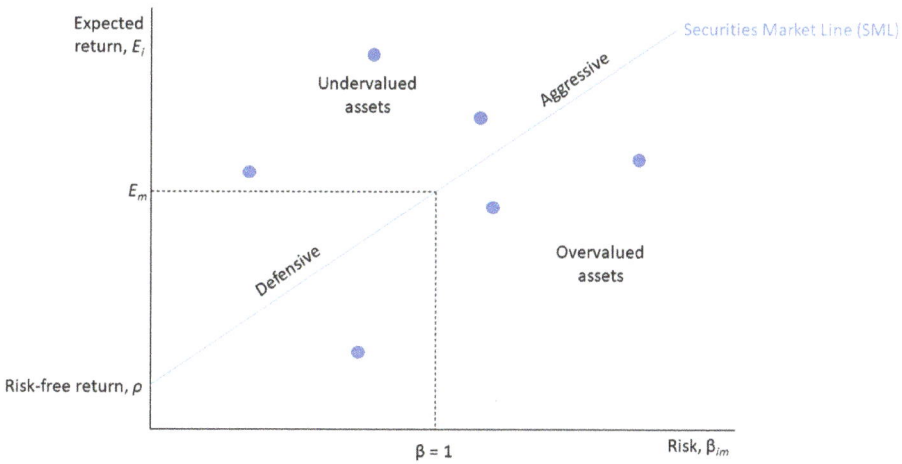

**Figure 18.3:** The Securities Market Line.

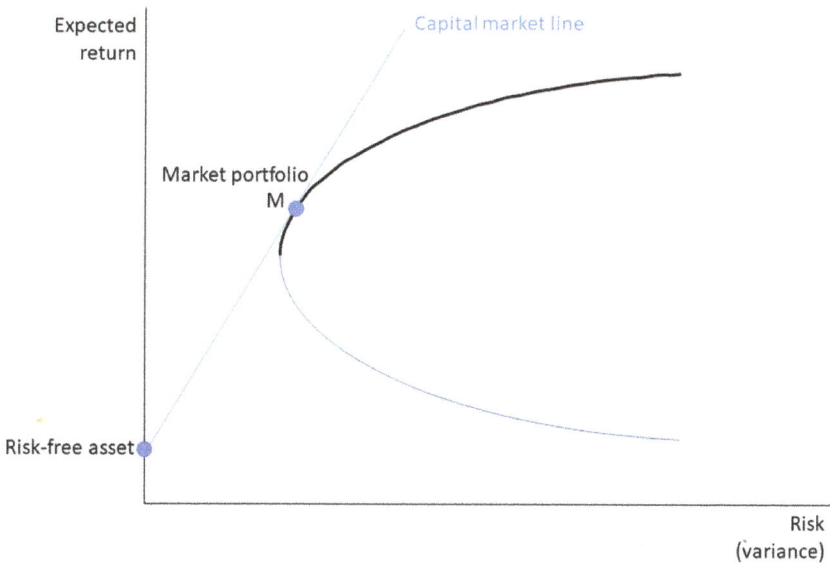

**Figure 18.4:** The Market Portfolio and Capital Market Line.

M is one of the portfolios that lie on the Markowitz efficient frontier. By definition, the risk of a market portfolio must be beta ($\beta = 1$); its return will be the risk-free return plus the appropriate risk premium. In the Markowitz model, investors who want a different combination of risk and return would select a different portfolio on the efficient frontier. CAPM suggests that a superior strategy – offering higher returns for the same or lower risk – is for investors who want less risk (and so willing to accept lower expected return) to create a portfolio that combines the market portfolio and the risk-free asset. For investors who want a higher risk–return combination, they should borrow at the risk-free rate in order to buy more of the market portfolio. All the combinations of the market portfolio and the risk-free asset (either holding it or borrowing at that rate) are located on the capital market line in Figure 18.4.

In recent times, other approaches to portfolio construction – often dubbed Post-Modern Portfolio Theory – have emerged, but MPT still continues to have considerable influence.

# Practitioner Tools and Techniques

The theories outlined in the previous section underpin some widely adopted tools and techniques used by the intermediaries with whom retail investors commonly interact and by some private investors, too.

## Fundamental Analysis

Investment analysts based in, for example, brokerage firms and investment fund management companies, most commonly use fundamental analysis as the basis for selecting which equities or other individual assets to buy.

The aim of fundamental analysis is to estimate the intrinsic value of an asset, which can be compared with its market price to establish whether the market price is less than intrinsic value (a buy signal) or greater than intrinsic value (a sell signal).

Fundamental analysis is grounded in the discounted cash flow (DCF) equation. Analysts will conduct substantial research to try to arrive at their judgment of the likely future income flows from a security (equities or bonds), including, for example: analysis of a company's accounts, operations, earnings trajectory, dividend policy, ambitions, and ethos; prospects for the sector or industry within which it operates; the effect of regulation; and the impact of wider economic, social, and political factors. Even if analysts have access to the same information, they will weigh and interpret it differently, so analysts' forecasts and recommendations will vary. It is common to see these divergent views collated into an average, called a broker consensus.

DCF is supplemented and informed by other commonly used metrics, such as price–earnings (PE) ratio for equities, which provides a shorthand for comparing market price with earnings to see whether it exceeds or falls short of some benchmark level, such as the historic average for the sector. (A high PE ratio may indicate a company that is expected to grow strongly.) Also important is dividend cover (earnings divided by most recent dividend payments) since ultimately the cash flow to a shareholder is not the earnings of the company but the part passed on in dividends and cover is an indicator of ability to sustain those payouts in the future.

The seminal work on fundamental analysis is *Security Analysis* first written in 1934 by Anglo-U.S. economist Benjamin Graham (1894–1976) and U.S. economist and financial analyst David Dodd (1895–1988), which is still updated (by later writers), published, and used today (see Graham and Dodd, 2009).

Fundamental analysis implicitly denies Fama's (1970) strong and semi-strong forms of the efficient market hypothesis by assuming that there is information that has not already been absorbed into the current market price that can be used to identify mispriced assets. On the other hand, fundamental analysis does rely on the notion that an asset mispriced today will nevertheless reflect its intrinsic value sometime in the future – called mean reversion – suggesting a belief that markets tend toward efficiency even though prices may fluctuate in the short or medium term.

## Technical Analysis

Technical analysts (also called chartists) use time-series data of price and trading volume to construct resourceful charts from which they identify trends and turning points for an asset price or market index. The foundation of technical analysis is credited to U.S. financial journalist Charles H. Dow (1851–1902) as evolved through his editorials in *The Wall Street Journal* that Dow cofounded (Bishop, 1961), although its modern-day version is somewhat different.

The underlying premise of technical analysis is that investors react to situations and information in consistent ways so that repeated and observable patterns occur in price data that can be an indicator of what happens next. In particular, once a turning point has been identified, the new trend (upwards or downwards) is likely to persist at least in the short-term – called momentum. This collective market behavior may be emotional rather than rational – much as Keynes (1936) suggested and the field of behavioral finance offers possible explanations. For example, Kahneman and fellow Israeli psychologist Amos Tversky (1937–1996), established that people are in general about twice as likely to seek to avoid losses as they are to seek gains (Kahneman and Tversky, 1979); this can help to explain a "support level" below which an asset price seems not to fall as investors shy away from crystallizing losses by selling.

The idea that patterns in past data can be an aid to predicting where asset prices go next breaches even Fama's weak-form test for an efficient market.

## Passive and Active Fund Management

Personal investors do not only have direct holdings of financial assets, such as bonds and equities. Many hold these assets indirectly through, for example, mutual funds, exchange-traded funds, investment-type life insurance products, and pension plans, collectively referred to here as "investment funds".

Investment fund managers fall into two overarching types – active managers and passive managers. In an actively managed fund, the managers try to construct portfolios that will produce superior returns – in other words, generate alpha. This means identifying portfolios that lie on the Markowitz efficient frontier and data providers do crunch the numbers for all possible portfolios to identify the efficient frontier – something that, given the state of computing power, was not possible when Markowitz first developed his theory. However, the efficient frontier suggests that the only way to generate higher returns is to take on additional risk. Fund managers aim to "beat the market" through skill at picking stocks and timing their trades, but research suggests they do not succeed. For example, average U.K. funds have been found to underperform the market, although with some tendency for funds that perform well in one quarter to persist in doing so in the next (Blake and Timmermann, 1998). Moreover, active fund charges tend to be relatively high both because of the managers' fees and the trading costs involved in a high turnover of assets in the portfolio.

Passive funds – also called "trackers" – are grounded in the CAPM approach. Rather than try to beat the market, a better strategy it is claimed is simply to hold the market portfolio, in other words, a fund that aims simply to track a particular stock-market index either with market-weighted direct holdings of all the assets in the index or replicating the performance of the index using derivatives. Because passive funds trade less frequently and have less manager input, their charges are typically lower than for active funds.

Fund data providers publish a wide range of metrics to help investors select and compare investment funds, including measures of alpha and beta based directly on CAPM.

## Applications

The standard approach to personal financial planning is to work through a hierarchy of needs. Once any debts are on a manageable footing and protection needs have been met through insurance and/or saving, individuals and households can turn to longer-term needs, in particular retirement saving, and more substantial wants, for example, school fees planning and inheritance. All of these latter goals are likely to involve investments.

Historical evidence supports the general pattern of relative returns shown in Figure 18.1 above, with equities consistently outperforming bonds and cash – for example, with a probability for the U.K. of 77 percent and 91 percent, respectively over a 10-year timeframe (Barclays, 2018). Importantly, equities beat inflation by a significant margin – for example, U.S. equities returned an average inflation-adjusted return of 6.5 percent a year over the period 1900 to 2019 (compared with 2.0 percent for bonds but with lower volatility), while real equity returns in selected other territories were: U.K. 5.5 percent, Europe 4.3 percent, and Japan 4.2 percent (Credit Suisse Research Institute, 2020, p. 23). Thus, long-term investors are more likely to protect the buying power of their store of value against inflation and to achieve large long-term goals if they invest in equities, but this entails taking on additional risk.

Strategies for managing the extra risk depend on an investor's goal and stage of life. This is clearly seen in retirement planning, which involves two stages: Accumulation during the working years; and decumulation once the individual is ready to start drawing income.

During the accumulation phase, short- and medium-term fluctuations in markets may create paper losses but, provided there is no need to sell assets, the investor can ride out the dips and stay focused on longer-term rising trends.

Capital risk becomes more significant during the decumulation phase. For many pensioners, it is not feasible or desirable to rely on the "natural income" (dividends and interest payments) produced by their investments, since this would require a large fund and leave substantial unused assets after death. A typical strategy involves withdrawing a mix of natural income and the proceeds from gradually cashing in the investments. Cashing in when the market is in a downturn means crystallizing paper losses as actual losses that will not be recouped in a subsequent upswing. As a result, many advisers suggest that pensioners include in their portfolio enough cash assets to cover, say, two years' spending so that cashing in investments can be suspended during a downtrend.

Another option for pensioners is to diversify at least part of their savings into a lifetime annuity (an income that is guaranteed to continue for as long as the person lives). This is an insurance product that protects against longevity risk – the risk of living longer than the savings last. The intrinsic value of an annuity can be readily calculated using a DCF equation weighting each payment by the probability of survival. However, even when annuity prices match or are lower than the intrinsic value, investors are resistant to buying annuities (Lowe, 2014). Research suggests this is due to behavioral factors with individuals framing annuities not as insurance but as investments and giving high weight to a fear of dying soon after buying an annuity (Brown, 2007).

A further strategy for the decumulation phase is to consider portfolio diversification in the widest terms, including not just formal retirement savings, but also, for example, human capital, if the pensioner is willing and able to continue doing some paid work, and the home, which could finance income through downsizing to a cheaper property or staying put but using equity release.

# Discussion

Economic theories that begin with the assumption of efficient markets – let alone CAPM's homogenous investors and ability of all to borrow at the risk-free rate – are clearly not precise reflections of the real world, but they serve to illuminate how markets could work, under what conditions and, since the turn toward neoliberalism from the 1970s, provide a compass that commonly underpins regulation both nationally and globally in asset markets and the real economy. However, the idealizing of free markets at the heart of neoliberalism is often at odds with social goals. Moreover, governments while espousing efficient markets on the one hand are sometimes with the other introducing major distortions, contributing to asset price bubbles that benefit some investors while shutting out others.

## Policy Issues

Efficient markets are prized because standard economic theory from Adam Smith (1776) onwards teaches that they allocate resources in the "best" way, optimizing the outcomes for society as a whole. While it is clear that few markets in the real world conform to this ideal, the goal of policymakers is typically to work toward efficiency by addressing the market failures that stand in its way.

A market is essentially an information-signaling mechanism – prices encapsulate the preferences and intentions of buyers and sellers, the relative abundance and scarcity of supply, and the collective view of where resources should be directed. One of the key reasons for market failure is that market participants do not have perfect information or that information is asymmetric (known to some but not to others).

In stock markets, where bonds and equities are traded, a key focus of policy is to tackle information failures. Thus, stock markets generally have strict rules around the release of new information to ensure that all participants potentially have simultaneous access and laws against the exploitation of "insider information," meaning information that is not publicly available; investment funds are required to communicate with investors in fair, transparent, and not misleading ways. However, regulations such as these do not ensure a level playing field for all – there is a cost to acquiring information in money, time, and cognitive effort (Lowe, 2017). Moreover, there are often incentives in real-world markets working against information transparency, for example, to gain or increase market power (Stiglitz, 2001). Most private investors are simply not in a position to acquire, and act on, perfect information, despite regulation.

The micro-regulation of markets may be confounded by wider macroeconomic policies. Kindleberger and Alber (2005) described credit as fueling bubbles, but the necessary liquidity can also come from the unconventional monetary policies that have been practiced by central banks since the 2008 global financial crisis. For example, the Bank of England's quantitative-easing program has involved buying government bonds deliberately to push up their price, which (as the DCF equation predicts) pushes down their expected return. The lower interest rates ripple through the economy with the aim of stimulating borrowing and economic growth (Bank of England, 2020). However, the stimulus can create bubbles in the price of assets, such as equities and housing (Blot et al., 2017).

Similarly, social policies aimed at increasing homeownership, for example, through grants, government-backed loans, and reductions in purchase taxes, stoke demand and, in the absence of policies to also increase supply, can create house price bubbles. This has the dual effect of producing excess returns for those who already own property but making it harder for some aspiring new owners to enter the market.

A major social policy issue is the extent to which individuals and households should take responsibility for their own security and well-being, importantly in the areas of housing and retirement income. The key is having access to the relevant markets, bearing in mind that demand constitutes those who are willing *and able* to buy. Households on low incomes or with low savings are often excluded in predominantly market-based systems.

# Future Directions

The single issue that is likely to loom largest for investors in the future is climate change. The effects have been predicted since the 1970s, but the escalation in extreme weather events since the start of the 2000s and hard-hitting research, such as that of Stern (2007), has raised awareness of the urgency to act. With this has come a growing attention to economic, social, and governance (ESG) issues, being driven by regulators and fund managers, with many of the latter becoming signatories to the United Nations' *Principles for Responsible Investment* (2019).

Increasingly, firms are being required to publish their ESG credentials. Many fundamental analysts are adapting and overlaying their DCF calculations with ESG information and shifting stock selection to greener industries and companies or alternatively applying direct pressure as shareholders on the boards of companies to shift to more environmentally sustainable practices.

It is predicted that the transition to a low-carbon future will not be a smooth one for investors, with the risk of sudden shifts in assets valuations, seeing "carbon assets" potentially stranded as they fall from favor and bubbles developing around emerging green technologies (see, for example, Semieniuk et al., 2020).

# Conclusion

Investment theory and practice are all about value. This may be some intrinsic value that can be calculated using the tools of economics, albeit based on a host of assumptions, or alternatively whatever the next speculative buyer is willing to pay that draws on the theories grounded in psychology. There is a general belief that, in the long term, asset prices tend toward their intrinsic value (reversion to mean) but fluctuate around it in the short to medium term, with trends (momentum) and more extreme deviations (bubbles) being driven by the collective behavior of investors.

Seminal work in the middle of the last century laid the foundations of portfolio construction that still dominate the way professional and private investors manage risk and return today. These techniques can be readily applied to the pursuit of long-term goals, particularly if the aim is simply to accumulate assets. However, the challenge for investors is greater if they need gradually to decumulate their assets – for example, to provide retirement income – because of the need to weather price downturns. The volatility of asset prices can be exacerbated by central bank monetary policies and government social policies, and may increase further in the future as financial markets adjust to climate change.

In largely market-based systems, individuals and households need to engage with asset markets in order to secure their financial well-being. However, a key social policy issue is that not everyone has access to these markets, particularly low-income households.

# References

Bank of England. (2020). *What is quantitative easing?* Accessed July 2021. https://www.banko fengland.co.uk/monetary-policy/quantitative-easing

Barclays. (2018). *Barclays equity gilt study 2018.* Accessed July 2021. https://www.scribd.com/ document/383879981/Barclays-Equity-Gilt-Study-2018

Bishop, G. W. (1961). Evolution of Dow theory. *Financial Analysts Journal, 17*(5), 23–26.

Blake, D., and Timmermann, A. (1998). Mutual fund performance: Evidence from the U.K. *European Finance Review, 2*(1), 57–77.

Blot, C., Hubert, P., and Labondance, F. (2017). *Monetary policy and asset price bubbles.* Université Paris Nanterre. Accessed July 2021. https://www.aeaweb.org/conference/2018/preliminary/ paper/S83RNNBs

Brown, J. R. (2007). *Rational and behavioural perspectives on the role of annuities in retirement planning* (NBER Working Paper No. 13537). National Bureau of Economic Research. https://www.nber.org/papers/w13537

Credit Suisse Research Institute. (2020). *Summary edition Credit Suisse global investment returns yearbook 2020.* Accessed July 2021. https://www.credit-suisse.com/media/assets/corporate/ docs/about-us/research/publications/credit-suisse-global-investment-returns-yearbook-2020-summary-edition.pdf

Fama, E. (1970). Efficient capital markets: A review of theory and empirical works. *Journal of Finance, 25*(2), 383–417.

Fisher, I. (1930). *The theory of interest.* Macmillan Company. https://oll-resources.s3.us-east-2. amazonaws.com/oll3/store/titles/1416/Fisher_0219_EBk_v6.0.pdf

Graham, B., and Dodd, D. L. (2009). *Security analysis* (6th ed.). McGraw-Hill Education.

Kahneman, D. (2011). *Thinking fast and slow.* Penguin.

Kahneman, D., and Tversky, A. (1979). Prospect theory: An analysis of decision under risk. *Econometrica, 47*(2), 263–292.

Keynes, J. M. (1936). *The general theory of employment, interest and money.* Macmillan Company.

Kindleberger, C. P., and Alber, R. Z. (2005). *Manias, panics, and crashes. A history of financial crises* (5th ed.). Palgrave Macmillan.

Lowe, J. (2014). Whither UK annuities? Why lifetime annuities should still be part of good financial advice in the post-pension-liberalisation world. *The International Longevity Centre UK.* https://ilcuk.org.uk/wp-content/uploads/2018/10/ILC-Whither-annuities-2.pdf

Lowe, J. (2017, March 6). *Consumers and competition: Delivering more effective consumer power in retail financial markets* [Senior Lecturer in Economics and Personal Finance]. The Open University. https://www.fscp.org.uk/sites/default/files/fscp_consumers_and_competition_ thinkpiece_finalpp_jtl_20170306.pdf

Markowitz, H. (1952). Portfolio selection. *Journal of Finance, 7*(1), 77–91.

Mazzucato, M., Lowe, J., Shipman, A., and Trigg, A. (2010). *Personal investment: Financial planning in an uncertain world.* Palgrave Macmillan.

Principles for Responsible Investment (2019). *A blueprint for responsible investment.* https://www. unpri.org/pri/a-blueprint-for-responsible-investment

Reinhart, C. M., and Rogoff, K.S. (2011). *This time is different: Eight centuries of financial folly.* Princeton University Press.

Semieniuk, G., Campiglio, E., Mercure, J-F., Volz, U., and Edwards, N. R. (2020). Low-carbon transition risks for finance [In review]. *Wiley Interdisciplinary Reviews: Climate Change, 12*(1), 1–24. https://doi.org/10.1002/wcc.678

Smith, A. (1776). *An inquiry into the nature and causes of the wealth of nations.* Methuen & Co.

Stanovich, K. E., and West, R. F. (2000). Individual differences in reasoning: Implications for the rationality debate. *Behavioural and Brain Sciences, 23*(5), 645–726. http://pages.ucsd.edu/~ mckenzie/StanovichBBS.pdf

Stern, N. (2007). *The economics of climate change: The stern review.* Cambridge University Press. https://doi.org/10.1017/CBO9780511817434

Stiglitz, J. E. (2001, December 8). *Information and the change in the paradigm in economics* [Nobel Prize lecture]. Columbia Business School, Columbia University. https://www.nobelprize.org/ uploads/2018/06/stiglitz-lecture.pdf

Part III: **Financial Security**

John E. Grable, Michelle Kruger

# 19 The Role of Insurance as a Household Financial Management Tool

**Abstract:** The insurance industry has evolved greatly from its early beginnings in the 14th century. Over time, market consolidation has occurred, and insurance companies have continued to become even larger. The purpose of this chapter is to provide a broad overview of commonly used insurance products and services from a personal and household financial management perspective. This chapter concludes by describing future insurance trends and research opportunities. Those interested in research opportunities focusing on the insurance industry should consider exploring problems such as moral hazard and adverse selection that can lead to market failure. Future research should also examine the relationship between insurance product choice and financial risk tolerance.

**Keywords:** insurance, risk, uncertainty, risk management

## Introduction

The term "insurance" is both ubiquitous and equivocal. As noted by Ewold (1991), insurance can be used to describe private and nationalized institutions, social security schemes, sharing risks through mutual and stock societies and organizations, or a hedging technique designed to minimize investment losses, as well as other specialized endeavors. When conceptualized in the context of personal finance, insurance is primarily a tool used by individuals, families, and households to manage risk. In this regard, according to the U.S. Consumer Financial Protection Bureau (2021), when a household purchases insurance, the household is purchasing protection against unexpected financial losses.

The notion of risk underlies all aspects of insurance. According to Ewold (1991), risk has three distinct characteristics. First, risk is calculable. This means that a priori, a financial decision maker must be able to evaluate the probability of a loss with a high degree of confidence. This makes risk distinct from the notion of uncertainty (Knight, 1921). Uncertainty refers to a situation in which the outcomes of a behavior, choice, or task are unknown and potentially negative. Insurance generally cannot be used to protect against uncertainty. Second, risk is collective. This means that while individuals incur losses, risk is something that affects a population. As such,

John E. Grable, University of Georgia
Michelle Kruger, Elwood & Goetz, LLC

https://doi.org/10.1515/9783110727692-019

insurance, as described in this chapter, cannot be used to protect a decision maker when wagering or taking chances that are unique to that decision maker. Third, risk is what Ewold called capital. Insurance does not make whole an injury but rather indemnifies only the loss of capital resulting from damage, injury, and loss.

In addition to insurance, which is a form of risk-sharing and transfer, households use three other techniques to manage risk. The simplest way to manage risk is to avoid behaviors that lead to potential losses. A more complex way to manage risk is to reduce or mitigate hazards[1] that can cause or worsen a loss. A third risk management strategy is called risk retention. With this strategy, a household accepts the possibility of risk and budgets for a potential loss in the future.

The purpose of this chapter is to provide an overview of insurance – as a risk transfer mechanism – in relation to individual, family, and household financial management tasks and behaviors. The chapter begins by describing the historical development of insurance as a risk management tool. This is followed by a brief overview of the most important and widely used forms of insurance. The chapter concludes with a discussion of the challenges and opportunities embedded in the insurance marketplace today with a focus on research possibilities.

## Historical Perspective

The challenge associated with writing a brief history of insurance is that the insurance literature is fragmented and distinctly regional. This is how Hellwege (2016), quoting Koch (2012), described the focus of insurance history:

> Even though the idea of insurance is international, its implementation shows many regional peculiarities . . . The insurance business found its special characteristic features in a local setting by the implementation of the idea of insurance and combining it with independent local ideas.[2]                                                                                            (p. 68)

The following narrative is overly simplified. Those who are interested in tracing the deeper origins and growth of the worldwide insurance industry are encouraged to review Ferguson (2009), Jenkins and Yoneyama (2000), Manes (1942), Masci et al., (2007), Pearson (2004), and Trenerry (1926). The outline that follows is based on Masci's (2011) historical framework that divides the history of insurance into seven periods.

---

1 Whereas a hazard is a factor that may lead to or worsen a loss, a peril is an event or factor that can cause a loss. Examples of perils include fire, windstorms, lightning, smoke, and vandalism.
2 In support of this assertion, Hellwege (2016) pointed out that in Germany, the origins of insurance are thought to be related to the development of maritime, life, and fire insurance distinctly, whereas in England the roots of insurance are generally thought to be singularly associated with the development of maritime insurance.

# 1 The Prehistory of Insurance

The origins of insurance stretch from what Masci (2011) called ancient times until the end of the medieval period in the 14th century. It is thought the Chinese merchants were the first to apply the concept of diversification to protect shipments from loss. The development of caravan trade in Babylon, the most famous city in ancient Mesopotamia, is also thought to be a concurrent foundation of modern insurance. These mutual associations were developed to share risks. It was at this time that the notion of bottomry was introduced into the insurance lexicon. Bottomry describes the notion of combining loans with insurance. In ancient times, a banker would loan a merchant money using the merchant's ship as collateral. Upon the successful completion of a trip, the merchant would repay the banker, but if a loss occurred, the merchant would not be liable for the loan. In order to protect their investments, bankers typically insisted that merchants align efforts for mutual assistance (e.g., travel via caravans or convoys). A similar method of trade, loans, and insurance was used by the Phoenicians, the Egyptians, and the Greeks. It is worth noting that the mention of bottomry or insurance is absent from Roman law; however, it is known that the Romans did have a form of life insurance to help families offset the cost of burials.

# 2 Introduction of the Insurance Policy

The concept of sharing risks – a foundational element that forms the basis of modern insurance – was further refined in Europe with the development of medieval guilds. Guilds typically were comprised of workers' fraternities where artisans, merchants, and other workers banded together to "protect their members from loss by fire and shipwreck, to ransom them from captivity by pirates, and to provide decent support or burial in sickness, poverty, or death" (Masci, 2011, p. 29). During the Middle Ages, Italy and Spain took leading roles in codifying foundational elements of insurance contracts that originated with guilds. The Italians later separated insurance from lending practices associated with bottomry. Beginning in 1435, marine insurance, which originated in Barcelona, replaced mutual assistance cooperatives.[3]

---

3 It is worth noting that a special insurance scheme was introduced in France in the 17th century that remained popular until the early 20th century. Although not technically insurance as it is defined today, tontines (named after Lorenzo di Tonti) were an "early form of pension scheme" (Hellwege, 2016, p. 68). In their simplest form, a tontine works like an annuity. Individuals contribute a lump sum to a pooled fund. The individual then receives an annual dividend from the pool. As those in the fund die, the remaining shares are distributed to the survivors thus increasing the annual dividend. At the death of the last person in the pool, any remaining capital is typically released to a governmental organization.

The development of insurance hit a major roadblock during the ending stages of the Middle Ages. It was at this time that legislation, at the behest of religious authorities, began to outlaw gambling. During this period of time, some saw insurance as a sophisticated type of wagering, which led to the use of insurance declining dramatically. One positive outcome from this shift away from insurance as a speculative tool was the introduction of what has become a key concept embedded in most insurance contracts today: insurable interest. Religious and civil authorities did allow for individuals and groups to band together to help offset losses if the owner of an insurance policy could document that they would incur a financial loss resulting from the death, loss, or destruction of the object being insured. The notion of an insurable interest was thought to separate insurance from gambling.

## 3 The Rise of Insurance Companies

Throughout Europe, a resurgence in commerce and trade was underway by the 15th century. By this time, the focus of economic growth started to shift away from Italy and Spain to northern Europe, particularly England and the Netherlands (Masci, 2011). The term "underwriter" was introduced in the 17th century. Underwriters were individuals who wrote insurance, or cooperated with others in writing insurance contracts, for merchants (i.e., the individual signed their name under the written contract, thus guaranteeing the contract). Underwriters coined terms well known in the insurance industry today, including the concept of an insurance premium. Initially, insurance contracts were limited to a ship's cargo, but by the mid-17th century, insurers had expanded to write contracts for other risks, including fire. This is how the now well-known Lloyd's of London started doing business.

According to Masci (2011), "The first real insurance company was founded in 1667, the year after the Great Fire of London" (p. 32). Although several insurance firms were established in London and Paris, the first joint-stock maritime insurance firm was started in 1720. By the end of the 18th century, marine, life, livestock, and fire insurance companies were well established. The concept of insurance spread to North America at this time. Fire insurance was first introduced in the British colonies in Charleston in 1735 and Philadelphia in 1752. The origins of many of the world's largest insurers (e.g., Aetna, Travelers, the Hartford) can trace their origins to this time in history.

## 4 Firm Growth and Social Insurance

Europe and much of the world was undergoing significant political and social change by the middle of the 18th century. Medieval institutions and guilds had practically disappeared. This meant that individuals and families were no longer able to rely on the welfare of neighbors and workers' groups for support during times of trouble. As a result, the role of private insurance expanded dramatically. The use of insurance contracts, offered by insurance firms rather than individuals, expanded worldwide to include not only merchant activities but losses resulting from declines in health, disability, and death. Property insurance, both commercial and household, increased as well.

According to Masci (2011), the growth in the insurance industry during the 18th and 19th centuries resulted in greater professionalization and increased regulation. Firms moved toward insurance specialization while expanding operations beyond narrow regional boundaries. In order to facilitate this growth, firms introduced the concept of brokerage firms and insurance agencies, where the primary role of the broker and agent was to canvas underdeveloped and/or underrepresented populations. Many insurance firms opened branch offices worldwide. At the same time, community-based organizations, mutual associations, and cooperatives were formed to provide lower-cost policies to niche groups and organizations.

The explosion in insurance products and services had two side effects that can be seen to this day. First, it soon became apparent that pricing and information asymmetries existed, making it difficult for household financial decision makers to effectively discern differences between insurance companies and policies. Second, it quickly became apparent that a large portion of society, across countries and regions, were effectively required to self-insure because they were priced out of the private insurance marketplace. Masci (2011, p. 36) noted that, by this time, insurance was transitioning into a product designed for those in the "upper classes, big landowners, or traders and professional people." It is at this point that public policy initiatives were introduced to (a) establish minimum funding and premium standards across firms and policies and (b) introduce social insurance schemes to bring a baseline level of support to the working classes.

Otto von Bismarck, who served as the founding chancellor of the German Empire, is generally credited with establishing the first social insurance contracts at the state level. From 1884 to 1888, the German Reichstag implemented sweeping accident (i.e., workers' compensation), health, retirement, and disability insurance programs for all German citizens. The success and public support of these social insurance systems prompted nearly all other European, American, and Asian countries to implement similar forms of social insurance. Rather than rely solely on private insurance contracts as the foundation of governmental insurance mandates, nearly all social insurance programs administered (and continue to administer) premium and claim payments through nationalized offices.

## 5 Insurance Firm Consolidation

While conflicts between the private insurance and social insurance sectors did emerge during the 19th century, for the most part, both insurance sectors operated and expanded in unison. Policymakers around the world found that insurance firms provided a means to mobilize savings, and as such, insurance products were often given preferential tax and legislative treatment (Skipper, 2001). As a result, throughout Europe and the Americas, insurance firms morphed from a means of sharing risks to the primary financial intermediaries at the national and regional level. In this regard, insurance firms took on the role of linking savers (suppliers of funds) and borrowers (users of funds). According to Skipper (2001, p. 6), the intermediary system works like this: "thousands of individuals each pay relatively small life insurance premiums, part of which typically represents savings. The insurers then invest these amassed funds as loans and other investments. In performing this intermediation function, direct lending and investing by individual policyholders, which would be time-consuming and costly, is avoided." In other words, insurance firms create market liquidity by using money from policyholders to invest in long-term assets. Over time, and in many countries, insurance companies became the largest holders of national debt. As such, a symbiotic relationship between insurance firms and countries emerged at this time.

Given the growth in the number and size of insurance firms during the 19th century, mergers and acquisitions occurred at a hurried pace at the dawn of the 20th century. These mergers were encouraged by policymakers who envisioned even greater liquidity and economies of scale by having fewer but larger firms in the marketplace. At the same time, insurance companies started to apply organizational standards and procedures that resulted in horizontal and vertical integration of operations. Insurance companies also established specialized insurance units. In some cases, insurance firms, individually and jointly, abandoned certain markets based on diminished profit expectations. Following these moves, governments were often called upon to establish new social insurance programs to address gaps in coverage (life insurance for military personnel, crop insurance, etc.).

## 6 Government Regulation

The sixth stage of the insurance industry and product development saw an increase in government regulation. The role of private insurance companies in the world economy from 1900 through 1930 was pervasive. Insurance products, primarily life insurance contracts, were used as a foundational element of savings for millions of people worldwide. Insurance products also provided a foundational level of confidence that supported entrepreneurship. During and after the First World War, insurance companies were responsible for purchasing significant national debt obligations, and in this respect, insurance companies provided significant market liquidity that facilitated the rapid economic growth seen in the 1920s.

However, the symbiotic relationship between national governments and insurance companies began to change after the Great Depression. At that time, private firms were seen as contributing to speculative tendencies that created systemic economic imbalances that resulted in the collapse of stock prices, asset deflation, and the failure of numerous financial institutions. Insurance companies were at the center of this controversy. Some insurance products, and companies, were seen as predatory and discriminatory. Following the Great Depression, governments took steps to more closely regulate insurance companies through increased supervision and product pricing oversight. Governments also replaced some forms of private insurance through social insurance programs. For example, social security retirement schemes were slowly introduced across the globe to replace private plans offered by insurance companies. In some situations (e.g., in Latin America), governments replaced private insurance with social insurance as a way to direct funding to governmental favored industrialization projects (Masci, 2011).

## 7 A Global Market

The seventh stage of the insurance industry and product development, which marks the period beginning with the 21st century, can best be described by the notion of globalization. The financial sector is more interconnected today than at any time in the past, which means that insurance companies must be competitive in terms of product pricing, market expansion, and the allocation of firm resources. This competitiveness factor, coupled with the realization that nearly all of the largest insurance companies operating worldwide are publicly owned, means that insurance company managers sometimes feel pressured to take excessive risks. The American International Group, Inc. (AIG) illustrates the pressures insurance companies began to face at the outset of the 21st century. In the pursuit of higher profits, AIG and other insurance firms established subsidiaries that were unrelated to their core insurance businesses. Whereas the insurance business tends to be highly regulated, these subsidiaries were not widely or deeply supervised. The result was that an AIG subsidiary began investing in credit default swaps.[4] The subsidiary employed leverage to enhance potential profits. When the AIG subsidiary purchased the credit swaps, AIG was effectively insuring the bond payments; however, unlike traditional insurance where an insurance company has reserves available to pay claims, the AIG subsidiary did not have sufficient reserves to make good on contractual agreements in the event of a credit rating downgrade. The insurance arm of

---

**4** Credit swaps are financial derivates that act as an insurance contract on a bond.

AIG was forced to cover the obligations when a series of events occurred during the outset of the Great Recession in 2008. In the end, AIG lost approximately $99 billion as a result of actions taken by the under-regulated subsidiary. AIG went out of business but not before the Federal Reserve Bank of New York intervened by loaning AIG more than $85 billion. This single event brought intense regulatory oversight of the entire insurance industry. The repercussions resulting from the collapse of AIG continue to be felt to this day.

As an industry, the role and power of private insurance companies plateaued following the Great Depression, although the marketing scope of most insurance firms expanded in the decades following the depression. Rather than being the primary financial intermediary in a country or region, insurance firms now share this role with other sectors of the economy and with governmental agencies. As the story of AIG illustrates, the insurance industry today must grapple with issues related to managing the risks associated with the core insurance business, elevated regulation and public skepticism of the role of insurance in the marketplace, and the continuing trend to move away from private insurance to social insurance programs. As noted by Masci (2011), "The main challenge for the future in both emerging and mature markets is to create a public policy agenda to make insurance services open, available, and a market institution capable to promote entrepreneurship, as well as social and economic growth" (p. 59).

# Applications

While understanding the historical development of the insurance industry provides context for the products and services offered by insurance firms, those interested in personal finance topics are generally most interested in better understanding the products currently used by individuals, families, and households when managing risks. The following discussion provides a brief overview of the eight most widely used forms of insurance. It is important to note that the products discussed may not be available as described throughout the world, and that in some cases, general forms of a product or service will be modified to meet the needs of particular cultures, societies, and populations.

## Health Insurance

When viewed as a globally recognized type of insurance coverage, health insurance can be packaged as private policy, universal health coverage (i.e., social insurance), or a combination of the two. The World Health Organization (2021a) defines universal health coverage as something where "all people and communities can use the promotive, preventive, curative, rehabilitative and palliative health services they need, of sufficient quality to be effective, while also ensuring that the use of these services does not expose the user to financial hardship." The United States is the only industrialized country to not have a form of universal health coverage.[5] Canada and Taiwan are the only two countries that have fully implemented universal health coverage through a single-payer plan. All other countries use either an insurance mandate or a hybrid system that combines elements from private insurance plans with those of a governmental mandate plan.

The following types of health insurance plans dominate the private insurance marketplace:

- Indemnity Plan: An indemnity plan offers an insured the broadest number of choices in relation to doctors, services, specialists, and hospitals. Such plans typically require an insured to meet a deductible before services are covered through insurance. A copayment (i.e., a fixed dollar amount per medical treatment or visit) or coinsurance clause (i.e., a percent of medical expenses) is generally applied until a stop-loss limit is reached, at which point the insured is no longer responsible for medical expenses for the year.
- Exclusive Provider Organization (EPO): An EPO is a managed care plan[6] where non-emergency services are paid for only if the insured uses doctors, specialists, and hospitals in the EPO's network.
- Point of Service (POS) plan: A POS plan provides medical services at reduced costs when doctors, specialists, and hospitals within the POS network are used. POS plans require a POS referral in order to see a specialist.
- Preferred Provider Organization (PPO): A PPO provides medical services at reduced costs when doctors, specialists, and hospitals within the PPO network are used; however, unlike a POS plan, an insured may use an out-of-network specialist without a referral (although the cost will be higher)
- Health Maintenance Organization (HMO): An HMO is a managed care plan that limits coverage to care from physicians who work directly for the HMO or are contracted by the HMO.
- High-Deductible Health Plan (HDHP): An HDHP plan may take the form of an HMO, PPO, EPO, or POS, with the key difference being that the insured will incur much higher out-of-pocket expenses before the insurance plan contributes to the cost of care. In the United States, those who use an HDHP may open a

---

5 Medicare, which is available to those over the age of 65, is an exception, as is the U.S. Veteran's Administration hospital system. Medicare is a single-payer policy that fits the definition of universal health coverage.
6 A managed care plan is one in which the plan contracts with healthcare providers and medical facilities to provide care for members of the plan.

health savings account (HSA). An HSA[7] is a tax-advantaged account that is funded by the insured; money in the account may be used to pay for eligible medical expenses on a tax-free basis.
-   Insurance Marketplace Plans: Although health insurance is not mandated in the United States, eligible individuals may purchase health insurance coverage through government-administered marketplaces. Whereas the plans are offered by private insurance companies, the elements of each plan are mandated through federal and state statutes. Marketplace plans are offered as bronze (i.e., lowest cost), silver, gold, and platinum (i.e., highest cost).

## Workers' Compensation

Workers' compensation insurance has its roots in the development of social insurance programs that occurred in the late 19th century. Essentially, workers' compensation insurance pays benefits to those who become ill or injured while working for pay (in Europe, workers' compensation benefits may also be available to those injured while commuting to work). Benefits can include medical treatment, temporary and permanent disability payments, job displacement benefits, and death benefits.[8] Worldwide, two models dominate how workers' compensation insurance programs are funded. One model is based on employer contributions to an insurance pool (i.e., Bismarckian system). The other model is financed through taxes (i.e., Beveridgean system). Both models are based on a no-fault assumption, meaning that benefits are available regardless of whether the employee or employer is at fault. Depending on the state, region, and country, workers' compensation programs may be run either by private insurance companies or through public insurance programs.

## Long-term Care Insurance

Long-term care (LTC) insurance is a specialized form of health insurance. LTC insurance pays for nursing home care, acute care, and adult day services for those who are unable to independently perform two of the following activities of daily living:[9] (1) bathing, (2) dressing, (3) transferring from a bed or chair, (4) eating, (5) caring for incontinence. LTC benefits can also be received by those with degenerative forms of dementia. According to the World Health Organization (2021b), a significant share of

---

7 In the United States, it is also possible to save money for annual medical expenses through an employer-sponsored flexible spending account (FSA). Unlike an HSA, money held in an FSA will generally be forfeited if unused within a calendar year.
8 Non-economic losses (e.g., pain and suffering) are generally not covered.
9 A physician's diagnosis is required before LTC benefits become available.

spending on LTC services is covered by a country's universal health coverage mandate. In the Netherlands, for example, federal expenditures account for more than 3.7 percent of gross domestic product (GDP). In the United States, on the other hand, where LTC benefits are extremely limited and only provided for a short duration through Medicare,[10] federal LTC expenditures are less than 0.5 percent of GDP. In the United States, the majority of the population retains the risks associated with LTC needs, although some individuals and married couples purchase private LTC policies.

Developments in the LTC marketplace have made LTC policies difficult to obtain. When first introduced into the market, insurance companies significantly underpriced LTC policies. This resulted in several large companies exiting the market. In place of stand-alone policies, insurance companies have been increasingly marketing combination life insurance and LTC policies. A typical combination policy works this way: A consumer, while healthy, transfers a single premium to an insurance company. The insurance company guarantees an LTC benefit equal to approximately four or five times the premium paid. If LTC benefits remain unused, and the policy owner dies, the insurance beneficiary receives the face value of the policy, which will be approximately one and a half times the premium paid. If some amount of the policy is used to pay LTC benefits before death, the face value of the policy is adjusted downward. It may be possible, in a combo policy, to terminate the policy early and receive some of the initial premium back on a tax-free basis.

## Disability Insurance

Disability insurance is another specialized form of health insurance that provides income payments to the insured when the insured's income is stopped or interrupted because of sickness, illness, or accident.[11] The definition of disability is an important consideration when disability insurance is purchased in the private market. The broadest definition is called any occupation disability. Under this definition, an insured will only receive income benefits if they are permanently disabled and unable to work in any occupation in which they are suited by education, training, or experience. This is the definition used by the U.S. Social Security Administration. A more narrowly defined policy is called own occupation disability. Under this definition, an insured may receive income benefits when they cannot work in their usual occupation or their chosen field of employment. Because it is difficult to obtain an own-occupation definition policy, financial planners often recommend modified own-occupation disability coverage. With this type of policy, an insured

---

**10** Individuals who fall below the poverty line, who also have limited assets, may qualify for LTC benefits under Medicaid.
**11** Those who are disabled as a result of a workplace accident or event will most often receive income payments through a workers' compensation insurance program.

will receive income payments if they are unable to engage in their chosen occupation and unable to work in a reasonable alternative occupation, one for which they are qualified by education, training, or experience (Grable et al., 2019). In some countries and regions outside of North America, disability insurance coverage is provided through a national system that insures work incapacity, maternity, vocational rehabilitation, and healthcare (e.g., the Dutch model).

## Life Insurance

Life insurance is designed to pay money to a named beneficiary in the event the person named in the insurance policy (i.e., the insured) dies. Four parties must exist in the context of a life insurance contract. The first is the insured. This is the person whose life is being covered. The next is the beneficiary. This is the person who receives the payout from the insurance policy in the event the insured dies. The third is the policy owner. The owner of the policy must prove an insurable interest in the life of the insured; however, once a contract is issued, the policy owner may transfer ownership of the policy to another person, organization, or entity. The fourth party to the contract is the insurance company. All four parties can be different, but insurance companies tend to do extra underwriting work in these cases because of an increased possibility of fraud.

Before issuing a life insurance contract, an insurance company will almost always attempt to verify the health status of the insurance applicant. This evaluation may include a medical evaluation. Factors that may limit the issuance of a policy, or increase the premium, include: smoking, drinking to excess, having a history of drug use, being over-weight, having a negative family medical history, and/or having a preexisting medical condition. In some cases, non-health-related behavior may prompt denial of a policy, including a poor credit history, a bad driving record, or one or more criminal indictments.

The number and types of life insurance policies available worldwide are expansive. Nearly all life insurance, however, falls into one of the following categories:

– *Term Life Insurance*. Sometimes referred to as pure life insurance, term is a type of policy that is in force only during the "term" of the policy. Term policies are most often sold as 1-, 5-, 10-, 15-, 20-, 25-, or 30-year policies. Term life insurance tends to be relatively inexpensive, compared to other forms of life insurance; however, the premium paid will increase in line with the insured's age, making term policies very expensive for older individuals. Nearly all forms of employer-provided life insurance are term insurance, typically annually renewable term.
– *Endowment Life Insurance*. This type of policy is popular outside of North America. An endowment policy is one in which the policy beneficiary receives a lump-sum benefit if the insured outlives the term of the policy. A hybrid between term and endowment insurance is called return-of-premium term insurance. With this

type of policy, the beneficiary receives the face value of the insurance policy if the insured dies within the stated term of the contract; however, if the insured outlives the term, the policy owner receives all premiums paid into the contract.[12]

- *Whole Life Insurance*. Sometimes called permanent or cash value life insurance, whole life insurance continues in force until the insured dies or premiums stop being paid. Whole life insurance is exponentially more expensive than comparable term insurance; however, whole life insurance is unique in that a portion of every premium payment is allocated to a cash or savings account. Over time, this account can grow quite large. The policy owner may borrow against the cash held in a whole life policy (in the event of death, the beneficiary will receive the face value of the policy less all outstanding loans). The cash value can also be surrendered and taken as cash, or the value held in the policy can be used to purchase a paid-up whole or term life insurance policy.

- *Universal Insurance*. Disadvantages associated with whole life insurance include an inability to change the level of insurance coverage over time, a fixed premium, and a relatively low fixed rate of return. Universal life insurance is designed to address these issues. A universal policy allows a policy owner to increase or decrease the premium paid, which can result in more or less coverage over time. Also, the rate of return earned on the cash element of a universal policy tends to be higher than that offered on whole life insurance products. Additionally, unlike whole life insurance that pays only the net face value amount of the policy (i.e., Option A), a universal policy owner may opt to have the policy beneficiary receive the face value plus the value held in the cash account (i.e., Option B). The premium for an Option B universal policy will be higher than either an Option A universal life policy or a whole life policy, but the policy beneficiary may receive a greater payout at the insured's death.

- *Variable Insurance*. Whole and universal life insurance pay a fixed interest rate on cash held in the policy. A variable life insurance policy applies a variable interest rate, based on the cash element of the policy being invested in securities (e.g., mutual funds, exchange-traded funds, and other assets that have a degree of price variability), to the cash held in the policy. Both the annual premium and face value associated with a variable policy are fixed, although an Option B payout may be available.

- *Variable-Universal Insurance*. Variable universal life (VUL) insurance, as the name implies, combines elements of universal and variable life insurance. The premium and face value of a VUL can vary, as can the amount received by a policy beneficiary.

---

**12** In most jurisdictions around the world, proceeds from a life insurance policy are received on a tax-free basis. Returned premiums and endowment payouts are also received tax-free in most situations.

Table 19.1 summarizes the key features associated with the primary forms of life insurance.

**Table 19.1:** Comparison of Different Types of Life Insurance Policies.

| Type of Policy | Premium | Face Amount | Cash Value | Policy Loans |
|---|---|---|---|---|
| Term | Initially low but increases with age | Renewability based on health status | None | No |
| Whole | Level | Level; cannot be changed | Yes; fixed rate of return | Yes |
| Universal | Flexible | Level; can vary | Yes; fixed rate of return | Yes |
| Variable | Level | Level; cannot be changed | Yes; variable rate of return | Yes |
| Variable Universal | Flexible | Level; can vary | Yes; variable rate of return | Yes |

## Property Insurance

When viewed as a content element within personal finance, property insurance is most directly associated with homeowner's insurance and personal automobile policies. The following discussion outlines some of the most important aspects of these types of insurance.[13]

Homeowner's insurance combines property and casualty coverages with the intent of providing protection against risks arising out of the ownership of a home. Typical coverage includes damage to the home, the home's contents, and additional living expenses. Homeowner's insurance also provides coverage for personal liability. There are many types of homeowner's policies, with numerous differences arising across regions and country boundaries. In general, however, the type of policy used by a household coincides with the type of structure being occupied. The following list provides an overview of the most common types of policies found in the North American insurance marketplace:

- *Owner-Occupied*:These policies are issued either as Basic or Broad Form. These policies (i.e., HO-1 and HO-2) cover the structure for specified perils[14] shown in

---

13 Definitions and examples in this and the following section were adapted from public files provided by the California Department of Insurance.
14 Examples of perils include fire, lightning, smoke, glass breakage, windstorm or hail, theft, vandalism, and civil disruption.

the policy. Special Form policies (i.e., HO-3) cover the structure for all perils except those specifically excluded in the policy.

- *Condominium (Owner-Occupied)*: Those who own and live in a condominium need a specialized (i.e., HO-6) policy. Condominium policies provide limited coverage for the structure and primary coverage for the personal property and liability of the insured. These policies cover named perils, but a special endorsement can be purchased to broaden the policy to cover all perils except what is excluded in the contract. Nearly all such policies provide loss assessment coverage. This pays for the insured's share of expenses for a covered loss to common property.
- *Renters*: Although not a required policy, those who rent or lease property may purchase a renter's policy (i.e., HO-4) to cover losses to personal property, as well as losses that arise from personal liability.
- *Modified Coverage*: In some states and regions, such as Florida, an insured may only have access to a Modified Coverage Form (i.e., HO-8) policy. A modified coverage policy limits the amount of insurance based on specified perils while limiting maximum payouts based on the type and age of the structure.
- *Dwelling Form*: A Dwelling Form is a limited policy that is used when a property is historic or unique and in situations where an insured rents their property to others.
- *Mobile Home*: As personal property, mobile homes (e.g., trailers) need a special form of homeowner's coverage. In situations where coverage is unavailable, a Dwelling Form may be used.

Motor vehicle insurance is used to provide coverage for an automobile (i.e., sometimes called a personal automobile policy [PAP]), truck, van, motorcycle, or another kind of private passenger vehicle. In North America, the type and minimum level of required coverage vary by individual state. Insurance is usually sold as a split-limit policy. A 50/100/50 policy, for example, will pay up to $50,000 in medical expenses for one person (not including the insured) or $100,000 for one accident, with a maximum of $50,000 in property damage. Other forms of coverage and endorsements include:

- Uninsured Motorist Coverage (UMC) Coverage: This covers an insured if they are involved in an accident with a driver who does not have liability insurance.
- Uninsured Motorist Bodily Injury (UMBI): This coverage pays for injuries to the insured and any person in the insured's car when there is an accident with an uninsured driver who is at fault.
- Underinsured Motorist (UIM): This covers limited costs for bodily injury if the insured is involved in an accident with a driver who does not have enough insurance to pay for damages.

- Uninsured Motorist Property Damage (UMPD): This coverage pays for the damage to an insured's car from an accident with an uninsured driver who is at fault.
- Medical Payments Coverage. This coverage covers the cost of medical expenses if the insured or passengers in the insured's vehicle are injured.
- Physical Damage Coverage: Physical damage coverage consists of two elements:
  - Collision covers damage to an insured's vehicle caused by physical contact with another vehicle or an object.
  - Comprehensive covers damage to an insured's vehicle caused by something other than a collision (e.g., fire, theft, vandalism, windstorm, flood, falling objects). Coverage excludes costs associated with mechanical breakdown, normal wear and tear, or maintenance.
- Endorsements and Riders: It is possible to purchase insurance for other assets normally stored in or used as a part of a vehicle (e.g., stereos, custom wheels, navigation systems, and permanently installed cell phones), as well as towing and road service coverage.
- GAP insurance: This coverage pays off a vehicle loan when a vehicle is damaged and its fair market value is less than the amount owed on the vehicle loan.

Regardless of the type of property insurance purchased, an insured will be required to pay an ongoing premium and a deductible when a claim is made. A premium represents the amount the insured must pay to the insurance company to maintain coverage. A deductible is the amount an insured must pay, out of pocket, before the insurance company pays anything on a claim. The cost of insurance (i.e., premium) will be reduced as the deductible is increased.

## Other Insurance

As illustrated in this chapter, insurance, as a foundational element of personal finance, encompasses a wide variety of topics, products, and services. The following list shows additional forms of insurance that are used as risk management tools at the individual, family, and household levels.

- Business Owner's Policy (BOP): This policy covers the operations of small and medium-sized businesses. Business owner's policies consist of integrated property coverage, general liability coverage, and specialized forms of coverage unique to the business being insured.
- Commercial Multiple Peril: This is a package insurance policy that provides both liability and property coverage for businesses and other organizations.
- Commercial Property Coverage: This type of insurance applies to real property (e.g., buildings, factories, warehouses) and business personal property (e.g.,

furniture, fixtures, inventory). Commercial property coverage also provides for the loss of income.

- Crop Insurance: Although very specialized, crop insurance provides coverage for a loss or damage by insured named perils. In the United States, crop insurance is available from the Federal Crop Insurance Corporation as well as from private insurance companies.
- Dwelling Property: This coverage differs from a homeowner's policy in that liability must be added as a policy endorsement. Essentially, the policy provides coverage for property damage to a personal dwelling. This will include at least coverage for fire and lightning but can be enhanced to include additional property coverages such as water damage, smoke, and theft.
- Earthquake Insurance: This is a form of property insurance that pays the insured in the event of damage caused by an earthquake. The premium and deductible associated with earthquake insurance can make these policies cost prohibitive.
- Equipment Breakdown Insurance: Although typically beyond the scope of personal finance, equipment breakdown insurance is important as a tool to cover costly physical and financial damage that can result from a business equipment breakdown.
- Excess Liability Insurance: Also known as umbrella insurance coverage, excess liability insurance pays for legal and other expenses once the liability limits on other forms of property insurance have been exhausted. Although the premium for excess liability coverage is low, insurance companies do require that liability limits on other policies be maintained at certain levels.
- Flood Insurance: Similar to earthquake insurance, flood insurance helps offset expenses associated with flooding. The U.S. federal government is the primary writer of the coverage that offers insurance in federally designated flood areas. This is an important risk management tool because damage from floods is excluded from most homeowner's and dwelling fire policies.
- Indemnity Insurance: Indemnity insurance is a type of voluntary insurance policy that reimburses an insured after expenses are incurred. Voluntary insurance policies often pay for expenses not reimbursed through traditional health and disability policies (e.g., critical illness, unreimbursed hospital costs, accidents).
- Inland Marine Insurance: This is a broad category of property insurance generally covering loss to movable property or unusual risks. Inland Marine includes coverage for personal effects like jewelry, fine art, sports, or musical equipment. Inland Marine coverage is typically added to a policy through an endorsement.
- Livestock Coverage: This coverage is designated for horses and other farm animals if they are damaged or destroyed. The insurance includes registered cattle and herds, other farm livestock, and zoo animals.

- Loss of Use Coverage: This endorsement pays additional housing and living expenses if the insured must move out of their covered home temporarily while the home is being repaired or replaced.
- Other Structures Coverage: This coverage pays for damage to detached structures on a property (e.g., garages, sheds, fences, cottages).

## Annuities

Although not technically a health, life, or property risk-management tool, annuities – defined as a financial product that promises to pay an income to a beneficiary in the future or immediately – comprise a large and growing market for insurance companies and social insurance programs. Two types of annuities are common. The first is an immediate annuity in which someone pays a lump sum to an insurance company in return for periodic payments that begin immediately. The second is a deferred annuity. A deferred annuity is one where someone pays premiums to an insurance company over time. The money accumulates on a tax-deferred basis, and at a later date (e.g., retirement) the insurance company commences periodic payments for a set period of time or for the remainder of the beneficiary's life.

There are two basic types of deferred annuities: fixed and variable. Fixed annuities guarantee that an annuitant's money will accumulate at a minimum insurance-company specified rate of interest. Variable annuities allow the contract owner to direct the distribution of their money among several different investment accounts. Earnings from the accounts are then credited to the annuity. Other types of deferred annuities exist, including index-linked deferred annuities, that combine the characteristics of fixed and variable annuities.

Annuities serve an important risk management function; however, annuities are not without risk. For example, if a contract owner dies during the surrender charge period, the surrender charges will be deducted from the amount the beneficiary receives. If the annuitant dies during the accumulation phase of a deferred annuity, an amount usually at least equal to the amount they have accumulated will be paid to the annuity beneficiary. If, however, a contract owner cancels a contract, or withdrawals money from the annuity, surrender charges will be deducted from the accumulation value. Additionally, unless someone purchases a life annuity with a period certain feature (discussed below), the entire investment can be lost upon the early or premature death of the annuitant.

Unlike insurance payouts, some or all of an annuity payment will be taxable. Annuity payments can be received in the following ways:
- Life Annuity: The insurance company will make payments for the life of the beneficiary.
- Period Certain Annuity: The insurance company guarantees payments for a specified period of time (e.g., 5-, 10-, 20 years).

- Life Annuity with Period Certain: The insurance company will make payments for the life of the annuitant, but if the annuitant were to die before the period outlined in the contract, income will be paid to a beneficiary until the end of that period.
- Joint and Survivor Annuity: Used primarily by married couples, the insurance company will make payments during the life of the annuitant and then to the beneficiary after the annuitant's death. Typically, the beneficiary will receive a reduction in the initial payment (e.g., 50 percent or 75 percent).

# Future Directions

Insurance companies, privately owned, mutually owned, and publicly traded, serve an important role as financial intermediaries. As noted by Skipper (2001), insurance companies "help mobilize national saving to support greater national investment" (p. 36). Even in the context of this important role, the insurance industry faces challenges that will likely result in a shift in the way insurance products and services are provided in the future. Consider the situation as this chapter was written. The insurance marketplace, particularly in relation to life insurance, appears to be saturated. This means that insurance companies must compete aggressively for premium dollars. At the same time, however, the insurance industry is faced with what appears to be a long-term environment in which interest rates are and will continue to be low. The result is a tightening of profit margins, making some market segments unprofitable. Coupling this with increased regulatory scrutiny means that insurance companies must find new sources of revenue and new investment opportunities that provide a high degree of asset value stability and reasonable returns. Historically, corporate and government-issued bonds offered these characteristics. An important question that needs to be addressed is what alternatives exist if traditional investment opportunities can no longer support the funding needs of insurance companies? It will also be important to determine how policymakers will contend with market gaps when and if insurance companies leave certain insurance markets in the future. Answering these questions will provide insights into the ongoing relationship between additional regulation and potential insurance company insolvency.

It is worth noting that the insurance industry is also grappling with other factors that will likely determine the types of products and services offered in the future. For example, in 2019, Korean regulators announced plans to limit the commissions paid on certain types of insurance products (Korean Life Insurance Association, 2019). This is likely a worldwide trend. An important question arises when these types of policies are enacted. For instance, without a well-paid salesforce, will insurance companies be able to continue to build reserves to pay future liabilities? Additionally, what social costs will arise if insurers in the private sector can no longer afford to provide certain insurance products and services? It is likely that policymakers will be called upon to provide tax concessions and/or absorb certain insurance lines.

The opportunities for insurance research, as it relates to individuals, families, and households, holds great promise for those interested in the subject. Much of the insurance research that does exist tends to be policy-driven, regulatory in nature, or focused on the firm rather than the delivery of products and services. More research is needed to address problems that can lead to market failure. For example, the issues of moral hazards[15] and adverse selection[16] have not been fully explored in the personal finance literature. A general need also exists for research to better understand the relationship between insurance product choices and financial risk tolerance. More empirical work describing issues related to asymmetric information in contracts and sales presentation is also necessary.[17] Additionally, as noted by Skipper (2001), research is needed to better understand the "applications of new financial paradigms, such as contingent claims analysis, to the analysis of insurance firms, insurance markets and corporate risk management, a development which links more closely insurance economics to financial economics, and insurance to finance" (p. 30). From a policy perspective, cross-border research is needed to create guidelines that will help insurance companies enter markets outside of their territory without having to deal with varied standards, tax laws, and legal systems (Hellwege, 2016).

## Discussion

As highlighted in this chapter, insurance remains one of those concepts that has universal application but tends to be elusive in context and application. Not only does insurance describe specific products and services that can be used by individuals, families, households, and institutions to manage risk, insurance is sometimes used to define actions (e.g., investment hedging) and policies (e.g., social security). However, when viewed with a personal finance lens, the concept of insurance transforms into something more precise – namely, a tool used by individuals, families, and households to manage risk. As one of four risk management strategies,

---

15 A moral hazard occurs when one side of an insurance contract cannot verify or observe the action of the other party in the contract; this can increase the likelihood that the insured will act inappropriately.

16 Adverse selection occurs when a contract is made between two parties each of which holds a different level of information (e.g., an insurance applicant does not disclose the severity of a potential loss).

17 Masci (2011, p. 60) noted, "Most theoretical research has focused on the problems of adverse selection and moral hazard in the insurance market," but that asymmetric information between consumers and insurers is a topic that is ripe for further study.

insurance serves as a fundamental factor describing household financial stability and capacity. Individuals, families, and households that opt to retain risk must, without corresponding social insurance programs in place, bear possible losses in isolation. The ability to share risks associated with health, life, and property hazards reduces the costs associated with possible losses. Insurance, therefore, can be seen as an essential element of a prudent financial plan and as a foundational element of personal finance as a field of study and practice.

# Conclusion

As noted at the outset of this chapter, insurance is a tool used by individuals, families, and households to manage risk. Insurance can be used to protect against unexpected financial losses. In addition to defining insurance in the context of personal finance, this chapter provided a brief history of the development of insurance as a risk management tool. The chapter also outlined the types of insurance products and services that are used by individuals, families, and households. The chapter concluded with a discussion of the challenges and opportunities facing policymakers and researchers working in the domain of insurance.

# References

Consumer Financial Protection Bureau. (2021). *What is insurance?* Accessed July 2021. https://
files.consumerfinance.gov/f/documents/cfpb_building_block_activities_what-is-insurance
_handout.pdf

Ewold, F. (1991). Insurance and risk. In G. Burchell, C. Gordon, and P. Miller (eds.), *The Foucault effect: Studies in governmentality* (pp. 197–210). The University of Chicago Press.

Ferguson, N. (2009). *The ascent of money: A financial history of the world.* Penguin Books.

Grable, J. E., Sages, R. A., and Kruger, M. E. (2019). *The case approach to financial planning: Bridging the gap between theory and practice.* National Underwriter.

Hellwege, P. (2016). A comparative history of insurance law in Europe. *American Journal of Legal History, 56,* 66–75.

Jenkins, D., and Yoneyama, T. (2000). *The history of insurance, volumes 1 and 2.* Routledge.

Knight, F. (1921). *Risk, uncertainty and profit.* Houghton Mifflin Company.

Koch, P. (2012). *History of the insurance industry in Germany* (P. Hellwege, Trans). Verlag Versicherungswirtschaft GmbH.

Korean Life Insurance Association. (2019). *Life insurance business in Korea.* https://www.klia.or.
kr/eng/reportStatistics/annualStatistics.do

Manes, A. (1942). Outlines of a general economic history of insurance. *Journal of Business of the University of Chicago, 15*(1), 30–48.

Masci, P. (2011). The history of insurance: Risk, uncertainty and entrepreneurship. *Journal of the Washington Institute of China Studies, 5*(3), 25–68.

Masci, P., Tejerina, L., and Webb, I. (2007). *Insurance market development in Latin America and the Caribbean* (Sustainable Development Department Best Practices Series IFM-146). Inter-American Development Bank.

Pearson, R. (2004). *Insuring the industrial revolution: Fire insurance in Great Britain*, 1700–1850 *(Modern economic and social history)*. Routledge.

Skipper Jr., H. D. (2001). *Insurance and private pensions compendium for emerging economies, book 1 Part 1:7)b*. Organisation for Economic Co-operation and Development. https://www.oecd.org/finance/insurance/1815326.pdf

Trenerry, C. F. (1926). *The origin and early history of insurance*. P. S. King.

World Health Organization. (2021a). *Health systems: Universal health coverage*. https://www.who.int/healthsystems/universal_health_coverage/en/

World Health Organization. (2021b). *Ageing and long-term care*. https://www.oecd.org/els/health-systems/long-term-care.htm

Suzanne Bartholomae, Jonathan J. Fox

# 20 Health and Financial Well-Being

**Abstract:** Financial well-being is an established correlate in the scholarship of general well-being or happiness as well as with health outcomes. A diverse set of disciplines produce empirical work on financial and health indicators. This work has established a strong intersection between these two domains. Both longitudinal and life span studies document the link between financial measures and health indicators. Theoretical frameworks help contextualize and predict financial well-being and its consequence for health. This chapter provides a brief review of the interlink and crossover between the domains of health and financial well-being.

**Keywords:** health, financial well-being, financial security, financial stress, personal finance

## Introduction

For good reason, the nexus between health and finances has generated a great deal of interest across disciplines and professions. A person's financial well-being can enable and affect their health, and their health can enable and affect their financial well-being. Pairing these two domains has been on the rise for the past several decades because scholars, policymakers, and practitioners recognize the many intersections between health and financial well-being (American Institutes for Research, 2010; Hoffman and Risse, 2020; Hyland and Revere, 2018; Puri and Robinson, 2007; Smith, 1999).

Both financial and health behaviors are driven by similar human tendencies, attitudes, traits, and motivations. For example, optimism, level of self-control, and conscientiousness shape one's ability to engage in beneficial health and financial behaviors (Hoffmann and Risse, 2020; Puri and Robinson, 2007). Financial and health decisions involve a consumer's ability to evaluate risk and to understand the long-term consequences of short-term and day-to-day choices (Deng and Liu, 2017). Financial and health decisions require understanding technical and legal information, contending with issues of privacy and disclosure, and dealing with a lack of transparency in general and in relation to pricing or fee structures and profit motives or conflicts of financial and health providers (Finke and Huston, 2013; James et al., 2012; McCormack et al., 2009). Access to financial and health services and products is an issue in both domains. Financial and health systems are embedded in and influenced by structural, institutional, and political forces that create barriers or opportunities for

**Suzanne Bartholomae, Jonathan J. Fox,** Iowa State University

https://doi.org/10.1515/9783110727692-020

consumers that ultimately shape their health and financial well-being (Fu, 2020; Nete-meyer et al., 2020; Solar and Irwin, 2010).

In many ways, financial and health services and products are similar in nature. For example, whether reading a food label or a mutual fund disclosure, individuals must possess numeracy and literacy skills to digest and comprehend the information. Increased attention has focused on the effect that health literacy and financial literacy has on outcomes in their respective domains (American Institutes for Research, 2010; Kindig et al., 2004; Letkiewicz and Fox, 2014), especially given an increasing empha-sis on personal decision making and consumer choice in a variety of areas of life (e.g., Thaler and Sunstein, 2008). Health and financial literacy are both defined by a person's "capacity to obtain, process, and understand" information (Ratzan et al., 2000, n.p.) and capability (e.g., have "the skills, knowledge, and tools") to make de-cisions and take actions to meet their health and financial goals (U.S. Financial Liter-acy and Education Commission, 2020, p. 2). This capability is exercised within the context of accessing health and financial services and products.

Prior work has linked health literacy with physical health outcomes and general well-being (e.g., Berkman et al., 2011; Netemeyer et al., 2020) and financial literacy with dimensions of financial and general well-being (e.g., Lusardi and Mitchell, 2014; Brüggen et al. 2017). A growing body of scholarship examines the crossover of these domains (Gillen et al., 2020; Hoffman and Risse, 2020; James et al., 2012). For exam-ple, health and financial practices are highly correlated, and engaging in planning be-haviors and budgeting has been linked to higher scores on health and financial assessments (O'Neill et al., 2016, 2017).

Several disciplines have contributed to advancing theoretical frameworks that help contextualize and predict financial well-being and its consequence for health (Brüggen et al., 2017; CFPB, 2015; Dorsey et al., 2020). Brüggen et al. (2017) depicted the pathways of financial well-being on health outcomes such as general well-being, mental health, quality of life, and relationship quality at organizational and societal levels and its effects on the "collective level" of individuals and families (p. 4). This chapter largely focuses on health and financial well-being at the individ-ual and household level.

# Developing the Connection Between Health and Financial Well-being

Early scholarship on the connection between health and financial well-being largely examined the effect of poverty (Braveman et al., 2011) on general well-being and health. This research showed that a scarcity of money deprives a person of their basic needs such as a nutritious diet and safe housing, and a lack of these basic needs undermines conditions necessary to promote good health (Habibov et al., 2019; Solar and Irwin, 2010). This materialistic argument has been supported empirically but is largely viewed as an inadequate explanation of the association of socioeconomic status and health disparities (French and Vigne, 2019). Nevertheless, low socioeconomic status has been consistently linked to greater health disparities whereas greater wealth is linked with more favorable health outcomes (Braveman et al., 2018; Habibov et al., 2019; Hill-Briggs et al., 2021). As Deaton (2002) stated, "Poorer people die younger and are sicker than richer people; indeed, mortality and morbidity rates are inversely related to many correlates of socioeconomic status such as income, wealth, education, or social class" (p. 13), a pattern referred to as the health–wealth gradient. Systematic reviews have documented an association between socioeconomic measures and health outcomes like life expectancy, mental health, smoking, heart disease, obesity, diabetes, alcohol use, physical activity, and general health status (Braveman et al., 2011, 2018; Hill-Briggs et al., 2021; Petrovic et al., 2018).

Markers of socioeconomic status are also associated with health literacy and financial literacy. Higher levels of education have been associated with higher health literacy (e.g., Berkman et al., 2011; Davey et al., 2015) and financial literacy (e.g., Finke et al., 2016). Higher income has been associated with greater levels of health literacy (Berkman et al., 2011) and financial literacy (Lusardi and Mitchell, 2011, 2014; Sekita, 2011). Higher occupational status is also associated with elevated levels of health literacy (Murray et al., 2011) and financial literacy (Monticone, 2010), which may reflect greater exposure to the healthcare system and financial institutions via greater access to employment benefits such as health insurance and retirement plans. Having both health and financial literacy is necessary given the complexity of the marketplace, the abundance of choices, and the link between health needs and financial considerations. Relationships of reverse causation between socioeconomic measures and health outcomes have been supported (Kim and von dem Knesebeck, 2018; Knorst et al., 2021), though the study of health on wealth emerged later (Braveman et al., 2011).

Another area of the wealth and health connection scholarship focuses on the "stress pathway." When basic needs are not met, the natural response is stress, which can manifest itself physically, mentally, emotionally, and behaviorally. Low-resourced individuals often suffer from elevated stress levels whereas higher-resourced individuals have a buffer to protect themselves from the adverse effects of stress and its effect on health outcomes (Moran et al., 2019; Purnell and Hajat, 2017). The stress pathway is conceptually considered a psychosocial mechanism (Solar and Irwin, 2010). O'Connor et al. (2021) specified that prolonged stress takes a toll on the body "at the cardiovascular, metabolic, neural, behavioral, and cellular levels and increases the risk of developing disease because the bodily systems stop working effectively" (p. 666). Repeated and prolonged stress compromises the immune system, making one more susceptible to infections, or exacerbating existing conditions (Segerstrom and Miller, 2004).

A well-established literature demonstrates that financial stress as a chronic stressor has a negative toll on the well-being of individuals and interpersonal relationships, including marital and family well-being (Fonseca et al., 2016; French and Vigne, 2019). Individuals and households with low levels of financial well-being are more vulnerable to financial stress (Bartholomae and Fox, 2017). Financial stress has been linked to increased levels of anger, hostility, depression, anxiety, somatic complaints, and poor physical health in general, and specific to chronic conditions like diabetes and cardiovascular disease (Corwin et al., 2021; Drentea and Reynolds, 2012; French and Vigne, 2019; Moran et al., 2019). Financial toxicity, expanded upon later, occurs when someone suffers from financial stress because of the healthcare costs incurred during and after medical treatment (Desai and Gyawali, 2020).

Sources of financial stress include job loss, excessive debt, difficulty making ends meet, and more. Using the cardiovascular system as an illustration, high financial stress can cause elevated levels of stress hormones (e.g., adrenaline or cortisol), heart rate, and blood pressure – these stress signals to the body can cause a person's arteries to tighten and narrow, causing the heart to work harder to push blood through the body. The greater blood pressure and heart rate, particularly with prolonged financial stress, can weaken cardiovascular health and reduce its functioning that leads to heart attacks, heart failure, coronary heart disease, and other maladies (Moran et al., 2019). Stress, particularly when it is chronic, takes a toll on all systems in the human body, reducing their functioning (American Psychological Association, 2018).

Along with individual well-being, the quality of interpersonal relationships, such as marital and parent–child relationships, is diminished by financial stress through strained interactions, disruptions and changes in social activities, support, and networks (Conger et al., 2010; Dew, 2007; Fonseca et al., 2016). How individuals and families adapt to financial stress and whether they use healthy and/or unhealthy coping strategies, for example, excessive eating, smoking, or drinking, has implications for both health and financial conditions (Bartholomae and Fox, 2017; Siahpush et al., 2003). Healthy behaviors, such as physical exercise, social support, and managing one's stress versus unhealthy behaviors, like being sedentary, smoking, and a poor diet, are coping mechanisms used to deal with stress. The gradient seen in wealth and health has been explained as a behavioral pathway by which greater exposure to stress among low socioeconomic households spurs unhealthy behaviors, which then causes greater disparities in health outcomes (Solar and Irwin, 2010). Empirical work has also examined the bi-directionality of these relationships. For example, the cost of smoking cigarettes may undermine one's socioeconomic position, illustrating the financial ramifications of unhealthy behaviors (e.g., Siahpush et al., 2003).

In the past several decades, a deeper shift occurred in research and practice when the nexus between health and financial well-being was cast in the Social Determinants of Health (SDH) framework developed by the World Health Organization (WHO) (Adler and Stead, 2015; Braveman et al., 2011; Solar and Irwin, 2010). Fundamental to the SDH framework are the social factors and conditions that help explain the connection between health and finances. WHO defines the SDH as

> the conditions in which people are born, grow, live, work, and age. These circumstances are shaped by the distribution of money, power, and resources at global, national, and local levels. The social determinants of health are mostly responsible for health inequities – the unfair and avoidable differences in health status seen within and between countries.
>
> (Hill-Briggs et al., 2021, p. 259)

As shown in Figure 20.1, the SDH framework synthesizes several causal mechanisms to explain health and well-being (Solar and Irwin, 2010). In sum, the SDH model conceptualizes socioeconomic status and health disparities as being associated with deprived material circumstances as well as greater susceptibility to environmental stressors, psychosocial circumstances, and behavioral factors. The health system (e.g., access to healthcare) is also an important intermediary. Socioeconomic status and intermediating factors are embedded within various structures and policies that shape a person's health outcomes.

Figure 20.2 shows economic stability as one of five domains used to organize the SDH and the circumstances that affect health outcomes (U.S. Department of Health and Human Services, 2021), and financial well-being falls within this domain. As part of the SDH framework, the goal of economic stability is outlined as helping "people earn steady incomes that allow them to meet their health needs" (U.S. Office of Disease Prevention and Health Promotion, 2021). Regrettably, stagnant income, higher out-of-pocket spending and healthcare costs, and fewer people with employer-sponsored health insurance (Kirzinger et al., 2019; Smith and Medalia, 2014) are among the reasons why many individuals and households cannot attain this goal. In sum, a rich and robust research has developed over time and highlights the complex, bi-directional nature of health and financial well-being.

# Research and Policy Issues

When the SDH framework was developed, the hope was for it to "guide empirical work to enhance our understanding of determinants and mechanisms and guide policy-making to illuminate entry points for interventions and policies" (Solar and Irwin, 2010, p. 3). The SDH framework has helped researchers and policymakers organize the complex and intricate relationship between these two domains, however, it is the very complexity of the SDH that prompts continued empirical and policy efforts. Scholarship reaches across several disciplines, including public health, health economics, medicine, and personal finance, thus research is approached from both micro and macro levels. Some studies use population-level data, whereas others use household-level data to study outcomes creating a dispersion of knowledge and implications. With diverse disciplines publishing findings in

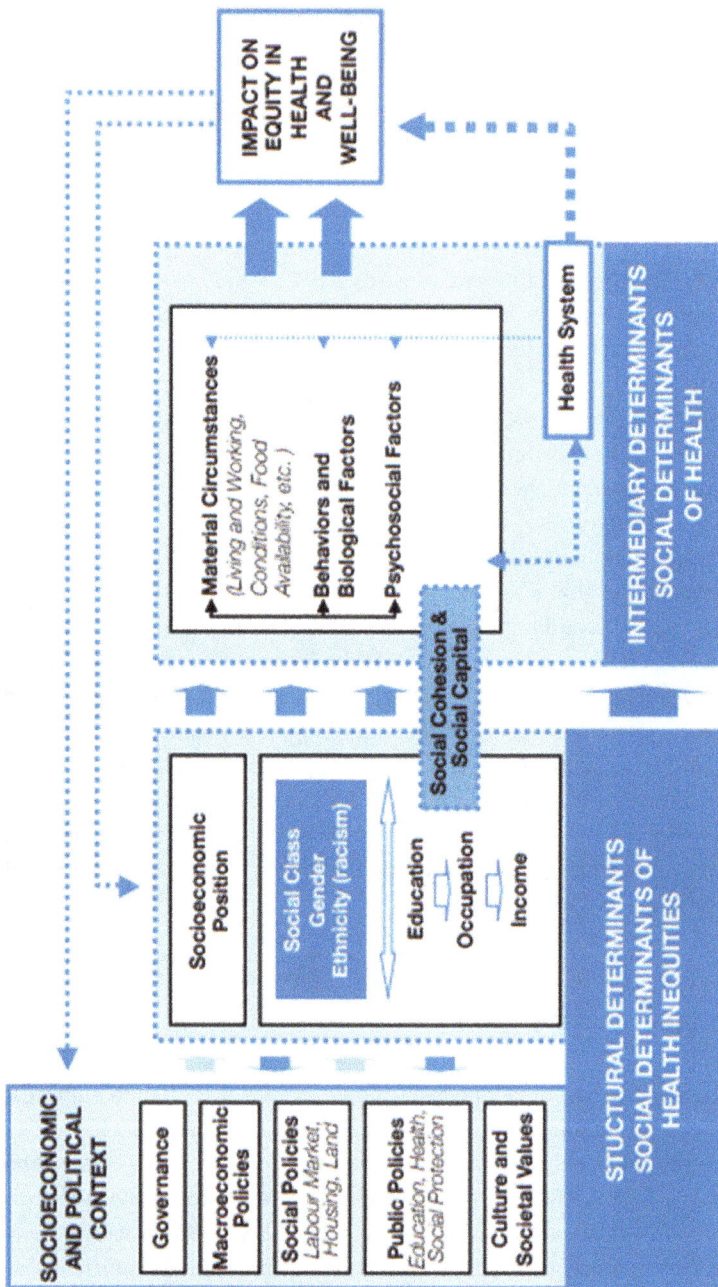

**Figure 20.1:** Social Determinants of Health Conceptual Framework.
*Source:* Solar and Irwin (2010).

# Social Determinants of Health

**Figure 20.2:** Five Domains of the Social Determinants of Health.
*Source*: U.S. Department of Health and Human Services (2021).

isolation, researchers and policymakers are challenged to synthesize the body of work from these two domains.

The presence of reverse causation is one issue that inhibits understanding the intersection of health and financial well-being, and whether a financial or health indicator is a cause or a consequence. According to Braveman et al. (2018) "While health can certainly affect the ability to generate both income and wealth, evidence from longitudinal studies confirms that health itself is strongly affected by both wealth and income" (p. 3). Indicators of socioeconomic status measures, such as education and income, are highly correlated, as are health indicators, such as being insured and healthy behavior. Health and financial indicators are also correlated with one another. As a result, it is difficult to identify mechanisms of association, establish causation, address multi-collinearity, and to inform policy (Fuchs, 2004).

Financial well-being gained traction after the global financial crisis and the passage of the Dodd-Frank Wall Street Reform and Consumer Protection Act in 2010, which created a new U.S. federal agency, the Consumer Financial Protection

Bureau (CFPB). The CFPB is the primary watchdog of the financial services industry in the United States and is tasked with consumer protection through regulation and enforcement, financial education and empowerment, and research. Consequently, their work has advanced research and policy-related issues related to consumer well-being and financial well-being in particular. For example, the CFPB produced an evidence-informed conceptualization of financial well-being and a ten-item survey to measure it, helping inform practice and research (CFPB, 2015).

The nexus of health and financial well-being bundles the objective (e.g., net worth or diabetes) and subjective (e.g., distress or worry) indicators of financial and health conditions, however, there is no measure that directly captures this intersection. Traditional financial indicators measure socioeconomic status, such as education, occupation, income, and net worth, with each behaving differently when linked to different health indicators (Deaton, 2002; Fuchs, 2004). The health literature will often report health measures at the population level, such as life expectancy and mortality (WHO, 2021). At the household level, a traditional measure of health is a self-report of general health status and/or the presence or absence of illness or chronic disease.

The CFPB defines financial well-being as "a state of being wherein a person can fully meet current and ongoing financial obligations, can feel secure in their financial future, and is able to make choices that allow enjoyment of life" (CFPB, 2015, p. 18). Several decades ago, the WHO defined health in their Constitution as "a state of complete physical, mental and social well-being and not merely the absence of disease or infirmity" (2020, p.1). Both the CFPB and WHO definitions distinguish or infer that on its own, the presence and/or absence of wealth or disease does not provide a complete definition, but rather the subjective or perceptual dimensions of how a person feels about his or her "state" of health and finances is essential. Agreement on definitions and the development of high-quality measurements is an important issue because policymakers draw on research to decide the best course of action, such as which programs to implement or which population to target.

The consumer skills, behaviors, and knowledge called upon to navigate and achieve optimal health and financial well-being are comparable. One approach to measurement would capture the behaviors and personality traits, such as self-control, that underlie both domains (Hoffmann and Risse, 2020). Health literacy and financial literacy are relevant measures, and both are linked to better health and financial outcomes, respectively. A related but underdeveloped measure that captures the nexus of health and wealth is consumer health insurance literacy, an area where consumers tend to have a deficit (Bartholomae et al., 2016). In late 2020, the U.S. Congress passed the No Surprises Act, which protects consumers from surprise medical bills (Adler et al., 2021). The CFPB has worked extensively to simplify financial decisions and to make financial information more transparent, such as their "Know Before You Owe" initiative that addresses mortgage loan options and provides tools for understanding home buying closing costs. Across the globe, many countries have established national strategies to address the financial capability of their citizens with policies that address consumer protection, like the CFPB initiative, and inclusion in financial markets. These strategies, typically paired with financial education, recognize and address the environmental challenges presented to consumers when making decisions related to financial products and services (Organisation for Economic Co-operation and Development, 2015).

Currently, consumer engagement with financial and health products and services is problematic. The availability of non-biased, simple, easy to understand information so consumers can make an optimal decision for their situation is rare (Bartholomae et al., 2016). The design and implementation of initiatives that address consumer skills should address consumer traits, particularly those that bolster beneficial health and financial behaviors (Hoffman and Risse, 2020). Legislative policy approaches of this nature have been shown to be successful. For example, consumer literacy was addressed with the U.S. Truth-in-Lending Act in 1968 and the U.S. CARD Act in 2009 that required credit card providers to improve their disclosure practices by providing standardized, simplified, and more transparent billing statements whose design was informed by consumer research (Jones et al., 2012). In sum, understanding the fluid relationship between these two domains, finding common definitions and measurements, and firmly establishing causal relationships between health and financial well-being are important areas of research and policy development.

## Practitioner Tools and Techniques

Health and financial resources are intertwined throughout life (e.g., Smith, 1999), and strong financial planning helps position households so they have the capacity to absorb a shock related to health, finances, or other areas. To increase effectiveness, financial service practitioners can regularly use consistent tools and techniques to assess their client's current health and financial status. This enables them to establish a baseline and evaluate progress toward or away from set goals. The CFPB's ten-item financial well-being measure is a promising tool since it captures objective and subjective aspects of financial well-being and is easy to implement and score relative to the wider population. The Center for Financial Services Innovation (CFSI) also provides a tool that can be used to measure financial health with eight items in four areas of behavior: (1) spending (spend less than their income and pay bills on time), (2) savings (sufficient liquid savings and long-term savings), (3) borrowing (manageable debt and has a prime credit score), and (4) planning (has appropriate insurance and plans ahead for expenses) (Garon et al., 2018). Despite health measures not being included, it would still be an effective practice to regularly administer these tools with financial services clients, especially when paired with health status questions.

Previous research using a health–wealth assessment found diet, sleep, and physical activity practices predicted financial behavior practices (O'Neill et al., 2018), and budgeting practices predicted health behavior practices (O'Neill et al., 2017). This is evidence that practitioners could glean client or patient information by collecting information from both domains and potentially demonstrating the value of services through health. Financial educators have created tools for practitioners, such as the Financial Check-Up (Burnett et al., 2021), which directs clients to assess their financial health as they would an annual physical examination. The Small Steps to Health and Wealth™ program integrates health with personal finance education (O'Neill and Ensle, 2014). Continuing to practice along the lines of medical services, using repeated measures of financial health, has the potential to further distinguish financial services professionals as members of the helping professions.

Healthcare costs are a strain on a household's budget, making it difficult to meet expenses and forcing individuals and families to make tough saving and spending decisions and creating distress and worry (Kirzinger et al., 2019; Pollitz et al., 2014). Practitioners would benefit from understanding that an element of the conceptualization of financial well-being is the ability to absorb shock, operationalized as having appropriate insurance coverage to address risk, emergency savings, and social capital (CFPB, 2015). A lack of savings and the inability to pay for emergency expenses are common problems related to people not being able to manage out-of-pocket costs (Bartholomae et al., 2020), practitioners can help individuals and families plan for expected and unexpected expenses. Many consumers are confused about deductibles and out-of-pocket costs, and over-estimate what their actual deductibles are, but tools are available to help solve this issue (Bartholomae et al., 2020; Politi et al., 2016). For example, "Show Me My Health Plans" is a decision aid shown to improve consumer health insurance literacy and decision self-efficacy (Politi et al., 2016). Practitioners can help clients understand the costs of medical treatments by introducing them to price comparison tools (e.g., Healthcare Bluebook) or help them save money by introducing them to cost-saving resources (e.g., GoodRx). Financial services practitioners who support clients by providing them with planning support and decision making tools could enable clients to make appropriate and quality decisions related to healthcare needs and insurance coverage.

## Applications

Households that experience problems with medical bills and debt tend to concurrently report an inability to meet necessities like food or rent. They also put off major household purchases, increase borrowing and credit card debt, cut spending on household items, and use all or most of their savings (Cohen and Kirzinger, 2014; Kirzinger et al., 2019). Medical debt has been associated with housing instability, such as missed mortgage or rent payments, disruptive moves, or eviction (Seifert, 2004). During interviews, adults who had health insurance and medical debt expressed emotional distress, shame, and embarrassment, and reported marital strain and dissolution (Pollitz et al., 2014). High healthcare costs and lost income due to missed work are the most common factors linked to bankruptcy (Himmelstein et al., 2019). Most bankruptcy cases, the most severe objective outcome of financial distress, are related to healthcare costs, medical bills, and/or debt (Himmelstein et al., 2019).

Nowhere is the interconnection between health and financial well-being more lucid than the scholarship examining medical financial hardship, also termed financial toxicity, financial burden, or out-of-pocket cost (Sharif et al., 2020; Zafar and Abernethy, 2013). Most often studied among cancer patients due to more expensive costs of treatment, financial toxicity examines the negative impact that diagnosis and treatment have on a patient's financial well-being (Lentz et al., 2019). This literature outlines three areas where financial toxicity has the consequence of "material loss, psychological distress, and/or maladaptive coping strategies" (Lentz et al., 2019, p. 85), concepts similar to the intermediary determinants in the SDH model.

Material loss includes direct costs such as "cost of drugs, surgery, radiation, procedures, imaging, and supportive needs (such as travel and hotels)," often paid out-of-pocket whereas indirect costs include depleted resources, loss of income due to time out of work, accumulation of debt, medical or otherwise, and bankruptcy (Lentz et al., 2019, p. 86). Financial toxicity has real psychological consequences through the reduction of quality of life and increased distress (Desai and Gyawali, 2020; Lentz et al. 2019; Zafar and Abernethy, 2013). Zafar and Abernethy (2013) quoted a patient with metastatic breast cancer: "We don't travel; we don't do anything now because it's a $100,000 illness. And it sucks. . . . What are you going to do? Caught between a rock and a hard spot" (p. 80).

Whether cancer or some other health crisis or condition, the burden of medical bills and debt among households has been on the rise. Before the Covid-19 pandemic, regardless of financial standing or health status, almost half of Americans worried about unaffordable, unexpected medical bills or high health insurance deductibles. Half had foregone needed medical or dental care in the previous year due to cost, with an even higher proportion (76 percent) of uninsured U.S. adults reporting they or family members had postponed medical care in the previous year (Kirzinger et al., 2019). A recent U.S. survey found almost 20 percent of adults indicated they would be unable to pay for quality healthcare if needed, with greater disparities among households of color and low-income (Witters, 2021). A recent National Health Interview Survey (Cha and Cohen, 2020) found 14 percent of American families experienced some problem paying for their medical bills in the previous year. Families at greater risk of experiencing problems associated with medical bills and medical debt include the uninsured, those with low or moderate income, and households with children (Cha and Cohen, 2020; Cohen and Kirzinger, 2014; Pollitz et al., 2014).

# Future Directions

There is growing interest in developing collaborative and integrative initiatives or partnerships that address financial conditions that affect health in the context of the healthcare system, such as financial well-being issues (Bell et al., 2020; Bibbins-Domingo, 2019; Dorsey et al., 2020). Karlawish (2016) termed the phrase "whealth-care" to denote the merge between medical and financial sectors, primarily to protect older adults from financial abuse. Dorsey et al. (2020) constructed a healthcare and financial well-being framework grounded in transformative service research that is a body of research that takes into account consumer well-being that results from inter-acting with the confluence of services from social work, education, healthcare, and financial services (Anderson et al., 2013). Health professionals recognize that finan-cial well-being influences their patients' health outcomes and healthcare access (Bartholomae et al., 2020). Patients have identified healthcare professionals as a more trusted source of financial information than financial advisors (Piette et al., 2005). The banking and financial sector sees the value of integrating their services with healthcare services (Hyland and Revere, 2018). Future research and practice should explore the feasibility of partnerships that address health and financial serv-ices together and what models work best.

Several studies suggest that consumers want to better understand health insur-ance terminology, plan costs, and the details of their health insurance benefits (CFPB, 2011; Kim et al. 2013). Many consumers report negative experiences that frame their expectations around a health insurance purchase, citing difficulty finding a plan they could afford that covered all their healthcare needs and understanding the details and fine print of a plan (Perry and Undem, 2013). Future work related to re-search, policy, and practice should address the complexity of healthcare decisions and health insurance purchases to reduce consumer challenges.

Research on the structural, institutional, and political factors that influence the health and financial system, and how those boost or constrain a consumer's health and financial well-being, can help inform policy interventions (Fu, 2020; Irwin and Solar, 2010). For example, studies could evaluate aspects of the decision-making process and focus on describing whether providing simple easy to understand infor-mation about products and services or designing the consumer experience using behaviorally informed practices (e.g., auto-enrollment or pre-populated forms) are efficacious and promote health and financial well-being. There are a number of ways health affects financial well-being, thus it is important for researchers, policy advocates, educators, and policymakers to be aware of these impacts.

# Conclusion

The inter-link between health and financial well-being has been examined by social scientists, including consumer scientists, economists, sociologists, and psychologists, as well as public policy, health, and personal finance researchers. This diverse set of disciplines has produced empirical work on financial and health indicators and established a strong intersection between these two domains. Several causal pathways have been offered and debated to explain the associations between health and financial well-being (Petrovic et al., 2018; Solar and Irwin, 2010).

Financial well-being can serve as a first line of defense to protect an individual's or household's health. This chapter provided a brief review of health disparities and their association with financial well-being. An important component of this body of work concerns the inequities of vulnerable and disadvantaged households who lack access to financial and health services and experience greater disparities in health and financial outcomes. The opportunity to achieve good health is a right that should be afforded to all individuals and households in a society. Future work that addresses these gaps, identifies the needs and priorities, and targets barriers that can be removed to help close these gaps should be imperative. To date, the most effective policies appear to be those that address household income, such as tax credits and other policy-derived incentives.

A robust body of research, both longitudinal and life span studies, has documented the association between financial measures and health indicators (Braveman et al., 2018; Fuchs, 2004). Financial well-being is an established correlate in the scholarship of general well-being and happiness (Diener and Seligman, 2018) as well as with health outcomes (Moran et al., 2019; Petrovic et al. 2018). So many complexities and intricacies occur at the intersection of an individual's and household's health and financial well-being. The bi-directional, correlational nature of these two domains makes the case for advancing the policy, practice, and research at this point of intersection.

# References

Adler, L., Fiedler, M., Ginsburg, P. B., Hall, M., Ippolito, B., and Trish, E. (2021). *Understanding the no surprises act*. Brookings. https://www.brookings.edu/blog/usc-brookings-schaeffer-on-health-policy/2021/02/04/understanding-the-no-surprises-act/

Adler, N. E., and Stead, W. W. (2015). Patients in context – EHR capture of social and behavioral determinants of health. *Obstetrical & Gynecological Survey*, *70*(6), 388–390. https://doi.org/10.1056/NEJMp1413945

American Institutes for Research. (2010). *Consumer education initiatives in financial and health literacy task 4: Deliverable 4, final report*. https://aspe.hhs.gov/system/files/pdf/76156/index.pdf

American Psychological Association. (2018). *Stress effects on the body.* https://www.apa.org/topics/stress/body

Anderson, L., Ostrom, A. L., Corus, C., Fisk, R. P., Gallan, A. S., Giraldo, M., . . . and Williams, J. D. (2013). Transformative service research: An agenda for the future. *Journal of Business Research, 66* (8),1,203–1,210. https://doi.org/10.1016/j.jbusres.2012.08.013

Bartholomae, S., Collins, J. M., Janney, C., Johnson, Kiss, D. E. (2020). Integrating and sustaining financial capability services in rural healthcare delivery: Consumers, healthcare providers, and systems perspectives. *Consumer Interests Annual, 66.* https://www.consumerinterests.org/assets/docs/CIA/CIA2020/BartholomaeSuzanneCIA2020.pdf

Bartholomae, S., and Fox, J. J. (2017). Coping with economic stress: A test of deterioration and stress-suppressing models. *Journal of Financial Therapy, 8*(1), 6. https://doi.org/10.4148/1944-9771.1134

Bartholomae, S., Russel, M. B., Braun, B., and McCoy, T. (2016). Building health insurance literacy: Evidence from the smart choice health insuranceTM program. *Journal of Family and Economic Issues, 37*(2), 140–155. https://doi.org/10.1007/s10834-016-9482-7

Bell, O. N., Hole, M. K., Johnson, K., Marcil, L. E., Solomon, B. S., and Schickedanz, A. (2020). Medical-financial partnerships: Cross-sector collaborations between medical and financial services to improve health. *Academic Pediatrics, 20*(2), 166–174. https://www.ncbi.nlm.nih.gov/pmc/articles/PMC7331932/

Berkman, N. D., Sheridan, S. L., Donahue, K. E., Halpern, D. J., Viera, A., Crotty, K., Holland, A., Brasure, M., Lohr, K. N., Harden, E., Tant, E., Wallace, I., and Viswanathan, M. (2011). Health literacy interventions and outcomes: An updated systematic review. *Evidence Report/Technology Assessment, 199*, 1–941.

Bibbins-Domingo, K. (2019). Integrating social care into the delivery of health care. *JAMA Network, 322*(18),1,763–1,764. https://doi.org/10.1001/jama.2019.15603

Braveman, P., Acker, J., Arkin, E., Proctor, D., Gillman, A., McGeary, K. A., and Mallya, G., (2018). *Wealth matters for health equity.* Robert Wood Johnson Foundation. https://www.rwjf.org/en/library/research/2018/09/wealth-matters-for-health-equity.html

Braveman, P., Egerter, S., and Williams, D. R. (2011). The social determinants of health: Coming of age. *Annual Review of Public Health, 32*, 381–398. https://doi.org/10.1146/annurev-publhealth-031210-101218.

Brüggen, E. C., Hogreve, J., Holmlund, M., Kabadayi, S., and Löfgren, M. (2017). Financial well-being: A conceptualization and research agenda. *Journal of Business Research, 79*, 228–237. https://doi.org/10.1016/j.jbusres.2017.03.013

Burnett, D., Latta, S., and Kiss, D. E. (2021). How are you doing? A financial checkup. *Kansas State University.* https://bookstore.ksre.ksu.edu/pubs/mf2721.pdf

Cha, A. E., and Cohen, R. A. (2020). *Problems paying medical bills, 2018.* Center for Disease Control and Prevention. https://www.cdc.gov/nchs/products/databriefs/db357.htm

Cohen, R. A., and Kirzinger, W. K. (2014). *Financial burden of medical care: A family perspective* (No. 2014). National Center for Health Statistics. https://pubmed.ncbi.nlm.nih.gov/24472320/

Conger, R. D., Conger, K. J., and Martin, M. J. (2010). Socioeconomic status, family processes, and individual development. *Journal of Marriage and Family, 72*(3), 685–704. https://doi.org/10.1111/j.1741-3737.2010.00725.x

Consumer Financial Protection Bureau (CFPB). (2011). *Building the CFPB: A progress report.* https://files.consumerfinance.gov/f/2011/07/Report_BuildingTheCfpb1.pdf

Consumer Financial Protection Bureau (CFPB). (2015). *Financial well-being: The goal of financial education.* https://files.consumerfinance.gov/f/201501_cfpb_report_financial-well-being.pdf

Corwin, T. R., Ozieh, M. N., Garacci, E., Palatnik, A., and Egede, L. E. (2021). The relationship between financial hardship and incident diabetic kidney disease in older US adults – a longitudinal study. *BMC Nephrology, 22*(1), 1–9. https://doi.org/10.1186/s12882-021-02373-3

Davey, J., Holden, C. A., and Smith, B. J. (2015). The correlates of chronic disease-related health literacy and its components among men: A systematic review. *BMC Public Health, 15*(1), 589. https://doi.org/10.1186/s12889-015-1900-5

Deaton, A. (2002). Policy implications of the gradient of health and wealth. *Health Affairs, 21*(2), 13–30. https://doi.org/10.1377/hlthaff.21.2.13

Deng, Z., and Liu, S. (2017). Understanding consumer health information-seeking behavior from the perspective of the risk perception attitude framework and social support in mobile social media websites. *International Journal of Medical Informatics, 105,* 98–109. https://doi.org/10.1016/j.ijmedinf.2017.05.014

Desai, A., and Gyawali, B. (2020). Financial toxicity of cancer treatment: Moving the discussion from acknowledgement of the problem to identifying solutions. *E Clinical Medicine, 20,* 100,269. https://doi.org/10.1016/j.eclinm.2020.100269

Dew, J. (2007). Two sides of the same coin? The differing roles of assets and consumer debt in marriage. *Journal of Family and Economic Issues, 28,* 89–104. https://doi.org/10.1007/s10834-006-9051-6

Diener, E., and Seligman, M. E. (2018). Beyond money: Progress on an economy of well-being. *Perspectives on Psychological Science, 13*(2), 171–175. https://doi.org/10.1177/1745691616689467

Dorsey, J. D., Hill, P., Moran, N., Nations Azzari, C., Reshadi, F., Shanks, I., and Williams, J. D. (2020). Leveraging the existing US healthcare structure for consumer financial well-being: Barriers, opportunities, and a framework toward future research. *Journal of Consumer Affairs, 54*(1), 70–99. https://doi.org/10.1111/joca.12274

Drentea, P., and Reynolds, J. R. (2012). Neither a borrower nor a lender be: The relative importance of debt and SES for mental health among older adults. *Journal of Aging and Health, 24*(4), 673–695. https://doi.org/10.1177/0898264311431304

Finke, M. S., Howe, J. S., and Huston, S. J. (2016). Old age and the decline in financial literacy. *Management Science, 63*(1), 213–230. https://doi.org/10.2139/ssrn.1948627

Finke, M. S., and Huston, S. J. (2013). Time preference and the importance of saving for retirement. *Journal of Economic Behavior and Organization, 89,* 23–34. https://doi.org/10.2139/ssrn.886554

Fonseca, G., Cunha, D., Crespo, C., and Relvas, A. P. (2016). Families in the context of macroeconomic crises: A systematic review. *Journal of Family Psychology, 30*(6), 687. https://doi.org/10.1037/fam0000230

French, D., and Vigne, S. (2019). The causes and consequences of household financial strain: A systematic review. *International Review of Financial Analysis, 62,* 150–156. https://doi.org/10.1016/j.irfa.2018.09.008

Fu, J. (2020). Ability or opportunity to act: What shapes financial well-being? *World Development, 128.* https://doi.org/10.1016/j.worlddev.2019.104843

Fuchs, V. R. (2004). Reflections on the socio-economic correlates of health. *Journal of Health Economics, 23*(4), 653–661. https://doi.org/10.1016/j.jhealeco.2004.04.004

Garon, T., Dunn, A., Golvala, K., and Wilson, E. (2018). *U.S. financial health pulse: 2018 baseline survey results.* Center for Financial Services Innovation. https://s3.amazonaws.com/cfsi-innovation-files-2018/wp-content/uploads/2018/11/20213012/Pulse-2018-Baseline-Survey-Results-11-16.18.pdf

Gillen, M., Yang, H., and Kim, H. (2020). Health literacy and difference in current wealth among middle-aged and older adults. *Journal of Family and Economic Issues*, *41*(2), 281–299. https://doi.org/10.1007/s10834-019-09648-w

Habibov, N., Auchynnikava, A., and Luo, R. (2019). Poverty does make us sick. *Annals of Global Health*, *85*(1). https://www.ncbi.nlm.nih.gov/pmc/articles/PMC6634464/

Hill-Briggs, F., Adler, N. E., Berkowitz, S. A., Chin, M. H., Gary-Webb, T. L., Navas-Acien, A., Thorton, P. L., and Haire-Joshu, D. (2021). Social determinants of health and diabetes: A scientific review. *Diabetes Care*, *44*(1), 258–279. https://doi.org/10.2337/dci20-0053

Himmelstein, D. U., Lawless, R. M., Thorne, D., Foohey, P., and Woolhandler, S. (2019). Medical bankruptcy: Still common despite the affordable care act. *American Journal of Public Health*, *109*(3), 431–433. https://doi.org/10.2105/AJPH.2018.304901

Hoffmann, A. O., and Risse, L. (2020). Do good things come in pairs? How personality traits help explain individuals' simultaneous pursuit of a healthy lifestyle and financially responsible behavior. *Journal of Consumer Affairs*, *54*(3), 1,082–1,120. https://doi.org/10.1111/joca.12317

Hyland, C. G., and Revere, C. J. (2018). *Health and financial wellbeing: Two good things that go better together: The case for credit union and health care collaboration*. National Credit Union Foundation. https://www.ncuf.coop/files/HealthAndFinWellBeing-1.pdf

Kindig, D. A., Panzer, A. M., and Nielsen-Bohlman. (2004). *Health literacy: A prescription to end confusion*. National Center for Biotechnology Information.

James, B. D., Boyle, P. A., Bennett, J. S., and Bennett, D. A. (2012). The impact of health and financial literacy on decision making in community-based older adults. *Gerontology*, *58*(6), 531–539. https://doi.org/10.1159/000339094

Jones, L. E., Loibl, C., and Tennyson, S. L. (2012). The effects of CARD act disclosures on consumers' use of credit cards. http://dx.doi.org/10.2139/ssrn.2034419

Karlawish, J. (2016). *Whealthcare: Or how we can assure older adults' cognitive and financial well being*. Whealthcare. http://www.whealthcare.org/

Kim, J., Braun, B., and Williams, A. D. (2013). Understanding health insurance literacy: A literature review. *Family and Consumer Sciences Research Journal*, *42*(1), 3–13.

Kim, T. J., and von dem Knesebeck, O. (2018). Income and obesity: What is the direction of the relationship? A systematic review and meta-analysis. *BMJ Open*, *8* (1),e019862. http://dx.doi.org/10.1136/bmjopen-2017-019862

Kirzinger, A., Munana, C., Wu, B., and Brodie, M. (2019). *Data note: Americans' challenges with health care costs*. Kaiser Family Foundation. https://www.kff.org/health-costs/issue-brief/data-note-americans-challenges-health-care-costs/

Knorst, J. K., Sfreddo, C. S., de F. Meira, G., Zanatta, F. B., Vettore, M. V., and Ardenghi, T. M. (2021). Socioeconomic status and oral health-related quality of life: A systematic review and meta-analysis. *Community Dentistry and Oral Epidemiology*, *49*(2), 95–102. https://doi.org/10.1111/cdoe.12616

Lentz, R., Benson III, A. B., and Kircher, S. (2019). Financial toxicity in cancer care: Prevalence, causes, consequences, and reduction strategies. *Journal of Surgical Oncology*, *120*(1), 85–92. https://doi.org/10.1002/jso.25374

Letkiewicz, J. C., and Fox, J. J. (2014). Conscientiousness, financial literacy, and asset accumulation of young adults. *Journal of Consumer Affairs*, *48*(2), 274–300. https://doi.org/10.1111/joca.12040

Lusardi, A., and Mitchell, O. S. (2011). Financial literacy around the world: An overview. *Journal of Pension Economics and Finance*, *10*(4), 497–508. https://www.nber.org/system/files/working_papers/w17107/w17107.pdf

Lusardi, A., and Mitchell, O. S. (2014). The economic importance of financial literacy: Theory and evidence. *Journal of Economic Literature*, *52*(1), 5–44. https://doi.org/10.1257/jel.52.1.5

Lusardi, A., Mitchell, O. S., and Curto, V. (2010). Financial literacy among the young. *Journal of Consumer Affairs*, *44*(2), 358–380. https://doi.org/10.1111/j.1745-6606.2010.01173.x

McCormack, L., Bann, C., Uhrig, J., Berkman, N., and Rudd, R. (2009). Health insurance literacy of older adults. *Journal of Consumer Affairs*, *43*(2), 223–248. https://doi.org/10.1111/j.1745-6606.2009.01138.x

Monticone, C. (2010). *Financial literacy and financial advice: Theory and empirical evidence* [Doctoral dissertation]. Universit`a degli Studi di Torino, Universit`a del Piemonte Orientale.

Moran, K. E., Ommerborn, M. J., Blackshear, C. T., Sims, M., and Clark, C. R. (2019). Financial stress and risk of coronary heart disease in the Jackson heart study. *American Journal of Preventive Medicine*, *56*(2), 224–231. https://doi.org/10.1016/j.amepre.2018.09.022

Murray, C., Johnson, W., Wolf, M. S., and Deary, I. J. (2011). The association between cognitive ability across the lifespan and health literacy in old age: The Lothian birth cohort 1936. *Intelligence*, *39*, 178–187. https://doi.org/16/j.intell.2011.04.001

O'Connor, D. B., Thayer, J. F., and Vedhara, K. (2021). Stress and health: A review of psychobiological processes. *Annual Review of Psychology*, *72*, 663–688. https://doi.org/10.1146/annurev-psych-062520-122331

O'Neill, B., and Ensle, K. (2014). Small steps to health and wealth™: Program update and research insights. *The Forum for Family and Consumer Issues*, *19*(1), 1–16. https://www.theforumjournal.org/wp-content/uploads/2018/05/Small-Steps-Program-Update.pdf

O'Neill, B., Xiao, J. J., and Ensle, K. (2016). Propensity to plan: A key to health and wealth? *Journal of Financial Planning*, *29*(3), 46–54.

O'Neill, B., Xiao, J. J., and Ensle, K. (2017). Positive health and financial practices: Does budgeting make a difference? *Journal of Family & Consumer Sciences*, *109*(2), 27–36. https://doi.org/10.14307/JFCS109.2.27

O'Neill, B., Xiao, J. J., and Ensle, K. (2018). Reading nutrition labels: A predictor of health and wealth? *Journal of Human Sciences and Extension*, *6*(3), 1–24.

Organisation for Economic Co-operation and Development. (2015). *National strategies for financial education: OECD/INFE policy handbook*. https://www.oecd.org/daf/fin/financial-education/National-Strategies-Financial-Education-Policy-Handbook.pdf

Netemeyer, R. G., Dobolyi, D. G., Abbasi, A., Clifford, G., and Taylor, H. (2020). Health literacy, health numeracy, and trust in doctor: Effects on key patient health outcomes. *Journal of Consumer Affairs*, *54*(1), 3–42. https://doi.org/10.1111/joca.12267.

Perry, M., and Undem, T. (2013). *Informing enroll America's campaign: Findings from a National Study*. Rep. Enroll America. https://enrollamerica.org/wp-content/uploads/2013/11/Informing-Enroll-America-Campaign.pdf.

Petrovic, D., de Mestral, C., Bochud, M., Bartley, M., Kivimäki, M., Vineis, P., Mackenbach, J., and Stringhini, S. (2018). The contribution of health behaviors to socioeconomic inequalities in health: A systematic review. *Preventive medicine*, *113*, 15–31. https://doi.org/10.1016/j.ypmed.2018.05.003

Piette J. D., Heisler, M., Krein, S., and Kerr, E. A. (2005). The role of patient-physician trust in moderating medication nonadherence due to cost pressures. *Arch. Intern. Med, 165* (15), 1,749–1,755. https://doi.org/10.1001/archinte.165.15.1749

Politi, M. C., Kuzemchak, M. D., Liu, J., Barker, A. R., Peters, E., Ubel, P. A., Kaphingst, K.A., McBride, T., Kreuter, M. W., Shacham, W., and Philpott, S. E. (2016). Show me my health plans: Using a decision aid to improve decisions in the federal health insurance marketplace. *MDM Policy & Practice*, (1). https://doi.org/10.1177/2381468316679998.

Pollitz, K., Cox, C., Lucia, K., and Keith, K. (2014). *Medical debt among people with health insurance*. The Henry J. Kaiser Family Foundation. https://www.kff.org/wp-content/uploads/2014/01/8537-medical-debt-among-people-with-health-insurance.pdf

Puri, M., and Robinson, D. T. (2007) Optimism and economic choice. *Journal of Financial Economics, 86*(1), 71–99. https://doi.org/10.3386/w11361

Purnell, J. Q., and Hajat, A. (2017). *The health and wealth connection: Opportunities for investment across the lifespan.* Asset Funders Network. https://assetfunders.org/wp-content/uploads/HealthandWealth_Brief_2017.pdf

Ratzan, S. C., Parker, R. M., and Zorn, M. (2000). *National library of medicine current bibliographies in medicine: Health literacy.* U.S. Department of Health and Human Services, National Institutes of Health.

Segerstrom, S. C., and Miller, G. E. (2004). Psychological stress and the human immune system: A meta-analytic study of 30 years of inquiry. *Psychological Bulletin, 130*(4), 601. https://doi.org/10.1037/0033-2909.130.4.601

Seifert, T. (2004). Understanding student motivation. *Educational Research, 46*(2), 137–149.

Sekita, S. (2011). Financial literacy and retirement planning in Japan. *Journal of Pension Economics & Finance, 10*(4), 637–656. https://doi.org/10.2139/ssrn.1809681

Sharif, S. P., Naghavi, N., Nia, H. S., and Waheed, H. (2020). Financial literacy and quality of life of consumers faced with cancer: A moderated mediation approach. *International Journal of Bank Marketing, 38* (5),1,009–1,031. https://doi.org/10.1108/IJBM-10-2019-0355

Siahpush, M., Borland, R., and Scollo, M. (2003). Smoking and financial stress. *Tobacco Control, 12*(1), 60–66. http://dx.doi.org/10.1136/tc.12.1.60

Smith, J. C., and Medalia, C. (2014). *Health insurance coverage in the United States: 2013.* United States Census Bureau. https://www.census.gov/library/publications/2014/demo/p60-250.html

Smith, J. P. (1999). Healthy bodies and thick wallets: The dual relation between health and economic status. *Journal of Economic Perspectives, 13*(2), 145–166. https://doi.org/10.1257/jep.13.2.145

Solar, O., and Irwin, A. (2010). *A conceptual framework for action on the social determinants of health.* World Health Organization. https://apps.who.int/iris/bitstream/handle/10665/44489/9789241500852_eng.pdf

Thaler, R., and Sunstein, C. R. (2008). *Nudge: Improving decisions about health, wealth, and happiness.* Yale University Press.

U.S. Department of Health and Human Services. (2021). *Healthy people 2030: Social determinants of health.* Accessed July 2021. https://health.gov/healthypeople/objectives-and-data/social-determinants-health

U.S. Financial Literacy and Education Commission. (2020). *U.S. national strategy for financial literacy 2020.* Accessed July 2021. https://home.treasury.gov/system/files/136/US-National-Strategy-Financial-Literacy-2020.pdf

U.S. Office of Disease Prevention and Health Promotion. (2021). *Economic stability.* Accessed July 2021. https://health.gov/healthypeople/objectives-and-data/browse-objectives/economic-stability

Witters, D. (2021). *In U.S., an estimated 46 million cannot afford needed care.* Gallup. https://news.gallup.com/poll/342095/estimated-million-cannot-afford-needed-care.aspx

World Health Organization. (2020). *Basic documents* (49th ed.). https://apps.who.int/gb/bd/pdf_files/BD_49th-en.pdf#page=1

World Health Organization. (2021). *World health statistics 2021: Monitoring health for the SDGs, sustainable development goals.* https://cdn.who.int/media/docs/default-source/gho-documents/world-health-statistic-reports/2021/whs-2021_20may.pdf?sfvrsn=55c7c6f2_8

Zafar, S. Y., and Abernethy, A. P. (2013). Financial toxicity, part I: A new name for a growing problem. *Oncology (Williston Park, NY), 27*(2), 80.

Vicki L. Bogan

# 21 Household Debt Behavior

**Abstract:** Trends in U.S. household debt levels, over the past 30 years, have generated increasing interest in household debt. Given the prevalence of household debt,
understanding household debt behavior is critical to understanding household finance. Further, the absolute levels of household debt make it a significant and important aspect of the U.S. economy. This chapter provides an overview of key
aspects of the theoretical and empirical literature on household debt and reviews
critical statistics on household debt composition, levels, and growth. This chapter
also discusses various household debt-related puzzles and opportunities for future
research. A central theme is the need to focus more on the liability side of the
household balance sheet in terms of both research and financial planning.

**Keywords:** household finance, debt, consumer debt, credit card

## Introduction

Rising U.S. household debt levels over the past 30 years (see Figure 21.1) have led to
increasing interest in household debt by academics, financial planning practitioners,
and policymakers alike (Barnes and Young, 2003; Zinman, 2015). The most recent statistics, from the 2019 Survey of Consumer Finances (SCF), provide an important picture of the prevalence, types, and levels of household debt (Bhutta et al., 2020).
Credit card debt continued to be the most prevalent type of debt in 2019, with more
than 45 percent of households reporting credit card balances after their last payment.
Of those households with credit car`d debt, the median household owed $2,700. The
2019 SCF data also indicate that more than 42 percent of households held debt se-
cured by a primary residence with the conditional median value of home-secured
debt being $134,800. In 2019, more than 21 percent of households had education
debt, and these student loans continued to be the greatest source, in dollar terms, of
non-mortgage debt owed by households in the 2019 SCF. Conditional median and
mean balances of education debt were $22,300 and $40,300, respectively, in 2019.
Almost 37 percent of households held vehicle loans and more than 10 percent of
households held other installment loans, which includes medical debt and purchases

**Note:** I would like to thank Cara Costich, Christian Karrer, George Lont, Dimitriy Nikolskiy, Jack Rong,
Chirag Shah, Margaret Szczerbicki, and Kristy Yang for research assistance. All errors are my own.

**Vicki L. Bogan,** Cornell University

https://doi.org/10.1515/9783110727692-021

of durable goods, like furniture and appliances. (See Figure 21.2 for an overview of statistics on household debt prevalence by debt type.)

Given the pervasiveness of household debt, understanding household debt behavior is critical to understanding household finance. Household debt affects the price of consumption when there is a wedge between borrowing costs and savings rates, making the understanding of debt behavior important for any life-cycle consumption-based economic model. Moreover, the absolute levels of household debt make it a fundamental aspect of the U.S. economy. However, much of the household finance literature focuses on saving and investing behavior (Zinman, 2015). This emphasis on the asset side of the household balance sheet to the exclusion of the liability side limits any potential to understand fully and completely household financial behaviors.

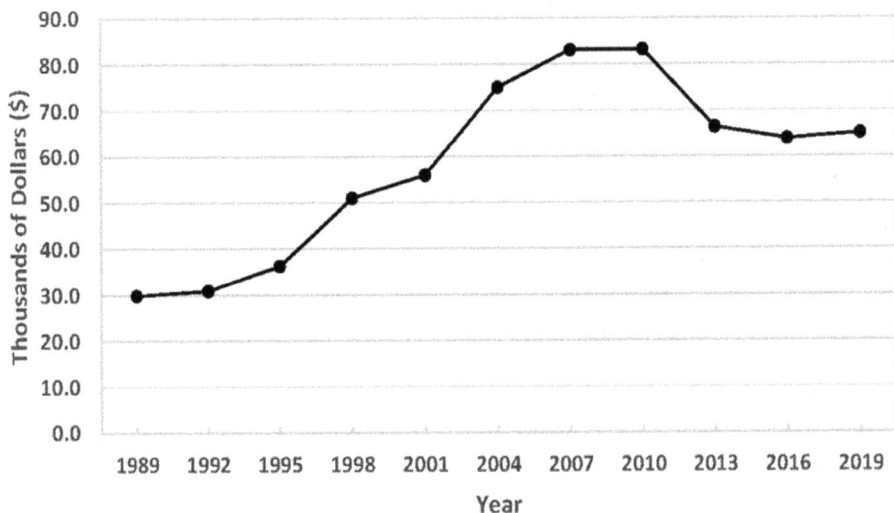

**Figure 21.1:** U.S. Median Household Debt Levels 1989–2019.
*Source*: Survey of Consumer Finances.

In this chapter, I will focus primarily on credit card debt; given it is the most common type of household debt. However, I also will discuss in detail the largest source of household debt in dollar terms, mortgage debt. Additionally, I will discuss various themes with regard to education debt. The last two sections of the chapter will include a discussion of future research directions followed by concluding remarks.

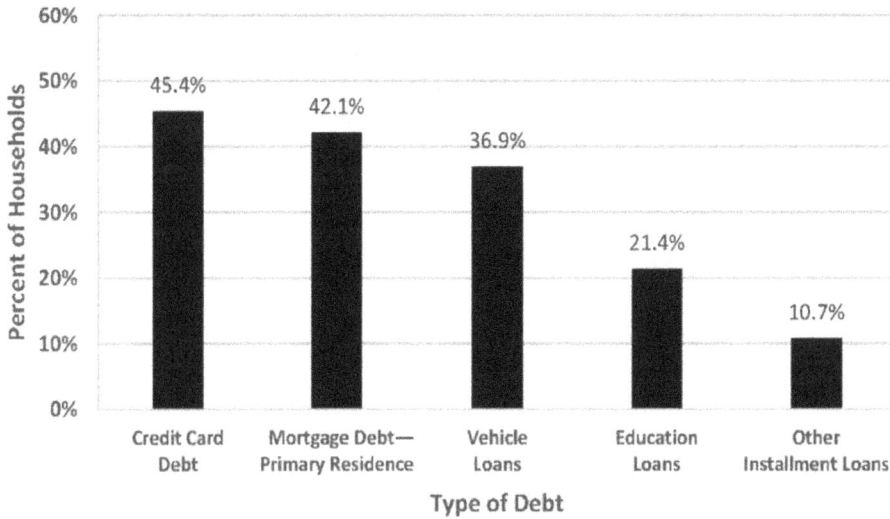

**Figure 21.2:** U.S. Household Debt Holding by Debt Type 2019.
*Source*: Survey of Consumer Finances.

# Credit Card Debt

## Trends and Topics

Credit cards have been around in a primitive form since the early 1900s, but the modern credit card structure was established in 1958 by American Express. Since then, the industry has evolved to become the primary method of purchase on nearly every continent. Usage convenience and availability have allowed an increasing number of consumers to access more revolving credit. Specifically in the United States, credit card usage is now a crucial function of the U.S. economy. Credit cards provide convenience in making purchases in stores and over the Internet and allow one to make purchases with almost a one-month grace period. The grace period, usually about 25 days, is the period of time during which one can pay back a credit card bill without paying a finance charge.[1] In reality, however, many cardholders are unable to take advantage of the grace period because they carry balances from month to month, paying finance charges that can be well over 20 percent.

    Empirical research has supported the notion of credit supply as a significant factor in regards to the level of debt taken on by consumers. From the end of 1992 to mid-1996, the United States experienced rapid growth in consumer credit with an

---

1 It is worth noting that with almost all credit cards, the grace period applies only if one is not carrying a current balance. In addition, the grace period does not apply to cash advances.

average annual growth rate over the three and a half year period of 12 percent (Yoo, 1997). Using three separate SCF waves (1983, 1989, and 1992), Yoo (1997) tried to explain the substantial increase in credit by separating changes in household debt from changes in the number of households with access to credit. Yoo (1997) concluded that the growth in credit card debt was primarily due to an increase in the credit card debt per household and not to an increase in the amount of households with access to credit cards. Furthermore, the research suggests, "households in the top half of the income distribution accounted for most of the changes in the growth of credit card debt" (p. 7).

Gross and Souleles (2002a) also examined how consumers change their decision making given changes in liquidity constraints. Two opposing theories were tested in their study: The Permanent Income Hypothesis (PIH) and the buffer-stock model of precautionary savings.[2] Gross and Souleles (2002a) determined that an increase in credit limits led to an increase in debt. This finding is inconsistent with the PIH, which theorizes that the marginal propensity to consume out of permanent income or "liquidity" is zero. The PIH predicts that an increase in the credit supply, or liquidity, should have no effect on additional debt consumption. However, this empirical research indicates that there is a significant relationship between credit limits and debt consistent with buffer-stock models of precautionary savings.

Ekici and Dunn (2010) suggested that, contrary to previous debt-consumption studies (McCarthy, 1997), the relationship between credit card debt and growth in consumption is negative. Furthermore, when they controlled for individual factors, such as individual age and income expectations, they still found a negative debt–consumption relationship. Chang (2006) also investigated the relationship between "greater access to credit and savings, investment, and consumption," and found that a discrepancy exists between revolving credit card debt and the level of savings among different economic classes. Chang (2006) showed that revolving credit card debt increases savings for high- and low-income classes, but decreases savings for lower-middle-income borrowers.

As shown in Figure 21.3, credit card default rates have been highly variable over the past three decades. Dunn and Kim (1999) suggested three key factors underlying credit default: (a) the ratio of household income to the total minimum required payment from all credit cards, (b) the percentage of the total credit line that has been used by the consumer, and (c) the number of credit cards on which the consumer has

---

**2** The Permanent Income Hypothesis, established by Milton Friedman, explained consumers' consumption patterns based upon their long-term income expectations. Friedman (1957) showed that the savings ratio is independent of the level of income. Carroll (1997) developed a theory in which consumers rationalize their consumption behavior according to a buffer-stock model of precautionary savings. This theory states that consumers set a target level of wealth and permanent income ratio such that if wealth is above the target, they tend to consume instead of saving; on the other hand, if wealth drops below the target, they are motivated to increase saving in order to accumulate wealth.

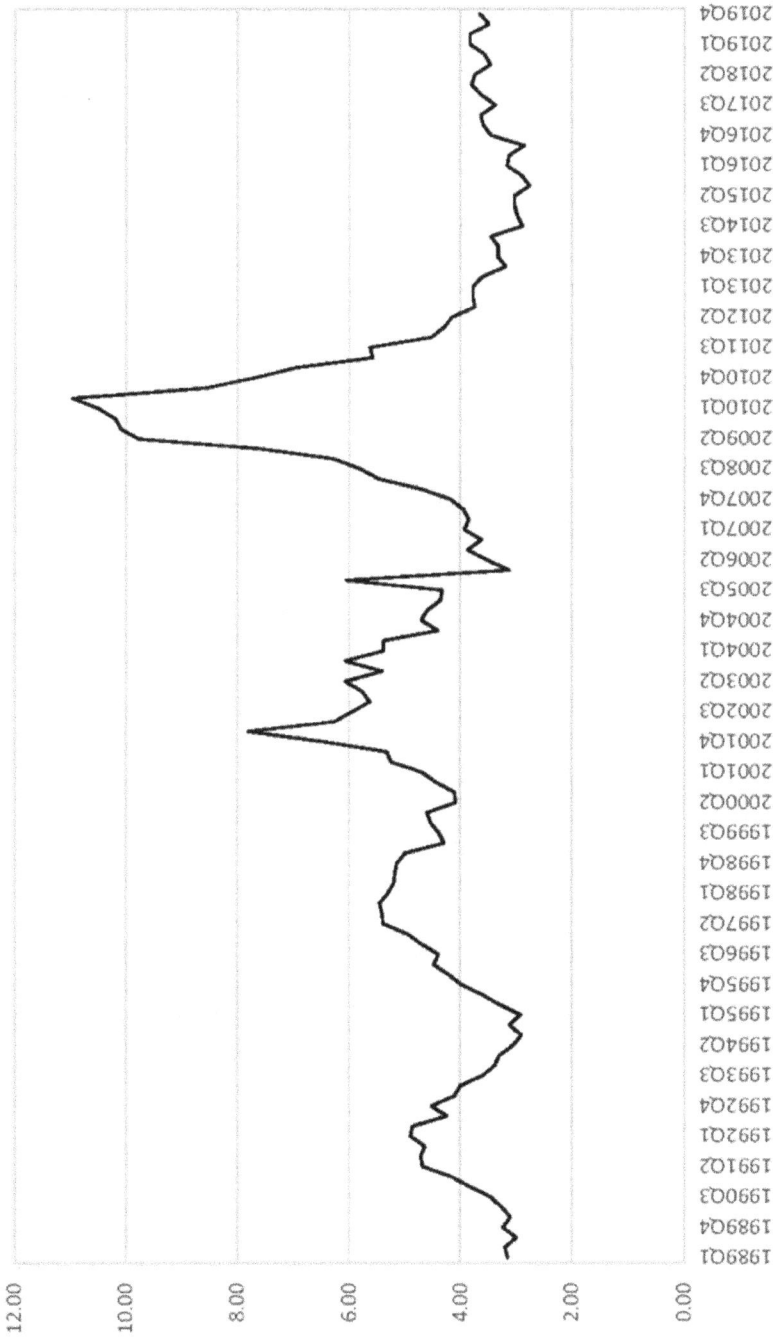

**Figure 21.3:** U.S. Credit Card Default Rates 1989–2019.
*Source:* Survey of Consumer Finances.

reached the borrowing limit. Lopes (2008) suggested that education level is also a significant factor in the probability of default.

Additionally, Lopes (2008) found that default rates are sensitive to changes in credit limits, such that higher default rates are associated with higher credit limits. This correlation between default rates and credit limits contrasts with Gross and Souleles (2002b) who found that increases in credit limits account for only a small part of the increase in default rates seen from 1995 to 1997. While Gross and Souleles (2002b) concluded that credit limits have only a small effect on default rates, their research points to another factor to account for the increase in defaults observed in the mid-1990s: The stigma effect. The stigma effect relates to the social stigma associated with filing for bankruptcy or defaulting on credit cards. Gross and Souleles (2002b) defined the relevant stigma as part of the cost of default, "both non-pecuniary (e.g., disgrace) and pecuniary (e.g., the consequences of a bad reputation)" (p. 320). They found that credit card default rates increased significantly, "even after controlling for risk-composition and other standard economic variables" (p. 322). Thus, the study concluded that the increase in default rates is largely dependent on a decrease in social stigmas surrounding default. The significance of the stigma effect in relation to default also is supported by other empirical studies (Bertaut et al., 2009).

While much research has pointed to the fact that the social stigma of defaulting has decreased significantly in recent years, some studies suggest that, while the stigma may be declining, the psychological cost of debt is still substantial. Using data from the British Household Panel Survey, Brown et al. (2005) evaluated the relationship between psychological well-being and debt. Their study found that "households who have outstanding credit and who have higher amounts of such debt are significantly less likely to report complete psychological well-being" (p. 642). This phenomenon, the study argued, points to the fact that there is a significant psychological cost placed on the consumer due to outstanding debt.

In addition to research related to usage and defaults, more recently, scholars have begun to investigate other important credit card behaviors. Keys and Wang (2019) found that behavioral biases significantly influence household credit card debt payment behavior. They documented that 29 percent of credit card holders regularly make payments at or near the minimum payment level.

With regard to the formulas used by credit card issuers to determine minimum payment levels, Keys and Wang (2019) found that 9 percent of the account holders responded to formula changes in a manner consistent with anchoring to a salient contractual term as opposed to liquidity constraints. Using a market experiment conducted by a U.S. bank, Agarwal et al. (2015) evaluated how often consumers make systematic mistakes in choosing credit card plans, and how costly these mistakes can be. They found that approximately 40 percent of consumers choose a sub-optimal plan, with the probability of choosing the sub-optimal plan decreasing as the cost of the incorrect choice increases. Furthermore, Agarwal et al. (2015) discovered that the mistakes made by consumers are not especially costly, as most consumers switch to the optimal plan after realizing the cost of their mistakes.

## Credit Card Debt Puzzles

While certain credit card mistakes are corrected once realized by consumers (Agarwal et al., 2015), there are some consumer credit card behaviors that persist despite being inconsistent with most standard life-cycle models. A substantial body of literature focuses on measuring and defining credit card debt-related puzzles.

## Underestimation Hypothesis

Ausubel (1991) was one of the first to document issues concerning individual credit card behavior. He developed what has become known as the "underestimation hypothesis," which states that consumers systematically miscalculate the extent of their current and future credit card borrowing. Ausubel (1991) suggested that consumers may be insensitive to credit card rates because they underestimate the probability that they will borrow on their credit cards or they believe the cost of switching to another credit card is large. This hypothesis implies that consumers' demand for credit card loans is inelastic. Yet, both Stavins (1996) and Gross and Souleles (2002a) tested and rejected this hypothesis. While it may not seem rational to borrow using high-interest rate credit cards, credit cards do have the additional benefit of allowing households to avoid opportunity costs of holding money.

## Credit Card Rate Stickiness

The fact that credit card rates do not seem to adjust to the cost of the underlying funds, the "stickiness" of credit card rates, is another well-documented credit card-related phenomenon (Mester, 1994). Calem and Mester (1995) empirically investigated three plausible explanations for credit card rate "stickiness": (a) cardholder search costs; (b) cardholders switching costs; and (c) firm adverse-selection problems from potentially reducing their interest rates unilaterally. Calem and Mester (1995) found that all of these factors contribute to the observed performance of the credit card market. Stavins (1996) also investigated the phenomenon and its relationship to consumer demand elasticities. She found that demand elasticities for delinquent consumer loans were significantly higher than for loans in the overall market. This discrepancy in elasticities forces an adverse selection problem upon the banks, such that if the banks were to lower interest rates, they would attract "disproportionately larger increases in delinquent loans" (Stavins, 1996, p. 53). Thus, banks have kept interest rates relatively high, despite the cost of funds, in order to mitigate their risks and protect against increases in delinquent loans.

## Revolving Debt While Holding Liquid Wealth

Interestingly, many individuals forego the benefits of the credit card grace periods as well as pay large finance charges, despite the fact that they have liquid wealth (i.e., checking and savings account balances) that exceed the value of their outstanding credit card balances. Gross and Souleles (2002a) showed that approximately one-third of households simultaneously carry credit card debt and hold liquid wealth that exceed one month of income. Conditional on credit card borrowing, 90 percent of households have some liquid assets in checking and savings accounts. Bertaut et al. (2009) documented the persistence of this credit card debt puzzle using four waves of SCF data. However, it is unclear whether the credit card debt puzzle is as large as previously defined, as both Zinman (2009b) and Karlan and Zinman (2008) provided evidence that individuals under-report data on consumer loans.

One of the most prominent explanations for the prevalence of this credit card debt puzzle is time-inconsistent preferences. Many scholars have proposed that a hyperbolic discounting model is well-suited to address this puzzle because it distinguishes between long-term and short-term preferences. Hyperbolic discounting could induce consumption situations in which households have substantial savings while sustaining high levels of credit card debt for the short term.

Using a standard life-cycle model, Laibson et al. (2003) identified a solution to this puzzle based on hyperbolic time preferences. Simulated hyperbolic consumers may act both patiently (when it comes to saving for retirement in the form of purchases of illiquid assets) and impatiently (when it comes to borrowing on the credit card market). By buying illiquid securities that do not allow consumption of invested money in the immediate period, households can engage in both significant long-term saving while engaging in high, immediate consumption. The authors argued that their hyperbolic life-cycle model, despite its inability to predict that high wealth households borrow at relatively low frequencies, is broadly consistent with empirical data. Nonetheless, their model fails to explain two important aspects of this credit card debt puzzle: (a) individuals carry high-interest rate credit card debt instead of switching to low-interest-rate cards; and (b) individuals simultaneously carry credit card debt and hold *liquid* wealth, which exceeds one month of income. While Kocherlakota (2001) argued that time-inconsistent agents specialize in their asset holdings and hold only liquid or only illiquid assets, the criticism of the illiquid asset assumption is one of the main objections brought against the Laibson et al. (2003) solution to this credit card debt puzzle.

Both Bertaut and Haliassos (2006) and Bertaut et al. (2009) developed accountant-shopper models to explain this credit card debt puzzle. In these models, revolving debt is used as a control mechanism to compensate for the consumption self-control problem. In Bertaut et al. (2009), they created an accountant-shopper model in which having a credit card allows consumption and saving decisions to be separated. The accountant self can exert control over the consumption decisions of the shopper self by revolving credit card debt to limit the value of new purchases the shopper self can make before reaching the credit limit. Since the card balance is used for control purposes, the accountant self also could find it optimal to save through lower return transaction accounts in order to finance future consumption.

Sprenger and Stavins (2008) analyzed 2005 Consumer Payment Preferences data to "explore the relationship between revolving credit card balances and payment use" (p. 6), finding that credit revolvers are more likely to use debit than credit compared to convenience users (those who pay their monthly credit card bills in full). Sprenger and Stavins (2008, p. 10) concluded that revolvers often regard debit as "superior to credit with respect to control over money and budgeting," while viewing credit as "superior with respect to ease of use and acceptability." Moreover, Zinman (2009a) found that debit use is higher among those who revolve debt, those who have a binding credit limit, and those without a credit card. These findings seem to point to the idea of self-control as an underlying cause of this credit card puzzle. People who revolve credit card debt may have difficulty controlling their credit expenditures, and consequently, they substitute from credit to debit as a stricter means of budgeting and financial control.

Lehnert and Maki (2007) argued that the favorable provisions of bankruptcy law in some states tend to raise the probability of holding simultaneously high amounts of credit card debt and liquid assets. Thus, strategic bankruptcy considerations could explain the debt revolving behavior of some households. Lopes (2008) investigated the effect of filing for bankruptcy on credit card debt. She found empirical evidence that supports the explanation of the credit card debt puzzle through bankruptcy exemption levels. Her study concluded that more consumers revolve high-cost credit card debt with low-yield liquid assets in states with higher exemption levels. However, Bertaut et al. (2009) challenged this explanation since they found empirical evidence that the puzzle is robust to controlling for strategic default and found that the behavior is widespread, particularly within the middle class.

Telyukova (2013) explained that the need for liquidity creates a situation in which households revolve credit card debt and have liquid wealth. In this model, households hold liquid assets (i.e., cash in savings accounts) that they expect to use for purposes for which a credit card could not be used. Telyukova (2013) showed that consumption in goods that require liquid payments could be somewhat large and unpredictable, creating a need for holding on to liquid assets instead of paying off debt.

# Mortgage Debt

## Trends and Topics

In dollar terms, mortgage debt is the largest source of debt on household balance sheets (Bhutta et al., 2020). Thus, over the last several decades, a large literature analyzing issues related to mortgage debt has been developed. In the 1980s, scholars began examining increases in housing prices and interest rates that took place during the 1970s that resulted in increases in household mortgage debt (Thrall, 1983). Early scholars in this area also began examining household characteristics, subjective measures, and psychological variables that could affect household mortgage-related decisions including whether to own a home, the home's value, and the amount of mortgage debt (Donkers and van Soest, 1999). Gerardi et al. (2007) looked specifically at debt related to mortgages, and used the relationship between housing spending and future income to determine if mortgage market developments, specifically deregulation, have helped households over time. Using data from the Panel Study of Income Dynamics (PSID), they concluded that households have become increasingly more able to buy homes that are consistent with the households' projected income forecasts. Furthermore, the relationship between size of housing purchase and future income increased significantly, with estimated sensitivity doubling from 1969 to 1999.

Campbell and Cocco (2003) examined the characteristics of a household that causes its preference for adjustable-rate mortgages (ARMs) over nominal fixed-rate mortgages (FRMs). They showed a strong negative correlation between FRM loans and the level of long-term interest rates. Campbell and Cocco (2003) proposed that this negative correlation exists because of the belief that long-term interest rates are mean-reverting, which rationalizes the tendency to attempt to obtain and maintain a relatively low-interest rate by obtaining an FRM. LaCour-Little (2007) found that mortgage choice is generally rational, with borrowers avoiding more expensive alternatives. Households with high debt levels or a need to close quickly tend to have increased non-prime product use. Low- and moderate-income households prefer loans with lower down payments, such as Federal Housing Administration (FHA) and special program loans.

The strong connections between mortgage debt behaviors and decision-making behavior for the asset side of a household's balance sheet has been a rich area for research. Brueckner (1997) combined the housing investment-consumption model of Henderson and Ioannides (1983) with the standard mean-variance portfolio framework of Fama and Miller (1972) and concluded that when an investment constraint is binding, the optimal portfolio of a homeowner is inefficient in a mean-variance respect and there is an over-investment in housing. Brueckner (1997) proffered that the result suggests households rationally balance consumption benefits with the portfolio distortion from housing investment. Brueckner (1997) also suggested that the findings would apply to any other asset that yields consumption benefits—such as jewelry or art.

The idea that households over-invest in housing also was echoed by Fratantoni (1998). Fratantoni (1998) showed that expenditures committed to homeownership cause households to hold their financial assets in safer investments. In particular, doubling the median homeowner's mortgage payment/income ratio decreases the risky share of their portfolios by 15 percent. Furthermore, Fratantoni (1998) emphasized that households that over-invest in housing hold highly non-diversified portfolios. Work by Englund et al. (2002) also supports the premise that households over-invest in housing. They found that for short time frames, the efficient portfolio contains no housing investment, while for longer periods, low-risk portfolios include 15 percent to 50 percent housing. Additionally, Cauley et al. (2007) analyzed the effect of household mortgage debt on households' investment portfolios. They investigated the impact of a "homeownership constraint" on an individual's optimal asset allocation decisions. They found that, for realistic parameter values, a homeownership constraint can have a large influence on an individual's asset allocation and influences the individual to invest a larger than optimal portion of the individual's wealth in a home.

Households earn pre-tax returns by contributing to their retirement accounts and pay after-tax rates on their mortgages, so households tend to benefit by contributing money to their tax-deferred accounts instead of their mortgage prepayment. However, mortgage debt has been found to cause households to have an inefficient allocation of mortgage prepayment versus retirement account contributions. Amromin et al. (2007) examined the choices that homeowners often make when deciding between contributing money to mortgage prepayment versus retirement accounts. Using data from the SCF, they found that households make decisions that are not cost-efficient, and a reallocation of their savings would allow them to save more. They calculated that the median gain of a reallocation of savings from mortgage prepayments to tax-deferred accounts could range from 11 to 17 cents per dollar. They related their findings to research that addresses the tradeoff between savings in taxable versus tax-deferred accounts (Dammon et al., 2004; Huang, 2008; Shoven and Sialm, 2004). Amromin et al. (2007) maintained that the misallocation is the result of households' hesitancy to take on debt. The inefficient behavior is explained by a self-reported debt aversion that makes households want to pay off their debt obligations early. Archer et al. (1996) found that income and collateral constraints, as well as other factors such as house value and family size and age, influence household mortgage prepayment behavior. However, they concluded that factors such as the age of the main family supporter, as well as family size, are only important in that they indicate whether or not a household is income-constrained or collateral-constrained.

Bernstein and Koudijs (2020) provided the first empirical evidence on the causal effects of mortgage amortization on wealth accumulation. They found nearly a one-for-one rise in net worth and little savings-debt fungibility. Findings hold for buyers with substantial liquid savings and across ages, suggesting general applicability beyond just individuals who are young or do not save. The findings suggest that homeownership, when combined with amortizing mortgages, is a key mechanism for household wealth building. While a large number of households have household debt and it is a means for wealth building, managing this debt is not always a household priority. Campbell (2006, p. 1590) discussed various 'investment mistakes,' and went on to assert that they are fundamental to household finance. He identified neglect of exercising mortgage refinancing options as a key household investment mistake.

## The Mortgage Crisis

The 2008 mortgage crisis highlighted other household mistakes with regard to household mortgage origination decisions. A few central themes emerged from the literature studying the mortgage crisis as it relates to household finance. Contrary to the widely purported narrative that subprime and poor borrowers were the main cause of the crisis, Adelino et al. (2016) highlighted the role of middle-class and borrowers with higher credit scores in the mortgage crisis. They found that middle-income, high-income, and prime borrowers all acutely increased their share of delinquencies during the crisis. Mocetti and Viviano (2017) examined delinquency rates for mortgages that originated before and after the mortgage crisis. They found that the credit risk models, generally used by lenders, systematically underestimate the connection between household income and the probability of mortgage default.

# Themes in Education Debt

While less than 22 percent of households have education debt, it is the largest type of nonmortgage household debt in dollar terms. As early as the 1980s, there was a robust discussion in the literature about a pending "student debt crisis" (Hansen and Rhodes, 1988). In recent years, the focus on the student loan debt crisis has intensified. However, Avery and Turner (2012) contended the claim that student borrowing is "too high" can be rejected, except with regard to for-profit colleges. Avery and Turner (2012) proffered that, under certain circumstances, "student loans can potentially improve the efficiency of the economy by raising the supply of college-educated workers in the labor market" (p. 167). They argued, since credit constraints are more likely to affect students from low-income households, student loans can serve to reduce both educational and income inequality among those within and across generations.

Dynarski (2015) also argued that there is no debt crisis. She maintained student debt levels are not large relative to the expected value of a college education in the United States. She asserted that there is not a student loan debt crisis but a repayment crisis because of the timing mismatch between receiving the benefits and incurring the costs of college. Since student loans must be paid when borrowers' earnings are lowest and most variable, Dynarski and Kreisman (2013) proposed to solve the repayment crisis with an income-based model of loan repayment in which student loan payments automatically rise and fall with a borrower's earnings.[3]

Mueller and Yannelis (2019) examined student loan defaults in the global financial crisis and found a compositional shift in loans that explains some of the rise in student loan defaults. The percent of nontraditional borrowers attending for-profit institutions and community colleges increased by 16.9 percent from 2006 to 2009. These borrowers were riskier and had higher default rates compared to traditional borrowers attending four-year colleges. Mueller and Yannelis (2019) calculated that this compositional shift in borrowers and the collapse in home prices during the global financial crisis can each account for approximately 30 percent of the increase in student loan defaults.

Looney and Yannelis (2015) examined student loan default and delinquency data from before and after the global financial crisis and found that borrowers from for-profit schools, two-year institutions, and certain other nonselective institutions account for most of the increase in default. These nontraditional borrowers are found to largely come from lower-income families, attend institutions with relatively weak educational outcomes, face poor labor market outcomes after leaving school, and have high default rates. They found the default rates of borrowers from four-year public and nonprofit private institutions remained constant. While these traditional borrowers have relatively high loan balances, they avoid adverse loan outcomes, due to higher earnings, low rates of unemployment, and greater family resources.

Cadena and Keys (2013), using the National Postsecondary Student Aid Study, investigated student loan take-up decisions for students who would receive their loan funds in cash. They found these students are significantly more likely to refuse the loan, since receiving loan funds in cash creates an especially tempting liquidity increase. They interpreted this finding to mean that consumers limit their liquidity generated by student borrowing as a way to avoid temptations to overspend.

## Future Research Directions

Research in the area of household finance has progressed in recent years. Yet, myriad issues relating to the debt side of the household balance sheet require further study. Fundamental questions remain open. For example, the role of other major debt types, like vehicle debt, on the household balance sheet remains underexplored. While not the focus of much research, over the past 30 years, consistently about one-third of households have held vehicle loans.[4] Given the large percentage of households with vehicle debt, more research is needed (Calem et al., 2020).

---

3 These plans now currently exist. https://studentaid.gov/manage-loans/repayment/plans.
4 https://www.federalreserve.gov/releases/g19/current/default.htm.

Interactions between household finance and the labor market is another key area for future research. For example, Donaldson et al. (2019) developed a theoretical model in which limited-liability debt on households' balance sheets creates a debt overhang problem. Indebted households in their model are hesitant to assume the cost of working because they will have to use their wages to repay debt. In this way, households act similarly to indebted firms in corporate finance, whose equity holders are reluctant to make new investments because the cash flows would be used to make repayments to existing creditors.

The degree to which credit markets develop and are shaped in the interest of households is also a crucial issue in need of further research and examination. Within the context of credit market products, Zinman (2015) highlighted another confounding puzzle with regard to the structure of the U.S. credit market. He drew attention to the "missing rungs in the lending ladder" (p. 258) between credit cards that have maximum annual percentage rates (APRs) of well over 20 percent and the next available type of credit, payday loans that have triple-digit APRs. He went on to comment that this gap is even more striking if maturities are taken into consideration. Maturities for credit cards can be very long because they are open-ended lines of credit with a small minimum required monthly payments. In contrast, maturities for payday loans are typically very short (e.g., one to four weeks).

## Conclusion

Financial opportunities for households have expanded over the past several decades. Chief among these opportunities has been the option of increased borrowing for households without strong collateral (Dynan, 2009). This can yield benefits, as the democratization of credit increases the possibilities for individuals to smooth consumption by borrowing against future income or accumulated home equity. However, recent economic times have dramatically illustrated that expanded financial opportunities can both increase household exposure to financial risks and have broader economic effects. For households, more borrowing means they can take on obligations that cannot be satisfied given their resources. For the economy as a whole, more borrowing to purchase assets can push asset prices to unsustainably high levels, and higher levels of leverage make subsequent price drops extraordinarily harmful to the economy (Dynan, 2009).

Much of the extant household finance literature focuses on saving and investing behavior, with a limited focus on household debt behaviors. This emphasis on the asset side of the household balance sheet to the exclusion of the liability side limits the personal finance field's ability to fully understand household financial behaviors and corresponding economic effects. Furthermore, while there is a robust financial planning industry that focuses on helping consumers with saving and investing decisions, more focus could be given to the liability side of the household balance sheet. There exists an opportunity in which financial advising services could help households make better choices with regard to debt. This also could provide significant benefits to both individual households and the economy as a whole.

# References

Adelino, M., Schoar, A., and Severino, F. (2016). Loan originations and defaults in the mortgage crisis: The role of the middle class. *The Review of Financial Studies*, *29*(7), 1635–1670.

Agarwal, S., Chomsisengphet, S., Liu, C., and Soueles, N. S. (2015). Do consumers choose the right credit contracts? *The Review of Corporate Finance Studies*, *4*(2), 239–257.

Amromin, G., Huang, J., and Sialm, C. (2007). The tradeoff between mortgage prepayments and tax-deferred retirement savings. *Journal of Public Economics*, *91*(10), 2014–2040.

Archer, W., Ling, D., and McGill, G. (1996). The effect of income and collateral constraints on residential mortgage terminations. *Regional Science and Urban Economics*, *26*(3–4), 235–261.

Ausubel, L. M. (1991). The failure of competition in the credit card market. *American Economic Review*, *81*, 50–81.

Avery, C., and Turner, S. (2012). Student loans: Do college students borrow too much—Or not enough? *Journal of Economic Perspectives*, *26*(1), 165–192.

Barnes, S., and Young, G. (2003). *The rise in U.S. household debt: Assessing its causes and sustainability* (Working Paper No. 206). Bank of England. http://dx.doi.org/10.2139/ssrn.597444

Bernstein, A., and Koudijs, P. (2020). *The mortgage piggy bank: Building wealth through amortization* (NBER Working Paper No. 28574). National Bureau of Economic Research. https://doi.org/10.3386/w28574

Bertaut, C. C., and Haliassos, M. (2006). Credit cards: Facts and theories. In G. Bertola, R. Disney, and C. Grant (eds.), *The economics of consumer credit* (pp. 181–237). MIT Press.

Bertaut, C. C., Haliassos, M., and Reiter, M. (2009). Credit card debt puzzles and debt revolvers for self control. *Review of Finance*, *13*(4), 657–692.

Bhutta, N., Bricker, J., Chang, A. C., Dettling, L. J., Goodman, S., Hsu, J. W., Moore, K. B., Reber, S., Volz, A. H., and Windle, R. A. (2020). Changes in U.S. family finances from 2016 to 2019: Evidence from the Survey of Consumer Finance. *Federal Reserve Bulletin*, *106*(5), 1–42.

Brown, S., Taylor, K., and Price, S. W. (2005). Debt and distress: Evaluating the psychological cost of credit. *Journal of Economic Psychology*, *26*(5), 642–663.

Brueckner, J. K. (1997). Consumption and investment motives and the portfolio choices of homeowners. *Journal of Real Estate Finance and Economics*, *15*(2), 159–180.

Cadena, B. C., and Keys, B. J. (2013). Can self-control explain avoiding free money? Evidence from interest-free student loans. *The Review of Economics and Statistics*, *95*(4), 1,117–1,129.

Calem, P., Ramasamy, C., and Wang, J. (2020). *What explains the post-2011 trends of longer maturities and rising default rates on auto loans?* (Discussion Paper No. 20–02). Federal Reserve Bank of Philadelphia.

Calem, P. S., and Mester, L. J. (1995). Consumer behavior and the stickiness of credit card interest rates. *The American Economic Review*, *85*(5), 1,327–1,336.

Campbell, J. (2006). Household finance. *The Journal of Finance*, *61*(4), 1,553–1,604.

Campbell, J. Y., and Cocco, J. F. (2003). House risk management and optimal mortgage choice. *The Quarterly Journal of Economics*, *118*(4), 1,449–1,494.

Carroll, C. D. (1997). Buffer-stock saving and the life cycle/permanent income hypothesis. *The Quarterly Journal of Economics*, *112*(1), 1–55.

Cauley, S. D., Pavlov, A. D., and Schwartz, E. S. (2007). Homeownership as a constraint on asset allocation. *Journal of Real Estate Finance and Economics*, *34*(3), 283–311.

Chang, B. (2006). *Access to consumer credit: Impact on low vs. high-income groups* (UMI No.3201125) [Doctoral dissertation, Fordham University]. ProQuest Dissertations and Theses Global.

Dammon, R. M., Spatt, C. S., and Zhang, H. H. (2004). Optimal asset location and allocation with taxable and tax-deferred investing. *The Journal of Finance*, *59*(3), 999–1,037.

Donaldson, J. R., Piacentino, G., and Thakor, A. (2019). Household debt overhang and unemployment. *The Journal of Finance*, *74*(3), 1,473–1,502.

Donkers, B., and van Soest, A. (1999). Subjective measures of household preferences and financial decisions. *Journal of Economic Psychology*, *20*(6), 613–642.

Dunn, L. F., and Kim, T. (1999). *An empirical investigation of credit card default* (Department of Economics Working Paper No. 99–13). Ohio State University.

Dynan, K. E. (2009). Changing household financial opportunities and economic security. *Journal of Economic Perspectives*, *23*(4), 49–68.

Dynarski, S. M. (2015). *An economist's perspective on student loans in the United States* (CESifo Working Paper No. 5579). Center for Economic Studies and IFO Institute.

Dynarski, S., and Kreisman, D. (2013, October 21). *Loans for educational opportunity: Making borrowing work for today's students*. Brookings. http://www.brookings.edu/research/papers/2013/10/21-student-loans-dynarski

Ekici, T., and Dunn, L. (2010). Credit card debt and consumption. *Applied Economics*, *42*(4), 455–462.

Englund, P., Hwang, M., and Quigley, J. M. (2002). Hedging housing risk. *Journal of Real Estate Finance and Economics*, *24*(1), 167–200.

Fama, E., and Miller, M. (1972). *The theory of finance*. Holt Rinehart and Winston.

Fratantoni, M. C. (1998). Homeownership and investment in risky assets. *Journal of Urban Economics*, *44*(1), 27–42.

Friedman, M. (1957). *A theory of the consumption function*. Princeton University Press.

Gerardi, K., Rosen, H. S., and Willen, P. (2007). *Do households benefit from financial deregulation and innovation? The case of the mortgage market* (NBER Working Paper No. 12967). National Bureau of Economic Research. https://www.doi.org/10.3386/w12967

Gross, D. B., and Souleles, N. S. (2002a). Do liquidity constraint and interest rates matter for consumer behavior? Evidence from credit card data. *The Quarterly Journal of Economics*, *117*(1), 149–185.

Gross, D. B., and Souleles, N. S. (2002b). Empirical analysis of personal bankruptcy and delinquency. *The Review of Financial Studies*, *15*(1), 319–347.

Hansen, W. L., and Rhodes, M. S. (1988). Student debt crisis: Are students incurring excessive debt? *Economics of Education Review*, *7*(1), 101–112.

Henderson, J., and Ioannides, Y. (1983). A model of housing tenure choice. *The American Economic Review*, *73*(1), 98–113.

Huang, J. (2008). Taxable and tax-deferred investing: A tax-arbitrage approach. *The Review of Financial Studies*, *21*(5), 2,179–2,207.

Karlan, D., and Zinman, J. (2008). Lying about borrowing. *Journal of the European Economic Association*, *6*(2–3), 510–521.

Keys, B. J., and Wang, J. (2019). Minimum payments and debt paydown in consumer credit cards. *Journal of Financial Economics*, *131*(3), 528–548.

Kocherlakota, N. R. (2001). Looking for evidence of time-inconsistent preferences in asset market data. *Federal Reserve Bank of Minneapolis Quarterly Review*, *25*(3), 13–24.

LaCour-Little, M. (2007). The home purchase mortgage preferences of low- and moderate-income households. *Real Estate Economics*, *35*(3), 265–290.

Laibson, D., Repetto, A., and Tobacman, J. (2003). A debt puzzle. In P. Aghion, R. Frydman, J. Stiglitz, and M. Woodford (eds.), *Knowledge, information, and expectations in modern economics: In honor of Edmund S. Phelps* (pp. 228–266). Princeton University Press.

Lehnert, A., and Maki, D. M. (2007). Consumption, debt, and portfolio choice: Testing the effect of bankruptcy law. In S. Agarwal, and B. W. Ambrose (eds.), *Household credit usage* (pp. 55–76). Palgrave Macmillan.

Looney, A., and Yannelis, C. (2015). A crisis in student loans? How changes in the characteristics of borrowers and in the institutions they attended contributed to rising loan defaults. *Brookings Papers on Economic Activity*, *2*, 1–89.

Lopes, P. (2008). Credit card debt and default over the life-cycle. *Journal of Money, Credit, and Banking*, *40*(4), 769–790.

McCarthy, J. (1997). Debt, delinquencies, and consumer spending. *Current Issues in Economics and Finance*, *3*(3), 1–6.

Mester, L. J. (1994). Why are credit card rates sticky? *Economic Theory*, *4*(4), 505–530.

Mocetti, S., and Viviano, E. (2017). Looking behind mortgage delinquencies. *Journal of Banking and Finance*, *75*, 53–63.

Mueller, H. M., and Yannelis, C. (2019). The rise in student loan defaults. *Journal of Financial Economics*, *131*, 1–19.

Shoven, J. B., and Sialm, C. (2004). Asset location in tax-deferred and conventional savings accounts. *Journal of Public Economics*, *88*(1–2), 23–38.

Sprenger, C., and Stavins, J. (2008). *Credit card debt and payment use* (Working Paper No. 08–2). Federal Reserve Bank of Boston.

Stavins, J. (1996, July). Can demand elasticities explain sticky credit card rates? *New England Economic Review*, 43–54.

Telyukova, I. A. (2013). Household need for liquidity and the credit card debt puzzle. *The Review of Economic Studies*, *80*(3), 1,148–1,177.

Thrall, G. I. (1983). The proportion of household income devoted to mortgage payments: A model with supporting evidence. *Annals of the Association of American Geographers*, *73*(2), 220–230.

Yoo, P. S. (1997). Charging up a mountain of debt: Accounting for the growth of credit card debt. *Federal Reserve Bank of St. Louis Review*, *79*(2), 3–13.

Zinman, J. (2009a). Debit or credit? *Journal of Banking and Finance*, *33*(2), 358–366.

Zinman, J. (2009b). Where is the missing credit card debt? Clues and implications. *The Review of Income and Wealth*, *55*(2), 249–265.

Zinman, J. (2015). Household debt: Facts, puzzles, theories, and policies. *The Annual Review of Economics*, *7*(1), 251–276.

Shinae L. Choi

# 22 Financial Security: Protecting the Health of Consumers

**Abstract:** Medical expenses and health insurance are important dimensions of policy and research debates in protecting the health of consumers. This chapter provides an overview of the large and growing body of literature exploring the determinants of medical expenses and health insurance in protecting the health of consumers in the context of financial security. This chapter highlights analyses of two distinct sets of evidence: (a) studies of medical expenses and health insurance; and (b) studies of job loss and financial insecurity, particularly the inability to pay medical bills resulting from the Covid-19 pandemic. As discussed in this chapter, implementing health policies and regulations plays a critical role in protecting the health of consumers. Thus, the chapter addresses recent U.S. legislation such as the Affordable Care Act (ACA) and the No Surprises Act, which could protect consumers both medically and financially. Reviewing an extensive body of literature on these issues, the chapter concludes with implications for both policy and practice, as well as for future research avenues.

**Keywords:** health, medical expenses, health insurance, Affordable Care Act, No Surprises Act

## Introduction

Medical expenses and health insurance are important dimensions of policy and in shaping ongoing research debates about the best way to protect the health of consumers (Choi and Blackburn, 2018). In the United States, health insurance coverage provides a primary means for financing healthcare expenses (U.S. Census Bureau, 2019).[1] Healthcare expenses have previously been shown to affect households' financial security and limit a person's capability to cope with unexpected expenses associated with

---

[1] As noted in Chapter 19, health insurance can be packaged as a private policy, universal health coverage (i.e., social insurance), or a combination of the two. The United States is the only industrialized country to not have a form of universal health coverage. Canada and Taiwan are the only two countries that have fully implemented universal health coverage through a single-payer plan. All other countries use either an insurance mandate or a hybrid system that combines elements from private insurance plans with those of a governmental mandate plan. Given the unique status of the United States, this chapter focuses primarily on health insurance issues from a U.S. perspective.

---

**Shinae L. Choi,** University of Alabama

https://doi.org/10.1515/9783110727692-022

medical events (Caraballo et al., 2020). Although health policy is often designed to help protect patients' financial security, there is limited understanding of the role medical debt plays in household finances (Batty et al., 2018). Medical bills can lead to serious financial consequences, resulting in depletion of savings or bankruptcy (Cook et al., 2010; Himmelstein et al., 2009; Richman and Brodie, 2014).

According to the U.S. Census Bureau (2020), in the United States, nearly all citizens have private health insurance, or they receive healthcare services under a federal program such as Medicare or Medicaid. Even so, approximately 30 million individuals, about 9.2 percent of the U.S. population, were uninsured in 2019 (U.S. Census Bureau, 2020).

Private health insurance is the predominant source of health insurance coverage in the United States (Rosso, 2021). In 2019, individuals, including those who were uninsured, health insurers, and federal and state governments spent nearly $3.6 trillion on various types of health consumption expenditures, which accounted for 16.8 percent of the nation's gross domestic product (GDP) (Centers for Medicare and Medicaid Services, 2020). Out-of-pocket spending (other than premiums) includes all amounts paid by the privately insured and other insured individuals for coinsurance, deductibles, and services not covered by insurance. It also includes any amounts paid by the uninsured for healthcare goods and services. Among all individuals, out-of-pocket spending totaled $407 billion in 2019 (Centers for Medicare and Medicaid Services, 2020). The ratio of total out-of-pocket spending for healthcare services and premiums to total family income is a significant financial burden nationally (Cunningham, 2010).

This chapter provides some evidence about what personal finance researchers know about protecting the health of consumers in the context of financial security. The chapter highlights two distinct sets of evidence: (a) studies of medical expenses and health insurance; and (b) studies of job loss and financial insecurity, particularly problems associated with the difficulty of paying medical bills during the Covid-19 pandemic.[2] Specifically, the chapter provides an overview of the large and growing body of literature exploring the determinants of medical expenses and health insurance premium payments (e.g., Choi and Blackburn, 2018) and medical debt and related financial consequences (e.g., Cook et al., 2010; Domowitz and Sartain, 1999; Duchon and Schoen, 2001; Himmelstein et al., 2009; Kielb et al., 2017; Richman and Brodie, 2014; Wiltshire et al., 2016). The chapter also addresses recent federal health legislation,

---

[2] The predominance of employment-based healthcare coverage in the United States reflects the realization that families may lose their health insurance when working parents change jobs, are laid off, or die (Institute of Medicine, 2002; Madrian, 1994). The Covid-19 pandemic has devastated the health, well-being, job security, and financial security of consumers and families in the United States and worldwide. Drawing from a nationally representative U.S. sample, the chapter will provide a review of new evidence on the loss of jobs and employer-sponsored health insurance plans by focusing on financial insecurity, particularly the inability to pay medical bills during the early months of the Covid-19 pandemic.

such as the Affordable Care Act (ACA) and the No Surprises Act, which were designed to protect consumers both medically and financially. Reviewing an extensive body of literature on consumers' and families' healthcare spending, the chapter concludes with implications for both policy and practice, as well as for future research avenues.

# Consumers' Medical Expenses and Health Insurance

Health insurance is a vital factor in promoting good health across household types. A growing body of literature documents that consumers' socioeconomic and demographic characteristics are linked to their medical expenses and health insurance premium payments. For example, Choi and Blackburn (2018) investigated household socioeconomic and demographic characteristics as predictors of patterns of health insurance premiums and medical expenses of consumers using the U.S. Consumer Expenditures Survey. The authors noted that the most common types of medical insurance were health maintenance organization plans and fee-for-service plans. Households that had a health maintenance organization plan spent more on health insurance premiums but less on payments for medical expenses. Nearly two-thirds of households obtained their policy as a group plan through their place of employment. Households who purchased a policy in the private marketplace spent more on both health insurance premiums and payments for medical expenses.

As demonstrated in a recent analysis by Choi and Blackburn (2018), socioeconomic and demographic characteristics are correlated with healthcare spending. Choi and Blackburn provided empirical support to testimonial evidence that older age, being married, educational attainment, and family income are associated with higher household spending on both health insurance premiums and medical expenses. Family size is only positively associated with the amount paid for health insurance premiums, whereas homeownership without a mortgage, and the number of owned vehicles, are only positively associated with the amount paid for medical expenses. On the other hand, government employment status is associated with lower spending on both health insurance premiums and medical expenses. The self-employed spend more on health insurance premiums and medical expenses since they have limited choices and are not able to take advantage of collective bargaining power when purchasing health insurance policies (Hong and Kim, 2000). Where a person lives also matters. Since Wennberg and Gittelsohn's (1973) research, many researchers have discussed regional variations in healthcare cost and delivery. Particular attention has been paid to differences seen in healthcare spending, health insurance coverage, and healthcare access for both children (Fisher et al., 2003; Kogan et al., 2010) and adults (Ozieh et al., 2016; Radley and Schoen, 2012) by geographic variation. Choi and Blackburn (2018) indicated that compared to households living in the Western United States, those living in the South paid higher levels of health insurance premiums while Northeastern residents paid lower levels on medical expenses.

Previous literature using both individual and population-level studies demonstrates that having health insurance promotes consumers' use of routine and appropriate care and facilitates a regular source of care, which eventually improves health-related outcomes through the life course (Institute of Medicine, 2002; Kuh et al., 2014; Kuruvilla et al., 2018). As examples of evidence- and rights-based global strategies, the World Health Organization (WHO, 2019) noted, "A life course approach provides a holistic view of individuals' health and well-being at all ages and prevents lifelong ill effects" (WHO, 2019, p. 1). The WHO (2019) report highlights the importance of early investment in health and well-being. For example, having well-childcare and seeing a regular healthcare provider are essential for monitoring a child's development and detecting potential problems early before they cause long-term negative health consequences (Institute of Medicine, 2002; Sawyer et al., 2012). Adolescents are particularly at risk of not having a regular source of care or any physician visits. This is particularly an issue in relation to mental health screening and treatment for drinking, other risky behaviors, and non-communicable diseases (Institute of Medicine, 2002; Sawyer et al., 2012; Sheehan et al., 2017). Greater attention to adolescent issues is required in order to maintain the robustness and success of any future public health initiatives (Sawyer et al., 2012; Sheehan et al., 2017). For pregnant persons, having health insurance is directly related to health outcomes for both the pregnant person and newborns. Prenatal care has been shown, for example, to be important in addressing low birth-weight complications (Tunçalp et al., 2015; WHO, 2016). Additionally, uninsured adults are more likely to receive no or delayed care, and they are at greater risk of hospitalization for conditions that could have been treated on an outpatient basis (Institute of Medicine, 2002). Roughly 30 percent of older adults are care-dependent because of functional impairments, high healthcare costs, and constraints to their continued contributions to family, community, and society (WHO, 2019).

Medical expenses have become burdensome for many Americans. In particular, the most vulnerable population – those with a low socioeconomic status and uninsured individuals – exhibit a high prevalence of financial hardship from medical bills, with deleterious consequences (Caraballo et al., 2020). These issues highlight not only the financial burden of healthcare expenditures on families but also their limited access to healthcare (Kielb et al., 2017). Indeed, using the 2011–2014 Medical Expenditure Panel Survey data, Kielb and colleagues (2017) confirmed that foregoing medical care is common among low-income populations. For those with low income in the privately insured population, Kielb et al. emphasized the importance of health insurance designed as a predictor of access and the need to expand the definition of financial barriers to care beyond expenditures. Research has been shown to suggest that low income, lack of health insurance, and poor health are related to a difficulty in paying medical bills (Richman and Brodie, 2014).

Regarding racial differences in medical debt, using a nationally representative cross-sectional data from the 2007 and 2010 U.S. Health Tracking Household Survey, Wiltshire et al. (2016) found evidence that Blacks had significantly higher odds of medical debt relative to Whites, and more than 40 percent of this debt was mediated by health status, income, and health insurance disparities. Wiltshire et al. also demonstrated that Blacks were more likely to borrow money because of medical debt and to be contacted by a collection agency compared with Whites.

Agarwal and Sommers (2020) showed that early diagnosis and treatment are essential to minimizing the severity of chronic illnesses, and that regular healthcare is important for promoting better overall health of consumers. However, persons who lack health insurance are often without a regular source of care (Gould, 2020) and tend to delay receiving healthcare. Compared with insured workers, uninsured individuals (and households) are more likely to have undiagnosed or untreated preexisting health conditions (Agarwal and Sommers, 2020).

The previous literature also suggests a family perspective that can be useful when examining the impact of having and/or not having health insurance on health-related outcomes. The Institute of Medicine (2002) reported that the financial burden of healthcare costs for uninsured families, and how these families cope with health outcomes in the context of the family, are important issues. Uninsured families are more likely than insured ones to face health costs that are high relative to their income (Duchon and Schoen, 2001; Institute of Medicine, 2002). Duchon and Schoen (2001) indicated that more than half of all uninsured working-age adults currently or in the recent past reported difficulties paying medical bills, compared with less than a quarter of insured adults.

Approximately 16 percent of U.S. consumers' credit reports included medical debt, defined as unpaid medical bills in collections, with more than $81 billion owed in 2016 (Batty et al., 2018). Although the relationship between high medical expenses and forms of financial stress, such as bankruptcy, is not clear, medical bills are a factor in nearly half of all bankruptcy filings (Domowitz and Sartain, 1999; Duchon and Schoen, 2001; Jacoby et al., 2000). Past studies have consistently shown that medical bills contribute to the large and increasing share of bankruptcies in the United States (Himmelstein et al., 2009). For example, Domowitz and Sartain (1999) estimated jointly qualitative choice models of consumers' decisions to file for bankruptcy and their choice of bankruptcy chapter by combining choice-based sampling techniques with a nested estimation procedure. Medical and credit card debt was found to be the strongest contributors to bankruptcy, but it is not known whether bankruptcy is more likely for uninsured families than for those with insurance coverage (Domowitz and Sartain, 1999; Duchon and Schoen, 2001; Institute of Medicine, 2002; Jacoby et al., 2000).

It is important to note, however, that most Americans take health insurance into account when making decisions about jobs and work (Institute of Medicine, 2002; Madrian, 1994). There is a large body of evidence demonstrating health insurance's relationship with labor market mobility. As preexisting conditions affected coverage prior to the ACA, health insurance might distort job mobility if employees decide to keep jobs they would rather leave for fear of losing coverage for preexisting conditions, a possibility that has been termed "job-lock" (Madrian, 1994). Using data from the National Medical Expenditure Survey, Madrian (1994) demonstrated that job-lock reduces the voluntary turnover rate of those with employer-provided health insurance by 25 percent, from 16 percent to 12 percent per year.

## Job Loss and Difficulty Paying Medical Bills During the Covid-19 Pandemic

The Covid-19 pandemic has devastated the health, well-being, job security, and financial security of consumers in the United States and worldwide. The loss of jobs, changes in income, and health insurance associated with the Covid-19 pandemic have exacerbated existing healthcare cost challenges for many consumers and families (King, 2020). During the Covid-19 pandemic, consumers experienced (and will likely continue to experience) financial hardships such as difficulty paying medical bills due to changes in employment status. The predominance of employment-based healthcare coverage in the United States reflects that families may lose their health insurance when working parents change jobs, are laid off, or die (Institute of Medicine, 2002; Madrian, 1994).

The economic impacts resulting from the Covid-19 pandemic for older adults have also been substantial. The landscape for older workers has also changed dramatically in recent decades (Coile, 2015). Older adults have been particularly vulnerable to the Covid-19 virus, accounting for more than 80 percent of all Covid-related deaths in the United States, although making up just 13 percent of the national population (Centers for Disease Control and Prevention, 2021). Older adults' vulnerability to the virus, along with social distancing practices, have impeded their ability to work and hastened retirement (Li and Mutchler, 2020). From January 2020 to September 2020, older workers experienced a substantial decrease in employment, with decreases most pronounced for those who already had relatively low earnings, such as personal care or service workers (Jacobson et al., 2020). Older adults also had new economic burdens placed on them, as they were called on to support younger family members, or as the economic supports they received from adult children diminished when the younger generation experienced job losses (Gilligan et al., 2020). Most importantly, widespread layoffs amid the pandemic threatened (and likely will continue to threaten) to cut off millions of people from their employer-sponsored health insurance plans (Agarwal and Sommers, 2020). Specifically, many Hispanic and Black workers, and workers in service industries, experienced job losses during the Covid-19 pandemic.

Using a nationally representative longitudinal survey of U.S. adults ages 51 years and older, the Health and Retirement Study (HRS), my colleagues and I (Choi et al., 2021) investigated job losses resulting from the Covid-19 pandemic and consumers' inability to pay medical bills. In 2020, a module on Covid-19 was administered to a 50 percent random subsample of households. One-half were released to fieldwork on June 11, 2020, with the second on September 24, 2020. The analytic sample included 3,191 persons from the earlier random subsample, comprising approximately 25 percent of the overall HRS sample (Health and Retirement Study, 2020). For the pandemic-related employment change variable, three mutually exclusive categories were created: (a) not working prior to the pandemic (reference group); (b) employed throughout the pandemic (i.e., work not affected by the pandemic, lost job but found new job); and (c) lost job in pandemic and did not find new work. Among older Americans, 26 percent were not working at the start of the pandemic. Three in five older Americans remained employed since the start of the pandemic, whereas 12 percent lost their job in the pandemic. Since the start of the pandemic, 4.2 percent stated that they could not pay medical bills. The results show a clear gradient in hardship outcomes; the proportion reporting an inability to pay medical bills increased as the number of functional limitations increased. Older adults with three or more functional limitations were roughly twice as likely as those with zero limitations to report an inability to pay medical bills (5.6 percent versus 2.5 percent).

Further, we estimated logistic regression models to predict financial hardships. Results showed that persons with three or more limitations were roughly twice as likely as those with no impairments to report that they missed regular bill payments (i.e., rent, mortgage, credit cards, other debt, utilities, or insurance) during the pandemic ($OR = 1.84$, $p < .001$). Similar patterns were found for difficulty paying medical bills, where those with one or two ($OR = 1.88$, $p < .01$) and three or more limitations ($OR = 2.25$, $p < .001$) being significantly more likely to face hardship relative to persons with no impairments. These results suggest that older adults with more functional limitations were, and continue to be, vulnerable to financial insecurity during and resulting from the pandemic, potentially exacerbating the physical and emotional health threats imposed by Covid-19. Persons who lost a job during the pandemic were observed to have significantly higher odds of financial insecurity. Relative to those who were not working at the start of the pandemic, older workers who lost their jobs were more likely to have missed regular bill payments ($OR = 4.64$, $p < .001$) and difficulty paying medical bills ($OR = 2.71$, $p < .001$).

Emerging research takes an intersectional approach to understanding disability, documenting that its economic and interpersonal costs are intensified for historically disadvantaged subpopulations, most notably racial and ethnic minorities and older adults (Brown and Moloney, 2019; Maroto et al., 2019). Thus, I further compared racial and ethnic groups on job loss and inability to pay medical bills during the early months of the Covid-19 pandemic. The proportion reporting each hardship increased across racial and ethnic minority groups. Hispanics suffered greater economic distress than their non-Hispanic White counterparts. Hispanic workers, particularly, faced devastating job losses during the Covid-19 pandemic. Hispanics were more than twice as likely as non-Hispanic Whites to report a job loss (29.4 percent versus 12.5 percent) during the early months of the Covid-19 pandemic. Concurrently, Hispanics were roughly three times as likely as non-Hispanic Whites to report an inability to pay medical bills (6.7 percent versus 2.5 percent) during the Covid-19 pandemic. Similarly, non-Hispanic Blacks also were more likely to report a job loss resulting from the pandemic (18.1 percent versus 12.5 percent) and were most likely to report an inability to pay medical bills (6.8 percent versus 2.5 percent), relative to non-Hispanic Whites during the Covid-19 pandemic. Despite the seemingly universal reach of the Covid-19 pandemic, these findings confirm that persons with a disability and some racial/ethnic groups faced disproportionate financial insecurity, particularly difficulties paying medical bills after a job loss during the pandemic.

# Protections for Consumers' Health: Policies and Legislation

Implementing health policies and regulations plays a critical role in protecting the health of consumers. In recent years, there has been a growing scientific interest in consumers' decision making to protect consumers medically and financially. The debate on how to determine the voluntary choice of a health insurance plan has become more common. The following discussion highlights how policymakers in the United States have recently enacted legislation designed to enhance health protections for consumers.

## The Affordable Care Act

The largest impact of the Affordable Care Act (ACA) has been on the health insurance industry, ensuring access for preexisting conditions (guaranteed issue), extending coverage for young adults, and lowering costs through regulations on premiums, preventive services, and prescription drugs (Patient Protection and Affordable Care Act, 2010). Given these changes, the price of insurance premiums is currently volatile as insurance companies have attempted to price products in line with regulations and increasing demand by enrollees for those companies offering plans in the health insurance marketplace and employer-sponsored plans.

Out-of-pocket costs for medical expenses vary for families based primarily on health insurance coverage and health status (Choi and Blackburn, 2018). Health insurance in the United States has been intertwined with employment since accident and health plans were developed in the late 1800s (Scofea, 1994). To prevent inflation during World War II, Congress enacted the Stabilization Act, which limited wage increases (Pub.L. 77–729, 56 Stat. 765). As a result, employers began offering additional compensation through health insurance plans and other benefits. Employer-based insurance peaked in the 1980s, then coverage began declining – by more than six percentage points from 1987 to 2004 (Enthoven and Fuchs, 2006). Due to the rising costs of health insurance in the last two decades, the cost of employer-sponsored insurance has increased by 59 percent since 2000 (Baicker et al., 2004; Cutler, 2003). Employers shifted some of the increasing costs of health insurance coverage to employees, which resulted in lower take-up during the 1990s and 2000s (Cutler, 2003; Gruber and McKnight, 2003). In 2019, health insurance coverage was held by approximately 49.6 percent of the U.S. population through an employer, or approximately 158 million non-elderly people (Kaiser Family Foundation, 2019). Other primary sources of health insurance coverage include Medicaid (19.8 percent of the U.S. population) and Medicare (14.2 percent of the U.S. population) (Kaiser Family Foundation, 2019).

Market competition and firm consolidation seem to contribute to the cost of non-public insurance premiums. Dafny (2010) first demonstrated that the lack of market competition leads to higher premiums, especially in areas with eight or fewer firms. Further work by Dafny and colleagues (2012) showed that from 1998 to 2006 the merger of Aetna and Prudential resulted in increased premiums by seven percentage points, which was equivalent to approximately $34 billion in additional spending (Dafny et al., 2012). Holahan (2014) also observed that after the first open enrollment in the ACA Marketplace, premiums were lowest in areas of high insurance company concentration. Among Medicare beneficiaries, out-of-pocket costs for premiums, copayments, and coinsurance grew from $3,293 on average annually to $4,734 from 2000 to 2010, a 44 percent increase (Cubanski et al., 2014).

Consumers' decision making on health insurance plans has been a core topic in national debates about health reform among researchers, practitioners, and policymakers. For instance, Mulligan and Castaneda (2017) showed how choice was experienced in this latest iteration of health reform utilizing four case studies derived from 180 enrollment observations at the Rhode Island health insurance exchange conducted from March 2014 through January 2017 and interviews with enrollees. Mulligan and Castaneda noted that consumers experienced choice as confusing and overwhelming. Although the ACA created new pathways to insurance coverage in the United States, consumers contended with confusing insurance terminology and a difficult-to-navigate website (Mulligan and Castaneda, 2017). That is, job insecurity, changes in income, existing health needs, and bureaucratic barriers shaped consumers' choices rather than exercising the power of consumer decision making through marketplaces where health insurance plans compete on quality, coverage, and price.

Nonetheless, before the ACA was implemented, people who lost their jobs had limited choices for health insurance (Agarwal and Sommers, 2020). Newly disabled people could apply for Medicaid if their savings and assets were low enough for them to qualify for Supplemental Security Income (SSI), or they could enroll in Medicare after receiving two years of benefits from Social Security Disability Insurance (Agarwal and Sommers, 2020). The SSI program provides monthly payments to more than eight million people who have limited income and few resources. The SSI is for those who are 65 years of age or older, as well as for those of any age, including children, who are blind or who have disabilities (Social Security Administration, 2021).

Approaches to implementing the ACA differ by state, but the law's consumer protections operate nationwide and nearly all states have taken responsibility for enforcing these reforms in their jurisdictions (Lucia et al., 2018). The ACA, having created several new options for health insurance unrelated to employment, may protect many recently unemployed people and their families from losing coverage. This is particularly true during and following the Covid-19 pandemic (Agarwal and Sommers, 2020). The insurance exchanges in most states have proven resilient in the face of significant change and uncertainty, with millions of Americans able to depend on individual health insurance to protect them medically and financially (Lucia et al., 2018).

## The No Surprises Act: New Protections for Consumers Against Surprise Medical Bills

Surprise medical bills can sometimes be enormous and result in severe financial distress, possibly even leading to bankruptcy, for unsuspecting patients. Surprise medical bills often arise in an emergency when a patient has no ability to select an ambulance provider, emergency room, or treating physician (Pollitz et al., 2020). After years of debate, on December 27, 2020, the No Surprises Act was signed into law as part of the Consolidated Appropriations Act of 2021 (H.R. 133; Division BB – Private Health Insurance and Public Health Provisions). The Act provides new federal consumer protections against surprise medical bills. The measure was included in omnibus legislation funding the federal government for the fiscal year 2021 (Congressional Research Service, 2019; Hoadley et al., 2020b; Kaiser Family Foundation, 2021). According to the American Hospital Association (2021) and the Congressional Research Service (2019), the No Surprises Act:

> Protects patients from receiving surprise medical bills resulting from gaps in coverage for emergency services and certain services provided by out-of-network clinicians at in-network facilities, including by air ambulances. Holds patients liable only for their in-network cost-sharing amount, while giving providers and insurers an opportunity to negotiate reimbursement. Allows providers and insurers to access an independent dispute resolution process in the event disputes arise around reimbursement. The legislation does not set a benchmark reimbursement amount. Requires both providers and health plans to assist patients in accessing health care cost information.

Although there is still debate on ground ambulance services, the No Surprises Act comprehensively protects consumers from unanticipated medical bills by promoting financial stability and reducing healthcare costs (Hoadley et al., 2020a). Under the No Surprises Act, insurers and providers are required to maintain up-to-date provider directory information and disclose price comparison tools for health plans. These requirements should improve consumers' access to information and empower consumers to evaluate more effectively their available medical service options (Kornreich et al., 2021). Beginning January 1, 2022, consumers have the benefit of these important measures.

Researchers have suggested that financial service providers and policymakers should pay more attention to growing surprise medical billing generated by the Covid-19 pandemic. The ongoing pandemic has intensified concern about affordability challenges related to surprise medical billing because of hospital staffing shortages and triage protocols that increase exposure to out-of-network physicians or facilities (King, 2020; Sheckter et al., 2020). King (2020) suggested that during the public health emergency, medical bills from out-of-network providers that exceed in-network cost-sharing limits for medical treatment received should be eliminated. Furthermore, lawmakers, state, and federal officials should continue addressing out-of-pocket expense concerns, such as cost-sharing and surprise medical billing to protect the health of consumers (King, 2020; Sheckter et al., 2020).

## Discussion and Implications

The chapter provided an overview of the large and growing body of literature exploring the determinants of medical expenses and health insurance in protecting the health of consumers in the context of financial security. Evaluating factors associated with medical expenses and health insurance premiums and highlighting the role of health insurance in household debt through a family lens underscores the long-term well-being of consumers, families, and communities (Institute of Medicine, 2002). Furthermore, the chapter explored job loss and financial insecurity, particularly the inability to pay medical bills during the Covid-19 pandemic. Over the last decade, a number of observational cohort studies, employing either theoretically based genealogical and ethnographic approaches, or empirically derived health insurance plans, have increasingly recognized that consumers' decision making on health insurance plans plays a critical role in shaping the health and financial well-being of consumers.

Research findings like those shared in this chapter are informative for both households in determining health insurance premiums and medical expenses throughout the life course as well as financial service providers who focus their work on healthcare issues (Choi and Blackburn, 2018). Further, as noted in this chapter, policymakers can play an important role in promoting well-being by legislatively applying research findings when recognizing the importance of factors associated with household healthcare decisions. Policymakers can use this information as the basis for providing guidelines for developing recommended strategies to improve healthcare service use among the U.S. population. Both policy decisions and market dynamics drive regional differences in the amount paid for healthcare services (American Hospital Association, 2021). Considering the regional variance in healthcare spending, policy decisions and educational programs might need to be more culturally sensitive to regional differences.

Since the start of the Covid-19 pandemic, those working in the personal finance field have witnessed the devastating impact of the public health emergency on people's lives. The Covid-19 pandemic unveiled widespread and persistent health disparities. Numerous studies have been undertaken to address household-level experiences with Covid-19. Documenting risk factors for economic hardships during the pandemic, and the factors that intensify these risks, is an important and policy-relevant goal, as these hardships may intensify long-standing economic and health disadvantages that have accumulated over the life course (Carr, 2019; Shandra, 2018; Wolfson et al., 2020). As noted in this chapter, the loss of jobs during the pandemic resulted in difficulties paying medical bills among older Americans. While recent policies and legislation to protect consumers' health have been implemented (e.g., the ACA and the No Surprises Act) more policy changes are likely in the future.

As noted above, legislation can play a vital role in protecting the health of consumers during unprecedented public health emergencies. In the current context of millions of Americans losing their jobs and the possibility that the pandemic may continue into the future, securing health insurance, particularly with new options created under the ACA, has become more important than ever to consumers, patients, and their caregivers (Agarwal and Sommers, 2020). Congress has passed several key pieces of legislation in response to the pandemic. The Families First Coronavirus Response Act (FFCRA) requires all private insurers, Medicare, Medicare Advantage, and Medicaid to cover Covid-19 testing and eliminate all cost-sharing associated with testing services during the public health emergency. Additionally, the Coronavirus Aid, Relief, and Economic Security (CARES) Act appropriations can now be used to cover hospital and provider reimbursement shortages (King, 2020).

During and after the pandemic, vulnerable consumers are making decisions between unpredictable healthcare spending and other essential household expenditures, such as paying regular monthly bills (e.g., rent, mortgage, utilities) and buying food. As many people lost their jobs or could not pay their health insurance premiums as a result of the pandemic, urgent policies and programs are needed to ensure that consumers can continue to access affordable care (King, 2020). As suggested by King (2020) and Sheckter et al. (2020), additional policies like extending the grace period for premium payments and freezing the insurance status of households are needed to help those who are most vulnerable maintain their health insurance coverage. It is likely that policymakers, in the United States and around the world, will take additional action in the wake of the Covid-19 pandemic. This action is likely to take the form of comprehensive investments in consumers' health, financial security, and well-being across the life course (Institute of Medicine, 2002; Kuh et al., 2014; Kuruvilla et al., 2018; Sheehan et al., 2017; WHO, 2019).

# Conclusion

The Covid-19 pandemic has produced an uncertain period for the worlds' economies and consumers' healthcare spending (Adams, 2020). Although this chapter discussed some recent evidence on medical expenses and health insurance, it is important to note that much of the health insurance literature was written prior to the Covid-19 pandemic. Future research should take into account consumers' medical expenses and health insurance premiums for healthcare in the context of the Covid-19 pandemic. Additionally, as noted in this chapter, older workers often face disproportionate health and economic challenges. This was most evident during the Covid-19 pandemic. Thus, future research is required to evaluate the consequences of job loss on health and health insurance coverage in the context of economic security at all ages using a life course approach. Finally, delayed care has been widely reported since the start of the Covid-19 pandemic. This was an unexpected outcome from the pandemic. Consumers delayed getting medical care for both serious medical problems and regular health checkups, such as pediatric visits, dental visits, and preventive care during the pandemic. Given the potential negative health consequences of delayed care (Findling et al., 2020), future research should explore household and societal costs associated with delayed care for serious medical problems and preventive care to protect the health of consumers.

# References

Adams, K. (2020). *Will the pandemic mean higher health care costs in the future?* Marketplace. Accessed July 2021. https://www.marketplace.org/2020/03/31/will-the-pandemic-mean-higher-health-care-costs-in-the-future/

Agarwal, S. C., and Sommers, B. D. (2020). Insurance coverage after job loss – The importance of the ACA during the Covid-associated Recession. *The New England Journal of Medicine, 383*, 1,603–1,606. https://doi.org/10.1056/NEJMp2023312

American Hospital Association. (2021). *Detailed summary of no surprises act.* American Hospital Association Legislative Advisory. Accessed July 2021. https://www.aha.org/system/files/media/file/2021/01/detailed-summary-of-no-surprises-act-advisory-1-14-21.pdf

Baicker, K., Chandra, A., Skinner, J. S., and Wennberg, J. E. (2004). Who you are and where you live: How race and geography affect the treatment of Medicare beneficiaries. *Health Affairs, 23*, 33–44. https://doi.org/10.1377/hlthaff.var.33

Batty, M, Gibbs, C, and Ippolito, B. (2018). Unlike medical spending, medical bills in collections decrease with patients' age. *Health Affairs, 37* (8), 1,257–1,264. https://doi.org/10.1377/hlthaff.2018.0349

Brown, R. L., and Moloney, M. E. (2019). Intersectionality, work, and well-being: The effects of gender and disability. *Gender & Society, 33*(1), 94–122. https://doi.org/10.1177/0891243218800636

Caraballo, C., Valero-Elizondo, J., Khera, R., Mahajan, S., Grandhi, G. R., Virani, S. S., Mszar, R., Krumholz, H. M., and Nasir, K. (2020). Burden and consequences of financial hardship from medical bills among nonelderly adults with diabetes mellitus in the United States. *Circulation: Cardiovascular Quality and Outcomes, 13*(2), e006139. https://doi.org/10.1161/CIRCOUTCOMES.119.006139

Carr, D. (2019). *Golden years? Social inequality in later life.* Russell Sage.

Centers for Disease Control and Prevention. (2021). *Older adults and COVID-19.* Accessed July 2021. https://www.cdc.gov/coronavirus/2019-ncov/need-extra-precautions/older-adults.html#anchor_1606159374271

Centers for Medicare and Medicaid Services. (2020). *National health expenditure accounts (NHEA) – National health expenditures by type of expenditure and program.* Accessed July 2021. https://www.cms.gov/Research-Statistics-Data-and-Systems/Statistics-Trends-and-Reports/NationalHealthExpendData

Choi, S. L., and Blackburn, J. (2018). Patterns and factors associated with medical expenses and health insurance premium payments. *Journal of Financial Counseling and Planning, 29*(1), 6–18. https://doi.org/10.1891/1052-3073.29.1.6

Choi, S. L., Carr, D., and Namkung E. H. (2021). Physical disability and older adults' perceived food and economic insecurity during the COVID-19 pandemic. *Journal of Gerontology: Social Sciences,* gbab162. https://doi.org/10.1093/geronb/gbab162

Coile, C. C. (2015). Economic determinants of workers' retirement decisions. *Journal of Economic Surveys, 29*(4), 830–853. https://doi.org/10.1111/joes.12115

Congressional Research Service. (2019). *H.R.3630 – No surprises act.* Accessed July 2021. https://www.congress.gov/bill/116th-congress/house-bill/3630

Cook, K., Dranove, D., and Sfekas, A. (2010). Does major illness cause financial catastrophe? *Health Services Research, 45*(2), 418–436. https://doi.org/10.1111/j.1475-6773.2009.01049.x

Cubanski, J., Swoope, C., Dmico, A., and Neuman, T. (2014). *How much is enough? Out-of-pocket spending among Medicare beneficiaries: A chartbook.* Kaiser Family Foundation. http://files.kff.org/attachment/how-much-is-enough-out-of-pocket-spending-among-medicare-beneficiaries-a-chartbook-report

Cunningham P. J. (2010). The growing financial burden of health care: National and state trends, 2001–2006. *Health Affairs, 29*(5), 1,037–1,044. https://doi.org/10.1377/hlthaff.2009.0493

Cutler, D. M. (2003). Employee costs and the decline in health insurance coverage. *Frontiers in Health Policy Research, 6*(1), 27–53.

Dafny, L. S. (2010). Are health insurance markets competitive? *American Economic Review, 100*(4), 1,399–1,431. https://doi.org/10.1257/aer.100.4.1399

Dafny, L. S., Duggan, M., and Ramanarayanan, S. (2012). Paying a premium on your premium? Consolidation in the U.S. health insurance industry. *American Economic Review, 102*(2), 1, 161–1,185. https://doi.org/10.1257/aer.102.2.1161

Domowitz, I., and Sartain, R. L. (1999). Determinants of the consumer bankruptcy decision. *Journal of Finance, 54*(1), 403–420. https://doi.org/10.1111/0022-1082.00110

Duchon, L. M., and Schoen, C. (2001). Experiences of working-age adults in the individual insurance market: Findings from the commonwealth fund 2001 health insurance survey. *The Commonwealth Fund, 514,* 1–4.

Enthoven, A. C., and Fuchs, V. R. (2006). Employment-based health insurance: Past, present, and future. *Health Affairs, 25*(6), 1,538–1,547. https://doi.org/10.1377/hlthaff.25.6.1538

Findling, M. G., Blendon, R. J., and Benson, J. M. (2020). *Delayed care with harmful health consequences – Reported experiences from national surveys during Coronavirus disease 2019.* JAMA Network. https://jamanetwork.com/channels/health-forum/fullarticle/2774358

Fisher, E. S., Wennberg, D. E., Stukel, T. A., Gottlieb, D. J., Lucas, F. L., and Pinder, E. L. (2003). The implications of regional variations in Medicare spending. Part 1: The content, quality, and accessibility of care. *Annals of Internal Medicine, 138*(4), 273–287. https://doi.org/10.7326/0003-4819-138-4-200302180-00006

Gilligan, M., Suitor, J. J., Rurka, M., and Silverstein, M. (2020). Multigenerational social support in the face of the COVID-19 pandemic. *Journal of Family Theory & Review, 12*(4), 431–447. https://doi.org/10.1111/jftr.12397

Gould, E. (2020). *Lack of paid sick days and large numbers of uninsured increase risks of spreading the Coronavirus.* Economic Policy Institute. https://www.epi.org/blog/lack-of-paid-sick-days-and-large-numbers-of-uninsured-increase-risks-of-spreading-the-coronavirus/

Gruber, J., and McKnight, R. (2003). Why did employee health insurance contributions rise? *Journal of Health Economics, 22*(6), 1,085–1,104. https://doi.org/10.1016/j.jhealeco.2003.06.001

Health and Retirement Study. (2020). *2020 HRS COVID-19 Project data description and usage.* The Institute for Social Research, The University of Michigan. https://hrsdata.isr.umich.edu/sites/default/files/documentation/data-descriptions/2020COVID_DD_0.pdf

Himmelstein, D. U., Thorne, D., Warren, E., and Woolhandler, S. (2009). Medical bankruptcy in the United States, 2007: Results of a national study. *The American Journal of Medicine, 122*(8), 741–746. https://doi.org/10.1016/j.amjmed.2009.04.012

Hoadley, J., Keith, K., and Lucia, K. (2020a, December 18). Unpacking the No Surprises Act: An opportunity to protect millions. *Health Affairs Blog.* https://doi.org/10.1377/hblog20201217.247010

Hoadley, J., Lucia, K., and Fuchs, B. (2020b, December 17). Surprise billing protections: Help finally arrives for millions of Americans. *The Commonwealth Fund.* https://www.commonwealthfund.org/blog/2020/surprise-billing-protections-cusp-becoming-law

Holahan, J. (2014). *Will premiums skyrocket in 2015?* Urban Institute. Accessed July 2021. http://www.rwjf.org/content/dam/farm/reports/issue_briefs/2014/rwjf413410

Hong, G.-S., and Kim, S. (2000). Out-of-pocket health care expenditure patterns and financial burden across the life cycle stages. *Journal of Consumer Affairs, 34*(2), 291–313. https://doi.org/10.1111/j.1745-6606.2000.tb00095.x

Institute of Medicine. (2002). *Health insurance is a family matter.* National Academies Press. https://doi.org/10.17226/10503

Jacobson, G., Feder, J., and Radley, D. C. (2020, October 6). COVID-19's impact on older workers: Employment, income, and Medicare spending. *The Commonwealth Fund.* https://www.commonwealthfund.org/publications/issue-briefs/2020/oct/covid-19-impact-older-workers-employment-income-medicare

Jacoby, M. G., Sullivan, T. A., and Warren, E. (2000). *Medical problems and bankruptcy filings.* Rochester, NY: Norton's Bankruptcy Advisor.

Kaiser Family Foundation. (2019). *Health insurance coverage of the total population.* http://kff.org/other/state-indicator/total-population/

Kaiser Family Foundation. (2021). *Surprise medical bills: New protections for consumers take effect in 2022.* https://www.kff.org/private-insurance/fact-sheet/surprise-medical-bills-new-protections-for-consumers-take-effect-in-2022/#

Kielb, E. S., Rhyan, C. N., and Lee, J. A. (2017). Comparing health care financial burden with an alternative measure of unaffordability. *Inquiry: The Journal of Health Care Organization, Provision, and Financing, 54,* 46958017732960. https://doi.org/10.1177/0046958017732960

King, J. S. (2020). Covid-19 and the need for health care reform. *The New England Journal of Medicine, 382*(26), e104. https://doi.org/10.1056/NEJMp2000821

Kogan, M. D., Newacheck, P. W., Blumberg, S. J., Heyman, K. M., Strickland, B. B., Singh, G. K., and Zeni, M. B. (2010). State variation in underinsurance among children with special health care needs in the United States. *Pediatrics, 125*(4), 673–680. https://doi.org/10.1542/peds.2009-1055

Kornreich, E., Siegel, E., and Weinstein, D. (2021, January 12). No surprises: Congress enacts surprise bill law and adds mandatory billing transparency. *JD Supra.* https://www.jdsupra.com/legalnews/no-surprises-congress-enacts-surprise-5695751/

Kuh, D., Cooper, R., Hardy, R., Richards, M., and Ben-Shlomo, Y. (2014). *A life course approach to healthy ageing.* Oxford University Press.

Kuruvilla, S., Sadana, R., Montesinos, E. V., Beard, J., Vasdeki, J. F., Araujo de Carvalho, I., Thomas, R. B., Drisse, M. B., Daelmans, B., Goodman, T., Koller, T., Officer, A., Vogel, J., Valentine, N., Wootton, E., Banerjee, A., Magar, V., Neira, M., Bele, J., . . . Bustreo, F. (2018). A life-course approach to health: Synergy with sustainable development goals. *Bulletin of the World Health Organization, 96*(1), 42–50. https://doi.org/10.2471/BLT.17.198358

Li, Y., and Mutchler, J. E. (2020). Older adults and the economic impact of the COVID-19 pandemic. *Journal of Aging & Social Policy, 32*(4–5), 477–487. https://doi.org/10.1080/08959420.2020.1773191

Lucia, K., Giovannelli, J., Corlette, S., Volk, J., Palanker, D., Kona, M., and Curran, E. (2018, March 29). State regulation of coverage options outside of the Affordable Care Act: Limiting the risk to the individual market. *The Commonwealth Fund.* https://www.commonwealthfund.org/publications/fund-reports/2018/mar/state-regulation-coverage-options-outside-affordable-care-act

Madrian, B. C. (1994). Employment-based health insurance and job mobility: Is there evidence of job-lock? *The Quarterly Journal of Economics, 109*(1), 27–54. https://doi.org/10.2307/2118427

Maroto, M., Pettinicchio, D., and Patterson, A. C. (2019). Hierarchies of categorical disadvantage: Economic insecurity at the intersection of disability, gender, and race. *Gender & Society, 33*(1), 64–93. https://doi.org/10.1177/0891243218794648

Mulligan, J. M., and Castaneda, H. (2017). *Unequal coverage: The experience of health care reform in the United States.* New York University Press.

Ozieh, M. N., Bishu, K. G., Walker, R. J., Campbell, J. A., and Egede, L. E. (2016). Geographic variation in access among adults with kidney disease: Evidence from medical expenditure panel survey, 2002–2011. *BMC Health Services Research, 16*, 585–594. https://doi.org/10.1186/s12913-016-1844-1

Patient Protection and Affordable Care Act of 2010, 42 U.S.C. § *18001 et seq.* (2010). https://www.congress.gov/111/plaws/publ148/PLAW-111publ148.pdf

Pollitz, K., Rae, M., Claxton, G., Cox, C., and Levitt, L. (2020, February 10). An examination of surprise medical bills and proposals to protect consumers from them. *Health System Tracker.* https://www.healthsystemtracker.org/brief/an-examination-of-surprise-medical-bills-and-proposals-to-protect-consumers-from-them-3/

Radley, D. C., and Schoen, C. (2012). Geographic variation in access to care – The relationship with quality. *The New England Journal of Medicine, 367*, 3–6. https://doi.org/10.1056/NEJMp1204516

Richman, I. B., and Brodie, M. (2014). A national study of burdensome health care costs among non-elderly Americans. *BMC Health Services Research, 14*, 435. https://doi.org/10.1186/1472-6963-14-435

Rosso, R. J. (2021). *U.S. health care coverage and spending.* Congressional Research Service. https://fas.org/sgp/crs/misc/IF10830.pdf

Sawyer, S. M., Afifi, R. A., Bearinger, L. H., Blakemore, S. J., Dick, B., Ezeh, A. C., and Patton, G. C. (2012). Adolescence: A foundation for future health. *The Lancet, 379*(9826), 1630–1640. https://doi.org/10.1016/S0140-6736(12)60072-5

Scofea L. A. (1994). The development and growth of employer-provided health insurance. *Monthly Labor Review, 117*(3), 3–10.

Shandra, C. L. (2018). Disability as inequality: Social disparities, health disparities, and participation in daily activities. *Social Forces, 97*(1), 157–192. https://doi.org/10.1093/sf/soy031

Sheckter, C. C., Singh, P., Angelos, P., and Offodile, A. C. (2020). Surprise billing in surgical care episodes – Overview, ethical concerns, and policy solutions in light of COVID-19. *Annals of Surgery, 272*(4), e264–e265. https://doi.org/10.1097/SLA.0000000000004152

Sheehan, P., Sweeny, K., Rasmussen, B., Wils, A., Friedman, H. S., Mahon, J., Patton, G. C., Sawyer, S. M., Howard, E., Symons, J., Stenberg, K., Chalasani, S., Maharaj, N., Reavley, N., Shi, H., Fridman, M., Welsh, A., Nsofor, E., and Laski, L. (2017). Building the foundations for sustainable development: A case for global investment in the capabilities of adolescents. *The Lancet, 390*(10104), 1,792–1,806. https://doi.org/10.1016/S0140-6736(17)30872-3

Social Security Administration. (2021). *A guide to supplemental security income (SSI) for groups and organization*s. https://www.ssa.gov/pubs/EN-05-11015.pdf

Tunçalp, Ö., Were, W. M., MacLennan, C., Oladapo, O. T., Gülmezoglu, A. M., Bahl, R., Daelmans, B., Mathai, M., Say, L., Kristensen, F., Temmerman, M., and Bustreo, F. (2015). Quality of care for pregnant women and newborns-the WHO vision. *BJOG: An International Journal of Obstetrics and Gynecology, 122*(8), 1,045–1,049. https://doi.org/10.1111/1471-0528.13451

U.S. Census Bureau. (2019). *Health insurance coverage in the United States: 2018*. Accessed July 2021. https://www.census.gov/content/dam/Census/library/publications/2019/demo/p60-267.pdf

U.S. Census Bureau. (2020). *Health insurance historical tables HIC ACS* (HIC-4_ACS. Health insurance coverage status and type of coverage by state – All persons: 2008 to 2019) [Data set]. Accessed July 2021. https://www.census.gov/data/tables/time-series/demo/health-insurance/historical-series/hic.html

Wennberg, J. E., and Gittelsohn, A. M. (1973). Small area variations in health care delivery. *Science, 182*(117), 1,102–1,108. https://doi.org/10.1126/science.182.4117.1102

Wiltshire, J. C., Elder, K., Kiefe, C., and Allison, J. J. (2016). Medical debt and related financial consequences among older African American and White adults. *American Journal of Public Health, 106*(6), 1,086–1,091. https://doi.org/10.2105/AJPH.2016.303137

Wolfson, J. A., Leung, C. W., and Kullgren, J. T. (2020). Food as a critical social determinant of health among older adults during the Coronavirus disease 2019 (COVID-19) pandemic. *JAMA Health Forum, 1*(7), e200925. https://doi.org/10.1001/jamahealthforum.2020.0925

World Health Organization (WHO). (2016). *Standards for improving quality of maternal and newborn care in health facilities*. https://www.who.int/maternal_child_adolescent/documents/improving-maternal-newborn-care-quality/en/

World Health Organization (WHO). (2019). *Promoting health through the life course: A life course approach to health, human capital and sustainable development*. Accessed July 2021. https://www.who.int/life-course/publications/life-course-brief-20190220.pdf?ua=1

Chia-Li Chien

# 23 Accounting for Retirement Asset Distributions during the Decumulation Stage of Life

**Abstract:** Retirement planning research is focused heavily on the portfolio of finan-cial assets, which may not be appropriate for all clients. Liabilities are affected by state of residence and scaling factors must be applied to determine accurate spend-ing projections and advice. Liquid assets may not be sufficient to offset unmitigated or unmanaged risks. In this chapter, retirement assets accumulated pre-retirement, post-retirement liabilities, and retirement risks are reviewed using the retirement balance sheet as a basis. The question underlying the work presented in this chap-ter is: To have 90 percent retirement success rates, what relationship, if any, exists between scaling factors, portfolio of financial assets (PFA)/net worth, and home eq-uity assets (HEA)/net worth ratios with or without a home equity conversion mort-gage (HECM) among the U.S. population? Using a proprietary dataset, PFA/NW and HEA/NW ratios were calculated for couples and singles households with and with-out HECM eligibility and use. A positive correlation between scaling factors and PFA/NW ratios and a negative correlation between scaling factors and HEA/NW ratios was observed. It was determined that as a personal finance tool, home equity conver-sion mortgages should be considered whenever the goal of a decumulation plan is to enhance retiree spending and retirement success.

**Keywords:** retirement decumulation, reverse mortgage, home equity assets, home equity conversion mortgage, retirement balance sheet

## Introduction

Retirement is a universal goal for individuals. Individuals put their savings into liq-uid assets like tax-advantaged retirement accounts, taxable brokerage accounts, or savings accounts before they retire. Individuals can also place their savings into il-liquid assets (tangible or intangible assets), such as a primary residence, rental real estate, or direct business ownership. The goal is to use both liquid and illiquid as-sets to fund retirement.

Saving for retirement or the accumulation stage during one's working years can be compared to climbing a mountain (Pfau, 2017). When individuals reach the top

**Chia-Li Chien,** California Lutheran University

https://doi.org/10.1515/9783110727692-023

of the mountain or their retirement age, they start to distribute their assets to fund their retirement lifestyle. Using mountain climbing as an analogy to describe an individual's personal finance lifecycle helps individuals see the big picture of the accumulation and decumulation stages of a savings plan. However, many experienced climbers would argue that the descent from a mountain top can present more risks than climbing up (Pfau, 2017).

Individuals need to be resourceful when they are in the decumulation stage of life, just like when one climbs down a mountain. Experienced climbers assess risks with a mitigation plan when they descend. Individuals planning for retirement, too, need to look at household assets and liabilities in their entirety, and assess retirement risks before they determine how to make distributions during the decumulation stage to avoid outliving their retirement resources. The purpose of this chapter is to provide empirical insights into how this can be accomplished.

# The Retirement Balance Sheet

The process of personal finance can be described as a seven-step practice. During the first two steps, a financial decision maker collects relevant data and establishes goals (Grable et al., 2020). These two factors can be used to help develop a retirement balance sheet. In the absence of a retirement balance sheet, it might not be easy to determine if household assets will be sufficient to guarantee a successful retirement. Many financial planning professionals (FPPs) use commercial planning software to perform simulations of retirement success rates, but if the financial planner does not utilize all asset options offered by the software, such as home equity assets, rental real estate assets, and business equity assets, planning opportunities will be missed. Table 23.1 illustrates a household balance sheet specifically for retirement. What follows is a review of the elements comprising this type of balance sheet.

**Table 23.1:** Retirement Balance Sheet.

| Assets | Liabilities |
| --- | --- |
| Human capital assets | Fixed expenses |
|     Continuing career |     Essential living needs |
|     Part-time work |     Taxes |
| |     Debt repayment |
| Home equity assets | Discretionary expenses |
|     Primary resident |     Travel and leisure |
|     Second home |     Lifestyle improvements |

**Table 23.1** (continued)

| Assets | Liabilities |
|---|---|
| Portfolio of financial assets | Contingencies |
|     Checking/Savings |     Long-term care |
|     Brokerage |     Health care |
|     Retirement plans |     Other spending shocks |
|     Insurance and annuities | |
| Social capital | Legacy goals |
|     Social security |     Family |
|     Medicare |     Community and society |
|     Company pension | |
|     Family and community | |
| Rental real estate assets | |
| Business assets | |

*Sources*: Author's table from Chien (2019) and Pfau (2017).

## Retirement Assets

Assets in the retirement balance sheet, if managed properly, can generate needed retirement income to meet the retirement liabilities that support life-income goals associated with a desired lifestyle and expected longevity. Ideally, enough assets can be accumulated over the lifespan to support the retirement liabilities of contingency (i.e., liquidity needs) and meet any legacy goals.

Retirees may generate retirement income from assets in the retirement balance sheet. The asset categories listed include human capital assets, home equity assets, portfolio of financial assets, social capital, rental real estate assets, and business assets. Some FPPs may narrowly focus on financial portfolio assets (Chien, 2019), including liquid assets, such as qualified retirement accounts (tax-advantaged), nonqualified accounts (taxable), or tax-free accounts like Roth IRAs or Roth 401(k)s in the United States (Chien, 2019). FPPs help clients measure probabilities (e.g., success rates) of generating retirement income from financial portfolio assets against retirement needs. It is, nonetheless, important that retirees be resourceful in looking to other retirement balance sheet asset areas to cover retirement income needs.

Using human capital assets to fund living expenses before retirement or to delay claiming Social Security (or other forms of social insurance) is common and achieved by working longer or part-time. For many retirees, a government pension is the major source of retirement income. Unfortunately, for many, this source of income may be insufficient to protect against retirement risks. Private pensions can also be disappointingly inadequate depending on an employer's defined-benefit or defined-contribution policy. However, when working longer is not an option, and with limited social capital assets, individuals may be able to borrow against housing equity assets to fund their spending needs.

It is worth noting that rental real estate assets and business assets have been shown in prior research to be riskier than residential real estate. Also, those assets may not be available as collateral in reverse mortgages (RM) or home equity lines of credit (HELOC). These risky assets are illiquid and may not meet the retirement need in a timely manner.

## Retirement Liabilities

Liabilities include fixed expenses, discretionary expenses, contingencies, and legacy goals. Table 23.1 itemizes fixed retirement liability expenses to include lifestyle living expenses, taxes, and debt payments, all of which are affected by homeownership. An increase in homeownership correlates with increasing trends in borrowing against home equity assets (Collins et al., 2020). Homeownership, unlike rent, can provide stable housing expenses. Mortgage interest can be tax deductible up to a limit. Finally, if there is a need, a home can be used to fund retirement living or health shock expenses (Collins et al., 2020). Home equity assets can be used to offset retirement liabilities; hence, retirees often prefer to remain in their homes. Home equity assets can provide needed retirement income when life retirement income falls short of needs.

As noted above, retirees generally prefer to maintain homeownership during retirement, especially those with limited social capital assets like pensions or defined benefits. Many individuals tend to leverage against their home equity assets (e.g., mortgage or line of credit but not a reverse mortgage) to generate necessary retirement income (Collins et al., 2020). Retirees with legacy goals tend to have limited liabilities against the home equity assets (Collins et al., 2020).

Financial planning professionals often recommend keeping debt to a minimum when approaching retirement or eliminating debt altogether when there is no income generated from human capital assets (Society of Actuaries, 2011). Reducing debt payments across fixed balance sheet liabilities helps relieve the fear of outliving retirement assets.

## Retirement Risks

Accumulating enough financial portfolio assets is one of the solutions leading to a successful retirement. If risks are not properly mitigated or managed, retirees may face the consequences of outliving their retirement assets (Milevsky and Abaimova, 2006). Table 23.2 lists risks associated with assets and liabilities in the retirement balance sheet. Human capital assets are subject to a retiree's ability to generate income. For some, the capacity to earn income may be reduced (Pfau, 2018) due to health shocks (Turner and Chien, 2020) or their attitude toward work (Quadagno, 2014). Inflation, deflation, or the economy could affect the value of home equity assets, rental real estate assets, business equity assets, portfolios of financial assets, and fixed expense liabilities. Purchasing power may erode the portfolio of financial assets (Pfau, 2018). Additionally, some retirees may feel limited to spending up to their ability to generate retirement income from the portfolio of financial assets (Pfau, 2018) to support the fixed expenses and discretionary liabilities.

**Table 23.2:** Risks Associated with Retirement Balance Sheet.

| Assets Risks | Liabilities Risks |
|---|---|
| Human capital assets | Fixed expenses |
|    Earning capacity |    Longevity |
|    Health shocks |    Inflation |
| |    Spending constraint |
| Home equity assets | Discretionary expenses |
|    Inflation |    Spending shocks |
| Portfolio of financial assets | Contingencies |
|    Investment risks |    Spending shocks |
|    Withdrawal risks |    Health shocks |
|    Inflation | |
| Social capital | Legacy goals |
|    Policy changes |    Competing objectives |
|    Benefits reduction | |
| Rental real estate assets | |
|    Economic changes | |
| Business assets | |
|    Economic changes | |

*Sources*: Chatterjee (2016), Chien (2019), Milevsky and Abaimova (2006), Pfau (2018).

The poor return or sequence of return risk (i.e., retire at the low or high of the market) will impact how much retirees can withdraw from their portfolio of financial assets (Pfau, 2018). If not careful, the withdrawal may deplete the portfolio of financial assets too early. Today, scientific advances enable retirees to live longer, but the longer the retiree lives, the smaller the amount that can be withdrawn from a portfolio of financial assets (Pfau, 2018). Often, the fear of outliving retirement assets is greater than the fear of death, sometimes unnecessarily inhibiting decumulation.

Spending shocks include rising healthcare costs, potential long-term care needs, and reductions in health status. Households may face additional spending shocks such as divorce, unforeseen home repairs, and elder scams. These spending shocks will unexpectedly deplete a portfolio of financial assets too early. Finally, retirees may potentially decrease their cognitive capability. The decrease in cognitive capability may result in making suboptimal or uninformed financial decisions (Quadagno, 2014).

# Historical Perspective

Much of the past research focuses on generating retirement income from a portfolio of financial assets (Chien, 2019). The effectiveness of generating retirement income includes safe withdrawal rates, allocation of investments, methods of testing future market risks, and longevity risks (Chien, 2019). For example, it has generally been reported that the SAFEMAX withdrawal rate is 4.15 percent using a deterministic method but not Monte Carlo simulations (Bengen, 2006) combined with the risks of 30 years of fixed longevity and sequence of returns. A guideline of asset allocation was tested to expand the SAFEMAX withdrawal rate by using Monte Carlo simulations with various asset allocation combinations with Ibbotson Associates data since 1962 from 10 to 40 years longevity (Pfau, 2012). It was determined that the 4.15 percent rule may be too aggressive. The SAFEMAX withdrawal rate, asset allocation, future market risks, and longevity risks become practical tools for financial decision makers in the context of retirement planning, but typical rules often fall short when decision makers only look at one retirement balance sheet asset – the portfolio of financial assets.

## The Use of Reverse Mortgage Globally

Homeowners may access home equity assets by using a mortgage, a second mortgage, a one-time loan, a home equity line of credit (HELOC), or a reverse mortgage, if qualified. A mortgage loan or HELOC requires the borrower to repay the amount owed plus interest. A reverse mortgage is a loan, but there is no repayment of the amount owed until the borrower dies, sells, or moves out of the home (Pfau, 2018).

Leveraging home equity assets is on the rise. In the United States, the number of people near retirement or in retirement using home mortgage debt tripled from 1980 to 2015 (Collins et al., 2020). Reasons that this trend will likely continue include (a) a low mortgage interest environment, (b) having often been advised not to pay off their mortgage, (c) tax-deductibility of mortgage interest, and (d) a need to fund consumption (Collins et al., 2020). In this regard, a reverse mortgage could help supplement fixed expenses (i.e., living expenses) and contingency expenses (e.g., healthcare or other spending shocks) in the liabilities section of the retirement balance sheet. In concept, a reverse mortgage is a logical choice for eligible households. The reverse mortgage is offered in many countries; however, countries like Singapore (Fong et al., 2020), India (Gupta and Kumar, 2017), and Australia (Australian Securities and Investment

Commission, 2018) have seen limited use of reverse mortgages. Tables 23.3 and 23.4 provide an overview of the RM product name, government oversight authority, and where consumers can obtain an RM.

**Table 23.3:** Reverse Mortgages in North America and Europe.

| Country (First Offered Year) | Types | Government Oversight | Offer by |
|---|---|---|---|
| U.S.A. (since 1961), HECM (1980s) | Home equity conversion mortgage or HECM | U.S. Department of Housing & Urban Development or HUD | Federal Housing Administration or FHA–approved lenders |
| Canada (since 1961) | Reverse mortgage | Financial Consumer Agency of Canada | 2 banks: HomeEquity Bank and Equitable Bank |
| UK (since 1965) | a. Equity release lifetime mortgage b. Home reversion plan | Investor's Compensation Scheme under Financial Conduct Authority | Approved banks or financial institutes |
| France | a. Viager occupe b. Viager libre | Ministry of the Economy, Finance and Recovery | Willing investors |

*Sources*: United States (Chen and Yang, 2020; Chien, 2019; Pfau, 2018); Canada (Canadian Centre for Elder Law Studies, 2006, 2007; Financial Consumer Agency of Canada, 2020); UK (Australian Securities and Investments Commission, 2018; Chou and Chang, 2014; Whait et al., 2019); France (Chou and Chang, 2014; Ministry of the Economy, Finance and Recovery, 2020).

**Table 23.4:** Reverse Mortgages in Asia.

| Country (First Offered Year) | Types | Government Oversight | Offer by |
|---|---|---|---|
| Australia (since 1990s) | a. Reverse mortgage b. Home reversion scheme c. Shared appreciation mortgage | Australian Securities & Investments Commission or ASIC | Banks |
| New Zealand | Reverse mortgage | Ministry of Social Development | Banks or approved-lenders |
| Singapore (since 1997) | Reverse mortgage | Housing Development Board | Insurance companies or banks |
| Korea (since 2010) | Joo Taek Yeon Keum or JTYK | The Korea Housing Finance Corporation or KHFC | Approved financial institutes |
| Taiwan (since 2013) | Reverse mortgage | Ministry of the Interior | Insurance companies or banks |

**Table 23.4** (continued)

| Country (First Offered Year) | Types | Government Oversight | Offer by |
|---|---|---|---|
| China–Hong Kong (since 2011) | Reverse Mortgage Programme or RMP | Hong Kong Mortgage Corporation or HKMC | HKMC Insurance Limited (HKMCI) |
| China (since 2014) | Reverse mortgage | The China Banking Regulatory Commission | Privatized |
| India (since 2007) | Reverse mortgage | National Housing Banks | Registered Primary Lending Institutions |

*Sources*: Australia (Australian Securities and Investments Commission, 2018; Whait et al., 2019); New Zealand (Australian Securities and Investments Commission, 2018); Singapore (Fong et al., 2020); Korea (Heo et al., 2016; Yang et al., 2020); Taiwan (Chou and Chang, 2014; Lu and Cai, 2018); China–Hong Kong (Han et al., 2017); China (Hanewald et al., 2020); India (Gupta and Kumar, 2017; National Housing Bank, 2020).

Home equity assets typically account for a large portion of a retiree's assets in the retirement balance sheet. They peak from the ages of 54 to 63. Home equity assets were 60 percent of the total net worth (median) in 2016 in the United States (Bricker et al., 2019). Singapore reported that 60 percent of an individual's total net worth was home equity assets in 2018 (Fong et al., 2020). In China, home equity assets represent 75 percent of an individual's total net worth in rural areas and 85 percent in urban areas (Hanewald et al., 2020). Retirement income planning with home equity assets or reverse mortgage use becomes an attractive alternative allowing retirees to remain in their home without repayment, if qualified.

## Reverse Mortgage Eligibility and Funding Features

The eligibility age for a reverse mortgage, for most borrowers, is 55 years for the countries listed in Tables 23.3 and 23.4. However, the U.S. minimum age limit is age 62 for an individual or the youngest of a couple (Pfau, 2018). In Korea, the age is set at 60 (Heo et al., 2016). Taiwan has the most flexibility depending on which bank offers the product; the minimum ages may be 55, 60, 63, or 65 (Lu and Cai, 2018).

A borrower's primary residence often is the underlying collateral. In the United States, the primary residence has to be a single home or an FHA-approved property such as a condo (Chien, 2019). Singapore has the most complex property eligibility rules due to 80 percent of the total population living in a Housing Development Board or HDB public housing program (Fong et al., 2020). The HDB public housing program grants 99 years of ownership under a leasehold system to allow rotation of ownership over time (Fong et al., 2020).

Tables 23.3 and 23.4 illustrate two different types of reverse mortgages. With the first type, retirees receive payment from their home equity assets. The second type is a sell and leaseback option. Australia (Australian Securities and Investments Commission, 2018), the UK (Whait et al., 2019), and France (Lu and Cai, 2018) have the sell and lease back option. Regardless of the type available, the majority of countries shown in the tables have the type of RM where retirees receive payments.

There are two categories of RM payments to retirees: lump sum and monthly payment. The monthly payment is most often used. However, a borrower's amount depends on the maximum dollar amount cap or a loan-to-value (LTV) cap. The maximum dollar amount cap in Singapore is 70 percent of the prevailing value throughout the loan tenure (Fong et al., 2020). In the United States, HECM was capped at $765,600 in 2020 (U.S. Department of Housing and Urban Development, 2020). Korea's JTYK caps at SKW$900 million or approximately USD 818,568 (Heo et al., 2016). Taiwan's RM caps range from NT$5.3 to NT$8.76 million or approximately USD 188,146 to USD 310,974 (Lu and Cai, 2018). In the UK and Australia, the LTV is capped at 50 percent. Life expectancy is used to determine the monthly tenure payment in most countries except Taiwan, which has a fixed number of years with a maximum cap of 30 years.

## The Limited Use of Reverse Mortgages

RMs have not been strategically used as a retirement planning tool worldwide (Knaack et al., 2020). Reasons for limited use worldwide include:
- Lack of policy to protect RM borrowers from default from unexpected spending shocks (Knaack et al., 2020); a decrease in cognitive capability may also result in default due to forgetting to pay property taxes (Chien, 2019) in the United States.
- Competing legacy goals; retirees generally prefer to pass on the home equity assets to heirs (Chatterjee, 2016), especially in Singapore (Fong et al., 2020), China (Han et al., 2017), China–Hong Kong, Korea (Han et al., 2017), Japan (Kobayashi et al., 2017), and Taiwan (Lu and Cai, 2018).
- Competing social benefits; in the United States, to qualify for social benefits such as Medicaid, the primary residence is an exempt asset (Chatterjee, 2016).
- Limited education or awareness of RMs; in the United States (Pfau, 2018), Korea (Yang et al., 2020), and New Zealand (Australian Securities and Investments Commission, 2018) listed in Tables 23.3 and 23.4, RM borrowers must obtain RM training and counseling to be eligible.

The target market of RMs tends to be low-income retirees in countries like Korea (Heo et al., 2016), Australia (Australian Securities and Investments Commission, 2018), China–Hong Kong (Han et al., 2017), Taiwan (Lu and Cai, 2018), and India (Gupta and Kumar, 2017). In India, in addition to low-income, the RM target market is focused on less-educated retirees (Gupta and Kumar, 2017). In the United States, less-educated retirees (lower than high school) are less likely to use RMs (Chatterjee, 2016).[1]

# A Research Study

Retirement strategies using home equity assets or RMs could improve retirement success rates. Retirement success has been defined as retirees maintaining a positive portfolio balance at death (Chien, 2019). There is limited research in retirement success rates when deploying all retirement assets from the retirement balance sheet. The retirement liabilities including fixed expenses, discretionary expenses, and contingency shocks could impact how fast a retiree depletes their retirement assets. Hence, how much retirees could spend depends on available retirement asset deployment to have a successful retirement. Scaling factors, defined as how much retirees could spend based on the state of residence and age group and still achieve successful retirement (Chien, 2019), help researchers evaluate financial readiness for retirement. There are reasons why FPPs do not advance reverse mortgages in financial plans, even though an RM could be easily accomplished in conjunction with the retirement balance sheet. Moreover, there is limited research into the extent of house-richness and cash-poorness. In this regard, the remainder of this chapter discusses results from a study that was undertaken to facilitate more knowledge about this topic.

## Distribution of Retirement Assets

The following research question was used to guide the study: To have 90 percent retirement success rates, what relationship, if any, exists between scaling factors, PFA/NW ratios, and HEA/NW ratios with or without RM (HECM) retirement strategies, in the U.S. retiree population? To answer this question it is first important to understand terms. The expression *house-rich* refers to the home equity assets of the retirement balance sheet as a significant part of net worth. The expression *cash-poor* often means the value of the portfolio of financial assets as a less significant part of

---

1 Home equity assets are the largest portion of net worth for low-income families living in the United States (Collins et al., 2020). In Korea, baby boomers are mostly house-rich and cash-poor. RM use becomes a form of retirement supplement due to limited government retirement income (Heo et al., 2016). The average borrowers of RMs in Australia are also house-rich and cash-poor. Low-income retirees could benefit from RMs to achieve a modest retirement lifestyle (Australian Securities & Investments Commission, 2018). Singapore has 90 percent homeownership, the largest in the world. Among those, the average portfolio of financial assets is approximately 15 percent. However, only about one-quarter of house-rich and cash-poor retirees have shown an interest in using RMs (Fong et al., 2020).

net worth. To see if an individual is (or a group are) house-rich, a ratio can be determined by dividing home equity asset value (HEA) by net worth (NW) or HEA/NW ratio. Cash-poor can similarly be determined using a ratio calculated by dividing the portfolio of financial assets (PFA) value by net worth or PFA/NW ratio.

It is safe to assume that every retiree wants to have a successful retirement. Successful retirement means that the retiree maintains a positive portfolio of financial assets at death. The retirement liabilities depend on a retiree's lifestyle (Chien, 2019). The relationship of how much retirees could spend (scaling factor) and house-rich (HEA/NW) or cash-poor (PFA/NW) ratios can provide a reference to success. The relationship of scaling factors and these ratios can help FPPs facilitate needed collaboration with clients using retirement balance sheets as part of a comprehensive financial plan or a modular retirement income plan.

## Data

Not every homeowner can qualify or should use home equity assets during retirement. The ideal net worth range is USD 250,000 to USD 499,999 to achieve 90 percent retirement success rates (Chien, 2019) for those qualified for RMs (HECM) in the United States. Chien (2019) extended past research from the Trinity study (Cooley et al., 1999) and the U.S. population asset study (Lichtenstein, 2012). Instead of using fictitious household retirement balance sheets, Chien (2019) used retirees' household retirement balance sheets from two major datasets (Chien, 2019). The primary retirees' household retirement assets data came from the U.S. retirees' population using the U.S. Census Survey of Income and Program Participation or SIPP (U.S. Census Bureau, 2011) in 2011. There were 7,563 households with 2,828 couples and 4,735 singles households age 62 and above who already claimed Social Security retirement benefits. Each of the SIPP households represented an estimated weighted population in their geographic area. The retirees' household liability data came from a consumer expenditure survey or CES (Bureau of Labor Statistics, 2011). CES was further divided into five different age groups (62–64, 65–69, 70–74, 75–79, and 80 and above) by each state. The age groups represented the various spending amount during retirement, not a fixed amount.

The market performance of stocks and bonds came from Morningstar from 1926 to 2016. The simulation did not use a fixed average market return, but instead a rolling market return to factor ups and downs of the economy or sequence of return risks. The allocation of the stocks and bonds ranged from 0 percent to 100 percent in increments of 25 percent instead of a fixed percentage. Additionally, instead of using 20- or 30-fixed retirement years for each retiree, the simulation used the U.S. Social Security Administration (SSA) Period Life Table (SSA, 2014) to determine the probability of survival for each age from age 62 up to age 119. Nine different retirement strategies were simulated to compare which one or combination of the retirement strategies achieved the highest scaling factors at 90 percent success rates. The scaling factor results expressed how much retirees could spend from 0 percent up to 300 percent in increments of 25 percent in retirees' domicile state lifestyle.

## Results

Datasets derived from Chien (2019) were used to calculate ratios of home equity assets to net worth and portfolio of financial assets to net worth. Table 23.5 shows that the national weighted average scaling factors for couples was 141.1 percent, and for singles was 110.7 percent, to achieve 90 percent success rates. The HEA/NW ratio was 39.9 percent for couples households and 52.1 percent for singles households. The PFA/NW ratio was 42.1 percent for couples and 31.9 percent for singles. Table 23.5 also displays the national weighted average for HECM (RM) eligible and not eligible households and the related ratios. Home equity assets households who were eligible for HECM were found to be more likely to have a successful retirement with a smaller portfolio of financial assets.

**Table 23.5:** Weighted Average Scaling Factors, PFA/NW, HEA/NW by Couples and Singles Households.

| | Couples Weighted Average | | | | | Singles Weighted Average | | | | |
|---|---|---|---|---|---|---|---|---|---|---|
| | Scaling Factors | PFA/ NW Ratio | HEA/ NW Ratio | N | % of N | Scaling Factors | PFA/ NW Ratio | HEA/ NW Ratio | N | % of N |
| HECM not eligible | 114.2% | 55.5% | 15.6% | 621 | 22% | 81.1% | 55.4% | 13.4% | 1,792 | 38% |
| HECM eligible | 148.7% | 40.4% | 42.9% | 2,207 | 78% | 128.3% | 28.5% | 57.7% | 2,943 | 62% |
| Total | 141.1% | 42.1% | 39.9% | 2,828 | | 110.7% | 31.9% | 52.1% | 4,735 | |

*Note.* HEA = home equity assets; NW = net worth; PFA = portfolio of financial assets.

Figure 23.1 illustrates couples households, whereas Figure 23.2 illustrates singles households. Each figure shows the correlation of the weighted average of PFA/NW and HEA/NW ratios with scaling factors with success rates set at 90 percent. Both Figures 23.1 and 23.2 show a positive correlation between scaling factors and PFA/ NW ratios and a negative correlation between scaling factors and HEA/NW ratios. The higher the scaling factors, the higher the PFA/NW ratio. However, the higher the scaling factors, the lower the HEA/NW ratio. In other words, to maintain the average state retirement lifestyle, PFA/NW and HEA/NW ratios do have a relationship or correlation with the scaling factors.

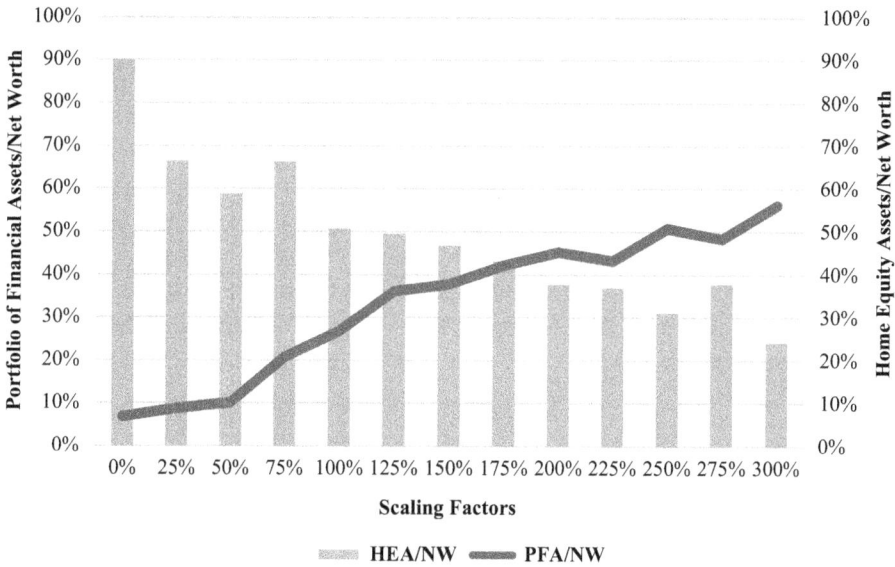

**Figure 23.1:** Weighted Average PFA/NW and HEA/NW Ratios by Scaling Factors for Couples Households.

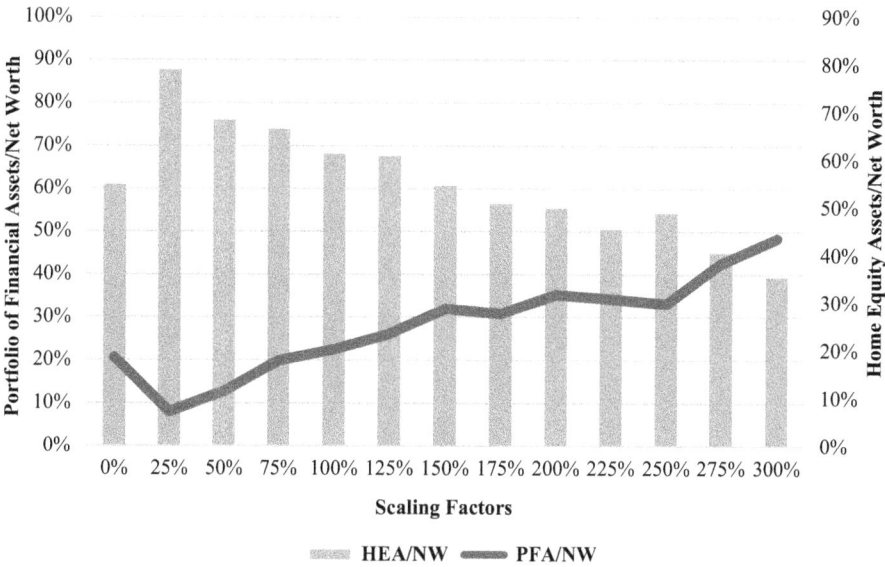

**Figure 23.2:** Weighted Average PFA/NW and HEA/NW Ratios by Scaling Factors for Singles Households.

Figures 23.3 (couples) and 23.4 (singles) illustrate the relationships between scaling factors, PFA/NW ratios, and HEA/NW ratios for the retiree households that owned their home and are HECM eligible. In Figure 23.3, regarding couples households with the HECM strategy, the weighted average of HEA/NW ratio was 57.1 percent compared to 50.6 percent when the scaling factor was at 100 percent in Figure 23.1, which does not use home equity assets. However, the PFA/NW ratio was 24.5 percent in Figure 23.3 using HECM strategy compared to without HECM strategy of 26.8 percent in Figure 23.1 when the scaling factor was at 100 percent. Couples and singles who expect or desire to spend more than the weighted average retirement lifestyle expense will need to have higher PFA/NW ratios but lower HEA/NW ratios to have successful retirements.

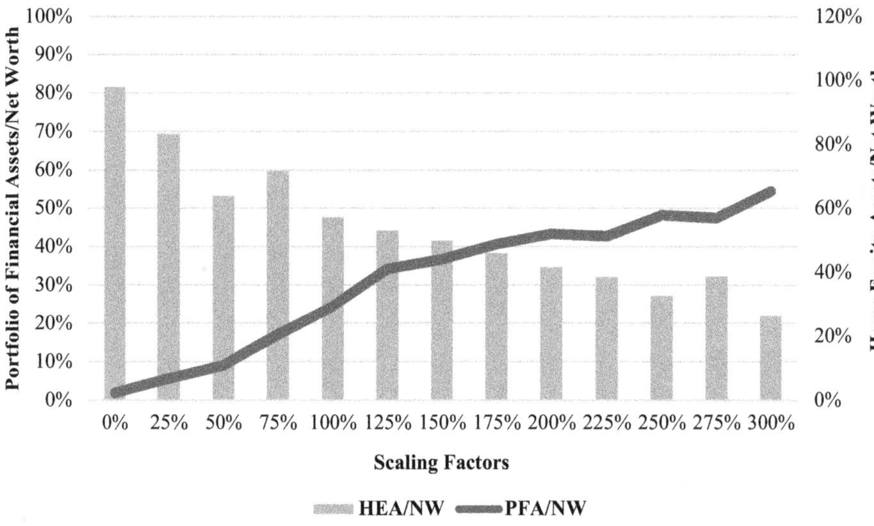

**Figure 23.3:** Weighted Average PFA/NW and HEA/NW Ratios by Scaling Factors of Couples Households with Owned Homes and HECM Eligibility.

Table 23.6 shows the weighted average for scaling factors less than 100 percent compared to equal and greater than 100 percent and up to 300 percent, along with the PFA/NW and HEA/NW ratios for couples and singles households. The weighted average PFA/NW ratio was 44.9 percent, whereas the weighted average HEA/NW ratio was 37.2 percent for couples households when the scaling factor was greater than and equal to 100 percent. For singles households that had scaling factors greater than and equal to 100 percent, the weighted average PFA/NW ratio was 35.1 percent and the weighted average HEA/NW ratio was 48.8 percent.

Scaling factors for households that were HECM eligible used the HECM during retirement in the simulation. The table is sorted by scaling factors from smallest to largest.

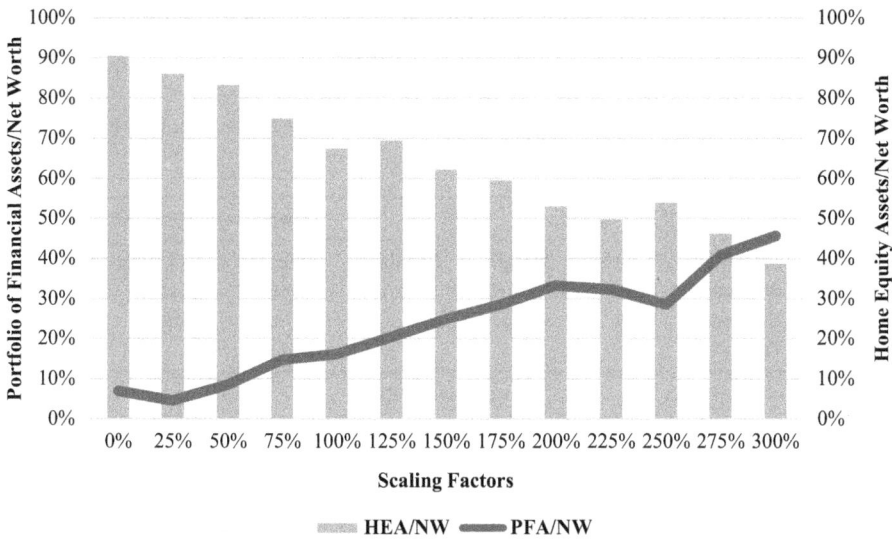

**Figure 23.4:** Weighted Average PFA/NW and HEA/NW Ratios by Scaling Factors of Singles Households with Owned Homes and HECM Eligibility.

**Table 23.6:** Weighted Average PFA/HW and HEA/HW Ratios by Scaling Factors for Couples and Singles Households.

| Scaling Factor | All Households | | Owned Home and HECM Eligible | |
|---|---|---|---|---|
| | Weighted PFA/NW Ratio | Weighted HEA/NW Ratio | Weighted PFA/NW Ratio | Weighted HEA/NW Ratio |
| | Couples | | | |
| <100% | 16.5% | 64.1% | 13.8% | 70.0% |
| ≥100% to 300% | 44.9% | 37.2% | 43.4% | 39.9% |
| | Singles | | | |
| <100% | 16.1% | 68.3% | 11.6% | 78.9% |
| ≥100% to 300% | 35.1% | 48.8% | 31.4% | 54.2% |

*Note.* HEA = home equity assets; PFA = portfolio of financial assets; NW = net worth.

Table 23.6 shows that couples and singles households who owned their home and were HECM eligible could afford a lower PFA/NW ratio and higher HEA/NW ratio than all households. It should be noted that the national weighted averages did not reflect state-specific lifestyle factors. Utilizing each state-specific scaling factor would clarify individual states' retirement liabilities to determine the efficacy of retirement spending options.

Table 23.7 provides the bottom and top five states for couples households sorted by scaling factors with PFA/NW and HEA/NW ratios.

**Table 23.7:** Weighted Average PFA/NW and HEA/NW Ratios by Scaling Factors for Couples Households Ranked by Bottom and Top Five States.

| Couples | All Households | | | Couples | Owned Home and HECM Eligible | | |
|---|---|---|---|---|---|---|---|
| | Weighted Average Scaling Factors | Weighted PFA/NW Ratio | Weighted HEA/NW Ratio | | Weighted Average Scaling Factors | Weighted PFA/NW Ratio | Weighted HEA/NW Ratio |
| | | | Bottom Five States | | | | |
| Alaska | 25.0% | 0.0% | 100.0% | Alaska | 25.0% | 0.0% | 100.0% |
| Wyoming | 95.1% | 4.3% | 87.4% | Maine | 105.6% | 45.9% | 40.8% |
| Alabama | 112.1% | 29.3% | 40.4% | Wyoming | 108.8% | 15.5% | 77.9% |
| Mississippi | 116.4% | 25.5% | 46.3% | Nebraska | 109.1% | 66.8% | 26.8% |
| Maine | 117.2% | 42.8% | 43.3% | Mississippi | 113.3% | 25.2% | 46.9% |
| | | | Top Five States | | | | |
| Oregon | 184.3% | 41.3% | 37.2% | Delaware | 171.8% | 33.7% | 29.4% |
| South Dakota | 188.2% | 54.5% | 19.8% | Iowa | 172.1% | 46.0% | 32.4% |
| Arizona | 190.7% | 39.2% | 39.0% | South Dakota | 179.4% | 54.6% | 19.7% |
| Nevada | 191.6% | 34.7% | 35.8% | Arizona | 187.9% | 46.7% | 32.1% |
| Delaware | 300.0% | 57.1% | 40.4% | DC | 300.0% | 57.1% | 40.4% |

*Note.* HEA = home equity assets; PFA = portfolio of financial assets; NW = net worth.

Scaling factors for households that were HECM eligible used the HECM during retirement in the simulation. The table is sorted by scaling factors from smallest to largest.

When comparing the popular retirement state of Arizona to all states, there is modestly more spending available using HECM strategies with PFA/NW and HEA/NW. Table 23.8 provides the bottom and top five states for singles households sorted by scaling factors with PFA/NW and HEA/NW ratios. The bottom five states (i.e., Alaska, Alabama, Arkansas, Louisiana, and Mississippi) did not reach 100 percent of the weighted scaling factors. With the HECM strategy, only three states (i.e., Alaska, Alabama, and Louisiana) were below 100 percent of the weighted scaling factors.

Scaling factors for households that were HECM eligible used the HECM during retirement in the simulation. The table is sorted by scaling factors from smallest to largest.

Figure 23.5 further breaks down the weighted average scaling factors into net worth groups. The figure shows the relation to PFA/NW and HEA/NW ratios for couples households who were HECM eligible. Figure 23.6 shows the same data for singles

**Table 23.8:** Weighted Average PFA/NW and HEA/NW Ratios by Success Rates for Singles Households Ranked by Bottom and Top Five States.

| Singles | All Households | | | Singles | Owned Home and HECM Eligible | | |
|---|---|---|---|---|---|---|---|
| | Weighted Average Scaling Factors | Weighted PFA/NW Ratio | Weighted HEA/NW Ratio | | Weighted Average Scaling Factors | Weighted PFA/NW Ratio | Weighted HEA/NW Ratio |
| | | | Bottom Five States | | | | |
| Alaska | 49.6% | 64.0% | 34.9% | Alaska | 40.5% | 0.0% | 97.5% |
| Alabama | 80.4% | 17.4% | 77.9% | Alabama | 89.5% | 17.0% | 78.5% |
| Arkansas | 86.0% | 19.1% | 55.4% | Louisiana | 92.4% | 26.5% | 56.0% |
| Louisiana | 86.6% | 31.6% | 50.0% | Mississippi | 101.6% | 13.7% | 69.8% |
| Mississippi | 88.1% | 12.6% | 66.1% | Arkansas | 103.7% | 17.7% | 56.0% |
| | | | Top Five States | | | | |
| Washington | 136.4% | 35.3% | 48.3% | Idaho | 170.2% | 52.7% | 35.2% |
| Utah | 137.1% | 17.5% | 61.9% | Arizona | 172.9% | 32.8% | 54.2% |
| New Hampshire | 145.1% | 60.9% | 32.3% | Washington | 177.6% | 31.6% | 53.9% |
| Arizona | 148.9% | 38.3% | 47.5% | New Hampshire | 189.9% | 57.0% | 35.1% |
| Nebraska | 174.9% | 53.6% | 29.2% | Delaware | 208.1% | 20.2% | 77.3% |

*Note.* PFA = portfolio of financial assets; HEA = home equity assets; NW = net worth.

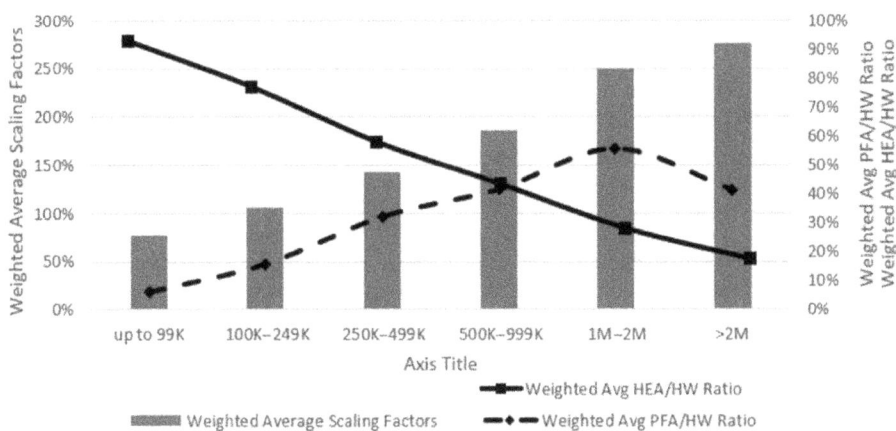

**Figure 23.5:** Weighted Average Scaling Factors by Net Worth, PFA/NW, and HEA/NW Ratios for Couples Households who are HECM Eligible.

households. It was determined that higher net worth households can afford to spend in line with the higher scaling factors but have lower house-rich or HEA/NW ratios. Lower net worth households tend to have higher HEA/NW ratios compared to higher net worth households with lower HEA/NW ratios. This shows that the "house-rich and cash-poor" assumption is not always correct when net worth is considered.

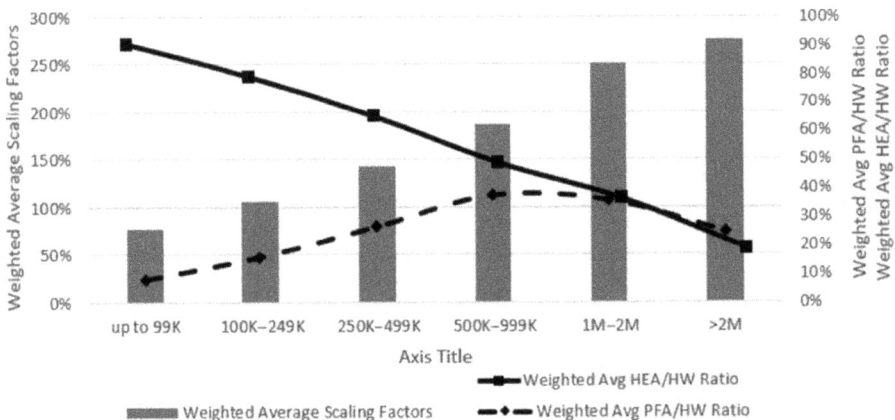

**Figure 23.6:** Weighted Average Scaling Factors by Net Worth, PFA/NW, and HEA/NW Ratios for Singles Households who are HECM Eligible.

## Conclusion

Results from the empirical analyses discussed above show how a reverse mortgage (RM) can be used as a way to enhance retirement outcomes. RMs can be a supplement for retirement liabilities in the retirement balance sheet. Nevertheless, the trend of using RMs is limited in many countries. This study found a positive correlation between scaling factors and PFA/NW ratios, but a negative correlation between scaling factors and HEA/NW ratios. The higher scaling factors were associated with a higher portfolio of financial assets to net worth ratio (PFA/NW) and a lower ratio of home equity assets to net worth (HEA/NW). Scaling factors or how much retirees spend can lead to the related ratios of house-rich (HEA/NW) and cash-poor (PFA/NW) when using the retirement balance sheet. In the United States, to spend above the state average retirement lifestyle liability, couples need to at least match the national weighted average of PFA/NW ratio of 43.4 percent, and HEA/NW ratio of 39.9 percent when HECM eligible compared to singles with 31.4 percent and 54.2 percent respectively.

# Discussion

As shown in this chapter, when U.S. retirees are in the house-rich and cash-poor category, a reverse mortgage can be a useful personal finance tool to help these retirees achieve retirement success. Let us walk through two U.S. household examples in the absence of financial planning but using the retirement balance sheet when considering an RM. In Household A, a married couple client wants a retirement lifestyle spending at 300 percent of California (CA) state averages. In this study, the CA state guideline is a PFA/NW of 54.4 percent and a HEA/NW of 26.3 percent. Household A has a $6 million net worth. Their PFA/NW ratio is 28.7 percent and HEA/NW ratio is at 71.3 percent, the opposite of the guidelines. Household A will not qualify for an RM due to a large outstanding mortgage balance and a high loan-to-value. The household is seriously house-rich and cash-poor and will not realize a successful retirement on their current course. Relocation, downsizing, or other attention to lifestyle to significantly reduce their retirement liabilities should be their primary focus.

Household B, a couple client, wants a retirement lifestyle spending at 125 percent of the North Carolina (NC) state average. The NC state shows a PFA/NW ratio of 34.1 percent and a HEA/NW ratio of 53 percent. Household B has a $2 million net worth. Household B has a PFA/HW of 82.0 percent and a HEA/NW of 18.0 percent. They will have a successful retirement on their current path because their ratios exceed the guidelines. Household B can qualify for a HECM but does not need to use an RM to supplement income.

These U.S. household examples demonstrate how using the retirement balance sheet to develop ratios for portfolios of financial assets and home equity assets can clarify strategies for meeting retirement liabilities. Lifestyle or retirement liabilities, not home equity assets, can be adjusted and will control the need for RMs.

# Future Directions

Reverse mortgages have been approached as a financial product transaction in many countries like Korea (Heo et al., 2016), Taiwan (Chou and Chang, 2014), Singapore (Fong et al., 2020), the UK (Whait et al., 2019), Australia (Australian Securities and Investments Commission, 2018), and even in the United States (Pfau, 2018). The retirement balance sheet can help financial institutions assess borrowers' eligibility for RMs. The implication for the financial institutions is which approach – financial transaction approach or financial planning approach – is ideal for helping clients to meet their retirement liabilities. The financial planning approach considers comprehensive planning areas of retirement, investment, risks, estate, tax, education, competing goals, client's risks and financial behavior preference, and overall economics (Grable et al., 2020). In the United States, the RM borrower needs to go through HECM training and counseling before applying for the HECM financial product (Pfau, 2018). The financial planning approach could put retirees at ease by looking at their entire retirement balance sheet to make an informed decision. Without the financial planning approach, how much retirees need to operate their household may be lost in the financial transaction. The financial planning approach can be part of the overall reverse mortgage policy in addition to the RM required education and counseling. The financial planning fee can be part of the RM product cost or subsidized by the RM government oversight agency.

In addition to developing a retirement balance sheet, alternative living arrangements must be part of the financial planning approach before recommending a reverse mortgage (Pfau, 2018). A deteriorating living environment can have a negative effect on the well-being of retirees (Quadagno, 2014). The alternative living arrangement may include group housing (co-habitat), assisted living facility, continuing care retirement community, active independent living community (Quadagno, 2014), on-the-road motor home (Solman, 2020), downsizing, or relocating to a lower cost of living state (or country). Some of the alternative living arrangements may significantly reduce retirement liabilities that could mitigate the house-rich and cash-poor situation.

In the end, several rules emerge when it comes to decumulating assets in retirement. First, conserve assets. Second, save more, and third, stay active and healthy while possible. For those retirees who have not saved enough and who may be house-poor, a corollary recommendation is to be nice to your children, families, and friends. They might be the last resort if retirement balance assets simply cannot meet the necessary retirement liabilities. But being aware of the value your home brings to the retirement equation in the form of a reverse mortgage may provide peace of mind, too.

# References

Australian Securities and Investments Commission. (2018). *Review of reverse mortgage lending in Australia*. Accessed July 2021. https://asic.gov.au/regulatory-resources/find-a-document/reports/rep-586-review-of-reverse-mortgage-lending-in-australia/

Bengen, W. P. (2006). Sustainable withdrawals. In H. Evensky, and D. B. Katz (eds.), *Retirement income redesigned: Master plans for distribution – An adviser's guide for funding boomers' best years*. Bloomberg Press.

Bricker, J., Moore, K. B., and Thompson, J. (2019). Trends in household portfolio composition. In A. Haughwout, and B. Mandel (eds.), *Handbook of US Consumer Economics* (pp. 53–96). Academic Press.

Bureau of Labor Statistics. (2011). *Consumer expenditure survey*. Accessed July 2021. https://www.bls.gov/cex/pumd_doc.htm#2011

Canadian Centre for Elder Law Studies. (2006). *Report on reverse mortgages* (CCELS Report No. 2). British Columbia Law Institute. Accessed July 2021. https://www.bcli.org/sites/default/files/Reverse_Mortgages_Rep.pdf

Chatterjee, S. (2016). Reverse mortgage participation in the United States: Evidence from a national study. *International Journal of Financial Studies*, 4(5), 1–10. https://doi.org/10.3390/ijfs4010005

Chen, K. S., and Yang, J. (2020). Housing price dynamics, mortgage credit and reverse mortgage demand: Theory and empirical evidence. *Real Estate Economics*, 48(2), 599–632. https://doi/org/10.1111/1540-6229.12230

Chien, C. L. (2019). *Enhancing retirement success rates in the united states: Leveraging reverse mortgages, delaying social security, and exploring continuous work.* Springer International Publishing. https://doi.org/10.1007/978-3-030-33620-2.

Chou, T. L., and Chang, C. J. (2014). Comparing of local government official website disclosure about home equity reverse mortgage pilot program in Taiwan. *Journal of Knowledge Management, Economics and Information Technology*, 4(5), 1–16.

Collins, J., Hembre, E., and Urban, C. (2020). Exploring the rise of mortgage borrowing among older Americans. *Regional Science and Urban Economics*, 83, 1–54. https://doi.org/10.1016/j.regsciurbeco.2020.103524

Cooley, P. L., Hubbard, C. M., and Walz, D. T. (1999). Sustainable withdrawal rates from your retirement portfolio. *Journal of Financial Counseling and Planning*, 10(1), 39–47.

Financial Consumer Agency of Canada. (2007). *Shopping around for a reverse mortgage.* Accessed July 2021. https://central.bac-lac.gc.ca/.item?id=FC5-8-2-2007E ⊕ pdf&app=Library

Financial Consumer Agency of Canada. (2020). *Reverse mortgages.* Accessed July 2021. https://www.canada.ca/en/financial-consumer-agency/services/mortgages/reverse-mortgages.html

Fong, J. H., Mitchell, O. S., and Koh, B. (2020). *Asset-rich and cash-poor: Which older adults value reverse mortgages?* (WPRC Working Paper No. 694). Wharton Pension Research Council. https://repository.upenn.edu/prc_papers/694

Grable, J. E., Kruger, M. E., and Ford, M. R. (2020). *The fundamentals of writing a financial plan* (1st ed.). National Underwriter.

Gupta, S., and Kumar, S. (2017). Investigating relationship between demand and awareness of reverse mortgage: An empirical analysis from India. *Journal for Studies in Management and Planning*, 3(13), 240–248.

Han, W., Wang, P., Xu, H., and Choi, J. S. (2017). Evaluation of the reverse mortgage option in Hong Kong. *Asian Economic Journal*, 31(2), 187–210.

Hanewald, K., Bateman, H., Fang, H., and Wu, S. (2020). Is there a demand for reverse mortgages in China? Evidence from two online surveys. *Journal of Economic Behavior and Organization*, 169, 19–37.

Heo, Y. C., An, S., and Hong, B. (2016). Reverse mortgage as an income stabilizer for the elderly in Korea. *Asian Social Work and Policy Review*, 10(1), 103–112.

Knaack, P., Miller, M., and Stewart, F. (2020). *Reverse mortgages, financial inclusion, and economic development potential benefit and risks* (Policy Research Working Paper No. 9134). World Bank Group. http://documents1.worldbank.org/curated/en/158231580411007157/pdf/Reverse-Mortgages-Financial-Inclusion-and-Economic-Development-Potential-Benefit-and-Risks.pdf

Kobayashi, M., Konishi, S., and Takeishi, T. (2017). The reverse mortgage market in Japan and its challenges. *Cityscape: A Journal of Policy Development and Research*, 19(1), 99–118.

Lichtenstein, J. (2012). *Financial viability and retirement assets: A look at small business owners and private sector workers.* U.S. Small Business Administration. https://www.sba.gov/sites/default/files/files/rs401tot%20(1).pdf

Lu, B., and Cai, P. (2018). *The Implementation of Reverse Mortgage Program in Taiwan: A Study on "Welfare Model" and "Commercial Model"* (Publication No. 104264002) [Master dissertation], National Chengchi University. http://nccur.lib.nccu.edu.tw/handle/140.119/117434

Milevsky, M. A., and Abaimova, A. (2006). Risk management during retirement. In H. Evensky, and D. B. Katz (Eds.), *Retirement income redesigned: Master plans for distribution – An adviser's guide for funding boomers' best years*. Bloomberg Press.

Ministry of the Economy, Finance and Recovery. (2020). *The life annuity: How does it work?* Accessed July 2021. https://www.economie.gouv.fr/particuliers/viager-comment-ca-marche

National Housing Bank. (2020). *Reverse mortgage loan (RML): Operational guidelines*. National Housing Bank. Accessed July 2021. https://nhb.org.in/RML/guidelines.php

Pfau, W. D. (2012). Capital market expectations, asset allocation, and safe withdrawal rates. *Journal of Financial Planning, 25*(1), 36–43.

Pfau, W. D. (2017). *How much can I spend in retirement?: A guide to investment-based retirement income strategies*. Retirement Researcher Media.

Pfau, W. D. (2018). *Reverse mortgages: How to use reverse mortgages to secure your retirement*. McLean Asset Management Corporation.

Quadagno, J. S. (2014). *Aging and the life course: An introduction to social gerontology* (6th ed.). McGraw-Hill Education.

Society of Actuaries. (2011). *Managing post-retirement risks: A guide to retirement planning*. Accessed July 2021. https://www.soa.org/globalassets/assets/files/research/projects/post-retirement-charts.pdf

Solman, P. (2020). *Unfinished business: These retirement-age nomads find work wherever the road takes them* [Video]. YouTube. https://youtu.be/9bJ0YjqALE0

Social Security Administration (SSA). (2014). *Period life table, 2014*. Accessed July 2021. https://www.ssa.gov/oact/STATS/table4c6.html

Turner, K., and Chien, C. L. (2020, September 30–October 1). *The Impact of mid-late career health shocks on retirement wealth* [Paper presentation]. Academy of Financial Services 34th Annual Meeting, Virtual Conference.

U.S. Census Bureau. (2011). *Survey of income and program participation (SIPP)*. Accessed July 2021. http://thedataweb.rm.census.gov/ftp/sipp_ftp.html#sipp14

U.S. Department of Housing and Urban Development. (2020, December 19). *How the HECM program works*. Accessed July 2021. https://www.hud.gov/program_offices/housing/sfh/hecm/hecmabou

Whait, R. B., Lowies, B., Rossini, P., McGreal, S., and Dimovski, B. (2019). The reverse mortgage conundrum: Perspectives of older households in Australia. *Habitat International, 94*, 102,073. https://doi.org/10.1016/j.habitatint.2019.102073

Yang, J., Min, D., and Kim, J. (2020). The use of big data and its effects in a diffusion forecasting model for Korean reverse mortgage subscribers. *Sustainability, 12*(3), 1–17. https://doi.org/10.3390/su12030979

Angela C. Lyons, Josephine Kass-Hanna

# 24 The Evolution of Financial Services in the Digital Age

**Abstract:** This chapter provides an overview of how digital technologies are transforming the financial services landscape. We highlight the latest in digital financial product and service offerings related to payments and transfers, savings and investments, borrowing, and risk management. We then consider how digitalization is impacting the delivery of financial advice – including virtual advisors, robo- and hybrid advisors, and personal finance communities. While many of these digital innovations were underway prior to Covid-19, the pandemic accelerated the transition raising concerns that some individuals and families may be at risk of being excluded from financial services due to growing socioeconomic and digital divides. We look at barriers to access and usage and emphasize the need for digital financial literacy. Legal and regulatory challenges are also examined. Particular attention is given to recent efforts by regulatory and supervisory authorities to balance innovation and competition with consumer protection. The insights from this chapter provide a useful starting place for scholars and practitioners who are interested in exploring in greater detail how digital technologies are impacting the financial services industry.

**Keywords:** digital financial services, advisory services, digitalization, fintech, financial inclusion, regulatory challenges

## Introduction

The digital revolution is changing the landscape of the financial services industry at an unprecedented rate. The emergence of FinTech (or financial technology) has fueled the development of a wide range of new digital financial products and services (DFS). While their emergence can be related to the recent FinTech movement, it is important to point out that the financial industry has a long history of reliance on technology. The industry has always been one of the prime users of technology-driven solutions, at least in developed markets (Arner et al., 2016). Technological advancements have transformed financial institutions' internal operations, from processing transactions to managing risks. Historically, they have also driven the digitalization of financial services and products. The introduction of the Automatic Teller Machine (ATM) in the late 1960s marked the beginning of digital innovations in financial services. The

**Angela C. Lyons,** University of Illinois at Urbana-Champaign
**Josephine Kass-Hanna,** Saint Joseph University of Beirut

https://doi.org/10.1515/9783110727692-024

emergence of the Internet in the 1990s took this evolution to the next level, especially in the developed world where regulated financial institutions increasingly offered online banking services (Arner et al., 2016). In an ever-evolving digital environment, the financial services sector is currently witnessing another surge in innovations that is revolutionizing the industry. A FinTech era has emerged that is characterized not only by a variety of new digital financial solutions but also by a wide range of new service providers. Beyond traditional banks, financial institutions, advisors, and planning firms, new market players now include technology firms, FinTechs, startup companies, mobile network operators (MNOs), among many others.

In addition, the recent Covid-19 pandemic has amplified the need for digital finance and further accelerated the expansion of DFS. Around the world, there has been a dramatic increase in individuals and businesses using the Internet and/or mobile devices to make payments and transfers, deposit and save money, finance and borrow, manage risks, and more recently, access financial and investment advice (GSMA, 2020; Mas, 2018). Mobile money, digital currencies, robo-advisors, crowdfunding, and peer-to-peer payments are just a few examples of the new DFS that have recently gained momentum.

Developing economies such as China, India, and Kenya have "leapfrogged" ahead of most others when it comes to harnessing the power of DFS (Lyons et al., 2021; Kass-Hanna et al., 2021; Sapovadia, 2018). Non-bank, technology-enabled innovators (e.g., FinTechs and MNOs) have been the driving force in developing countries. They have leveraged growing mobile and Internet penetration rates to offer more convenient and affordable financial products and services that serve as strong competitors to those offered by traditional providers. In contrast, the banking sector has led the shift to digitalization in advanced economies (AFI, 2019). Non-bank market players have only recently been involved in the digital transformation of financial services. The 2008 Global Financial Crisis was a turning point. Following the crisis, consumers' trust in traditional financial institutions fell dramatically. On the firm side, regulatory reforms burdened the banks and made lending difficult and expensive for them. While banks were focused on complying with new regulatory requirements, tech companies and start-ups were able to enter the market by offering financial services at lower costs and more efficiently (Arner et al., 2016; IFC, 2017). These new non-bank players have thrived and experienced rapid growth, as customers have quickly developed more trust and ease with tech-based financial solutions (AFI, 2020; IFC, 2017). Traditional financial institutions have responded to rising competition by acquiring or cooperating with FinTech start-ups (e.g., alliances, outsourcing of DFS) and/or by investing heavily in FinTech innovations internally (Clavijo et al., 2019; Sahay et al., 2020). There has also been the emergence of digital-only financial institutions.[1]

---

1 Examples of the largest digital-only banks include Nubank (Brazil), Chime (U.S.), SoFi (U.S.), Tinkoff (Russia), and Revolut (England).

Globally, the development of DFS has created opportunities to expand financial inclusion and reach wider segments of the population that have been unserved or underserved by traditional financial service providers. The promise of greater inclusion through DFS has been strengthened by the Covid-19 crisis. At the same time, the crisis also raised great awareness about the potential risks. These have included concerns that the transition to DFS might be widening gaps and exacerbating financial exclusion for vulnerable groups that could be left behind, especially those with lower socio-economic status and limited digital skills. The consequences of not being able to fully participate in the new digital financial system can exacerbate existing financial fragilities and limit one's ability to build financial resilience and long-run financial security. Concerns related to consumers' data privacy and security, regulatory arbitrage, fair competition, and financial stability have also been raised. These need to be addressed through legal frameworks that regulate the entry and activities of non-bank FinTech entities in a way that enables healthy competition in the marketplace, while simultaneously ensuring consumer protection. The approaches adopted so far have varied across geographical locations and financial activities.

Given the current environment, it is critically important that researchers and financial practitioners develop a deeper understanding of how DFS are evolving, along with the related benefits and risks. Few survey articles have attempted to take stock of the current state of digitalization within the financial services industry and the anticipated trends. This chapter sheds light on the digital evolution of financial services and financial advice and provides an overview of the most important trends that are (re)shaping the financial landscape. We first take stock of the different digital financial solutions currently available to individuals and businesses. To do this, we present the modus operandi for key DFS, while also providing specific examples of services and providers from different countries around the world. Challenges and opportunities brought about by the rapid development of DFS and FinTech are also discussed, including those related to digital financial inclusion and the need for digital financial literacy. Finally, we highlight key legal and regulatory issues and the growing need to better balance innovation and competition with stronger consumer protection measures. This chapter provides a useful starting place for researchers and financial practitioners who are interested in exploring further the promises that digital technologies hold for the financial services industry.

# Digital Financial Landscape: Providers, Products, and Services

Technological innovations have transformed the financial services landscape in several ways. The most obvious change has been the wider array of digital products and services that are now being offered to clients, especially those related to mobile and smartphone devices. Table 24.1 provides an overview of how technological innovations have impacted the evolution of financial products and services. It compares traditional product and service offerings to those brought about by the recent digitalization for: (1) payments and transfers, (2) savings and investments, (3) borrowing and financing, and (4) risk management. Some of the most influential financial innovations in recent years are highlighted below. For additional examples and discussion, see Gomber et al. (2017), International Monetary Fund and World Bank (2019), and Thakor (2020).

**Table 24.1:** Evolution of Financial Products and Services via Digitalization.

| Financial Services | Traditional Products and Services | New Digital Products and Services |
|---|---|---|
| Payments and transfers | – Cash/ATM<br>– Check<br>– Wire/MTO<br>– Debit/Credit cards | – Mobile payments, mobile money, mobile PoS<br>– Peer-to-peer (P2P) payments<br>– Business-to-business (B2B) transactions<br>– Digital wallets, e-wallets, mobile wallets<br>– Digital money, virtual currencies |
| Savings and investments | – Bank deposits<br>– Mutual funds<br>– Bonds<br>– Equities | – Mobile banking<br>– Micro-saving and micro-investing apps<br>– Mobile market funds<br>– Blockchain stocks and bonds<br>– Online brokers<br>– Mobile trading<br>– Crowdinvesting or equity crowdfunding<br>– Social trading |
| Borrowing and financing | – Bank loan<br>– Microcredit and microloans<br>– Bonds<br>– Mortgages<br>– Trade credit | – Crowdsourcing and alternative financing<br>– Crowdfunding (crowdlending, P2P lending, social lending)<br>– Online business lending<br>– Blockchain bonds<br>– Electronic or e-leasing<br>– Electronic or e-invoicing<br>– Electronic or e-factoring<br>– Credit scoring and modeling |

**Table 24.1** (continued)

| Financial Services | Traditional Products and Services | New Digital Products and Services |
|---|---|---|
| Risk management | – Insurance<br>– Brokerage underwriting<br>– Structured products<br>– Trading regulation<br>– Compliance KYC | – Digital or e-insurance<br>– Peer-to-peer (P2P) insurance<br>– Social insurance (Friendsurance)<br>– Online business insurance<br>– Smart contracts<br>– Regtech, Suptech<br>– Crypto-asset exchanges<br>– e-KYC<br>– Digital ID |

*Sources*: Gomber et al. (2017), International Monetary Fund and World Bank (2019), Thakor (2020).

## Payments and Transfers

The Covid-19 pandemic resulted in a rapid shift from cash to digital, spurring demand for digital payment and transfer solutions across the globe (Lyons et al., 2021). The usage of mobile money to conduct basic daily transactions has been the most impactful game-changer (Chu, 2018; Kass-Hanna et al., 2021; Lyons et al., 2020; Lyons et al., 2021). Mobile money is a digital technology that can be used to deposit or withdraw funds, pay bills, or transfer funds between financial accounts or people using a mobile phone. Mobile money is unique from other DFS because of its strong linkages to a wide range of collaborators, spanning mobile network operators (MNOs), FinTechs, banks, non-bank financial institutions, retailers, governments, and so on. As such, it is not surprising that it has rapidly become an integral part of the financial services landscape and a critical tool to effectively participating in today's digital economy. As of this publication, there are more than 1.2 billion registered mobile money accounts globally and 300 million monthly active accounts (GSMA, 2021). In 2020 alone, the number of registered mobile money accounts grew by about 13 percent, double the forecasted growth rate. More than $2 billion USD is being transacted every day, with this amount expected to climb to $3 billion USD by the end of 2022 (GSMA, 2021). In terms of transfers, international remittances sent via mobile phone have increased by 65 percent in the past year, with more than $1 billion USD being sent and received every month for the first time ever. Africa has the world's largest mobile money market, with the most successful provider being M-Pesa (M for mobile and *pesa* for money in Swahili) (Ndung'u, 2018).[2] M-Pesa was launched in 2007 by Kenya's leading MNOs – Vodafone Group and Safaricom. It is a branchless banking service that allows users to deposit, withdraw, transfer money, pay for goods and

---

2 https://www.vodafone.com/about-vodafone/what-we-do/consumer-products-and-services/m-pesa

services, and access credit and savings from a network of banking agents[3] with their mobile device.

Digital wallets (or e-wallets or mobile wallets) offer customers a means of storing money digitally on a mobile device. They are digital versions of a physical wallet made accessible typically via a smartphone or other smart device. Users store identification information (e.g., national ID card, driver's license, insurance cards), payment methods such as debit or credit cards, among other sources of digital information. Examples of popular digital wallets include Apply Pay (U.S.), Alipay (China), Paytm (China), and MobiKwik (India). Digital wallets are inherently safe. However, clients should take precautions to protect their information by locking their phones and wallet apps using separate codes or facial/thumbprint recognition software.

Peer-to-peer (P2P) or business-to-business (B2B) payment tools are another subcategory of digital payments, which allow clients to easily send money to retailers or family and friends. Examples include PayPal and Venmo, which are non-bank-centric models where individuals instruct a non-bank intermediary to transfer funds to another party. However, to use these services, clients must register using their bank account information, which can exclude those without an account and can also raise security concerns if the service provider has not yet established themselves.

Digital money (or digital currency, virtual currency, or e-money) has also garnered considerable attention in recent years. Note that digital payments refer to electronic payments using traditional fiat currencies, whereas digital money refers to a newly established digital currency that is a virtual medium of exchange independent of fiat currencies. Unlike traditional money, digital money exists only virtually. There is no central issuer (e.g., a central bank). Instead, the currency is based on a decentralized autonomous network. For example, a cryptocurrency is a digital currency that can be used to buy goods and services based on blockchain technologies, which is an online ledger system with strong cryptography to secure online transactions. The most well-known cryptocurrency is Bitcoin. Digital currencies such as Bitcoin are still considered highly risky investments. In 2021, Bitcoin had volatile price moves, reaching almost $65,000 USD in April before losing nearly half its value in May (Bovaird, 2021).

## Savings and Investments

The rise in smartphones has led to the emergence of mobile banking, as well as micro-saving and micro-investing applications such as Acorns and Qapital.[4] By paying a monthly subscription fee, Acorn members can round up purchases and invest their

---

**3** A banking agent is a retail or postal outlet that is contracted by a financial institution or a mobile network operator (MNO) to process clients' financial transactions.
**4** Acorns (https://www.acorns.com/); Qapital (https://www.qapital.com/)

spare change in a diversified portfolio to grow their wealth. Acorn also offers retirement savings accounts, debit cards, and other basic banking services to its customers at low fees. Qapital is a free micro-savings app that is designed to motivate users to save money in small increments by gamifying their spending behavior. Specifically, it directs users to set savings goals and then moves money from the user's checking account to a separate Qapital savings account when certain daily activities are completed (e.g., the user spends less money).

Digitalization has also resulted in a wide variety of DFS where clients can invest in the securities markets directly. For example, online brokers or "e-brokerages" are brokerage firms that operate on the Internet. Clients use a digital platform and specialized trading software provided by the firm to buy and sell securities and to obtain investment information. Clients manage their accounts by giving orders online rather than in person, which the brokerage firm then fills. Online brokerages usually charge lower commissions, but also offer more limited individual investment advisory services. In this sense, trading is largely self-directed by the client. The four biggest online brokers in the U.S. are Fidelity, Charles Schwab, TD Ameritrade, and E*Trade.[5]

In addition, online stock trading companies have also emerged that make it easy for both novice and sophisticated investors to participate in the capital markets using a mobile investment app. Examples of U.S.-based firms include Robinhood and Webull,[6] which allow their clients to trade U.S. stocks, exchange-traded funds (ETFs), cryptocurrencies, and options, and even engage in margin lending. Clients can also purchase foreign securities via equity securities called American Depository Receipts (ADRs).[7] One disadvantage is that apps such as Robinhood tend to offer only online customer service options, through a FAQ and email address with no telephone support of any kind. Webull is one of the few that offers FAQ and e-mail options, as well as a customer support telephone number where investors can speak with a live agent. Another downside has been the recent "Robinhood Effect," which is the term now used to describe irrational stock purchases by retail traders buying stocks without regard to their fundamentals (Lyons and Kass-Hanna, 2021). Such irrational purchases have given rise to greater uncertainty and volatility in the financial markets (Glossner et al., 2021). During the pandemic in 2020, Robinhood had more than 13 million active users in the U.S. and now is estimated to have more than 20 million – many of which have virtually no market experience (Curry, 2021; Popper, 2020).

Crowdinvesting or equity crowdfunding is yet another example of how digitalization is changing the investment markets globally. Crowdinvesting is a type of

---

5 Fidelity (https://www.fidelity.com/); Charles Schwab (https://www.schwab.com/); TD Ameritrade (https://www.tdameritrade.com/); E*Trade (https://us.etrade.com/)
6 Robinhood (https://robinhood.com/); Webull (https://www.webull.com/)
7 An American depositary receipt (ADR) is a certificate issued by a U.S. depositary bank that represents shares in a foreign company's stock. ADRs trade on U.S. stock markets as any domestic shares would. ADRs represent an easy, liquid way for U.S. investors to own foreign stocks.

crowdfunding used by private companies to raise money and capital online. The company sells securities to online investors via an online crowdinvesting platform. Businesses, especially start-ups and early stage companies, can use it instead of relying on a bank or establishing a corporation. There are several major risks to investors when it comes to equity crowdfunding. These are related to fraud, online security, a higher risk of business failure, and delayed returns on the initial investment. Still, a growing number of entrepreneurs and investors are using this new digital financial product to diversify, especially those who are looking for high-risk, high-reward investment opportunities. Among the top equity crowdfunding platforms in the world are AngelList, CircleUp, Fundable, Crowdfunder, EquityNet, and WeFunder.[8]

## Borrowing and Financing

Traditionally, banks have been the primary provider of financing for individuals and businesses. In recent years, digital financing has created new online opportunities to secure financing independently of mainstream lending products such as bank loans. These crowdsourcing (or crowdfunding, social lending, or alternative financing) platforms connect borrowers with investors. They thus improve access to credit for individuals and companies that have lower chances of receiving bank loans while also offering profitable digital lending opportunities. Peer-to-peer (P2P) lending is one type of crowdsourcing that connects cash-flushed investors to cash-strapped borrowers and allows the parties to set up lending agreements without the involvement of a traditional financial institution. P2P lenders operate similarly to traditional lenders in that borrowers' income, expenses, debt, and credit history are still taken into consideration. However, unlike traditional lenders, P2P lending companies allow individuals to obtain a loan, without any collateral and often at lower interest rates. Interested investors who loan to these borrowers usually believe they can earn more in interest payments than through other investments.

Other types of crowdsourcing platforms are linked with social lending. These include donation-based crowdfunding that focuses on connecting donors to charitable causes of their choice or reward-based crowdfunding that focuses on connecting donors to projects or businesses with the expectation of receiving a non-financial reward in return at a later stage (e.g., creative works, technology development, or community-driven projects). The top crowdfunding platforms in the world are all

---

**8** AngelList (https://angel.co/); CircleUp (https://circleup.com/); Fundable (https://www.fundable.com/); Crowdfunder (https://www.crowdfunder.com/); EquityNet (https://www.equitynet.com/); WeFunder (https://wefunder.com/)

based in the U.S. and include companies such as Kickstarter, Indiegogo, Patreon, and GoFundMe.[9]

Besides making loans more accessible and affordable, digitalization has also impacted other areas of lending. For instance, it has simplified the leasing process for acquiring assets such as cars (e-leasing), it has automated the invoicing process and improved the electronic transfer of invoice data (e-invoicing), and it has sped up the time it takes for businesses to access cash or money based on future income streams related to accounts receivable or business invoices (e-factoring). Digitalization has also improved traditional credit scoring models and led to the development of alternative credit scoring models. These give potential borrowers, whose credit risk profiles may be lacking, a chance to receive a loan by basing their score on alternative data sources such as rent or utility payments.

## Risk Management

Consider also the impacts of digitalization on risk management. Digital insurance is commonly defined as any insurance company that relies heavily upon digital technologies to sell and manage insurance policies and to interface with its clients. Digital insurance models typically include the following key features. Clients can research, compare, and purchase insurance online or through an app without having to speak directly to an agent. The pricing, risk evaluation, and/or claims handling are based on insurance-specific technologies and algorithms (i.e., insurtech). Also, coverage options are simplified to serve individuals with less robust insurance needs. E-insurance products and services related to auto, home, and life insurance are growing in popularity for their accessibility – being almost exclusively online or app-based – and their promise of greater affordability. In the U.S., Esurance has been identified among the top overall companies for digital insurance, including home, auto, life, and even pet coverage. Hippo and Lemonade have been identified among the top e-insurance companies for homeowners' and renters' insurance and Root and Metromile for auto insurance.[10] Most companies specializing in digital insurance operate using a hybrid model, where one arm of the business focuses on digital insurance and the other on traditional insurance practices.

The demand for more accessible and low-cost services in the insurance industry has also resulted in the development of peer-to-peer (P2P) insurance models. With P2P insurance, a group of individuals (or policyholders) create a risk-sharing network

---

9 Kickstarter (https://www.kickstarter.com/); Indiegogo (https://www.indiegogo.com/); Patreon (https://www.patreon.com/); GoFundMe (https://www.gofundme.com/).
10 Esurance (https://www.esurance.com/); Hippo (https://myhippo.com/); Lemonade (https://www.lemonade.com/); Root (https://www.joinroot.com/); Metromile (https://www.metromile.com/).

and pool their premiums together to insure against potential risk. If the pool of premiums is insufficient to pay for the claims of its members, the P2P provider pays the excess from its retained premiums and reinsurance. Conversely, if the pool exceeds the amount paid out in claims, the "excess" or "profit" is given back to the pool as a cash-back bonus or as a payout to a cause the pool members care about. P2P insurance companies earn money through a flat fee paid to them by the insurers or a commission fee that is paid when individuals purchase one of the insurers' products. The fees are independent of how many (or how few) claims are paid. The P2P model has been found to minimize the moral hazard problem by reducing the number of insurance claims, thereby also reducing members' annual insurance premiums. The P2P insurance model was first introduced in Germany in 2010 via the digital insurance company Friendsurance.[11] This digital insurance company was launched to reduce the high number of insurance claims that were being filed in Germany at the time. On average, Friendsurance members have been found to file 20 to 40 percent fewer claims than other companies, and more than 80 percent have received cash back totaling approximately 30 percent of the premiums paid (Sapona, 2016).

Digital technologies are also transforming risk management practices more generally in the financial services industry. For example, technology applications are regularly used to support compliance and reporting requirements by regulated financial institutions. They are also being used by the supervisory agencies themselves (regtech and suptech). Digital IDs and e-KYC (electronic Know Your Customer) processes have also revolutionized how financial institutions are able to electronically verify the credentials of their customers. The most well-known example of digital IDs and e-KYC can be found in India, where the Unique Identification Authority of India (UIDAI) issues residents a national ID number and card called an Aadhaar (UIDAI, 2021). Currently, Aadhaar is the largest biometric ID system in the world. An online electronic KYC verification service is used by UIDAI to rapidly identify an individual using the biometric and demographic data stored on the Aadhaar card, while still maintaining the person's privacy, security, and inclusion.

## Digital Delivery of Financial Advice

Globally, the number of clients who are using digital channels to access financial advice has increased dramatically, especially since the pandemic. Prior to Covid-19, the transition to digital delivery channels was already underway by the financial services industry. The pandemic accelerated the transition (Daub and Weisinger, 2015). In this section, we highlight a few key examples of how digitalization has changed the delivery of products and services for financial institutions and advisory firms.

---

11 Friendsurance (https://www.friendsurance.com/).

## Virtual Advisors

Given the increase in novice investors and how much money can be at stake, the ability to talk with a financial professional about a question or concern remains important – even in the digital age. Banking and financial planning services have traditionally been rooted in physical branch/office locations and in-person contact. In the post-pandemic environment, financial advisors have seized on the power of virtual platforms (such as Zoom and Microsoft Teams, among others) to facilitate "in-person" contact with clients remotely. More and more, the "virtual advisor" is replacing the brick-and-mortar advisory offices with centralized online platforms and videoconferencing, where practitioners can meet with their clients virtually to deliver advice and other services digitally. In many cases, virtual platforms are proving to be more efficient and convenient than face-to-face meetings in terms of both time and cost. From a practitioner's perspective, estimates have shown that switching to a virtual model can reduce costs by as much as 40 percent to 50 percent. Practitioners are also finding that virtual meetings have created an opportunity to reach client groups that they have previously found difficult to attract and serve – in particular, younger clients and those with assets from $100,000 to $1 million USD (Daub and Weisinger, 2015).

## Robo and Hybrid Advisors

In addition to the growth in virtual advisors, the financial industry has also seen the emergence of robo-advisors, which deliver and execute financial advice and investment management services using algorithms on digital platforms (Gerlach and Lutz, 2021; Iannarone, 2018; Tertilt and Scholz, 2018). The algorithms automatically allocate, manage, and optimize clients' investment portfolios according to their risk preferences and desired rates of return (D'Acunto et al., 2019; D'Acunto and Rossi, 2020). The robo-advising industry started as a FinTech disruptor to the financial services industry in an attempt to reach customer segments too small for traditional financial advisers. Robo-advisors offer an easily accessible and less expensive option than traditional brick-and-mortar financial advisory firms because they require moderate to minimal human intervention. Also, financial professionals often use rules of thumb and common approaches when advising their clients that can be subject to the advisor's own behavioral biases and cognitive limitations. Some argue that robo-advisors are less likely to be prone to these human and institutional biases (D'Acunto et al., 2019).

Following the global financial crisis of 2008, the usage of robo-advisors grew in popularity, especially among investors concerned about a potential conflict of interest and fraud within the financial industry (Brenner and Meyll, 2020; Phoon and Koh, 2017). Not surprisingly, they have become more prominent in developed countries, with the U.S. being, by far, the leading market. The rapid development of digital advisory models has fueled competition and incentivized traditional actors such as brokerage firms, asset managers, and even bank giants to offer their own automated advisory services (Abraham et al., 2019). Currently, Betterment, Wealthfront, and Vanguard Personal Advisor Services are among the largest robo-advisors in the U.S., with assets under management (AUM) totaling approximately $26.7 billion USD, $25 billion USD, and $231 billion USD, respectively (Friedberg, 2021).[12]

However, not all clients want a digital-only experience. To this end, a growing number of banks and financial firms now provide "hybrid" models that offer both human and digital advice to their clients. A growing number of clients are also looking for these hybrid models to go beyond savings and investments to seeking assistance with financial planning needs related to critical life decisions and work-life challenges that have arisen from the pandemic. The economic shock of the pandemic has significantly impacted how individuals are thinking about financial planning when it comes to preparing for retirement, healthcare expenses, and future emergencies. Financial advisors can help clients navigate these financial decisions, especially those related to disruptions in employment status, earnings, and the number of household earners (Benz, 2020). For example, demand has increased for digital financial advisory tools that help clients make more informed decisions about whether to continue working from home or what is the best financial option when it comes to childcare. As countries transition back to work, many families are weighing the affordability of daycare services versus a parent deciding to cut back on work hours and provide stay-at-home childcare.

## Personal Finance Communities

Finally, it is important to acknowledge the increasingly important role that social networks are playing in the transmission of financial advice and the adoption of new DFS and FinTech. Clients are spending an increasing amount of time on social media platforms discussing their finances with friends and family worldwide (Daub and Weisinger, 2015). In fact, individuals are increasingly becoming more likely to make investment decisions using the information they acquire from social media platforms such as Facebook and Twitter instead of from a qualified financial professional (Gomber et al., 2017). Terms such as "trading community," "investment community," and "stock community" are emerging that describe online communities that discuss and share information on stocks and investments (e.g., Yahoo Finance, Google Finance,

---

12 Betterment (https://www.betterment.com/); Wealthfront (https://www.wealthfront.com/); and Vanguard Digital Advisor (https://investor.vanguard.com/advice/digital-advisor/).

ragingbull.com). The use of such social networks facilitates interaction among buyers and sellers, while also improving financial literacy and inclusion.

Take, for example, the recent case of Reddit and GameStop. Retail investors used the social media platform Reddit to exchange investment information. Reddit users created a short squeeze by buying up shares of the struggling video game retailer GameStop, taking on institutional investors who were betting the company would fail.[13] People in the Reddit community purchased stock on no-fee online trading platforms such as Robinhood and Webull. On January 28, 2021 this "social trading" community was able to push up GameStop's share price to nearly 30 times its valuation. Institutional investors who had bet against the company lost billions of dollars. This coordinated buying frenzy by retail investors is considered one of the first such events driven by social media. It has since led to concerns that retail investors could do this again, creating a new level of risk and uncertainty for institutional investors – all of which has been brought about by digitalization and the increased inclusiveness of financial services.

## DFS and Financial Inclusion

The digital transformation has impacted all persons, but not every person equally. In the last decade and especially post-Covid, researchers and practitioners have begun to focus on the digitalization of financial products and services within the context of financial inclusion, especially for populations traditionally excluded from mainstream financial markets (Barajas et al., 2020). In this section, we explore gaps in access and usage of DFS and solutions to improve financial inclusiveness and bridge the digital divides.

Financial inclusion is most often defined as having universal access to a full range of safe, secure, and affordably priced financial products and services. Globally, the public and private sectors have concentrated their efforts on promoting financial inclusion through basic account ownership.[14] However, leveraging digital technologies to offer low-cost and easily accessible financial services and products goes beyond account ownership. These technologies have long had the potential to promote

---

13 https://www.nytimes.com/2021/01/29/technology/roaring-kitty-reddit-gamestop-markets.html

14 As of 2018, it was estimated that about 47 countries had implemented a national financial inclusion strategy while an additional 22 countries had strategies that were in various stages of development (AFI, 2018). The World Bank's *Global Findex* has come to be the most well-known data source for measuring the state of financial inclusion worldwide. The *Global Findex* collected cross-sectional data in 2011, 2014, and 2017 from approximately 150,000 households across 140 countries (Demirgüç-Kunt et al., 2018). The findings provide evidence that financial inclusion has improved in the last decade. The percentage of adults holding a financial account has increased from 51.0 percent on average in 2011 to 69.0 percent in 2017.

"inclusion" across many dimensions of the financial services industry – payments, savings, investments, borrowing, and insurance. Still, progress remains uneven across population groups and countries (Demirgüç-Kunt et al., 2018; Lyons et al., 2021). Not only are the developing and emerging economies facing this challenge, but advanced economies as well (Barboni et al., 2017; Demirgüç-Kunt et al., 2018; Dostov et al., 2019; Fernández-Olit et al., 2020). The most recent estimates from the World Bank's *Global Findex* database reveal that approximately 6 percent of the world's unbanked (53 million) live in high-income developed countries (Patwardhan, 2018). Further- more, there is a larger share of the population in developed countries classified as underbanked. In the U.S. alone, the Federal Deposit Insurance Corporation (2018) esti- mates that more than 25 percent of households are underserved by the financial mar- kets (32.6 million adults) – 6.5 percent are unbanked (8.4 million households) and 18.7 percent are underbanked (24.2 million households).

With the expansion of mobile broadband networks and almost half of the world's population now using mobile Internet (GSMA, 2020; Mas, 2018), there is the expecta- tion that the transition to DFS will result in greater reach and a deepening of financial inclusion that will build a more equitable distribution of financial services worldwide. However, it is not yet clear that this will be the case. The Covid-19 pandemic acceler- ated the transition to DFS and exacerbated financial and digital disparities at increas- ing rates (United Nations Department of Economic and Social Affairs, 2021). Also, unequal access to the Internet and mobile phones has led to new forms of exclusion (GSMA, 2020). Even with greater access, some population groups, especially those with low digital literacy, cannot keep up with the rapid shifts in digitalization (Lyons and Kass-Hanna, 2021). They also are unable to reap the benefits of more complex digi- tal financial solutions to save and prepare for emergencies and future goals, borrow to smooth consumption or start a business, and protect against risk. Lack of knowledge and confidence thus have also hindered access to and usage of DFS, as well as the adoption of behaviors that build financial resilience (Kass-Hanna et al., 2021). These concerns have been at the core of recent studies and discussions among researchers and practitioners aimed at improving the uptake of DFS and the achievement of finan- cial resilience and long-run financial security for all (Lyons and Kass-Hanna, 2021).

## Access to and Usage of DFS: Barriers and (dis)Connections

DFS has the potential to address traditional barriers to access. Demand-side con- straints have been associated with: (1) high service fees and costs, (2) the distance to financial institutions, (3) lack of personal identification and other required documen- tation, and (4) emotional barriers related to financial confidence and trust in the fi- nancial industry. Supply-side problems have been related to: (1) high operating costs, (2) the continued usage of legacy business models, (3) information asymmetries, (4) gaps in geographical coverage, and (5) lack of competition and innovation. The FinTech revolution has catalyzed the emergence of new business models that are able to offer financial services to larger customer bases at reduced costs and with fewer requirements. These new DFS providers have been able to reach excluded populations while generating profits (Agur et al., 2020; Davis, 2021). Expanding access to DFS thus holds the promise of enhancing financial inclusion.

With this said, lack of access to digital connectivity and mobile and data services have long been perceived to hinder digital financial inclusion. While some countries still need to invest in digital and financial infrastructure, issues related to Internet and mobile access are proving to be lesser challenges (GSMA, 2020, 2021). The major obstacle has been driving and sustaining the usage of DFS. In fact, removing barriers to access does not mean that individuals will necessarily use DFS. Nor does initial adoption, even when voluntary, imply regular usage (Kass-Hanna et al., 2021; Lyons and Kass-Hanna, 2021; Lyons et al., 2021; Lyons et al., 2020). The literature investigating the linkages between access to and consistent usage of DFS is still nascent. A recent study has found evidence that FinTech development is improving access to financial services, especially account ownership from banks and non-bank financial institutions (NBFIs) (Lyons et al., 2021). Yet, when it comes to savings and borrowing, they find that access may not translate into greater usage. Research highlights other persisting barriers to the usage of digital and non-digital financial services. These are related to perceived benefits of usage, capabilities and confidence, trust in service providers, and cultural factors, among others.

Also, in countries such as the U.S., individuals can appear to have access to a wider range of conventional financial products and services, even when digital connectivity is not an issue. Yet, they may still be denied access to those products and services due to socioeconomic divides (e.g., income and employment volatility, poor credit histories). Research points to socioeconomic barriers driving racial/ethnic divides in access to financial services in the U.S. A recent study found that, while Black and Hispanic households see value in using financial planning services, most of them still do not seek advice. This appears to be due to large gaps in income and wealth relative to White and Asian households (White and Heckman, 2016). Once socioeconomic factors were accounted for, Black households were more likely to use a financial planner. The findings suggest that gaps in financial services access and usage could be improved if there was a more level playing field that better accounted for socioeconomic divides.

Generational views and preferences also vary when it comes to DFS and digital financial advisory services. Until recently, demand for DFS was largely driven by younger, tech-savvy persons who had no or limited access to traditional financial services and financial planners and advisors (Lopez et al., 2016). Vanguard recently conducted an online survey of a nationally representative sample of U.S. adults to understand how preferences have changed after Covid-19 and the corresponding volatilities in the financial markets (Vanguard, 2020). Younger clients were more likely than older generations to use a robo-advisor and to express interest in receiving professional financial advice online (Daub and Weisinger, 2015; Vanguard, 2020). This is not surprising, since they have grown up in a technology-driven world, having had greater exposure to the Internet, mobile phones, artificial intelligence (AI) and automation, and social media. They are thus more comfortable accessing and using digital technologies. However, other groups are increasingly discovering the convenience of DFS as well. Consider those who might not normally engage in investing because of limited funds or long distance, or simply because they feel intimidated by human advisors (Abraham et al., 2019). Traditional clients are even being motivated to switch to digital services given the reduction in costs and efficiencies in accessibility and design. These solutions also allow clients to connect and engage with practitioners more easily. They also facilitate clients' ability to research, compare, and purchase various types of financial products and services.

## From Financial Literacy to Digital Financial Literacy

Financial literacy has long been recognized as a key tool to improving financial inclusion and individuals' financial resilience, among researchers and practitioners alike. Practitioners' focus has been on designing more effective financial planning and counseling interventions that enhance clients' literacy levels. Researchers' focus has been on examining the determinants of financial literacy and analyzing their relationship with financial behaviors (Lyons and Kass-Hanna, 2021). Key factors include the awareness, knowledge, and ability to make appropriate financial decisions and use available financial services.

With the rapid expansion of DFS triggered by FinTech and hastened by Covid-19, financial literacy is no longer enough. Digital skills have also become prerequisites to access and use DFS. To ensure that individuals are able to use DFS effectively and responsibly, they need to have awareness and capabilities that cover aspects of both financial and digital literacy (Lyons and Kass-Hanna, 2021). In other words, they need to be equipped with "digital financial literacy," which additionally involves specific aspects relevant to the features and risks inherent to DFS. Lyons and Kass-Hanna (2021) described a multidimensional framework for digital financial literacy that identifies five core dimensions: (1) basic financial knowledge and digital skills; (2) awareness of available DFS; (3) practical know-how of how to use and operate DFS applications; (4) ability to make appropriate financial decisions within the digital context; and (5) self-protection from online scams and frauds. Financial professionals are in a unique position to provide not only financial advisory services but also digital knowledge and skills related to how to effectively access and use financial products and services. As Lyons and Kass-Hanna (2021) point out, financial practitioners need to design online and offline educational resources to teach their clients about how to access and use DFS. New digital counseling strategies also need to be developed to assist practitioners in how to effectively communicate with their clients about DFS and related topics.

Also, digital financial literacy provides individuals greater autonomy and confidence, and thus can be an effective means to increase the uptake and usage of DFS. Moreover, it can play an important role in fostering positive financial attitudes toward DFS and related resilience-building financial behaviors (Kass-Hanna et al., 2021; Lyons and Kass-Hanna, 2021). In this way, digital financial literacy constitutes an essential pathway to reducing vulnerabilities and achieving long-run financial security (Barajas et al., 2020; Lyons et al., 2021). Financial practitioners should take digital financial literacy into consideration when assisting clients, especially those most at risk of being left behind due to the rapid shifts in digitalization. Lyons and Kass-Hanna (2021) and Kass-Hanna et al. (2021) have identified several client groups that may have the most difficulty in transitioning to DFS. These include those with lower literacy levels and socioeconomic status, the elderly, women, those inclined toward certain behavioral biases and cognitive limitations, persons with disabilities. and those living in remote areas.

Practitioners should identify which of their clients find it challenging to transition to digital solutions and choose from a broad range of DFS. For example, clients who are planning for retirement may need general financial advice related to savings and investments, taxation, and insurance. They may also need digital financial literacy on how to choose the most appropriate digital products and services to save and invest, pay taxes, and insure against risk. Education and counseling may also be needed to assist them in better understanding the risk and return trade-offs of specific DFS. Additionally, older clients close to, or in retirement, may require more specialized education and counseling on how to use digital devices and digital financial products and services. Financial practitioners can also raise clients' awareness about data privacy and account security to empower them to detect and protect against identity theft, scams, and frauds, especially those who may be more vulnerable.

Clients are more focused and motivated to learn and apply acquired knowledge when they are in a position where they need to use DFS (e.g., check online the allocations within their retirement portfolio). Practitioners can create and tailor digital learning opportunities and related digital solutions to address clients' needs at teachable moments. In designing these educational and counseling resources, practitioners should take into consideration clients' risk profiles, preferences, and cognitive biases (see Lyons and Kass-Hanna (2021) for more examples).

# DFS and Regulatory Challenges

The transition to DFS also brings with it several risks and challenges related to legal and regulatory frameworks. These are unique across jurisdictions. Regulatory approaches aimed at keeping up with fast-paced innovations in DFS differ across countries – and even within countries. Still, they all seek to strike a balance between (1) stimulating innovation and competition among existing and new DFS providers; and (2) ensuring customer protection and trust (Bank for International Settlements and World Bank Group, 2016). FinTech regulation focuses on two areas of digital financial solutions – digital banking operations and digital advisory services. Research has contributed to ongoing discussions in these areas to better inform the design of legal and regulatory frameworks that advance DFS development and adoption. This section highlights some of the most pressing challenges and key solutions to address them.

## Digital Banking and Related Financial Services

The rise of technology-enabled providers of services related to deposit-taking, credit intermediation, and capital raising has prompted central banks and other financial authorities to reassess existing regulatory frameworks. When it comes to digital banking, most jurisdictions currently apply existing banking laws and regulations, regardless of the technologies used (Financial Stability Institute, 2020). While a few jurisdictions have designed specific regulatory frameworks for digital banks and related activities, they still follow requirements that are similar to those for traditional banks. One difference is that regulatory authorities do not impose restrictions on digital banks that pertain to physical bank branches. Also, digital banks may be restricted in terms of the market segments they are allowed to serve.

When it comes to regulating the entry of non-bank DFS providers (e.g., FinTechs, start-ups, MNOs), authorities may: (1) require a partnership with a bank; (2) grant a special license of financial service provision to start-ups and companies' subsidiaries; or (3) grant a license to non-financial sector entities (Pazarbasioglu et al., 2020). Despite being risky and uncommon, the latter illustrates the case of Kenya's Vodafone Group and Safaricom. Both of these are MNOs, not banks, but were still allowed by the Central Bank of Kenya (CBK) to operate the mobile money service M-Pesa. In terms of regulating this service, the CBK adopted a "test and learn" approach, allowing M-Pesa to function under a custom framework with close supervision. To ensure flexibility and encourage innovations, regulators in other countries have preferred the "wait and see" approach that allows new business models to function, while monitoring them from afar and gradually introducing changes. For example, the People's Bank of China (PBOC) used this approach to help AliPay and WeChat innovate and rapidly grow the mobile money market. However, the market grew faster than PBOC had anticipated, which allowed several fraudulent providers to enter the market and take advantage of consumers. The PBOC had to intervene and require that all e-money balances be maintained with the PBOC. Several other countries have recently experimented with regulatory sandboxes and innovation hubs, even smaller economies such as Sierra Leone, Rwanda, and Jordan (Pazarbasioglu et al., 2020). Regulatory sandboxes are set up by regulators to allow FinTechs, start-ups, and other innovators to conduct live experiments in a controlled environment under regulators' supervision. Innovation hubs provide them the workspace and other infrastructure to interact, create, and innovate, while navigating the regulatory, supervisory, and legal environments.

Ensuring competition and creating a level playing field are also key challenges facing regulators. This includes the prevention of regulatory arbitrage to block banks and non-banks from seizing on loopholes to circumvent unfavorable regulations. This also includes improving access to existing data, technologies, and infrastructures for all DFS players. To this end, regulators are encouraging incumbent banks to provide technology and communication companies with more open access to financial infrastructure. For example, the Reserve Bank of India required access to payment infrastructure for non-bank e-money issuers (Pazarbasioglu et al., 2020). Similarly, technology and communication companies are encouraged to provide banks with more open access to their data platforms and telecommunication services (Pazarbasioglu et al., 2020).

On the consumer protection front, regulators are working to improve on the DFS delivery side the following: (1) the electronic disclosure of terms and conditions related to DFS, (2) the security of electronic funds and transactions, (3) DFS providers' responsibilities and liabilities, and (4) consumers' recourse mechanisms in the event of fraud, scams, and bad business practices. DFS and other related technologies are often being adopted by new users with little understanding of the costs and benefits, and without any in-person assistance from a financial professional as to their suitability and security. This can easily expose consumers to abuse and fraud, thereby reducing trust in DFS and undermining their adoption. TransUnion (2021a, 2021b), a U.S. consumer credit reporting agency, highlighted a sharp rise in the rate of suspected digital fraud attempts on financial service transactions.[15]

Regulatory authorities and supervisory agencies have been adapting regulations to ensure transparency and timely disclosure by standardizing total-cost metrics and providing pricing information before users of DFS complete a transaction. Some regulators are requiring explicit warnings about the risks associated with digital products and services. They are also limiting providers' usage of "one-click" processes, and instead are requiring them to include more intermediate steps for the consumer to

---

15 These rose by 149 percent globally and by 109 percent for the U.S., when comparing the last four months of 2020 (September 1–December 31) to the first four months of 2021 (January 1–May 1). These global fraud insights are based on data collected from billions of transactions detected by TruValidate™, which is TransUnion's risk-based authentication and fraud analytics solution suite.

minimize aggressive marketing practices (Pazarbasioglu et al., 2020). Product suitability and provider liability laws and regulations are also being adapted to include DFS. In addition, regulators and supervisory agencies are increasingly introducing new laws and regulations related to data protection and privacy. Providers are being required to inform their clients about how their data is being accessed, stored, used, and discarded, as well as shared between various service providers. Users must provide informed consent and be able to have control over what information providers are accessing and how that information may be shared.

## Digital Advisory Services

Similar to digital banking regulation, data privacy and security challenges are major regulatory concerns in the automated advisory space. General legal requirements that address these challenges and prevent fraudulent and abusive practices are thus essential to regulating digital advisory services. But they are not enough. The nature of these services adds another layer of risk. The consequences of poor financial advice can be serious not only at the individual client level but also on a large scale. The growth of the industry raises the concern of a greater possibility of systemic risk, especially if a certain robo-advisor were to gain massive market share, or if the models underlying different robo-advisors were to be similar (Baker and Dellaert, 2018; Magnuson, 2018).

Even though the robo-advice industry is still at an early stage, policymakers are paying more attention to the importance and specificities of its regulation and supervision (Financial Stability Institute, 2020; Financial Industry Regulatory Authority, 2016). So far, robo-advisors have been subject to existing regulations applied to financial intermediaries such as brokers. For instance, in the U.S., they are subject to the same securities laws and regulations as traditional brokers. Like human advisors, they are required to register with the Securities and Exchange Commission (SEC). Most are also members of the Financial Industry Regulatory Authority (FINRA), which is the self-regulatory organization for member brokerage firms and exchange markets.

Traditional goals of the regulation of intermediaries revolve around ensuring: (1) competence of intermediaries to provide appropriate advice and related services; (2) honesty with customers through disclosure; and (3) suitability of the financial advice or service recommended to the client (Baker and Dellaert, 2018). To ensure robo-advisors are "well-designed" to meet these regulatory goals, financial authorities are increasingly recognizing the importance of investing in new areas of expertise. Beyond expertise in law, economics, and behavioral science, regulators need to develop technical skills in computer and data science. This equips them with the necessary expertise to assess the algorithms and data incorporated in the automated advisors, the choice architecture through which the advice is delivered, and the underlying IT infrastructures (Baker and Dellaert, 2018). This process paves the way for formulating strategies that mitigate the potential risks linked with robo-advisors reaching a mass-market scale.

Moreover, changes to current regulations are also suggested to limit the vulnerability to systemic risk (Magnuson, 2018). This includes adopting measures that incentivize digital advice providers to share information about their businesses and processes. Regulators should be given the authority to limit contagion from adverse shocks related to DFS, both ex-ante and ex-post. Financial authorities across countries and jurisdictions are also encouraged to collaborate in designing more effective regulations on an international level (Magnuson, 2018).

# Conclusions and Future Directions

In this chapter, we looked at how digital technologies have been transforming the financial services landscape. We highlighted the latest in digital financial product and service offerings related to payments and transfers, savings and investments, borrowing and financing, and risk management. We took an additional step to show how virtual advisors, robo- and hybrid advisors, and personal finance communities have been creating new opportunities for the industry to deliver financial advice and other related educational and counseling services. While many of these digital advancements were underway prior to Covid-19, the pandemic accelerated the transition, raising concerns that some individuals and families may be at risk of being excluded from financial services due to growing socioeconomic and digital divides. We looked at barriers to access and usage and emphasized the need for digital financial literacy. Legal and regulatory challenges were also examined, which highlighted recent efforts by regulatory and supervisory authorities to balance innovation and competition with consumer protection.

This chapter provides a useful starting place for researchers and financial practitioners who are interested in exploring further the promises that digital technologies hold for the financial services industry. The impacts of digital technologies are ever-changing – both in terms of products and services and the delivery of financial advice. By the time this chapter goes to print, there will likely be several new developments. Thus, it is important for researchers and financial practitioners to have a basic understanding of how DFS are evolving, as well as a general sense of the future trajectory of innovations to come. Research that examines the relationships between DFS, FinTech, and individuals' financial outcomes is still at an early stage, and there are ample opportunities to more rigorously investigate the issues raised in this chapter from both a research and practitioner point of view. Researchers can use this chapter as a foundation for forming research questions that are of interest to academics and practitioners alike such as:

- Are digital technologies increasing access and usage of financial services? If so, how and for whom? If not, why and who is most likely to be excluded?
- What factors are influencing the uptake and usage of digital financial services in comparison to traditional financial services?
- What are the benefits and risks related to digital financial services? How do they compare to traditional financial services?
- What factors drive client demand for digital financial advisory services (e.g., robo- and hybrid advisors)? What factors hinder demand? How do these factors differ from those related to the demand for traditional in-person financial advice?

Analysis that provides insights into these and other issues would help scholars and practitioners to build their own knowledge base of DFS so as to better understand the opportunities and challenges associated with DFS that have been outlined in this survey article. In this way, practitioners can better assist their clients in navigating the increasingly complex digital financial services landscape today and into the future.

# References

Abraham, F., Schmukler, S. L., and Tessada, J. (2019). *Robo-advisors: Investing through machines*. World Bank Group. Accessed July 2021. https://documents1.worldbank.org/curated/en/275041551196836758/pdf/Robo-Advisors-Investing-through-Machines.pdf

Agur, I., Peria, S. M., and Rochon, C. (2020, July). Digital financial services and the pandemic: Opportunities and risks for emerging and developing economies [Special series]. *International Monetary Fund*, 1–13.

Alliance for Financial Inclusion (AFI). (2018). *National financial inclusion strategies: Current state of practice*. Accessed July 2021. https://www.afi-global.org/sites/default/files/publications/2018-06/National%20Financial%20Inclusion%20Strategies.pdf

Alliance for Financial Inclusion (AFI). (2019). *The digital financial services ecosystem in Latin America and the Caribbean*. Accessed July 2021. https://www.afi-global.org/publications/3061/The-Digital-Financial-Services-Ecosystem-in-Latin-America-and-the-Caribbean

Alliance for Financial Inclusion (AFI). (2020). *Creating enabling FinTech ecosystems: The role of regulators*. Accessed July 2021. https://www.afi-global.org/publications/3181/Creating-Enabling-Fintech-Ecosystems-The-Role-of-Regulators

Arner, D. W., Barberis, J., and Buckley, R. P. (2016). The evolution of Fintech: A new post-crisis paradigm. *Georgetown Journal of International Law, 47*(4), 1271–1320.

Baker, T., and Dellaert, B. (2018). Regulating robo advice across the financial services industry. *Iowa Law Review, 103*(713), 713–749.

Bank for International Settlements and World Bank Group. (2016). *Payment aspects of financial inclusion*. World Bank Group. Accessed July 2021. http://documents.worldbank.org/curated/en/806481470154477031/pdf/107382-WP-REPLLACEMENT-PUBLIC-PAFI-Report-final-in-A4.pdf

Barajas, A., Beck, T., Belhaj, M., and Naceur, S. B. (2020). Financial inclusion: What have we learned so far? What do we have to learn? *International Monetary Fund, 20*(157), 1–51.

Barboni, G., Cassar, A., and Demont, T. (2017). Financial exclusion in developed countries: A field experiment among migrants and low-income people in Italy. *Journal of Behavioral Economics for Policy*, *1*(2), 39–49.

Benz, C. (2020, October 13). What the Coronavirus means for the future of financial planning. *Morningstar*. https://www.morningstar.com/features/what-covid-means-for-the-future-of-financial-planning

Bovaird, C. (2021, June 2). Bitcoin price volatility reached its highest in a year during May. *Forbes*. Accessed July 2021. https://www.forbes.com/sites/cbovaird/2021/06/02/bitcoin-price-volatility-reached-its-highest-in-a-year-during-may/?sh=547a3b7d39e7

Brenner, L., and Meyll, T. (2020). Robo-advisors: A substitute for human financial advice? *Journal of Behavioral and Experimental Finance*, *25*, 1–8.

Chu, A. B. (2018). Mobile technology and financial inclusion. In D. L. K. Chuen, and R. Deng (eds.), *Handbook of blockchain, digital finance, and inclusion, volume 1* (pp. 131–144). Academic Press.

Clavijo, S., Vera, N., Beltran, D., and Londoño, J. D. (2019). Digital financial services (FinTech) in Latin America. Accessed July 2021. http://dx.doi.org/10.2139/ssrn.3334198

Curry, D. (2021, May 6). Robinhood revenue and usage statistics. *Business of Apps*. Accessed July 2021. https://www.businessofapps.com/data/robinhood-statistics/

D'Acunto, F., Prabhala, N., and Rossi, A. G. (2019). The promises and pitfalls of robo-advising. *The Review of Financial Studies*, *32*(5),1,983–2,020.

D'Acunto, F., and Rossi, A. G. (2020). Accessed July 2021. Robo-advising. http://dx.doi.org/10.2139/ssrn.3545554.

Daub, M., and Weisinger, A. (2015, March 1). Acquiring the capabilities you need to go digital. *McKinsey & Company*. Accessed July 2021. https://www.mckinsey.com/business-functions/mckinsey-digital/our-insights/acquiring-the-capabilities-you-need-to-go-digital

Davis, C. (2021, March 30). Driving purpose and profit through financial inclusion: Strong together. Accessed July 2021. *Deloitte Insights*. https://www2.deloitte.com/us/en/insights/industry/financial-services/purpose-through-inclusive-finance.html

Demirgüç-Kunt, A., Klapper, L., Singer, D., Ansar, S., and Hess, J. (2018). *The global findex Database 2017: Measuring financial inclusion and the FinTech revolution*. The World Bank. Accessed July 2021. https://elibrary.worldbank.org/doi/abs/10.1596/978-1-4648-1259-0

Dostov, V., Shust, P., and Khorkova, A. (2019). New trends in financial inclusion policies: Role of digital technologies and digital inclusion. *Advances in Economics, Business and Management Research*, *104*, 502–514.

Federal Deposit Insurance Corporation. (2018). *FDIC national survey of unbanked and underbanked households*. Accessed July 2021. https://www.fdic.gov/analysis/household-survey/2017/2017report.pdf

Fernández-Olit, B., Martín, J. M. M., and González, E. P. (2020). Systematized literature review on financial inclusion and exclusion in developed countries. *International Journal of Bank Marketing*, *38*(3), 600–626. https://doi.org/10.1108/IJBM-06-2019-0203

Financial Industry Regulatory Authority. (2016). *Report on digital investment advice*. Accessed July 2021. https://www.finra.org/sites/default/files/digital-investment-advice-report.pdf

Financial Stability Institute. (2020). *Regulating FinTech financing: Digital banks and FinTech platforms*. Accessed July 2021. https://www.bis.org/fsi/publ/insights27.pdf

Friedberg, B. A. (2021, May 3). Robo-advisors with the most assets under management-2021. *Robo-advisor Pros*. Accessed July 2021. https://www.roboadvisorpros.com/robo-advisors-with-most-aum-assets-under-management/

Gerlach, J. M., and Lutz, J. K. (2021). Digital financial advice solutions – Evidence on factors affecting the future usage intention and the moderating effect of experience. *Journal of Economics and Business*, forthcoming. https://doi.org/10.1016/j.jeconbus.2021.106009

Glossner, S., Matos, P., Ramelli, S., and Wagner, A. F. (2021). Do institutional investors stabilize equity markets in crisis periods? Evidence from Covid-19. *Swiss Finance Institute Research Paper No. 20–56*. http://dx.doi.org/10.2139/ssrn.3655271

Gomber, P., Koch, J. A., and Siering, M. (2017). Digital finance and FinTech: Current research and future research directions. *Journal of Business Economics*, *87*(5), 537 –580.

GSMA. (2020). *The state of mobile internet connectivity 2020*. Accessed July 2021. https://www.gsma.com/r/wp-content/uploads/2020/09/GSMA-State-of-Mobile-Internet-Connectivity-Report-2020.pdf

GSMA. (2021). *State of the industry report on mobile money 2021*. Accessed July 2021. https://www.gsma.com/mobilefordevelopment/wp-content/uploads/2021/03/GSMA_State-of-the-Industry-Report-on-Mobile-Money-2021_Full-report.pdf

Iannarone, N. G. (2018). Computer as confidant: Digital investment advice and the fiduciary standard. *Chicago-Kent Law Review*, *93*(1), 141 –164.

International Finance Corporation (IFC). (2017). *Digital financial services: Challenges and opportunities for emerging market banks*. World Bank Group. Accessed July 2021. https://openknowledge.worldbank.org/bitstream/handle/10986/30368/118736-BRI-EMCompass-Note-42-DFS-Challenges-and-Opportunities-PUBLIC.pdf?sequence=1&isAllowed=y

International Monetary Fund and World Bank. (2019). *FinTech – The experience so far*. Accessed July 2021. https://www.elibrary.imf.org/view/journals/007/2019/024/007.2019.issue-024-en.xml?Tabs=citedBy-102778

Kass-Hanna, J., Lyons, A. C., and Liu, F. (2021). Building financial resilience through financial and digital literacy in South Asia and Sub-Saharan Africa. *Emerging Markets Review*. http://doi.org/10.1016/j.ememar.2021.100846

Lopez, J. C., Babcic, S., and De La Ossa, A. (2016). Advice goes virtual: How new digital investment services are changing the wealth management landscape. *The Journal of Financial Perspectives*, *3*(3), 1–18.

Lyons, A. C., and Kass-Hanna, J. (2021). A methodological overview to defining and measuring "digital" financial literacy. *Financial Planning Review*, *4*(2), e1113. https://doi.org/10.1002/cfp2.1113

Lyons, A. C., Kass-Hanna, J., and Fava, A. (2021). Fintech development on savings, borrowing, and remittances: A comparative study of emerging economies. *Emerging Markets Review*. http://doi.org/10.1016/j.ememar.2021.100842

Lyons, A. C., Kass-Hanna, J., and Greenlee, A. (2020). Impacts of financial and digital inclusion on poverty in South Asia and Sub-Saharan Africa. https://dx.doi.org/10.2139/ssrn.3684265

Magnuson, W. (2018). Regulating FinTech. *Vanderbilt Law Review*, *71*(4), 1,167–1,226.

Mas, I. (2018). Using broadband to enhance financial inclusion. In D. L. K. Chuen, and R. Deng (eds.), *Handbook of blockchain, digital finance, and inclusion, volume 1* (pp. 91–129). Academic Press.

Ndung'u, N. (2018). The M-Pesa technological revolution for financial services in Kenya: A platform for financial inclusion. In D. L. K. Chuen, and R. Deng (eds.), *Handbook of blockchain, digital finance, and inclusion, volume 1* (pp. 37–56). Academic Press.

Patwardhan, A. (2018). Financial inclusion in the digital age. In D. L. K. Chuen, and R. Deng (eds.), *Handbook of blockchain, digital finance, and inclusion, volume 1* (pp. 57–89). Academic Press.

Pazarbasioglu, C., Mora, A. G., Uttamchandani, M., Natarajan, H., Feyen, E., and Saal, M. (2020). *Digital financial services*. World Bank Group. Accessed July 2021. http://pubdocs.worldbank.org/en/230281588169110691/Digital-Financial-Services.pdf

Phoon, K., and Koh, F. (2017). Robo-advisors and wealth management. *The Journal of Alternative Investments*, *20*(3), 79–94.

Popper, N. (2020, July 8). Robinhood has lured young traders, sometimes with devastating results. *The New York Times*. Accessed July 2021. https://www.nytimes.com/2020/07/08/technology/robinhood-risky-trading.html

Sahay, R., von Allmen, U. E., Lahreche, A., Khera, P., Ogawa, S., Bazarbash, M., and Beaton, K. (2020). *The promise of FinTech: Financial inclusion in the post COVID-19 era*. International Monetary Fund. Accessed July 2021. https://www.imf.org/en/Publications/Departmental-Papers-Policy-Papers/Issues/2020/06/29/The-Promise-of-Fintech-Financial-Inclusion-in-the-Post-COVID-19-Era-48623

Sapona, I. (2016, June). *Peer-to-peer insurance models: Sharing economy adds [new] tech twist to [old] risk pooling*. Insurance Institute of Canada. Accessed July 2021. https://www.insuranceinstitute.ca/en/cipsociety/information-services/advantage-monthly/0616-peertopeer

Sapovadia, V. (2018). Financial inclusion, digital currency, and mobile technology. In D. L. K. Chuen, and R. Deng (eds.), *Handbook of blockchain, digital finance, and inclusion, volume 2* (pp. 361–385). Academic Press.

Tertilt, M., and Scholz, P. (2018). To advise, or not to advise – How robo-advisors evaluate the risk preferences of private investors. *The Journal of Wealth Management*, 21(2), 70–84.

Thakor, A. V. (2020). Fintech and banking: What do we know? *Journal of Financial Intermediation*, 41, 100, 833. https://doi.org/10.1016/j.jfi.2019.100833

TransUnion. (2021a, March 23). *Global fraud trends: Device insights highlight increased threats since onset of pandemic*. Accessed July 2021. https://www.transunion.com/blog/global-fraud-trends-Q1-2021

TransUnion. (2021b, June 3). *Rate of suspected financial services digital fraud attempts rise nearly 150% worldwide as digital transactions increase*. Accessed July 2021. https://www.transunion.com/blog/global-fraud-trends-Q2-2021?utm_campaign=q2-quarterly-fraud-report&utm_content=blog&utm_medium=press-release&utm_source=press-release&utmsource=press-release

Unique Identification Authority of India (UIDAI). (2019). *Aadhaar paperless offline e-KYC*. Accessed July 2021. https://uidai.gov.in/ecosystem/authentication-devices-documents/about-aadhaar-paperless-offline-e-kyc.html

United Nations Department of Economic and Social Affairs. (2021). *Leveraging digital technologies for social inclusion*. Accessed July 2021. https://www.un.org/development/desa/dspd/wp-content/uploads/sites/22/2021/02/PB_92-1.pdf

Vanguard (2020). *Generational views on financial advice, investing, and retirement*. Accessed July 2021. https://pressroom.vanguard.com/nonindexed/DigitalAdvisorSurveyExecutiveSummary08262020.pdf

White, K. J. Jr., and Heckman, S. J. (2016). Financial planner use among Black and Hispanic households. *Journal of Financial Planning*, 29(9), 40–49.

Part IV: **Future Directions**

Angela C. Lyons, Josephine Kass-Hanna

# 25 Behavioral Economics and Financial Decision Making

**Abstract:** Behavioral economics provides insights into how people process information and make decisions. It also helps to explain why and how people tend to make decisions that are not in their best interest, as opposed to what rational choice theory would suggest. This chapter introduces behavioral economics and highlights its relevance to understanding and influencing financial decision making. The chapter explores major cognitive biases that commonly lead to mistakes in financial decisions, such as confirmation bias, overconfidence bias, loss aversion, the endowment effect, and status quo bias. The chapter also highlights the challenges brought about by choice overload, that is the multiplicity of options that overwhelms people and undermines their ability to make appropriate financial decisions. The chapter then discusses how choice architecture and nudges can be used to address the limitations resulting from cognitive biases and choice overload. In particular, we examine default choices, pre-commitment mechanisms, framing, and priming approaches and discuss how these can foster positive financial behaviors. This chapter thus represents a useful starting point for researchers and practitioners interested in developing and applying behavioral economics principles and tools to prompt financial decisions that lead to long-run financial security.

**Keywords:** behavioral economics, cognitive biases, choice architecture, nudges, financial decisions

## Introduction

How and why do people make the financial decisions that they do? From a macro perspective, those working in the field of personal finance have largely focused on addressing this question and in showing how various financial decisions matter to long-run financial well-being and security. In an ideal world, people's decisions would be the result of a careful weighing of costs and benefits and informed by existing preferences. However, human beings are prone to flawed decision making and perhaps subject to irrational behavior.

The economist Gary Becker outlined "rational choice" theory in his 1976 book *The Economic Approach to Human Behavior*. The theory assumes that when making

**Angela C. Lyons,** University of Illinois at Urbana-Champaign
**Josephine Kass-Hanna,** Saint Joseph University of Beirut

https://doi.org/10.1515/9783110727692-025

decisions individuals engage in unemotional maximizing behavior based on their preferences. As long as individuals are able to understand the full consequences of their decisions, they tend to make "rational choices." This theory assumes, though, that individuals have unbounded rationality, unbounded willpower, and unbounded selfishness, which are three unrealistic traits. Unbounded rationality implies that human beings have an unlimited capacity to process information and solve problems. Even if someone has more information available in the age of the Internet and big data, they cannot physically process all of that information every time they need to make a decision. As for unbounded willpower and selfishness assumptions, we know that people often lack self-control and willpower (O'Donoghue and Rabin, 1999, 2001), and they often exhibit social preferences that are not inherently selfish. Consider for example the person who eats a 3,000-calorie hamburger. They know that it is not in the best interest of their health to do so, but still, they eat it anyway. Consider also the two-player ultimatum game, whereby splitting an amount of money is decided by the first player, while the second decides whether to accept or reject the share of money offered. If the second player refuses the offer, both players receive nothing. Rational choice theory predicts that, whatever amount the first player offers, the second player should accept, because something is better than nothing. However, experiments have found that the second player typically rejects offers of less than 20 percent, because they feel that anything less is unfair (Camerer, 2011). How do researchers explain such decisions that appear to be irrational according to traditional economic theory?

Behavioral economics provides an alternative approach to rational choice theory to explain why and how people's behavior does not follow the predictions of rational choice theory. Behavioral economics – and the related field of behavioral finance – is focused on studying the effects of psychological, social, cognitive, and emotional factors on the economic and financial decisions of individuals. Additionally, it helps to explain why people may not be the "rational beings" that rational choice theory would have us believe. You can think of behavioral economics as how people *do* behave and rational choice theory as a model for how people *should* behave in an ideal world.

In this chapter, we shed light on major concepts and tools of behavioral economics and focus on how these relate to the process of financial decision making. We begin by exploring how decisions are generally made and why human beings are prone to making errors. We highlight several cognitive biases that can negatively impact financial decisions. We then discuss how choice architecture and nudges can be useful tools to helping individuals overcome cognitive limitations and to fostering more positive financial behaviors. Specifically, we discuss the role of default choices, pre-commitment mechanisms, framing, and priming. Examples from the field of financial planning are provided throughout to illustrate core behavioral concepts.

# Decision Making and Heuristics

When processing information to make decisions, individuals use generalized rules called heuristics to manage information and solve problems. Heuristics are simple, efficient mental rules, learned or hard-wired by evolutionary processes. They allow people to make decisions, come to judgments, and solve problems when faced with complex or incomplete information. Heuristics are not guaranteed to be optimal or perfect, but sufficient to assist individuals in making timely decisions to reach their goals.

People tend to use three common heuristics (Tversky and Kahneman, 1974): anchoring ("anchoring and adjustment"), availability, and representativeness ("the similarity heuristic"). The anchoring heuristic refers to the human tendency to accept and rely on pre-existing information or the first piece of information found before making decisions. That piece of information becomes an "anchor" or reference point that influences subsequent decisions. For instance, a price of $100 might seem expensive for a new T-shirt, but if the price was marked 50 percent off from the original price of $200, you might feel that you are getting a good deal. In this example, the original price of $200 serves as an anchor. The availability heuristic is a mental shortcut that relies on immediate examples that come to a person's mind when evaluating a decision. Under the availability heuristic, people tend to heavily rely on the most recent information when making decisions. For example, people are more likely to purchase insurance after a natural disaster they have just experienced than they are to purchase insurance before the disaster happens (Simonsohn et al., 2008). Finally, the representativeness heuristic is a mental shortcut used to determine the similarity of items or events and then organize them into categories based on existing prototypes of what already exists in one's mind. For example, investors might be tempted to forecast a company's future earnings using a short history of the company's most recent earnings growth. These estimates may then be used to price the company's stock, which could lead to overpricing if recent growth has trended higher than the average growth of the company since its inception.

# Cognitive Limitations and Biases

From the examples presented above, one can begin to see how the use of heuristics, such as anchoring, availability, and representativeness, can lead to systematic biases or mistakes in how information is processed when making decisions. Researchers call these cognitive biases. A cognitive bias is a subconscious systematic error in thinking that occurs when individuals process and interpret the information they are receiving using their own subjective perceptions of the world around them. For instance, suppose we want to purchase a car. We could go to every dealership and test drive every car that exists. However, it is not practical to do so. Instead, we use mental shortcuts to narrow down the choices. Given our preferences, we might decide we would like to purchase a red sub-compact sport utility vehicle (SUV). We might even decide we want to buy a specific brand of vehicle because we previously had a good experience with the brand. By narrowing down our choices to a specific brand of red sub-compact SUV, we are using heuristics to assist in making a choice more efficiently. But in doing so, we could make a mistake. It is possible that, if we tested every car at every dealership, we might discover that we made a suboptimal decision and we might even decide to purchase a different vehicle. However, we will never know what the best decision is, because we are not physically able to research every vehicle available on the market.

Nearly 200 cognitive biases affect daily decision making. Benson and Manoogian sorted and grouped these biases into four large categories of what they referred to as "cognitive conundrums" or problems that impact human decision making (Benson, 2017). We have already mentioned the first two conundrums. The first is that there is too much information in the universe that we are missing and will continue to miss, and the second is that we do not have enough cognitive capacity to store and process all of the information. The third conundrum is that processing the raw information into something meaningful requires making connections between the limited information received and the mental models, beliefs systems, symbols, and so forth created and stored based on our previous experiences. Gathering information and making these connections necessitate considerable time and resources, which brings us to the final conundrum. We do not have unlimited time and resources to analyze all the information and possible choices available to us when making decisions. Even artificial intelligence (AI) is currently unable to do this.

According to Benson (2017), the complete list of cognitive biases has been arranged in an algorithmic layout called the *Cognitive Bias Codex*.[1] Next, we discuss five of the biases that most commonly impact financial decision making: (1) confirmation bias, (2) overconfidence bias, (3) loss aversion, (4) endowment effect, and (5) status quo bias. From the diagram, you can see that there are many more.

## Confirmation Bias

Confirmation bias refers to the tendency of people to seek out information that supports what they already think or believe. They ignore information that contradicts those existing beliefs, which distorts the reality from which they draw evidence. Various social media platforms, such as Facebook, use algorithms that reinforce confirmation bias by feeding us stories that we are likely to agree with (Pariser, 2011). An example of confirmation bias that is specific to the domain of personal finance occurs

---

1 https://upload.wikimedia.org/wikipedia/commons/6/65/Cognitive_bias_codex_en.svg.

when financial planning clients focus on information that confirms their hypothesis about an investment or supports the investment outcome they desire. This could have a negative impact on their portfolio if they ignore essential facts or data that signal that it is time to rebalance their portfolio or even sell or avoid purchasing a particular investment. Financial advisors estimate that 82 percent of their clients are affected by confirmation bias and 24 percent are significantly affected, with younger clients being more likely than those who are older to be hindered by their own pre-existing beliefs and opinions (Cerulli Associates, 2020). Financial professionals can help clients overcome confirmation bias by providing them with up-to-date information gathered from a variety of reputable sources so that they have a more balanced view of the pros and cons associated with various investments.

## Overconfidence Bias

Another common behavioral bias is overconfidence bias. This occurs when individuals exhibit irrational exuberance or over-optimism in the quality of the information they have and their ability to act on the information. Individuals are more likely to overestimate the likelihood of experiencing a positive event while underestimating the likelihood of a negative event (Weinstein, 1980). In financial planning, for example, overconfidence bias can lead clients to overestimate their understanding of financial market outcomes or specific investments. Over-optimism is perhaps best illustrated by examples related to herd behavior in the financial markets, where individuals collectively act as part of a group creating an asset bubble that results in panic buying and selling and then a market crash. Take, for example, the 2008 global financial crisis when investors became overly optimistic that housing prices would continue to soar and that they would continue to see unprecedented growth in the financial markets. Investors were blindsided by the growing economic bubble and overlooked the pending financial crash that was looming as a result of the financial industry's engagement in the trading of risky derivatives (Sharot, 2011). Financial professionals can help clients avoid overconfidence bias by working with them to develop financial plans that include an annual review and portfolio rebalancing based on actual market conditions and reliable forecasting models. For those clients who may be overly exuberant about particular investments, financial professionals may want to take both an outside perspective to help their clients analyze the decision and a post-mortem approach to predict problems that could arise after making a particular financial decision (Kahneman, 2013).

## Loss Aversion

Loss aversion is another cognitive bias that describes how individuals make choices taking into consideration the perceived likelihood of different options and the probable losses and gains associated with each (Kahneman and Tversky, 1979, 1984). In their landmark study, Kahneman and Tversky (1979) used subjective probabilities to show that people tend to feel the pain of a loss twice as intensively as the equivalent pleasure of a gain. This is a fundamental concept of prospect theory, which posits that individuals evaluate losses and gains in an asymmetric fashion. When making a decision, they focus more on what they might lose rather than on what they could gain. In the context of personal financial planning, loss aversion may lead investors to focus on investment *losses more* than gains and to hold on to investments that are losing value longer than they should. This can result in inaction that stagnates or negatively impacts the growth of their portfolios. Additionally, insurance companies use loss aversion to persuade potential buyers to purchase insurance to avoid future losses and risks so as to guarantee that they will be covered in the event of a negative shock. Loss aversion is the result of many factors including mainly an individual's preferences and tolerance for risk, socioeconomic status, and cultural background. One way in which financial professionals can help their clients tackle loss aversion is to ask them what the worst possible outcome would be for a given financial scenario. Usually, this helps individuals put loss, and their associated feelings of a potential loss, into perspective to better rationalize if an investment is worth the risk. Also, financial practitioners can help their clients to better understand and accept that losing money is an inevitable part of investing and that having a diversified portfolio and a predetermined exit strategy are key to minimizing risk and potential losses.

## Endowment Effect

While loss aversion maintains that people dislike losses more than they like gains, the endowment effect seems to show that people put a higher price on losing something than gaining it. The endowment effect describes people's tendency to value items that they own more highly than they otherwise would if the items did not belong to them (Thaler, 1980). In a seminal study by Knetsch (1989), a group of people were randomly assigned to two groups – one group received a coffee mug and the other group did not. Those that received a mug were then asked what the lowest price was that they would sell the mug for, while those that did not receive a mug were asked what would be the highest price they would be willing to pay for the mug. The study showed that sellers' minimum selling price was two to three times higher, on average, than the maximum price buyers were willing to pay. The endowment effect happens because sellers often try to charge more for an item than its average market value – thereby, creating a gap between a buyer's willingness to pay and a seller's willingness to accept a certain price. Consider financial decision makers who are selling their house and want to set the price higher than what similar homes are going for on the market. In this case, the endowment effect can lead to opportunity costs (i.e., gains that the clients miss out on), especially if it causes them to overprice their house to the point that they are unable to sell it. In such cases, clients can end up holding on to investments longer than they would have or even should have.

## Status Quo Bias

The status quo bias describes an individual's general tendency to prefer their current situation such that they are resistant to change their position. Deviating from the status quo and choosing an alternative – in their minds – comes with uncertainty and involves risk. Samuelson and Zeckhauser (1988) were among the first to introduce and study the concept of status quo bias. According to their theory, when individuals consider alternative options, they assign greater weight to potential losses and lesser weight to potential gains. In doing so, they may fail to see that choosing an alternative might lead to a more favorable outcome. The status quo bias often results because people are uncertain of which decision to make. They may also feel overwhelmed by the number of options or information presented to them. In these instances, people are more likely to maintain the status quo because it is familiar or to choose the "default option" because it is easier. Kempf and Ruenzi (2006) examined the extent to which status quo bias influences individuals' investment decisions and found that investors prefer to stick with prior mutual fund choices, even if they are no longer the optimal choice and better mutual funds are made available. Thus, people's preference for the status quo over alternatives can have significant negative financial consequences. Financial professionals can assist their clients in overcoming status quo bias by simplifying the choices so that a decision is less daunting. Financial practitioners can also frame choices according to what could be lost by staying with the current investment strategy and by explaining and quantifying the expected benefits that could be gained by switching.

# Choice Overload

Up until now, we have touched on how the brain works when faced with choices and explored common cognitive biases that are typically made unconsciously. Overcoming these biases requires that individuals take action to train their minds to become more aware of their cognitive limitations and to adopt new patterns of thinking that help to reduce the negative impacts that these biases can have on financial decision making.

In this section, we take a closer look at why people have a harder time making decisions when they have many options presented to them.

Is there such a thing as too many options? The short answer is yes – individuals can be faced with too many choices. Can more choices lead to worse financial decisions and outcomes? The answer to this question is a bit more complicated. Traditional rational choice theory, and conventional wisdom, suggest that more choice is a good thing. The "paradox of choice," however, is that sometimes "more" is actually less (Schwartz, 2004). Research has shown that people have a harder time choosing when presented with a larger array of options (e.g., Chernev et al., 2015; Iyengar and Lepper, 2000; Schwartz, 2004). The more options that are available, the more taxing it is on people's cognitive systems to process the information such that people experience decision fatigue. In behavioral economics, researchers use the concept of "choice overload" to describe how people get overwhelmed when they are presented with too many options, especially if the choices are complex and detail oriented (Chernev et al., 2015).

"The Jam Experiment" was among the first studies to examine choice overload (Iyengar and Lepper, 2000). Researchers conducted two jam tasting sessions at a local grocery store. In one session, shoppers encountered a tasting booth that included an extensive selection of 24 jams from which they could sample. In another session, shoppers were presented with a more limited selection of only six jams. The first session that included the 24 jams attracted 60 percent of store shoppers. On average, shoppers sampled two flavors. However, only 3 percent of shoppers bought jam. When shoppers were presented with six jams, only 40 percent of shoppers were attracted to the session. While shoppers still sampled on average two flavors, more people purchased jam; in fact, 30 percent of shoppers bought jam. This study has since been replicated numerous times within a variety of contexts, and most have found that more options can delay people in making choices. More choices can also deter them from taking any action at all – even when it comes to important decisions.

Researchers have also found that more choices can negatively impact individuals' ability to make appropriate financial decisions, which can ultimately be quite costly to individuals in the long run. For example, Iyengar and Kamenica (2010) conducted three experiments to determine how increasing the size of the choice set can impact individuals' decisions related to their 401(k) retirement plans. They found that the more mutual fund options employees had to choose from, the more likely they were to be deterred from enrolling in the plan. Conditional on participation, they also found that – for every 10 additional funds included in the plan – allocation to equity funds decreased by 3.3 percentage points. Moreover, there was a 2.9 percentage point increase in the probability that participants allocated nothing at all to equity funds. Other studies related to healthcare coverage have found similar results – with more choices resulting in lower enrollment rates and suboptimal financial outcomes (Abaluck and Gruber, 2011; McWilliams et al., 2011).

# Choice Architecture and Nudges

Chernev and associates (2015) conducted a meta-analysis of 99 behavioral studies on choice and found that four key factors primarily influence cognitive biases within the context of choice overload. These four factors are related to (1) the complexity of the choice set, (2) the difficulty of the decision task, (3) the degree to which an individual knows about their preferences related to the decision, and (4) the extent to which the individual has a clear understanding of what the ultimate goal is and why they are gathering information and comparing different choices. In this section, we examine some common methods that financial practitioners can use to package and present choices to clients in ways that make it easier for them to make more appropriate and optimal decisions when faced with cognitive limitations such as choice overload. This might mean helping clients to better structure their information search and assist them in streamlining choices and understanding their preferences, especially when it comes to riskier decisions.

Choice architecture, a term coined by Thaler and Sunstein (2009), refers to the different ways in which choices can be presented to individuals to influence their decisions. In choice architecture, the design and presentation of choices matter. A common example is how food is displayed in cafeterias, where offering healthy food at the beginning of the line or at eye level can contribute to healthier choices (Mancino and Guthrie, 2009). Choice architecture includes many tools that can assist behavioral economists in structuring choice sets and describing available choices within a personal finance context. These can include but are not limited to creating default options, using framing and priming when describing the attributes of various choices, limiting the number of choices, restructuring complex choices, and creating incentives and pre-commitment mechanisms. Ultimately, the aim is to create choice architecture that "nudges" individuals toward choices that are in their best interest without limiting choice or significantly changing the economic incentives of the various options.

Nudges are words or visual prompts used to "prod" individuals to "voluntarily" do something. A nudge is any aspect of choice architecture that is used to influence people's choices or behaviors, by altering the environment so that their cognitive processes are triggered to favor the desired outcome (Thaler and Sunstein, 2009). Successful nudges do not explicitly prohibit behavior. Instead, they incentivize individuals to change their behavior by highlighting the consequences that may follow from maintaining it. In recent years, nudge theory has come to be viewed as an effective and popular means to influencing individuals' decisions and behaviors – that is, when used ethically. Critics have challenged nudging for being paternalistic and diminishing an individual's autonomy and freedom of choice (Smith et al., 2013; Sunstein, 2016). Critics of nudge theory argue that nudging, in the wrong hands, has the potential to be used in a manipulative manner to sway people into making decisions that are not in their best interest and that they may later regret. According to Thaler (2015), three principles should guide the use of nudges. First, all nudging should be transparent and never misleading. Second, it should be as easy as possible to opt-out of a nudge. Third and finally, there should be a good reason to believe that the behavior being encouraged will improve the welfare of those being nudged.

## Default Choices

When it comes to nudging, "default" choices have been found to be powerful tools. A default option is defined as a choice frame in which one selection is pre-selected and active steps must be taken to select another option. Default choices can take many forms such as automatic enrollment into a particular choice or forced choice. In forced choice, there is no default option per se, instead, the individual must actively make a decision or they will be denied access to a particular service, product, or situation. Default choices can also come in the form of a specific option that is set up to go into effect if the individual does not "opt-out" or if an alternative is not selected. A large body of research has found that individuals have a strong tendency to choose default options when they are made available (e.g., Benartzi and Thaler, 2007; Bernheim et al., 2015; Brown et al., 2016; Brown and Previtero, 2020; Davidai et al., 2012; Madrian and Shea, 2001). There are several reasons why individuals tend to select default choices. Many of these are related to cognitive biases discussed earlier, such as loss aversion, the endowment effect, the status quo bias, and choice overload. Other reasons are related to the amount of time and effort required to opt out of the default or make an alternative decision, as well as those associated with time inconsistency and procrastination (O'Donoghue and Rabin, 1999, 2001) and a lack of financial literacy (Thaler and Sunstein, 2009).

One of the most famously cited studies on the power of defaults was conducted by Davidai and associates (2012). They investigated the impact that "opt-out" versus "opt-in" donor registration programs had on countries' organ donation rates. In countries such as Austria, organ donation is the default option for all citizens, and, as such, people must explicitly "opt out" if they do not wish to be an organ donor. In countries such as the United States and Germany, people must explicitly "opt in" if they want to donate their organs. The difference in organ donation rates between the two groups of countries is quite staggering. In the *opt-out countries,* more than 90 percent of people have registered to donate their organs, whereas in the *opt-in* countries, fewer than 15 percent of people have registered to be a donor.

Other studies have found that default options have a similar and powerful impact on financial decisions, especially those related to savings and retirement planning (e.g., Benartzi and Thaler, 2007). In one study, Madrian and Shea (2001) showed how using a default option could significantly increase enrollment in a company's 401(k) plan. When the framing orientation of the participation decision was changed from "Do you want to participate?" to "You will participate unless you choose not to," the retirement-plan participation rate among new hires increased from 37 percent before automatic enrollment to 86 percent after automatic enrollment was introduced.

Savings for retirement is a complex problem, and most individuals have some level of difficulty when it comes to making decisions about whether to participate in a savings plan, how much to contribute, and how the contributions should be invested. Rational choice theory assumes that people are able to accurately calculate how much they need to save for retirement. The theory also assumes that people have enough willpower to implement the appropriate savings plan to reach the desired savings goal. However, researchers now know that people do not have unbounded rationality; they also do not have unbounded willpower. Therefore, it should not be surprising that individuals will tend to opt into the default choice when it comes to retirement savings plans, especially when they are faced with too many complex and confusing choices. Employers and financial practitioners can improve the savings outcomes of their employees and clients by thoughtfully crafting sensible default options that are low cost in terms of both time and money. Once individuals are enrolled in a plan, additional opportunities can be created that provide a more "hands-off" approach using software and algorithms that automatically increase clients' savings rates and rebalance portfolios. This again builds on the power of default choice by creating more passive rather than active investment strategies that require minimal client engagement.

## Pre-commitment Mechanisms

Pre-commitment mechanisms are another type of choice architecture that can be used to nudge individuals to change their financial behaviors. Pre-commitment strategies tend to work because they help individuals overcome human tendencies toward loss aversion and status quo bias, among others. They also help people to align long-term goals, such as saving for retirement, with short-term decisions, such as how much to save each month in order to reach their ultimate retirement savings goal. One of the most well-known examples of a successful pre-commitment mechanism is that used by the *Save More Tomorrow*$^{TM}$ program (SMT). SMT was pioneered by Thaler and Benartzi (2004) to foster participation in savings plans and increase savings rates overall. The program was launched in 1998 at a midsize manufacturing firm and studied over a four-year period. Employees were first offered the option to meet with a financial advisor. Note that a small percentage of employees chose not to meet with an advisor (approximately 10 percent). These individuals saved about 6 percent of their income when the program started; their savings rate did not change over the four years. The vast majority of employees (about 90 percent), however, chose to meet with an advisor, who generally recommended that they increase their savings by five percentage points of their pay. On average, their savings rate went from 4 percent to 9 percent after the first pay raise and then stayed constant the next few years. About

25 percent of employees accepted this offer. Others said they could not afford the cut in pay and were offered the SMT program. Of this group, 78 percent chose to enroll in SMT. Contribution rates started lower at about 3.5 percent of income and then steadily went up by three percentage points after each pay raise to 13.6 percent by the end of the four-year period (pay raises were typically from 3.25 percent to 3.5 percent). By pre-committing to an automatic escalation of payments, the SMT participants were able to save the most money – 13.6 percent compared to only 6 percent and 9 percent for the other employees, respectively.

Another successful pre-commitment model that is often cited is *StickK.com*.[2] The platform uses commitment contracts to help individuals set goals and change behavior using loss aversion and accountability. The user selects a goal – like losing weight – and pledges a certain amount of money toward achieving it. Then a referee – often a friend – is chosen and a contract signed. If the goal is achieved, the participant gets the money back. If the goal is not achieved, they forfeit their pledge to a charity, friend, or even an "anti-charity."

## Framing Effect

One of the key assumptions of rational choice theory is that people have well-defined and stable preferences that guide their decisions. However, we have seen from behavioral economics that preferences can be easily influenced by various choice architecture schemes. In fact, the language used to present and describe choices can create powerful nudges that influence people's decisions. This is referred to as the "framing effect." Framing does not change the choice itself, be it a product, service, or situation. Instead, it changes how individuals interact with it or experience it. Consider the following example based on the work of Tversky and Kahneman (1981). Suppose you need an operation. Doctor A tells you: "Of 100 patients who have this operation, 90 are alive after five years." Now suppose you go to Doctor B for a second opinion and Doctor B tells you: "Of 100 patients who have this operation, 10 are dead after five years." Which doctor do you think most people will tend to prefer? Of course, Doctor A. However, traditional rational choice theory would say that, all other things being equal, it should not matter how the situation is framed to the patient – the probability of survival is the same in both cases. But, in reality, words matter. The way information is worded can influence people's choices more than the information itself.

When it comes to framing, research has found that more often than not: (1) using positive messaging is more effective than using negative messaging (Cialdini et al., 2006); (2) focusing on the desirability of the activity/behavior is more effective than focusing on the undesirability (Perkins et al., 2010); and (3) informational messaging

---

2 https://www.stickk.com/.

can be more effective when combined with an emotional nudge (Schultz et al., 2007). In the latter case, consider the following study where researchers monitored the home energy consumption of nearly 300 residents in San Marcos, California (Schultz et al., 2007; Thaler and Sunstein, 2009). All of the households were given information about their energy usage and how it compared to the average energy usage of other households in their neighborhood. In the following weeks, households that were on average using more energy decreased their energy usage. However, those that were using less energy significantly increased their usage. This finding is referred to as the "boomerang effect," where an attempt to persuade individuals to decrease their energy consumption resulted in more energy usage for those that had previously been using less than their neighbors. Additionally, a subset of the households also received an emotional nudge. Specifically, those households that had consumed more energy than the average household received an unhappy "emoticon" or "frowny face" on their utility bill, while those that consumed less energy received a happy "emoticon" or "smiley face." Interestingly, households that consumed more energy ended up reducing their energy consumption by even more when they received the unhappy emoticon. Moreover, for households that consumed less energy, the boomerang effect completely disappeared when they received the happy emoticon. These findings demonstrate the additional power informational messaging can have when combined with an emotional nudge.

With regards to personal financial planning, Tversky and Kahneman (1981) explained framing using prospect theory. Recall that individuals tend to be more influenced by the possibility of a loss than the prospect of an equivalent gain. Simply stated, the theory posits that a sure gain is preferable to a probable gain, and a probable loss is preferable to a sure loss. The way financial choices are framed can influence a person's certainty about whether the various choices will bring either a gain or a loss (Levin et al., 1998). Given this, individuals will find financial choices more attractive when the positive features of the option are highlighted instead of the negative ones. Financial practitioners can also think about the framing of probable losses and gains within the context of clients' preferences and tolerance for risk.

## Priming

Priming is another powerful tool of choice architecture that uses words, but also objects, images, and smells to influence decision making. Priming occurs when an individual is exposed to certain stimuli that influence the individual's response to subsequent stimuli. For example, priming has been used to help people lose weight, exercise more, vote, and even get vaccinated. Asking people a series of questions about what they intend to do and how they plan to do it is a common method used to "prime" individuals. The questions are used to "plants seeds" that encourage them to change a particular behavior without directly telling them that they *should* change their behavior.

In a cutting-edge experiment, Hershfield et al. (2011) posited that young people would be motivated to save more and consume less if they were able to connect better with their future selves. Participants were given virtual reality (VR) goggles and then were sent into a VR laboratory where they were able to view a three-dimensional version of themselves. Half of the participants saw a virtual version of their older "future selves," while the other half saw a version of their "current selves." The researchers prompted people to actively engage with their virtual image while asking them questions that prompted them to connect even more with their virtual image. Later, participants were asked a series of questions about finances and retirement. Those who had seen their older selves were willing to allocate significantly more money toward retirement than those who had seen their current selves – almost twice as much.

In 2012, the *Merrill Edge Face Retirement* app was built on this concept. The app used 3D technology to morph a client's photograph into a life-like image of what they might look like at a few key times during their life span (Tausche and Bergman, 2012). The goal was to connect them to their future self so as to nudge them to start planning for their retirement today. A tab at the bottom of the app pulled up a landing page, which showed them how much they needed to start investing now to retire. While this app is no longer available, it provided a useful example of how behavioral economic research can have direct implications for financial professionals in practice. In this case, the research was used to design an app that used behavioral concepts such as priming and framing to nudge clients to start thinking about retirement planning.

## Conclusions and Future Directions

Rational choice theory provides a general and tractable framework for analyzing how individuals should make decisions in an ideal world. The model is helpful in explaining some behaviors. However, it cannot fully explain all behaviors, especially those that are seemingly irrational. Behavioral economics differs from traditional economics by incorporating insights from human psychology to explain why people deviate from rational action when they are making decisions. In this way, behavioral economics presents a more realistic picture of what people actually do in the real world.

This chapter explored some of the most fundamental concepts associated with behavioral economics and explained how those concepts can be used to better understand how people make financial decisions and why these decisions are not always in their best interest. As described in this chapter, people make systematic mistakes due to cognitive biases that influence their perceptions and decisions. It was also shown that different types of choice architecture and nudges can have a significant and positive impact on individuals' financial decisions and preferences, and ultimately on their long-run financial security. There are many other behavioral economic concepts, cognitive biases, and choice architecture and nudges that could not be included in this chapter that deserve further exploration, including present bias, myopic preferences, time inconsistency, and mental accounting, to name a few. Researchers, practitioners, and policymakers who are interested in further exploring the linkages between behavioral economics and financial decision making can use this chapter as an introduction to some of the most well-known studies and seminal research in the field.

With this said, it is important to recognize that behavioral economics also has limitations. First, individuals may respond differently to information and have varying responses to different types of choice architecture and nudges when making decisions. For example, a specific type of framing may work well as a nudge to positively change some people's behaviors but not others. Second, it can be difficult for researchers and practitioners to definitively determine whether choice architecture and nudges are, in fact, improving financial decision making. Experimental design can assist in establishing causality via the usage of treatment and control groups. However, even these studies have their shortcomings, as they may be unable to adequately simulate the real-world conditions under which individuals are making decisions. There may also be confounding factors, which make it difficult to isolate the true effect of the behavioral intervention.

Finally, behavioral economics is still relatively in its infancy, compared to other economic fields of study. At present, it is largely comprised of hundreds of different concepts – mostly behavioral biases – that are largely a set of exceptions to the rules of standard economic theory. As such, there remain considerable definitional and conceptual gaps in core concepts and theories. From this vantage point, researchers and practitioners should focus on synthesizing existing ideas and creating more structure, theories, and modeling around those ideas. From here, more formal hypotheses can be established and rigorously tested and compared to those of standard economic theory.

# References

Abaluck, J., and Gruber, J. (2011). Choice inconsistencies among the elderly: Evidence from plan choice in the Medicare part D program. *American Economic Review, 101*(4), 1180–1210.

Becker, G. S. (1976). *The economic approach to human behavior*. University of Chicago Press.

Benartzi, S., and Thaler, R. (2007). Heuristics and biases in retirement savings behavior. *Journal of Economic Perspectives, 21*(3), 81–104.

Benson, B. (2017, March 25). 4 basic problems cause all the cognitive biases that screw up our judgement. *Insider*. https://www.businessinsider.com/4-basic-problems-cause-all-the-cognitive-biases-that-screw-up-our-judgment-2017-3

Bernheim, B. D., Fradkin, A., and Popov, I. (2015). The welfare economics of default options in 401(k) plans. *American Economic Review, 105*(9), 2798–2837.

Brown, J. R., Farrell, A. M., and Weisbenner, S. J. (2016). Decision-making approaches and the propensity to default: Evidence and implications. *Journal of Financial Economics*, *121*(3), 477–495.

Brown, J. R., and Previtero, A. (2020). *Saving for retirement, annuities and procrastination* (Working Paper). Accessed July 2021. http://www.aleprevitero.com/wp-content/uploads/2020/06/ 027_Previtero_WP_Procrastination.pdf

Camerer, C. F. (2011). *Behavioral game theory: Experiments in strategic interaction*. Princeton University Press.

Cerulli Associates. (2020). *The evolving role of behavioral finance 2020*. Cerulli Associates, Charles Schwab Investment Management, and Investments & Wealth Institute. Accessed July 2021. https://info.cerulli.com/rs/960-BBE-213/images/SchwabBeFi%20Whitepaper%20-%20Evolv ing%20Role%20of%20Behavioral%20Finance%202020.pdf

Chernev, A., Böckenholt, U., and Goodman, J. (2015). Choice overload: A conceptual review and meta-analysis. *Journal of Consumer Psychology*, *25*(2), 333–358.

Cialdini, R. B., Demaine, L. J., Sagarin, B. J., Barrett, D. W., Rhoads, K., and Winter, P. L. (2006). Managing social norms for persuasive impact. *Social Influence*, *1*(1), 3–15.

Davidai, S., Gilovich, T., and Ross, L. D. (2012). The meaning of default options for potential organ donors. *Proceedings of the National Academy of Sciences*, *109*(38), 15201–15205.

Hershfield, H. E., Goldstein, D. G., Sharpe, W. F., Fox, J., Yeykelis, L., Carstensen, L. L., and Bailenson, J. N. (2011). Increasing saving behavior through age-progressed renderings of the future self. *Journal of Marketing Research*, *48*(SPL), S23–S37.

Iyengar, S. S., and Kamenica, E. (2010). Choice proliferation, simplicity seeking, and asset allocation. *Journal of Public Economics*, *94*(7–8), 530–539.

Iyengar, S. S., and Lepper, M. R. (2000). When choice is demotivating: Can one desire too much of a good thing? *Journal of Personality and Social Psychology*, *79*(6), 995–1006.

Kahneman, D. (2013). *Thinking, fast and slow*. Farrar, Straus and Giroux.

Kahneman, D., and Tversky, A. (1979). Prospect theory: An analysis of decisions under risk. *Econometrica*, *47*, 263–291.

Kahneman, D., and Tversky, A. (1984). Choices, values, and frames. *American Psychologist*, *39*(4), 341–350.

Kempf, A., and Ruenzi, S. (2006). Status quo bias and the number of alternatives: An empirical illustration from the mutual fund industry. *The Journal of Behavioral Finance*, *7*(4), 204–213.

Knetsch, J. L. (1989). The endowment effect and evidence of nonreversible indifference curves. *American Economic Review, 79* (5), 1277–1284.

Levin, I. P., Schneider, S. L., and Gaeth, G. J. (1998). All frames are not created equal: A typology and critical analysis of framing effects. *Organizational Behavior and Human Decision Processes,76*(2), 149–188.

Madrian, B. C., and Shea, D. F. (2001). The power of suggestion: Inertia in 401(k) participation and savings behavior. *The Quarterly Journal of Economics*, *116* (4), 1149–1187.

Mancino, L., and Guthrie, J. F. (2009). When nudging in the lunch line might be a good thing. *Amber Waves*, *7*(1), 32–38.

McWilliams, J. M., Afendulis, C. C., McGuire, T. G., and Landon, B. E. (2011). Complex Medicare advantage choices may overwhelm seniors – especially those with impaired decision making. *Health Affairs, 30* (9), 1786–1794.

O'Donoghue, T., and Rabin, M. (1999). Doing it now or later. *American Economic Review*, *89*(1), 103–124.

O'Donoghue, T., and Rabin, M. (2001). Choice and procrastination. *The Quarterly Journal of Economics*, *116*(1), 121–160.

Pariser, E. (2011). *The filter bubble: What the internet is hiding from you*. The Penguin Group.

Perkins, H. W., Linkenbach, J. W., Lewis, M. A., and Neighbors, C. (2010). Effectiveness of social norms media marketing in reducing drinking and driving: A statewide campaign. *Addictive Behaviors*, *35*(10), 866–874.

Samuelson, W., and Zeckhauser, R. (1988). Status quo bias in decision making. *Journal of Risk and Uncertainty*, *1*(1), 7–59.

Schultz, P. W., Nolan, J. M., Cialdini, R. B., Goldstein, N. J., and Griskevicius, V. (2007). The constructive, destructive, and reconstructive power of social norms. *Psychological Science*, *18*(5), 429–434.

Schwartz, B. (2004). *The paradox of choice: Why more is less*. Harper-Collins Publishers.

Sharot, T. (2011). The optimism bias. *Current Biology*, *21*(23), R941–R945.

Simonsohn, U., Karlsson, N., Loewenstein, G., and Ariely, D. (2008). The tree of experience in the forest of information: Overweighing experienced relative to observed information. *Games and Economic Behavior*, *62*(1), 263–286.

Smith, N. C., Goldstein, D. G., and Johnson, E. J. (2013). Choice without awareness: Ethical and policy implications of defaults. *Journal of Public Policy & Marketing*, *32*(2), 159–172.

Sunstein, C. R. (2016). *The ethics of influence: Government in the age of behavioral science*. Cambridge University Press.

Tausche, K., and Bergman, J. (2012, December 19). Your "face" and your retirement at 100. *CNBC*. https://www.cnbc.com/id/100327174

Thaler, R. (1980). Toward a positive theory of consumer choice. *Journal of Economic Behavior & Organization*, *1*(1), 39–60. https://doi.org/10.1016/0167-2681(80)90051-7

Thaler, R. (2015, October 31). The power of nudges, for good and bad. *The New York Times*. Accessed July 2021. https://www.nytimes.com/2015/11/01/upshot/the-power-of-nudges-for-good-and-bad.html

Thaler, R. H., and Benartzi, S. (2004). Save more tomorrow™: Using behavioral economics to increase employee saving. *Journal of Political Economy*, *112*(S1), S164–S187.

Thaler, R. H., and Sunstein, C. R. (2009). *Nudge: Improving decisions about health, wealth, and happiness*. The Penguin Group.

Tversky, A., and Kahneman, D. (1974). Judgment under uncertainty: Heuristics and biases. *Science*, *185*(4,157), 1124–1131.

Tversky, A., and Kahneman, D. (1981). The framing of decisions and the psychology of choice. *Science*, *211* (4,481), 453–458.

Weinstein, N. D. (1980). Unrealistic optimism about future life events. *Journal of Personality and Social Psychology*, *39*(5), 806–820.

Jinhee Kim, Isha Chawla

# 26 The Role of Socialization in Shaping Personal Finance Attitudes and Behaviors

**Abstract:** Financial socialization is a key process of developing financial values, attitudes, knowledge, and behaviors that contribute to individuals' financial well-being and financial capability. This chapter provides a critical review of the financial socialization literature and theoretical frameworks. Empirical research review has been organized by the components of financial socialization: (a) socio-demographic factors (e.g., race/ethnicity, gender, and income), (b) socialization agents (e.g., peers, parents, and media), and (c) type of learning mechanism. The chapter presents some limitations in the existing literature and concludes with recommendations for researchers, policymakers, and personal finance practitioners.

**Keywords:** socialization, financial socialization, financial literacy, financial behavior

## Introduction

Socialization refers to the ways in which individuals are involved within a community or as a group. In the socialization process, experienced or authoritative group members influence newer or less influential members in infusing social norms, rules, and attitudes into their behavior (Gudmunson et al., 2016). In recent years, scholars, educators, and policymakers have brought their attention to socialization in the context of money and personal finance. The concept of financial socialization is defined as "the process of acquiring and developing values, attitudes, standards, norms, knowledge, and behaviors that contribute to the financial viability and individual well-being" (Gudmunson and Danes, 2011, p. 645). The increasing focus on financial socialization is attributed to concerns related to individuals' and families' inadequate financial literacy and financial hardships. This concern was highlighted at the National Symposium on Financial Literacy and Education, which concluded that financial socialization is one of the most critical research topics that need to be addressed in the future (Solheim et al., 2011).

Given the predominance of complex financial products and services offered by businesses, it has become imperative to establish a link between financial education programs and contextually driven financial socialization (Gudmunson et al., 2016). Moreover, relevant insight into the financial socialization processes and the development of children's and adolescents' financial values, attitudes, and behaviors

**Jinhee Kim, Isha Chawla,** University of Maryland

https://doi.org/10.1515/9783110727692-026

are thought to be vital for a successful transition into adulthood (Kim et al., 2011). In particular, financial socialization is known to impact financial decision making (Jorgensen et al., 2017; Rea et al., 2019) and financial well-being during adulthood (Ullah and Yusheng, 2020). For example, childhood financial socialization experiences positively relate to beneficial financial practices, financial asset ownership (Kim and Chatterjee, 2013), and preparation for retirement in adulthood (Payne et al., 2014). Thus, the purpose of this chapter is to review existing research on financial socialization and offer future directions in research and recommendations for personal finance practitioners and policymakers.

This chapter starts with a review of the evolution of financial socialization by describing the progression and importance of financial socialization as a field. The chapter further describes the fundamental theoretical approaches used to explain the financial socialization process and elaborates on existing research related to the type of financial socialization, socialization agents, gender, and race/ethnic differences in financial socialization. This chapter also evaluates the limitations present in recent literature. The chapter concludes with recommendations for researchers, educators, and policymakers.

## Historical Perspective

Financial socialization has been a continuous focus of scholars across the past several decades. Researchers have explored different factors that affect socialization, including literacy, attitudes, beliefs, norms, roles, skills, standards, and values. Further, these factors and their antecedents are dynamic and have evolved over the years, affecting financial decision making outcomes (Danes, 1994). Over time, financial socialization has helped contextualize financial behavior and decision making and has complemented the existing literature to expand the personal finance field's understanding of several underlying mechanisms. For example, neoclassical economics has provided the rationale for variability in financial decisions due to financial literacy, but traditional economics models have been limited in providing a holistic explanation, primarily because widely used models have failed to account for financial socialization (Gudmunson and Danes, 2011; Lunt, 1996).

There has been increasing acknowledgment that financial decision making and financial behavior stem from individuals' characteristics affected by social and psychological influences (Danes, 1994). Moschis (1987) stressed the notion that family influence in the socialization process is related to several important decisions. In this regard, Danes (1994) noted the following: "Socialization is the process by which individuals acquire the knowledge, skills, and value dispositions that enable them to participate as more or less effective members of groups and society" (p. 127).

Additionally, researchers have focused on the mode of exchange of several aspects of financial socialization, such as communication. According to Moschis et al. (1984), communication assists individuals in grasping the content, logic, and operation of financial systems. Mugenda et al. (1990) demonstrated that family characteristics impact the form of communications about money, resulting in improved financial behaviors (see also Gudmunson and Danes, 2011). Ivan and Dickson (2008) provided a comprehensive view of the influence exerted by family members, through verbal and nonverbal communication, on intermediate outcomes, such as the development of money attitudes associated with financial behaviors and well-being.

The last decade has seen several important theoretical developments in the conceptualization of financial socialization. Family financial socialization theory has been developed and refined (e.g., Danes, 1994; Ivan and Dickson, 2008; Ward, 1974). Gudmunson and Danes (2011), for example, presented family financial socialization as a theory and offered a cohesive framework in this field of study (Danes and Yang, 2014; LeBaron and Kelley, 2020).

Despite these developments, scholars continue to argue that there is still scope to understand the unique socializing role of social agents, including families, peers, and society, in influencing several aspects of financial socialization, such as promoting financial literacy (Jorgensen and Savla, 2010; LeBaron and Kelley, 2020). Researchers also suggest that a gap exists in understanding the underlying mechanisms of the exchange of social values, especially financial ethics, saving habits, and economic pressure. Additionally, limited information is available about how the effects of social agents and subjects vary by different demographic and socioeconomic groups. Also, limited research is available about the long-term impacts of financial socialization using longitudinal data. There is an opportunity to expand or extend existing theories to further the personal finance field's understanding of some of the critical aspects mentioned above.

# Theoretical Perspective

Financial socialization theory and social learning theory comprise the primary frameworks used for research and practice among those interested in the topic of socialization. The following discussion reviews both theories.

## Family Financial Socialization (FFS) Theory

Bandura's (1977) social learning theory suggests that people acquire behavior and attitudes by observing important people in their lives. The learning process, which occurs by noticing the behavior and attitudes of other individuals, is known as modeling.

Social learning theory has been utilized widely for examining changes in behavior. Most behavior is learned either through deliberate or unintended socialization. According to Bandura (1977), behavior can be changed effectively and efficiently through modeling. Consumer socialization literature centered on social learning theory suggests that behaviors can be acquired through socialization agents such as family and peers during adolescence and can also be transferred further to the following generations (Churchill and Moschis, 1979; Valence et al., 1988).

Gudmunson and Danes' (2011) family financial socialization theory posits that children's learning related to money takes place in a social setting, where family is the primary socialization unit. Financial learning influences financial outcomes during childhood and even in adulthood. FFS ties together the family unit characteristics and interactions, with financial socialization outcomes, including behaviors and well-being, through financial attitudes, knowledge, and capabilities (Payne et al., 2014). While some financial socialization occurs deliberately, a considerable portion of learning and teaching occurs when family members observe the behaviors of others. Such socialization is linked with the advancement of financial management capabilities, defined as financial attitudes, knowledge, and capabilities. FFS theory is based on the assumption that financial socialization's effect on individuals and families varies by life stage and in terms of socialization agents and contexts. Family processes are determined by individual and family characteristics, including age, gender, socioeconomic, and marital status. Observing parental financial behaviors, children acquire internalized lessons and messages that form their financial attitudes and behavior. The quality of relationships with parents determines purposive and financial socialization outcomes. In other words, a healthy parent–child relationship is more likely to result in successful purposive socialization. Thus, both implicit and deliberate financial socialization affect financial attitudes, knowledge, and capabilities. Regarding the outcomes of financial socialization, Gudmunson and Danes (2011) argued that family socialization processes are further related to financial behavior and subsequently affect financial well-being. Financial well-being involves subjective indicators, such as financial satisfaction and financial stress, and objective indicators, such as income, savings, and credit score. Thus, financial well-being integrates family financial socialization processes over the life course, especially during childhood and adolescence (LeBaron and Kelley, 2020). Since its inception, scholars have widely used the FFS theory to study the financial socialization processes in families. In addition to utilizing the FFS theory, future research could focus on critically reviewing the theory and seeking more creative, innovative, and collaborative efforts for future modifications or integration of different theoretical frameworks.

## Other Theories

To further increase understanding of the financial socialization process, it is crucial to study environmental and attitudinal factors. The theory of planned behavior (Ajzen, 1991) and the theory of family resource management (Deacon and Firebaugh 1981) are considered relevant in explaining financial socialization (Van Campenhout, 2015). The theory of planned behavior (TPB) is the most cited explanation of human behavior. TPB provides a theoretical basis and posits that human behavior is shaped by someone's behavioral intentions, attitudes, subjective norms, and perceived control, describing individuals' decision-making processes. TPB has been widely applied in finance-related contexts, such as investments (Kurland, 1995), insurance (Cuccinelli et al., 2016), and financial behavior (Shim et al., 2012).

Deacon and Firebaugh (1981) developed family resource management theory to explain resource expansion, distribution, and management within the family. Family resource management theory uses four stages to explain how financial behaviors are influenced by existing resources and personal characteristics (Jorgensen and Savla, 2010). The stages of the model (i.e., inputs, throughputs, outputs, and feedback loop) describe the basis of financial decisions and behaviors. Jorgensen and Savla (2010) utilized this framework to demonstrate the influence of existing inputs, including environmental factors, such as parents, on the financial behavior of young adults. This theory, and the other theories discussed above, provide essential insights into the financial socialization process and pave the way for future research by those interested in the topic.

# Empirical Research on Financial Socialization

The scholars who have been instrumental in the development of socialization models tend to stress the importance of three components of financial socialization: (a) socioeconomic factors (e.g., gender, race/ethnicity), (b) socialization agents (e.g., peers, parents, media), and (c) type of learning mechanism (Carlson and Grossbart, 1988; Garrison and Gutter, 2010; Mascarenhas and Higby, 1993). These elements are crucial to explaining socialization processes and offer a broader overview of financial socialization. Each is described in more detail below.

## Socio-demographic Factors

There is ample evidence of a positive association between parents' socioeconomic status and positive financial outcomes (Destin and Oyserman, 2009; Kim and Chatterjee, 2013; Shanks, 2007). Wealth is not only associated with financial independence but wealth is also considered to be a cushion against adverse economic outcomes (Destin and Oyserman, 2009). Moreover, financial struggles may adversely affect emotions, behaviors, and parental beliefs, resulting in a negative influence through parental socialization. Similarly, financial difficulties can have an adverse effect on parents' emotions, behaviors, and beliefs, which in turn can negatively influence parenting practices and socialization strategies (Conger and Conger, 2002). Transitioning to adulthood may require financial support from parents due to the addition of emerging adulthood as a life stage. Parental resources relate to the sense of security for children and influence parent–child interactions about finances and spending (Anderson, 2018). Disparities in access to financial services can influence the level of financial knowledge as well as financial capabilities. Minority groups and low-income youths are less likely to have access to mainstream financial systems and lack checking or savings accounts, investments, and insurance coverages (Sherraden et al., 2018). Owning a bank account is an important aspect of financial socialization. Parents' access to a bank account is important because children cannot open an account without their parents.

In a study of youth and financial capability, White students scored relatively higher (55.0 percent) than Hispanics (46.8 percent) and African Americans (44.7 percent) on a financial literacy test, and students from the higher income group (i.e., more than $80,000 per year) scored significantly higher than lower-income students (Sherraden et al., 2018). Inadequate financial knowledge due to less exposure to mainstream financial institutions, and other contextual factors, may further inhibit financial socialization, especially among low to moderate-income households (Sherraden, 2013). Low-income or low asset families may lack access to savings accounts due to these barriers. Due to the existing inequities in financial access, financial socialization through experiential learning is likely limited for many young people of color (Hudson, 2016).

## Gender

Gender difference in the context of risk-taking has been extensively studied (Hallahan et al., 2004; Watson and McNaughton, 2007). In much of the extant literature, women have been found to be more risk-averse than men in terms of investing and, in general, are less engaged in investing their money (Garrison and Gutter, 2010). According to Sohn (2021), the average life expectancy in the United States was 75.1 for men, while it was 80.5 years for women during the first half of 2020. Aside from outliving their male counterparts, women experience increasing poverty levels. According to Firestone et al. (1999), earnings are found to be lower in female-dominated occupations. Garrison and Gutter (2010) found that female college students have considerably more conversations with their parents and friends regarding saving and investing their money than male college students. Although females have had more interactions about saving and investing, females have been found to pursue conservative saving and investment strategies more frequently.

Theories related to gender development suggest that female and male children may experience varying forms of financial socialization in their immediate environment (i.e., home), which leads to varying financial behaviors and knowledge in adulthood. According to Danes and Haberman (2007), females are taught to embrace safety rather than risk-taking. There seems to be gender bias in how parents interact with their children related to financial matters. Agnew and Cameron-Agnew (2015) demonstrated that 14-year-old females, on average, had their first financial discussions with their parents later than their male counterparts. Therefore, parents' role in this process should not be undervalued, as opinion-related financial discussions are formed in the home and translated in their later years of life (Agnew et al., 2018; Shim et al., 2011). Discussions with parents about financial matters that lead to greater financial knowledge may be subjected to gender bias (Agnew et al., 2018). Overall, there is ample evidence of gender bias in financial socialization and risk tolerance of women; however, there is little known about whether the gender bias in financial socialization affects future intrahousehold decisions. It is reasonable to hypothesize that early age financial discussions with daughters within an immediate setting can impact their bargaining power and intrahousehold resource allocation after marriage.

## Race/Ethnicity

According to the U.S. Census Bureau, in 2019, Americans who identified their race or ethnicity as other than non-Hispanic White altogether comprised 40 percent of the population, with this percentage expected to increase to 50 percent by 2044. There have been documented significant wealth and income disparities by race and ethnicity. The racial gap has increased in the past couple of decades. Lower levels of socioeconomic status such as education and income explain some of the disparities. However, there have also been documented social and structural barriers to building wealth for people of color (Kim et al., 2016; Shapiro et al., 2013).

The consumer socialization theory posits that social class, race, and ethnicity influence socialization by learning processes. Race and ethnicity influence socialization within a group, influencing financial literacy and behavior (Jorgensen et al., 2017). Gurney (1988) argued that the meaning associated with money is also determined by cultural background and religion, along with the influence of parents, teachers, and life goals. According to Tang (1993), socio-political and religious beliefs are significant contributors to financial attitudes, indicating that financial attitudes may differ from region to region. Bailey et al. (1994) found that a person's nation of origin outweighed the shared experience, norms, and expectations predicting Americans', Canadians', and Australians' financial attitudes. In exploring racial/ethnic differences in financial socialization, White et al. (2020) found that specific financial messages related to a person's family origin and that saving, banking, and investing were positively associated with shaping the financial management behaviors and attitudes among Latinos. In one study, it was determined that African American students who were motivated to save experienced reduced financial stress compared to Asian American students who were encouraged to save money (Hudson et al., 2017). Compared to other racial and ethnic groups, African American people face various barriers to attaining financial well-being and have faced numerous challenges in accessing financial services (Baity, 2020; Billingsley, 1968). Family financial socialization may play a key role in navigating structural barriers for African American families. Due to racism and racial injustices, Black families may sometimes focus on socializing members to surviving social constructs of race and racism while under-socializing members in financial matters (Baity, 2020). As this discussion highlights, there is a need for future studies to focus on the racial/ethnic groups when studying financial socialization processes.

Moreover, Danes et al. (2008) suggested that cultural differences among different racial and ethnic groups may influence financial outcomes in purposive financial socialization. According to Hofstede (2015), cultural values are typically acquired in childhood and established across generations through the transmission by important financial socialization agents, including parents. Jorgensen et al. (2017), utilizing the family financial socialization model framework, stressed differences by geographical location when examining the differences in financial achievement and power attitudes and spending behavior. They found that financial achievement attitudes, financial power attitudes, and responsible behavior vary across four regions in the United States (Jorgensen et al., 2017). Notwithstanding the greater prominence of the impact of culture on financial socialization, there is limited research that examines differences in the financial socialization process. Even fewer have explored racial or ethnic differences in financial socialization processes (Gudmunson and Danes, 2011; White et al., 2020). Advancement in the financial socialization field can be made by increasing attention to racial or ethnic differences (and similarities) and by investigating why these factors influence financial outcomes (Gudmunson and Danes, 2011; White et al., 2020).

## Socialization Agents

The socialization process incorporates both socialization agents and learning in socialization processes (Moschis and Churchill Jr., 1978). The existing literature has centered on family, peers, school, and media as the significant agents of consumer socialization. This literature has revealed that each agent interacts differently throughout the life-cycle (Sohn et al., 2012). These four agents are widely emphasized in the consumer socialization literature (Ward, 1974). Each is described in more detail below.

*Parents.* Amidst different sets of socialization agents, parents are considered to play a crucial role in financial socialization (Churchill and Moschis, 1979; Sohn et al., 2012). Parents are found to be primary socialization agents for youth in shaping money or saving attitudes (Rettig, 1985), credit behaviors (Norvilitis et al., 2006), and seeking financial information (Lyons, 2008). On surveying high-school and college students who participated in financial education workshops, one study found that about 77 percent of the students had turned to their parents to seek financial information (Lyons, 2008). Parents' role in financial socialization at an early stage of childhood is of profound importance (Van Campenhout, 2015). Family, mothers, and fathers, in particular, contribute to the financial beliefs and attitudes of youths, meaning that the children acquire the symbolic meaning of money from their parents and other family members (Gutter et al., 2010; Hira, 1997). While almost all research focuses on parents, limited research is available about the roles of caregivers or other critical family members for individuals from non-traditional families in the U.S.

*Financial education.* According to Bernheim et al. (2001), mandated school financial education significantly increases saving rates and wealth levels throughout life. Moreover, a well-designed financial curriculum can enhance high-school students' financial knowledge and behavior (Sohn et al., 2012; Varcoe et al., 2005). Studies gauging the impact of high-school financial curriculums have found that after completing a financial education course, the school participants reported an increase in financial knowledge and confidence in their financial management and short-term savings abilities (Danes and Brewton, 2014; Danes et al., 1999; Deenanath et al., 2019). In addition, high-school and college financial education are known to be positively related to increasing financial capabilities (Xiao and O'Neill, 2016). Currently, 24 U.S. states require high schools to offer an economics course, and 19 states require personal finance courses (CEE, 2016). Mandated financial education is conducted through lectures in a classroom setting or online (Mandell, 2006). While results of evaluation studies on school-based financial education are mixed, most of such education programs are found to be effective in enhancing students' financial literacy, behaviors, and attitudes toward money (Jin and Chen, 2019). While the effect of financial education on financial outcomes is significant, there is a need for additional research that turns its attention to other agents and considers the moderating or mediating role of financial education.

*Media.* Media is an important socialization agent for children and adolescents. Lyons et al. (2006) found that 33 percent of high-school and college students had used media and the Internet to acquire financial information. The existing literature has demonstrated that television viewership is positively correlated with purchase decisions, brand recognition, materialistic attitudes, and financial behaviors (Buijzen and Valkenburg, 2003; Churchill and Moschis, 1979; Hira and Loibl, 2005). Moreover, media, including newsletters, publications, software as information sources for money management, is positively related to healthy financial practices and financial satisfaction (Hira and Loibl, 2005). Hira and Loibl (2005) claimed that these media sources effectively assist self-directed learning in adults' financial learning (Sohn et al., 2012). A person's self-directed initiative to acquire financial knowledge may vary from one life stage to another. Additional research to explore media use at different life stages may provide more insights.

*Peers.* Scholars have also observed that peers' influence plays a role in shaping a young adult's financial behavior (Kretschmer and Pike, 2010; Masche, 2010; Moore and Bowman, 2006). In their exploration of adolescents' propensities to gamble, Delfabbro and Thrupp (2003) found that part of youths' gambling behavior was attributed to peer socialization. The influences of peers increases as individuals grow older and shift from parents to peers. Peer effects are stronger in cases of ineffective parental communication and an unstable family environment (John, 1999). Peers become critical socialization agents as an individual reaches adolescent age. According to Abramovitch and Grusec (1978), children from age 4 years to 11 years are significantly influenced by their peers as they, in the study conducted by Abromovitch and Grusec (1978), mimicked 19 behaviors of peers in a natural setting for a time duration of one hour (Mohamed, 2017). Regarding financial socialization, children are more likely to learn financial management skills if they more often observe and interact with parents and their peers (Gutter et al., 2009; Mohamed, 2017). Using data on Pakistan adults with a maximum age of 40 years, Ullah and Yusheng (2020) demonstrated that financial socialization through peers exhibited a negative effect on financial well-being. This indicates that financial well-being is reduced for those who discuss and observe the financial behaviors of their peers. It is also evident that individuals who mimic and observe the financial decisions of their peers experience difficulties in managing their finances. According to Beshears et al. (2015), peer information support negatively influences savings. Overall, the existing literature alludes to the possibility that peers could affect decision-making processes that may not always result in positive financial outcomes.

With the advancement of financial technology, peers' socialization may be crucial in using financial technology and applications. However, there is little research showing the role of peers in opting for the latest financial technology applications. Thus, additional research is needed on the roles and interrelationships of peers and other financial socialization agents.

## Type of Family Financial Socialization

To fully understand the process of socialization, it is important to understand the type of learning mechanisms that govern financial socialization. Family financial socialization theory posits that financial socialization between children and parents occurs within the family through purposive and unintentional socialization processes (Gudmunson and Danes, 2011). Money being an essential resource, family interactions and discussions center on procurement, distribution, and allocation of resources to a large extent (Deenanath et al., 2019). Children acquire knowledge unintentionally by observing their parents and modeling observed behaviors (Deenanath et al., 2019). On noticing their parents' discussion about money issues, children learn without much deliberation. Involvement in discussions and seeking clarification helps generate confidence in children in terms of managing money (Gudmunson and Danes, 2011). Jorgensen and Savla (2010) demonstrated a significant effect of discussing money with parents on young adults' financial knowledge and financial behavior. In addition, college students who got involved in conversations related to money with their parents became skilled in financial management during their college years (Shim et al., 2010). The studies in financial socialization have primarily stressed parent–child communications to examine unintentional socialization. The influence of other socialization agents, including media, should not be underestimated. Media commercials related to financial products and services may be an important contributor to enhancing one's financial knowledge.

Purposive socialization can occur when parents deliberately teach children about financial concepts and behavior (Gudmunson and Danes, 2011). Intended socialization should necessarily involve access to money and making financial decisions. Parents can encourage children to look for part-time job opportunities or provide them with a regular allowance to induce a purposive learning environment (Deenanath et al., 2019). Simple financial management practices, such as opening a savings account, may amount to purposive financial socialization. The extant literature suggests that children who had an allowance through a job source or were provided an allowance by their parents were more sophisticated about their finances in later life (Abramovitch et al., 1991) and were less worried about money (Kim and Chatterjee, 2013), saved up to 16 percent of their income (Bucciol and Veronesi, 2014), and had a higher level of financial literacy (Deenanath et al., 2019; Worthington, 2006). While most research in family financial socialization has focused on deliberate teaching and unintended modeling of financial behavior, there has been a less explicit focus on experiential learning. It is suggested that experience-based, practical learning can help children learn about managing money, enhance their confidence, and improve their financial well-being in adulthood (Ullah and Yusheng, 2020). Experiential learning is the process of acquiring knowledge through life experiences (Kolb, 2014). Experiential learning theory suggests that children can learn about money through their own experience with money (Kolb, 2014; LeBaron et al., 2019). Financial expertise may enhance financial literacy (Chen and Volpe, 1998), resulting in increased financial responsibility and confidence when making financial decisions (Jorgensen and Savla, 2010). The existing literature has studied the importance of financial experience and has implicitly examined experiential learning; however, there is a need to explore experiential learning more extensively in terms of past experiences with financial products and the context of the financial socialization framework. Thus, more research in this direction could potentially bridge the gap in the literature.

# Implication for Future Researchers, Policy Makers, and Personal Finance Professionals

Financial socialization is an ongoing process that involves several socialization agents, which together influence later-life financial outcomes, including financial well-being. The critical role of financial socialization on consequential decision making such as saving, budgeting, and investing may be worth noting for educators, researchers, personal finance professionals, and policymakers.

## Implications for Educators

Financial socialization takes place throughout one's lifetime in different contexts and environments. Family and schools play a critical role in shaping one's financial norms, attitudes, behaviors, and future financial well-being. Despite substantial research on the importance of several aspects of financial socialization in day-to-day practice, its use has been limited. This chapter offers important recommendations for financial socialization stakeholders, especially school-based financial teachers and parents. Some recommendations for teachers and parents include:

*Teachers.* Integrating purposive and experiential learning with financial education programs for youth and children can significantly improve young people's financial behavior and well-being. Batty et al. (2015) suggested that experiential financial education is an effective strategy for teaching financial literacy as it promotes financial socialization. Experiential financial learning models include student-run banks or credit unions, savings programs for students, assignments on making small deposits, and so forth (Batty et al., 2015; Choi, 2009; Johnson and Sherraden, 2007).

*Practitioners as educators.* Apart from teachers, personal finance practitioners can impact financial socialization and education as well. They can share pertinent examples and tools for children or family members to improve engagement with children at an early stage. They can target elementary school students and their families and educate them on integrating purposive role modeling techniques.

*Parents.* It is evident from the literature that parents play an important role in influencing their children's financial behavior; however, many parents may not have the necessary financial literacy and access to financial services themselves to effectively teach and guide their children. Parents should ensure that they have access to resources, such as specific tools and information that will be helpful for them to engage and influence their children positively. Furthermore, parents need to reinforce what children learn in school. It is critical to acknowledge that many children may not have the same opportunities for financial socialization and education as others; this is especially true for people of color and immigrants or other economically disadvantaged groups. There is well-documented evidence of a wealth divide by race and ethnicity in the U.S. (and European) society. Therefore, educators, especially teachers, need to focus appropriate financial education efforts on more vulnerable groups.

## Implications for Personal Finance Professionals

This chapter reinforces and highlights the importance of financial socialization as a tool for personal finance practitioners to connect and better serve clients. Financial practitioners can significantly impact the financial socialization journey of their clients at all stages of the client's life development. However, findings reported in the literature suggest that practitioners need to be aware of several things, such as:

- They need to take into account the background and the life experiences of their clients. Understanding a client's earlier experiences with money can offer useful insights into their financial socialization journey and how socialization has influenced their financial behavior and decisions.
- They should leverage the sociodemographic characteristics of their clients to understand and account for their childhood experiences with money. For example, financial counselors can tailor their dealings with female clients by suggesting lucrative yet less risky options for channelizing savings. Some female clients, due to childhood conditioning, may find risk-averse opportunities more attractive. In another example, for immigrant families, personal finance practitioners can adopt a multi-generational strategy wherein they connect with their client's family across generations. This can be effective for immigrants because they often pool resources or reside in multi-generational households. For clients of color, especially those with lower socioeconomic status, it might be more valuable to increase the frequency of interactions and focus on building trust, growing resources and access, and increasing their confidence in financial decision making.
- Further, personal finance practitioners can take steps to incorporate customized client education and marketing material, or curriculum related to financial counseling, for client relatability and promote clients' practice and apply their financial knowledge to financial decision making in various settings based on experiential learning.

## Implications for Policymakers

This chapter highlights several issues around financial socialization that have important implications for policymakers. First, to promote healthy financial behavior, policymakers should focus their attention on increasing financial capability and wealth building at a very early age. Providing financial education and resources for parents will be beneficial for their financial well-being and their children and generations to come. Another consideration is mandating financial education for children as part of formal education and providing financial access through child accounts for parents who are currently unbanked or underbanked. Second, policymakers should also focus their attention on devising policies that provide financial education to parents. Third, policymakers should consider making financial education a mandatory component of formal education programs. Finally, policymakers should further formulate policies that provide economically vulnerable consumers with affordable and appropriate financial services products, including investment, insurance, and other products. These policies should also focus on spreading awareness about the importance of financial socialization among families and help address various barriers to financial socialization.

## Implications for Future Research

Financial socialization research is still being conceptualized. Many opportunities for future work exist. First, future research needs to address the limitations of the existing literature. Accordingly, there should be more studies on the long-term impacts of financial socialization among different populations in different countries. The effect of financial socialization among older adults (i.e., individuals beyond college age) needs much more attention. There needs to be more longitudinal studies that use multiple data points and data sources.

Second, the FFS model needs to be tested with empirical data from diverse family structures, such as single-parent and lesbian, gay, bisexual, transgender and queer or questioning (LGBTQ) groups, low to moderate-income households, different geographic areas, and people of color. Studies have been conducted using data from different countries (e.g., Sirsch et al., 2020; Ullah and Yusheng, 2020), but these data tend to be primarily European and American. Recent research on Black families has shed insights into how racism and racial structures interact with finances in families. Research focusing on Latinx, immigrants, Native Americans, and other groups has been minimal. Because of structural barriers and income and wealth gaps, Black families living in the United States, for example, are known to have fewer financial resources for financial socialization (Fulk and White, 2018). Additionally, they may have to prioritize parental socialization for their children's survival or navigating racism (Baity, 2020). There is limited research on how these factors affect the financial socialization process and outcomes for Black families. Traditional measures in personal finance research have been mainly developed and tested with White/Caucasian and middle-class families. Those measures may not capture other aspects of financial socialization in immigrant families. The impacts of the Covid-19 pandemic should also be addressed in future research because low- to moderate-income communities and people of color have been disproportionately affected by the pandemic (Clark et al., 2020; Yancy, 2020).

Third, the FFS model can be further empirically tested with diverse populations in different situations. Researchers should consider connecting the theory with other theoretical frameworks as a way to consider the roles psychological and contextual factors play in moderating or mediating financial socialization and financial outcomes. FFS focuses on financial attitudes, financial knowledge, and financial capabilities. However, studies have identified the role of psychological and attitudinal factors, such as financial self-efficacy and locus of control, and socioeconomic contexts such as unemployment, births and death, unemployment, health, and sickness as contextual factors that influence one's financial well-being (Consumer Financial Protection Bureau, 2017). It is important to understand how FFS may influence these factors or interact with these factors in predicting financial behaviors and financial well-being.

Fourth, research evaluating the effectiveness of financial education socialization programs needs to be conducted. There is a strong need to understand the performance of existing policies and programs. Understanding the effectiveness of these programs will help policymakers target policy initiatives in a more focused and customized fashion. Moreover, studying the impact of socialization programs can help policymakers understand common barriers, required resources, and prevalent engagement mechanisms. More research is needed to know how financial education programs impact the diffusion of different aspects of financial socialization.

Fifth, existing research has provided substantial evidence of the positive influence of parent–child interactions related to money in creating financial socialization; however, the early negative experiences of children with their caretakers, such as insecure attachment, abusive relationships, parent separation, parent incarceration, or foster care, can also critically shape financial socialization and adulthood financial well-being. Future studies could examine the impact of adverse childhood experiences on aspects of financial socialization.

Sixth, previous studies have extensively focused on parent–child dyads when examining the constructs of financial socialization, but these studies have been limited in exploring the impact of other relationship influences, such as siblings, romantic partners, and grandparents. This presents an opportunity for future researchers to explore and expand. Additionally, the literature is limited in utilizing theories to explain the underlying mechanism(s) of financial socialization. For example, despite several advantages, family system theory has not been leveraged enough to explain the impact of family hierarchy, economic enmeshment, and financial decision making.

In this regard, researchers should use several frameworks to explain financial socialization processes. The existing literature has mainly focused on the influence of financial socialization on more general financial outcomes, including financial literacy, financial capability, and financial behavior; however, there is a need to understand which aspects (savings, investment, etc.) of these general outcomes are affected by financial socialization. Future studies should focus on gaining a deeper understanding of these outcomes. Further studies should attempt to gather data from multiple family members. A multi-informant study can capture a variety of family dynamics, which could be vital in understanding the socialization process

(Lanz et al., 2020). Future research should, therefore, consider including a father, mother, children, and/or siblings when studying household outcomes. Qualitative or mixed-methods approaches may particularly be effective in gauging these family perspectives. The existing literature presents some limitations that can be improved in future research.

## Conclusion

As discussed in this chapter, the process of general socialization and financial socialization provides a unique way to conceptualize the way individuals develop how to feel about, think, and manage personal finance. Numerous research opportunities exist for those interested in better understanding relationships between and among financial socialization, financial behaviors, and well-being. Future research will help policymakers better understand the dynamics that shape financial behavior at the personal and household level. As noted by the National Symposium on Financial Literacy and Education, financial socialization is a topic that will undoubtedly grow in importance in future years.

## References

Abramovitch, R., Freedman, J. L., and Pliner, P. (1991). Children and money: Getting an allowance, credit versus cash, and knowledge of pricing. *Journal of Economic Psychology*, *12*(1), 27–45. https://doi.org/https://doi.org/10.1016/0167-4870(91)90042-R.

Abramovitch, R., and Grusec, J. E. (1978). Peer imitation in a natural setting. *Child Development*, *49*(1), 60–65. https://doi.org/10.2307/1128593

Agnew, S., and Cameron-Agnew, T. (2015). The influence of consumer socialisation in the home on gender differences in financial literacy. *International Journal of Consumer Studies*, *39*(6), 630–638. https://doi.org/https://doi.org/10.1111/ijcs.12179

Agnew, S., Maras, P., and Moon, A. (2018). Gender differences in financial socialization in the home – An exploratory study. *International Journal of Consumer Studies*, *42*(3), 275–282. https://doi.org/https://doi.org/10.1111/ijcs.12415

Ajzen, I. (1991). The theory of planned behavior. *Organizational Behavior and Human Decision Processes*, *50*(2), 179–211. https://doi.org/10.1016/0749-5978(91)90020-T

Anderson, R. E. (2018). And still WE rise: Parent–child relationships, resilience, and school readiness in low-income urban Black families. *Journal of Family Psychology*, *32*(1), 60.

Bailey, W., Johnson, P., Adams, C., Lawson, R. J., Williams, P. K., and Lown, J. M. (1994). An exploratory study of the money beliefs and behaviors scale using data from three nations. *Consumer Interests Annual*, *40*, 178–185.

Baity, C. S. (2020). *Family financial socialization in Black families: An exploratory study* [Doctoral dissertation, Florida State University]. ProQuest Dissertations and Theses Global.

Bandura, A. (1977). *Social learning theory*. General Learning Press.

Batty, M., Collins, J. M., and Odders-White, E. (2015). Experimental evidence on the effects of financial education on elementary school students' knowledge, behavior, and attitudes. *Journal of Consumer Affairs*, *49*(1), 69–96. https://doi.org/https://doi.org/10.1111/joca.12058

Bernheim, B. D., Garrett, D. M., and Maki, D. M. (2001). Education and saving: The long-term effects of high school financial curriculum mandates. *Journal of Public Economics*, *80*(3), 435–465. https://doi.org/https://doi.org/10.1016/S0047-2727(00)00120-1

Beshears, J., Choi, J. J., Laibson, D., Madrian, B. C., and Milkman, K. L. (2015). The effect of providing peer information on retirement savings decision. *The Journal of Finance*, *70*(3), 1161–1201.

Billingsley, A. (1968). *Black families in White America*. Englewood Cliffs.

Bucciol, A., and Veronesi, M. (2014). Teaching children to save: What is the best strategy for lifetime savings? *Journal of Economic Psychology*, *45*, 1–17. https://doi.org/10.1016/j.joep.2014.07.003

Buijzen, M., and Valkenburg, P. M. (2003). The effects of television advertising on materialism, parent–child conflict, and unhappiness: A review of research. *Journal of Applied Developmental Psychology*, *24*(4), 437–456. https://doi.org/https://doi.org/10.1016/S0193-3973(03)00072-8

Carlson, L., and Grossbart, S. (1988). Parental style and consumer socialization of children. *Journal of Consumer Research*, *15*(1), 77–94. https://doi.org/10.1086/209147

Chen, H., and Volpe, R. P. (1998). An analysis of personal financial literacy among college students. *Financial Services Review*, *7*(2), 107–128. https://doi.org/https://doi.org/10.1016/S1057-0810(99)80006-7

Choi, L. (2009). Bank accounts and youth financial knowledge: Connecting experience and education. *The Federal Reserve Bank of San Francisco*. https://www.frbsf.org/community-development/publications/working-papers/2009/september/bank-accounts-youth-financial-education/

Churchill, G. A., Jr., and Moschis, G. P. (1979). Television and interpersonal influences on adolescent consumer learning. *Journal of Consumer Research*, *6*(1), 23–35. https://doi.org/10.1086/208745

Clark, R. L., Lusardi, A., and Mitchell, O. S. (2020). *Financial fragility during the Covid-19 pandemic* (NBER Working Paper No. 28207). National Bureau of Economic Research. http://www.nber.org/papers/w28207

Conger, R. D., and Conger, K. J. (2002). Resilience in Midwestern families: Selected findings from the first decade of a prospective, longitudinal study. *Journal of Marriage and Family*, *64*(2), 361–373.

Consumer Financial Protection Bureau. (2017). *Financial well-being in America*. https://files.consumerfinance.gov/f/documents/201709_cfpb_financial-well-being-in-America.pdf

Council for Economic Education (CEE) (2016). *Survey of the states: Economic and personal finance education in our nation's schools*. https://www.councilforeconed.org/wp-content/uploads/2014/02/2014-Survey-of-the-States.pdf.

Cuccinelli, D., Gandolfi, G., and Soana, M.-G. (2016). Customer and advisor financial decisions: The theory of planned behavior perspective. *International Journal of Business and Social Science*, *7*(12), 80–92.

Danes, S. M. (1994). Parental perceptions of children's financial socialization. *Journal of Financial Counseling and Planning*, *5*(1), 127–149.

Danes, S. M., and Brewton, K. E. (2014). The role of learning context in high school students' financial knowledge and behavior acquisition. *Journal of Family and Economic Issues*, *35*(1), 81–94. https://doi.org/10.1007/s10834-013-9351-6

Danes, S. M., and Haberman, H. R. (2007). Teen financial knowledge, self-efficacy, and behavior: A gendered view. *Journal of Financial Counseling and Planning*, *18*(2), 48–60.

Danes, S. M., Huddleston-Casas, C., and Boyce, L. (1999). Financial planning curriculum for teens: Impact evaluation. *Journal of Financial Counseling and Planning*, *10*(1), 26.

Danes, S. M., Lee, J., Stafford, K., and Heck, R. K. Z. (2008). The effects of ethnicity, families and culture on entrepreneurial experience: An extension of sustainable family business theory. *Journal of Developmental Entrepreneurship*, *13*(3), 229–268. https://doi.org/10.1142/s1084946708001010

Danes, S. M., and Yang, Y. (2014). Assessment of the use of theories within the journal of financial counseling and planning and the contribution of the family financial socialization conceptual model. *Journal of Financial Counseling and Planning*, *25*(1), 53–68.

Deacon, R. E., and Firebaugh, F. M. (1981). *Family resource management: Principles and applications*. Allyn and Bacon. https://books.google.com/books?id=-JDzAAAAMAAJ

Deenanath, V., Danes, S., and Jang, J. (2019). Purposive and unintentional family financial socialization, subjective financial knowledge, and financial behavior of high school students. *Journal of Financial Counseling and Planning*, *30*, 83–96. https://doi.org/10.1891/1052-3073.30.1.83

Delfabbro, P., and Thrupp, L. (2003). The social determinants of youth gambling in South Australian adolescents. *Journal of Adolescence*, *26*(3), 313–330. https://doi.org/https://doi.org/10.1016/S0140-1971(03)00013-7

Destin, M., and Oyserman, D. (2009). From assets to school outcomes: How finances shape children's perceived possibilities and intentions. *Psychological Science*, *20*(4), 414–418.

Firestone, J. M., Harris, R. J., and Lambert, L. C. (1999). Gender role ideology and the gender based differences in earnings. *Journal of Family and Economic Issues*, *20*(2), 191–215. https://doi.org/10.1023/A:1022158811154

Fulk, M., and White, K. J. (2018). Exploring racial differences in financial socialization and related financial behaviors among Ohio college students. *Cogent Social Sciences*, *4*(1), 151,4681.

Garrison, S. T., and Gutter, M. (2010). Gender differences in financial socialization and willingness to take financial risks. *Journal of Financial Counseling and Planning*, *21*(2), 60–72.

Gudmunson, C. G., and Danes, S. M. (2011). Family financial socialization: Theory and critical review. *Journal of Family and Economic Issues*, *32*(4), 644–667. https://doi.org/10.1007/s10834-011-9275-y

Gudmunson, C. G., Ray, S. K., and Xiao, J. J. (2016). Financial socialization. In J. J. Xiao (ed.), *Handbook of consumer finance research* (pp. 61–72). Springer. https://doi.org/10.1007/978-3-319-28887-1_5

Gurney, K. (1988). *Your money personality: What it is and how you can profit from it*. Doubleday.

Gutter, M., Copur, Z., and Garrison, S. T. (2009). *Which students are more likely to experience financial socialization opportunities? Exploring the relationship between financial behaviors and financial well-being of college students* (NFI Working Paper No. 2009-WP). Networks Financial Institute at Indiana University. https://www.indstate.edu/business/sites/business.indstate.edu/files/Docs/2009-WP-07_Gutter_Copur_Garrison.pdf

Gutter, M. S., Garrison, S., and Copur, Z. (2010). Social learning opportunities and the financial behaviors of college students. *Family and Consumer Sciences Research Journal*, *38*(4), 387–404.

Hallahan, T. A., Faff, R. W., and McKenzie, M. D. (2004). An empirical investigation of personal financial risk tolerance. *Financial Services Review*, *13*(1), 57–78.

Hira, T. K. (1997). Financial attitudes, beliefs and behaviours: Differences by age. *Journal of Consumer Studies and Home Economics*, *21*(3), 271–290. https://doi.org/10.1111/j.1470-6431.1997.tb00288.x

Hira, T. K., and Loibl, C. (2005). Understanding the impact of employer-provided financial education on workplace satisfaction. *Journal of Consumer Affairs, 39*(1), 173–194. https://doi.org/https://doi.org/10.1111/j.1745-6606.2005.00008.x

Hofstede, G. J. (2015). Culture's causes: The next challenge. *Cross Cultural Management: An International Journal, 22*(4), 545–569.

Hudson, C., Young, J., Anong, S., Hudson, E., and Davis, E. (2017). African American financial socialization. *The Review of Black Political Economy, 44*(3–4), 285–302.

Hudson, P. (2016). Forming the mentor-mentee relationship. *Journal of Mentoring and Tutoring, 24*(1), 30–43.

Ivan, B., and Dickson, L. (2008). Consumer economic socialization. In Xiao, J. J. (ed.), *Handbook of consumer finance research* (pp. 83–102). Springer.

Jin, M., and Chen, Z. (2019). Comparing financial socialization and formal financial education: Building financial capability. *Social Indicators Research, 149*, 641–656.

John, D. R. (1999). Consumer socialization of children: A retrospective look at twenty-five years of research. *Journal of Consumer Research, 26*(3), 183–213. https://doi.org/10.1086/209559

Johnson, E., and Sherraden, M. S. (2007). From financial literacy to financial capability among youth. *Journal of Sociology and Social Welfare, 34*, 119.

Jorgensen, B. L., Foster, D., Jensen, J. F., and Vieira, E. (2017). Financial attitudes and responsible spending behavior of emerging adults: Does geographic location matter? *Journal of Family and Economic Issues, 38*(1), 70–83.

Jorgensen, B. L., and Savla, J. (2010). Financial literacy of young adults: The importance of parental socialization. *Family Relations, 59*(4), 465–478.

Kim, J., and Chatterjee, S. (2013). Childhood financial socialization and young adults' financial management. *Journal of Financial Counseling and Planning, 24*(1), 61–79.

Kim, J., Kim, J. E., and Moon, U. J. (2016). Differences in bank account ownership among White, Black, and Latino children and young adults. *Journal of Financial Counseling and Planning, 27*(2), 212–230.

Kim, J., Lataillade, J., and Kim, H. (2011). Family processes and adolescents' financial behaviors. *Journal of Family and Economic Issues, 32*(4), 668–679. https://doi.org/10.1007/s10834-011-9270-3

Kolb, D. A. (2014). *Experiential learning: Experience as the source of learning and development.* FT Press.

Kretschmer, T., and Pike, A. (2010). Associations between adolescent siblings' relationship quality and similarity and differences in values. *Journal of Family Psychology, 24*(4), 411–418. https://doi.org/10.1037/a0020060

Kurland, N. B. (1995). Ethical intentions and the theories of reasoned action and planned behavior. *Journal of Applied Social Psychology, 25*(4), 297–313.

Lanz, M., Sorgente, A., and Danes, S. M. (2020). Implicit family financial socialization and emerging adults' financial well-being: A multi-informant approach. *Emerging Adulthood, 8*(6), 443–452. https://doi.org/10.1177/2167696819876752

LeBaron, A. B., and Kelley, H. H. (2020). Financial socialization: A decade in review. *Journal of Family and Economic Issues, 42*, 195–206. https://doi.org/10.1007/s10834-020-09736-2

LeBaron, A. B., Runyan, S. D., Jorgensen, B. L., Marks, L. D., Li, X., and Hill, E. J. (2019). Practice makes perfect: Experiential learning as a method for financial socialization. *Journal of Family Issues, 40*(4), 435–463.

Lunt, P. (1996). Discourses of savings. *Journal of Economic Psychology, 17*(6), 677–690.

Lyons, A. C. (2008). Risky credit card behavior of college students. In J. J. Xiao (ed.), *Handbook of consumer finance research* (pp. 185–207). Springer. https://doi.org/10.1007/978-0-387-75734-6_11

Lyons, A. C., Chang, Y., and Scherpf, E. (2006). Translating financial education into behavior change for low-income populations. *Journal of Financial Counseling and Planning, 17*(2), 27–45.

Mandell, L. (2006). Financial literacy: If it's so important, why isn't it improving? *Networks Financial Institute Policy Brief*. 2006-PB-08.

Mascarenhas, O. A. J., and Higby, M. A. (1993). Peer, parent, and media influences in teen apparel shopping. *Journal of the Academy of Marketing Science, 21*(1), 53–58. https://doi.org/10.1177/0092070393211007

Masche, J. G. (2010). Explanation of normative declines in parents' knowledge about their adolescent children. *Journal of Adolescence, 33*(2), 271–284. https://doi.org/https://doi.org/10.1016/j.adolescence.2009.08.002

Mohamed, N. A. (2017). Financial socialization: A cornerstone for young employees' financial well-being. *Reports on Economics and Finance, 3*(1), 15–35.

Moore, E., and Bowman, G. (2006). Of friends and family: How do peers affect the development of intergenerational influences? *ACR North American Advances*.

Moschis, G. P. (1987). *Consumer socialization: A life-cycle perspective*. Lexington Books.

Moschis, G. P., and Churchill Jr, G. A. (1978). Consumer socialization: A theoretical and empirical analysis. *Journal of Marketing Research, 15*(4), 599–609.

Moschis, G. P., Moore, R. L., and Smith, R. B. (1984). The impact of family communication on adolescent consumer socialization. *ACR North American Advances, 11*, 314–319.

Mugenda, O. M., Hira, T. K., and Fanslow, A. M. (1990). Assessing the causal relationship among communication, money management practices, satisfaction with financial status, and satisfaction with quality of life. *Lifestyles, 11*(4), 343–360.

Norvilitis, J. M., Merwin, M. M., Osberg, T. M., Roehling, P. V., Young, P., and Kamas, M. M. (2006). Personality factors, money attitudes, financial knowledge, and credit-card debt in college students 1. *Journal of Applied Social Psychology, 36* (6), 1395–1413.

Payne, S. H., Yorgason, J. B., and Dew, J. P. (2014). Spending today or saving for tomorrow: The influence of family financial socialization on financial preparation for retirement. *Journal of Family and Economic Issues, 35*(1), 106–118. https://doi.org/10.1007/s10834-013-9363-2

Rea, J. K., Danes, S. M., Serido, J., Borden, L. M., and Shim, S. (2019). Being able to support yourself: Young adults' meaning of financial well-being through family financial socialization. *Journal of Family and Economic Issues, 40*(2), 250–268.

Rettig, K. (1985). Consumer socialization in the family. *Journal of Consumer Education, 3*(1), 1–7.

Shanks, T. R. W. (2007). The impacts of household wealth on child development. *Journal of Poverty, 11*(2), 93–116.

Shapiro, T., Meschede, T., and Osoro, S. (2013). The roots of the widening racial wealth gap: Explaining the Black-White economic divide. *Brandeis University Institute on Assets and Social Policy*. http://iasp.brandeis.edu/pdfs/Author/shapiro-thomas-m/racialwealthgapbrief.pdf

Sherraden, M. (2013). Building blocks of financial capability. In J. Birkenmaier, M. Sherraden, and J. Curley (eds.), *Financial Education and Capability: Research, Education, Policy, and Practice* (pp. 3–43). Oxford University Press.

Sherraden, M., Birkenmaier, J., and Collins, J. M. (2018). *Financial capability and asset building in vulnerable households: Theory and practice*. Oxford University Press.

Shim, S., Barber, B. L., Card, N. A., Xiao, J. J., and Serido, J. (2010). Financial socialization of first-year college students: The roles of parents, work, and education. *Journal of Youth and Adolescence, 39* (12),1,457–1,470. https://doi.org/10.1007/s10964-009-9432-x

Shim, S., Serido, J., and Barber, B. L. (2011). A consumer way of thinking: Linking consumer socialization and consumption motivation perspectives to adolescent development. *Journal of Research on Adolescence, 21*(1), 290–299.

Shim, S., Serido, J., and Tang, C. (2012). The ant and the grasshopper revisited: The present psychological benefits of saving and future oriented financial behaviors. *Journal of Economic Psychology, 33*(1), 155–165. https://doi.org/https://doi.org/10.1016/j.joep.2011.08.005

Sirsch, U., Zupančič, M., Poredoš, M., Levec, K., and Friedlmeier, M. (2020). Does parental financial socialization for emerging adults matter? The case of Austrian and Slovene first-year University students. *Emerging Adulthood, 8*(6), 509–520.

Sohn, R. (2021). U.S. life expectancy fell by a year in the first half of 2020, CDC report finds. *STAT.* https://www.statnews.com/2021/02/18/u-s-life-expectancy-fell-by-a-year-in-the-first-half-of -2020-cdc-report-finds/#:~:text=Among%20males%2C%20life%20expectancy%20at,2019% 20to%205.4%20in%202020.

Sohn, S.-H., Joo, S.-H., Grable, J. E., Lee, S., and Kim, M. (2012). Adolescents' financial literacy: The role of financial socialization agents, financial experiences, and money attitudes in shaping financial literacy among South Korean youth. *Journal of Adolescence, 35*(4), 969–980. https://doi.org/https://doi.org/10.1016/j.adolescence.2012.02.002

Solheim, C. A., Zuiker, V. S., and Levchenko, P. (2011). Financial socialization family pathways: Reflections from college students' narratives. *Family Science Review, 16*(2), 97–112.

Tang, T. L.-P. (1993). The meaning of money: Extension and exploration of the money ethic scale in a sample of university students in Taiwan. *Journal of Organizational Behavior, 14*(1), 93–99. https://doi.org/https://doi.org/10.1002/job.4030140109

Ullah, S., and Yusheng, K. (2020). Financial socialization, childhood experiences and financial well-being: The mediating role of locus of control. *Frontiers in Psychology, 11*(2,162). https://doi.org/10.3389/fpsyg.2020.02162

Valence, G., d'Astous, A., and Fortier, L. (1988). Compulsive buying: Concept and measurement. *Journal of Consumer Policy, 11*(4), 419–433.

Van Campenhout, G. (2015). Revaluing the role of parents as financial socialization agents in youth financial literacy programs. *Journal of Consumer Affairs, 49*(1), 186–222. http://www.jstor.org/stable/43861592

Varcoe, K., Martin, A., Devitto, Z., and Go, C. (2005). Using a financial education curriculum for teens. *Journal of Financial Counseling and Planning, 16*(1), 63–71.

Ward, S. (1974). Consumer socialization. *Journal of Consumer Research, 1*(2), 1–14.

Watson, J., and McNaughton, M. (2007). Gender differences in risk aversion and expected retirement benefits. *Financial Analysts Journal, 63*(4), 52–62.

White, K., Watkins, K., McCoy, M., Muruthi, B., and Byram, J. L. (2020). How financial socialization messages relate to financial management, optimism and stress: Variations by race. *Journal of Family and Economic Issues, 42*, 237–250 https://doi.org/10.1007/s10834-020-09704-w

Worthington, A. C. (2006). Predicting financial literacy in Australia. *University of Wollongong Research Online.* https://ro.uow.edu.au/commpapers/116

Xiao, J. J., and O'Neill, B. (2016). Consumer financial education and financial capability. *International Journal of Consumer Studies, 40*(6), 712–721. https://doi.org/https://doi.org/10.1111/ijcs.12285

Yancy, C. W. (2020). COVID-19 and African Americans. *Journal of the American Medical Association, 323*(19), 1,891–1,892.

Dee Warmath

# 27 Measuring and Applying Financial Literacy

**Abstract:** While financial literacy is hailed as the promised antidote or remedy to poor financial decision making, there is mixed evidence for the ability of financial literacy to deliver on this promise and a lack of consensus as to what financial literacy is. The dominant view equates financial literacy with knowledge of financial concepts and calculations. Numerous studies suggest that financial knowledge alone is insufficient to improve financial outcomes. Despite attempts to conceptualize financial literacy as more than mere knowledge, there remains a misalignment between the concept and its measures. There is an opportunity to clarify and potentially expand what is needed to make effective financial decisions (i.e., what financial literacy is) as well as produce stronger evidence of the role of (or lack of a role for) financial literacy in financial outcomes.

**Keywords:** financial literacy, financial knowledge, financial decision making

## Introduction

The importance of money management for an individual or household has been recognized for at least as long as the money economy has been in place. For hundreds of years, learning how to make effective decisions about money most likely came through socialization experiences with family and friends or through trial and error in the marketplace (Zinn, 1980). Beginning in the 1700s, sporadic publications would address opportunities to solidify one's financial position through wise financial decisions. One example of such a publication was a Poor Richard post from Benjamin Franklin titled "Hints for those that would be Rich," which described the ways in which credit, interest, and spending habits influence one's financial situation (Poor Richard, 1737). Another example is the publication "Ten Minutes' Advice about Keeping a Banker" by James Gilbart (1839). Gilbart was a banker who sought to remove barriers to bank accounts by increasing awareness and familiarity of what it was like to be in a bank and work with a banker. Beginning in the early 1900s, the disciplines of home and consumer economics taught primarily female students how to run a household, including the money management decisions required for effective home management (Elias, 2010). While not typically described as financial literacy, these and other forms of consumer education intended to build "competency for managing

**Dee Warmath,** University of Georgia

https://doi.org/10.1515/9783110727692-027

money" (Remund, 2010, p. 279). These disciplines also studied what it meant to be a consumer and to establish a standard of living through consumption habits (Kyrk, 1923). At about the same time, cooperative extension programs began offering financial education focused primarily on building money management abilities (United States Department of Agriculture, 2021). Thus, the importance of understanding the financial system and how to manage money effectively was recognized long before our modern discussion of financial literacy.

The modern view of financial literacy seems to operate from a qualitatively different perspective than home and consumer economics early in the 20th century. Home and consumer economics emphasized decision making ability, skill, and confidence alongside knowledge in managing money for the household. Financial literacy as a concept and measure today almost exclusively emphasizes knowledge of financial concepts and calculations (Huston, 2010). Financial education to build literacy seeks to increase participant stores of explicit knowledge given the belief that this knowledge leads to more favorable financial behaviors and outcomes (Collins and O'Rourke, 2010; Fernandes et al., 2014). Home and consumer economics viewed financial education from the perspective of a prudent and natural element of development. Today, financial literacy tends to be viewed as remedial or a race against time in an increasingly complex marketplace with fewer protections and a woefully unprepared decision maker (Boshara et al., 2010; Hastings et al., 2013; Mason and Wilson, 2000; Mandell, 2006; Nicolini and Haupt, 2019; Remund, 2010). Interestingly, the home and consumer economics efforts were met with criticism for enforcing conformity in behavior to support efficiency in the financial system whereas the modern efforts seem to be couched in a self-help message with implications for the financial system a distant secondary theme (Fox et al., 2005; Klapper and Lusardi, 2020; Mandell, 2006).

The financial literacy story over the past few decades is a complex narrative with strong beliefs, poorly developed constructs, a proliferation of measures, mixed evidence of what matters, and an emerging agreement that knowledge alone is insufficient. Many of the questions surrounding financial literacy are not new (Cude, 2010; Huston, 2010: Remund, 2010), yet little progress has been made to resolve the limitations (Nicolini and Haupt, 2019). There is still no clear, accepted definition of financial literacy as a complete construct distinct from its antecedents and consequences and aligned with its measures (Fernandes et al., 2014; Goyal and Kumar, 2021). There has been little progress in resolving the question of whether financial literacy matters to an individual's financial behavior and outcomes (Adams, and Rau, 2011; Collins and O'Rourke, 2010; Fernandes et al., 2014; Hastings et al., 2013; Kaiser et al., 2020).

Despite these limitations and open questions, studies continue to bemoan the paucity of data showing a clear link between financial literacy as financial knowledge. Financial education programs continue to be offered or, in some cases, mandated (Mandell, 2004). On the one hand, there is fear that millions are unprepared for their financial future (Hung et al., 2009). On the other hand, there is handwringing brought about by a fear of being unprepared (Lusardi, 2019). Yet, a recent study by Capital One

(2020) found that while 77 percent of American adults are anxious about their financial situation, their anxiety can be reduced merely by focusing on their situation and goals.

While it is difficult to imagine that financial literacy (and the education to build it) cannot be the promised antidote or remedy (Hastings et al., 2013), it is important to consider whether financial literacy as financial knowledge will deliver on that promise. Does financial literacy (perhaps as more than just financial knowledge) deserve the attention being given or should the personal finance profession move on? Answering this question has implications for enhancing financial and overall well-being at the individual and household level (Consumer Financial Protection Bureau, 2015; Netemeyer et al., 2018).

The purpose of this chapter is to consider what financial literacy is and might be in the context of its origin, evolution, and potential. The historical perspective considers (1) the ways in which the current understanding of financial literacy is largely driven by the measures employed, (2) whether there is evidence to conclude that financial literacy matters, and (3) the evolutionary avenues that research and practice have suggested. Against this backdrop, the remainder of the chapter will consider the implications and opportunities for research, policy, and practice. The chapter concludes with suggestions for future directions.

# Historical Perspective

The study of financial literacy is a story with three interrelated parts: (a) what financial literacy is, (b) whether financial literacy matters, and (b) whether there is more to financial literacy than is currently understood. These three issues are discussed below.

## Financial Literacy Defined

A common, underlying construct is key to the development of a valid, reliable, consensus measure and the positive outcomes of such a construct and measure for research, policy, and practice (Remund, 2010). Defining the construct should be the *first* step in construct development and a critical step in determining whether measures of the construct are valid and reliable (Churchill, 1979; Nicolini et al., 2013). As of 2010, 72 percent of financial literacy studies did not even offer a definition (Huston, 2010). Since that time, financial literacy has largely been defined by the measures used to assess its presence and level (Fernandes et al., 2014).

Most measures of financial literacy are tests of an individual's stored knowledge of financial concepts. These measures range from three to more than 70 questions and employ methods ranging from writing an exam to item response modeling

(Chen and Volpe 1998; Fernandes et al., 2014; Hilgert et al., 2003; Hung et al., 2009; Knoll and Houts, 2012; Lusardi and Mitchell, 2007, 2008; Lusardi and Tufano, 2015; Mandell, 2004). Two tests written by Lusardi and Mitchell, and now dubbed the "Big 3" (Table 27.1) and the "Big 5" (Table 27.2), are the most often employed measures perhaps simply because of their brevity (Lusardi, 2019; Lusardi and Mitchell, 2007). The use of the "Big" descriptor in financial literacy seems to be based on the frequency of use (Hastings et al., 2013). The measures have most often been criticized for their focus on a narrow set of financial knowledge topics (Huston, 2010; Nicolini et al., 2013).

**Table 27.1:** The Big 3 Financial Literacy Test.

| Question | Response Options |
|---|---|
| 1) "Suppose you had $100 in a savings account and the interest rate was 2% per year. After 5 years, how much do you think you would have in the account if you left the money to grow?" | More than $102; Exactly $102; Less than $102; Don't know; Refuse to answer |
| 2) "Imagine that the interest rate on your savings account was 1% per year and inflation was 2% per year. After 1 year, with the money in this account, would you be able to buy . . . ?" | More than today; Exactly the same as today; Less than today; Don't know; Refuse to answer |
| 3) "Do you think the following statement is true or false? Buying a single company stock usually provides a safer return than a stock mutual fund." | True; False; Don't know; Refuse to answer |

*Source*: https://gflec.org/education/questions-that-indicate-financial-literacy/.

**Table 27.2:** The Big 5 Financial Literacy Test.

| Question | Response Options |
|---|---|
| 1) Suppose you had $100 in a savings account and the interest rate was 2% per year. After 5 years how much do you think you would have in the account if you left the money to grow? | More than $102; Exactly $102; Less than $102; Don't know; Prefer not to say |
| 2) Imagine that the interest rate on your savings account was 1% per year and inflation was 2% per year. After 1 year how much would you be able to buy with the money in this account? | More than today; Exactly the same; Less than today; Don't know; Prefer not to say |
| 3) If interest rates rise what will typically happen to bond prices? | They will rise; They will fall; They will stay the same; There is no relationship between bond prices and the interest rate; Don't know; Prefer not to say |

**Table 27.2** (continued)

| Question | Response Options |
|---|---|
| 4) A 15-year mortgage typically requires higher monthly payments than a 30-year mortgage but the total interest paid over the life of the loan will be less. | True; False; Don't know; Prefer not to say |
| 5) Buying a single company's stock usually provides a safer return than a stock mutual fund. | True; False; Don't know; Prefer not to say |

There are many other measures used, with some being constructed from the knowledge being taught in a particular financial education course (e.g., Yetter and Suiter, 2015) and others emerging from the study of the test items that produce an estimate of stored knowledge (e.g., Knoll and Houts, 2012). Some measures view financial literacy as a broad, singular construct (e.g., Fernandes et al., 2014) while others focus on individual domains of knowledge (e.g., saving or investing [Nicolini et al., 2013]). Some measures attempt to separate basic knowledge (i.e., numeracy, compound interest, inflation, time value of money, and inflation/money illusion) from what they term "sophisticated" knowledge (i.e., stock market, mutual funds, relative risk of stocks versus bonds, long-term returns, fluctuation/volatility, and risk diversification [Lusardi et al., 2009]). Debates about these measures often center on whether a particular realm of knowledge (e.g., investing) is too prominent in the test.

The common thread among financial literacy measures is an almost exclusive focus on assessing an individual's store of knowledge related to financial concepts and calculations. In the world of financial literacy, that similarity has been sufficient to back into a definition of the construct, perhaps stated most succinctly in a recent article titled, "Financial Literacy is a Measure of Performance on a Financial Knowledge Test" (Kaiser et al., 2020, p. 7). In fact, financial literacy has become synonymous with financial knowledge with some studies using the terms interchangeably (Goyal and Kumar, 2021; Huang et al., 2013; Nicolini and Haupt, 2019).

Financial education, the dominant tool to build financial literacy, has predominantly focused on building stores of financial knowledge (Cole and Shastry, 2009; Huston, 2010). In fact, it has been suggested that improvement in knowledge is the goal of financial education (Hastings et al., 2013; Kaiser et al., 2020; Lusardi and Mitchell, 2014). Thus, when someone says that a person or population has low financial literacy, what they are really saying is that the person is not able (or, with "don't know" responses, perhaps not willing) to calculate compound interest, to determine the effect of inflation on buying, or to select the riskiest investment from a list without consulting the Internet or other source.

## Insights on Whether Financial Literacy as Financial Knowledge Matters

The second part of the financial literacy story has to do with whether financial literacy matters. Given the current understanding and measures of financial literacy, this part of the story considers whether greater stores of financial knowledge equip an individual to make better financial decisions and produce better financial outcomes. In reality, studies address two distinct questions often without clarity regarding which question is being addressed: (1) Does financial literacy as financial knowledge promote more favorable financial behaviors and outcomes? and (2) Does a financial education program improve financial knowledge and downstream behaviors? The first question is an assessment of financial literacy. The second question is an evaluation of a given financial education program intended to examine whether the program is working (Lyons et al., 2006). Most studies use a more descriptive approach while an increasing number of studies seek to incorporate some element of experimental design as suggested by Fox et al. (2005). The number of available studies using experimental design increased from 13 in the Fernandes et al. (2014) study to 68 in the Kaiser et al. (2020) study.

It is not unfair to state that the evidence for the effectiveness of financial literacy as financial knowledge is mixed, with some studies suggesting that financial literacy/knowledge plays little role in shaping financial behavior or outcomes (CFPB, 2017; Fernandes et al., 2014; Mandell, 2006; Mandell and Klein, 2009; Willis, 2008, 2009) and other studies suggesting that it plays an important role (Allgood and Walstad, 2016; Kaiser et al., 2020; Lusardi, 2003). Some studies conclude that financial knowledge alone is not sufficient to produce the desired financial behaviors and outcomes (CFPB, 2015; Kempson et al., 2013; Lee, Lee, and Kim, 2020).

As examples, consider the following studies. In a cross-sectional study, Hilgert et al. (2003) found that greater knowledge of a particular financial content area was associated with higher levels of positive behaviors in that area. Hira and Loibl (2005) found that taking a financial education course was associated with higher levels of financial literacy and that higher levels of financial literacy were associated with greater confidence in one's future financial situation. Cole and Shastry (2009) found that state mandates regarding financial education seem to have no effect on financial market participation while general education and cognitive ability mattered. Hung et al. (2009) found that financial literacy seems to be strongly predictive of consumers' intentions but less so for actual outcomes as contextual and other factors may interfere with the translation of knowledge and intention into action. Fernandes et al. (2014) found that, while statistically significant, the effect of financial education on downstream financial behavior is miniscule and tends to decay. Kaiser et al. (2020) reported strong positive effects of financial education both on financial knowledge with no evidence of decay and on a large number of financial behaviors.

The methods used may contribute to the mixed findings (Collins and O'Rourke, 2012; Fernandes et al., 2014; Kaiser et al., 2020). The descriptive approach, referred to as *measured financial literacy*, measures the store of financial knowledge and examines its relationship with behaviors and outcomes (Fernandes et al., 2014). The alternative approach, *manipulated financial literacy*, attempts to change the financial literacy of a treatment group and then compare their behavior and outcomes to an untreated group (Fernandes et al., 2014). There is evidence to suggest that the magnitude of the relationship between financial education and financial literacy or downstream behaviors depends on the methods employed with descriptive studies finding much stronger relationships than experiments or quasi-experiments (Collins and O'Rourke, 2012; Fernandes et al., 2014). There is a general belief that evaluations of financial education courses that involve an experimental design are inherently better assessments of the effect of financial literacy (Fernandes et al., 2014; Kaiser et al., 2020). This may not be true in all cases as the financial education programs being evaluated are rarely designed a priori to test an important hypothesis related to financial literacy and often use inconsistent measures (Huston, 2010; Lyons et al., 2006). It seems that these studies are almost always an evaluation of the education first and an assessment of manipulated financial literacy second.

Does financial literacy matter? The only defensible answer is that 'we don't know' (Hastings et al., 2013, p. 352). It is premature to claim that "financial illiteracy is onerous and jeopardizes the financial health of people" (Goyal and Kumar, 2021, p. 92). Most, but not all studies of financial education programs designed to increase financial knowledge report that financial knowledge increases through participation (Goyal and Kumar, 2021; Hastings et al., 2013). That finding, however, says little about the role of financial literacy in describing an individual's financial health. Demonstrating clear and consistent effects of increased stores of financial knowledge on downstream financial behavior and outcomes is needed to determine whether financial literacy, as financial knowledge, is sufficient or at least matters. Such efforts necessitate a willingness to report findings whether they support or do not support the effectiveness of financial knowledge (Kaiser et al., 2020).

## Financial Literacy as More than Financial Knowledge

The third part of the story is whether financial literacy is something more than stored knowledge of financial concepts and calculations. When compared to other forms of literacy, financial literacy is unique in its exclusive focus on knowledge (Remund, 2010; Warmath and Zimmerman, 2019). This observation in no way implies that financial knowledge cannot be an important component of financial literacy. Instead, it merely suggests that the current financial literacy construct as financial knowledge might be shortsighted or simply a proxy for a larger construct

(Goyal and Kumar, 2021; Nicolini and Haupt, 2019). An examination of the proposed definitions of financial literacy offers several avenues for evolution.

One common theme in many definitions is an individual's ability to use knowledge rather than just their existing store of knowledge. Consider these definitions, respectively, from Hung et al. (2009) and Huston (2010):

> Financial literacy: knowledge of basic economic and financial concepts, as well as the ability to use that knowledge and other financial skills to manage financial resources effectively for a lifetime of financial well-being. (Hung et al., 2009, p. 12)

> Financial literacy could be conceptualized as having two dimensions – understanding (personal financial knowledge) and use (personal finance application). (Huston, 2010, p. 306)

The central idea is that individuals who are financially literate will be able to apply financial knowledge to make financial decisions (Huston, 2010). The challenge with the notion of ability to use is the tendency to incorporate behaviors and outcomes (e.g., money management and financial security) in the definition of financial literacy (Hung et al., 2009; Huston, 2010; Organisation for Economic Co-operation and Development, 2014; Remund, 2010). This incorporation is problematic as it requires that constructs such as money management and financial security be included in the determination of financial literacy levels.

Financial literacy should be defined and measured independent from such related constructs so their empirical relationships can be studied (Hung et al., 2009; Huston, 2010). There is also the suggestion that financial literacy might be measured by actual financial behavior through administrative records (Hastings et al., 2013). Thus, whereas ability to use appears to be an important component of financial literacy, further development is needed to establish an understanding and measure of financial literacy including ability to use without reference to behavior.

Another suggested element of financial literacy is confidence (OECD, 2014; Remund, 2010) or self-efficacy (Warmath and Zimmerman, 2019). Consider this definition proposed by Remund (2010):

> Financial literacy is a measure of the degree to which one understands key financial concepts and possesses the ability and confidence to manage personal finances through appropriate, short-term decision-making and sound, long-range financial planning, while mindful of life events and changing economic conditions. (p. 284)

Confidence and self-efficacy are related, yet distinct constructs with both including a sense of firm belief but only self-efficacy including direction or intention (Bandura, 1986, 1990). From this perspective, confidence would be one's belief in their ability as has been explored through studies of subjective knowledge as an indicator of confidence (Lind et al., 2020) while self-efficacy would be one's belief that they would be successful if they acted in financial matters (Warmath and Zimmerman, 2019).

One other potential element of financial literacy is *knowing how versus knowing what*. In other words, being able to find and use information to make decisions when needed versus having a store of knowledge. In this regard, Mason and Wilson (2000) defined financial literacy as:

> an individual's ability to obtain, understand, and evaluate the relevant information necessary to make decisions with an awareness of the likely financial consequences. (p. 31)

Rather than emphasizing an individual's store of financial knowledge, there is a general realization on many fronts that financial literacy should focus more on decision-making ability, including the ability to do "just in time" research when needed (Fernandes et al., 2014; Willis, 2011). A related consideration is whether financial literacy precedes or follows financial behavior. The current view of financial literacy assumes that an individual builds their store of financial knowledge through financial education and then makes a financial decision. Through extensive qualitative research, however, the CFPB discovered that the opposite occurs as well. Individuals gain financial knowledge, decision-making ability, and confidence through their decisions, especially when those decisions result in mistakes (Consumer Financial Protection Bureau, 2015). Cross-sectional studies, as most studies of financial literacy are, cannot say which came first – the knowledge or the decision (Hilgert et al., 2003). As Hastings et al. (2013) asked, "Does financial literacy lead to better economic outcomes? Or does being engaged in certain types of economic behaviors lead to greater financial literacy?" (p. 10).

Warmath and Zimmerman (2019) proposed the following definition of financial literacy that incorporates several of these suggested elements.

> Financial literacy can be defined simply as one's capacity to make effective financial decisions, where "capacity" refers to knowledge, skill, and self-efficacy. (pp. 1609–1610)

Modeled after Bloom and associates' (1956) three domains of knowledge (i.e., cognitive, affective, and psychomotor), this perspective of financial literacy emphasizes an individual's preparation to make financial decisions as a composite of knowledge, abilities, and beliefs. Warmath and Zimmerman (2019) proposed a formative measure of financial literacy in which increases in any of these three components (i.e., knowledge, skill, or self-efficacy) will improve an individual's capacity to make decisions.

## Summary

Although financial literacy has been heralded as the remedy for poor financial decision making and the negative outcomes that often are the result, there is mixed evidence to date for its ability to deliver on this promise (Allgood and Walstad, 2016; Consumer Financial Protection Bureau, 2017; Fernandes et al., 2014; Hastings et al.,

2013; Kaiser et al., 2020; Lusardi, 2003; Mandell, 2006; Mandell and Klein, 2009; Willis, 2008, 2009). Yet the evidence available is built on a myopic view of financial literacy as financial knowledge alone (Warmath and Zimmerman, 2019). Unless one concludes that financial literacy is nothing more than the ability to pass a financial knowledge test (Kaiser et al., 2020), the existing literature must be viewed not as an assessment of financial literacy but of explicit knowledge of financial concepts and calculations. Despite several suggested expansions of the construct (Hung et al., 2009; Huston, 2010; Organisation for Economic Co-operation and Development, 2014; Remund, 2010; Warmath and Zimmerman, 2019), little progress has been made to broaden the study of financial literacy beyond knowledge or to consider the implications for financial education programs, practices and/or policy. Yet financial education programs continue to be offered.

The following takeaways emerge from a careful reading of the literature:
- Financial literacy is defined largely by its current measure (i.e., a financial knowledge test).
- Evidence of the importance of financial knowledge in downstream behaviors and outcomes is mixed and seems to depend on the design of the study.
- Other constructs (e.g., ability to use, confidence, and self-efficacy) are included in some definitions of financial literacy but not considered in measures or in the design of financial education programs.

Based on these takeaways the following are questions to consider:
- How has the "financial literacy as financial knowledge" influenced the approaches included (or excluded) in the design of financial education?
- What are the potential benefits and challenges of refocusing financial literacy on the ability to make sound financial decisions?
- How might questions related to the importance of financial literacy be resolved?

## Research and Policy Issues

Research, policy, and practice in the domain of financial literacy share a common goal of reducing the mistakes that consumers make in their financial decisions (Huston, 2010). It is generally thought that fewer mistakes will lead to higher levels of financial well-being and to a more efficient and predictable economic system (Consumer Financial Protection Bureau, 2015; Fox et al., 2005; Klapper and Lusardi, 2020; Mandell, 2006). Financial literacy is valuable only to the extent it supports these outcomes (Hastings et al., 2013). There are several implications of these statements for research and policy.

First, there is the need to develop a consensus as to what financial literacy is (Remund, 2010). Currently, there are two general schools of thought as outlined above: (1) financial literacy is knowledge of financial concepts and calculations as evidenced by one's score on a financial knowledge test (Kaiser et al., 2020; Lusardi and Mitchell, 2007, 2008; Lusardi and Tufano, 2009), and (2) financial literacy is a combination of knowledge, decision making ability, and self-efficacy or confidence that supports more effective financial decisions (Allgood and Walstad, 2016; Fernandes et al., 2014; Hadar et al., 2013; Huston, 2010; Remund, 2010; Warmath and Zimmerman, 2019). If financial literacy is nothing more than an individual's ability to pass a financial knowledge test, perhaps the concept of financial literacy is superfluous. Financial knowledge would be a clearer and simpler way to describe the construct. Then research on financial knowledge could focus on determining whether financial knowledge matters and is sufficient to produce the desired financial outcomes. The primary role of policy in this scenario might be establishing the imperative to evaluate the ability of programs to improve financial knowledge as well as the methods and measures that guide such evaluation (Kaiser et al., 2020; Lyons et al., 2006).

Another benefit of calling financial knowledge "financial knowledge" is the space created for the development of (a) financial literacy as a more complete construct and (b) the measures to support the expanded definition (Fernandes et al., 2014; Huston, 2010). An expanded view of financial literacy would likely include a focus on decision-making ability as well as the knowledge and confidence required to make effective decisions (Allgood and Walstad, 2016; Huston, 2010; Knoll and Houts, 2012; Remund, 2010; Warmath and Zimmerman, 2019). As the financial literacy construct evolves, there is a related need to evolve how financial literacy is measured. Such a shift in the definition and measurement of financial literacy is and will not be easy (Remund, 2010). It requires researchers to conduct studies to define and measure financial literacy as more than knowledge. It requires editors and reviewers who are willing to consider expanded views on what constitutes financial literacy. It also requires communication practitioners who are designing and evaluating programs to build financial literacy. If this path is adopted, policy has a role in breaking financial literacy free from mere financial knowledge and establishing a mandate to examine other aspects of financial literacy that might support a reduction in financial mistakes. Policy might also play the roles of convener and communicator in a process that resembles the work of the U.S. Consumer Financial Protection Bureau (CFPB) to define, measure, and disseminate the concept of financial well-being (Consumer Financial Protection Bureau, 2015, 2017, 2018).

Another implication is the need for a shift in thinking from financial knowledge or literacy as the desired outcome to an objective financial situation or financial well-being as the desired outcome (Consumer Financial Protection Bureau, 2015). This shift requires a willingness to admit that financial literacy might not matter in comparison to other potential actions to improve financial well-being (Hastings et al., 2013). The currently shared intuition is that financial literacy reduces financial mistakes and increases financial well-being (Collins and O'Rourke, 2010;

Fernandes et al., 2014; Lyons et al., 2006). Yet, many studies do not measure these ultimate outcomes and, for those that do, there is no consistent approach to the measurement (Lyons et al., 2006; Remund, 2010). Often, studies use financial education as a proxy for financial literacy without validating that the particular approach to financial education in fact produces higher levels of financial literacy (Hung et al., 2009). Studies that do assess the downstream effects of financial literacy on financial behavior or other outcomes tend to be correlational in nature (Collins and O'Rourke, 2010; Fernandes et al., 2014). There is a need for more causal evidence of impact, especially long-run impact (Hastings et al., 2013; Kaiser et al., 2020; Remund, 2010). Qualitative research offers an interesting method for humanizing the study of financial literacy through an understanding of the lived financial experiences that produce higher (or lower) levels of financial well-being (Consumer Financial Protection Bureau, 2015; Goyal and Kumar, 2021). Actual financial narratives provide examples that might reinforce current assumptions or reveal blind spots in working models.

Then there are implications related to financial education as the primary method of building financial literacy. Policy should consider setting a higher bar for approval of financial literacy education courses based on evidence to support likely financial outcomes at an individual and a societal level. Following methods established by the Department of Education, policy can support the exploration of innovative approaches to financial literacy education while setting clear standards for acceptance of such approaches for broader implementation. Policy can define the intended outcomes of efforts to build financial literacy and establish criteria for what constitutes an approved or accepted form of financial education. Policy could also incentivize explorations of alternatives to financial education (Fernandes et al., 2014). Through regulation and/or incentives, policies could support the identification of optimal approaches to improving financial literacy and to removing barriers that limit its effect on financial outcomes. If financial literacy is as important for the well-being of individual citizens and society as some existing studies suggest, this level of attention and oversight seems warranted to ensure the promise of financial literacy is realized, if possible.

Research and policy also have roles to play in considering that financial knowledge or financial literacy is not the optimal path to better financial outcomes. As most financial literacy education programs do not report program costs, there is incomplete knowledge on the resources being devoted to building financial knowledge with little to no understanding of the benefits of higher levels of financial literacy. If the goal is better financial outcomes, there must be a willingness to ask whether financial knowledge or financial literacy matter. If not, resources should be directed toward activities with a greater demonstrated effect on desired outcomes.

## Practitioner Tools and Techniques

From a personal finance practitioner perspective, the state of knowledge on financial literacy should inspire caution and optimism. A sense of caution should lead practitioners to review their program logic, theory of change, and evaluation plan to ensure, first, that they have these elements in place and, second, that they are grounded in the available evidence. A sense of optimism should offer practitioners an invitation to innovate. Some practitioners are already moving beyond building stores of financial knowledge to identifying novel approaches to creating safe experiences that build confidence and decision-making ability, including the ability to do research when needed (Willis, 2011). Approaches to consider include experience and exposure, ability to practice, safe just-in-time research spaces, and opportunities to learn from the outcomes of decisions made by others. It will be important that practitioners document what they are doing and measure how it is working.

## Future Directions

If the goal is to explore financial literacy as more than knowledge, there are several steps that might offer a way forward.
- Acknowledge the contributions and limitations of the current approach to financial literacy as financial knowledge.
- Complete the development of the financial literacy construct.
- Develop a measure based on this complete understanding of the construct.
- Design and test programs that build financial literacy in its evolved form using consistent measures.
- Test and improve the programs over time based on their performance.

## Discussion

While financial literacy is not a new topic, its current form has a greater sense of self-help or remediation. This sense is somewhat driven by the increasing complexity of the financial marketplace and the shift of financial responsibility and risk to the individual household. Despite the believed importance of financial literacy, its conceptual development is lacking and driven primarily by its measures rendering financial literacy as nothing more than financial knowledge (Fernandes et al., 2014; Huston, 2010; Kaiser et al., 2020; Remund, 2010). Yet, research suggests that financial knowledge alone is likely insufficient to improve financial decision making and outcomes (Consumer Financial Protection Bureau, 2017; Kempson et al., 2013; Lee et al., 2020). Other potential components of financial literacy include confidence or self-efficacy, the ability to apply knowledge in decision making, and the ability to conduct research on a financial decision. Is an individual able to use the knowledge they have effectively? When they do not possess the knowledge needed, are they able to recognize this fact and seek trustworthy sources? Do they have the belief that they will be successful if they take action?

## Conclusion

Despite the mixed evidence and misalignment related to financial literacy as financial knowledge, there is a steady stream of publications following the current order. A Google Scholar search for financial literacy on May 9, 2021 returned more than 5,400 publications in 2021 alone. Financial literacy's current trajectory risks irrelevance as there is already evidence to suggest that some are replacing it with other constructs such as financial capability (Organisation for Economic Co-operation Development, 2014). There are many suggestions in the existing literature for improving the financial literacy construct and research to determine its importance. While knowledge of financial concepts and calculations is not likely to hurt financial decision making, such knowledge alone appears insufficient to improve such decisions. The ability to gather and use information in financial decisions as well as the sense of self-efficacy that encourages an individual to take action is important as well. There is also the suggestion that what matters is not whether a high percentage of adults can answer financial knowledge questions correctly. Instead, it is their ability to achieve and maintain high levels of financial well-being (Consumer Financial Protection Bureau, 2015). The opportunity is to encourage an evidence-based consensus definition, to demonstrate the effectiveness of financial literacy in financial outcomes, and to identify the methods that build the form of financial literacy that leads to desired outcomes.

## References

Adams, G. A., and Rau, B. L. (2011). Putting off tomorrow to do what you want today: Planning for retirement. *American Psychologist, 66*(3), 180–192.

Allgood, S., and Walstad, W. B. (2016). The effects of perceived and actual financial literacy on financial behaviors. *Economic Inquiry, 54*(1), 675–697.

Bandura, A. (1986). The explanatory and predictive scope of self-efficacy theory. *Journal of Social and Clinical Psychology, 4*(3), 359–373.

Bandura, A. (1990). Perceived self-efficacy in the exercise of personal agency. *Journal of Applied Sport Psychology, 2*(2), 128–163.

Bloom, B. S., Engelhart, M. D., Furst, E. J., Hill, W. H., and Krathwohl, D. R. (1956). *Taxonomy of educational objectives, Handbook 1: Cognitive domain*. Longmans.

Boshara, R., Gannon, J., Mandell, L., Phillips, J. W. R., and Sass, S. (2010). Consumer trends in the public, private, and nonprofit sector. *National Endowment for Financial Education Quarter Century Project*, 1–34.

Capital One. (2020, January). *Big-picture thinking leads to the right money mindset*. Accessed July 2021. https://www.capitalone.com/about/newsroom/mind-over-money-survey/

Chen, H., and Volpe, R. P. (1998). An analysis of personal financial literacy among college students. *Financial Services Review*, 7(2), 107–128.

Churchill Jr., G. A. (1979). A paradigm for developing better measures of marketing constructs. *Journal of Marketing Research*, 16(1), 64–73.

Cole, S. A., and Shastry, G. K. (2009). *Smart money: The effect of education, cognitive ability, and financial literacy on financial market participation*. Harvard Business School.

Collins, J. M., and O'Rourke, C. M. (2010). Financial education and counseling – Still holding promise. *Journal of Consumer Affairs*, 44(3), 483–498.

Consumer Financial Protection Bureau. (2015). *Financial well-being: The goal of financial education*. Accessed July 2021. https://www.consumerfinance.gov/data-research/research-reports/financial-well-being/

Consumer Financial Protection Bureau. (2017). *CFPB financial well-being scale development technical report*. Accessed July 2021. https://www.consumerfinance.gov/data-research/research-reports/financial-well-being-technical-report/

Consumer Financial Protection Bureau. (2018). *Financial well-being in America*. Accessed July 2021. https://www.consumerfinance.gov/data-research/research-reports/financial-well-being-america/

Cude, B. J. (2010). Financial literacy 501. *Journal of Consumer Affairs*, 44(2), 271–275.

Elias, M. J. (2010). *Stir it up: Home economics in American culture*. University of Pennsylvania Press.

Fernandes, D., Lynch, Jr., J. G., and Netemeyer, R. G. (2014). Financial literacy, financial education, and downstream financial behaviors. *Management Science*, 60 (8),1861–1883.

Fox, J., Bartholomae, S., and Lee, J. (2005). Building the case for financial education. *Journal of Consumer Affairs*, 39(1), 195–214.

Gilbart, J. W. (1839). "Ten Minutes of Advice About Keeping a Banker." The Financial System in Nineteenth-Century Britain. Ed. Mary Poovey. Oxford: Oxford UP, 2003. 231–38

Goyal, K., and Kumar, S. (2021). Financial literacy: A systematic review and bibliometric analysis. *International Journal of Consumer Studies*, 45(1), 80–105.

Hadar, L., Sood, S., and Fox, C. R. (2013). Subjective knowledge in consumer financial decisions. *Journal of Marketing Research*, 50(3), 303–316.

Hastings, J. S., Madrian, B. C., and Skimmyhorn, W. L. (2013). Financial literacy, financial education, and economic outcomes. *Annual Review of Economics*, 5(1), 347–373.

Hilgert, M. A., Hogarth, J. M., and Beverly, S. G. (2003). Household financial management: The connection between knowledge and behavior. *Federal Reserve Bulletin*, 89, 309.

Hira, T. K., and Loibl, C. (2005). Understanding the impact of employer-provided financial education on workplace satisfaction. *Journal of Consumer Affairs*, 39(1), 173–194.

Huang, J., Nam, Y., and Sherraden, M. S. (2013). Financial knowledge and child development account policy: A test of financial capability. *Journal of Consumer Affairs*, 47(1), 1–26.

Hung, A., Parker, A. M., and Yoong, J. (2009). *Defining and measuring financial literacy* (Rand Working Paper No. 708). RAND Corporation. https://www.rand.org/content/dam/rand/pubs/working_papers/2009/RAND_WR708.pdf

Huston, S. J. (2010). Measuring financial literacy. *Journal of Consumer Affairs*, 44(2), 296–316.

Kaiser, T., Lusardi, A., Menkhoff, L., and Urban, C. J. (2020). *Financial education affects financial knowledge and downstream behaviors* (NBER Working Paper No. w27057). National Bureau of Economic Research. https://www.nber.org/papers/w27057

Kempson, E., Perotti, V., and Scott, K. (2013). *Measuring financial capability: a new instrument and results from low-and middle-income countries*. World Bank. https://openknowledge.world bank.org/bitstream/handle/10986/16296/798060WP020Mea0Box0379791B00PUBLIC0.pdf? sequence=1

Klapper, L., and Lusardi, A. (2020). Financial literacy and financial resilience: Evidence from around the world. *Financial Management, 49*(3), 589–614.

Knoll, M. A., and Houts, C. R. (2012). The financial knowledge scale: An application of item response theory to the assessment of financial literacy. *Journal of Consumer Affairs, 46*(3), 381–410.

Kyrk, H. (1923). *A theory of consumption*. Houghton Mifflin Company.

Lee, J. M., Lee, J., and Kim, K. T. (2020). Consumer financial well-being: Knowledge is not enough. *Journal of Family and Economic Issues, 41*(2), 218–228.

Lind, T., Ahmed, A., Skagerlund, K., Strömbäck, C., Västfjäll, D., and Tinghög, G. (2020). Competence, confidence, and gender: The role of objective and subjective financial knowledge in household finance. *Journal of Family and Economic Issues, 41*(4), 626–638.

Lusardi, A. (2003). *Saving and the effectiveness of financial education* (Wharton Pension Research Council Working Paper No. 430). Oxford University Press. https://repository.upenn.edu/cgi/viewcontent.cgi?article=1431&context=prc_papers

Lusardi, A. (2019). Financial literacy and the need for financial education: Evidence and implications. *Swiss Journal of Economics and Statistics, 155*(1), 1–8.

Lusardi, A., and Mitchell, O. S. (2007). Baby boomer retirement security: The roles of planning, financial literacy, and housing wealth. *Journal of Monetary Economics, 54*(1), 205–224.

Lusardi, A., and Mitchell, O. S. (2008). Planning and financial literacy: How do women fare? *American Economic Review, 98*(2), 413–417.

Lusardi, A., and Mitchell, O. S. (2014). The economic importance of financial literacy: Theory and evidence. *Journal of Economic Literature, 52*(1), 5–44.

Lusardi, A., Mitchell, O. S., and Curto, V. (2009). *Financial literacy and financial sophistication among older Americans* (NBER Working Paper No. w15469). National Bureau of Economic Research. https://www.nber.org/papers/w15469

Lusardi, A., and Tufano, P. (2015). Debt literacy, financial experiences, and overindebtedness. *Journal of Pension Economics & Finance, 14*(4), 332–368.

Lyons, A. C., Palmer, L., Jayaratne, K. S. U., and Scherpf, E. (2006). Are we making the grade? A national overview of financial education and program evaluation. *Journal of Consumer Affairs, 40*(2), 208–235.

Mandell, L. (2004). Financial literacy: Are we improving? Results of the 2004 national Jump$tart survey. *Jumpstart Coalition for Personal Financial Literacy*.

Mandell, L. (2006). Financial literacy: If it's so important, why isn't it improving? *Networks Financial Institute Policy Brief*, 2006-PB 08.

Mandell, L., and Klein, L. S. (2009). The impact of financial literacy education on subsequent financial behavior. *Journal of Financial Counseling and Planning, 20*(1), 15–24.

Mason, C. L. J., and Wilson, R. M. S. (2000). *Conceptualising financial literacy* (Occasional Paper No. 2000:7). Loughborough University.

Netemeyer, R. G., Warmath, D., Fernandes, D., and Lynch Jr., J. G. (2018). How am I doing? Perceived financial well-being, its potential antecedents, and its relation to overall well-being. *Journal of Consumer Research, 45*(1), 68–89.

Nicolini, G., Cude, B. J., and Chatterjee, S. (2013). Financial literacy: A comparative study across four countries. *International Journal of Consumer Studies*, *37*(6), 689–705.

Nicolini, G., and Haupt, M. (2019). The assessment of financial literacy: New evidence from Europe. *International Journal of Financial Studies*, *7*(54), 1–20.

Organisation for Economic Co-operation and Development. (2014). *PISA 2012 results: Students and money (Volume VI): Financial literacy skills for the 21st century*. OECD Publishing.

Poor Richard. (1737). *Founders online*. National Archives. Accessed July 2021. https://founders. archives.gov/documents/Franklin/01-02-02-0028

Remund, D. L. (2010). Financial literacy explicated: The case for a clearer definition in an increasingly complex economy. *Journal of Consumer Affairs*, *44*(2), 276–295.

United States Department of Agriculture. (2021). *National extension money management*. Accessed July 2021. https://nifa.usda.gov/national-extension-money-management-1

Warmath, D., and Zimmerman, D. (2019). Financial literacy as more than knowledge: The development of a formative scale through the lens of bloom's domains of knowledge. *Journal of Consumer Affairs*, *53* (4), 1602–1629.

Willis, L. E. (2008). Against financial-literacy education. *Iowa Law Review*, *94*, 197–285.

Willis, L. E. (2009). Evidence and ideology in assessing the effectiveness of financial literacy education. *San Diego Law Review*, *46*(2), 415–458.

Willis, L. E. (2011). The financial education fallacy. *American Economic Review*, *101*(3), 429–434.

Yetter, E. A., and Suiter, S. (2015). Financial literacy in the community college classroom: A curriculum intervention study (Working Paper No 2015-001). *Federal Reserve Bank of St. Louis*. https://www.stlouisfed.org/~/media/education/papers/financial-literacy-in-the-community-college-classroom.pdf

Zinn, H. (1980). The influence of home environments on the socialization of children. *Ekistics*, *47*(281), 98–102.

Adrian Furnham, Simmy Grover

# 28 Money Psychology: Beliefs and Behaviors about Investing, Saving, and Spending

**Abstract:** This chapter provides a comprehensive and topical overview of the studies that have set out to measure money beliefs and behaviors. Papers reviewed were those that documented studies of money attitudes and included the measures used, where the studies were conducted, and which demographic correlates were investigated. The chapter also looks at the concepts and measures of financial capability, literacy, and well-being that are currently attracting a good deal of attention in both the academic and practitioner world. The chapter also examines a number of tools that are used to help both clients and their advisors understand their money beliefs and behaviors. The chapter concludes with developments and limitations in this research.

**Keywords:** money beliefs, pathology, financial literacy, saving, spending

## Introduction

Why are some people irrationally compulsive savers and other people profligate spenders? Why are others, especially well-educated people, ignorant to the point of phobia about their personal finances? How should financial organizations try to persuade and "sell to" potential clients of their services in a way that is tailored to the individual?

Long before the emergence of behavioral economics, psychologists from many different areas (e.g., cognitive, clinical, differential, social) had been interested in money. All, in their different ways, had known that the prototypic cool, rational, "homo-economicus" never existed. They were confronted by their patients, laboratory subjects, and small groups whose heart ruled their head – those who were a-rational, rather than irrational, but whose money-related behavior could be explained and predicted.

As a result, there is a clinical, differential, educational, and social psychology of money (Furnham, 2014). Even evolutionary psychologists have been interested (Hantula, 2003) as well as experimental psychologists (Vohs et al., 2006; Zhou and Wei, 2020). Of course, there are many other disciplines interested in how people think about and use their money, including anthropology, economics, finance, marketing, political science, public policy, and sociology.

**Adrian Furnham,** Norwegian School of Management
**Simmy Grover,** University College London

https://doi.org/10.1515/9783110727692-028

The sort of issues that psychologists have focused on include the following: (a) to what extent money is an effective motivator at work; (b) how money beliefs and behaviors are acquired; (c) the causes and cures of those with "money problems"; (d) how best to assess/measure money attitudes; (e) the relationship between money and happiness; and (f) most importantly, how people make money decisions. Each area remains contentious with arguments between those in different disciplines (e.g., the Easterlin hypothesis that disputed the relationship between money and happiness) (Furnham, 2014).

There are also a number of institutions and individuals (e.g., banks, financial planners) who are interested in the financial literacy and preferences of their clients. They want to understand clients better so they are able to advise and sell to them more effectively. There are also journals (*Financial Planning Review, Journal of Financial Planning, Journal of Financial Therapy, Journal of Financial Counseling and Planning*) dedicated to understanding some of the issues in this field (Furnham et al., 2014; Horwitz et al., 2019; Klontz et al., 2019; Larrabee and Klontz, 2019).

Indeed, there is now a discipline called "financial psychology," which looks at issues like how an individual's "money scripts" influence their financial behavior (Klontz and Britt, 2012). There is a particular interest in financial ignorance, disorders, and well-being (Santos, and Campos, 2019) as well as more specific topics like investing in stocks (Keller and Siegrist, 2006) and savings (Maison et al., 2019). However, the theoretical origin (i.e., economics or psychology) is often clearly apparent in the way researchers frame their questions and conduct their research. The purpose of this chapter is to extend the personal finance field's understanding of money psychology by providing a comprehensive and topical overview of the studies that have set out to measure money beliefs and behaviors.

# Historical Perspective

## The Psychology of Money

Over the past several decades there has been an increasing interest in the psychology of money (Belsky and Gilovich, 1999; Bodnar, 1993; Cohen et al., 2019; Cone and Gilovich, 2010; Dakin and Wampler, 2008; Ealy and Lesh, 1998; Engelberg and Sjoberg, 2006; Furnham, 2014; Furnham and Cheng, 2019; Furnham and Grover, 2019; Lea and Webley, 2006; Lemroává, et al, 2014; Mumford and Weeks, 2003; Qamar et al., 2016; Rick et al., 2008; Tang, 2010; Tang et al., 2006; Tatarko and Schmidt, 2012; Wang et al., 2020). There is also an interest in the measurement of money attitudes and beliefs (Furnham and Murphy, 2019; Furnham and Grover, 2019; Lay and Furnham, 2019; Taylor et al., 2016) as well as money and well-being (Netemeyer et al., 2018).

Table 28.1 details the results of several noteworthy studies that have attempted to measure money attitudes, beliefs, and behaviors. A few observations should be made from this table. First, work on this topic goes back fifty years. Second, research has been done all around the world with, however, the usual predominance of English-speaking countries. Third, while the number of measures has increased over the years, there is considerable overlap in the specific attitudes and beliefs that have been measured.

It appears that there are a number of money-types, or more accurately money themes, which all researchers have identified, although the precise number and labeling differ, as if found in personality theories. The factors are usually labelled. Examples include: Achievement and Success, Power and Status, Mindful and Responsible, Saving Concerns and Financial Literacy Worries. Some, however, have talked about money being associated with four factors: Freedom, Love, Power, and Security (Furnham, 2014). Goldberg and Lewis (1978) showed that money can represent security (a primary way of staving off anxiety), power (a method to gain importance, dominance, and control), love (a manifestation of and substitute for affection), and freedom (a necessity to acquire what you want). Although this classification has been supported empirically (Furnham, 2014; Furnham et al., 2012; Klontz et al., 2012) it only examines the positive effects or bright side of money. In a more recent study, Lay and Furnham (2019) devised a robust measure that has a financial worries measure and taps into the potential dark side of money and the negative emotions that may be caused when individuals perceive they do not have enough money.

## Demography and Ideology

Many have been interested in demographic correlates of money beliefs and behaviors (Edwards et al., 2007; Potrich et al., 2018; Walczak and Pieńkowska-Kamieniecka, 2018). We know that men rather than women, older rather than younger, better educated rather than less educated, higher rather than lower social class, and richer rather than poorer people are better informed about financial affairs and more sensible and responsible with respect to their money. That is, they are more likely to become savers than spenders (Furnham, 2014). These variables are often highly correlated (e.g., education, income, work status), and recent studies have tried to look at the relative contribution of these factors. For instance, Fenton-O'Creevy and Furnham (2020) found that age, followed by education and then gender, were related to a range of financial variables. It has also been established that religious and political beliefs, here called ideology, are related to money beliefs and behaviors. Fenton-O'Creevy and Furnham (2020) found political beliefs, more than religion, accounted for a small but consistent amount of variance in financial beliefs and behaviors.

**Table 28.1:** Empirical Studies: Methodological Characteristics and Demographic and Personality Factors That Do and Do Not Influence Money Attitudes.

| Empirical Studies | Scale Used | N | Sample | Location | Factors that Influence Money Attitudes |
|---|---|---|---|---|---|
| Wernimont and Fitzpatrick (1972) | Modified Semantic Differential (MSD) | 533 | College students, engineers, religious sisters, etc. | Large U.S. Midwestern City | Work experience, socioeconomic level, and gender |
| Yamauchi and Templar (1982) | Money Attitude Scale (MAS) | 300 | Adults from different professions | Los Angeles and Fresno, CA | |
| Furnham (1984) | Money Beliefs and Behavior Scale (MBBS) | 256 | College students | England, Scotland, and Wales | Income, gender, age, and education |
| Bailey and Gustafson (1986) | MBBS | NA | College students | U.S. Southwestern City | Gender |
| Gresham and Fontenot (1989) | Modified MAS | 557 | College students and their parents | U.S. Southwestern Cities | Gender |
| Bailey and Gustafson (1991) | Modified MBBS | 472 | College students | U.S. Southwestern City | Sensitivity and emotional stability |
| Hanley and Wilhelm (1992) | MBBS | 143 | NA | Phoenix, Tucson, Denver, and Detroit | Compulsive behavior |
| Tang (1992) | Money Ethic Scale (MES) | 769 | College students, faculty, managers, etc. | Middle Tennessee City | Age, income, work ethic, social, political, and religious values |
| Bailey and Lown (1993) | Money in the Past and Future Scale (MPFS) | 654 | College students, their relatives, and other professionals | Western U.S. States | Age |

| Author (year) | Scale | Sample size | Sample | Country/Location | Topic |
|---|---|---|---|---|---|
| Tang (1993) | MES | 68 and 249 | College students | Taiwan | |
| Wilhelm et al. (1993) | MBBS | 559 | Adult Americans | U.S.A. | Gender, financial progress |
| Bailey et al.(1994) | MBBS | 344, 291, and 328 | Employed adults related to college students | U.S.A., Australia, and Canada | Geographical location |
| Lim and Teo(1997) | MBBS MAS | 200 | Students | Singapore | Gender differences |
| Roberts and Sepulveda(1999) | MAS | 273 | Adults | Mexican | Compulsive buying |
| Ozgen and Bayoglu (2005) | MPFS | 300 | Turkish students | Ankara, Turkey | Gender, age, family type |
| Burgess (2005) | Modified MAS | 221 | Urban South Africans | Major Metropolitan Cities | Values and culture |
| Engelberg and Sjoberg (2006) | MAS | 212 | Swedish students | Sweden | Emotional intelligence |
| Christopher et al. (2004) | MPPS | 204 | Students | American | Materialism |
| Klontz et al.(2012) | KMSI | 422 | Adults | American | Sex, age, race education, gross income |
| Tatarko and Schmidt (2012) | MPPS | 634 | Adults | Russian | Social capital |

(continued)

**Table 28.1** (continued)

| Empirical Studies | Scale Used | N | Sample | Location | Factors that Influence Money Attitudes |
|---|---|---|---|---|---|
| Furnham et al. (2012) | Short Money Type Measure (SMTM) | 400 | Adults | English | Age, ethnicity, salary, education, politics |
| Von Stumm et al. (2013) | SMTM | 109472 | Adults | British | Education, income, financial habits |
| Taylor et al.(2011) | KMSI-R | 326 | Students | American | Sex, age, education, etc. |
| Lay and Furnham (2019) | NMAQ | 268 | Adults | British | Sex, age, ideology, work success |
| Furnham and Murphy (2019) | Money Mindset | 3285 | Adults | Australian | Sex, age, wealth spender-saver |
| Furnham and Grover (in press) | NMBQ | 402 | Adults | British | Sex, age, wealth |

## Money Attitudes

A number of studies have examined how attitudes to money act as direct and mediator effects on financial outcomes (Abdullah et al., 2019; Gasiorowska, 2015). Various clinicians have been particularly interested in money attitudes labeled pathology/insanity and "neuroses" (Fenton-O'Creevy and Furnham, 2019; Forman, 1987; Furnham 2019; Goldberg and Lewis, 1978; Matthews, 1991; Phau and Woo, 2008). Numerous studies have been conducted over the last 20 years using some of these measures (Baker and Hagedorn, 2008; Christopher et al., 2004; Durvasula and Lysonski, 2010; Henchoz et al., 2019; Inseng, 2019; Jia et al., 2013; Kamis et al., 2020; Rose et al., 2016; Rose and Orr, 2007). The question that researchers have been interested in, other than the validity of money attitude tests, is what behaviors are robustly related to money attitudes as well as where the attitudes come from and whether they can easily be modified.

## Personality

Research in this area is also concerned with the relationship between bright- and dark-side personality and money beliefs and behaviors. Studies have looked at the relationship between the Big Five traits and money (Brown and Taylor, 2014). Both Donnelly et al. (2012) and Xu et al. (2015) found that the trait Conscientiousness was negatively, and Neuroticism positively, correlated with young adults' financial distress. Looking at personality disorder correlates of money attitudes, Furnham (2019) found that individuals who score higher on Avoidant, Narcissistic, and Sadistic, and lower on Antisocial and Self-Defeating, were more likely to associate money with achievement and success. Those who were more likely to view money as Power and Prestige tended to be male, high on Dependent, Histrionic, Narcissistic, and Sadistic but low on Depressive. Regarding the Mindful and Responsible money attitude, individuals who tended to endorse this money attitude were more likely to be those scoring high on Obsessive Compulsive and lower on Antisocial.

It is probably true to say that no one theoretical or empirical approach dominates this highly interdisciplinary area. However, perhaps the most interesting and important development is using big data to explore some of these questions (Gladstone et al., 2019; Matz et al., 2016). This tends not to use self-report but rather details on actual money transactions as well as social media to determine personality. Big data methodologies offer the advantages of escaping the cross-sectional, self-report data from relatively small and unrepresentative social groups that limit a great deal of social science research.

## Financial Capability, Literacy, and Wellbeing

There has been a great deal of interest around the world on the important topics of financial well-being (Abdullah et al., 2019; Bruggen et al., 2017), capability (Atkinson et al., 2006; Taylor, 2011), risk-taking (Blais and Weber, 2006; Dohmen et al., 2011; Keller and Siegrist, 2006), and satisfaction (Gasiorowska, 2015). Parents and teachers are interested in teaching financial literacy and those in the financial world, as well as politicians, are concerned about financial literacy, knowing how important it is to personal well-being.

Many have looked at attitudinal, demographic, and financial correlates of financial factors, some concentrating particularly on young people (Ali et al., 2014; Garg and Singh, 2018; Loh et al., 2019; Lusardi et al., 2010; Lusardi, 2015; Mandell and Klein, 2009; Sohn et al., 2012; Tavares et al., 2019). The issue is more about their knowledge than attitudes, the idea being that financial literacy is one of the most obvious and important determinants of financial well-being. It is known that the better-informed make better decisions. Various authors have concentrated on how to measure it (Huston, 2010; Knoll and Houts, 2012) and there remains no consensus as to a clear operational definition of (adequate, appropriate) financial knowledge.

Reviews have appeared in this growing area like that of Kebede and Kuar (2015) who showed that people, even in the developed world, lack basic knowledge, skills, and attitudes for optimal personal financial management decisions. They reported that studies from emerging and developing countries have confirmed a low level of financial literacy. Lower financial literacy has been associated with being female, unemployed, having low educational attainment, low income, and living in rural areas.

The determinants of adult financial capability, distress, knowledge, and welfare are important as they can have a considerable impact on a person's health and welfare (Fenton-O'Creevy and Furnham, 2020). Many have been concerned with developing and validating a new and comprehensive measure of financial literacy and well-being (Bruggen et al., 2017; Folke et al., 2019). Others have taken an interest in how to educate people to become more literate and capable (Blue et al., 2014; Fernandes et al., 2014).

One large sample study is illustrative of the key issues in this space. Von Stumm et al. (2013) were interested in financial capability, which is essentially the ability to manage living on the resources available and to make sensible financial decisions. Five key elements of financial capability were identified: (a) adequate management of available financial resources; (b) monitoring one's personal financial status; (c) financial precautions taken for the immediate future; (d) care in selecting financial products; and (e) engagement with current economic developments. They found that socioeconomic status was associated with financial capabilities but not with money attitudes, which were independent of financial capabilities. While they found financial capabilities to be greater risk factors for adverse financial outcomes compared to money attitudes, they concluded the latter important and likely targets to be changed by education and other interventions.

There are a number of interesting issues here. The first is the extent to which people are insightful about their financial literacy – that is, the degree to which they are accurate in their appraisal about the specific and general ignorance and knowledge, which is determined by examining their actual knowledge from their self-appraisal of their knowledge. The second is how easily and efficiently to increase financial literacy; this is an educational issue deciding on what are the key points to convey and how that is best done. The third is the major consequences of knowledge or ignorance for the individual and the individual's family.

It remains unclear, however, as to what are the fundamentals of financial literacy and whether this may vary by population and culture. That is, whether literacy in a first-world, developed economy is quite different from that in a developing country.

Some researchers and policymakers are more attracted to literacy rather than attitudes because it appears the former is able to be measured more accurately in the sense that people do, or do not, have specific and correct knowledge. However, the central question for many is what determines economic behavior and where to invest effort to increase the financial literacy and well-being of whole groups in a society.

# Practitioner Tools and Techniques: Classifying Potential Investors

Many involved in selling financial products and services are inevitably interested in understanding their client's needs and preferences to make the sales experience more efficient for both parties (Horwitz and Klontz, 2013). As a consequence, various groups have attempted to develop tests that indicate potential investor preferences and styles. These can be administered in various ways, including an online questionnaire or by an interviewer. The idea is to get a profile of an individual's financial needs and wants so that they can be advised/sold a particular product. These tests could, also, be used for counselling for those individuals or couples who are struggling with money issues.

Consider, for example, Money Habitudes, a measure devised by Soloman and Gimpel, which offers a free online measure. Those who take it receive a free, thorough 27-page report. Money Habitudes says it is "a fun, easy way to understand your money personality. It helps you think about money in new ways and talk about your finances." Within the Money Habitudes framework, there are six money types, each with a "money message": Security (stay safe and secure), Planning (act intentionally), Spontaneous (Enjoy the moment), Status (make a good impression), Giving (help others), and Carefree (not to be a priority). The following feedback notes highlight responses from those who have used Money Habitudes:

> Everyone is a combination of Money Habitudes types and each one is good. There's no "perfect" combination. Overusing or underusing any Habitude can be challenging. Your Habitudes can change over time depending on circumstances or if you intentionally decide to change. Many people will have one or two Habitudes that are dominant. That means that when they get money, the first thought they will have is the message related to their dominant Habitude (s). The most important thing to think and talk about is what your results mean to you. Are you satisfied with your combination? If yes, that's great! If not, would you benefit from using one Habitude more or less? (Soloman and Gimpel, n.d., p. 3)

The first author of this chapter took the test and scored very high on *Planning* and very low on *Carefree*. Certainly, it seemed from someone who was hopefully monetarily self-aware, and knowledgeable about psychometrics fairly accurate and descriptively sensitive.

Each comes with personal recommendations and warnings about over- and under-using that mindset. For example, the following recommendations apply to *Planning*:

> OVERUSING. *Learn communication skills to use when pressured by others to spend in ways that conflict with your values or goals. Identify and explore money messages from your past. Ask yourself if your goals reflect your wants and needs – or are they actually others' expectations of what you "should" do. Be supportive and giving to others. Take a break from being productive and goal oriented. Be spontaneous, relax, enjoy life. Try new activities outside your comfort zone. Take some risks. Be tolerant and patient with people whose lifestyles and values are different. See things from their perspective to learn what works for them.*

> UNDERUSING. *Write down what would add value to you this year (vacation, pay off debt, etc.) and what you want in the future (own a home, start a business, etc.). It's the start of short- and long-term plans. Make a list of how you spent money last year (or last month). Mark items with a "+" if they were necessary or a good use of money; mark those that weren't with an "x." Make a list of necessary expenses (housing, food, transport, etc.). Include items billed quarterly or annually. Circle those that change by month (utilities, food, credit cards, gifts, etc.). Use this information to make a realistic spending and savings plan. Set up automatic payments and deductions to stick to your plan.*

> The feedback notes: *"We use Money Habitudes to help identify underlying emotional factors that may support or sabotage the development and implementation of a realistic, individualised financial plan from basic money management to complex investment strategies."*

Another example is the Klontz Money Behavior Inventory (KMBI), which is a multi-scale measure that assesses eight distinct money disorders. In their review, Taylor et al. (2016) argue that the results from the KMBI can be used to inform both mental healthcare professionals and financial planners. Using this instrument, researchers have found KMBI money behaviors to be associated with income, net worth, money scripts, and other aspects of financial health (Klontz et al., 2008, 2014). The eight types are: Compulsive Buying, Gambling Disorder, Hoarders, Workaholism, Financial Dependence, Financial Enabling, Financial Denial, Financial Enmeshment, and Financial Infidelity. Four are of particular interest and described in more detail below:

- Financial Enabling occurs when people put themselves at financial risk in an effort to help others. They have trouble saying "no" to financial requests from children, friends, and/or family members and may avoid making clear arrangements for repayment of loans. They often feel taken advantage of by others and may feel resentment or anger after giving money to others.
- Financial Denial is when people try to cope with financial stress by simply not thinking about money or by trying to avoid dealing with it. Rather than addressing financial situations or problems, they try to ignore them. While offering psychological relief in the short term, such avoidance leads to a worsening of one's financial situation. Chronic financial avoidance leads to long-term financial difficulties and leads to a lack of financial planning and preparedness.
- Financial Enmeshment involves the blurring of boundaries between adults and minor children around money. It involves the "use" of children by adults to bear unreasonable responsibility for or worry about adult financial situations. It may include parents asking children to act as go-betweens in arguments or decisions about money, sharing too much financial information with children such that they feel worried or overwhelmed while the parent may feel a sense of relief after talking to the child about the details of a troubling financial situation.
- Financial Infidelity includes lying about, hiding, or omitting information about one's financial behaviors from one's spouse or partner. Financial infidelity includes secret spending, saving, investing, giving, borrowing, receiving, gambling, or income. People who engage in acts of financial infidelity often do so to cover up problematic money behaviors and/or avoid conflicts with their partners.

A rather different approach has been taken by Furnham and Grover (in press) who developed a three-dimensional model based on whether a person is a saver versus a spender, a money worrier or not, and how financially informed they are. As shown in Table 28.2, this is thus a 2 × 2 × 2 model generating eight types.

Using this tool, people are invited to complete a short 20-item questionnaire that measures all three factors. They are then categorized depending on whether they score below or above average on each factor.

These different methods are used to help financial advisers as well as ordinary individuals to get some insight into their money beliefs and behaviors, so that they can get advice as to how to deal with their current financial situation or improve it. This may be no more than gaining insight and self-help as well as getting formal clinical, financial, or therapeutic advice. They are designed to be helpful for non-experts rather than diagnostic tools. However, they do present for researchers the opportunity to do more investigation of the antecedents and consequences of these money types.

**Table 28.2:** The Grover–Furnham Financial Process Grid.

| | Worry | | |
|---|---|---|---|
| Saver<br>**Money is security/<br>love** | Saver, Savvy, Non-Worrier<br>**Interested in financial affairs,<br>small-time investor** | Saver, Savvy, Worrier<br>**Pessimist, small-time investor,<br>maybe a bit obsessional** | Not<br>Savvy |
| | Saver, Non-savvy, Non-Worrier<br>**Careful but not thoughtful,<br>habitual patterns, not ambitious** | Saver, Non-savvy, Worrier<br>**Skimper and saver, self-deny,<br>irrational behavior** | |
| Spender<br>**Money is power/<br>achievement/freedom** | Spender, Savvy, Non-Worrier<br>**Clued up, hedonistic, can cope,<br>high roller, optimistic** | Spender, Savvy, Worrier<br>**Ambitious for more, social<br>climber** | Savvy |
| | Spender, Non-savvy, Non-Worrier<br>**Spendthrift; live for the day; easy<br>come, easy go** | Spender, Non-savvy, Worrier<br>**No savings, impulsive, not<br>planful** | |

# Future Directions

This research is at the intersection of different social science disciplines, including economics, education, finance, and psychology. It is also of practical interest to many in the financial services profession. There are a number of questions for researchers in this area. They include:

- What are the major factors that determine money attitudes and financial literacy?
- Can we agree on a comprehensive and parsimonious list of money/financial types and how they are related?
- How can we best go about teaching people to become financially literate?

One major development lies in the use of big data supplied by banks and other financial institutions. While there are certain ethical issues to be confronted, what is available is the detailed records of who spends what and where. Anyone who owns a credit, store, or other loyalty card is supplying, on a daily basis, a great deal of data on their income, spending, or saving behavior. This may not cover cash and other transactions (bartering), however, with recent trends, such as retail and hospitality businesses becoming cashless and younger generations concentrating their spending electronically, this is less likely to be an issue. Regardless, this source of spending information provides wonderful data to explore various hypotheses without the typical concerns associated with self-report. Many organizations are storing data that can be matched up to provide an invaluable, detailed, and unique record of financial transactions and money habits.

Inevitably all researchers know that with cross-disciplinary boundaries comes divergence about the most appropriate research methods. Yet, cross-disciplinary applied research can be extremely interesting, fulfilling, and insightful. In many ways, this volume illustrates where we are and where we hope to go on these important issues.

# Conclusion

Understanding people and their money is the concern of many different disciplines. Psychologists have been involved in many issues from the design of currency to maximizing recognition, through advice about how to socialize children, to adults with serious money problems. While those working in the area appear to have been in a small cottage research industry, developments in the field have seen great growth in trying to understand how to measure and explore money beliefs and behaviors. This has been led by practitioners, as much as academics, and the results of this exploration are likely to provide considerable benefit for individuals, organizations, and the wider society.

# References

Abdullah, N., Fazil, S., and Arif, A. (2019). The relationship between attitude toward money, financial literacy and debt management with young worker's financial well-being. *Pernatika Journal of Social Science and Humanities, 27*, 361–378.

Ali, P., Anderson, M., McRae, C., and Ramsay, I. (2014). The financial literacy of young Australians: An empirical study and implications for consumer protection and ASIC's national financial literacy strategy. *Company and Securities Law Journal, 32*(5), 334–352.

Atkinson, A., McKay, S., Kempson, E., and Collard, S. (2006). Levels of financial capability in the UK: Results of a baseline survey (Consumer Research Paper No. 47). *Financial Service Authority*.

Bailey, W., and Gustafson, W. (1986). Gender and gender-role orientation differences in attitudes and behaviors toward money. In K. Kitt (Ed.), *Proceedings of the Fourth Annual Conference of the Association for Financial Counseling and Planning Education* (pp. 11–20).

Bailey, W., and Gustafson, W. (1991). An examination of the relationship between personality factors and attitudes to money. In R. Frantz, H. Singh, and J. Gerber (eds.), *Handbook of behavioural economics* (pp. 271–285). JAI Press.

Bailey, W., Johnson, P., Adams, C., Lawson, R., Williams, P., and Lown, J. (1994). An exploratory study of money beliefs and behaviours scale using data from 3 nations. *Consumer Interests Annual, 40*, 178–185.

Bailey, W., and Lown, J. (1993). A cross-cultural examination of the aetiology of attitudes toward money. *Journal of Consumer Studies and Home Economics, 17*, 391–402.

Baker, P. M., and Hagedorn, R. B. (2008). Attitudes to money in a random sample of adults: Factor analysis of the MAS and MBBS scales, and correlations with demographic variables. *Journal of Socio-Economics, 37*(5), 1803–1814.

Belsky, G., and Gilovich, T. (1999). *Why smart people make big money mistakes – and how to correct them*. Simon and Schuster.

Blais, A. R., and Weber, E. U. (2006). A domain-specific risk-taking (DOSPERT) scale for adult populations. *Judgment and Decision Making*, *1*(1), 33–47.

Blue, L., Grootenboer, P., and Brimble, M. (2014). Financial literacy education in the curriculum: Making the grade or missing the mark? *International Review of Economics Education*, *16*, 51–62. https://doi.org/10.1016/j.iree.2014.07.005

Bodnar, J. (1993). *Dr. Tightwad's money: Smart kids*. Random House.

Brown, S., and Taylor, K. (2014). Household finances and the "big five" personality traits. *Journal of Economic Psychology*, *45*, 197–212. https://doi.org/10.1016/j.joep.2014.10.006

Brüggen, E. C., Hogreve, J., Holmlund, M., Kabadayi, S., and Löfgren, M. (2017). Financial well-being: A conceptualization and research agenda. *Journal of Business Research*, *79*, 228–237. https://doi.org/10.1016/j.jbusres.2017.03.013

Burgess, S. M. (2005). The importance and motivational content of money attitudes: South Africans with living standards similar to those in industrialised Western countries. *South African Journal of Psychology*, *35*(1), 106–126.

Christopher, A. N., Marek, P., and Carroll, S. M. (2004). Materialism and attitudes toward money: An exploratory investigation. *Individual Differences Research*, *2*(2), 109–117.

Cohen, D., Shin, F., and Liu, X. (2019). Meanings and functions of money in different cultural milieus. *Annual Review of Psychology*, *70*(1), 475–497. https://doi.org/10.1146/annurev-psych-010418-103221

Cone, J., and Gilovich, T. (2010). Understanding money's limits. *Journal of Positive Psychology*, *5*(4), 294–301. https://doi.org/10.1080/17439760.2010.498620

Dakin, J., and Wampler, R. (2008). Money doesn't buy happiness, but it helps. *American Journal of Family Therapy*, *36*(4), 300–311. https://doi.org/10.1080/01926180701647512

Dohmen, T., Falk, A., Huffman, D., Sunde, U., Schupp, J., and Wagner, G. G. (2011). Individual risk attitudes: Measurement, determinants, and behavioral consequences. *Journal of the European Economic Association*, *9*(3), 522–550. https://doi.org/10.1111/j.1542-4774.2011.01015.x

Donnelly, G., Iyer, R., and Howell, R. (2012). The big five personality traits, material values, and financial well-being of self-described money managers. *Journal of Economic Psychology*, *33*(6), 1,129–1,142. https://doi.org/10.1016/j.joep.2012.08.001

Durvasula, S., and Lysonski, S. (2010). Money, money, money – how do attitudes toward money impact vanity and materialism? The case of young Chinese consumers. *Journal of Consumer Marketing*, *27*(2), 169–179.

Ealy, C. D., and Lesh, K. (1998). *Our money ourselves: Redesigning your relationship with money*. Amacom.

Edwards, R., Allen, M., and Hayhoe, C. (2007). Financial attitudes and family communication about students' finances: The role of sex differences. *Communication Reports*, *3*(2), 90–100. https://doi.org/10.1080/08934210701643719

Engelberg, E., and Sjoberg, L. (2006). Money attitudes and emotional intelligence. *Journal of Applied Social Psychology*, *36*(8), 2,027–2,047. https://doi.org/10.1111/j.0021-9029.2006.00092.x

Fenton-O'Creevy, M., and Furnham, A. (2019). Money attitudes, personality and chronic impulse buying. *Applied Psychology: An International Review*, *69*(40), 1,557–1,572. https://doi.org/10.1111/apps.12215

Fenton-O'Creevy, M., and Furnham, A. (2020). Personality, ideology and money attitudes as correlates of financial literacy and competence. *Financial Planning Review*, *3*(1), 1–14. https://doi.org/10.1002/cfp2.1070

Fernandes, D., Lynch Jr, J., and Netemeyer, R. (2014). Financial literacy, financial education, and downstream financial behaviors. *Management Science, 60*(8), 1,861–1,883. https://doi.org/10.1287/mnsc.2013.1849

Folke, T., Gjorgjiovska, J., Paul, A., Jakob, L., and Ruggeri, K. (2019). Asset: A new measure of economic and financial literacy. *European Journal of Psychological Assessment, 37*, 65–80. https://doi.org/10.1027/1015-5759/a000575

Forman, N. (1987). *Mind over money*. Doubleday.

Furnham, A. (1984). Many sides of the coin: The psychology of money usage. *Personality and Individual Differences, 5*(5), 501–509.

Furnham, A. (2014). *The new psychology of money*. Routledge.

Furnham, A. (2019). The personality disorders and money beliefs and behaviours. *Financial Planning Review, 2*(2), 1–9. https://doi.org/10.1002/cfp2.1046

Furnham, A., and Cheng, H. (2019). Factors influencing adult savings and investment: Findings from a nationally representative sample. *Personality and Individual Differences, 151*, 1–6.

Furnham, A., and Grover, S. (2019). A new money behaviour quiz. *Journal of Individual Differences, 41*(4), 17–29. https://doi.org/10.1027/1614-0001/a000299

Furnham, A., and Grover, S. (in press). *Correlates of financial literacy and well-being*.

Furnham, A., and Murphy, T. A. (2019). Money types, money beliefs and financial worries: An Australian study. *Australian Journal of Psychology, 71*(2), 193–199. https://doi.org/10.1111/ajpy.12219

Furnham, A., von Stumm, S, and Fenton-O'Creevy, M. (2014). Sex differences in money pathology in the general population. *Social Indicators Research, 123*(3), 701–711. https://doi.org/10.1007/s11205-014-0756-x

Furnham, A., Wilson, E., and Telford, K. (2012). The meaning of money: The validation of a short money-type measure. *Personality and Individual Differences, 52*(6), 707–711. https://doi.org/10.1016/j.paid.2011.12.020

Garg, N., and Singh, S. (2018). Financial literacy among youth. *International Journal of Social Economics, 45*(1), 173–186. https://doi.org/10.1108/IJSE-11-2016-0303

Gasiorowska, A. (2015). The impact of money attitudes on the relationship between income and financial satisfaction. *Polish Psychological Bulletin, 46*(2), 197–208. https://doi.org/10.1515/PPB-2015-0026

Gladstone, J., Matz, S., and Lemaire, A. (2019). Can psychological traits be inferred from spending? Evidence from transaction data. *Psychological Science, 30*(7), 1087–1096.

Goldberg, H., and Lewis, R. (1978). *Money madness*. Springwood Books.

Gresham, A., and Fontenot, G. (1989). The differing attitudes of the sexes toward money: An application of the money attitude scale. *Advances in Marketing, 8*, 380–384.

Hanley, A., and Wilhelm, M. (1992). Compulsive buying: An exploration into self-esteem and money attitudes. *Journal of Economic Psychology, 13*(1), 5–18.

Hantula, D. (2003). Evolutionary psychology and consumption. *Psychology and Marketing, 20*, 757–763.

Henchoz, C., Coste, T., and Wernli, B. (2019). Culture, money attitudes and economic outcomes. *Swiss Journal of Economics and Statistics, 155*(1), 1–13.

Horwitz, E. J., Bradley, T., Klontz, B., and Zabek, F. (2019). A financial psychology intervention for increasing employee participation in and contribution to retirement plans: Results of three trials. *Journal of Financial Counselling and Planning, 30*(2), 262–276.

Horwitz, E. J., and Klontz. B.T. (2013). Understanding and dealing with client resistance to change. *Journal of Financial Planning, 26*(11), 27–31.

Huston, S. J. (2010). Measuring financial literacy. *Journal of Consumer Affairs, 44*(2), 296–316.

Inseng, H. D. (2019). Symbolic money attitudes and compulsive buying: Are they all bad for happiness? *African Journal of Business and Economic Research, 14*(1), 31–48.

Jia, S., Zhang, W., Li, P., Feng, T., and Li, H. (2013) Attitude toward money modulates outcome process: An ERP study. *Social Neuroscience, 8*(1), 43–55.

Kamis, J., Samad, A. N., Pheng, S. L., Rasli, S., Hajali, M. S. H., and Peing, F. S. E. (2020). The influence of money attitude towards spending behaviour among university Selangor (Unisel) students. *Selangor Science & Technology Review, 4*(1), 6–13.

Kebede, M., and Kuar, J. (2015). Financial literacy and management of personal finance: A review of recent literatures. *Research Journal of Finance and Accounting, 6*(13), 92–106.

Keller, C., and Siegrist, M. (2006). Investing in stocks: The influence of financial risk attitudes and values-related money and stock market attitudes. *Journal of Economic Psychology, 27*(2), 285–303. https://doi.org/10.1016/j.joep.2005.07.002

Klontz, B. T., Bivens, A., Klontz, P. T., Wada, J., and Kahler, R. (2008). The treatment of disordered money behaviors: Results of an open clinical trial. *Psychological Services, 5*(3), 295–308.

Klontz, B. T., and Britt, S.L. (2012). How clients' money scripts predict their financial behaviors. *Journal of Financial Planning, 25*(11), 33–43.

Klontz, B., Britt, S., Archuleta, K., and Klontz, T. (2012). Disordered money behaviours. *Journal of Financial Therapy, 53*(3), 17–43.

Klontz, B. T., Seay, M. C., Sullivan, P., and Canale, A. (2014). The psychology of wealth: Psychological factors associated with high income. *Journal of Financial Planning, 27*(12), 46–53.

Klontz, B. T., Zabek, F., Taylor, C., Bivens, A., Horwitz, E., Klontz, P. T., Tharp, P., and Lurtz, M. (2019). The sentimental savings study: Using financial psychology to increase personal savings. *Journal of Financial Planning, 32*(10), 44–55.

Knoll, M., and Houts, C., (2012). The financial knowledge scale: An application of item response theory to the assessment of financial literacy. *Journal of Consumer Affairs, 46*(3), 381–410.

Larrabee, L., and Klontz, B, (2019). Using financial psychology to better serve female clients. *Journal of Financial Planning, 32*(9), 24–27.

Lay, A., and Furnham, A. (2019). A new money attitudes questionnaire. *European Journal of Psychological Assessment, 35*(6), 813–822. https://doi.org/10.1027/1015-5759/a000474

Lea, S. E. G., and Webley, P. (2006). Money as tool, money as drug: The psychology of a strong incentive. *Behavioural and Brain Sciences, 29*(2), 161–209. https://doi.org/10.1017/S0140525X06009046

Lemroává, S., Reiterová, E., Fatěnová, R., Lemr, K., and Tang, T. L. P. (2014) Money is power: Monetary intelligence – love of money and temptation of materialism among Czech university students. *Journal of Business Ethics, 125*(2), 329–348.

Lim, V. K., and Teo, T. S. (1997). Sex, money and financial hardship: An empirical study of attitudes towards money among undergraduates in Singapore. *Journal of Economic Psychology, 18*(4), 369–386.

Loh, A., Peong, K., and Peong, K. (2019). Determinants of personal financial literacy among young adults in Malaysian accounting firms. *Global Journal of Business Social Science Review, 7*(1), 8–19. https://ssrn.com/abstract=3352465

Lusardi, A. (2015). Financial literacy: Do people know the ABCs of finance? *Public Understanding of Science, 24*(3), 260–271. https://doi.org/10.1177/0963662514564516

Lusardi, A., Mitchell, O. S., and Curto, V. (2010). Financial literacy among the young. *Journal of Consumer Affairs, 44*(2), 358–380. https://doi.org/10.1111/j.1745-6606.2010.01173.x

Maison, D., Marchlewska, M., Sekścińska, K., Rudzinska-Wojciechowska, J., and Łozowski, F. (2019). You don't have to be rich to save money: On the relationship between objective versus subjective financial situation and having savings. *PLoS ONE, 14*(4), e0214396. https://doi.org/10.1371/journal.pone.0214396

Mandell, L., and Klein, L., (2009). The impact of financial literacy education on subsequent financial behavior. *Journal of Financial Counseling and Planning*, *20*(1), 15–24.

Matthews, A. (1991). *If I think about money so much, why can't I figure it out?* Summit.

Matz, S. C., Gladstone, J. J., and Stillwell, D. (2016). Money buys happiness when spending fits our personality. *Psychological Science*, *27*(5), 715–725.

Mumford, D., and Weeks, G. (2003). The money genogram. *Journal of Family Psychotherapy*, *14*(3), 33–45.

Netemeyer, R. G., Warmath, D., Fernandes, D., and Lynch Jr., J. G. (2018). How am I doing? Perceived financial well-being, its potential antecedents, and its relation to overall well-being. *Journal of Consumer Research*, *45*(1), 68–89. https://doi.org/10.1093/jcr/ucx109

Ozgen, O., and Bayoglu, A. (2005). Turkish college students' attitudes towards money. *International Journal of Consumer Studies*, *29*(6), 493–501.

Phau, I., and Woo, C. (2008). Understanding compulsive buying tendencies among young Australians: The roles of money attitude and credit card usage. *Marketing Intelligence and Planning*, *26*(5), 441–458.

Potrich, A., Vieira, K., and Kirch, G., (2018). How well do women do when it comes to financial literacy? Proposition of an indicator and analysis of gender differences. *Journal of Behavioral and Experimental Finance*, 17, 28–41. https://doi.org/10.1016/j.jbef.2017.12.005

Qamar, M. A. J., Khemta, M. A. N., and Jamil, H. (2016). How knowledge and financial self-efficacy moderate the relationship between money attitudes and personal financial management behavior. *European Online Journal of Natural and Social Sciences*, *5*(2), 296–308.

Rick, S., Cryder, C., and Loewenstein, G. (2008). Tightwads and spendthrifts. *Journal of Consumer Research*, *34*(6), 767–782. https://doi.org/10.1086/523285

Roberts, J., and Sepulveda, C. (1999). Money attitudes and compulsion buying. *Journal of International Consumer Marketing*, *11*(4), 53–79.

Rose, G.M., Bakir, A., and Gentina, E. (2016) Money meanings among French and American adolescents. *Journal Consumer Marketing*, *33*(5), 364–375.

Rose, G. M., and Orr, L. M. (2007). Measuring and exploring symbolic money meanings. *Psychology and Marketing*, *24*(9), 743–761.

Santos, E., and Campos, A. (2019). Symbolic uses of money and disorders of financial consumption. *Journal of Psychiatry and Behaviour Therapy*, *2*(1), 1–3.

Sohn, S. H., Joo, S. H., Grable, J. E., Lee, S., and Kim, M. (2012). Adolescents' financial literacy: The role of financial socialization agents, financial experiences, and money attitudes in shaping financial literacy among South Korean youth. *Journal of Adolescence*, *35*(4), 969–980. https://doi.org/10.1016/j

Tang, T. L. P. (1992). The meaning of money revisited. *Journal of Organizational Behavior*, *13*(2), 197–202.

Tang, T. L. P. (1993). The meaning of money: Extension and exploration of the money ethic scale in a sample of university students in Taiwan. *Journal of Organizational Behavior*, *14*(1), 93–99.

Tang, T. L. P. (2010). Money, the meaning of money, management, spirituality and religion. *Journal of Management, Spirituality and Religion*, *7*(2), 173–189. https://doi.org/10.1080/14766081003746448

Tang, T. L. P., Tang, T. L. N., and Homaifar, B. (2006). Income, the love of money, pay comparison and pay satisfaction. *Journal of Managerial Psychology*, *21*(5), 476–491. https://doi.org/10.1108/02683940610673988

Tatarko, A., and Schmidt, P. (2012). *Social capital and attitudes towards money* (HSE Working Paper No.7). National Research University Higher School of Economics Research.

Tavares, F., Almeida, L., and Cunha, M. N., (2019). Financial literacy: Study of a university students sample. *International Journal of Environmental & Science Education*, *14*(9), 499–510.

Taylor, C., Klontz, B., and Britt, S. (2016) Internal consistency and convergent validity of the Klontz money behavior inventory (KMBI). *Journal of Financial Therapy*, *6*, 14–31.

Taylor, M. (2011). Measuring financial capability and its determinants using survey data. *Social Indicators Research*, *102*(2), 297–314.

Vohs, K., Mead, N., and Goode, M. (2006). The psychological consequences of money. *Science*, *314*(5,802), 1,154–1,156.

Von Stumm, S., Fenton O'Creevy, M., and Furnham, A. (2013). Financial capability, money attitudes and socioeconomic status. *Personality and Individual Differences*, *54*(3), 344–349. https://doi.org/10.1016/j.paid.2012.09.019

Walczak, D., and Pieńkowska-Kamieniecka, S. (2018). Gender differences in financial behaviours. *Engineering Economics*, *29*(1), 123–132. https://doi.org/10.5755/j01.ee.29.1.16400

Wang, X., Chen, Z., and Krumhuber, E.G. (2020) Money: An integrated review and synthesis from a psychological perspective. *Review of General Psychology*, *24*(2), 172–190.

Wernimont, P., and Fitzpatrick, S. (1972). The meaning of money. *Journal of Applied Psychology*, *56*(3), 248–261.

Wilhelm, M., Varese, K., and Friedrich, A. (1993). Financial satisfaction and assessment of financial progress. *Journal of Financial Counselling and Planning*, *4*(1), 181–199.

Xu, Y., Beller, A., Roberts, B., and Brown, J. (2015). Personality and young adult financial distress. *Journal of Economic Psychology*, *51*, 90–100. https://doi.org/10.1016/j.joep.2015.08.010

Yamauchi, K. T., and Templer, D. J. (1982). The development of a money attitude scale. *Journal of Personality Assessment*, *46*(5), 522–528.

Zhou, H., and Wei, X. M. (2020). The influence of different meanings of money priming on consumer's comparative decision making. *Open Journal of Social Sciences*, *8*(3), 180–193. https://doi.org/10.4236/jss.2020.830

Kristy L. Archuleta

# 29 Financial and Relationship Satisfaction

**Abstract:** Couple relationships are complex and uniquely intertwined with personal finances. According to theory and empirical research, the intersectionality of multiple factors impacts the relationship and financial satisfaction of intimate partner couples. This chapter conceptualizes financial and relationship satisfaction and illustrates the connection between the two. This chapter also introduces the growing field of financial therapy and how financial therapy modalities can help practitioners improve relationship and financial satisfaction for their couple clients.

**Keywords:** relationship satisfaction, financial satisfaction, family systems theory, systemic financial therapy, solution-focused financial therapy, financial therapy, couples and finances theory

## Introduction

Couple relationships are complex. Multiple factors contribute to this complexity. Money is a complicated factor as well. Most people would like to think about money as a tool used rationally that is needed to access necessities like food, shelter, and clothing. However, the impact money has on individuals' emotions, thoughts, and behavior is deep-seated, making money's impact on intimate partner relationships unique (Ford et al., 2020) when compared to other relationship issues. Most couples want to work toward having both a satisfying relationship and financial situation.

Relationship and financial satisfaction can be seen as outcomes of financial and relationship processes with the interplay between the two being multifaceted, interdependent, and dynamic (Archuleta, 2013; Archuleta and Burr, 2015). Neither relational nor financial satisfaction can be viewed in isolation. However, when differences concerning money occur within the relationship, couples and helping professionals tend to view relational and financial processes as separate. In fact, research has indicated that for couples who seek help with finances, about one-third are also experiencing relationship problems (Aniol and Synder, 1997). Likewise, for couples who seek help with their relationship, about one-third report having financial issues.

In recent years, financial services practitioners, other help providers, and researchers have recognized that relationships and money and relationship and financial satisfaction are important to helping couples achieve successful outcomes and their ultimate goals. Dew (2008, 2016) reviewed money and marriage literature,

**Kristy L. Archuleta,** University of Georgia

https://doi.org/10.1515/9783110727692-029

noting in 2016 that the update was extensive due to the increased amount of research. This chapter is not meant to be a replication or extension of Dew's work; rather, this chapter focuses more closely on literature pertaining to financial satisfaction and relationship satisfaction as outcomes and the interplay between the two concepts. This chapter also connects theory, research, and practice by examining theory and theoretically informed approaches that can help couples move toward increased relational and financial satisfaction (Britt et al., 2015).[1]

# Conceptual and Definition Background

## Financial Satisfaction

Financial satisfaction has been defined by researchers as how satisfied one is with their current financial situation (Joo and Grable, 2004). It is often used as a global measure of subjective satisfaction related to personal finances. Financial satisfaction has also been applied to more specific aspects of one's personal financial situation, such as with "income, money for family necessities, ability to handle financial emergencies, amount of money owed, level of savings, and money for future needs" (Joo, 2008, p. 25). While financial satisfaction has been used as a proxy for more comprehensive concepts such as financial well-being, financial wellness, or financial health, financial satisfaction captures the subjective nature of these terms.

Joo (2008) proposed the notion that financial satisfaction is a component of personal financial wellness in which personal financial wellness is comprised of objective and subjective factors. These factors include objective status (e.g., income and financial ratios), financial satisfaction, financial behaviors, and subjective perceptions (e.g., financial attitudes and perceived financial knowledge). Moreover, personal financial wellness was one component of overall well-being.

In Joo and Grable's (2004) seminal paper they proposed and then tested a framework for financial satisfaction. Their framework included demographic factors like age, income, race/ethnicity, marital status, and education as well as financial solvency, financial behaviors, risk tolerance, and financial stress. All of these factors were found to be directly or indirectly associated with financial satisfaction. More recent studies have helped to support Joo and Grable's framework. For example, financial ratios have been used to further understand how objective household cash flow and net worth measures are associated with financial satisfaction. Garrett and James (2013) used financial solvency (measured as assets/debt) as a proxy for financial distress and found this ratio of assets to debt to be a significant contributor to financial satisfaction while

---

1 Readers are also encouraged to read Dew's 2008 and 2016 reviews.

holding income and wealth constant. They found that financial solvency was more important than liquidity (measured with the ratio: liquid assets/monthly income) in predicting financial satisfaction and changes in one's investment ratio (measured as investment assets/net worth), with solvency being positively associated with changes in one's financial satisfaction.

What one knows (i.e., objective financial knowledge) and what one thinks they know (i.e., subjective financial knowledge) about personal finance are important concepts to understand as they relate to financial satisfaction. Interestingly, researchers have found that subjective financial knowledge is more important than objective financial knowledge when it comes to how one perceives their financial situation (Lind et al., 2020; Woodyard and Robb, 2016). It is possible that when individuals exhibit higher objective financial knowledge, they recognize that their financial situation could be better (Woodyard and Robb, 2016). However, subjective financial knowledge as the most significant factor impacting financial satisfaction could be in part because both are measures of self-perception. The issue has raised concerns among researchers in regards to the accuracy of such a perception, as it relates to how one's household is doing financially from an objective standpoint (Woodyard and Robb, 2016). Dare and colleagues (2020) found that financial confidence was the most significant variable when predicting financial satisfaction via financial behavioral control. Over-confidence in one's own financial knowledge may lead to an inaccurate understanding of one's financial reality, which helps explain the oft-quoted phrase, "ignorance is bliss." Conversely, under-confidence may also lead to a lower but skewed sense of financial satisfaction.

It should be no surprise that positive financial behaviors are associated with financial satisfaction. Numerous studies have linked these two variables together (Dare et al. 2020; Lind et al., 2020). When individuals engage in positive or sound financial behaviors, they tend to view their financial situation more positively. Further, women tend to engage in positive financial behaviors more than men, but they are also less likely to feel as confident in their knowledge (Lind et al., 2020).

While much of the research on financial satisfaction has been conducted with individuals, Totenhagen et al. (2018) explored husbands' and wives' day-to-day financial satisfaction. They found financial satisfaction fluctuates daily with more within-person variability for women. Boyle (2012) studied perceived money ownership. Boyle found when couples considered their money ownership as shared, their financial satisfaction increased. Boyle also discovered that the relationship between perceived money ownership and financial satisfaction was mediated by negative communication, meaning that when couples had negative communication interactions, the relationship between perceived money ownership and financial satisfaction disappeared. In other words, the way in which couples interact with each other matters.

## Relational Satisfaction

Similar to financial satisfaction, relationship satisfaction looks at one's perception of satisfaction in their relationship with their intimate partner or spouse. Researchers have studied relational satisfaction more broadly among couples (i.e., considered in an intimate relationship, cohabiting, or married) and among specific groups like married couples and/or cohabiting couples (Lawson, 2019; Totenhagen et al., 2018; 2019). Relational satisfaction, relationship happiness, relationship adjustment, relationship stability, and relationship quality are concepts researchers have studied over several decades within the domains of family science, marriage and family therapy, psychology, and related areas. Today, the word "marital" is often substituted for "relationship" when studying couples who are legally married. Sometimes these terms are used interchangeably in the literature, but are often considered distinct concepts yet correlated. As a result, marital quality has generated multiple definitions. However, nearly all researchers agree that relationship satisfaction, happiness, adjustment, and instability can be viewed as aspects of a more global concept of relationship quality or marital quality that is multidimensional.

Johnson et al. (1992) described marital quality as multi-dimensional, including marital happiness, amount of interaction, amount and intensity of disagreement, behavioral attributes that cause problems in a relationship, and divorce proneness. They observed in their longitudinal study that marital quality declines over time. Other research has suggested that marital quality or marital satisfaction resembles a U-shaped curve (i.e., a curvilinear relationship) where marital quality tends to be high in the earliest years of marriage and then lower during the parenting years with an increase in later life (Glenn, 1990; Orbuch et al., 1996) when children have left the home and assets tend to be higher. Yet, other research indicates that marital quality or marital satisfaction is high early in the marriage, then decreases to a certain level, ultimately plateauing for the remainder of the marriage (VanLaningham et al., 2001).

Research often cites household work, finances, and parenting issues as top sources of conflict for couples. Amato and Previti (2003) found that a husband's housework decreased the husband's marital quality, whereas it increased the marital quality of the person's spouse. Conflict over housework is notable as it can represent the presence of gender role norms within the relationship and the expectations that arise from those roles. For example, in a relationship with the presence of traditional gender role expectations, female partners may have the expectation of themselves and/or by their male partners to take on the majority of housework. There may be a need or desire for the female partner to contribute to the household financially, which takes away from time that can be spent on housework. The competition among responsibilities, values, and expectations may yield individual and couple stress. When female partners are breadwinners, Mendiola et al. (2017) found that they are more likely to perceive their partners as not meeting their expectations and use blame language, which can result in being less likely to use "togetherness" language when describing relationship arguments compared to females who earned the same or less than their male partner. While exploring the impact of earnings on a couple relationship is outside the scope of this chapter, highlighting how expectations within the relationship can set the tone for couple interactions is germane to the topic because couple interactions are known to have an impact on financial and relational satisfaction.

Housework aside, a common anecdote that is often cited is that money is the top cause of divorce. It is worth noting that while this makes a good headline, research investigating the association between money and divorce is limited (Dew, 2016). While marital instability is conceptually different than relationship or marital satisfaction, research focused on marital instability and/or divorce proneness are often conducted concurrently with marital instability and marital satisfaction studied together (Boyle, 2012; Ross et al., 2016). When reviewing the literature, one can safely assume that there will be an absence of marital satisfaction when marital instability exists. Britt and Huston (2012) found that financial arguments were a significant predictor of relationship satisfaction but not for divorce. They noted that an increased frequency of financial conflict early in the marriage was a predictor of divorce. Dew et al. (2012) argued that financial disagreements are a stronger predictor of divorce than other types of marital disagreements. Papp and colleagues (2009) noted that financial arguments do not always prompt the most frequent fights; however, financial arguments do tend to be the most intensely fought about issue within a relationship. These findings imply that money is an emotionally charged issue that is different from other marital issues, and therefore, couples may go about arguing about them differently.

How couples communicate about money has been an important topic within the literature. Much of the literature suggests that communication tactics, partner support, and shared perceptions, goals, and values around money impact couples' relationship satisfaction. Wilmarth and colleagues (2014) noted that positive and negative communication produce different impacts on relationship satisfaction. In their study, negative communication mediated the relationship between financial wellness and relationship satisfaction. In other words, changes in financial wellness affected relationship satisfaction through communication patterns. Other research has shown that conflict tactics and marital satisfaction fully mediate the relationship between financial disagreements and divorce proneness (e.g., Dew et al., 2012). While not surprising, individuals who exhibit higher levels of warmth more often have spouses who report higher levels of marital quality (Lawson, 2019; Ross et al., 2017). Yet, individuals with higher levels of concern about financial management within the relationship express lower levels of warmth toward their partner. Ross and colleagues (2017) noted that subjective aspects of financial stress, like concern for financial management, may be more important than actual stress, like living paycheck to paycheck, in regards to marital quality. Economic stress appears to impact relationship satisfaction and marital quality negatively (Ross et al., 2016; Spuhlera and Dew, 2019). When couples do feel economic stress, marital quality and marital instability are affected via both husbands' and wives' marital support. Again, these insights seem to point to money as an emotionally charged issue within a couple relationship.

From the outset of their relationship, couples may find money a source of conflict because, as the age-old adage goes, "opposites attract." "Spenders" and "tightwads" often attract each other (Rick et al., 2011). Over time, these different personalities can lead to greater conflict. Britt and colleagues (2017) found that for husbands, sources of conflict were associated with having a "spendy" wife, financial worries, lower income, three or more children, and having a wife that thinks the husband is too spendy. For wives, sources of financial conflict were having husbands who think the wife is too spendy, lack of communication with husbands, low income, and holding perceptions that her husband spends too much.

To date, most research has focused on married heterosexual couples. A growing number of studies have focused on cohabiting couples or have included cohabiting couples within the sample being studied. In regards to cohabiting couples, unions are on the rise, having increased by approximately 900 percent in the last 60 years (Kuperberg, 2014). Rates of cohabiting couples in first union type relationships rose from 33 percent in 1995 to 48 percent in 2010 (Copen et al., 2012). Research has typically shown that those who cohabit prior to marriage exhibit an increased likelihood for divorce and negative financial and relationship outcomes (Copen et al., 2012). More recent research indicates that there is little difference between cohabiting couples and couples who do not cohabit, especially in regards to economic well-being and relationship satisfaction (Lawson, 2019). These more recent findings may indicate that an increased cultural acceptance of cohabitation exists and that couples are waiting longer to marry until they are more financially established.

## Connecting Financial and Relational Satisfaction

The connection between money and relationships has been studied for several decades (Archuleta et al., 2013; Glenn et al., 2019). Researchers have reported that financial behaviors, shared goals and values, financial management roles, and financial knowledge are associated with both financial satisfaction and relational satisfaction (e.g., Archuleta, 2013; Archuleta et al., 2013; Britt et al., 2017; Dew and Xiao 2013; Totenhagen et al., 2018). When couples view money as shared, marital satisfaction and financial satisfaction increase, ultimately lowering marital instability (Boyle, 2012). Shared goals and values around money have been shown to have a positive association with financial and relational satisfaction (Archuleta et al., 2013; Baisden et al., 2018). Financial management practices and behaviors also have been shown to have a positive relationship with financial and relationship satisfaction. Archuleta (2013) reported that when it comes to whom does what in regards to financial roles in a relationship, satisfaction with that role is more important to relationship satisfaction (see also Archuleta and Grable, 2012). Positive financial behaviors have also been linked to relationship satisfaction and vice-a-versa. Dew et al. (2021) argued that the relationship between marital satisfaction and sound financial behaviors may be bi-directional. In their study, sound financial behaviors were negatively associated with marital conflict. Moreover, husbands' sound financial behavior was negatively related to economic stress.

## The Role of Financial Therapy

Since the birth of the Financial Therapy Association and its sponsored scholarly publication, *Journal of Financial Therapy,* research related to specific financial constructs (financial satisfaction, financial well-being, financial behaviors, financial knowledge, etc.) and relationship satisfaction/quality (e.g., marital satisfaction and marital quality) have multiplied (Glenn et al., 2019). Financial therapy helps people to think, feel, and act differently in regards to money to improve individual, couple, and family well-being (Financial Therapy Association, n.d.). Dare et al. (2020) described financial therapy practitioners as tending "to combine financial planning services with mental health treatment, meaning that their clients process feelings, experiences, and beliefs about money while working on plans to reach their goals (e.g., retirement, savings, and investments)" (p. 18). Financial therapy scholars and researchers in related fields study the intersection of cognition, emotion, behavior, relationships, and personal finance with the ultimate outcome being to help clients to reach their goals and outcomes successfully and improve their overall well-being.

# Theoretical Perspectives

Social Exchange Theory (Anderson, 2000; Sabatelli, 1982) and Becker's Theory of Marriage (Becker, 1973) are commonly used theories among those who study financial and relationship satisfaction and related concepts (Boyle, 2012; Britt and Huston, 2012; Mendiola et al., 2017; Totenhagen et al., 2018). Considering the complexities embedded in couple dynamics (Johnson et al., 1992), these theories fall short as they conceptualized couple and financial functioning as linear. The associations are, in fact, not necessarily linear; rather, they are bi-directional or even circular, as noted in the literature. Couples and Finances Theory (CFT) (Archuleta, 2008, 2013) was proposed as a way for both scholars and practitioners to understand the complex dynamics of money within a couple relationship.[2] The theory was initially developed by Archuleta (2008), utilizing inductive theory development techniques based on existing empirical research available at the time. This theoretical framework is rooted in family systems theory and family resource management theory. One of the main assumptions of family systems theory is that the whole is greater than the sum of its parts, meaning individuals cannot be viewed alone but rather as part of larger contexts that intersect (Becvar and Becvar, 2017; Gale et al., 2020). Family systems theory is described in more depth later in the chapter.

CFT not only links financial satisfaction with relationship/marital quality, including relationship satisfaction, but also shows the complexities of the interrelationships among these two concepts and couples' relational characteristics and financial management practices. Couple relationship characteristics can be described as how a couple relates to each other through such mechanisms as communication styles and conflict management strategies. Financial management practices, such as financial behaviors and financial management roles, focus on how couples manage money. CFT suggests that these relational and financial factors are set within individual and social-ecological contexts. In other words, the ways in which couples interact, manage their money, and are satisfied within their relationship and with their financial situation are influenced by individual attributes and characteristics, such as ethnicity, age, and personality. Additionally, social-ecological aspects, such as one's community, culture, religion, and the economy, are thought to influence both individual and couple outcomes.

As the body of knowledge has expanded, CFT has evolved. In 2015, Archuleta and Burr updated the framework to demonstrate that the relationship between relational and financial processes cannot be considered in isolation. While individual factors were included in the initial model, Archuleta and Burr showed that the same factors can impact both relational and financial processes and the interactions between the two. Furthermore, Archuleta and Lutter (2020) extended the concept of financial satisfaction to include financial well-being as an increasing number of studies included multidimensional measures of how one perceives their financial situation. Financial well-being in this sense is both subjective (i.e., perception) and objective (i.e., observed). While CFT has evolved, the growing body of research continues to support the bi-directional and circular relationships among the concepts in the model (see Figure 29.1). Figure 29.1 illustrates how CFT is conceptualized, the circular relationships among the constructs, and how it is applied in research and practice.

---

2 See Archuleta (2013), Archuleta and Burr (2015), and Archuleta and Lutter (2020) for a more in-depth description of Couples and Finances Theory.

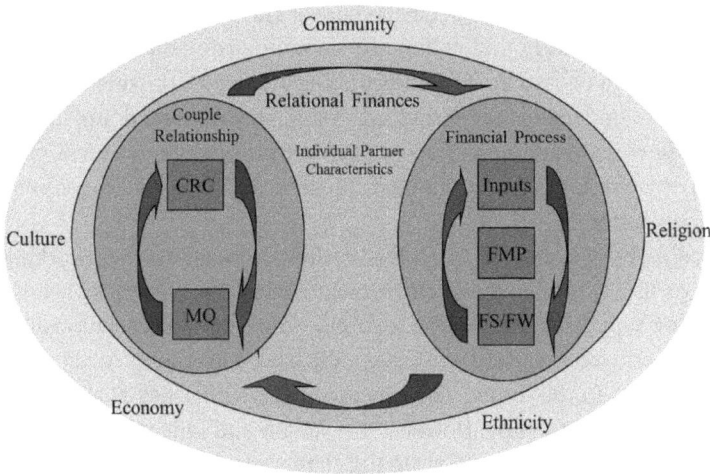

**Figure 29.1:** Couples and Finances Theory.
*Source*: Archuleta and Burr (2015).

# Tools and Techniques to Improve Financial Satisfaction and Relationship Satisfaction

Theory and empirical knowledge are not enough to help those who are in pursuit of gaining a greater understanding of relational and financial satisfaction. Financial help providers need to know how to integrate theory and research into their work with couples who are experiencing either or both financial and relational issues. As a result, practitioners and scholars have been called on to work together to identify effective strategies to help not only understand the dynamics at play but how to change how one thinks, feels, behaves, and relates to others in regard to money (Archuleta and Grable, 2011; Britt et al., 2015). In other words, it is important to know what works in helping couples meet their goals.

The field of financial therapy has led the way in developing evidence-based practices to help facilitate client change in one or more areas of cognition, emotion, behavior, or relational interactions to enhance financial well-being. Borrowing from the disciplines in clinical mental health (e.g., psychology, marriage and family therapy, and clinical social work), multiple modalities exist that are rooted in theory to understand how the intersection of cognition, emotion, behavior, relational dynamics, and money play a role in describing the attitudes and behaviors exhibited by individuals. Some examples include cognitive-behavioral, emotionally focused, experiential, family systems therapy, feminist, narrative, solution-focused, and psychodynamic therapies, to name a few (Klontz et al., 2014). These modalities align theory and interventions, sometimes referred to as tools and techniques in the personal finance literature, to motivate or encourage client change. Theoretically informed modalities offer a way to consistently and coherently communicate and interact with "clients" to help move them toward goal fulfillment. The modalities provide a framework to help providers to understand what they are doing, why they are doing it, and when to do something when working with clients. As a result, when a professional gets "stuck" and does not know what to do next, theoretically informed modalities offer ways to move forward.

The typical steps, broadly speaking, that a financial therapist takes when working with clients to change, as a way to create or move toward better life outcomes or client goals, include building rapport or developing a strong client–therapist relationship, assessment, diagnosis, and treatment. In most cases, the goal is for clients to not need the therapist at some point in the future. The concept of self-sufficiency is a foundational element within financial therapy. However, the length and intensity of therapy depends on several factors like the type of issue the client presents to therapy, readiness to change, therapist and client preferences, and the theoretical orientation from which the clinician works. The following discussion highlights some commonly used theories as they relate to the practice of financial therapy.[3]

## Systemic Financial Therapy

Two theoretically informed approaches that have been tested in the financial therapy literature, that have specific implications for professionals working with couples, are systems theory, financial therapy, and solution-focused financial therapy (Archuleta and Burr, 2015; Archuleta et al., 2015; Smith et al., 2016). Family systems theory is the basis for the profession of marriage and family therapy. While multiple modalities exist within the profession, the modalities have some roots within systems theory that views individuals as part of larger socio-ecological contexts (e.g., family, culture, community, socioeconomics, politics, race, gender, and religion) (Gale et al., 2020). The field of financial therapy has adopted a systemic foundation due to the intersectionality of multiple disciplines and contexts that inherently exist.

Family systems theory was developed from von Bertalanffy's (1968) General Systems Theory and cybernetics and applied to the interplay of family dynamics. To help make sense of family systems theory, key concepts and assumptions are helpful to understand. Important concepts associated with family systems theory include systems, sub-systems, suprasystems, homeostasis, boundaries, circularity, and equifinality. Assumptions that family systems theory makes include holism, systems are hierarchically organized, living systems are open, human systems are self-reflective,

---

3 These theoretical approaches can be adapted for use in a broader personal finance context and whenever personal financial advice is provided to others after proper training has occurred.

reality is constructed, and feedback loops can be negative or positive (Jurich and Myers-Bowman, 1998).

Per its namesakes, members of a family are viewed as part of a family system, while the family system is thought to be comprised of multiple sub-systems. Consider a traditional family comprised of a mother and father and two children. This family is considered a system. The subsystems that make up this family system include a parent subsystem and a child/sibling subsystem. This family system is part of a larger extended family system that is also comprised of subsystems, the family being one of those subsystems along with a grandparent subsystem, aunt and uncle subsystems, cousin subsystems, etc. Systems are hierarchically organized where systems are nested within systems. Parent and child subsystems are nested within the family system and the family system is nested within the extended family system and subsystems. These systems operate within suprasystems, which include neighborhoods, culture, schools, cities, etc. Systems, subsystems, and suprasystems are interrelated and none can be considered alone. Becvar and Becvar (2017) described the interaction and behavior among subsystems this way: "all behavior must be considered relative to context, as both antecedent and subsequent behavior of other family members. All events of a family must be considered simultaneously to antecedent and subsequent behaviors" (p. 5). This is referred to as holism where the system or family is understood as a whole rather than by its individual parts (Smith-Acuna, 2010).[4]

The application of family systems theory in financial therapy occurs over the course of four stages (Archuleta and Burr, 2015; Nichols, 2010). During these four stages, two hallmark techniques are typically used: genograms and process questions. Genograms can be utilized as an assessment tool to help understand the dynamics of a client's family system and as an intervention tool to help clients' unconscious emotions become conscious so that clients can process, and as a result, alter thoughts, feelings, and behavior on a conscious level.[5] The genogram provides a visual representation of family members with a focus on the relational dynamics of the family. Process or circular questions can be asked of the client to help the client understand their own family dynamics. Demographic (age, race/ethnicity, education level, employment, socioeconomic status, career, religious affiliation, etc.) information, in addition to birth and death dates, marriage and divorce dates, and physical and mental health abilities, are added for each person to help give context. Information specifically regarding money, such as money attitudes (e.g., spender versus saver), money scripts, and money disorders, can help professionals who are helping their clients work through financial-related issues. The visual representation can then be used to facilitate process-oriented

---

4 For a more in-depth understanding of family systems theory, refer to Smith-Acuna (2010) and Becvar and Becvar (2017).
5 For more information about genograms, refer to McGolderick, Gerson, and Petry (2020). For more information about how genograms can be used in a personal finance context, refer to Archuleta and Burr (2015), Archuleta and Ross (2015), and Mumford and Weeks (2003).

discussions. An example of a process question in regards to money is, "What did it look like when Mom was anxious about money?" Mumford and Weeks (2003, p. 40) recommended asking questions such as, "When there was a conflict about money, how was it resolved? Was there a pattern in either the conflict areas or who won?"

## Relational Financial Therapy

The collaborative relational model of financial therapy, or relational financial therapy, was initially tested by Kim and associates (2011). In this model, a financial practitioner and marriage and family therapist collaboratively work together to integrate family systems theory and the six-step financial planning process[6] over the course of five sessions. The goals of the model were: (a) helping clients improve couple communication, (b) strengthening relationship stability, (c) decreasing financial distress, (c) increasing financial management skills, (f) creating an economic internal locus of control, and (g) improving overall well-being (Kim et al., 2011). The model was initially developed to be used when working with couples near or below the poverty line; however, the model has evolved in its design to include work with individuals, couples, and families across income levels (Seay et al., 2015). Kim and colleagues reported that in a pilot study, the approach appeared to improve financial well-being, financial locus of control, and positive relationship changes, including increased communication about money, knowing where a household's money goes and planning for the future.

Ford and colleagues (2020) applied the relational financial therapy work described by Seay et al. (2015) and Kim and colleagues (2011) into a three-session model. While the objective of the approach was similar – to help couple clients gain financial and relational insights – they utilized the same dyad of practitioners (i.e., marriage and family therapist and financial planner) who worked with all clients and a team of marriage and family therapist and financial planners as observers. From observations of video recordings, the researchers developed practice and outcome themes. They discovered that client participants reported improvements in relationship dynamics and financial outcomes, including relationship enhancement, increased frequency of financial communication, understanding of the impact money has on a relationship and awareness of their financial situation(s). The researchers noted that the approach tended to produce positive financial behavioral change.

---

6 The six-step financial planning process, as prescribed by the Financial Planning Standards Board, includes: (a) determining your current financial situation, (b) developing financial goals, (c) identifying alternative courses of action, (d) evaluating alternatives, (e) creating and implementing a financial action plan, and (f) reevaluating and revising the plan. CFP Board has expanded the process to include seven steps. For more information, see https://www.fpsb.org/about-financial-planning/

The relational financial therapy approach has also been extended to create a group psychoeducational program, pairing complementary professionals of a financial counselor and couples therapist. (Falconier, 2015). This has come to be known as the "TOGETHER" program. The program is the first of its kind to help couples facing financial strain improve their communication, coping, and financial management skills. Results from an initial pilot study of the program indicated that couples may reduce their partners' financial strain and improve financial management skills. Moreover, Falconier (2015) found that there was an increase in men's relationship satisfaction and a decrease in their psychological aggression upon completion of the program. Client participants also reported being highly satisfied with the program.

## Solution-Focused Financial Therapy

Another approach to working with couples and money that has been supported in the literature is solution-focused therapy or solution-focused financial therapy (Archuleta and Burr, 2015; Archuleta et al., 2020; Smith et al., 2016). Solution-focused therapy (SFT) was first developed by Insoo Kim Berg and Steve deShazer in the early 1980s. SFT is rooted in social constructionism, family systems theory, and Whittgenstein thought (DeShazer et al., 2007). SFT was developed pragmatically after observing hundreds of clients in treatment for substance abuse. Since then, it has been applied in various disciplines like healthcare, business consulting, and financial therapy. SFT has been found to be effective in producing positive client outcomes (Archuleta and Burr, 2015; Archuleta et al., 2020). Key principles and assumptions embedded in SFT include: (a) if it's not broke, don't fix it; (b) if it isn't working, do something different; (c) if it is working, do more of it; (d) small steps can lead to big changes; (d) the solution is not necessarily directly related to the problem; (e) clients are the experts of their own lives; (f) the language for solution development is different from that needed to describe a problem; (g) no problems happen all the time and there are always exceptions that can be utilized; and (h) the future is both created and negotiable (de Shazer et al., 2007, Nichols and Schwartz, 2000). SFT, in a financial setting, has shown promise in improving individual clients' mental health functioning, financial anxiety symptoms, financial behaviors, and subjective financial knowledge (Archuleta et al., 2015; Archuleta et al., 2020).

Similar to family systems theory, there are several interventions associated with this modality, but two hallmark interventions discussed here are the miracle question and scaling questions. In short, the miracle question asks those going through financial therapy treatment to envision going through their nightly routine, falling asleep, and a miracle occurring in the night. The person is asked to imagine waking up in the morning and noticing what would be different about themselves and how others would know that a miracle happened. In relation to a financial therapy session, a client may describe waking up and feeling "free" or worry-free and others would notice that they are smiling more or they would be more agreeable. The goal of the miracle question is to ask as much detail as possible to help the client gain a clear picture of what life would look like and imagine themselves being in that position. The more someone can gain clarity about what they are working toward, the more realistic their future vision may seem. A briefer way to help clients envision their future is to ask about their best hopes for their financial future (Archuleta et al., 2020). Asking the question within the frame of "best hopes" is a technique adapted from the Brief Group in the United Kingdom.[7]

Scaling questions can be used as assessment tools to find out someone's perceptional status in relation to the goal they are working toward. Scale questions can also be used in subsequent sessions to measure progress toward goals. Scaling questions can also be used as interventions to help clients recognize their own strengths and to capitalize on those strengths by doing more of what is good for them or finding an alternative that may work better in their own lives. An example of scaling questions to be used in conjunction with or after the miracle or best hopes question may be framed as follows: "On a scale from 0 to 10, 0 representing *not at all* and 10 representing *I am doing all that I can do*, how confident are you in your ability to realize your best hopes?" Of course when asking such questions, it is important to mirror the clients' language and how they describe their "miracle" or their best hopes. The client may respond that they are a 3 on the scale from 0 to 10. A follow-up question by the professional should then be, "Why so high?" or "Why a three and not a two?" The key for the financial therapist asking "why so high" is to help the client reframe their situation from a perspective of failure to one of relative strength.

Smith and colleagues (2016) specifically applied SFT to couples undergoing financial counseling. In their approach, they integrated solution-focused techniques within a five-step model that aligned with stages in the Transtheoretical Model of Change and appropriate financial education strategies. The five steps in their model – in relation to each stage in the Transtheoretical Model of Change – and solution-focused intervention are outlined in Table 29.1.

While Systemic Financial Therapy and Solution-Focused Financial Therapy are not the only two modalities that exist, they are two within the financial therapy literature that have been found to be particularly valuable for couples. Other approaches that have been shown to be efficacious for couples in traditional psychology and marriage and family therapy include cognitive-behavioral therapy (CBT), narrative therapy, emotionally focused therapy, experiential therapy, and acceptance and commitment therapy (Klontz et al., 2014). Most important to remember is that helping professionals who implement any of these approaches with their clients, regardless of discipline, should not do so unless the approach and the concerns are within the practitioner's

---

**7** See Archuleta et al. (2020) for more information on the best hopes question as it relates to one's financial future, and how it can be asked in a financial setting.

**Table 29.1:** Integration of Five-Step Solution-Focused Financial Therapy for Couples Model.

| | Stage | Transtheoretical Model of Change Stage | Financial Education Tasks | Solution-Focused Therapy Technique |
|---|---|---|---|---|
| 1. | Want | Pre-contemplation | Deciding intentionality, Discussing goals | Scaling questions, Miracle Questions, Exceptions, Challenge question |
| 2. | Need | Contemplation | Deciding intentionality, Discussing needs | Scaling questions, Miracle questions, Exceptions, Revisit Challenge question, Compliment clients' strengths |
| 3. | Have | Preparation | Compile documents, Identify heuristics | Scaling questions, Miracle Questions, Exceptions, Revisit Challenge question Compliment Clients' Strengths |
| 4. | Do | Action | Create a budget | Scaling questions, Miracle Question, Crystal Ball exercise Exceptions, Compliment Clients' Strengths |
| 5. | Plan | Maintenance | Create a financial plan | Scaling questions, Miracle Questions, Exceptions, Compliment Clients' Strengths |

*Source*: Smith et al. (2016).

scope of practice. When clients' emotions, behaviors, thinking, or relational dynamics are beyond one's scope of practice, it is prudent for the professional to make a referral or to collaborate with another professional (Goetz and Gale, 2014).[8]

# Conclusion: Future Directions

The study of financial and relational satisfaction within the context of couples and families is complex, particularly as it relates to the domains of personal and household finance. Considering the multiple dynamics, contexts, and nuances that exist, the body of literature needs to continue to expand. However, the lack of large, generalizable, and longitudinal datasets that include all of the relevant relationship and financial concepts continues to hamper research in this field. In recent years, advanced statistical methods have helped researchers gain a better understanding of dyadic relationships while simultaneously considering multiple contextual factors.

---

**8** See Goetz and Gale (2014) for models of collaborations for complementary professionals.

However, qualitative research should also be expanded to understand the how and why of couple dynamics and intersectionality as described by Gale et al. (2020).

Theoretically informed modalities should be tested for their effectiveness with couples. To date, only a few modalities and approaches, as outlined by Klontz and colleagues (2014), have been empirically tested in relation to working in financial settings or with financial issues, and even fewer have been tested with couples. This is due in part to the financial and time constraints associated with conducting clinical research, whether within a clinic or real-world setting, and limited funding opportunities available. While this chapter has focused primarily on couples, considering overall family well-being and the effectiveness these modalities and approaches may provide in terms of improving family outcomes should also be considered. Personal finance professionals working with couples deal with estate planning questions may find this particularly useful (Archulea and Ross, 2015). For practitioners who are working with couple and family clients, knowing what works and why certain techniques work is helpful. For those who are interested in studying financial and relational satisfaction, the opportunities to expand the literature in meaningful ways are almost unlimited. There is much work yet to be done.

# References

Amato, P. R., and Previti, D. (2003). People's reasons for divorcing: Gender, social class, the life course, and adjustment. *Journal of Family Issues, 24*(5), 602–626.

Anderson, J. D. (2000). *Financial problems as predictors of divorce: A social exchange perspective* [Doctoral dissertation]. Utah State University. https://digitalcommons.usu.edu/etd/2445

Aniol, J. C., and Snyder, D. K. (1997). Differential assessment of financial and relationship distress: Implications for couple therapy. *Journal of Marital and Family Therapy, 23*(3), 347–352.

Archuleta, K. L. (2008). *The impact of dyadic processes and financial management roles on farm couples* [Doctoral dissertation]. Kansas State University. http://hdl.handle.net/2097/929

Archuleta, K. L. (2013). Couples, money, and expectations: Negotiating financial management roles to increase relationship satisfaction. *Marriage & Family Review, 49*(5), 391–411.

Archuleta, K. L., and Burr, E. A. (2015). Systemic financial therapy. *Financial therapy: Theory, research, and practice* (pp. 217–234). Springer.

Archuleta, K. L., Burr, E. A., Carlson, M. B., Ingram, J., Kruger, L. I., Grable, J. E., and Ford, M. R. (2015). Solution-focused financial therapy: A brief report of a pilot study. *Journal of Financial Therapy, 6*(1), 1–16. https://doi.org/10.4148/1944-9771.1081

Archuleta, K. L., and Grable, J. E. (2011). The future of financial planning and counseling: An introduction to financial therapy. *Financial planning and counseling scales* (pp. 33–59). Springer.

Archuleta, K. L., and Grable, J. E. (2012). Does it matter who makes the financial decisions? An exploratory study of married couples' financial decision-making and relationship satisfaction. *Financial Planning Review, 5*(4), 1–15.

Archuleta, K. L., Grable, J. E., and Britt, S. L. (2013). Financial and relationship satisfaction as a function of harsh start-up and shared goals and values. *Journal of Financial Counseling and Planning, 24*(1), 3–14.

Archuleta, K. L., and Lutter, S. (2020). Utilizing family systems theory in financial therapy. *Financial Planning Review, 3*(1), e1073.

Archuleta, K. L., Mielitz, K. S., Jayne, D., and Le, V. (2020). Financial goal setting, financial anxiety, and solution-focused financial therapy (SFFT): A quasi-experimental outcome study. *Contemporary Family Therapy, 42*(1), 68–76.

Archuleta, K. L., and Ross, D. B. (2015). Marriage and family therapy applications to financial planning. In C. Chaffin (Ed.), *Financial planning competency handbook* (pp. 763–777). Wiley.

Baisden, E. D., Fox, J. J., and Bartholomae, S. (2018). Financial management and marital quality: A phenomenological inquiry. *Journal of Financial Therapy, 9*(1), 47–71. https://doi.org/10.4148/1944-9771.1153

Becker, G. S. (1973). A theory of marriage: Part I. *Journal of Political Economy, 81*(4), 813–846.

Becvar, R. J., and Becvar, D. S. (2017). *Systems theory and family therapy: A primer.* Rowman & Littlefield.

Boyle, J. (2012). *Shared money, less conflict, stronger marriages: The relationship between money ownership perceptions, negative communication, financial satisfaction, marital satisfaction and marital instability* [Doctoral dissertation]. Kansas State University.

Britt, S. L., Archuleta, K. L., and Klontz, B. T. (2015). Theories, models, and integration in financial therapy. In B. T. Klontz, S. L. Britt, and K. L. Archuleta (eds.), *Financial therapy: Theory, research, and practice* (pp. 15–22). Springer.

Britt, S. L., Hill, E. J., LeBaron, A. B., Lawson, D. R., and Bean, R. A. (2017). Tightwads and spenders: Predicting financial conflict in couple relationships. *Journal of Financial Planning, 30*(5), 36–42.

Britt, S. L., and Huston, S. J. (2012). The role of money arguments in marriage. *Journal of Family and Economic Issues, 33*(4), 464–476.

Copen, C. E., Daniels, K., Vespa, J., and Mosher, W. D. (2012). *First marriages in the United States: Data from the 2006–2010 national survey of family growth* (No. 49). National Center for Health Statistics. https://www.cdc.gov/nchs/data/nhsr/nhsr049.pdf

Dare, S. E., van Dijk, W. W., van Dijk, E., van Dillen, L. F., Gallucci, M., and Simonse, O. (2020). The road to financial satisfaction: Testing the paths of knowledge, attitudes, sense of control, and positive financial behaviors. *Journal of Financial Therapy, 11*(2), 1–30. https://doi.org/10.4148/1944-9771.1240

De Shazer, S., Dolan, Y., Korman, H., McCollum, E., Trepper, T., and Berg, I. K. (2007). *More than miracles: The state of the art of solution-focused brief therapy.* Haworth Press.

Dew, J. (2008). Marriage and finance. In *Handbook of consumer finance research* (pp. 337–350). Springer.

Dew, J. (2016). Revisiting financial issues and marriage. In *Handbook of consumer finance research* (pp. 281–290). Springer.

Dew, J., Barham, C., and Hill, E. J. (2021). The longitudinal associations of sound financial management behaviors and marital quality. *Journal of Family and Economic Issues, 42*(1), 1–12.

Dew, J., Britt, S., and Huston, S. (2012). Examining the relationship between financial issues and divorce. *Family Relations, 61*(4), 615–628.

Dew, J., and Xiao, J. J. (2013). Financial declines, financial behaviors, and relationship happiness during the 2007–2009 recession. *Journal of Financial Therapy, 4*(1), 1–20.

Falconier, M. K. (2015). Together–A couples' program to improve communication, coping, and financial management skills: Development and initial pilot-testing. *Journal of Marital and Family Therapy, 41*(2), 236–250.

Financial Therapy Association (n.d.) Retrieved March 31, 2021, from https://financialtherapyassociation.org

Ford, M. R., Ross, D. B., Grable, J., and DeGraff, A. (2020). Examining the role of financial therapy on relationship outcomes and help-seeking behavior. *Contemporary Family Therapy*, *42*(1), 55–67.

Gale, J., Ross, D. B., Thomas, M. G., and Boe, J. (2020). Considerations, benefits and cautions integrating systems theory with financial therapy. *Contemporary Family Therapy*, *42*(1), 84–94.

Garrett, S., and James III, R. N. (2013). Financial ratios and perceived household financial satisfaction. *Journal of Financial Therapy*, *4*(1), 39–62.

Glenn, C., Caulfield, B., McCoy, M. A., Curtis, J. R., Gale, N., and Astle, N. (2019). An annotated bibliography of financial therapy research: 2010 to 2018. *Journal of Financial Therapy*, *10*(2), 1–92. https://doi.org/10.4148/1944-9771.1218

Glenn, N. D. (1990). Quantitative research on marital quality in the 1980s: A critical review. *Journal of Marriage and the Family*, *52*(4), 818–831.

Goetz, J., and Gale, J. (2014). Financial therapy: De-biasing and client behaviors. *Investment behavior: The psychology of financial planning and investing* (pp. 227–244). John Wiley & Sons.

Johnson, D. R., Amoloza, T. O., and Booth, A. (1992). Stability and developmental change in marital quality: A three-wave panel analysis. *Journal of Marriage and the Family*, *54*(3), 582–594.

Joo, S. H. (2008). Personal financial wellness. In J. J. Xiao (ed.), *Handbook of consumer finance research* (pp. 21–33). Springer.

Joo, S. H., and Grable, J. E. (2004). An exploratory framework of the determinants of financial satisfaction. *Journal of Family and Economic Issues*, *25*(1), 25–50.

Jurich, J. A., and Myers-Bowman, K. S. (1998). Systems theory and its application to research on human sexuality. *Journal of Sex Research*, *35*(1), 72–87.

Kim, J. H., Gale, J., Goetz, J., and Bermúdez, J. M. (2011). Relational financial therapy: An innovative and collaborative treatment approach. *Contemporary Family Therapy*, *33*(3), 229–241.

Klontz, B. T., Britt, S. L., and Archuleta, K. L. (eds.). (2014). *Financial therapy: Theory, research, and practice*. Springer.

Kuperberg, A. (2014). Age at coresidence, premarital cohabitation, and marriage dissolution: 1985–2009. *Journal of Marriage and Family*, *76*(2), 352–369. https://doi.org/10.1111/jomf. 12092

Lawson, D. R. (2019). *Cohabitation as a young adult: Examining relationship interactions & outcomes and financial characteristics and economic well-being* [Doctoral dissertation]. Kansas State University. http://hdl.handle.net/2097/40247

Lind, T., Ahmed, A., Skagerlund, K., Strömbäck, C., Västfjäll, D., and Tinghög, G. (2020). Competence, confidence, and gender: The role of objective and subjective financial knowledge in household finance. *Journal of Family and Economic Issues*, *41*(2), 626–638.

McGoldrick, M., Gerson, R., and Petry, S. (2020). *Genograms: Assessment and treatment*. W.W. Norton & Company.

Mendiola, M., Mull, J., Archuleta, K. L., Klontz, B., and Torabi, F. (2017). Does she think it matters who makes more? Perceived differences in types of relationship arguments among female breadwinners and nonbreadwinners. *Journal of Financial Therapy*, *8*(2), 42–62. https://doi. org/10.4148/1944-9771.1147

Mumford, D. J., and Weeks, G. R. (2003). The money genogram. *Journal of Family Psychotherapy*, *14*(3), 33–44.

Nichols, M. P. (2010). *Family therapy: Concepts and methods* (9th ed.). Pearson.

Nichols, M. P., and Schwartz, R. C. (2000). *Family therapy: Concepts and methods* (5th ed.). Allyn & Bacon.

Orbuch, T. L., House, J. S., Mero, R. P., and Webster, P. S. (1996). Marital quality over the life course. *Social Psychology Quarterly*, *59*(2), 162–171.

Papp, L. M., Cummings, E. M., and Goeke-Morey, M. C. (2009). For richer, for poorer: Money as a topic of marital conflict in the home. *Family Relations, 58*(1), 91–103.

Rick, S. I., Small, D. A., and Finkel, E. J. (2011). Fatal (fiscal) attraction: Spendthrifts and tightwads in marriage. *Journal of Marketing Research, 48*(2), 228–237.

Ross, D. B., Gale, J., and Goetz, J. W. (2016). Ethical issues and decision making in collaborative financial therapy. *Journal of Financial Therapy, 7*(1), 17–37. https://doi.org/10.4148/1944-9771.1087

Ross, D. B., O'Neal, C. W., Arnold, A. L., and Mancini, J. A. (2017). Money matters in marriage: Financial concerns, warmth, and hostility among military couples. *Journal of Family and Economic Issues, 38*(4), 572–581.

Sabatelli, R. M. (1982). *Marital cohesiveness and family life transitions: A social exchange perspective* [Paper presentation]. The Annual Conference of the National Council on Family Relations, Washington, D.C., United States.

Seay, M., Goetz, J. W., and Gale, J. (2015). Collaborative relational model. In B. T. Klontz., S. L. Britt, and K. L. Archuleta (eds.), *Financial therapy: Theory, research, and practice* (pp. 161–172). Springer.

Smith, T. E., Shelton, V. M., and Richards, K. V. (2016). Solution-focused financial therapy with couples. Journal of Human Behavior in the Social Environment, *26*(5), 452–460.

Smith-Acuna, S. (2010). *Systems theory in action: Applications to individual, couple, and family therapy.* John Wiley & Sons.

Spuhlera, B. K., and Dew, J. (2019). Sound financial management and happiness: Economic pressure and relationship satisfaction as mediators. *Journal of Financial Counseling and Planning, 30*(2), 157–174.

Totenhagen, C. J., Wilmarth, M. J., Serido, J., and Betancourt, A. E. (2018). Do day-to-day finances play a role in relationship satisfaction? A dyadic investigation. *Journal of Family Psychology, 32*(4), 528.

Totenhagen, C. J., Wilmarth, M. J., Serido, J., Curran, M. A., and Shim, S. (2019). Pathways from financial knowledge to relationship satisfaction: The roles of financial behaviors, perceived shared financial values with the romantic partner, and debt. *Journal of Family and Economic Issues, 40*(3), 423–437.

VanLaningham, J., Johnson, D. R., and Amato, P. (2001). Marital happiness, marital duration, and the U-shaped curve: Evidence from a five-wave panel study. *Social Forces, 79*(4), 1,313–1,341.

von Bertalanffy, L. (1968). *General system theory: Foundations, development, applications.* George Braziller.

Wilmarth, M. J., Nielsen, R. B., and Futris, T. G. (2014). Financial wellness and relationship satisfaction: Does communication mediate? *Family and Consumer Sciences Research Journal, 43*(2), 131–144.

Woodyard, A. S., and Robb, C. A. (2016). Consideration of financial satisfaction: What consumers know, feel, and do from a financial perspective. *Journal of Financial Therapy, 7*(2), 41. https://doi.org/10.4148/1944-9771.1102

Michelle Cull
# 30 The Growing Role of FinTech and Robo-advisors

**Abstract:** This chapter provides a summary of key findings from the literature on the growing role of FinTech and robo-advisors in the personal finance space. The chapter describes the various types of FinTech and robo-advice and provides a historical review of the development of FinTech. It outlines the benefits of FinTech and robo-advice relating to accessibility, compliance, efficiencies, and cost savings while also exploring some of the challenges in terms of consumer protection, cybersecurity, and data privacy. The chapter discusses a range of tools and techniques being used by practitioners along with how FinTech and robo-advice have disrupted the financial advice market and the impact on the traditional role of the financial advisor. The chapter also discusses the main issues facing researchers and policymakers in the areas of FinTech and robo-advice during a period of rapid change. The future direction of FinTech is discussed, including the increased sophistication of machine learning and artificial intelligence (AI) and how continued disruption will influence customer behavior, business models, and the long-term structure of the financial services market.

**Keywords:** financial advice, financial planning, FinTech, robo-advice

## Introduction

The digital revolution has fundamentally changed how people live. It has impacted not only the landscape of the financial system but also on how people manage their finances. This chapter takes stock of the impact that FinTech has had on consumers, financial advisors, and society more broadly. It also considers the implications for all stakeholders in the financial system, including the important role of regulators.

While the Internet provided a fertile environment for the development of FinTech, the smartphone has enabled FinTech applications to significantly change the way financial institutions interact with their customers. Global investment in financial technology has reached approximately $150.4 billion USD globally (KPMG, 2020a) and although traditional financial institutions are the major users of this technology, FinTech has opened the gates to thousands of new businesses, increasing competition and creating new markets. FinTech applications (apps) have had the greatest impact on society as they have realized efficiencies, reduced costs to

**Michelle Cull,** Western Sydney University

https://doi.org/10.1515/9783110727692-030

the client, and improved accessibility. Further, the rapid technological innovation of both FinTech and robo-advice has challenged the traditional roles of financial institutions and financial advisors in addition to the legislative framework that supports them.

While this chapter provides a historical perspective of the development of FinTech and discusses the main research and policy issues in the areas of FinTech and robo-advice, the remainder of this section introduces FinTech and robo-advice by defining the terms and describing the various forms and types of this technology.

## FinTech

The word FinTech is an abbreviation for the words financial technology. While FinTech has become more prevalent and more advanced in the last decade, the use of the term FinTech was originally defined by Bettinger (1972) as "an acronym which stands for financial technology, combining bank expertise with modern management science techniques and the computer" (p. 62). In the 1970s, FinTech mainly related to programs created to assist with solving daily banking problems, such as bond valuations, discounted cash flow analysis, credit analysis, and buy versus lease scenarios. More recently, FinTech has been described as "a living body with a flexible and changing nature rather than a stable notion that is transparent and clearly understood by both academia and the media" (Zavolokina et al., 2016, p. 12). Generally speaking, FinTech can be described as sophisticated technology that automates the delivery and use of financial products and services to achieve efficiencies for both organizations and consumers. FinTech continues to utilize the latest innovative technology by incorporating software and algorithms used in computers, smartphones, and other digital devices to improve accessibility and streamline processes relating to financial management. Examples of FinTech include cryptocurrencies, digital advisory services, peer-to-peer lending, digital and mobile payment systems, asset management, brokerage services, and other personal financial management technology (Philippon, 2016), such as budgeting and credit monitoring.

According to Knewtson and Rosenbaum (2020), the FinTech industry can be organized into four broad areas that reflect the structure of traditional financial services: (a) Monetary Alternatives, (b) Capital Intermediation, (c) InvestTech, and (d) Infrastructure. The four areas are shown in Figure 30.1 and adopted to facilitate the discussion below.

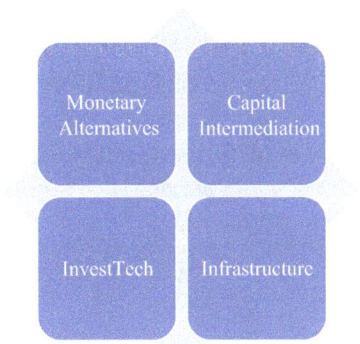

**Figure 30.1:** Four Areas of FinTech.
Adapted from Knewtson and Rosenbaum (2020, p. 1050).

## Monetary Alternatives

Monetary alternatives comprise items such as cryptocurrency (e.g., bitcoin), digital cash, and bank payment systems. Digital payment systems can be used for individual consumer payments as well as for business-to-business (B2B) payments. Digital payment systems are found in various mobile phone apps as well as web-based payment systems. Examples include Apple Pay, Google Pay, PayPal, Stripe, and Venmo (peer-to-peer payments). From 2019 to 2020, the total transaction value of digital payments grew by approximately $1.1 trillion USD from $4.1 trillion USD to $5.2 trillion USD (Andjelic, 2021).

## Capital Intermediation

The broad area of capital intermediation includes FinTech that competes with traditional banking services and insurance companies and focuses on lending and insurance, including digital banks, InsurTechs, and LendTechs (Knewtson and Rosenbaum, 2020), as described below.

– Digital banks – these are banks with no physical branches that offer banking services exclusively through digital platforms, such as mobiles, tablets, and computers. For example, Ally Bank, Chime, NuBank, and Varo Bank in the United States, Revolut in the United Kingdom, and ING and Volt Bank in Australia.

– InsurTechs – this refers to insurance technology that simplifies and streamlines policy issuance, underwriting, and claims through risk assessment and data analysis using artificial intelligence (AI) and machine learning, which enables products to be priced more competitively. Examples include BIMA (Sweden), Huddle (Australia), Lemonade (United States), Slice (Canada, United Kingdom, and the United States), and Zego (United Kingdom).

- LendTechs – these offer lending services without the need for physical locations by utilizing mobile phone technology, text messages, and digital contracts. Some LendTechs target specific markets and risk categories that are not often serviced by traditional banks. Such markets may include small loans, loans for small businesses and entrepreneurs, or specific types of businesses, as well as loans for applicants in areas of the world that are under-serviced by banks. Some examples include Avant, Opploans, Prosper, and Tala.

## InvestTech

The InvestTech category includes FinTechs that provide equity valuation, equity issuance, portfolio planning, and advisory services related to financial planning. It includes algorithmic trading, crowdfunding, financial intelligence, and investment apps.

Crowdfunding through InvestTechs enables small and medium enterprises (SMEs) to raise funds for their operations and retail investors to invest small amounts in projects that match their interests by facilitating the investment of small amounts of money from a large number of people via the Internet. This provides an alternative method of raising funds for start-up businesses, with some platforms enabling equity crowdfunding. Examples of crowdfunding InvestTechs include Crowdcube (United Kingdom), FrontFundr (Canada), Kickstarter, Patreon (United States), Seedrs (United Kingdom), and VentureCrowd (Australia). Crowdfunding platforms can also assist in raising money for charitable causes and non-profit campaigns and endeavors (e.g., Causes and GoFundMe).

Investment apps (e.g., Acorns, Fidelity, Robinhood, and TD Ameritrade) can assist both retail and institutional investors in establishing investments. While this category may also include some forms of robo-advice, the rapid development of robo-advisors in the last two years has given robo-advice some distinct features that set it apart from other forms of FinTech. As a result, robo-advice is discussed in more detail under a separate heading later in this section.

## Infrastructure

FinTechs in this group includes those that act as intermediaries for financial institutions and include CreditTechs, Financial Application Programming Interface (API) Techs (APITechs), and RegTechs.

- CreditTechs – these utilize technology that automates the sourcing of alternative sources of consumer data (e.g., analysis of bank statements, Internet searches, social media posts) to predict default risk, review spending habits, and to assist creditors to assess the ability of consumers to repay a loan. It can enable consumers to receive credit they otherwise may not access. Examples include Credit Karma and CredoScore.

- APITechs – these provide the infrastructure between a bank and an investment app (Knewtson and Rosenbaum, 2020) in order to provide customers with the information they require. APITechs link a bank's database with different applications or programs to enable services, payments, and products to be available to the end-user. For example, Plaid connects banks with apps such as Venmo (peer-to-peer payments), Betterment (automated investing), and Chime (online banking). Other Financial APITech examples include Eurobits Technologies and Yodlee.
- RegTechs – this technology seeks to assist financial services firms with compliance requirements, such as regulatory reporting, risk management, transaction analysis, anti-money laundering (AML), and anti-fraud screening as well as Know Your Client (KYC) procedures (Deloitte, 2021; KPMG, 2020b). Examples include Ascent, ComplyAdvantage, Hummingbird, and Suade.

As with most technology, the consumers who use FinTech tend to be younger. The focus of FinTech markets has been more heavily on Millennials who are tech-savvy (Terry et al., 2015). The number of FinTechs continues to increase globally with the Americas producing the most FinTech start-ups (5,779), followed by Europe, the Middle East and Africa combined (3,583), and the Asia Pacific (2,849) (FinancesOnline, 2021). Global FinTech investment was estimated to have reached a total of $150.4 billion USD in 2019 (KPMG, 2020a), and as of March 2021, there were a total of 144 FinTech unicorns[1] worldwide (Fintech Live, 2021).

While FinTech provides advantages to consumers in terms of access, and convenience, it is often also more affordable than using traditional methods. However, as FinTech continues to innovate and expand products and markets, new threats such as privacy breaches and cybercrime are also increasing. With their heavy reliance on technology infrastructure, FinTech businesses are faced with additional threats when compared to traditional financial services as they are more vulnerable to technological failure. As a result, FinTech businesses need to continually invest in their business by ensuring that they have the latest risk management systems in place. Employing the right people who possess the required capabilities is also critical to these businesses as they continue to innovate and evolve.

FinTech businesses face the additional risk of regulatory changes that continue to evolve as the FinTech market evolves. Thus, the right systems and procedures need to be in place to ensure that FinTech businesses keep up to date with the latest changes and understand their responsibilities in different countries should they operate internationally. Many of the advantages to consumers as well as the additional risks and challenges that apply to FinTech also apply to robo-advice, which is discussed below.

---

1 Unicorns are start-up companies valued at $1 billion USD or more.

# Robo-advice

Robo-advice (also known as automated advice, digital advice, and AdviceTech) is the provision of automated financial product advice using algorithms and technology that is addressed to a specific individual, without the direct involvement of a human advisor. It can comprise general or personal advice, ranging from advice that is narrow in scope (e.g., advice about portfolio construction) to a comprehensive financial plan (Australian Securities and Investment Commission, 2016). Examples of robo-advisors include Betterment (United States), Moneybox (United Kingdom), Nutmeg (United Kingdom), SixPark (Australia), QuietGrowth (Australia), Vanguard (United States), and Wealthsimple (Canada).

Robo-advice represents the second wave of financial service digitalization (Jung et al., 2018) being more advanced than other FinTech platforms. Robo-advice provides a more comprehensive service than that provided by investment apps in that it collects additional information from the client and attempts to match the individual client's needs and circumstances with the investment advice provided. Through the use of algorithms rather than humans, robo-advisors monitor and evaluate investment trends, and based on the client's risk tolerance, financial goals, and other preferences, make investment recommendations. Further, robo-advisors continue to manage and monitor the portfolio once the investment has been made, noting market changes and changes of asset characteristics (Jung et al., 2019). By automating the advice process, robo-advisors lower the cost of advice and increase accessibility to investment advice for consumers with smaller amounts to invest. Robo-advice is now also expanding into other areas with consumers able to obtain guidance on additional finance-related issues, including taxes, mortgage financing, education funds, and retirement planning (Woodyard and Grable, 2018).

Robo-advisors have radically disrupted the financial advice market by serving non-traditional markets, such as low-budget investors and Millennials who are not discouraged by technology like some older investors (Sironi, 2016). This has also provided an opportunity for new robo-advice firms to enter the market. Global assets under management by robo-advisors were almost $1.1 trillion USD in 2020, with the United States having the highest assets under management in robo-advice, expected to reach $937,109 million USD in 2021 (Statista, 2021). Further, some financial planners have begun to augment their advice process to include some aspects of robo-advice as a means of taking advantage of the cost efficiencies and accessibility it offers.

It has been considered that robo-advisors may be an option for those not presently seeking financial-planning services (Todd and Seay, 2020), however, some consumers have indicated that they would prefer to discuss options with a human advisor, utilize human expertise, or lack trust in an online platform (Northwestern Mutual, 2016).

Robo-advice faces similar threats to FinTech in terms of privacy and data breaches, and is more exposed to regulatory risk than FinTech, with regulators in some countries now heavily focusing their attention on robo-advice to ensure that consumers are not being manipulated into investing in products that are unsuitable for their individual circumstances and that robo-advisors are abiding by their licensing requirements. Research and policy issues are discussed later in the chapter.

While this section has introduced the growing role of FinTech and robo-advice, the next section provides a historical perspective of the development of FinTech and robo-advice. This is followed by a discussion of the various issues facing researchers and policymakers in the FinTech and robo-advice environment and then proceeds to describe how FinTech and robo-advice tools and techniques are being used by consumers for financial management and by financial advice practitioners in the provision of financial advice. Further, the chapter provides a commentary on future directions for FinTech and robo-advice and a discussion of implications for personal finance.

## Historical Perspective

The development of FinTech has been described by some as a sequence of "waves" (Goldman Sachs, 2020; Mirchandani et al., 2020; Myers, 2016) with Arner et al. (2015) describing the evolution of FinTech in versions, from FinTech 1.0 through to FinTech 3.5. These versions, along with a proposed additional version assist in understanding the historical perspective of FinTech and robo-advice and are discussed below.

Arner et al. (2015) argued that FinTech 1.0 (1866–1967: from analogue to digital) began in the late 19th century with the advent of technology, such as the telegraph, railroads, canals, and steamships that enabled the first financial interlinkages across borders. This same period saw the introduction of credit cards and the use of the telex machine with the financial calculator introduced in 1967. This links into the next phase, FinTech 2.0 (1967–2008), which initially included complex calculations in the back end of established financial institutions as defined by Bettinger (1972) as well as the use of automated telling machines (ATMs), the establishment of the National Association of Securities Dealers Automated Quotations (NASDAQ), and the use of the Internet for financial transactions.

FinTech 3.0 covers the period from 2008 to the time that the paper by Arner and colleagues (2015) was written and includes the use of technology for crowdfunding, venture capital, private equity, private placements, public offerings, listings, and the 1990s tech bubble through to some areas of robo-advice. The paper also discusses FinTech 3.5 as the emerging FinTech developments in markets in Asia and Africa.

With the technological advancements since 2015, a new version of FinTech has now evolved, and following the version examples introduced by Arner et al. (2015), this latest version may be referred to as FinTech 4.0 (or the fourth wave). FinTech 4.0 includes the use of artificial intelligence, machine learning, and sophisticated algorithms to assist both consumers and finance professionals with financial management and investment services. With this innovation in technology, robo-advice has also taken on a more sophisticated dimension and FinTech has become more embedded in mainstream finance (Mirchandani et al., 2020), extending its reach to a range of sectors, including retail banking, investment management, education, fundraising, and non-profit organizations, serving both business-to-business needs and consumer needs. The focus has increasingly shifted from back-end system technology to user-facing technology, aided by the personalized niche services, data-driven solutions, innovative culture, and nimble organization provided by FinTech startups (Lee and Shin, 2018).

The period from 2010 through the end of 2019 has also been referred to as the FinTech Revolution (Imerman and Fabozzi, 2020) and the Fourth Industrial Revolution (Schwab, 2017) with the Global Financial Crisis (GFC) seen as the catalyst for digital transformation to the financial services industry. This is also reflected in academic papers where the usage of the term FinTech has grown twenty-five fold since 2008 to more than 1,000,000 works per year in 2019 (Knewtson and Rosenbaum, 2020). The Covid-19 pandemic may also be viewed as a major catalyst for change in the sector, being cited as the determining factor for the success or failure of FinTech innovations (Imerman and Fabozzi, 2020).

Lee and Shin (2018) identified five main groups of participants in the FinTech ecosystem: (a) FinTech startups, (b) technology developers, (c) regulators, (d) financial customers, and (e) traditional financial institutions. Each of these participants has worked together as part of the continual development of FinTech through facilitating innovation, economic stimulus, collaboration, and competition in the financial industry.

While traditional financial institutions have financial resources and can take advantage of economies of scale, FinTech start-ups are more agile in that they are able to offer stand-alone, specialized products and services to match the needs of consumers and have completely changed how people save, borrow, invest, move, spend, and protect money (Lee and Shin, 2018). As a result, FinTech start-ups have been the main disruptors in the FinTech space with investment in FinTech growing each year as companies mature and new entrants enter the space. In 2013, FinTech companies were attracting as much as $12 billion USD in investments (Mention, 2019) and by 2019, FinTech investment was estimated to have reached a total of USD $150.4 billion (KPMG, 2020a) with a total of 144 FinTech unicorns worldwide (Fintech Live, 2021). The impact of FinTech has been so great that the total transaction value of digital payments alone was $5.2 trillion USD in 2020 (Andjelic, 2021). Large financial institutions have recognized the threat posed by FinTechs and have begun to collaborate with FinTech start-ups (Lee and Shin, 2018). This allows them to draw on the insights of start-ups and to keep up to date with the latest developments in technology (Yang, 2015).

Like other sectors of the financial services industry, insurance companies are also relying on technological innovation to provide key data that can assist in determining life insurance or car insurance premiums. InsurTech is expected to have the greatest impact of FinTech disruption due to the emergence of online insurance marketplaces and homogenization of risks (McWaters, 2015), which is demonstrated by global investment in the InsurTech sector reaching $7.1 billion USD in 2020 (Olano, 2021). Innovation in the insurance space has led to the collection and analysis of more granular data relating to health, lifestyle, and driving patterns for example, which enables insurers to predict risk more accurately. This results in more accurate underwriting and allows customized insurance premium calculations. The growing use of telemedicine and the associated payment integration and insurance claims systems have also contributed to the rise of InsurTech solutions (Imerman and Fabozzi, 2020). This has also provided an opportunity for InsurTech developments to partner with current financial institutions (Wilamowicz, 2019) and FinTechs.

While tech-savvy Millennials have mostly driven the growth of FinTech (Lee and Shin, 2018), older wealthier clients are contributing to the growth of the wealth management area of FinTech as they become more comfortable with the technology, aided by the reduction in face-to-face meetings with financial advisors due to the Covid-19 pandemic (Imerman and Fabozzi, 2020). While robo-advice began with a much slower growth rate, robo-investing is now the fastest growing area of wealth management, predicted to grow to more than 1.26 trillion USD by 2023 (Snell, 2019). In 2020, global assets under management by robo-advisors were almost $1.1 trillion USD (Statista, 2021).

The first forms of robo-advice utilized a series of client questions to recommend investment products, and the client was then required to implement the recommendations themselves (Deloitte, 2016b). Over the years, robo-advice has become much more sophisticated by collecting more information from a client and automating the advice process by using algorithms to formulate an investment strategy and manage the client's portfolio. Further, some offer additional related services, including taxation advice (Lightbourne, 2017). While machine learning has enabled robo-advisors to manage portfolios with no human oversight, the algorithms are limited by the questions asked and information provided by the client. As a result, some robo-advisors allow clients to engage with a human advisor such as by online chat, phone, or video call (BlackRock, 2016). A more hybrid approach to robo-advice is also being adopted where a professional advisor may manage long-term investment allocations and the human dimension of advice while an algorithm rebalances the portfolio based on certain parameters (Bhatnagar, 2016). Of course, the fees charged in each case are dependent on the complexity of the advice and the level of human involvement, with the fully automated systems making advice more accessible and affordable.

While some may consider robo-advice a threat to the work undertaken by "human" professional financial advisors, the use of robo-advisors can complement the work of professional advisors who adapt and embrace the technology as part of a hybrid offering. There is also work for professional advisors in assisting with testing and refining the algorithms used in robo-advice. Further, as robo-advice attracts clients who may otherwise not seek professional advice, it encourages them to engage with their finances, in some cases leading them to also seek out personal advice from a financial advisor. This increased demand is evidenced by the reported steady increase in assets under management, with a five-year compound annual growth rate of 7.4 percent from 2014 to 2018 (Charles Schwab, 2021).

Financial advisors who adapt and evolve to take advantage of FinTech are able to offer increased services to their clients and improve operational efficiencies. Similarly, the RegTech area of FinTech offers significant efficiencies to financial advisors by assisting them to better comply with regulations (Anagnostopoulos, 2018; Arner et al., 2015). Benefits of RegTech in financial advice include the speed of processing, timely reporting, and enhanced analytics, which is also less costly and enables data-driven compliance and pro-active risk management (Brummer, 2015; Deloitte, 2016a). While RegTech is able to help financial services organizations build a culture of compliance, and save time and money, it can also support regulators and contribute to positive consumer outcomes (Australian Securities and Investment Commission, 2021). This has resulted in financial and other support being provided by government to RegTech start-ups in Australia (Australian Securities and Investment Commission, 2021) and the United Kingdom (Financial Conduct Authority, 2020a). As the regulatory environment can directly affect the ability of organizations to grow and innovate, it is in the regulators' interests to move beyond compliance and encourage innovation in RegTech as a means of improving economic growth (World Government Summit, 2018). Sixty percent of the current RegTech market is occupied by three countries: the United States (29 percent), the United Kingdom (18 percent), and Australia (13 percent) (Wray et al., 2020).

## Research and Policy Issues

The evolution of FinTech and robo-advice has brought a range of benefits for businesses, consumers, financial advisors, and regulators, but it has also raised a number of research and policy issues. Some of these issues that will need to be addressed involve privacy issues, data security, and fraud prevention (Pettipas, 2017). While these issues are common concerns for all stakeholders, consumers are mainly concerned about the misuse of their personal information and financial data with regulation being the main concern among governments as FinTechs move quickly to disrupt the financial services sector.

Although governments have generally provided a favorable regulatory environment for FinTech since the 2008 financial crisis (Terry et al., 2015), different governments have different levels of regulation, with some relaxing regulations to stimulate FinTech innovation and contribute to economic growth. This is done in a number of ways such as granting financial service licenses, relaxing capital requirements, providing tax incentives, or providing innovation support hubs.

To facilitate FinTech innovation, some governments introduced regulatory sandboxes. These regulatory sandboxes provide licenses to FinTechs to enter the financial services market without undergoing the usual burdensome process or high regulatory entry costs. However, this has also brought with it some concern about the potential for regulatory arbitrage (Allen, 2020). Regulatory sandboxes have been used successfully in Australia under the Corporations (FinTech Sandbox Australian Financial Services Licence Exemption) Regulations 2020 and the National Consumer Credit Protection (FinTech Sandbox Australian Credit Licence Exemption) Regulations 2020 (Australian Securities Investment Commission, 2020) as well as Canada (Financial and Consumer Services Commission, 2017) and across six cohorts in the United Kingdom (Deloitte, 2018; Financial Conduct Authority, 2020b). While there was also a failed attempt to establish similar sandboxes in the United States at a federal level, some states such as Arizona, Florida, Utah, West Virginia, and Wyoming have now begun utilizing them (Native American Financial Services Association, 2020).

Sandboxes can assist regulators to monitor FinTechs and protect the public interest (Knewtson and Rosenbaum, 2020). The use of regulatory sandboxes also enables FinTech organizations to develop products, services, or business models that are regulatory compliant from the design phase, which can help to avoid potential legal risks later on from non-compliance (Lim and Low, 2019) by ensuring FinTech start-ups properly understand the regulations that may affect their service provisions. FinTech start-ups that have not understood their legal obligations have been found to produce undesirable results for both themselves and consumers. For example, LendUp, a payday loan FinTech company, violated consumer protection laws in the United States and was fined $3.63 million USD (Lee and Shin, 2018) while Zenefits, (which was valued at more than a billion U.S. dollars) allowed unlicensed brokers to sell its products and underwrite insurance policies, being penalized $7 million USD by California's Department of Insurance (Dickey, 2016). Meanwhile, in Australia, FinTech giant Tyro Payments sent 150,000 emails and SMS messages to consumers without including an unsubscribe function, putting them in breach of the Spam Act (Sadler, 2020).

As innovation in the FinTech industry is moving so fast and has become so diverse, it is difficult for regulatory authorities to keep up and to form an overarching comprehensive approach. In many cases, the adaptation and customization of existing regulations are required to help regulate the areas impacting on or from FinTech. Some of these areas that regulators need to consider, as identified by McWaters and Galaski (2017) in their report for the World Economic Forum, include:

- abuse of market power by distributors, especially in open platforms where distributors control the customer shopping experience
- sharing of data
- use of data
- consumer control, education and understanding of how their data is used and shared
- global convergence versus localized regulations.

Other regulatory and consumer protection issues relate to the potential of lower quality credit risk assessments and possible lowering of lending/credit benchmarks by FinTech lenders that utilize alternative sources of consumer data lending criteria to that of traditional markets (Anagnostopoulos, 2018).

In terms of robo-advice, there has been some debate concerning whether robo-advisors should be required to meet the same fiduciary standard as that required of registered financial advisors, and investment advisors, and who should bear the cost when a robo-advisor does not meet the standard. A legal fiduciary duty applies in varying degrees to financial advisors in Australia, Canada, the United Kingdom, and the United States (Skultety et al., 2020); however, regulation was initially designed with human advisors in mind. Advisors are required to provide advice that is in the best interests of their clients, disclose any conflicts of interest, and provide recommendations that are tailored to the client's specific needs. It has been suggested that investment strategies proposed through robo-advice are not personalized and consistently provided disclaimers that attempt to avoid fiduciary duties (Fein, 2015). However, Lightbourne (2017) challenged these assumptions stating that "properly designed robo-advisers are not inherently unable to meet the fiduciary duty any more than human advisers are" (p. 665), although Lightbourne acknowledged (Fein, 2015) that "robo-advisors do not provide the same level of personalized investment advice as an ideal human adviser" (p. 666). As a result, Lightbourne (2017) proposed that robo-advisors should therefore be expected to register/be licensed accordingly to ensure that liability can be properly attributed. However, the challenge of applying the same legal framework to both robo-advisors and human advisors still exists and will only become more difficult as machine algorithms grow in sophistication. Regulators in Europe have addressed this by designing a dedicated legal regime for autonomous machines (European Parliament, 2017), which could potentially include a compensation fund for any victims of robo-advice, funded by a levy on robo-advice practices/organizations.

Further regulatory issues revolve around societal norms, changing values, and structural changes that require orderly markets and public welfare (Anagnostopoulos, 2018). The impact of FinTech and associated business models have not yet been tested and further research into both the technology itself as well as the users and application of the technology is required before any conclusions can be made.

## Practitioner Tools and Techniques

While the rapid development of innovations in FinTech could be perceived by some as a threat to professional financial advice practitioners, it has also provided several tools and techniques that can improve efficiencies for financial advisors, reduce costs, and improve the services provided to clients. Some advancements in technology are able to directly support the advisor–client relationship while others are able to provide back-end support and compliance.

Clients expect their financial advisors to use some form of digital tools just as the same type of tools permeates all other aspects of their lives. The most common digital tools used by financial advisors relate to the following:
- customer relationship management (CRM) software
- simulation and visualization software
- social media marketing software (e.g., Hootsuite)
- data storage systems (e.g., Google Drive, Dropbox)
- time management software and appointment scheduling (e.g., Bookeo)
- website management
- online data collection/fact finders
- text-messaging
- video conferencing (e.g., Zoom, Teams, Skype)

These digital tools can assist in reducing overhead and improve efficiencies for advisors by automating processes. This in turn provides value for money for clients and offers clients greater convenience and flexibility as they are able to access and review their information and portfolios remotely at times that suit them. Such tools can also be used to communicate with clients whether this be via automated reminders, appointment scheduling, online meetings, investment updates, or newsletters. The ease in which digital tools allow advisors to have more frequent communication with their clients can also assist in building and maintaining trust as frequent communication has been found to be an important factor for trust and commitment in the advisor–client relationship (Christiansen and DeVaney, 1998). However, results from an experimental study found that outdated regulations that have not kept up with technological advances can influence communication technology adoption among financial advisors and may discourage the use of technological communications mediums that provide permanent records of communication with clients (Tharpe, 2020).

Automated "in-house" asset allocation and portfolio management tools, such as Monte Carlo simulations, have been utilized by advisors in the advice process for some time. More recent FinTech innovations, such as budgeting and cash-flow management tools and client portals, are now also used by financial advisors to improve the client experience and reduce costs while digital payment systems can streamline payment of fees by clients. In addition, financial advisors can utilize RegTech to close the gap between compliance and efficiency through technology and automation and reduce compliance costs for regulatory reporting, risk management, and screening for money laundering and fraud. RegTech can also provide digital Know Your Client checks, facilitate remote client onboarding, and expose cross-sell opportunities by highlighting where documentation has not been provided.

While there are a range of technologically advanced tools available to practitioners, ultimately, it is up to the individual advisor or practice to determine the technology to implement that is most suited to their client base. For example, younger clients may prefer that advisors incorporate technology into their practices, with 53 percent of Gen X/Y millionaires saying they would seek out a new advisor if their current advisor was not satisfactorily using technology, while only 29 percent of Baby Boomer millionaires reported the same expectation (Fidelity Investments, 2017). However, advisors need to be wary of using multiple technological platforms that do not integrate with one another as this could cause problems, inefficiencies, and frustration from both advisors and clients. The challenge for financial advisors is to balance client preferences with knowing which area of the business is best to apply technology. The main objective is to minimize repetitive processes, gain key data insights, and ensure that all systems can be integrated into one streamlined process. As described by Hendy (2020), "Ultimately, advisers are craving an integrated ecosystem where they can produce documentation, run a CRM and execute on their platform with as few keystrokes as possible, reducing inefficiencies and providing a richer experience and a transparent wealth picture to clients" ("A New Level of Service" section).

Some financial advisors have also taken advantage of the cost benefits provided by robo-advice by offering a hybrid version of financial advice that incorporates both robo-advice and personal "human" advice. For example, WealthO2 is a robo-advice platform designed to be used in consultation with human financial advisors. The founder, Shannon Bernasconi, stated that this allows for costs to be kept low for clients while also providing oversight for the irrational and emotional factors of investing through ongoing, comprehensive advice from a qualified human professional, which is better able to consider the client's best interests (Vickovich, 2020). This is supported by Polansky et al. (2018) who noted that many clients do not understand the basics of risk and reward, let alone more complicated concepts such as probability that is factored into most robo-advice models. As a result, clients may require the assistance of a human advisor to interpret and explain the information that robo-advisors provide. Further, the complexities of the decumulation phase of the lifecycle can be more difficult to cater for clients using strictly robo-only advice. Polansky and associates (2018) found that effective financial planning for retirement requires a far broader view of a client's circumstances, to include both quantitative information (e.g., assets, social security and pension eligibility, liabilities) and qualitative information (e.g., personal and family health history, how they will spend their time during retirement, possible cognitive decline), which requires interaction with a human advisor.

## Applications

FinTech offers a large variety of options that specifically target the financial behavior of consumers, with the capability to improve the personal finances of households (Li, 2009). It is common for this type of FinTech to be available through smartphone applications (apps). There are thousands of FinTech apps available for both Android and iOS platforms. Some of the more popular apps include (but are in no way limited to) Chime (mobile banking), Coinbase (cryptocurrency exchange/broker), Credit Karma (credit score monitoring), Mint (budgeting), Nubank (expense classification and payments), Planto (financial management), Prism (tracks bills and payments), Chime (mobile banking), and Robinhood (brokerage/trading). As with apps in other industries, such as health and fitness that involve self-tracking, these apps are able to help users reach their goals by tracking against a specific target and providing additional insights along the way (Rooksby et al., 2014).

Prior to the advent of FinTech, business owners and entrepreneurs/start-ups would have physically visited a bank to secure financing. For businesses to be able to accept payments via credit card or electronic funds transfer for that matter, they would need to pay for expensive infrastructure, high transaction fees, and seek approval from a bank. Mobile technology, specifically smartphones, has now allowed businesses to be more responsive to customers and provide a more seamless service experience. Further, consumers are now able to apply for credit without leaving their homes or obtaining physical documentation and some can obtain approval of credit within 24 hours. The application of FinTech to the everyday lives of consumers no longer limits financial activity to the opening hours of a bank with financial activity now able to take place 24 hours a day, seven days a week.

It has been established that FinTech applications are more likely to be adopted earlier by younger people. Similarly, robo-advice is more likely to be used by younger clients as well as clients with lower amounts to invest. Those on higher incomes are less likely to have used a robo-advisor (Todd and Seay, 2020) as those with higher incomes are more likely to be able to afford the services of a personal "human" financial advisor than those on lower incomes. Some robo-advisors can provide investment advice from beginning to end with no human interaction and are thus less costly than human advisory firms as they can save on fixed costs, such as the salaries of expensive financial advisors or the maintenance of a physical office (Abraham et al., 2019) and are thus suited to those on lower incomes who otherwise would not be able to afford advice. The application of robo-advice can be done remotely where clients are asked about their goals and time horizons, complemented by questions to assess the client's risk tolerance (Lam, 2016).

InsurTech can also provide greater convenience to clients by reducing the need for physical appointments or paperwork and increasingly relying on other forms of data to ascertain risk. This can assist in tailoring coverage for the client and simplifying claims processes (Organisation for Economic Co-operation and Development, 2017). It also assists insurance firms as they have access to a wider range of data to assist in determining risk and calculating the appropriate premiums that reflect this risk. However, the application of InsurTech also raises issues with regard to policyholder choices and rights in terms of data protection and the possibility that segments of the population may become uninsurable (Organisation for Economic Co-operation and Development,

2017). As with the application of all forms of FinTech, ensuring that consumers are fairly treated and appropriately protected when the implications of certain innovations and technologies are uncertain will be important going forward.

## Future Directions

Traditionally, financial services institutions were able to offer clients a "one-stop shop" in terms of providing a variety of services (e.g., borrowing, financial and investment advice, lending, trading, payments) in one location. FinTech has unbundled these services to provide a range of individual service offerings that enable efficiencies and cost savings. Further, many of these innovations are now offered via the convenience of a smartphone, with no need for fancy offices, glossy brochures, computers, or tedious paperwork.

The disruption that has taken place in financial services through FinTech and robo-advice has substantially transformed both the way that financial service institutions do business and also the way people now live their lives. However, while so much has changed, there is still much more change on the horizon.

The investment in FinTech alone has brought about change that has seen the success and failure of thousands of start-ups globally but, more recently, the traditional institutions have taken note and begun to claw back some of the market by investing heavily to become more like the nimble companies that seek to disrupt them while others have found new ways to collaborate with them. However, the future of FinTech is much deeper than increased investment in financial technology. It will involve new ways of thinking, new process improvements, changes to the way decisions are made and evaluated and new business structures that allow for design thinking and the agility that thriving businesses have learned to rely upon.

The future of FinTech will allow for more refined data matching to reduce fraud and to raise real-time alerts where breaches have occurred. There will be an increased use of chat bots, which will lower staffing costs as they service clients with their immediate needs and triage them accordingly. Machine learning and artificial intelligence will continue to become more sophisticated, allowing for predictive behavioral analytics where apps will engage users in gamification to learn the habits of users (often unknown or "hidden" to the users themselves) and use these to nudge consumers to make better spending and saving decisions. Further development of artificial intelligence technology will also have a role in supporting advisors, with the use of robo-advisors expected to grow at an annual rate of 25.6 percent (Statista, 2021). Advisors will continue to be forced to adapt to changes to the way that advice is delivered and will be forced to embrace technology as a partner in delivering value to their clients.

Further, as more customers elect to provide personal information through linking their smartphones and other technological devices, insurers are more able to be more proactive in their approach and manage future risks; this might be through scheduling health appointments for customers or providing warnings about driving conditions or weather patterns. This also provides further value of an insurance policy to the client (McWaters, 2015).

As FinTech in its various forms continues to grow in sophistication, the legal framework in which it operates will also need to become more sophisticated. In addition, this will require the design of new regulatory funding models and innovative ways to compensate those who might potentially fall victim to FinTech that is not in their best interests. It is worth remembering that disruption in financial services is not a one-off affair but rather "a continuous force to innovate that will influence customer behaviour, business models, as well as the long-term structure of the financial services" (McWaters, 2015, p. 13).

# Conclusion

Disruption to the financial services industry has been happening since as far back as 1866 with the advent of technology, such as the telegraph, railroads, canals, and steamships that enabled the first financial interlinkages across borders. Known as FinTech 1.0, this period saw the move from the analogue to the digital. Today, FinTech investment exceeds $150.4 billion USD globally (KPMG, 2020a), and the impact of FinTech has been so great that the total transaction value of digital payments in 2020 was approximately $5.2 trillion USD (Andjelic, 2021).

FinTech has included the development of digital banks, APITech, CreditTech, InsurTech, InvestTech, LendTech, RegTech, and robo-advice, which have radically disrupted financial advice, financial management, and financial services. The advent of the Internet and the use of smartphones has facilitated the growth of FinTech to date with machine learning and artificial intelligence leading the way of the future.

FinTech provides a range of benefits to both financial advisors and their clients. It enables advisors to manage more clients, improve the client experience, and keep costs down. At the same time, FinTech can make advice more affordable and accessible to clients, and it has been able to improve how clients engage with their finances. However, FinTech has also challenged the role of the human advisor and how financial advisors can best utilize technology as part of the advice process. Specifically, RegTech has assisted advisors with compliance matters, timely reporting, enhanced analytics, and proactive risk management (Brummer, 2015; Deloitte, 2016a).

Further, FinTech has presented a number of issues with regards to consumer protection, sharing and use of data, and cybercrime, with appropriate regulation at the center of these issues. Regulation has in many cases struggled to keep up with the rapid pace of FinTech development, with Australia, Canada, the United Kingdom, and some states in the United States introducing regulatory sandboxes to address these issues. Europe has gone a step further by designing a dedicated legal regime for autonomous machines (European Parliament, 2017).

As FinTech continues to evolve, and machine algorithms grow in sophistication, financial advisors will need to continue to adapt their services to meet the increasing needs of clients, although it is unlikely that FinTech will be able to ever completely replace the human advisor. Clients will always need someone to explain and interpret information for them and to consider qualitative information, such as their personal and family health history, their changing needs and circumstances during different phases in their lifecycle, pension eligibility, and possible cognitive decline. Issues will continue to revolve around societal norms, changing values, and structural changes (Anagnostopoulos, 2018), and regulation will need to be continually revised and updated to ensure the smooth functioning of markets and that the needs of broader society are met. Further research into the use, function, and application of various new financial technologies is required to test the impact on its users and inform the future use and regulation of FinTech as the personal finance field embarks on FinTech 5.0.

# References

Abraham, F., Schmukler, S. L., and Tessada, J. (2019). *Robo-advisors: Investing through machines.* World Bank Group. http://documents1.worldbank.org/curated/en/275041551196836758/pdf/ Robo-Advisors-Investing-through-Machines.pdf

Allen, H. J. (2020). Sandbox boundaries. *Vanderbilt Journal of Entertainment & Technology Law, 22* (2), 299–322. https://scholarship.law.vanderbilt.edu/cgi/viewcontent.cgi?article=1017&con text=jetlaw

Anagnostopoulos, I. (2018). FinTech and RegTech: Impact on regulators and banks. *Journal of Economics and Business, 100,* 7–25.

Andjelic, J. (2021, February 5). These FinTech statistics show an industry on the rise. *Fortunly.* https://fortunly.com/statistics/FinTech-statistics/#gref

Arner, D. W., Barberis, J. N., and Buckley, R. P. (2015). The evolution of FinTech: A new post-crisis paradigm? *Georgetown Journal of International Law, 47,* 1271–1316.

Australian Securities and Investment Commission. (2016). *Regulatory guide 255: Providing digital financial product advice to retail clients.* https://www.asic.gov.au/media/3994496/rg255-pub lished-30-august-2016.pdf

Australian Securities and Investment Commission. (2020). *Enhanced regulatory sandbox regulations.* https://asic.gov.au/for-business/innovation-hub/enhanced-regulatory-sandbox/ enhanced-regulatory-sandbox-regulations/

Australian Securities and Investment Commission. (2021). *ASIC and RegTech.* https://asic.gov.au/ for-business/innovation-hub/asic-and-regtech/

Bettinger, A. (1972). FinTech: A series of 40 time shared models used at manufacturers Hanover trust company. *Interfaces, 2*(4), 62–63. http://www.jstor.org/stable/25058931

Bhatnagar, A. (2016). How robo technology is changing wealth management. *Journal of Financial Planning, 29*(5), 22–25.

BlackRock. (2016). *Digital investment advice: Robo advisors come of age*. https://www.blackrock.com/corporate/literature/whitepaper/viewpoint-digital-investment-advice-september-2016.pdf

Brummer, C. (2015). Disruptive technology and securities regulation. *Fordham Law Review, 84*(3), 977–1,051.

Charles Schwab. (2021). *Focusing on fundamentals helps advisors succeed*. https://advisorservices.schwab.com/focusing-on-fundamentals

Christiansen, T., and DeVaney, S. (1998), Antecedents of trust and commitment in the financial planner–client relationship. *Journal of Financial Counselling and Planning, 9*(2), 1–10.

Deloitte. (2016a). *RegTech is the new FinTech: How agile regulatory technology is helping firms better understand and manage their risks*. https://www2.deloitte.com/content/dam/Deloitte/ie/Documents/FinancialServices/IE_2016_FS_RegTech_is_the_new_FinTech.pdf.

Deloitte. (2016b). *The expansion of robo-advisory in wealth management*. https://www2.deloitte.com/content/dam/Deloitte/de/Documents/financial-services/Deloitte-Robo-safe.pdf

Deloitte. (2018). *A journey through the FCA regulatory sandbox: The benefits, challenges, and next steps*. https://www2.deloitte.com/content/dam/Deloitte/uk/Documents/financial-services/deloitte-uk-fca-regulatory-sandbox-project-innovate-finance-journey.pdf

Deloitte. (2021). *RegTech universe 2021: Take a closer look at who is orbiting in the RegTech space*. https://www2.deloitte.com/lu/en/pages/technology/articles/regtech-companies-compliance.html

Dickey, M. (2016, November 29). Zenefits penalized $7 million in California for insurance licensing violations. *Tech Crunch*. https://techcrunch.com/2016/11/28/zenefits-penalized-7-million-in-california-for-insurance-licensing-violations/

European Parliament. (2017, February 16). *Civil law rules on robotics*. https://www.europarl.europa.eu/doceo/document/TA-8-2017-0051_EN.html

Fein, M. (2015). Robo-advisors: A closer look. https://papers.ssrn.com/abstract_id=2658701

Fidelity Investments. (2017). *The tipping point: Will the coming wave of wealth value advice?* [Video]. Brainshark. https://www.brainshark.com/1/player/fidelityiws?pi=zFrzFX650zIWXsz0&nodesktopflash=1&fb=0

FinancesOnline. (2021). *81 Key FinTech statistics 2021/2022: Market share & data analysis*. https://financesonline.com/FinTech-statistics/

Financial and Consumer Services Commission. (2017). *The Canadian securities administrators launches a regulatory sandbox initiative*. https://fcnb.ca/en/news-alerts/the-canadian-securities-administrators-launches-a-regulatory-sandbox-initiative

Financial Conduct Authority. (2020a). *Innovate and innovation hub*. https://www.fca.org.uk/firms/innovate-innovation-hub

Financial Conduct Authority. (2020b). *Regulatory sandbox – cohort 6*. https://www.fca.org.uk/firms/regulatory-sandbox/regulatory-sandbox-cohort–6

Fintech Live. (2021). *FinTech unicorns of the 21st century*. https://FinTechlabs.com/FinTech-unicorns-of-the-21st-century/

Goldman Sachs. (2020). *COVID-19's impact on the future of FinTech*. https://www.goldmansachs.com/insights/pages/from_briefings_03-june-2020.html

Hendy, N. (2020, November 10). Advice tech works, but only when it fits. *Professional Planner*. https://www.professionalplanner.com.au/2020/11/advice-tech-works-but-only-when-it-fits/

Imerman, M. B., and Fabozzi, F. J. (2020). Cashing in on innovation: a taxonomy of FinTech. *Journal of Asset Management, 21*, 167–177. https://doi.org/10.1057/s41260-020-00163-4

Jung, D., Dorner, V., Glaser, F., and Morana, S. (2018). Robo-advisory. *Business & Information Systems Engineering, 60*(1), 81–86.

Jung, D., Glaser, F., and Köpplin, W. (2019). Robo-advisory: Opportunities and risks for the future of financial advisory. In V. Nissen (ed.), *Advances in consulting research* (pp. 405–427). Springer.

Knewtson, H. S., and Rosenbaum, Z. A. (2020). Toward understanding FinTech and its industry. *Managerial Finance, 46*(8), 1043–1060. https://doi-org.ezproxy.uws.edu.au/10.1108/MF-01-2020-0024

KPMG. (2020a). *Pulse of Fintech H1 2020.* https://assets/kpmg/contect/dam/kpmg/xx/pdf/2020/09/pulse-of-FinTech-h1-2020.pdf

KPMG. (2020b). *The RegTech revolution is here.* https://home.kpmg/au/en/home/insights/2020/03/embracing-regtech-revolution.html

Lam, J. (2016). *Robo-Advisors: A portfolio management perspective* [Senior thesis]. Yale College. https://economics.yale.edu/sites/default/files/files/Undergraduate/Nominated%20Senior%20Essays/2015-16/Jonathan_Lam_Senior%20Essay%20Revised.pdf

Lee, I., and Shin, Y. J. (2018). FinTech: Ecosystem, business models, investment decisions, and challenges. *Business Horizons, 61*(1), 35–46.

Li, I. (2009, October 4–7). *Designing personal informatics applications and tools that facilitate monitoring of behaviors* [Conference session]. UIST 2009, Victoria, BC, Canada. https://uist.acm.org/archive/adjunct/2009/pdf/doctoral_symposium/paper154.pdf

Lightbourne, J. (2017). Algorithms & fiduciaries: Existing and proposed regulatory approaches to artificially intelligent financial planners. *Duke Law Journal, 67*, 651–679.

Lim, B., and Low, C. (2019). Regulatory sandboxes. In J. Madir (ed.), *FinTech: Law and regulation* (pp. 302–325). Edward Elgar Publishing.

McWaters, J. (2015). *The future of financial services: How disruptive innovations are reshaping the way financial services are structured, provisioned and consumed.* World Economic Forum. http://www3.weforum.org/docs/WEF_The_future__of_financial_services.pdf

McWaters, J., and Galaski, R. (2017). *Beyond FinTech: A pragmatic assessment of disruptive potential in financial services.* World Economic Forum. https://www2.deloitte.com/content/dam/Deloitte/pl/Documents/Reports/pl_beyond_FinTech_a_pragmatic_assessment_of_disruptive_potential_inf_inancial_services.pdf

Mention, A. L. (2019). The future of FinTech. *Research-Technology Management, 62*(4), 59–63.

Mirchandani, A., Gupta, N., and Ndiweni, E. (2020). Understanding the FinTech wave: A search for a theoretical explanation. *International Journal of Economics and Financial Issues, 10*(5), 331–343.

Myers, C. (2016, October 3). FinTech's "third wave" is coming, and it will change everything. *Forbes.* https://www.forbes.com/sites/chrismyers/2016/10/03/FinTechs-third-wave-is-coming-and-it-will-change-everything/?sh=7e386a766026

Native American Financial Services Association. (2020). *More states establishing regulatory sandboxes for FinTechs.* https://nativefinance.org/news/more-states-establishing-regulatory-sandboxes-for-FinTechs/

Northwestern Mutual. (2016). *2016 planning and progress study.* https://news.northwesternmutual.com/planningand-progress-study–2016

Olano, G. (2021, January 29). Record-high InsurTech funding tops AU$9 billion in 2020. *Insurance Business.* https://www.insurancebusinessmag.com/au/news/technology/recordhigh-insurtech-funding-tops-au9-billion-in-2020-244885.aspx

Organisation for Economic Co-operation and Development. (2017). *Technology and innovation in the insurance sector.* https://www.oecd.org/finance/Technology-and-innovation-in-the-insurance-sector.pdf

Pettipas, C. (2017). *The future of financial advising in a FinTech world* [Doctoral dissertation]. Swiss Management Center University.

Philippon, T. (2016). *The FinTech opportunity* (NBER Working Paper No. 22476). National Bureau of Economic Research. https://www.nber.org/papers/w22476

Polansky, S., Chandler, P., and Mottola, G. R. (2018). *The big spenddown: Digital investment advice and decumulation* (Working Paper No. WP2018-18). Wharton School and Pension Research Council. https://repository.upenn.edu/prc_papers/4.

Rooksby, J., Rost, M., Morrison, A., and Chalmers, M. (2014, April 26–May 1). *Personal tracking as lived informatics* [Conference session]. The ACM Conference on Human Factors in Computing System Conference. Toronto, ON, Canada. https://doi.org/10.1145/2556288.2557039

Sadler, D. (2020, December 21). FinTech giant breaches spam laws: Sent 150,000 messages without an unsubscribe option. *Information Age*. https://ia.acs.org.au/article/2020/FinTech-giant-breaches-spam-laws.html

Schwab, K. (2017). *The Fourth Industrial Revolution*. Penguin Random House.

Sironi, P. (2016). *FinTech innovation: From robo-advisors to goal based investing and gamification.* Wiley.

Skultety, C., Kavalamthara, P. J., and Cull, M. (2020). *Financial planning education and regulatory requirements: A cross country comparison between Australia, Canada, United Kingdom and United States of America*. Western Sydney University. https://doi.org/10.26183/5e9e7d3663232

Snell, R. (2019, May 22). In 2023, robots will invest $1.26 trillion of our money. *Barron's*. https://www.barrons.com/articles/alphabet-and-uber-are-top-net-reopening-plays-for-morgan-stanley-51616691056

Statista. (2021). *Robo-advisors*. https://www.statista.com/outlook/dmo/FinTech/personal-finance/robo-advisors/united-states

Terry, H. P., Schwartz, D., and Sun, T. (2015). *The future of finance: The socialization of finance*. Goldman Sachs. https://www.planet-FinTech.com/downloads/The-future-of-Finance-the-Socialization-of-Finance-Golman-Sachs-march-2015_t18796.html

Tharpe, D. (2020). Potential consumer harm due to regulation on financial advisory communication in the FinTech age. *Journal of Financial Counseling and Planning*, *31*(1), 146–161.

Todd T. M., and Seay, M. C. (2020). Financial attributes, financial behaviors, financial advisor-use beliefs, and investing characteristics associated with having used a robo-advisor. *Financial Planning Review*, 3, e1104. https://doi.org/10.1002/cfp2.1104

Vickovich, A. (2020, April 30). Amid the virus, have robo-advisers found their moment? *The Australian Financial Review*. https://www.afr.com/wealth/investing/amid-the-virus-have-robo-advisers-found-their-moment-20200420-p54lh6)

Wilamowicz, A. (2019). The great FinTech disruption: InsurTech. *Banking & Finance Law Review*, *34*(2), 215–238.

Woodyard, A., and Grable, J. (2018). Insights into the users of robo-advisory firms. *Journal of Financial Service Professionals*, *72*(5), 56–66.

World Government Summit. (2018). *RegTech for regulators: Re-architect the system for better regulation*. https://www.worldgovernmentsummit.org/api/publications/document?id=5ccf8ac4-e97c-6578-b2f8-ff0000a7ddb6

Wray, P., Mackay, W., Loh, I., Young, D., and Ang, Y. (2020, October 27). Australia's global RegTech hub poised for growth. *Boston Consulting Group*. https://www.bcg.com/en-au/publications/2020/australia-global-regtech-hub-poised-for-growth

Yang, S. (2015, March 21). Why Wall Street is pouring money into companies that want to eat its lunch. *Business Insider Australia*. https://www.businessinsider.com.au/wall-street-invests-in-FinTech-startups-2015-3

Zavolokina, L., Dolata, M., and Schwabe, G. (2016). The FinTech phenomenon: Antecedents of financial innovation perceived by the popular press. *Financial Innovation*, *2*(1), 1–16.

Lu Fan

# 31 The Use of Financial Advice: Consumers' Financial Advice-Seeking

**Abstract:** This chapter provides an overview of the research on consumers' financial advice-seeking decisions and behavior. The overview includes a comprehensive review of studies from a historic perspective, theoretical foundations, research and policy issues, and practitioner tools and techniques. This chapter also discusses potential limitations in the literature and understanding of consumers' financial advice-seeking behavior. The chapter concludes with future directions for research on the consumers' demand and usage of financial advice.

**Keywords:** advice-seeking, help-seeking, financial stress, financial advice

## Introduction

Understanding individuals' and households' demand for financial advice is of importance to researchers, financial practitioners, and policymakers. The past decades have seen an increased awareness among consumers regarding personal financial management issues, including wealth, debt, tax, insurance, investments, and estate planning. However, the complexity of financial markets and products have made financial decision making burdensome for unsophisticated individual investors. It is a growing concern that the nationwide (as well as worldwide) lack of financial literacy could induce financial vulnerability for the overall population. Meanwhile, the coronavirus pandemic that began in 2019–2020, and the resulting economic recession, have created opportunities for online and mobile financial service delivery. FinTech has emerged rapidly as a powerful set of tools and platforms for providing financial services, products, and advice to consumers. Notably, other than professional financial advice and service providers, consumers may also rely on personal social networks to seek financial advice. These sources are not mutually exclusive, meaning multiple advice sources can be used simultaneously or in various combinations. There could also exist interconnections among the financial advice source alternatives.

Questions about consumer financial advice-seeking include but are not limited to (a) *Do people need financial advice?* (b) *Why seek financial advice and help?* (c) *What advice sources are available?* (d) *What affects people's choices among financial advice source alternatives?* and (d) *What can financial advice provide?* This chapter provides a holistic overview from a historical perspective of the financial advice-

**Lu Fan,** University of Georgia

https://doi.org/10.1515/9783110727692-031

seeking literature, theoretical foundations and frameworks, and research and policy issues as well as practical tools and technology applications. The chapter concludes with a discussion of future directions of consumer financial advice-seeking research.

# Historical Perspective

The following discussion provides a systematic overview of financial advice-seeking behavior, including a review of past literature. The topics covered include the development of a definition of financial advice-seeking and its relationship to general help-seeking behavior. This chapter also discusses the theoretical foundations for financial advice-seeking and introduces readers to the seminal theoretical and conceptual frameworks that can be used for studying financial advice-seeking behavior. Furthermore, this chapter discusses financial-advice-related sources and the value that financial advice provides for consumers.

## Development of the Concept

The development of financial advice- and help-seeking research helps in building a historical understanding of how the concept has been established and defined. A five-stage decision-making process framework of financial help-seeking is reviewed and evaluated. The key financial advice sources and their value are also summarized and compared.

Financial advice-seeking can be defined as problem-solving behaviors with the purpose to resolve individual and family financial concerns (Grable and Joo, 2003). This definition stems from the understanding of general advice-seeking behavior, which has been documented in many other disciplines such as health and psychology studies. In general, help-seeking behavior refers to the "communication about a problem or troublesome event, which is directed toward obtaining support or assistance in times of distress" (Gourash, 1978, p. 414). It may consist of a complex set of decision-making activities, including understanding the problem and seeking advice, information, or treatments that may involve challenges to individuals' abilities (Cornally and McCarthy, 2011; Rickwood et al., 2005). Advice- and help-seeking behavior often starts with a realized concern in life that is difficult to resolve using available resources (Burks, 2001; Cornally and McCarthy; 2011; Hinson and Swanson, 1993). Such behavior is usually problem-focused, with intentional and active actions, and involves interpersonal interactions (i.e., between the help-seeker and the helper).

A widely used financial help-seeking framework (FHSF), proposed by Grable and Joo (1999, 2001, see Figure 31.1) and inspired by health psychological research, conceptualizes a five-stage decision-making process for individuals' and households' financial advice-seeking. According to FHSF, a person typically starts the financial advice-seeking decision process by (a) realizing a financial concern or exhibiting a certain financial behavior, followed by (b) evaluating the concern or behavior, (c) identifying the causes, then (d) making the decision to seek advice or not. If the decision is to seek advice, the next decision-making step is to (e) choose among financial advice providers or alternatives. The decision to seek financial advice or not can bring feedback or consequences to the initial financial concern or behavior. The FHSF proposes that financial stressors, knowledge, and attitudes, along with psychographic, socioeconomic, and demographic characteristics, can play a role in this decision-making process.

Under the guidance of the FHSF, a large number of existing studies have explored the fourth and fifth stages of the FHSF, which are related to two questions: (1) whether to seek financial advice and (2) among advice seekers, which financial advice providers and alternatives have been used? For instance, it has been suggested that young, non-homeowners, and those who have engaged in riskier financial behaviors and had more financial stressor experiences, are more likely to see financial help and advice (Grable and Joo, 1999). Furthermore, when financial advice alternatives are separated as professional and nonprofessional, being a homeowner and having higher levels of financial satisfaction are indicative of being more likely to seek financial retirement advice from professionals (Grable and Joo, 2001). The following sections will review more details about financial advice sources and individuals' and households' characteristics as they relate to financial advice-seeking decisions and behavior.

## Financial Advice Source Alternatives

The types of personal financial matters for which individuals and households seek advice can include, but are not limited to, financial goal assessment, emergency fund preparation, retirement planning, education saving, investment, taxes, estate, mortgages, insurance, debt and credit management, and bankruptcy (Sherraden, 2013; Warschauer and Sciglimpaglia, 2012).When consumers seek financial advice, they will find various "information intermediaries" or choice alternatives such as financial advisors, insurance agents, media, and the Internet (Lee and Cho, 2005). There are also various ways to inspect financial advice source alternatives, for example, professional versus nonprofessional or personal versus nonpersonal.

Grable and Joo (2001) categorized personal financial advice sources into professional and nonprofessionalalternatives. Professional alternatives include, for example, financial planners and financial counselors, insurance agents, financial therapists, and stockbrokers, whereas nonprofessional alternatives include family, friends, and colleagues. Kwon (2004) grouped the financial advice sources into personal (i.e., financial professionals, friends, and family members) and nonpersonal (i.e., news and advertising), where friends and families were found to be the most significant advice sources for savings and investment-related help and

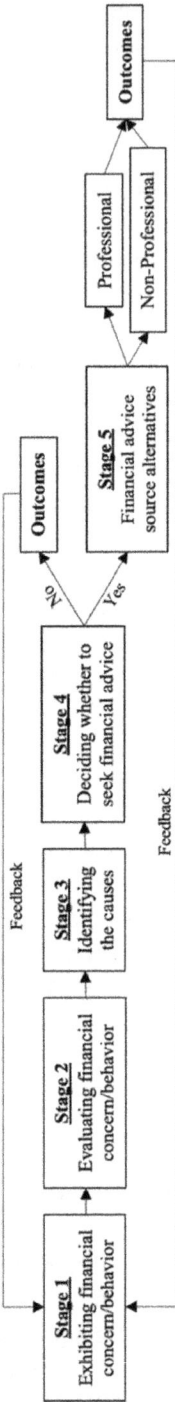

**Figure 31.1:** Adapted Illustration of the Financial Help-Seeking Framework.

advice. These personal financial advice sources were preferred by lower-net-worth households, whereas professional sources were more likely to be selected by higher net-worth households (Chang, 2005). Among these advice sources, financial professionals, families, and friends are mainly studied in the literature.

Two models of personal financial planning service delivery exist: (a) a specialist model, where a client may work individually with multiple financial professionals; and (b) a planner model, where a client often works with a financial planner who serves as an intermediary between the client and other financial professionals (Black et al., 2002; Elmerick et al., 2002). Consumers' choices between these two models vary based on the amount and types of advice needed as well as consumer characteristics (Elmerick et al., 2002). Consumers value personal financial services differently, depending on specific financial needs and concerns, their individual characteristics, and available service types.

## Value of Financial Advice

The benefits of seeking professional financial advice and help can be seen primarily in three areas: increasing wealth, preventing losses, and smoothing consumption (Hanna and Lindamood, 2010). Warschauer and Sciglimpaglia (2012) suggested that the value of comprehensive financial advice can be seen in overall net worth accumulation by providing more effortful planning; further, the demand for such comprehensive advice depends on individual and household characteristics. For example, household income, net worth, education levels, holding positive debts, and being Black, young, an unmarried female, and employed make one more likely to seek comprehensive financial advice, which could, in turn, help households to accumulate net worth. Using quantifiable measures (e.g., gamma and zeta), researchers found that the value of financial advisors and financial planners also includes increased portfolio efficiency and reduced wealth volatility (Blanchett and Kaplan, 2013; Grable and Chatterjee, 2014).

On the other hand, friends, families, and relatives, categorized as nonprofessional financial advice sources in the FHSF, are of equal importance. Research shows that friends and families are the most commonly used information sources when individuals are in need of saving and investment advice (Kwon, 2004). Women (Loibl and Hira, 2007) and households with a lower net worth (Chang, 2005) are known to be more likely to seek financial advice from friends and families. The high preference toward families and friends as financial advice sources may be because close personal relationships are more cost-efficient and trustworthy sources for seeking financial advice (Lachance and Tang, 2012); however, advice-seeking and information-searching behaviors may stop when individuals find a reliable advice source (Lee and Hogarth, 2000). In fact, close personal networks are popular advice-providing sources in general, and advice- and help-seeking from these sources are considered informal (Rickwood et al., 2005).

From a social capital perspective, personal social networks, including families, relatives, and friends, are considered important sources of social capital that provide emotional support; these networks are also especially important for older populations and their overall life satisfaction. Social networks, including friends, coworkers, and community-based organizations (Yeo and Lee, 2019), are considered significant sources of social capital in life and can also be utilized as an alternative to financial advice sources. Other studies have also confirmed the significant roles of close personal networks, including friends and family members, when seeking investment advice (Abreu and Mendes, 2012; Shin et al., 2020).

Developments in the FinTech industry have necessitated a new area of research that focuses on consumers' utilization of financial technologies when seeking financial advice. As FinTech has pervasively permeated the daily lives of individuals, families, and households, recent findings have revealed a negative relationship between the adoption of robo-advisors and the need for human advisors (Brenner and Meyll, 2020). The literature shows that investors with higher risk tolerance and subjective financial knowledge (Fan and Chatterjee, 2020b), those who are independent financial decision makers (Kim et al., 2019a, 2019b), and investors who are wealthier (Fulk et al., 2018) and have higher investment confidence (Phoon and Koh, 2017) are more likely to use robo-advisors. Robo-advisors are preferred financial service providers by those who are younger, with more investable assets, and individuals looking for time-efficient (Fan and Chatterjee, 2020b) and cost-efficient (Phoon and Koh, 2017) wealth management services. Moreover, the use of a robo-advisor is largely determined by trust in robo-advisory services, which can be included in trust in vendors and trust in technologies in general (Cheng et al., 2019).

# Theoretical Foundations for Financial Advice-Seeking Research

Two main streams of theoretical models guide the research on financial advice-seeking behavior. One stream stems from a traditional economic perspective, which examines the costs and benefits of information search behavior (Stigler, 1961). This approach explains the demand for financial advice as a rational choice. The consumer information search framework (Beales et al., 1981) follows this modality by presenting a categorization method of information and advice-seeking sources that can be internal and external. The other theoretical perspective (i.e., stress-coping theories) provides a new lens to view advice- and help-seeking as a coping mechanism triggered by stressor events (Lazarus and Folkman, 1984). Both streams provide the rationale to understand the motivations of individuals' and households' financial advice- and help-seeking behavior.

## Information Search Theories

Consumer information search sources can be internal and external. Internally, individuals can use their own knowledge, memories, and skills to assist in decision making. Externally, they can actively seek advice from professionals or use media to acquire new knowledge (Beales et al., 1981). Stigler (1961) provided an information search theory that considers information search activities using a cost–benefit analysis approach. According to the information search theory, the search activities continue until the marginal cost of the search is equal to or higher than the marginal benefit. The motivations of individuals or households to seek financial advice include reduced extensive search costs and increased benefits from the collected information.

This theoretical framework provides solid support for research on financial advice- and help-seeking behavior, which can be a form of information-search behavior. Indeed, the economic approach is recognized as one of the three important theoretical paradigms for consumer external information search, along with psychological motivation and consumer information processing (memory) approaches (Srinivasan, 1990). Black et al. (2002) suggested that seeking professional financial advice can potentially reduce costs for consumers to search and seek information, make transactions, and monitor financial status. Those who provide personal finance advice can provide customized counsel that can potentially reduce the marginal cost of information search for consumers (Collins, 2012). Notably, the financial delegation literature closely aligns with stages four and five in the FHSF.

Information search theories have provided theoretical insights for research on financial delegation that captures the consumer–financial professional engagement when making financial decisions. In the financial decision delegation literature, there has been debate regarding the substitution or complementarity relationship between consumers' own financial literacy and seeking externally for professional financial advice (e.g., Calcagno and Monticone, 2015; Collins, 2012; Robb et al., 2012). Kim et al. (2016) argued that the decision to engage in financial delegation is motivated by considerations of time costs, efficiency gains, and beliefs over professional expertise. Tang and Hu (2019) separately examined three investment decision-making approaches: (a) self-investment without any advice; (b) consulting advisors to assist decision making; and (c) delegation fully to financial advisors. Kim et al. found that individuals' financial literacy plays an important role in this decision-making process. Thus, the demand for professional financial advice appears to be related to a consumer's personal financial literacy. Contrarily, Kramer (2016) posited that it is financial confidence, rather than financial literacy, that drives people to seek financial advice; Fan (2017) also found a negative relationship between perceived financial ability (or financial confidence) and the likelihood of seeking professional advice.

## Stress-Coping Theories

According to the commonly used financial advice- and help-seeking definition and the FHSF, the decision to seek financial advice often happens as a consequence of realizing a financial concern, which could potentially be triggered by certain stressor events. Stress-coping theories study individuals' coping strategies and behavior from a stressor–stress–cope angle. This stream of theories provides a theoretical background in which to examine financial advice- and help-seeking behavior under specific circumstances (i.e., the occurrence of stressor events). Coping is defined as "constantly changing cognitive and behavioral efforts to manage specific external and/or internal demands that are appraised as taxing or exceeding the resources of the person" (Lazarus and Folkman, 1984, p. 141). The main purpose of advice- and help-seeking, in general, is to cope with negative life events and stress induced by stressful events (Wills, 1987). Coping strategies can be problem- or emotion-focused (Lazarus and Folkman, 1984).

While financial professionals are believed to provide problem-solving solutions, seeking financial advice from close personal networks (i.e., spouse, parents, children, friends, etc.) could possibly provide emotional support. Under the stress-coping theoretical perspective, Lakey and Cohen (2000) suggested that financial professionals are capable of providing expertise and advice for personal financial management and social support, which can help maintain health and well-being. Given different types of stressors, consumers may choose various coping strategies. For example, financial strains are economic stressors that can be negatively associated with mental health (Asebedo and Wilmarth, 2017). Over-indebtedness, bankruptcy, income shocks, and unpaid medical bills are also examples of financial stressor events that are significantly associated with seeking professional financial advice (Fan, 2021).

# Factors Associated with Financial Advice-Seeking

The literature has provided rich evidence on the factors associated with financial advice-seeking behavior. Empirical research using national and international data sets has analyzed individuals' and households' characteristics, including financial literacy, capability, and psychological factors as well as socioeconomic and demographic characteristics.

## Financial Advice- and Help-Seeking

Financial advice-seeking behavior has been analyzed primarily using national secondary data sets, including the National Financial Capability Study (NFCS) and the Survey of Consumer Finances (SCF), which provides an array of measures for financial advice sources in their cross-sectional questionnaire waves. For example, in the 2009 and 2012 waves of the NFCS, consumers' preferences and choices on professional financial services were included. Empirical analyses showed that trust in human advisors (Lachance and Tang, 2012), financial satisfaction, financial confidence, risk tolerance (Robb et al., 2012), financial capability, financial stressors, and perceived debt (Fan, 2021) are significant indicators of the propensity to seek professional advice that may be provided for saving/investment, insurance, tax, debt, and loan management. Other studies on financial advice-seeking have also used two waves of the NFSC (e.g., Collins, 2012; Kramer, 2016; Xiao and Porto, 2016). However, the set of financial advice questions in the NFCS was dropped starting from the 2015 wave. In fact, the Investor Survey supplemental survey of the NFCS, starting from 2015 started to incorporate survey questions relating to investors' preferences over investment information sources.

Another large-scale national data set that contains survey questions on financial advice sources is the SCF. Although the advice source options included in the SCF feature a wide range, including, for example, newspapers, mailed materials, media and online, friends, relatives, bankers, brokers, or financial planner, most studies using this data set have been more interested in consumers' propensity to hire financial planners. For instance, consumption of financial services (Elmerick et al., 2002), risk tolerance (Hanna, 2011), portfolio performance (Lei and Yao, 2016), and portfolio diversification (Shin et al., 2020) have been linked to seeking investment advice from financial planners across different waves of the SCF. As already noted, most previous studies have tended to focus on the use of financial planners and have not fully reflected the advice-seeking behavior associated with other financial professionals (e.g., financial advisors and counselors) or nonprofessional advice sources.

National data sets are also available internationally to study household finance and advice-seeking behavior. For example, the Panel on Household Finances (PHF) dataset, administered by the Deutsche Bundesbank starting in 2010–2011, has been used to examine the relationships among consumers' financial literacy, financial behavior, and the use of financial professionals' advice among German households (see Stolper and Walter, 2017). Chinese households' stock market participation and its relationship with seeking financial advice have been analyzed using the Consumer Finance Survey for Urban China Households (CFS) (see Pan et al., 2020). Additionally, CentERpanel and the DHB Household Survey have been utilized to study psychological and economic aspects of Dutch households, including the use of financial advice (see Von Gaudecker, 2015).

## Personal Characteristics

To date, various studies have assessed indicators of financial advice- and help-seeking behavior. The literature has indicated that consumers' personal characteristics, such as financial literacy and capability factors, psychological and attitudinal traits, and cognitive abilities, are significantly related to the individuals' and households' propensity to seek financial advice. For example, studies show that financial knowledge (in some studies interchangeably used with financial literacy) is a strong predictor of seeking professional financial advice (Calcagno and Monticone, 2015; Collins, 2012; Fan, 2017, 2021; Finke et al., 2011; Gerrans and Hershey, 2017; Perry and Morris, 2005; Robb et al., 2012). In addition, financial stress and hardship variables, including debt stress of college students (Lim et al., 2014), perceived over-indebtedness and financial stressors (Fan, 2021), financial anxiety (Gerrans and Hershey, 2017; Westermann et al., 2020), and so forth, have also been found to be significantly associated with the likelihood of seeking professional financial advice and help. These individuals are more likely to seek professional financial advice due to mental stress related to personal finance issues, which creates a negative self-evaluation of their money management capability and reduced financial well-being (Archuleta et al., 2013; Grable et al., 2015).

Furthermore, risk tolerance, perceived financial knowledge, financial confidence (Kramer, 2016), financial overconfidence (Porto and Xiao, 2016), risk tolerance (Hanna and Lindamood, 2010), personality (Fan and Chatterjee, 2020a), self-efficacy (Lim et al., 2014), advisor trust (Lachance and Tang, 2012; Westermann et al., 2020), and advisor anxiety (Van Dalen et al., 2017) are also influential factors describing whether to seek financial advice. Lastly, given the aging worldwide population, older individuals' financial advice-seeking and well-being are of interest because cognitive decline is a common barrier against making sound financial decisions. Recent studies show that cognitive abilities are significantly associated not only with whether to seek financial advice (Fan and Chatterjee, 2020a; Fan and Lim, 2019; Gamble et al., 2015; Kim et al., 2019a, 2019b) but also with the preference of advice sources (Fan and Lim, 2019).

## Research and Policy Issues

Research findings on financial advice- and help-seeking have emphasized the significant role of financial knowledge, literacy, and capability. In particular, the positive influences of financial literacy on positive financial management practices (e.g., Hilgert et al., 2003; Perry and Morris, 2005) and seeking professional financial advice (e.g., Robb et al., 2012) have called for public policy development, implementation, and reinforcement of national strategies to promote financial literacy. The benefits and value of financial advice and service providers that can help consumers cope with adverse financial stressors include gaining self-confidence in financial management, being more financially responsible, and improving financial well-being. However, research shows that wealthier individuals and families with higher income are more likely to seek professional financial advice (e.g., Collins, 2012). Therefore, more reachable, affordable, and accessible financial advice and services should be provided to lower-income and rural communities and households as well as to minority groups and those facing large income shocks and unemployment.

Another line of research on the accountability, misconduct, trust, and fiduciary issues of professional financial advice providers (Redhead, 2011; Tharp et al., 2020) has also raised policy concerns. Integrated and compressive regulations and ethical standards are needed at federal and state levels for all financial advice source alternatives (financial advisors, financial planners, financial counselors, robo-advisory, etc.). Regulations on the financial advice market are of interest for policymakers worldwide, because "rather than helping consumers by bridging gaps in knowledge and facilitating transactions, professional financial advice stands accused of helping to exploit consumers' lack of financial literacy and inexperience" (Hackethal and Inderst, 2013, p. 213). A lack of ability to de-bias retail investors' portfolios was also observed among financial advisers in an audit study (Mullainathan et al., 2012). Moreover, consumers with low financial literacy may find it difficult to understand or adhere to financial advice and the underlying conflict of interest in the financial advice received from professionals. Consumer-focused policy is particularly in high demand given the rapid development of FinTech, where system and cost transparency, fiduciary versus suitability standards, and information reliability (Fein, 2015; Rühr, 2020) could potentially put consumers at financial risk.

# Practitioner Tools, Techniques, and Applications

Besides research findings from the consumers' perspective, from the practitioners' standpoint, financial advice- and help-seeking studies can provide insights into the appropriate applications of tools and techniques that can be used to assist in evaluating consumers' attitudes and intentions to seek advice. The application of financial planning tools and technologies can also help attract potential clients and understand current clients' satisfaction toward advice and services provided. Grable et al. (2011) summarized survey instruments developed to measure consumers' commitment, trust, preference, willingness, and satisfaction of advice sought from financial professionals. Some relevant survey scales include the preference for financial planner index (i.e., financial planners' traits, skills, and abilities) (Bae and Sandager, 1997), the attitudes toward financial planning scale (i.e., the need and value of financial planning) (Godwin and Koonce, 1992), the willingness to seek financial counseling scale (Lown and Cook, 1990), the commitment to and trust in financial planner scale (Sharpe et al., 2007), the investment advice use scale (Li et al., 2002), and so forth. Practitioners are encouraged to adopt these useful research-based tools.

Financial planning software is an efficient way to establish client and practitioner relationships and is often used to present and showcase financial advice, project future wealth growth, and monitor clients' financial status. In addition, practitioners often use financial planning software, other than traditional survey questionnaires, to collect and assess a client's risk and psychological profile in order to better provide customized financial advice and services based on clients' psychological traits and financial needs.

## Future Directions

A greater focus on constructing overarching theoretical frameworks is needed to provide a solid and comprehensive level of support guiding research in this domain of personal finance. The FHSF illustrates the stages that a typical consumer would follow when there is a financial concern. Each stage within the FHSF can be expanded and deepened to further study the nuances of the decision-making process, with the incorporation of enriched rational and irrational decision-making mechanisms. Because most of the current research is centered on studying stages four and five of the FHSF, considerably more work will, therefore, be needed to examine the other stages of FHSF. In addition, the theoretical approaches such as consumer memory, information-seeking, motivational and psychological approaches, other than the traditional economic approach, can provide foundations for financial advice-seeking research.

That said, more national and publicly accessible data sets (cross-sectional or panel) are needed that include individual- and household-level information regarding financial advice-seeking attitudes, intentions, source-selection criteria, behavior, and satisfaction. Researchers can also explore survey instruments and experimental designs to provide more insights into this field of study. Lastly, given the trend of FinTech, it is also suggested that more research be carried out on the usage of robo-advisory and other FinTech tools as financial advice-seeking sources.

More cross-national comparisons can also be conducted to expand the research on financial advice-seeking topics to a broader context. As suggested by Badarinza et al. (2016) and Badarinza et al. (2019), cross-country analyses of household finance can provide a deeper insight into the impacts of differences in culture, economy, and institutional arrangements on individuals' and households' financial outcomes, especially for the emerging countries with rapidly growing economies and the increasing demand for financial advice.

## Conclusion

Research on consumers' financial advice-seeking decisions and behaviors is a continuing topic within the personal finance discipline, as there has been a rapid increase in the demand for professional financial services and advice. Furthermore, making financial advice easily accessible, along with designing policies and programs aimed at reducing the barriers against consumers' accessing professional financial advice, can play an important role in building a more financially resilient society in the future. It is crucial for researchers, financial practitioners, and public policymakers to further investigate this subject to promote consumers' financial security and well-being.

# References

Abreu, M., and Mendes, V. (2012). Information, overconfidence and trading: Do the sources of information matter? *Journal of Economic Psychology*, *33*(4), 868–881.

Archuleta, K. L., Dale, A., and Spann, S. M. (2013). College students and financial distress: Exploring debt, financial satisfaction, and financial anxiety. *Journal of Financial Counseling and Planning*, *24*(2), 50–62.

Asebedo, S. D., and Wilmarth, M. J. (2017). Does how we feel about financial strain matter for mental health? *Journal of Financial Therapy*, *8*(1), 62–80.

Badarinza, C., Balasubramaniam, V., and Ramadorai, T. (2019). The household finance landscape in emerging economies. *Annual Review of Financial Economics*, *11*, 109–129. https://doi.org/10.1146/annurev-financial-110118-123106

Badarinza, C., Campbell, J. Y., and Ramadorai, T. (2016). International comparative household finance. *Annual Review of Economics*, *8*, 111–144.

Bae, S. C., and Sandager, J. P. (1997). What consumers look for in financial planners. *Journal of Financial Counseling and Planning*, *8*(2), 9–16.

Beales, H., Mazis, M. B., Salop, S. C., and Staelin, R. (1981). Consumer search and public policy. *Journal of Consumer Research*, *8*(1), 11–22. https://doi.org/10.1086/208836

Black Jr, K., Ciccotello, C. S., and Skipper Jr, H. D. (2002). Issues in comprehensive personal financial planning. *Financial Services Review*, *11*(1), 1–9.

Blanchett, D., and Kaplan, P. (2013). Alpha, beta, and now . . . gamma. *The Journal of Retirement*, *1*(2), 29–45.

Brenner, L., and Meyll, T. (2020). Robo-advisors: A substitute for human financial advice? *Journal of Behavioral and Experimental Finance*, *25*, 100,275. https://doi.org/10.1016/j.jbef.2020.100275

Burks, K. J. (2001). Intentional action. *Journal of Advanced Nursing*, *34*(5), 668–675.

Calcagno, R., and Monticone, C. (2015). Financial literacy and the demand for financial advice. *Journal of Banking & Finance*, *50*, 363–380.

Chang, M. L. (2005). With a little help from my friends (and my financial planner). *Social Forces*, *83*(4), 1,469–1,498.

Cheng, X., Guo, F., Chen, J., Li, K., Zhang, Y., and Gao, P. (2019). Exploring the trust influencing mechanism of robo-advisor service: A mixed method approach. *Sustainability*, *11*(18), 4,917.

Collins, J. M. (2012). Financial advice: A substitute for financial literacy? *Financial Service Review*, *21*(4), 307–322.

Cornally, N., and McCarthy, G. (2011). Help-seeking behavior: A concept analysis. *International Journal of Nursing Practice*, *17*(3), 280–288. https://doi.org/10.1111/j.1440-172X.2011.01936.x

Elmerick, S. A., Montalto, C. P., and Fox, J. J. (2002). Use of financial planners by US households. *Financial Services Review*, *11*(3), 217–231.

Fan, L. (2017). *The influences of financial help-seeking and other information sources on consumer's financial management behavior* [Unpublished doctoral dissertation]. University of Georgia.

Fan, L. (2021). A conceptual framework of financial advice-seeking and short- and long-term financial behaviors: An age comparison. *Journal of Family and Economic Issues*, *42*(1), 90–112.

Fan, L., and Chatterjee, S. (2020a). *Financial help-seeking behavior and life satisfaction among the U.S. elderly: The roles of personality, cognitive ability, and risk tolerance* [Conference presentation]. 2020 Academic Research Colloquium for Financial Planning, Arlington, VA, United States.

Fan, L., and Chatterjee, S. (2020b). The utilization of robo-advisors by individual investors: An analysis using diffusion of innovation and information search frameworks. *Journal of Financial Counseling and Planning*, *31*(1), 130–145.

Fan, L., and Lim, H. (2019). *The relationship between cognitive abilities and financial help-seeking behavior* [Conference presentation]. 2019 Association for Financial Counseling and Planning Education, Portland, OR, United States.

Fein, M. L. (2015). Robo-advisors: A closer look. Accessed July 2021. https://papers.ssrn.com/sol3/papers.cfm?abstract_id=2658701

Finke, M. S., Huston, S. J., and Winchester, D. D. (2011). Financial advice: Who pays. *Journal of Financial Counseling and Planning*, *22*(1), 18–26.

Fulk, M., Grable, J. E., Watkins, K., and Kruger, M. (2018). Who uses robo-advisory services, and who does not? *Financial Services Review*, *27*(2), 173–188.

Gamble, K. J., Boyle, P. A., Yu, L., and Bennett, D. A. (2015) Aging and financial decision making. *Management Science*, *61*(11), 2,603–2,610. https://doi.org/10.1287/mnsc.2014.2010

Gerrans, P., and Hershey, D. A. (2017). Financial adviser anxiety, financial literacy, and financial advice seeking. *Journal of Consumer Affairs*, *51*(1), 54–90.

Godwin, D. D., and Koonce, J. C. (1992). Cash flow management of low-income newlyweds. *Journal of Financial Counseling and Planning*, *3*(1), 17–42.

Gourash, N. (1978). Help-seeking: A review of the literature. *American Journal of Community Psychology*, *6*(5), 413–423. https://doi.org/10.1007/BF00941418

Grable, J. E., Archuleta, K. L., and Nazarinia, R. R. (2011). Measures for professional aspects of the financial helping relationship. In J. E. Grable, K. L. Archuleta, and R. R. Nazarinia (eds.), *Financial Planning and Counseling Scales* (pp. 577–631). Springer.

Grable, J. E., and Chatterjee, S. (2014). Reducing wealth volatility: The value of financial advice as measured by zeta. *Journal of Financial Planning*, *27*(8), 45–51.

Grable, J., Heo, W., and Rabbani, A. (2015). Financial anxiety, physiological arousal, and planning intention. *Journal of Financial Therapy*, *5*(2). https://doi.org/10.4148/1944-9771.1083

Grable, J. E., and Joo, S. H. (1999). Financial help-seeking behavior: Theory and implications. *Journal of Financial Counseling and Planning*, *10*(1), 14–25.

Grable, J. E., and Joo, S. H. (2001). A further examination of financial help-seeking behavior. *Journal of Financial Counseling and Planning*, *12*(1), 55–74.

Grable, J. E., and Joo, S. H. (2003). A snapshot view of the help-seeking market. *Journal of Financial Planning*, *16*(3), 88–94.

Hackethal, A., and Inderst, R. (2013). How to make the market for financial advice work. In O. S. Mitchell and K. Smetters (eds.), *The market for retirement financial advice* (pp. 213–228). Oxford University Press.

Hanna, S. D. (2011). The demand for financial planning services. *Journal of Personal Finance*, *10*(1), 36–62.

Hanna, S. D., and Lindamood, S. (2010). Quantifying the economic benefits of personal financial planning. *Financial Services Review*, *19*(2), 1–21.

Hilgert, M., Hogarth, J., and Beverley, S. (2003). Household financial management: The connection between knowledge and behavior. *Federal Reserve Bulletin*. https://heinonline.org/HOL/LandingPage?handle=hein.journals/fedred89&div=90&id=&page=

Hinson, J. A., and Swanson, J. L. (1993). Willingness to seek help as a function of self-disclosure and problem severity. *Journal of Counseling and Development, 71*(4), 465–470. https://doi.org/10.1002/j.1556-6676.1993.tb02666.x

Kim, H. H., Maurer, R., and Mitchell, O. S. (2016). Time is money: Rational life cycle inertia and the delegation of investment management. *Journal of Financial Economics, 121*(2), 427–447.

Kim, H. H., Maurer, R., and Mitchell, O. S. (2019a). *How cognitive ability and financial literacy shape the demand for financial advice at older ages* (NBER Working Paper No. w25750). National Bureau of Economic Research. Accessed July 2021. https://www.nber.org/papers/w25750

Kim, S. D., Cotwright, M., and Chatterjee, S. (2019b). Who are robo-advisor users? *Journal of Finance Issues, 18*(2), 33–50.

Kramer, M. M. (2016). Financial literacy, confidence, and financial advice seeking. *Journal of Economic Behavior & Organization, 131*(A), 198–217. https://doi.org/10.1016/j.jebo.2016.08.016

Kwon, J. (2004). Clustering users of multiple sources of information for saving and investment. *Journal of Personal Finance, 3*(4), 33–48.

Lachance, M. E., and Tang, N. (2012). Financial advice and trust. *Financial Services Review, 21*(3), 209–226.

Lakey, B., and Cohen, S. (2000). Social support theory and measurement. In S. Cohen, L. G. Underwood, and B. H. Gottlieb (eds.), *Social support measurement and intervention: A guide for health and social scientists* (pp. 29–52). Oxford University Press. https://doi.org/10.1093/med:psych/9780195126709.003.0002

Lazarus, R. S., and Folkman, S. (1984). *Stress, appraisal, and coping*. Springer Publishing Company.

Lee, J., and Cho, J. (2005). Consumers' use of information intermediaries and the impact on their information search behavior in the financial market. *Journal of Consumer Affairs, 39*(1), 95–120.

Lee, J., and Hogarth, J. M. (2000). Relationships among information search activities when shopping for a credit card. *Journal of Consumer Affairs, 34*(2), 330–360.

Lei, S., and Yao, R. (2016). Use of financial planners and portfolio performance. *Journal of Financial Counseling and Planning, 27*(1), 92–108.

Li, Y. M., Lee, J., and Cude, B. J. (2002). Intention to adopt online trading: Identifying the future online traders. *Journal of Financial Counseling and Planning, 13*(2), 49–64.

Lim, H., Heckman, S. J., Letkiewicz, J. C., and Montalto, C. P. (2014). Financial stress, self-efficacy, and financial help-seeking behavior of college students. *Journal of Financial Counseling and Planning, 25*(2), 148–160.

Loibl, C., and Hira, T. K. (2007). New insights into advising female clients on investment decisions. *Journal of Financial Planning, 20*(3), 68–75.

Lown, J. M., and Cook, J. (1990). Attitudes toward seeking financial counseling: Instrument development. *Journal of Financial Counseling and Planning, 1*(1), 93–112.

Mullainathan, S., Noeth, M., and Schoar, A. (2012). *The market for financial advice: An audit study* (NBER Working Paper No. w17929). National Bureau of Economic Research. doi: 10.3386/w17929

Pan, X., Wu, W., and Zhang, X. (2020). Is financial advice a cure-all or the icing on the cake for financial literacy? Evidence from financial market participation in China. *International Review of Financial Analysis, 69*, 101,473.

Perry, V. G., and Morris, M. D. (2005). Who is in control? The role of self-perception, knowledge, and income in explaining consumer financial behavior. *Journal of Consumer Affairs, 39*(2), 299–313.

Phoon, K., and Koh, F. (2017). Robo-advisors and wealth management. *The Journal of Alternative Investments, 20*(3), 79–94.

Porto, N., and Xiao, J. J. (2016). Financial literacy overconfidence and financial advice seeking. *Journal of Financial Service Professionals, 70*(4), 78–88.

Redhead, K. (2011). Behavioral perspectives on client mistrust of financial services. *Journal of Financial Service Professionals, 65*(6), 50–61.

Rickwood, D., Deane, F. P., Wilson, C. J., and Ciarrochi, J. (2005). Young people's help-seeking for mental health problems. *Australian e-Journal for the Advancement of Mental Health, 4*(3), 218–251.

Robb, C. A., Babiarz, P., and Woodyard, A. (2012). The demand for financial professionals' advice: The role of financial knowledge, satisfaction, and confidence. *Financial Services Review, 21*(4), 291–305.

Rühr, A. (2020, June 15–17). Robo-advisor configuration: An investigation of user preferences and the performance-control dilemma [Conference session]. *29$^{th}$ European Conference on Information System,* Online conference. https://aisel.aisnet.org/ecis2020_rp/94

Sharpe, D. L., Anderson, C., White, A., Galvan, S., and Siesta, M. (2007). Specific elements of communication that affect trust and commitment in the financial planning process. *Journal of Financial Counseling and Planning, 18*(1), 3–17.

Sherraden, M. S. (2013). Building blocks of financial capability. In J. Birkenmaier, M. Sherraden, and J. Curley (eds.), *Financial education and capability: Research, education, policy, and practice* (pp. 3–43). Oxford University Press.

Shin, S. H., Kim, K. T., and Seay, M. (2020). Sources of information and portfolio allocation. *Journal of Economic Psychology, 76,* 102,212. https://doi.org/10.1016/j.joep.2019.102212

Srinivasan, N. (1990). Pre-purchase external search for information. *Review of marketing, 4,* 153–189.

Stigler, G. J. (1961). The economics of information. *The Journal of Political Economy, 69*(3), 213–225.

Stolper, O. A., and Walter, A. (2017). Financial literacy, financial advice, and financial behavior. *Journal of Business Economics, 87*(5), 581–643.

Tang, N., and Hu, X. (2019). *Financial literacy and the use of financial advice – a non-monotonic relationship.* Teachers Insurance Annuity Association of America Institute. Accessed July 2021. https://origin-www.tiaainstitute.org/sites/default/files/presentations/2019-08/TIAA%20Insti tute_Financial%20literacy%20and%20the%20use%20of%20financial%20advice_T%26I_ Tang_August%202019.pdf

Tharp, D. T., Camarda, J., Lee, S. J., and de Jong, P. J. (2020). Do CFP® professionals engage in less misconduct? Exploring the importance of job classification when comparing misconduct rates among financial service professionals. *Applied Economics Letters,* 1–6.

Van Dalen, H. P., Henkens, K., and Hershey, D. A. (2017). Why do older adults avoid seeking financial advice? Adviser anxiety in the Netherlands. *Ageing and Society, 37*(6), 1–23.

Von Gaudecker, H. M. (2015). How does household portfolio diversification vary with financial literacy and financial advice? *The Journal of Finance, 70*(2), 489–507. https://www.jstor.org/ stable/43611039

Warschauer, T., and Sciglimpaglia, D. (2012). The economic benefit of personal financial planning: An empirical analysis. *Financial Service Review, 21*(3), 195–208.

Westermann, S., Niblock, S. J., Harrison, J. L., and Kortt, M. A. (2020). Financial advice seeking: A review of the barriers and benefits. *Economic Papers, 39*(4), 367–388. https://doi.org/10. 1111/1759-3441.12294

Wills, T. A. (1987). Help-seeking as a coping mechanism. In C. R. Snyder and C. E. Ford (eds.), *Coping with negative life events* (pp. 19–50). Springer.

Xiao, J. J., and Porto, N. (2016). Which financial advice topics are positively associated with financial satisfaction? *Journal of Financial Planning, 29*(7), 52–60.

Yeo, J., and Lee, Y. G. (2019). Understanding the association between perceived financial well-being and life satisfaction among older adults: Does social capital play a role? *Journal of Family and Economic Issues, 40*(4), 592–608.

Claire Matthews

# 32 The Future of Payments: Cash, Cryptocurrencies, and Peer-to-Peer Payments

**Abstract:** Access to some form of money is essential to participate in the economy, but money today takes a wide range of forms from traditional cash to cryptocurrencies. Although cash still represents the payment of choice for the majority of transactions globally, the importance of alternative payment platforms is growing, particularly peer-to-peer 'payments'. The new kid on the block is cryptocurrency, and the jury is still out on whether it will disrupt the sector. Researchers and policymakers are interested in what drives the choices consumers make between the payment platforms available to them, with technology being a key driver on the supply side, and demographic factors and personal preferences on the demand side. Understanding these drivers can assist in encouraging behavioral changes, for example where a payment method is being removed. Policymakers are also interested in issues such as cybersecurity, given the increasing use of electronic payment options, and encouraging competition, via open banking and management of network effects. Considerable ongoing research on payments means researchers and policymakers have access to a range of data. It is unlikely that cash will disappear any time soon, but the development of new payment platforms continues to offer additional options for consumers while providing new avenues of research.

**Keywords:** bitcoin, cash, cryptocurrency, payments, peer-to-peer

## Introduction

While money has been described as the root of all evil, access to money in some form is essential in the modern world. Being able to make payments to purchase goods and services is fundamental to participating in economic life in most countries around the world. However, while the foundation of payments is money, there is now a variety of available payment types, and electronic payments, particularly peer-to-peer payments via smartphone apps, which are becoming more dominant. The development of payment platforms continues to offer new payment options, some of which disrupt the payment sector and result in long-lasting change while others show promise but fail to live up to the hype that accompanies their launch.

**Claire Matthews,** Massey University

https://doi.org/10.1515/9783110727692-032

PayPal is a good example of a platform that changed the way payments are made, while Mondex is a good case study of a new platform that did not deliver. In this chapter, I will review the development of payments over time and the issues of interest to researchers and policymakers.

## Historical Perspective

Today, although money is more often used in some digital form, most people still think of it as physical cash comprising notes and coins of different denominations. The existence of money dates to about 5000 BC, and originally took the form of shells, stones, and a variety of other objects. The move to the use of metal coins is attributed to the Lydians in approximately 700 BC, while paper money followed much later, being introduced in China in the 11th century. A subsequent key development came in the 17th century when the central banks of Sweden and England introduced money issued by central banks, which carried a guarantee of value that enhanced its acceptability.

While many currencies have used non-decimal systems in the past, almost all currencies now have a decimal base. Countries that have had long-standing decimal currencies include the United States and France. During the latter part of the 20th century, several countries with non-decimal systems went through a decimalization process to move to a decimal base, including the United Kingdom (in 1971) and Australia (in 1966). Most countries today use a mix of notes and coins for their currency, with the denominations of each varying between countries and changing over time. Smaller denomination coins have been discontinued where inflation has eroded their value, while smaller denomination notes have been changed to coins to enhance their longevity. "Paper" banknotes today are increasingly made from a polymer plastic that provides a longer life and allows the inclusion of a range of security features against counterfeiting.

Recent decades have seen a move away from the use of physical cash for payments to electronic payments systems, even in less developed countries (Bagnall et al., 2016). This means cash now represents one of a range of payment choices available to consumers. Other payment methods include cheques (checks), debit cards, credit cards, and electronic payments.[1] Figure 32.1 shows the average number of transactions per inhabitant in the countries covered by the BIS Committee on Payments and Market Infrastructures and the increase since 2012.[2]

---

[1] Cheques are a written instruction to the payer's financial institution to withdraw funds from the payer's account and transfer it to the payee's account at their financial institution. Debit and credit cards are both plastic cards, with the difference being that payment is taken from the payer's bank account with a debit card, while a debt is incurred with a credit card. Electronic payments include direct payments, standing orders, Internet banking payments, and phone banking payments.
[2] The increase for Spain is from 2014 rather than 2012.

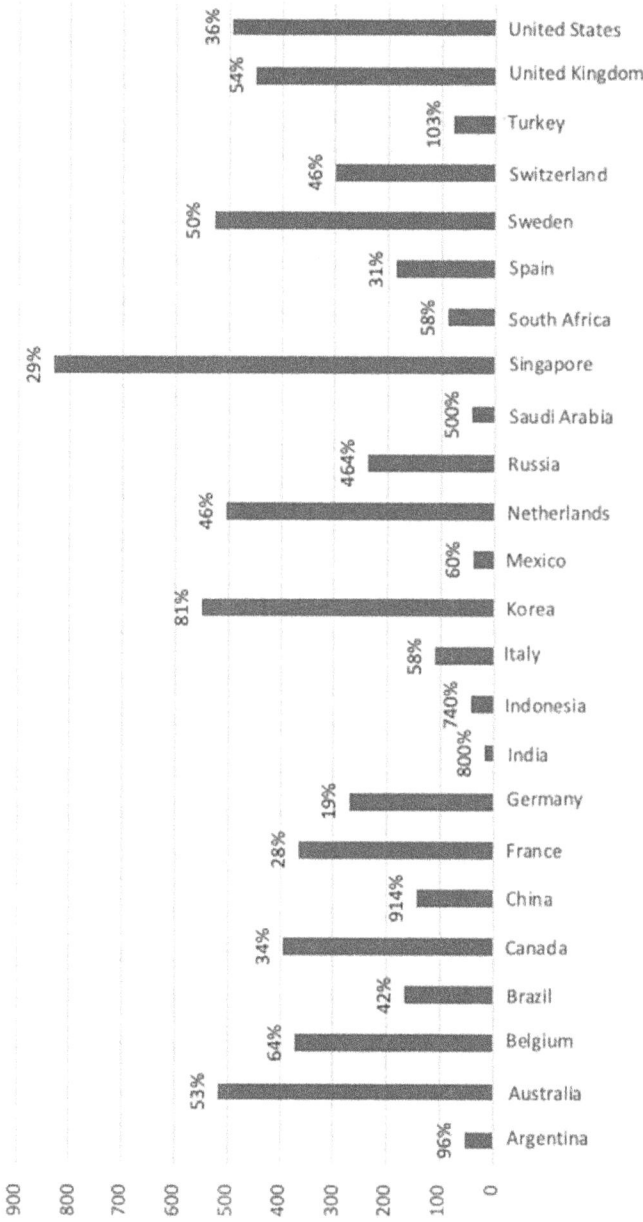

**Figure 32.1:** The Average Number of Cashless Payments Per Inhabitant in 2018 and the Percentage Change Since 2012.[3]

**3** Source of data: Table CT5 (Use of Payment Services/Instruments: Volume of Cashless Payments) from the BIS Committee on Payments and Market Infrastructures (https://stats.bis.org/statx/srs/table/CT5).

A feature of these payments is the involvement of at least one, and frequently two, financial institutions, usually a bank or credit union, as an intermediary in the transaction. The payer issues a payment instruction to the financial institution and the financial institution then makes the payment to the payee, via their financial institution. In 1998, this model was disrupted with the establishment of PayPal, widely regarded as the pioneer in peer-to-peer payments. A key difference with peer-to-peer payments is that the payer does not need to know the payee's bank account details, rather the payment is based on knowing their email address, phone number, or username. PayPal has developed to include a suite of brands offering and supporting peer-to-peer payments, including Venmo and Xoom. A variety of other providers have subsequently sprung up, including Square, Zelle, Google Pay, and Apple Pay, as well as Alipay in China, Paytm in India, M-Pesa in Africa, and KakaoPay in South Korea. In addition, some social media networks such as FB Messenger and WeChat in China also enable peer-to-peer payments.

The most recent addition to the payments sector is cryptocurrency, which is primarily attributed to the creation of Bitcoin in 2009, although it can be argued that its origins date back to the 1980s.[4] Bitcoin's development followed the publication of a white paper that outlined the basis for a cryptocurrency, and it is argued that it was a response to the 2008 global financial crisis (see Dupont, 2019), which led to a loss of trust in central financial authorities. A cryptocurrency is a form of digital money that is distinguished by the use of cryptographic security, which means it is almost impossible to counterfeit. The underlying cryptography uses a distributed ledger, with the best-known type being blockchains. Another distinguishing feature is the lack of a central authority to verify and maintain records of the cryptocurrency; rather verification and record-keeping are undertaken via cryptographic technology. While Bitcoin is the best-known of the cryptocurrencies, there are others, with the next largest by market capitalization including Ethereum, Tether, Binance Coin, and Cardana. An increasing number of businesses are accepting payment by Bitcoin, with one of the most notable being Tesla from February 2021, although it soon suspended Bitcoin acceptance in May 2021 over environmental concerns related to Bitcoin mining and transactions. Cryptocurrencies can also be used for peer-to-peer payments. The peak for cryptocurrency transactions was during the crypto-boom of late 2017 and early 2018, although 2021 also saw an increased level of interest, perhaps reflecting the economic uncertainty related to the global Covid-19 pandemic. A notable development in the acceptability of cryptocurrencies was the decision in mid-2021 by El Salvador to recognize Bitcoin as legal tender alongside the U.S. dollar, accompanied by the promised issue of $30 in Bitcoin to all adult citizens when they downloaded and registered the government's cryptocurrency app when it became available.

---

4 Some of the technologies that enable the development of cryptocurrencies date back to the 1970s (Grabowski, 2019).

# Research and Policy Issues

The nature of consumer payments means a number of issues have been raised for researchers and policymakers. Of particular interest is seeking to understand the choice consumers make between the types of payments available to them, what drives these choices, and to what extent can these choices be influenced by regulation?

Stavins (2017) noted that the choice of payment method may be driven by factors on the supply side of the transaction or the demand side. On the supply side, a key driver is technology, which expands the suite of available options. As discussed previously, the choice available has expanded from some form of cash to the current profusion of options ranging from cash to cryptocurrencies. Stavins explained that regulation is another supply-side driver of payment choice although its impact on consumers is indirect, being specifically targeted at financial institutions and merchants. The impact of regulation is via the third supply-side driver of payment choice – cost. The effect of cost to consumers, which may be affected by regulation, will depend on the extent to which merchants pass that cost on. The cost for merchants may include security and storage (for physical cash), transaction fees (cards and electronic payments), the purchase or lease of equipment (cards), and utility expenses, such as electricity or Internet access. Costs for the consumer may include any fees charged by the merchant, such as surcharges for using credit cards or discounts for using debit cards, ongoing charges for access to the payment method, such as annual fees for credit cards or mobile payment apps, transaction fees charged by the provider, and the burden of the payment method, such as holding cash or a card.

On the demand side of the transaction, a key factor is an individual's demographic characteristics, with age, education, and income having the strongest impact (Connolly and Stavins, 2015). Also on the demand side, payment choice is driven by a consumer's assessment of the attributes of the payment method and their personal preferences. The consumer's assessment of and preference for a payment method will consider several attributes, including security, privacy, risk aversion, personal experiences, exogenous events, and the influence of others. The Covid-19 pandemic provided a timely example of an exogenous shock affecting payment choice, with a noticeable increase in the use of contactless cards, with 41 percent of consumers reporting using contactless cards for the first time in 2020 (Capgemini Research Institute, 2020).

An enigma is the continued growth in cash issuance by central monetary authorities (Fish and Whymark, 2015; Gerst and Wilson, 2011) despite the availability and growing use of alternative payment methods. Fish and Whymark (2015) suggested the growth in demand for cash is driven by domestic demand for transactions and "hoarding," the overseas market, and the shadow economy.[5] They suggested that

---

5 The shadow economy comprises "illegal activities, as well as legitimate activities that are unlawfully concealed from the authorities" (Fish and Whymark, 2015, p. 220).

cash held overseas or used in the shadow economy is primarily used as a store of value. Fish and Whymark argued that the total cash on issue for a domestic transaction has grown but represents a diminishing portion of the total cash on issue. However, they also highlighted a key challenge associated with understanding cash use, in that the untraceable nature of cash makes it difficult to validate calculations of cash volumes, which includes the number, size, and frequency of cash transactions.

While these issues are of interest to policymakers, there are other issues related to payments that concern them. The first is ensuring the application of anti-money laundering (AML) requirements, which may be more challenging with the new payment options, particularly peer-to-peer payments and cryptocurrencies. Banks and credit unions are experienced at meeting AML requirements, particularly at the point that cash enters or leaves the financial system. Determining the extent to which AML requirements apply to peer-to-peer providers and cryptocurrencies has been the subject of considerable discussion.

A related issue is the cybersecurity threat associated with the growing reliance on electronic payments, in all their forms. Any system that is reliant on technology is vulnerable to cyberattacks, and financial system entities are particularly attractive due to the access they provide to financial resources. The weakest link in most systems is people, and in the case of payments systems, the number of people involved – which includes consumers – offers a substantial opportunity for criminals. Understanding how to guard against attacks and limit the impact of those that do occur is the subject of ongoing work by policymakers, individually and collectively.

Another key issue that concerns policymakers is supporting open banking development to encourage competition in financial services. Investopedia (2021) defines open banking as a practice that provides third-party financial service providers with open access to consumer banking, transactions, and other financial data from financial institutions through the use of application programming interfaces (APIs). Open banking offers opportunities for the development of new payment platforms. However, policymakers must balance these opportunities against the risks to consumers of having their data more widely available. It also creates additional opportunities for cybercriminals by providing additional pathways into financial institutions.

One final issue that concerns policymakers, and is also of interest to researchers, is that of network effects and switching costs. Farrell and Klemperer (2007) explained that a "good exhibits direct network effects if adoption by different users is complementary so that each user's adoption payoff, and his incentive to adopt, increases as more others adopt" (p. 1974). Network effects apply to payments systems because a consumer's access to and interest in using a particular payment method is influenced by others' adoption and use of that method. As more consumers use a particular payment method, it becomes more attractive to a merchant to offer that payment method, and as the network of merchants accepting the payment grows it becomes more attractive to consumers. The issue for policymakers is the need for a new payments platform to achieve an unknown threshold of users and merchants to provide long-term viability. A related issue is that of switching costs, which has the effect of discouraging a consumer from using an alternative service provider. "A product has classic switching costs if a buyer will purchase it repeatedly and will find it costly to switch from one seller to another" (Farrell and Klemperer, 2007, p. 1972). Switching costs and network effects combine to provide an incumbent with advantages over a new entrant, potentially giving them greater market power by restricting competition. Switching costs can be limited if it is easy to switch between payment platforms. Wheatley (2017) suggested that the "M-Pesa mobile payment service took off in Kenya because there was one dominant mobile operator" (p. 33).

## Research Data and Opportunities

The size of the consumer payments market, its widespread use by consumers globally, and the issues discussed above mean that it is the subject of ongoing and extensive research. There are challenges in undertaking this research as it involves seeking to understand individuals' behaviors and attitudes as reflected in the choices they make about payments. While it is possible to ask people directly about their attitudes and behaviors, they may not be accurate in their responses. This inaccuracy may stem from a desire to provide what they perceive to be a socially acceptable response, an inability to articulate their motivation for their preferences and choices, or simply an inability to accurately recall their past actions. To overcome these potential problems, several research approaches have been developed.

A common technique is to ask consumers to keep a diary of all their payment transactions for a period of time. In the United States, the Federal Reserve runs the annual Diary of Consumer Payment Choice (DCPC),[6] which collects data over three consecutive days. The Reserve Bank of Australia undertakes a triennial Consumer Payments Survey,[7] which collects data about all transactions made over a week, followed by a questionnaire on preferences and attitudes. Similar surveys have been undertaken in other countries including Canada, Austria, France, Germany, and the Netherlands (Bagnall et al., 2016). This is a very demanding exercise for participants, which restricts its use.

There are a number of public databases available that include consumer payment data, particularly in the United States. These include:
- the Survey of Consumer Finances (SCF), a triennial cross-sectional survey sponsored by the Federal Reserve Board and the Department of Treasury

---

6 Information about the DCPC and links to related publications can be found at: https://www.atlantafed.org/banking-and-payments/consumer-payments/diary-of-consumer-payment-choice.
7 Information about the most recent survey can be found at: https://rba.gov.au/payments-and-infrastructure/consumer-payments-survey/.

- the National Financial Capability Study, commissioned by the FINRA Investor Education Foundation in the United States, including some payment-related data
- the annual Survey of Consumer Payment Choice (SCPC), a project of the Federal Reserve Bank of Atlanta, which complements the DCPC

Another option for consumer-level data is to undertake a tailored survey of individuals to answer a specific research question of interest. This has the advantage of collecting the specific data needed for the research, but it can be expensive to find a suitably representative sample with sufficient participants to provide statistically significant data. These days such a survey would almost certainly be conducted online, which can cause issues with bias due to the exclusion of those without Internet access. When designing a survey, it is important to take care in the way questions are asked and the questionnaire is designed, with Dillman's Tailored Design Method providing an effective survey design approach (Smyth et al., 2014).

A further source of data is the statistical data published by a central monetary authority in many countries. For example, the Reserve Bank of Australia publishes monthly and quarterly statistics on the Australian payments system, as does Pay UK for the UK market and Payments Canada for the Canadian market. In addition, the Committee on Payments and Market Infrastructures (CPMI) of the Bank for International Settlements (BIS) publishes a range of data on payments for 26 countries and the Euro area. The disadvantage of these databases is that the data provided is at the aggregate level and does not provide information about individuals' choices. Nevertheless, they are useful in providing information on trends in the absolute and relative use of different payment methods.

## Future Directions

The future of payments is difficult to predict, as it is almost impossible to foresee the development of something completely new, such as cryptocurrency before it happens. While there have long been predictions of the disappearance of cash, and its use is diminishing, the volume of cash on issue continues to rise in most countries. The continued importance of cash for transactions was noted by Delaney (2020) who argued that cash remains the most common form of payment globally despite worldwide increases in cashless transactions. Delaney suggested the reason for the continued widespread use of cash includes the proportion of the population that remains unbanked, particularly in less developed economies, for whom other payment choices are limited, and cultural reasons, such as the traditional giving of koha during events in New Zealand and the Asian cultures that exchange lucky red envelopes as part of the Lunar New Year celebrations. It is therefore unlikely that cash will completely disappear in the short term.

The future of consumer payments likely lies in mobile or peer-to-peer payments, with users projected to increase from 2.3 billion globally in 2019 to 4 billion by 2024 (Capgemini Research Institute, 2020). While much of this growth will occur in existing payment platforms, new platforms can also be expected to appear.[8] Those new platforms are likely to be particularly focused on cryptocurrencies as they become more mainstream. However, it will be interesting to observe the evolution of cryptocurrencies. Will they live up to the promise of providing a real alternative for cash or will they turn out to be another dot-com bubble? One possibility that may support the longevity of cryptocurrencies is the creation of a central bank digital currency (CBDC). China has tested a digital renminbi and the launch of a digital Euro has also been announced, while the Federal Reserve has announced plans to also explore a CBDC issuance.

# Discussion

In the United States, cash dropped to the second most used payment method after debit cards in 2018 at 26 percent (down from 31 percent in 2016) according to the annual Diary of Consumer Payment Choice research conducted by the Federal Reserve and stayed at that level in 2019 (Kim et al., 2020). The drop has been more dramatic in the United Kingdom (from 58 percent in 2009 to 23 percent in 2019 according to U.K. Finance 2020) and Australia (69 percent in 2007 down to 27 percent in 2019 [Caddy et al., 2020]). Cash is used primarily for smaller transactions, with the DCPC research reporting that cash was used in 2019 for 47 percent of transactions less than $10 (down from 49 percent a year earlier) but only 7 percent of transactions of $100 or more. Similarly, Caddy et al. (2020) reported that by value cash represented just 10 percent of all transactions in Australia in 2019 (down from 40 percent in 2007). However, Wheatley (2017) suggested that globally 85 percent of payments are made in cash.

Chen et al. (2019) found that the burden of receiving coins as change influenced payment choice at particular transaction value thresholds, which they attributed to the denomination structure. Price discounts and surcharges have also been found to have some effect on payment choice (Stavins and Wu, 2017), although the authors noted that the frequency with which price incentives occurred was limited.

Cheques are used with reduced frequency, dropping from 7 percent in 2016 to 5 percent in 2019 in the United States (Kim et al., 2020), while in 2019 cheques represented

---

**8** The growth of peer-to-peer payments is likely to result in reduced use of other payment methods, with cheques likely to be phased out relatively soon due to the high processing costs involved as discussed below.

just 0.68 percent of transactions in the United Kingdom (U.K. Finance, 2020) and 0.2 percent in Australia (Caddy et al., 2020). The low volume of cheques, and the processing costs, have seen cheques discontinued as a payment method by the major banks in New Zealand over 2020/2021 and were discontinued in Sweden several years ago.

Credit cards are unusual because they are both a means of payment and a form of lending. Credit cards continue to increase in use for payments, albeit slowly, as they are particularly suited to online purchases. However, the growth in credit card payment volumes has not kept pace with the growth in online purchases as they are being replaced by online debit cards and Internet banking payments that have the benefit of not incurring debt. The number of credit card providers is usually seen as a sign of a competitive market, but Chandran et al. (2005) found consumer awareness of the pricing of credit card services in New Zealand to be very low, suggesting that the extent of actual effective competition in the New Zealand market may be overstated.

Debit cards have become the dominant payment method in many countries, primarily due to the convenience they offer. Debit cards became the most popular payment method in the United States in 2018, in the United Kingdom in 2017, and in Australia in 2019 but had been the most popular non-cash payment method for at least a decade longer. Debit cards linked to credit card schemes, such as Debit MasterCard and Visa Debit, have extended the use of debit cards to online purchases, further increasing their popularity.

Direct debits and standing orders have provided a useful option for regular payments such as rent and utilities, and therefore assist financial management, but are not a payment method that can be chosen for purchases, which is the primary focus of the discussion of payments. Direct debits have the advantage of managing the variable payment amount associated with utility payments and the like, while standing orders mean the payer has greater control. They are a useful aid to personal financial management by helping ensure payments are made on time. A standing order is for a payment of a set amount at a specified frequency and can only be amended by the payer. Once a payer authorizes a direct debit, the amount and timing of the payment are managed by the payee, albeit with advance notice to the payer, and the payer's control is limited to cancelling the direct debit instruction to their financial institution. The use of direct debits is limited to approved organizations.

Internet and phone banking payments are more recent additions to the suite of payment options available to consumers. Initially, the introduction of phone banking allowed consumers to make payments to any organization or individual, provided the payer had the payee's bank account detail. The introduction of Internet banking extended this option by allowing individuals to set up payees online themselves,[9] which increased the convenience of this option. As consumers have become more trusting of these arrangements, and the use of Internet banking has become more widespread, the growth of this category of payments has increased, although it is still a relatively small proportion of non-cash payments.

Research has explored how differences in personal characteristics influence payment choice, as well as examining the effect of characteristics of the transaction on a consumer's choice. For example, studies have found that older people are more likely to use cash (Kim et al., 2020; Lockhart et al., 2004) while cash is more likely to be used at some merchants, such as food and personal care supplies merchants (Kim et al., 2020) and for smaller transactions (Bagnall et al., 2016; Kim et al., 2020; Reserve Bank of Australia, 2019; U.K. Finance, 2020). Research into factors that influence consumers in their choice of EFTPOS or credit cards as a means of payment found that age, convenience, transaction size, and the interest-free period are key factors in consumers' decisions (Liu et al., 2004).

Use of a peer-to-peer payment service involves downloading an app, originally onto a computer but today it is more likely to be on a smartphone. An account is created, which is linked to a debit or credit card or a traditional bank account. The app can then be used to make payments to another individual who uses the same app. A key advantage of this form of payment is that it is almost instantaneous, occurring within seconds. The simplicity of making a payment using limited information, such as an email address, also makes it an attractive payment method. In 2018, 44 percent of U.S. debit and credit card users had used peer-to-peer payments (Statista, 2021). The value of peer-to-peer payments in the United States in 2015 was approximately $16 billion and was forecast to reach at least $86 billion by 2018 (Statista, 2021).

The anonymity of cryptocurrency transactions means they can be used for illegal activities, including money laundering. Governments have introduced Know Your Customer (KYC) and AML regulation for cryptocurrency exchanges as a result (Nuryyev et al., 2021). Cryptocurrencies are increasingly sought as payment in ransomware cyberattacks, due to the lack of traceability they provide. This is not to suggest that AML concerns do not apply to traditional payments. Money laundering in the United States was estimated at 200 billion USD in 2017 (Nuryyev et al., 2021). One of the complications with cryptocurrencies is that they are like credit cards in having two functions: payments and investment. The limited use of cryptocurrencies for payments means that to date most of the focus of research has been on the investment function in terms of the returns that can be achieved and the drivers of value. One study into the dynamics of the cryptocurrency industry included data on 1,082 coins and 725 tokens (Gandal et al., 2021) demonstrating the breadth of the market.

---

**9** Setting up payees for phone banking is generally done by the financial institution on the payer's behalf.

## Conclusion

The creation of cash in about 5000 BC was the first step in the ongoing development of payment options, which has accelerated since the middle of the 20th century. The plethora of payment options means that the question of the choices consumers make around payments generates a lot of interest from researchers and policy-makers. Researchers are interested in what drives those choices, while policy-makers are interested in ensuring a secure and competitive market.

Cash remains king, and still accounts for the majority of transactions globally, but is under growing threat, particularly from peer-to-peer payments. The prospects for the latest entrant into this market, cryptocurrency, remains unknown but has promise, as demonstrated by the interest in CBDCs.

## References

Bagnall, J., Bounie, D., Huynh, K. P., Kosse, A., Schmidt, T., and Schuh, S. (2016). Consumer cash usage: A cross-country comparison with payment diary survey data. *International Journal of Central Banking*, *12*(4), 1–61.

Caddy, J. Delaney, L., Fisher, C., and Noone, C. (2020). Consumer payment behaviour in Australia. *Reserve Bank of Australia Bulletin*. https://www.rba.gov.au/publications/bulletin/2020/mar/consumer-payment-behaviour-in-australia.html

Capgemini Research Institute. (2020). *World payments report 2020*. Accessed July 2021. https://worldpaymentsreport.com/wp-content/uploads/sites/5/2020/10/World-Payments-Report-2020.pdf

Chandran, C., Matthews, C., and Tripe, D. (2005). Competition in the New Zealand credit card market from the consumer perspective. *Journal of Asia-Pacific Business*, *6*(1), 59–74

Chen, H., Huynh, K. P., and Shy, O. (2019). Cash versus card: Payment discontinuities and the burden of holding coins. *Journal of Banking and Finance*, *99*, 192–201.

Connolly, S., and Stavins, J., (2015). Payment instrument adoption and use in the United States, 2009–2013, by consumers' demographic characteristics (Research Data Report No. 15–6). *Federal Reserve Bank of Boston*.

Delaney, A. (2020, March 30). Are we heading to the end of cash? *Chartered Accountants Australia and New Zealand*. Accessed July 2021. https://www.acuitymag.com/business/are-we-heading-to-the-end-of-cash

DuPont, Q. (2019). *Cryptocurrencies and blockchains*. John Wiley & Sons.

Farrell, J., and Klemperer, P. (2007). Coordination and lock-in: Competition with switching costs and network effects. In M. Armstrong and R. Porter (eds.), *Handbook of industrial organization* (pp. 1967–2072). North-Holland.

Fish, T., and Whymark, R. (2015). How has cash usage evolved in recent decades? What might drive demand in the future? *Bank of England Quarterly Bulletin*, *2015*(Q3), 216–227.

Gandal, N., Hamrick, J. T., Moore, T., and Vasek, M. (2021). The rise and fall of cryptocurrency coins and tokens. *Decisions in Economics and Finance*. https://doi.org/10.1007/s10203-021-00329-8

Gerst, J., and Wilson, D. J. (2011). What's in your wallet? The future of cash. *FRBSF Economic Letter*, *2011–33*, 1–4.

Grabowski, M. (2019). *Cryptocurrencies: A primer on digital money*. Routledge.

Investopedia (2021). *Open Banking*. Accessed July 2021. https://www.investopedia.com/terms/o/open-banking.asp

Kim, L., Kumar, R., and O'Brien, S. (2020). *2020 Findings from the diary of consumer payment choice*. Federal Reserve Bank of San Francisco. Accessed July 2021. https://www.frbsf.org/cash/publications/fed-notes/2020/july/2020-findings-from-the-diary-of-consumer-payment-choice/

Liu, C., Matthews, C. D. and Tripe, D. W. (2004, September 30-October 1). *Preferred payment methods for consumers – Credit card or EFTPOS?* 9th AIBF Banking and Finance Conference, Melbourne, Australia.

Lockhart, M., Matthews, C. D., and Tripe, D. W. (2004). *Cash – Is the end nigh?* 17th Australasian Finance and Banking Conference, Sydney, Australia.

Nuryyev, G., Savitski, D. W., and Peterson, J. E. (2021). The microeconomics of cryptocurrencies. In J. M. Munoz and M. Frenkel (eds.), *The economics of cryptocurrencies* (pp. 35–42). Routledge.

Reserve Bank of Australia. (2019). *The 2019 consumer payments survey*. https://rba.gov.au/payments-and-infrastructure/consumer-payments-survey/

Smyth, J. D., Christian, L. M., and Dillman, D. A. (2014). *Internet, phone, mail, and mixed-mode surveys: The tailored design method*. Wiley.

Statista. (2021). *Financial services*. Accessed July 2021. https://www.statista.com/markets/414/topic/459/financial-services/#overview

Stavins, J. (2017). How do consumers make their payment choices? (Research Data Report No. 17–1). *Federal Reserve Bank of Boston*. Accessed July 2021. https://www.bostonfed.org/publications/research-data-report/2017/how-do-consumers-make-their-payment-choices.aspx

Stavins, J., and Wu, H. (2017). *Payment discounts and surcharges: the role of consumer preferences* (Working Papers No. 17–4). Federal Reserve Bank of Boston. Accessed July 2021. https://www.bostonfed.org/publications/research-department-working-paper/2017/payment-discounts-and-surcharges-the-role-of-consumer-preferences.aspx

U.K. Finance. (2020). *UK payments markets summary 2020*. Accessed July 2021. https://www.ukfinance.org.uk/system/files/UK-Payment-Markets-Report-2020-SUMMARY.pdf

Wheatley, A. (2017). Cash is dead, long live cash. *Finance & Development, 54*(2), 32–35.

Part V: **Summarization**

Jing Jian Xiao

# 33 Personal Finance Research: An Editor's Perspective

**Abstract:** As a research field, the purpose of personal finance is to improve consumer financial capability and well-being. In this chapter, the term "consumers" refers to individuals and families. This chapter describes the past, present, and future of personal finance research. Personal finance is a research field historically rooted in the tradition of land grant universities in the United States. At the present time, personal finance is a common research topic (personal finance is sometimes referred to by various other names, such as household finance, consumer finance, behavioral finance, and family finance) contributed to by researchers from almost all other social science disciplines especially economics, business, and consumer science. In the future, personal finance research will continue to expand with new data, methods, contexts, and theories to address challenging issues faced by consumers.

**Keywords:** behavioral finance , consumer finance , family finance , financial capability, financial well-being , household finance, personal finance

## Introduction

I was asked to write a historical review of personal finance from an editor's perspective for this handbook. I may be qualified in some way. For 11 years I served as the editor of *Journal of Family and Economic Issues* (2001–2011), and since 2014 I have served as the editor of *Journal of Financial Counseling and Planning*. I also edited *Handbook of Consumer Finance Research* for two editions (Xiao, 2008, 2016). This book covered a broad range of research topics in personal finance. However, readers should be aware that my experiences also show a limitation of this chapter in that the material reflects only my preferences and biases regarding the topic discussed.

For convenience, it is important to note that in this chapter the term "consumers" refers to individuals and families. Personal finance research covers various topics, including budgeting, spending, borrowing, insuring, saving, investing, and donating.

**Note:** I wish to thank the book editors, John Grable and Swarn Chatterjee, for their helpful guidance and suggestions on earlier versions of this chapter. I also thank two anonymous reviewers and Nilton Porto for their constructive comments and suggestions, and Beatrix Lavigueur for her able research assistance.

**Jing Jian Xiao,** University of Rhode Island

https://doi.org/10.1515/9783110727692-033

About 15 years ago, personal finance research was mostly conducted by consumer science researchers who were housed in traditional land grant universities in the United States. Consumer science is a loosely defined term that includes topics relevant to family economics, consumer economics, and consumption economics (for definitions of these terms, see Abdel-Ghany, 2001). Some researchers also labeled work in this area as family finance research if they were interested in financial issues in a family setting. Since the middle of the 2000s, several influential papers on financial literacy and financial capability have been published by researchers in economics, business, and social work (e.g., Atkinson et al., 2007; Lusardi and Mitchell, 2007; Johnson and Sherraden, 2007). Research on financial literacy and financial capability has exploded in recent years. Much of this work has overlapped topics covered in personal financial research. This overlap can be seen in review papers on financial literacy (Goyal and Kumar, 2020), financial capability (Xiao and Huang, 2020), and personal financial management behavior (Goyal et al., 2021). In addition, personal finance research has also become a common topic in other fields, especially in economics and business. Economists and business/finance researchers often refer to personal finance as household finance and consumer finance (see a review by Xiao and Tao, 2020). The term *household finance* was proposed by a financial economist who was concerned about households as a sector contributing to the economy (Campbell, 2006). The term *consumer finance* was first used in a popular dataset beginning in 1983: the Survey of Consumer Finance and its companion reports (Avery et al., 1984). Later, this term was used in a book title, *Handbook of Consumer Finance Research,* which was a compilation of original material contributed by mostly consumer science researchers (Xiao, 2008). A finance professor from a business school published a review on consumer finance (Tufano, 2009) and argued that consumer finance is an important research topic and that finance researchers in business schools should pay adequate attention to it (Tufano, 2016). In recent years, household finance has become a dominant descriptor in economics and business fields. Today, it is quite common to see household finance session titles at major economics and finance conferences. The term was assigned a code (G5) in the economics coding system managed by *Journal of Economic Literature (JEL)*. Note that *JEL* has another code under microeconomics that also describes research on the broad topic of personal and household finance (i.e., D14 Household saving; personal finance). In addition, many research topics in behavioral economics and behavioral finance are also about personal finance. Recently, economics and business researchers have started to use the term *personal finance* when teaching and conducting research. Many top universities have also started to offer personal finance courses (Carpenter, 2019). Some business journals even publish special issues on personal finance. For example, *Journal of Accounting and Public Policy* recently issued a call for papers for a special issue on "Accounting and Personal Finance." Thus, when researchers search for literature regarding personal finance, they may use these terms to locate specific research literature.

# Historical Review: The Past

Personal finance research has long historical roots tracing back more than 200 years (Abdel-Ghany, 2001). The first systematic collection of family receipts and expenditures was the work of a clergyman, David Davies, in England. In his book titled *The Case of Labourers in Husbandry Stated and Considered*, Davies reported in detail the budgets of 135 families (Davies, 1795). His chief proposal was the enactment of a minimum-wage law (Stigler, 1954).

In the United States, the purpose of personal finance research has tended to focus on ways to improve quality of life through systematic research at land grant universities. Land grant universities were created after several major legislative acts were passed about 160 years ago. In 1862, the Morrill Act was passed and the U.S. Department of Agriculture was established. The Act enabled higher education to evolve from being a privileged good of the minority to a right of the majority. Land grant universities came to be recognized as peoples' universities. The Act authorized the establishment of a land grant institution in each state to educate citizens in agriculture, home economics, mechanical arts, and other practical professions (Abdel-Ghany, 2001; Liston, 1993). In 1887, the Hatch Act was passed by Congress. This Act provided $15,000 annually to establish agricultural experiment stations in connection with land grant institutions. Due to the Hatch Act and the tremendous research contributions and discoveries by the stations, the mission of land grant institutions expanded from imparting information to the creation of knowledge (Abdel-Ghany, 2001; Liston, 1993). Farmers living closer to these stations benefited more through increased productivity (Kantor and Whalley, 2019). In 1914, the Smith–Lever Act was passed by Congress. This Act established the system of cooperative extension services to bring to the general population benefits of current developments in the fields of agriculture, home economics, and related subjects. Federal funds were to be available in amounts not to exceed 50 percent of the cost of extension; the rest was to be provided by state, county, and local authorities. This mechanism of joint funding is in keeping with the term *cooperative extension*. The Smith–Lever Act expanded the mission of land grant institutions to include public service through outreach activities (Abdel-Ghany, 2001; Liston, 1993).

Personal finance research has been promoted by several professional organizations in the United States. In the early years, the United States was an agricultural country. Farmers accounted for a majority of the population and farms were (and continue to be) considered both production and living entities. Training housewives was an important task at the time, which resulted in the formation of home economics as an academic field. In the early years, it was common to see colleges of home economics in land grant universities. In 1909, the American Home Economics Association was established (Abdel-Ghany, 2001; Liston, 1993). In a typical college of home economics, department names included home management, child development, textile and interior design, food and nutrition, and housing where all topics were centered on household life. Home management departments later changed names to family resource management or consumer economics. This change occurred in leading academic institutions. Personal finance research was typically conducted by faculty and students in this type of department. During the last three decades, as agriculture's role in the U.S. economy has declined, home economics as a field has also changed. In the late 1980s and early 1990s, home economics colleges were merged with other colleges across the land grant landscape. If they stayed independent, they changed names to reflect new norms. Examples of name changes include colleges of human ecology, human services, and human-environment science. At the department level, in some universities, the names of departments of family resource management were changed to personal financial planning and consumer science. At the national level, in 1993, the American Home Economics Association (AHEA) changed its name to the American Association of Family and Consumer Science. As a result, the field changed its name from home economics to family and consumer science. Personal finance is now most commonly conceptualized as a subtopic of family resource management, which is a subfield of home economics. This subfield is changing in two major directions. One is to focus on training future financial planners and financial counselors, with many programs affiliating with the Certified Financial Planner (CFP) Board of Standards and the Association for Financial Counseling and Planning Education (AFCPE). Universities following this path include the University of Georgia, Texas Tech University, Kansas State University, University of Missouri, and Utah Valley University. Among other land grant universities, home management or similar departments have merged with other departments, such as human development and family science (this was the case at the University of Rhode Island where I am working and many other universities, such as the Ohio State University, Iowa State University, and Utah State University). This type of department's goal is to move in a way that contributes literature to the broad topic of well-being, integrating health and finance research into research and teaching. In addition, these departments tend to recruit faculty from diverse fields, such as economics, business, and other social sciences. This approach makes this field interdisciplinary (Schuchardt et al., 2007).

Numerous academic organizations have many members who conduct personal finance research. The American Council on Consumer Interests (ACCI), for example, is an academic organization founded in 1954 with financial support provided by Consumers Union, a consumer advocacy organization. In the early years of ACCI, the membership included researchers from diverse fields such as economics, business, psychology, and home economics, and research topics in its annual conferences covered broad themes relevant to consumer issues. Since it had limited space for those interested in personal finance topics, a group of researchers launched another organization called the Association for Financial Counseling and Planning Education (AFCPE) in 1984 (Burns, 2008). This organization has a diverse membership that includes both researchers and practitioners. In 1993, AFCPE created the Accredited Financial Counselor (AFC) certification program that has attracted more practitioners from the personal finance profession. The creation of AFCPE was considered a significant indicator of the establishment of personal finance as a field of study and practice (Schuchardt et al., 2007). Another informal organization called the Asian Consumer and Family Economics Association held its first conference in 1996. This conference-based organization has held biennial conferences at different locations in Asia and the United States. This organization has had close connections with U.S. researchers since its co-founding presidents and several past presidents were consumer science professors from the United States. A major move forward for the study of personal finance was taken by the CFP Board of Standards, Inc. in 2017. This organization established what has since become an annual academic research colloquium that attracts researchers from around the world. In addition, several other organizations have conferences providing presentation opportunities for personal finance research, including the Academy of Financial Services and the Financial Therapy Association.

From a historical perspective, personal finance has been and continues to be a topic of interest to researchers, consumers (individuals and families), practitioners, and policymakers. Based on a literature review of family resource management publications from 1930 to 1990 (i.e., a review of 201 papers published in five consumer and family journals, *Journal of Home Economics, Journal of Marriage and the Family, Journal of Consumer Affairs, Home Economics Research Journal,* and *Journal of Consumer Studies and Home Economics/International Journal of Consumer Studies*), 34 percent of published papers were relevant to personal and household financial management (author calculation based on Table 1, Israelsen, 1990). The author of the review also checked themes by decades, with the theme of financial management appearing in four out of six decades (Israelsen, 1990). Another literature review of consumer science papers published in the 1980s and 1900s compared the trend changes during the two decades. Based on papers reviewed in four journals (*Family and Consumer Science Research Journal, Journal of Consumer Affairs, Journal of Family and Consumer Science,* and *Journal of Family and Economic Issues*), during the 1980s, JCA was the most frequent outlet for articles on consumer economics; HERJ published the most articles on family economics and family financial planning and financial counseling; JCSHE published an equal number of articles devoted to consumer economics and family economics, whereas JFEI articles focused mainly on family economics. In the 1990s, JCA was the most frequent outlet for articles on consumption economics. The majority of articles published in FCSRJ focused on consumer economics and family economics, whereas JCSHE was by far the most frequent outlet for articles on consumer economics. JFEI published the most articles relating to family economics, as well as the greatest number of articles dealing with household management. JFEI and JCSHE published nearly an equal number of articles devoted to family financial planning and financial counseling (Abdel-Ghany, 2001).

In the research on personal finance, besides annual conferences sponsored by previously mentioned organizations, many special forums have been conducted to discuss and disseminate personal finance research. For example, in October 2008,

29 scholars from public and private universities, non-profit organizations, and the federal government participated in a National Research Symposium on Financial Literacy and Education in Washington, DC. The purpose of the meeting was to identify critical research questions that could inform outcomes-based financial education, relevant public policy, and effective practice leading to personal and family financial literacy. Following the symposium, the U.S. Department of Treasury released a comprehensive report. The identification of topics was informed by *Handbook of Consumer Finance Research* (Xiao, 2008). Prior to the symposium, each participant chose a topic and prepared a brief paper summarizing research related to that particular area. A group facilitator for each topic was responsible for summarizing key themes from the individual papers and preparing a topic area summary. The topics included behavior theory application, consumer economic socialization, financial education and program evaluation, and financial risk assessment (Schuchardt et al., 2009). Similar national expert forums were also conducted on personal finance research (see Hira, 2009) and financial education research (see Walstad et al., 2017). Both of these forums were sponsored by the National Endowment on Financial Education.

# The Present

## Organizations

Currently, several national and international professional organizations sponsor annual or biennial conferences for scholars to present personal finance research. As mentioned in the previous section, three organizations that have included personal finance researchers are ACCI, AFCPE, and ACFEA. These organizations were highlighted in the context of this chapter because they have had the most direct impact on the lives of researchers working in the United States and throughout Asia including myself. ACCI is an academic organization and most current members are personal finance researchers. Besides consumer science, ACCI has members from other disciplines, such as economics, business, social work, and other social science fields. Contrasted to ACCI, AFCPE has both researchers and practitioners in its membership. AFCPE's annual symposium has sessions for both researchers and practitioners. ACFEA is a conference-based organization. Its biennial conferences attract scholars from many countries, especially those from Asian countries. Since many personal finance researchers in the United States have Asian roots, they are very active in ACFEA conferences. Other organizations having personal finance researchers include the Academy of Financial Services (AFS), the Financial Therapy Association (FTA), and the Financial Planning Association (FPA). In addition, more personal finance research papers are increasingly seen at larger conferences, such as the Applied Social Science Association (ASSA) conference that includes the American Economic Association, the American Finance Association, and dozens of other economics associations, which usually attract more than 10,000 attendees on an annual basis. Personal finance research papers can be seen in sessions titled household finance, behavioral finance, saving behavior, and borrowing behavior.

## Journals

Several journals specialize in the publication of personal finance research. The *Journal of Financial Counseling and Planning*, the official research journal of AFCPE, publishes original research papers relevant to personal finance researchers, practitioners, and policymakers, especially those interested in financial counseling, financial planning, and financial education. Most authors are from traditional land grant universities. In recent years, more authors from other fields such as economics, business, social work, and other relevant fields have also published their works in JFCP. The number of non-U.S. authors has also grown over the past few years (Xiao et al., 2020). The *Journal of Consumer Affairs*, owned by ACCI, publishes research papers promoting the consumer interest. Papers range from consumer health to consumer finance. Most authors are from business schools, especially marketing. In recent years, more authors from personal finance and other relevant fields have been publishing papers in JCA. The *Journal of Family and Economic Issues* is another journal focusing on the interaction between the economic environment and family functioning. Authors working in both personal finance and family studies contribute to the journal. The *International Journal of Consumer Studies* is another journal that publishes personal finance and other consumer behavior topics contributed by authors from around the world. The journal has become extremely competitive in recent years. Based on an internal communication, the editor of the journal informed editorial board members that by October 2020, more than 1,300 papers had been submitted. It is important to note that several other journals publish personal finance research papers. The *Journal of Personal Finance* is sponsored by the International Association of Registered Financial Consultants (IARFC). The *Family and Consumer Science Research Journal*, affiliated with the American Association of Family and Consumer Sciences, also publishes research articles contributed by a diverse group of researchers. The *Journal of Financial Therapy* sponsored by the Financial Theory Association also publishes papers relevant to personal finance. The *Financial Planning Review*, sponsored by the CFP Standard Board, publishes papers on financial planning and other personal finance-related topics.

## Common Topics and Themes

Across journals, a variety of personal finance topics and themes can be seen, including money management, spending, borrowing, saving/investing, and insuring (Xiao and Tao, 2020). In addition, several topics continue to draw the attention of researchers from multiple disciplines. These topics include financial literacy (Goyal and Kumar, 2020), financial capability (Xiao and Huang, 2020), financial behavior (Goyal et al., 2021), financial well-being (Xiao, 2015), risk tolerance (Grable, 2016), retirement planning (Hanna et al., 2016), financial education (Bartholomae and Fox, 2016), financial socialization (Gudmunson et al., 2016; Kim and Chatterjee, 2013), financial parenting (Serido and Deenanath, 2016), finance and marriage (Dew, 2016), financial planning (Browning and Finke, 2016), financial counseling (Delgadillo, 2016), financial coaching (Collins and Olive, 2016), financial therapy (Archuleta et al., 2016), and financial social work (Sherraden et al., 2016). Personal finance topics have also been (and continue to be) examined among special populations, such as high-school students (Walstad et al., 2016), college students (Cude et al., 2016), older adults (DeVaney, 2016), low-income families (Nielsen et al., 2016), business-owning families (Danes et al., 2016), women (Loibl and Hira, 2016), Hispanics (Porto, 2016), Blacks (Anong, 2016), Asians (Yao, 2016), workers (Kim, 2016), and military personnel (Carlson et al., 2016).[1]

## Common Theories

Theories used by personal finance researchers come mainly from two sources: economics and psychology (Schuchardt et al., 2007). The most commonly used theory from economics is the lifecycle hypothesis (Modigliani, 1986). Because of the advance of behavioral economics, the behavioral life cycle hypothesis (Shefrin and Thaler, 1988; Thaler and Shefrin, 1981) is also commonly used in personal finance research. In addition, personal finance researchers who are interested in identifying factors predicting consumer financial behavior have applied the Theory of Planned Behavior (Ajzen, 1991). Researchers who are interested in how consumers change behaviors to achieve a better quality of life have used the transtheoretical model of behavior change (TTM) (Prochaska et al., 1992).

---

1 See the two editions of *Handbook of Consumer Finance Research* (Xiao, 2008, 2016) for details about these and other topics.

## Common Datasets Used

In the United States, many publicly available datasets are used as the basis of personal finance research. The most commonly used dataset is the Survey of Consumer Finances (SCF). The SCF is a triennial survey sponsored by the Federal Reserve System. The data are cross-sectional but occasionally panel data between two time periods are available. Since 2009, another national dataset, the National Financial Capability Survey (NFCS), a biennial survey sponsored by FINRA Investor Education Foundation, has been frequently used by personal finance researchers. The Foundation sometimes collects additional data for special populations, such as the disabled, military personnel, and investors. Another dataset used by personal finance researchers is the Panel Study of Income Dynamics (PSID). The PSID is a long-term panel data series. Recent versions of the PSID include data collected from children of the respondents. Two additional companion panel datasets (i.e., the Supplemental to Children and Transition to Adulthood) are also widely used. The PSID occasionally offers special topic surveys on topics such as financial literacy and well-being, making this dataset attractive to personal finance researchers. With the onset of the Covid-19 pandemic 2020, a new survey series called the Household Pulse Survey (HPS) has been collected by the U.S. Census Bureau. The survey was conducted every two weeks during the pandemic with close to 70,000 observations in each survey. The large sample sizes, collection frequencies, and topic currency of this dataset are attractive to personal finance researchers.

## The Future

Personal finance researchers have historical roots in conducting research designed to improve the quality of life. In the past, personal finance researchers have contributed their research expertise and publications to enrich the literature. To make broader and greater impacts on society through personal finance research, researchers need to devote time and energy to address challenging issues facing consumers throughout the world. At the current time, major issues faced by consumers include the effects of pandemics across all aspects of life, the balance between safety and economy, and social justice between consumers at different resource levels. When researchers start a new project, they need to ask themselves how their research models and hypotheses are related to these important and broad questions in the special social contexts.

Consumer finance capability refers to a consumer's ability to apply appropriate financial knowledge and perform desirable financial behavior for achieving financial and overall well-being (Xiao et al., 2014; Xiao and O'Neill, 2016; Xiao and Porto, 2017). Because of this, personal finance researchers could propose interesting research questions asking what factors are associated with financial capability and what effects are associated with the factors contributing to consumer financial and overall well-being. This approach can provide a unique perspective compared to researchers in other fields who mainly provide policy implications for governments or business school researchers providing strategies for commercial companies.

Personal finance research methodologies tend to be diverse. All quantitative and qualitative methods can be used to address important research questions. As a quantitative researcher, I use both secondary data and primary data. How to use secondary data innovatively and effectively and how to collect unique and reliable primary data with limited resources are challenges for many personal finance researchers. Additionally, how to effectively conduct qualitative research exploring personal finance questions that cannot be answered by secondary data, and then publishing the results in top journals, are challenges for personal finance researchers. For quantitative studies, besides data available from the United States, data from other countries may also be used to better understand consumer financial capability and well-being. For example, some commonly used datasets in China are described in Xiao and Tao (2020). Besides using survey data, other types of research methods can also be used, such as experimental research. Experimental research has always been popular in economics (e.g., experimental economists won Nobel prizes twice in recent years). Personal finance researchers could use this approach to better understand the causes and effects between consumer financial capability and well-being.

To help make personal finance a research field that grows continuously, researchers need to exchange ideas with researchers from other disciplines, such as economics, business, social work, and other related fields. Many personal finance researchers have been doing this by attending conferences and publishing articles in economics, business, social work, and other related disciplines, and inviting scholars from other fields to attend conferences and publish papers in the personal finance field. Because financial literacy is now a hot topic in economics and business, more economic and business conferences and journals appear to be more willing to publish personal finance-related articles. Similarly, since financial capability has arisen to be a popular topic in social work, more conferences and journals in social work also appear willing to publish papers on financial capability and personal finance. Personal finance researchers should take these opportunities to interact with researchers in other fields even working with them to produce unique findings to enrich the research literature on a larger scale and make greater impacts through their scholarship.

FinTech offers a new topic for those interested in personal finance research. FinTech refers to technology applications in the financial service industry. Advances in FinTech provide unique opportunities and challenges for personal finance researchers. Because of FinTech, many boundaries in traditional financial services have disappeared or are changing. For example, in China, a popular online superstore is called Alibaba. Using FinTech technologies, the company offers financial services through its payment channel, Zhifubao. Through this tool, consumers not only use Alibaba to make payments but also to earn interest on account balances. They can also borrow money from the site. The company even created a product for insurance, offering very low premiums to attract customers. The application of FinTech is showing a strong degree of competitiveness. All these are new topics for personal finance researchers to examine. Ultimately, personal finance research is needed to answer this important question: What are the financial products consumers should use, and what are the benefits and pitfalls associated with new FinTech products? Additionally, more research is needed to determine what capabilities (i.e., knowledge and behavior) consumers should possess to use FinTech products and services effectively.

## Conclusion

As noted at the outset of this chapter, I was asked by the editors of this handbook to provide a review of personal finance research from an editor's perspective. Over the years, I have seen the types of studies submitted for publication change. What has remained constant, however, is the purpose of personal finance, which is to improve consumer financial capability and well-being. In this chapter, I reviewed the historical origins of personal finance and provided context for the growth of personal finance research. Regardless of what personal finance is referred to in distinct disciplines (e.g., family finance, consumer finance, household finance), one commonality links those who are interested in how consumers interact with the economy – namely, a desire to expand the field with new data, methods, contexts, and theories to address challenging issues faced by consumers. In this context, publication opportunities in leading journals are likely to continue to grow over the next few decades.

## References

Abdel-Ghany, M. (2001). The evolution of research in consumer science: A 200-year perspective. *Family and Consumer Sciences Research Journal, 30*(2), 223–239.

Ajzen, I. (1991). The theory of planned behavior. *Organizational Behavior and Human Decision Processes, 50*, 179–211.

Anong, S. T. (2016). Financial issues of African Americans. In J. J. Xiao (ed.), *Handbook of consumer finance research* (2nd ed., pp. 215–224). Springer.

Archuleta, K., Britt, S. L., and Klontz, B. T. (2016). Financial therapy. In J. J. Xiao (ed.), *Handbook of consumer finance research* (2nd ed., pp. 73–82). Springer.

Atkinson, A., McKay, S., Collard, S., and Kempson, E. (2007). Levels of financial capability in the UK. *Public Money and Management, 27*(1), 29–36. https://doi:10.1111/j.1467-9302.2007. 00552.x

Avery, R. B., Elliehausen, G. E., and Canner, G. B. (1984). Survey of consumer finances, 1983. *Federal Reserve Bulletin, 70*, 679–692.

Bartholomae, S., and Fox, J. J. (2016). Advancing financial literacy education using a framework for evaluation. In J. J. Xiao (ed.), *Handbook of consumer finance research* (2nd ed., pp. 45–60). Springer.

Browning, C., and Finke, M. S. (2016). Conducting research in financial planning. In J. J. Xiao (ed.), *Handbook of consumer finance research* (2nd ed., pp. 103–114). Springer.

Burns (2008). Promoting applied research in personal finance. In J. J. Xiao (ed.), *Handbook of consumer finance research* (pp. 411–418). Springer.

Campbell, J. Y. (2006). Household finance. *Journal of Finance, 61*(4), 1553–1604.

Carlson, M. B., Nelson, J. S., and Skimmyhorn, W. L. (2016). Military personal finance research. In J. J. Xiao (ed.), *Handbook of consumer finance research* (2nd ed., pp. 251–264). Springer.

Carpenter, J. (2019, May 18). Even Harvard is now teaching personal finance. *Wall Street Journal.* https://www.wsj.com/articles/even-harvard-is-now-teaching-personal-finance-11558171800#: ~:text=In%20his%20day%20job%2C%20Harvard's,asset%20pricing%20and%20consumer% 20protection.&text=The%20move%20to%20teach%20personal,wider%20range%20of%20fi nancial%20backgrounds

Collins J. M., and Olive, P. (2016). Financial coaching: Defining an emerging field. In J. J. Xiao (ed.), *Handbook of consumer finance research* (pp. 93–102). Springer.

Cude, B. J., Danns, D., and Kabaci, M. J. (2016). Financial knowledge and financial education of college students. In J. J. Xiao (ed.), *Handbook of consumer finance research* (2nd ed., pp. 141–154). Springer.

Danes, S. M., Haynes, G. W., and Haynes, D. C. (2016). Business-owning families: Challenges at the intersection of business and family. In J. J. Xiao (ed.), *Handbook of consumer finance research* (2nd ed., pp. 179–194). Springer.

Davies, D. (1795). *The case of labourers in husbandry stated and considered.* Bath.

Delgadillo, L. M. (2016). Financial counseling and financial wealth. In J. J. Xiao (ed.), *Handbook of consumer finance research* (2nd ed., pp. 83–92). Springer.

DeVaney, S. A. (2016). Financial issues of older adults. In J. J. Xiao (ed.), *Handbook of consumer finance research* (2nd ed., pp. 155–166). Springer.

Dew, J. P. (2016). Revisiting financial issues and marriage. In J. J. Xiao (ed.), *Handbook of consumer finance research* (2nd ed., pp. 281–290). Springer.

Goyal, K., and Kumar, S. (2020). Financial literacy: A systematic review and bibliometric analysis. *International Journal of Consumer Studies. 45*(1), 80–105. https://doi.org/10.1111/ ijcs.12605

Goyal, K., Kumar, S., and Xiao, J. J. (2021). Antecedents and consequences of personal financial management behavior: A systematic literature review and future research agenda. *International Journal of Bank Marketing, 39*(7), 1166–1207. https://doi.org/10.1108/IJBM-12- 2020-0612

Grable, J. E. (2016). Financial risk tolerance. In J. J. Xiao (ed.), *Handbook of consumer finance research* (2nd ed., pp. 19–32). Springer.

Gudmunson, C. G., Ray, S. K., and Xiao, J. J. (2016). Financial socialization. In J. J. Xiao (ed.), *Handbook of consumer finance research* (2nd ed., pp. 19–32). Springer.

Hanna, S. D., Kim, K. T., and Chen, S. C. (2016). Retirement savings. In J. J. Xiao (ed.). *Handbook of consumer finance research* (2nd ed., pp. 33–44). Springer.

Hira, T. K. (2009). Personal finance: Past, present and future. *Networks Financial Institute at Indiana State University Policy Brief,* 2009-PB-10. https://papers.ssrn.com/sol3/papers.cfm? abstract_id=1522299

Israelsen, C. L. (1990). Family resource management research: 1930–1990. *Journal of Financial Counseling and Planning, 1*(1), 1–37.

Johnson, E., and Sherraden, M. S. (2007). From financial literacy to financial capability among youth. *Journal of Sociology and Social Welfare, 34*(3), 119–145.

Kantor S., and Whalley A. (2019). Research proximity and productivity: Long-term evidence from agriculture. *Journal of Political Economy, 127*(2), 819–854.

Kim, J. (2016). Financial issues of workers. In J. J. Xiao (ed.), *Handbook of consumer finance research* (2nd ed., pp. 239–250). Springer.

Kim, J., and Chatterjee, S. (2013). Childhood financial socialization and young adults' financial management. *Journal of Financial Counseling and Planning, 24*(1), 61–79.

Liston, M. I. (1993). *History of family economics research: 1862–1962*. Iowa State University Research Foundation.

Loibl, C., and Hira, T. K. (2016). Financial issues of women. In J. J. Xiao (ed.), *Handbook of consumer finance research* (2nd ed., pp. 195–204). Springer.

Lusardi, A., and Mitchell, O. S. (2007). Baby boomer retirement security: The roles of planning, financial literacy, and housing wealth. *Journal of Monetary Economics, 54*(1), 205–224.

Modigliani, F. (1986). Life cycle, individual thrift, and the wealth of nations. *American Economic Review, 76*(3), 297–313.

Nielsen, R. B., Fletcher, C. N., and Bartholomae, S. (2016). Consumer finances of low-income families. In J. J. Xiao (ed.), *Handbook of consumer finance research* (2nd ed., pp. 167–178). Springer.

Porto, N. (2016). Financial issues of Hispanic Americans. In J. J. Xiao (ed.), *Handbook of consumer finance research* (2nd ed., pp. 205–214). Springer.

Prochaska, J. O., DiClemente, C. C., and Norcross, J. C. (1992). In search of how people change: Applications to addictive behaviors. *American Psychologist, 47*, 1102–1114.

Reynolds, L. M., and Abdel-Ghany, M. (2001). Consumer sciences research: A two-decade comparison, 1980s and 1990s. *Family and Consumer Sciences Research Journal, 29*, 382–440.

Schuchardt, J., Durband, D., Bailey, W. C., DeVaney, S. A., Grable, J. E., Leech, I. E., Lown, J. M., Sharpe, D. L., and Xiao, J. J. (2007). Personal finance: An interdisciplinary profession. *Journal of Financial Counseling and Planning, 18*(1), 61–69.

Schuchardt, J., Hanna, S. D., Hira, T. K., Lyons, A. C., Palmer, L., and Xiao, J. J. (2009). Financial literacy and education research priorities. *Journal of Financial Counseling and Planning, 20*(1), 84–94.

Serido, J., and Deenanath, V. (2016). Financial parenting: Promoting financial self-reliance of young consumers. In J. J. Xiao (ed.). *Handbook of consumer finance research* (2nd ed., pp. 291–300). Springer.

Shefrin, H. M., and Thaler, R. H. (1988). The behavioral life-cycle hypothesis. *Economic Inquiry, 26*(4), 609–643.

Sherraden, M. S., Frey, J. J., and Birkenmaier, J. (2016). Financial social work. In J. J. Xiao (ed.), *Handbook of consumer finance research* (2nd ed., pp. 115–127). Springer.

Stigler, G. J. (1954). The early history of empirical studies of consumer behavior. *Journal of Political Economy, 62*(2), 95–113.

Thaler, R. H., and Shefrin, H. M. (1981). An economic theory of self-control. *Journal of Political Economy, 89*(2), 392–406.

Tufano, P. (2009). Consumer finance. *Annual Review Financial Economics, 1*(1), 227–247.

Tufano, P. (2016). Foreword. In J. J. Xiao (ed.), *Handbook of consumer finance research* (2nd ed., pp. v–vii). Springer.

Walstad, B. W., Tharayil, A., and Wagner, J. (2016). Financial literacy and financial education in high school. In J. J. Xiao (ed.), *Handbook of consumer finance research* (2nd ed., pp. 131–140). Springer.

Walstad, W., Urban, C., Asarta, C. A., Breitbach, E., Bosshardt, W., Heath, J., O'Neill, B., Wagner, J., and Xiao, J. J. (2017). Perspectives on evaluation in financial education: Landscape, issues, and studies. *The Journal of Economic Education*, *48*(2), 93–112.

Xiao, J. J. (2008). *Handbook of consumer finance research*. Springer.

Xiao, J. J. (2015). *Consumer economic wellbeing*. Springer.

Xiao, J. J. (2016). *Handbook of consumer finance research* (2nd ed.). Springer.

Xiao, J. J., Chen, C., and Chen, F. (2014). Consumer financial capability and financial satisfaction. *Social Indicators Research*, *118*(1), 415–432.

Xiao, J. J., and Huang, J. (2020). *Financial capability: A conceptual review, extension, and synthesis.* SSRN: http://dx.doi.org/10.2139/ssrn.3943629

Xiao, J. J., Lavigueur, B., Izenstark, A., Hanna, S., and Lawrence, F. C. (2020). Three decades of the *Journal of Financial Counseling and Planning. Journal of Financial Counseling and Planning*, *31*(1), 5–13. https://doi.org/10.1891/JFCP–20–00010

Xiao, J. J., and O'Neill, B. (2016). Consumer financial education and financial capability. *International Journal of Consumer Studies*, *40*(6), 712–721.

Xiao, J. J., and Porto, N. (2017). Financial education and financial satisfaction: Financial literacy, behavior, and capability as mediators. *International Journal of Bank Marketing*, *35*(5), 805–817.

Xiao, J. J., and Tao, C. (2020). Consumer finance/household finance: The definition and scope. *China Finance Review International*, *11*(1), 1–25. https://doi.org/10.1108/CFRI-04-2020-0032

Yao, R. (2016). Financial wellbeing of Asian Americans. In J. J. Xiao (ed.), *Handbook of consumer finance research* (2nd ed., pp. 225–238). Springer.

Swarn Chatterjee, John E. Grable

# 34 The Future of Personal Finance: An Educational and Research Agenda

**Abstract:** The purpose of this chapter is to synthesize much of what has been presented in this handbook and provide a discussion on the future of personal finance from an educational and research perspective. The discussion in this chapter focuses on the following points:

- Future financial security and well-being remains a major concern for millions of individuals worldwide.
- Personal financial education will continue to play an important role in teaching people to make informed financial decisions, and in enhancing the financial resiliency.
- A need exists to help underserved populations and individuals from minority racial and ethnic groups deal with financial struggles.
- Future research is needed to further identify delivery methods and policies that can make personal financial education more accessible to those living in underserved communities.
- The general personal finance curricula needs to be constantly updated to keep up with the innovations happening in the financial marketplace, and to inform students of the benefits, risks, and opportunities new products and services can provide in enhancing financial well-being.
- Finally, there is a need for consensus across disciplines related to the basic core principles that should be covered in a personal finance curriculum to provide consistency for the delivery of this subject area across academia and beyond.

**Keywords:** asset location, behavioral economics, financial capability, financial education, financial well-being, personal finance, public policy

## Introduction

Personal finance is an evolving discipline. As new findings from the areas of behavioral economics and household finance, as well as marketing, psychology, and the human sciences, continue to broaden the personal finance field's understanding of the antecedents of financial behavior and financial decision making (Thaler, 2018), integration of relevant key concepts within the personal finance curriculum will emerge. Likewise, strategies designed to improve personal financial planning decisions made at the

**Swarn Chatterjee, John E. Grable,** University of Georgia

https://doi.org/10.1515/9783110727692-034

household level will continue to evolve, as will the types of resources used to train and educate future generations of consumers and financial service providers (Federal Deposit Insurance Corporation, 2021; Grable and Palmer, 2018; Jump$tart, 2021; National Endowment for Financial Education, 2021). We concur with Bodie (2006) in believing that future curriculum offerings in personal finance need to include the following four principles:[1]

(1) Financial markets are efficient [to some extent], household financial decision makers abide by the "*law of one price*," and financial decision making is always a *trade-off* between different outcomes with opportunity costs.
(2) Financial decisions should be framed in the context of lifetime expected income and consumption goals, which implies that the present value of future expected consumption cannot exceed the present value of future expected income.
(3) Investment and portfolio decisions should be framed from the perspective of maximizing investors' utility by matching an investor's risk tolerance to the risk of their asset positions and invested portfolios through investment diversification.
(4) Environmental factors must be accounted for when financial decisions are made at the household level. Specifically, the consequences of *taxes and transaction costs* when optimizing the outcome of a financial decision must be a primary concern.

In relation to the last point, as the discipline of personal finance evolves, the awareness of the importance of taxes and transaction costs will continue to remain an important issue in the context of investment decision making. As noted by Ciccotello (2016), the need to create greater awareness of the strategic concept of asset location for optimizing individuals' tax-adjusted investment outcomes will likely grow in importance in the future.

As noted throughout this handbook, the importance of personal financial education continues to be recognized by a wide range of stakeholders, including those from academic institutions and non-profit groups involved in improving financial resiliency among vulnerable communities to policymakers, government agencies, and financial institutions. However, the prevalent lack of financial literacy has been shown to impede the development, participation, and speed of adoption of sophisticated financial products and services. Ignorance of personal finance-related concepts and topics also hampers the financial well-being and resiliency of wide segments of society (Hira, 2009; Lusardi et al., 2020a). In this regard, Lusardi et al. (2020a) found that financial fragility among minority socio-demographic groups,

[1] We also acknowledge that, as suggested in Thaler (2018), financial decision makers do not always (or often) act rationally and adhere to the four core principles suggested by Bodie (2006). Nonetheless, these principles should be taught as a normative foundation of personal finance but supplemented with the integration of concepts from behavioral finance to provide a complete description of personal finance behavior.

such as African Americans, lower-income households, and other underserved communities, is associated with a lack of financial literacy. Reports in this handbook confirm what Lusardi et al. (2020a) noted. Households with lower levels of financial education and literacy appear to be more likely to make problematic financial decisions. They are also less likely to have the skills needed to successfully navigate through periods of economic uncertainty (e.g., the global financial crisis and the Covid-19 pandemic).

According to Hira (2009), the successful development and delivery of personal financial education in institutions of higher education needs to involve offering personal finance courses at both graduate and undergraduate levels. Future academic programs teaching personal finance need to focus on preparing students to become proficient financial decision makers who exhibit skillsets needed to fulfill the numerous and growing responsibilities of managing household financial tasks. For some, this may evolve into a career as a financial service professional. When considering the future of personal finance, Hira (2009) also emphasized the need for creating a research-based informed body of knowledge, with teaching and research faculty becoming more professionally engaged with policy groups, financial institutions, and professional and academic organizations. Faculty outreach efforts to the profession can inform non-academic stakeholders and help them in designing better financial services and products that can benefit society as a whole. The remainder of the chapter focuses on some key issues that can improve the content, delivery, access, and adoption of personal financial tools and techniques across diverse audiences, and foster research and growth in the academic body of knowledge related to personal finance.

# The Future Curriculum in Personal Finance

Academic research related to the topic of personal financial literacy, conducted over the past three decades, indicates that low levels of financial capability and knowledge are significant factors affecting the financial well-being and financial resiliency of households across the globe (Cutler and Devlin, 1996; Fan et al., 2021; Greenspan, 2002; Lusardi, 2009; Lusardi et al., 2020b; Tennyson and Nguyen, 2001). The existing literature suggests that several factors influence the poor financial outcomes and decisions made by some households. Some adverse outcomes can be explained by a lack of awareness of personal finance tools and techniques, including a lack of awareness related to interest rates, diversification, portfolio management, and general use of financial products and services (Abreu and Mendes, 2010; Fan and Chatterjee, 2017; Lusardi et al., 2020b; Polkovnichenko, 2003; Von Gaudecker, 2015; Warschauer, 2002). One way to help household financial decision makers overcome personal finance decision making obstacles is to standardize what is universally taught in schools, colleges, and universities.

A perusal of the most widely used textbooks and course materials written in the domain of personal finance (e.g., Bajtelsmit; 2019; Gitman et al., 2014; Grable and Palmer, 2018; Jump$tart, 2021; Kapoor et al., 2020; National Endowment for Financial Education, 2021) shows that the following topics are considered to be foundational elements of all well-designed personal finance curriculums:

- Basics of time-value of money
- Cash flow management
- Personal tax planning
- Debt management
- Housing decisions
- Vehicle ownership decisions
- Basics of saving and investing
- Retirement planning
- Risk management
- Estate and long-term care planning

Going forward, it will be important to expand this core content list to include topics that help increase the financial literacy and capabilities of household financial decision makers. Most of the currently available personal finance-related textbooks and course materials focus on the importance of planning and managing one's finances. However, findings from recent research, as described throughout this handbook, reveal a shift in the field's understanding of what financial decision makers consider when deciding between choices and options. It is now known that people assign greater weight to some factors that normatively should be underweighted. Financial decision makers are increasingly seen to violate normative economic recommendations and instead rely on heuristics and other decision-making shortcuts when making financial decisions. As the world's financial markets become more complex and interrelated, household decision makers will need more than simple heuristic strategies to increase their households' financial well-being. Table 34.1 describes some key changes and developments, as described throughout this handbook, that should be further developed and incorporated into personal finance educational textbooks, course materials, and policy and practice models and intervention approaches.

## Future Needs and Opportunities

Along with core financial literacy-related topics, the study and practice of personal finance can be informed, as noted by Bodie (2006), through the inclusion of behavioral economics-related topics such as framing, risk tolerance (aversion), and information on the trade-offs involving taxation and transaction costs associated with holding assets in various investment accounts and when utilizing different investment assets.

**Table 34.1:** Important New Concepts in Personal Finance.

| Personal Financial Decisions | Example of Current Understanding | Future Perspective |
| --- | --- | --- |
| Inter-temporal Financial Decisions | Maximize wealth and meet retirement goals | Subjective Well-being and Financial Satisfaction (Asebedo et al., 2020; Bruggen et al., 2017; Chatterjee and Fan, 2021; Chen et al., 2020; Fan et al., 2021). |
| Psychological Factors | Consideration of risk tolerance in personal financial decisions | Consideration of personality, cognitive biases, human and social capital, time orientation, and other biopsychosocial factors along with risk tolerance (Fan et al., 2021; Grable et al., 2021; Grable, 2000; Thanki et al., 2020). |
| Choice of Popular Investment Vehicles | Stocks, bonds, mutual funds, and ETFs Derivative strategies and hedge funds for accredited investors | Emergence of automated investment platforms, risks and returns associated with block-chain and crypto-currencies, structured contracts and annuities, goal-specific accounts (child saving accounts, ABLE savings accounts, health savings accounts, etc.). |
| Portfolio Management | Knowledge of asset allocation and diversification | Emphasis on *asset location*, along with asset allocation, and diversification (Ciccotello, 2016). |
| Personal Debt Management | Mortgages, personal loans, and credit card debt as major debt-related factors | Emergence of student loan debt and medical debt as important additional debt-related factors (Lusardi et al., 2020b; Robb et al., 2019). |
| Financial Service Providers | Banks, brokerages, insurance companies, and other traditional financial services institutions. | Emergence of FinTech as a competing option to traditional brick and mortar financial service providers. |
| Professional Help-Seeking Options | Financial counselors, financial planners, financial/investment advisors, bankers, accountants, attorneys, and brokers | Emergence of financial therapists as a help-seeking option for providing professional advice. |

Practical management techniques can also elevate the practice of personal finance. Ciccotello (2016), for instance, noted the importance of creating greater awareness among household financial decision makers of the concept of asset location as a tool to improving the financial performance of individual investment portfolios.

Recent research can also inform the development of personal finance curricula. For example, an understanding of what creates greater satisfaction for households has broadened with the emergence of new research from the fields of behavioral economics and social psychology. The focus has been gradually shifting from teaching individuals to simply manage their personal financial situation to the broader paradigm of helping individuals maximize the perception of their subjective well-being and financial satisfaction. Similarly, incorporating information on the roles of factors such as personality traits, psychological biases and heuristics, and biopsychosocial factors in shaping household financial decision making will, we believe, enable students enrolled in personal finance classes to broaden their understanding of the rationale (and mistakes) that people make when engaging in financial decision making.

Moreover, the emergence of artificial intelligence (AI), inventions of more efficient optimization algorithms, and other innovations in the financial services sector have resulted in making available greater choices of investment products and tools for consumers engaging in saving, investment planning, and credit management (Asebedo et al., 2020; Fan et al., 2021; Grable, 2000; Grable et al., 2021; Thanki et al., 2020). Those who are interested in personal finance will benefit from learning about these newly available financial services options. The following additional opportunities exist to improve personal finance curricula (see Financial Literacy and Education Commission, 2020):

- documenting the availability of options and strategies for obtaining basic needs such as food, shelter, healthcare, and utilities when experiencing financial hardship from income shocks or unexpected expenses
- presenting information on accessing various social programs, such as unemployment insurance benefits and economic impact payments
- documenting information on accessing and understanding information on provisions available for running a small business, and information on the various mortgage and housing assistance options when experiencing financial hardship
- increasing knowledge of family and medical leave options and other workplace protections when experiencing personal and family emergencies
- recognizing and avoiding financial frauds and scams, and knowing where victims of frauds and scams can seek help
- increasing knowledge of the resources and options that are available for managing credit card debt, student loans, auto loans, and other forms of indebtedness

The way financial decision makers seek help can also be informed by research and developments in the financial services field. It is already well known that seeking professional financial counseling and advice can help ease the stress that people feel when they have to deal with financial topics, particularly when dealing with topics they do not completely understand (Joo and Grable, 2001). Students of personal finance learn about the availability of professional help providers (financial counselors, financial planners, investment brokers, etc.) in a variety of ways. Yet, to date, no clearinghouse or central registry exists, in any country, to help consumers compare and contrast financial service providers and offerings. Consider the burgeoning field of financial therapy. Financial therapists provide another option for individuals who need more specialized therapeutic help for alleviating their financial stress (Britt et al., 2015; Ford et al., 2020; Grable et al., 2020; Kim et al., 2011), yet few consumers know that financial therapy is available. According to a report by the U.S. Financial Literacy Education Commission (Financial Literacy and Education Commission, 2020), vulnerable populations can especially benefit from inclusion therapeutic services, but until the average consumer can obtain valid information about help providers, information asymmetry will continue to exist, which will place limits on the well-being of individuals and families.

## Improving the Delivery and Design of Personal Finance Curricula

Although personal finance education is generally delivered in a more traditional setting or through an online format, pedagogical research continues to reveal that personal finance education delivered using a service-learning or experiential learning approach might be beneficial in creating greater student engagement, helping generate better learning outcomes, and creating greater financial self-efficacy among students. Goetz et al. (2011) found in a survey of college students that there is a preference for receiving personal financial education through a combination of on-campus one-on-one financial counseling, online financial management resources, and in-person educational workshops. When service-learning or experiential learning is integrated into a personal finance class curriculum, students have the opportunity to help answer personal finance-related questions of their peers and provide solutions under the supervision of their mentor faculty, while receiving credit for the course (Annis et al., 2010). Emerging literature has found that teaching a college-level personal finance class using an experiential learning format not only creates greater engagement and financial socialization among participating students (LeBaron et al., 2019), but this approach also builds greater financial self-efficacy (White et al., 2019). A FLEC (2020) study recommended that there be a steady increase in the quality, training, and standards for personal financial educators over time. In this regard, the FLEC study recommended (a) creating benchmarks for improving the quality of educators teaching personal finance courses, (b) creating capacity for making more one-to-one education and counseling programs accessible to vulnerable populations, and (c) developing greater accountability for personal financial education programs through better management of resources and regular assessment of the outcomes related to the delivery of such programs.

## Extending Access to and Reach of Personal Finance

Scholars, policymakers, and personal finance stakeholders have thus far struggled to make personal financial resources and education more effective and accessible for the general population, including underserved households and minority racial-ethnic groups – those who need this type of information and education most desperately. This is not just a U.S. issue. Lack of access to useful personal finance information and education is a phenomenon encountered worldwide. Worse, this issue is likely to persist into the near future. As a solution to this issue, one option could be to build regional resource hubs for personal financial education and to utilize grass-roots social networks and community groups to make access to personal finance resources transparent, affordable, and meaningful for those living in underserved communities. A similar solution was suggested by Lusardi et al. (2020a, 2020b) as a strategy for making financial information more accessible to people during the Covid-19 pandemic.

The idea of making personal financial information, resources, education, and services more readily accessible by tapping into various community-based resources that people trust and visit frequently is something being explored by the Consumer Financial Protection Bureau (CFPB). The multi-faceted strategy that CFPB is pursuing, with the goal of building financial resiliency within communities, includes providing personal finance-related resources focusing on various population groups, including military service members and veterans, young adults, older adults, caregivers, and economically marginalized households (Consumer Financial Protection Bureau, 2020). The CFPB is currently working on building a permanent system of delivery for personal financial education by using the infrastructure that is already in place in local communities. These community-based strategies involve collaborating with local and regional library systems. Other grass-roots-level educational outreach strategies include collaborating with local non-profits and social service-related organizations, Army Officer Training Corps (ROTC) offices, workplaces, state and local government agencies, university extension offices, and identifying and training educators in the area of personal finance (Consumer Financial Protection Bureau, 2020).[2] Additionally, the CFPB is collaborating with

2 Some of the ideas that CFPB has developed with the goal of creating greater access to personal financial information, resources, education, and services include collaboration with local libraries, where librarians are provided with personal finance-related outreach materials and are provided the opportunity to connect with local personal finance educators. Thus, libraries can become an important resource for personal finance-related information for the local community. Another CFPB program is called the Your Money, Your Goals (YMYG) Train-the-Trainer program. This program consists of a personal financial education-related toolkit that helps train local educators to provide personal financial education in their community. The YMYG toolkits are distributed in every state and U.S. territory including Puerto Rico and Guam (Consumer Financial Protection Bureau, 2020). In addition, the CFPB has started collaborating with the Internal Revenue Service (IRS) sponsored Voluntary Income Tax Assistance (VITA) program to distribute educational materials that encourage savings at tax time. These recent initiatives are expected to build greater financial resiliency in the population over time.

the Financial Literacy Education Commission (FLEC) to synergistically offer financial education curricula in local communities. If these efforts prove effective, the CFPB model could be used as a guide for similar programs worldwide.

Xiao et al. (2020) suggested that it might be more efficient to unbundle content typically found in a personal finance curriculum and customize the content based on the specific needs of stakeholders. For example, those individuals who are struggling to manage student loans or credit card debt would probably benefit most from receiving personal financial education related to debt management rather than learning about a wide assortment of other personal finance topics. Similarly, for individuals who are just beginning their investment journey, a deeper dive into learning about the basics of saving and investing might be more useful than other types of personal finance topic education. In a field experiment conducted in emerging economies, one study found that providing incentives for individuals to participate in personal finance coursework was associated with an increase in individual participation (Cole et al., 2009). It is possible that following a similar strategy (e.g., offering incentives) could increase motivation among individuals from underserved populations to participate in personal finance courses being offered through local community centers.

## Opportunities for Future Research

A frequent limitation of research examining the efficacy of personal financial education is that a majority of these studies were based on convenience sampling of college students – who, by virtue of being in college, already possess higher educational attainment than those individuals who have lower educational attainment and would benefit most from learning the concepts and tools of personal finance. A further limitation is that most of these research participants are majors in business, financial planning, economics, or other business fields, and are therefore likely to be more knowledgeable about some personal finance-related concepts than other non-business or non-financial planning majors. There is a need for research focused on nationally and internationally representative samples to examine the true benefits associated with the delivery and use of personal finance education. Such research should move beyond university students and other convenience samples. In a recent report, Financial Literacy and Education Commission (2020) also identified the need for more data that can help in making more informed policy decisions. Analyses of such data will help in identifying the topics within a personal financial education curriculum that are most beneficial in generating favorable financial outcomes over the short-, intermediate-, and long-term. Furthermore, FLEC staff noted that current gaps in the literature and unavailability of related data are major limitations in determining the effectiveness of the personal financial education programs.

608 — Swarn Chatterjee, John E. Grable

Another limitation of the literature on personal finance-related issues is that nearly all previous studies were conducted using cross-sectional data. There is very little information available on the association between receiving personal financial education and individual well-being across time. Future studies need to address this gap in the literature. An extension of this need relates to the issue of endogeneity and causation (Grable and Lyons, 2018). While researchers and personal finance practitioners sometimes make causal inferences, very little data exists, in terms of published empirical studies, showing causal mechanisms from personal finance education, interventions, or tools to behaviors or outcomes.

Tangential opportunities for research also exist. For example, individuals have different learning styles. Some people are visual information processors, while others are auditory or kinesthetic processors (i.e., learners); some individuals are global thinkers while others are analytical thinkers; some individuals learn inductively, whereas others are deductive learners (Hatami, 2013). However, there is currently a paucity of literature available to inform personal finance stakeholders on what type of course or service delivery format is most beneficial for different information processing types. Future research is needed to help develop pedagogical approaches that will cater to the wide assortment of learning styles, particularly in an international context (e.g., taking into account aspects of locus of control, self-esteem, and mastery). It is also not known whether a personal finance class taken in elementary, middle, or high school is more or less beneficial to an individual when compared to a personal education class taken in college or the workplace. Future research is needed to shed light on the benefits associated with the timing and delivery of personal financial education. More information is also needed to understand whether the benefits of providing personal financial education courses catering to specific needs based on different lifecycle stages are better than offering personal finance education courses at one point in time.

More broadly, future research is needed to improve the field's understanding of whether and to what extent receiving personal finance-related education improves financial decision making, financial resiliency, and the well-being of households. To design more efficient personal finance curricula, as well as to develop, deliver, and regulate personal finance products and services, it will also be important for future research to examine the topic areas that people consider most frequently when making routine financial decisions. Studies should also examine whether receiving personal financial education is most beneficial in improving peoples' short-term financial decision making, long-term financial decision making, or both. Additional research is also needed to determine whether certain pedagogical techniques – in-person format, online format, or experiential learning format – benefits the learning, and subsequent well-being, of underserved groups and minority households.[3] The CFPB is currently working on developing various scales of financial well-being to measure the association between receiving personal financial education and financial well-being of households, and to translate the findings of their research in developing a personal financial education-related curriculum for distribution to local communities (Consumer Financial Protection Bureau, 2020). A financial well-being scale developed by the CFPB was recently included in the Federal Reserve System's Survey of Household Economics and Decision Making (SHED) beginning with the 2017 wave of the SHED dataset. This provides future opportunities for examining the association between receiving personal financial education and measuring their financial well-being of households using a national dataset (Collins and Urban, 2020). Even so, more domain-specific datasets are needed, with the application of additional qualitative and experimental methodologies.

# Conclusion

This chapter discussed and summarized the core principles and topic areas that are commonly included in personal finance-related curricula at the present time, which match to a great extent the chapter topics in this handbook. This chapter also discussed changes and innovations taking place in the financial marketplace. To keep up with these changes, this chapter suggested some important personal finance-related topics that should be included in future personal finance educational programs and incorporated into service delivery activities. As noted in this chapter, the pedagogical techniques and course delivery formats that are currently in use were discussed. This chapter also explored emerging formats and educational delivery techniques, such as providing experiential learning opportunities within a personal finance curriculum, and a strategy for unbundling the personal finance curriculum and providing customized educational content based on the needs of specific consumers. Pathways to extend the reach of personal finance and a discussion of potential strategies for making personal financial education more accessible to marginalized communities were included. The various limitations of our current understanding of the benefits of providing personal financial education and how it translates into better financial decision making were reviewed. Opportunities for future research that can contribute to the growing

---

**3** A counter-argument to providing personal finance education has been that some people learn about personal finance through experience (Frijns et al., 2014). However, no previous research has measured the expected direct and indirect effects of receiving personal finance-related education through a curriculum vis-à-vis learning through experience on financial decision making and financial well-being of individuals across time, and whether providing personal financial education through an experiential learning format provides the best of both opportunities. There is a need for future research to examine these differences.

body of literature on personal finance and provide valuable insight for making the delivery of personal financial education more efficient for all stakeholders in the future were discussed.

# References

Abreu, M., and Mendes, V. (2010). Financial literacy and portfolio diversification. *Quantitative Finance, 10*(5), 515–528.

Annis, P. M., Palmer, L., and Goetz, J. (2010). Service-learning in the financial planning curriculum: Expanding access to the community. *Journal of Family & Consumer Sciences, 102*(3), 16–21.

Asebedo, S. D., Seay, M. C., Little, T. D., Enete, S., and Gray, B. (2020). Three good things or three good financial things? Applying a positive psychology intervention to the personal finance domain. *The Journal of Positive Psychology*, 1–11.

Bajtelsmit, V. (2019). *Personal finance* (2nd ed.). John Wiley & Sons.

Bodie, Z. (2006). A note on economic principles and financial literacy. *Networks Financial Institute Policy Brief* (2006-PB), 07. Accessed July 2021. http://dx.doi.org/10.2139/ssrn.923561

Britt, S. L., Klontz, B. T., and Archuleta, K. L. (2015). Financial therapy: Establishing an emerging field. In B. T. Klontz, K. L. Archuleta, and S. L. Britt (eds.), *Financial therapy: Theory, research, and practice* (pp. 3–13). Springer.

Brüggen, E. C., Hogreve, J., Holmlund, M., Kabadayi, S., and Löfgren, M. (2017). Financial well-being: A conceptualization and research agenda. *Journal of Business Research, 79*, 228–237.

Chatterjee, S., and Fan, L. (2021). Older adults' life satisfaction: The roles of seeking financial advice and personality traits. *Journal of Financial Therapy, 12*(1), 51–78.

Chen, F., Hsu, C. L., Lin, A. J., and Li, H. (2020). Holding risky financial assets and subjective wellbeing: Empirical evidence from China. *The North American Journal of Economics and Finance, 54*, 101,142.

Ciccotello, C. (2016). Financial planning issues in the era of asset location. *Journal of Financial Service Professionals, 70*(2), 74–80.

Cole, S. A., Sampson, T. A., and Zia, B. H. (2009). *Financial literacy, financial decisions, and the demand for financial services: evidence from India and Indonesia* (Working Paper No. 09-117). Harvard Business School.

Collins, M. J., and Urban, C. (2020). Measuring financial well-being over the lifecourse. *The European Journal of Finance, 26*(4–5), 341–359.

Consumer Financial Protection Bureau (2020). *Financial literacy annual report*. Accessed July 2021. https://files.consumerfinance.gov/f/documents/cfpb_financial-literacy_annual-report_2020.pdf.

Cutler, N. E., and Devlin, S. J. (1996). A framework for understanding financial responsibilities among generations. *Generations: Journal of the American Society on Aging, 20*(1), 24–28.

Fan, L., and Chatterjee, S. (2017). Borrowing decision of households: An examination of the information search process. *Journal of Financial Counseling and Planning, 28*(1), 95–106.

Fan, L., Chatterjee, S., and Kim, J. (2021). An integrated framework of young adults' subjective well-being: the roles of personality traits, financial responsibility, perceived financial capability, and race. *Journal of Family and Economic Issues*, 1–20. https://doi.org/10.1007/s10834-021-09764-6

Federal Deposit Insurance Corporation. (2021). *Money smart: A financial education program*. Accessed July 2021. https://www.fdic.gov/resources/consumers/money-smart/index.html.

Financial Literacy and Education Commission. (2020). *U.S. national strategy for financial literacy*. Accessed July 2021. https://home.treasury.gov/system/files/136/US-National-Strategy-Financial-Literacy-2020.pdf

Ford, M. R., Ross, D. B., Grable, J., and DeGraff, A. (2020). Examining the role of financial therapy on relationship outcomes and help-seeking behavior. *Contemporary Family Therapy*, *42*(1), 55–67.

Frijns, B., Gilbert, A., and Tourani-Rad, A. (2014). Learning by doing: The role of financial experience in financial literacy. *Journal of Public Policy*, *34*, 123–154.

Gitman, L. J., Joehnk, M. D., and Billingsley, R. S. (2014). *Personal financial planning* (13th ed.). Cengage.

Goetz, J., Cude, B. J., Nielsen, R. B., Chatterjee, S., and Mimura, Y. (2011). College-based personal finance education: Student interest in three delivery methods. *Journal of Financial Counseling and Planning*, *22*(1), 27–42.

Grable, J. E. (2000). Financial risk tolerance and additional factors that affect risk taking in everyday money matters. *Journal of Business and Psychology*, *14*(4), 625–630.

Grable, J. E., Archuleta, K. L., Ford, M. R., Kruger, M., Gale, J., and Goetz, J. (2020). The moderating effect of generalized anxiety and financial knowledge on financial management behavior. *Contemporary Family Therapy*, *42*(1), 15–24.

Grable, J. E., Heo, W., and Rabbani, A. (2021). Characteristics of random responders in a financial risk-tolerance questionnaire. *Journal of Financial Services Marketing*, *26*(1), 1–9.

Grable, J. E., and Lyons, A. C. (2018). An introduction to big data. *Journal of Financial Services Professionals*, *72*(5), 17–20.

Grable, J. E., and Palmer, L. (2018). *Introduction to personal finance: Beginning your financial journey*. John Wiley & Sons.

Greenspan, A. (2002). Financial literacy: A tool for economic progress. *The Futurist*, *36*(4), 37.

Hatami, S. (2013). Learning styles. *Elt Journal*, *67*(4), 488–490.

Hira, T. K. (2009). Personal finance: Past, present and future. *Networks Financial Institute Policy Brief*, 2009-PB-10. http://dx.doi.org/10.2139/ssrn.1522299

Joo, S. H., and Grable, J. E. (2001). Factors associated with seeking and using professional retirement-planning help. *Family and Consumer Sciences Research Journal*, *30*(1), 37–63.

Jump$tart. (2021). *Jump$tart coalition for personal financial literacy*. Accessed July 2021. https://jumpstartclearinghouse.org

Kapoor, J. R., Dlabay, L. R., and Hughes, R. J. (2020). *Personal finance* (13th ed.). McGraw-Hill Education.

Kim, J. H., Gale, J., Goetz, J., and Bermúdez, J. M. (2011). Relational financial therapy: An innovative and collaborative treatment approach. *Contemporary Family Therapy*, *33*(3), 229–241.

LeBaron, A. B., Runyan, S. D., Jorgensen, B. L., Marks, L. D., Li, X., and Hill, E. J. (2019). Practice makes perfect: Experiential learning as a method for financial socialization. *Journal of Family Issues*, *40*(4), 435–463.

Lusardi, A. (2009). Planning for retirement: The importance of financial literacy. *Public Policy and Aging Report*, *19*(3), 7–13.

Lusardi, A., Hasler, A., and Yakoboski, P. J. (2020a). Building up financial literacy and financial resilience. *Mind & Society*, 1–7. https://doi.org/10.1007/s11299-020-00246-0

Lusardi, A., Mitchell, O. S., and Oggero, N. (2020b). Debt and financial vulnerability on the verge of retirement. *Journal of Money, Credit and Banking*, *52* (5),1,005–1,034.

National Endowment for Financial Education. (2021). *Cash course*. https://www.nefe.org/initiatives/cashcourse.aspx.

Polkovnichenko, V. (2003). *Household portfolio diversification* (Working Paper Vol. 88). University of Minnesota and The Federal Reserve Bank of Minnesota.

Robb, C. A., Chatterjee, S., Porto, N., and Cude, B. J. (2019). The influence of student loan debt on financial satisfaction. *Journal of Family and Economic Issues*, *40*(1), 51–73.

Tennyson, S., and Nguyen, C. (2001). State curriculum mandates and student knowledge of personal finance. *Journal of Consumer Affairs*, *35*(2), 241–262.

Thaler, R. H. (2018). From cashews to nudges: The evolution of behavioral economics. *American Economic Review*, *108* (6),1,265–1,287.

Thanki, H., Karani, A., and Goyal, A. K. (2020). Psychological antecedents of financial risk tolerance. *The Journal of Wealth Management*, *23*(2), 36–51.

Von Gaudecker, H. M. (2015). How does household portfolio diversification vary with financial literacy and financial advice? *The Journal of Finance*, *70*(2), 489–507.

Warschauer, T. (2002). The role of universities in the development of the personal financial planning profession. *Financial Services Review*, *11*(3), 201–216.

White, K. J., Park, N., Watkins, K., McCoy, M., and Thomas, M. G. (2019). The relationship between financial knowledge, financial management, and financial self-efficacy among African-American students. http://dx.doi.org/10.2139/ssrn.3468751

Xiao, J. J., Porto, N., and Mason, I. M. (2020). Financial capability of student loan holders who are college students, graduates, or dropouts. *Journal of Consumer Affairs*, *54*(4), 1,383–1,401.

# List of Figures

https://doi.org/10.1515/9783110727692-035

# List of Tables

https://doi.org/10.1515/9783110727692-036

# About the Editors

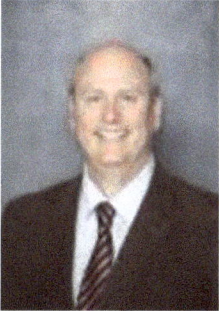

Professor **John E. Grable** teaches and conducts research in the Certified Financial Planner™ Board of Standards Inc. undergraduate and graduate programs at the University of Georgia where he holds an Athletic Association Endowed Professorship. He is currently co-editor of *Financial Planning Review*.

Professor **Swarn Chatterjee** is the Bluerock Professor of Planning at the University of Georgia. He currently serves as associate editor for the *Journal of Financial Counseling and Planning* and *Financial Services Review* and is on the editorial review board of the *Journal of Financial Planning*.

https://doi.org/10.1515/9783110727692-037

# Index

https://doi.org/10.1515/9783110727692-038

www.ingramcontent.com/pod-product-compliance
Lightning Source LLC
Chambersburg PA
CBHW081211220326
41598CB00037B/6742